ALSO BY ANDREW SOLOMON

A Stone Boat

The Irony Tower:
Soviet Artists in a Time of Glasnost

The Noonday Demon

An Atlas *of* Depression

Andrew Solomon

SCRIBNER

New York   London   Toronto   Sydney   Singapore

SCRIBNER
1230 Avenue of the Americas
New York, NY 10020

SCRIBNER and design are trademarks of Macmillan Library Reference USA, Inc.,
used under license by Simon & Schuster, the publisher of this work.

For information regarding special discounts for bulk purchases,
please contact Simon & Schuster Special Sales at 1-800-456-6798 or
business@simonandschuster.com

DESIGNED BY ERICH HOBBING

Set in Janson

Manufactured in the United States of America

1   3   5   7   9   10   8   6   4   2

Library of Congress Cataloging-in-Publication Data
Solomon, Andrew, 1963–
The Noonday demon : an atlas of depression / Andrew Solomon.
p. cm.
Includes bibliographical references and index.
1. Depression, Mental. 2. Solomon, Andrew, 1963–.
3. Depressed persons—Case studies. I. Title.

RC537.S598 2001
616.85'27'0092—dc21
[B]   2001018884

ISBN 0-684-85466-X

The copyright page continues after the index.

For my father,
who gave me life not once, but twice

Contents

Everything passes away—suffering, pain, blood, hunger, pestilence. The sword will pass away too, but the stars will still remain when the shadows of our presence and our deeds have vanished from the earth. There is no man who does not know that. Why, then, will we not turn our eyes toward the stars? Why?
—Mikhail Bulgakov, *The White Guard*

The
Noonday
Demon

A Note on Method

The writing of this book has been my life for the past five years, and it is sometimes hard for me to trace my own ideas back to their various sources. I have attempted to credit all influences in the notes at the back of the book, and not to distract readers with a cascade of unfamiliar names and technical jargon in the main text. I asked my subjects to allow me to use their actual names, because real names lend authority to real stories. In a book one of the aims of which is to remove the burden of stigma from mental illness, it is important not to play to that stigma by hiding the identities of depressed people. I have, however, included the stories of seven people who wished to remain pseudonymous and who persuaded me that they had significant reason to do so. They appear in this text as Sheila Hernandez, Frank Rusakoff, Bill Stein, Danquille Stetson, Lolly Washington, Claudia Weaver, and Fred Wilson. None of them is a composite personality, and I have taken pains to change no details. The members of Mood Disorders Support Groups (MDSG) use first names only; these have all been changed in keeping with the private nature of the meetings. All other names are actual.

I have allowed the men and women whose battles are the primary subject of this book to tell their own stories. I have done my best to get coherent stories from them, but I have not in general done fact-checking on their accounts of themselves. I have not insisted that all personal narrative be strictly linear.

I have often been asked how I found my subjects. A number of professionals, as noted in the acknowledgments, helped me to gain access to their patients. I met an enormous number of people in my ordinary life who volunteered, upon learning of my subject, their own copious histories, some of which were extremely fascinating and ultimately became source material. I published an article about depression in *The New Yorker* in 1998 and received over a thousand letters in the months imme-

11

diately following publication. Graham Greene once said, "I sometimes wonder how all those who do not write, compose, or paint can manage to escape the madness, the melancholia, the panic fear which is inherent in the human situation." I think he vastly underestimated the number of people who do write in one way or another to alleviate melancholia and panic fear. In responding to my flood of mail, I asked some people whose correspondence had been particularly moving to me whether they would be interested in doing interviews for this book. Additionally, I spoke at and attended numerous conferences where I met consumers of mental health care.

I have never written on any subject about which so many people have so much to say, nor on any subject about which so many people have chosen to say so much to me. It is frighteningly easy to accumulate material about depression. I felt in the end that what was missing in the field of depression studies was synthesis. Science, philosophy, law, psychology, literature, art, history, and many other disciplines have independently taken up the cause of depression. So many interesting things are happening to so many interesting people and so many interesting things are being said and being published—and there is chaos in the kingdom. The first goal of this book is empathy; the second, which has been for me much more difficult to achieve, is order: an order based as closely as possible on empiricism, rather than on sweeping generalizations extracted from haphazard anecdotes.

I must emphasize that I am not a doctor or a psychologist or even a philosopher. This is an extremely personal book and should not be taken as anything more than that. Though I have offered explanations and interpretations of complex ideas, this book is not intended to substitute for appropriate treatment.

For the sake of readability, I have not used ellipsis marks or brackets in quotations, from spoken or written sources, where I felt that the omitted or added words did not substantially change meaning; anyone wishing to reference these sources should go back to the originals, which are all cataloged at the end of this book. I have also avoided use of "[sic]" in the eighth chapter, where historical sources use obsolete spellings. Quotations for which citations are not furnished are from personal interviews, most of which were conducted between 1995 and 2001.

I have used those statistics that come out of sound studies and have been most comfortable with statistics that have been extensively replicated or frequently cited. My finding, in general, is that statistics in this field are inconsistent and that many authors select statistics to make an attractive ensemble in support of preexisting theories. I found one major study, for example, that showed that depressed people who abuse substances nearly always choose stimulants; and another, equally convincing one that demonstrated that depressed people who abuse substances invariably use opiates. Many authors derive a rather nauseous air of invincibility from statistics, as though showing that something occurs 82.37 percent of the time is more palpable and true than showing that something occurs about three out of four times. It is my experience that the hard numbers are the ones that lie. The matters that they describe cannot be defined so clearly. The most accurate statement that can be made on the frequency of depression is that it occurs often and, directly or indirectly, affects the lives of everyone.

It is hard for me to write without bias about the pharmaceutical companies because my father has worked in the pharmaceutical field for most of my adult life. As a consequence of this I have met many people in that industry. It is fashionable at the moment to excoriate the pharmaceutical industry as one that takes advantage of the sick. My experience has been that the people in the industry are both capitalists and idealists—people keen on profit but also optimistic that their work may benefit the world, that they may enable important discoveries that will put specific illnesses into obsolescence. We would not have the selective serotonin reuptake inhibitors (SSRIs), antidepressants that have saved so many lives, without the companies that sponsored the research. I have done my best to write clearly about the industry insofar as this is part of the story of this book. After his experience of my depression, my father extended the reach of his company into the field of antidepressants. His company, Forest Laboratories, is now the U.S. distributor of Celexa. To avoid any explicit conflict of interest, I have not mentioned the product except where its omission would be ostentatious or misleading.

I was frequently asked, as I wrote this book, whether the writing was cathartic. It was not. My experience conforms to that of others who have written in this field. Writing on depression is painful, sad, lonely, and stressful. Nonetheless, the idea that I was doing something that might be useful to others was uplifting; and my increased knowledge has been useful to me. I hope it will be clear that the primary pleasure of this book is a literary pleasure of communication rather than the therapeutic release of self-expression.

I began by writing about my depression; then about the similar depression of others; then about the different depression of others; and finally about depression in completely other contexts. I have included three stories from outside the first world in this book. The narratives of my encounters with people in Cambodia, Senegal, and Greenland are provided in an attempt to counterbalance some of the culturally specific ideas of depression that have circumscribed many studies in the area. My trips into unknown places were adventures tinged with a certain exoticism, and I have not suppressed the fairy-tale quality of those encounters.

Depression, under various names and in various guises, is and has always been ubiquitous for biochemical and social reasons. This book strives to capture the extent of depression's temporal and geographical reach. If it sometimes seems that depression is the private affliction of the modern Western middle classes, that is because it is in this community that we are suddenly acquiring new sophistication to recognize depression, to name it, to treat it, and to accept it—and not because we have any special rights to the complaint itself. No book can span the reach of human suffering, but I hope that by indicating that reach, I will help to liberate some men and women who suffer from depression. We can never eliminate all unhappiness, and alleviating depression does not assure happiness, but I hope the knowledge contained in this book will help to eliminate some pain for some people.

CHAPTER I

Depression

Depression is the flaw in love. To be creatures who love, we must be creatures who can despair at what we lose, and depression is the mechanism of that despair. When it comes, it degrades one's self and ultimately eclipses the capacity to give or receive affection. It is the aloneness within us made manifest, and it destroys not only connection to others but also the ability to be peacefully alone with oneself. Love, though it is no prophylactic against depression, is what cushions the mind and protects it from itself. Medications and psychotherapy can renew that protection, making it easier to love and be loved, and that is why they work. In good spirits, some love themselves and some love others and some love work and some love God: any of these passions can furnish that vital sense of purpose that is the opposite of depression. Love forsakes us from time to time, and we forsake love. In depression, the meaninglessness of every enterprise and every emotion, the meaninglessness of life itself, becomes self-evident. The only feeling left in this loveless state is insignificance.

Life is fraught with sorrows: no matter what we do, we will in the end die; we are, each of us, held in the solitude of an autonomous body; time passes, and what has been will never be again. Pain is the first experience of world-helplessness, and it never leaves us. We are angry about being ripped from the comfortable womb, and as soon as that anger fades, distress comes to take its place. Even those people whose faith promises them that this will all be different in the next world cannot help experiencing anguish in this one; Christ himself was the man of sorrows. We live, however, in a time of increasing palliatives; it is easier than ever to decide what to feel and what not to feel. There is less and less unpleasantness that is unavoidable in life, for those with the means to avoid. But despite the enthusiastic claims of pharmaceutical science, depression cannot be wiped out so long as we are creatures conscious of our own selves. It can at best be contained—and containing is all that current treatments for depression aim to do.

Highly politicized rhetoric has blurred the distinction between depression and its consequences—the distinction between how you feel and how you act in response. This is in part a social and medical phenomenon, but it is also the result of linguistic vagary attached to emotional vagary. Perhaps depression can best be described as emotional pain that forces itself on us against our will, and then breaks free of its externals. Depression is not just a lot of pain; but too much pain can compost itself into depression. Grief is depression in proportion to circumstance; depression is grief out of proportion to circumstance. It is tumbleweed distress that thrives on thin air, growing despite its detachment from the nourishing earth. It can be described only in metaphor and allegory. Saint Anthony in the desert, asked how he could differentiate between angels who came to him humble and devils who came in rich disguise, said you could tell by how you felt after they had departed. When an angel left you, you felt strengthened by his presence; when a devil left, you felt horror. Grief is a humble angel who leaves you with strong, clear thoughts and a sense of your own depth. Depression is a demon who leaves you appalled.

Depression has been roughly divided into small (mild or disthymic) and large (major) depression. Mild depression is a gradual and sometimes permanent thing that undermines people the way rust weakens iron. It is too much grief at too slight a cause, pain that takes over from the other emotions and crowds them out. Such depression takes up bodily occupancy in the eyelids and in the muscles that keep the spine erect. It hurts your heart and lungs, making the contraction of involuntary muscles harder than it needs to be. Like physical pain that becomes chronic, it is miserable not so much because it is intolerable in the moment as because it is intolerable to have known it in the moments gone and to look forward only to knowing it in the moments to come. The present tense of mild depression envisages no alleviation because it feels like knowledge.

Virginia Woolf has written about this state with an eerie clarity: "Jacob went to the window and stood with his hands in his pockets. There he saw three Greeks in kilts; the masts of ships; idle or busy people of the lower classes strolling or stepping out briskly, or falling into groups and gesticulating with their hands. Their lack of concern for him was not the cause of his gloom; but some more profound conviction—it was not that he himself happened to be lonely, but that all people are." In the same book, *Jacob's Room*, she describes how "There rose in her mind a curious sadness, as if time and eternity showed through skirts and waistcoats, and she saw people passing tragically to destruction. Yet, heaven knows, Julia was no fool." It is this acute awareness of transience and limitation that constitutes mild depression. Mild depression, for many years simply accommodated, is increasingly subject to treatment as doctors scrabble to address its diversity.

Large depression is the stuff of breakdowns. If one imagines a soul of iron that weathers with grief and rusts with mild depression, then major depression is the startling collapse of a whole structure. There are two models for depression: the dimensional and the categorical. The dimensional posits that depression sits on a continuum with sadness and represents an extreme version of something everyone has felt and known. The categorical describes depression as an illness totally separate from other emotions, much as a stomach virus is totally different from acid indigestion. Both are true. You go along the gradual path or the sudden trigger of emotion and then you get to a place that is genuinely different. It takes time for a rusting iron-framed building to collapse, but the rust is ceaselessly powdering the solid, thinning it, eviscerating it. The collapse, no matter how abrupt it may feel, is the cumulative consequence of decay. It is nonetheless a highly dramatic and visibly different event. It is a long time from the first rain to the point when rust has eaten through an iron girder. Sometimes the rusting is at such key points that the collapse seems total, but more often it is partial: this section collapses, knocks that section, shifts the balances in a dramatic way.

It is not pleasant to experience decay, to find yourself exposed to the ravages of an almost daily rain, and to know that you are turning into something feeble, that more and more of you will blow off with the first strong wind, making you less and less. Some people accumulate more emotional rust than others. Depression starts out insipid, fogs the days into a dull color, weakens ordinary actions until their clear shapes are obscured by the effort they require, leaves you tired and bored and self-obsessed—but you can get through all that. Not happily, perhaps, but you can get through. No one has ever been able to define the collapse point that marks major depression, but when you get there, there's not much mistaking it.

Major depression is a birth and a death: it is both the new presence of something and the total disappearance of something. Birth and death are gradual, though official documents may try to pinion natural law by creating categories such as "legally dead" and "time born." Despite nature's vagaries, there is definitely a point at which a baby who has not been in the world is in it, and a point at which a pensioner who has been in the world is no longer in it. It's true that at one stage the baby's head is here and his body not; that until the umbilical cord is severed the child is physically connected to the mother. It's true that the pensioner may close his eyes for the last time some hours before he dies, and that there is a gap between when he stops breathing and when he is declared "brain-dead." Depression exists in time. A patient may say that he has spent certain months suffering major depression, but this is a way of imposing a measurement on the immeasurable. All that one can really say for certain is that one has known major depression, and that one does or does not happen to be experiencing it at any given present moment.

The birth and death that constitute depression occur at once. I returned, not long ago, to a wood in which I had played as a child and saw an oak, a hundred years dignified, in whose shade I used to play with my brother. In twenty years, a huge vine had attached itself to this confident tree and had nearly smothered it. It was hard to say where the tree left off and the vine began. The vine had twisted itself so entirely around the scaffolding of tree branches that its leaves seemed from a distance to be the leaves of the tree; only up close could you see how few living oak branches were left, and how a few desperate little budding sticks of oak stuck like a row of thumbs up the massive trunk, their leaves continuing to photosynthesize in the ignorant way of mechanical biology.

Fresh from a major depression in which I had hardly been able to take on board the idea of other people's problems, I empathized with that tree. My depression had grown on me as that vine had conquered the oak; it had been a sucking thing that had wrapped itself around me, ugly and more alive than I. It had had a life of its own that bit by bit asphyxiated all of my life out of me. At the worst stage of major depression, I had moods that I knew were not my moods: they belonged to the depression, as surely as the leaves on that tree's high branches belonged to the vine. When I tried to think clearly about this, I felt that my mind was immured, that it couldn't expand in any direction. I knew that the sun was rising and setting, but little of its light reached me. I felt myself sagging under what was much stronger than I; first I could not use my ankles, and then I could not control my knees, and then my waist began to break under the strain, and then my shoulders turned in, and in the end I was compacted and fetal, depleted by this thing that was crushing me without holding me. Its tendrils threatened to pulverize my mind and my courage and my stomach, and crack my bones and desiccate my body. It went on glutting itself on me when there seemed nothing left to feed it.

I was not strong enough to stop breathing. I knew then that I could never kill this vine of depression, and so all I wanted was for it to let me die. But it had taken from me the energy I would have needed to kill myself, and it would not kill me. If my trunk was rotting, this thing that fed on it was now too strong to let it fall; it had become an alternative support to what it had destroyed. In the tightest corner of my bed, split and racked by this thing no one else seemed to be able to see, I prayed to a God I had never entirely believed in, and I asked for deliverance. I would have been happy to die the most painful death, though I was too dumbly lethargic even to conceptualize suicide. Every second of being alive hurt me. Because this thing had drained all fluid from me, I could not even cry. My mouth was parched as well. I had thought that when you feel your worst your tears flood, but the very worst pain is the arid pain of total violation that comes after the tears are all used up, the pain that stops up every space through which you once metered the world, or the world, you. This is the presence of major depression.

I have said that depression is both a birth and a death. The vine is what is born. The death is one's own decay, the cracking of the branches that support this misery. The first thing that goes is happiness. You cannot gain pleasure from anything. That's famously the cardinal symptom of major depression. But soon other emotions follow happiness into oblivion: sadness as you had known it, the sadness that seemed to have led you here; your sense of humor; your belief in and capacity for love. Your mind is leached until you seem dim-witted even to yourself. If your hair has always been thin, it seems thinner; if you have always had bad skin, it gets worse. You smell sour even to yourself. You lose the ability to trust anyone, to be touched, to grieve. Eventually, you are simply absent from yourself.

Maybe what is present usurps what becomes absent, and maybe the absence of obfuscatory things reveals what is present. Either way, you are less than yourself and in the clutches of something alien. Too often, treatments address only half the problem: they focus only on the presence or only on the absence. It is necessary both to cut away that extra thousand pounds of the vines and to relearn a root system and the techniques of photosynthesis. Drug therapy hacks through the vines. You can feel it happening, how the medication seems to be poisoning the parasite so that bit by bit it withers away. You feel the weight going, feel the way that the branches can recover much of their natural bent. Until you have got rid of the vine, you cannot think about what has been lost. But even with the vine gone, you may still have few leaves and shallow roots, and the rebuilding of your self cannot be achieved with any drugs that now exist. With the weight of the vine gone, little leaves scattered along the tree skeleton become viable for essential nourishment. But this is not a good way to be. It is not a strong way to be. Rebuilding of the self in and after depression requires love, insight, work, and, most of all, time.

Diagnosis is as complex as the illness. Patients ask doctors all the time, "Am I depressed?" as though the result were in a definitive blood test. The only way to find out whether you're depressed is to listen to and watch yourself, to feel your feelings and then think about them. If you feel bad without reason most of the time, you're depressed. If you feel bad most of the time with reason, you're also depressed, though changing the reasons may be a better way forward than leaving circumstance alone and attacking the depression. If the depression is disabling to you, then it's major. If it's only mildly distracting, it's not major. Psychiatry's bible—the *Diagnostic and Statistical Manual,* fourth edition *(DSM-IV)*—ineptly defines depression as the presence of five or more on a list of nine symptoms. The problem with the definition is that it's entirely arbitrary. There's no particular reason to qualify five symptoms as constituting depression; four symptoms are more or less depression; and five symptoms are less severe than six. Even one symptom is unpleasant. Having slight versions of all the symptoms may be less of a problem than having severe versions of two symptoms. After enduring diagnosis, most people seek causation, despite the fact that knowing why you are sick has no immediate bearing on treating the sickness.

Illness of the mind is real illness. It can have severe effects on the body. People who show up at the offices of their doctors complaining about stomach cramps are frequently told, "Why, there's nothing wrong with you except that you're depressed!" Depression, if it is sufficiently severe to cause stomach cramps, is actually a really bad thing to have wrong with you, and it requires treatment. If you show up complaining that your breathing is troubled, no one says to you, "Why, there's nothing wrong with you except that you have emphysema!" To the person who is experiencing them, psychosomatic complaints are as real as the stomach cramps of someone with food poisoning. They exist in the unconscious brain, and often enough the brain is sending inappropriate messages to the stomach, so they exist there as well. The diagnosis—whether something is rotten in your stomach or your appendix or your brain—matters in determining treatment and is not trivial. As organs go, the brain is quite an important one, and its malfunctions should be addressed accordingly.

Chemistry is often called on to heal the rift between body and soul. The relief people express when a doctor says their depression is "chemical" is predicated on a belief that there is an integral self that exists across time, and on a fictional divide between the fully occasioned sorrow and the utterly random one. The word *chemical* seems to assuage the feelings of responsibility people have for the stressed-out discontent of not liking their jobs, worrying about getting old, failing at love, hating their families. There is a pleasant freedom from guilt that has been attached to *chemical.* If your brain is predisposed to depression, you need not blame yourself for it. Well, blame yourself or evolution, but remember that blame itself can be understood as a chemical process, and that happiness, too, is chemical. Chemistry and biology are not matters that impinge on the "real" self; depression cannot be separated from the person it affects. Treatment does not alleviate a disruption of identity, bringing you back to some kind of normality; it readjusts a multifarious identity, changing in some small degree who you are.

Anyone who has taken high school science classes knows that human beings are made of chemicals and that the study of those chemicals and the structures in which they are configured is called biology. Everything that happens in the brain has chemical manifestations and sources. If you close your eyes and think hard about polar bears, that has a chemical effect on your brain. If you stick to a policy of opposing tax breaks for capital gains, that has a chemical effect on your brain. When you remember some episode from your past, you do so through the complex chemistry of memory. Childhood trauma and subsequent difficulty can alter brain chemistry. Thousands of chemical reactions are involved in deciding to read this book, picking it up with your hands, looking at the shapes of the letters on the page, extracting meaning from those shapes, and having intellectual and emotional responses to what they convey. If time lets you cycle out of a depression and feel better, the chemical changes are no less particular and complex than the ones that are brought about by taking antidepressants. The external determines the internal as much as the internal invents the external. What is so unattractive is the idea that in addition to all other lines being blurred, the boundaries of what makes us ourselves are blurry. There is no essential self that lies pure as a vein of gold under the chaos of experience and chemistry. Anything can be changed, and we must understand the human organism as a sequence of selves that succumb to or choose one another. And yet the language of science, used in training doctors and, increasingly, in nonacademic writing and conversation, is strangely perverse.

The cumulative results of the brain's chemical effects are not well understood. In the 1989 edition of the standard *Comprehensive Textbook of Psychiatry*, for example, one finds this helpful formula: a depression score is equivalent to the level of 3-methoxy-4-hydroxyphenylglycol (a compound found in the urine of all people and not apparently affected by depression); minus the level of 3-methoxy-4-hydroxymandelic acid; plus the level of norepinephrine; minus the level of normetanephrine plus the level of metanepherine, the sum of those divided by the level of 3-methoxy-4-hydroxymandelic acid; plus an unspecified conversion variable; or, as *CTP* puts it: "D-type score = C_1 (MHPG) - C_2 (VMA) + C_3 (NE) - C_4 (NMN + MN)/VMA + C_0." The score should come out between one for unipolar and zero for bipolar patients, so if you come up with something else—you're doing it wrong. How much insight can such formulae offer? How can they *possibly* apply to something as nebulous as mood? To what extent specific experience has conduced to a particular depression is hard to determine; nor can we explain through what chemistry a person comes to respond to external circumstance with depression; nor can we work out what makes someone essentially depressive.

Although depression is described by the popular press and the pharmaceutical industry as though it were a single-effect illness such as diabetes, it is not. Indeed, it is strikingly dissimilar to diabetes. Diabetics produce insufficient insulin, and diabetes is treated by increasing and stabilizing insulin in the bloodstream. Depression is *not* the consequence of a reduced level of anything we can now measure. Raising levels of serotonin in the brain triggers a process that eventually helps many depressed people to feel better, but that is *not* because they have abnormally low levels of serotonin. Furthermore, serotonin does *not* have immediate salutary effects. You could pump a gallon of serotonin into the brain of a depressed person and it would not in the instant make him feel one iota better, though a long-term sustained raise in serotonin level has some effects that ameliorate depressive symptoms. "I'm depressed but it's just chemical" is a sentence equivalent to "I'm murderous but it's just chemical" or "I'm intelligent but it's just chemical." Everything about a person is just chemical if one wants to think in those terms. "You can say it's 'just chemistry,'" says Maggie Robbins, who suffers from manic-depressive illness. "I say there's nothing 'just' about chemistry." The sun shines brightly and that's just chemical too, and it's chemical that rocks are hard, and that the sea is salt, and that certain springtime afternoons carry in their gentle breezes a quality of nostalgia that stirs the heart to longings and imaginings kept dormant by the snows of a long winter. "This serotonin thing," says David McDowell of Columbia University, "is part of modern neuromythology." It's a potent set of stories.

Internal and external reality exist on a continuum. What happens and how you understand it to have happened and how you respond to its happening are usually linked, but no one is predictive of the others. If reality itself is often a relative thing, and the self is in a state of permanent flux, the passage from slight mood to extreme mood is a glissando. Illness, then, is an extreme state of emotion, and one might reasonably describe emotion as a mild form of illness. If we all felt up and great (but not delusionally manic) all the time, we could get more done and might have a happier time on earth, but that idea is creepy and terrifying (though, of course, if we felt up and great all the time we might forget all about creepiness and terror).

Influenza is straightforward: one day you do not have the responsible virus in your system, and another day you do. HIV passes from one person to another in a definable isolated split second. Depression? It's like trying to come up with clinical parameters for hunger, which affects us all several times a day, but which in its extreme version is a tragedy that kills its victims. Some people need more food than others; some can function under circumstances of dire malnutrition; some grow weak rapidly and collapse in the streets. Similarly, depression hits different people in different ways: some are predisposed to resist or battle through it, while others are helpless in its grip. Willfulness and pride may allow one person to get through a depression that would fell another whose personality is more gentle and acquiescent.

Depression interacts with personality. Some people are brave in the face of depression (during it and afterward) and some are weak. Since personality too has a random edge and a bewildering chemistry, one can write everything off to genetics, but that is too easy. "There is no such thing as a mood gene," says Steven Hyman, director of the National Institute of Mental Health. "It's just shorthand for very complex gene-environment interactions." If everyone has the capacity for some measure of depression under some circumstances, everyone also has the capacity to fight depression to some degree under some circumstances. Often, the fight takes the form of seeking out the treatments that will be most effective in the battle. It involves finding help while you are still strong enough to do so. It involves making the most of the life you have between your most severe episodes. Some horrendously symptom-ridden people are able to achieve real success in life; and some people are utterly destroyed by the mildest forms of the illness.

Working through a mild depression without medications has certain advantages. It gives you the sense that you can correct your own chemical imbalances through the exercise of your own chemical will. Learning to walk across hot coals is also a triumph of the brain over what appears to be the inevitable physical chemistry of pain, and it is a thrilling way to discover the sheer power of mind. Getting through a depression "on your own" allows you to avoid the social discomfort associated with psychiatric medications. It suggests that we are accepting ourselves as we were made, reconstructing ourselves only with our own interior mechanics and without help from the outside. Returning from distress by gradual degrees gives sense to affliction itself.

Interior mechanics, however, are difficult to commission and are frequently inadequate. Depression frequently destroys the power of mind over mood. Sometimes the complex chemistry of sorrow kicks in because you've lost someone you love, and the chemistry of loss and love may lead to the chemistry of depression. The chemistry of falling in love can kick in for obvious external reasons, or along lines that the heart can never tell the mind. If we wanted to treat this madness of emotion, we could perhaps do so. It is mad for adolescents to rage at parents who have done their best, but it is a conventional madness, uniform enough so that we tolerate it relatively unquestioningly. Sometimes the same chemistry kicks in for external reasons that are not sufficient, by mainstream standards, to explain the despair: someone bumps into you in a crowded bus and you want to cry, or you read about world overpopulation and find your own life intolerable. Everyone has on occasion felt disproportionate emotion over a small matter or has felt emotions whose origin is obscure or that may have no origin at all. Sometimes the chemistry kicks in for no apparent external reason at all. Most people have had moments of inexplicable despair, often in the middle of the night or in the early morning before the alarm clock sounds. If such feelings last ten minutes, they're a strange, quick mood. If they last ten hours, they're a disturbing febrility, and if they last ten years, they're a crippling illness.

It is too often the quality of happiness that you feel at every moment its fragility, while depression seems when you are in it to be a state that will never pass. Even if you accept that moods change, that whatever you feel today will be different tomorrow, you cannot relax into happiness as you can into sadness. For me, sadness always has been and still is a more powerful feeling; and if that is not a universal experience, perhaps it is the base from which depression grows. I hated being depressed, but it was also in depression that I learned my own acreage, the full extent of my soul. When I am happy, I feel slightly distracted by happiness, as though it fails to use some part of my mind and brain that wants the exercise. Depression is something to do. My grasp tightens and becomes acute in moments of loss: I can see the beauty of glass objects fully at the moment when they slip from my hand toward the floor. "We find pleasure much less pleasurable, pain much more painful than we had anticipated," Schopenhauer wrote. "We require at all times a certain quantity of care or sorrow or want, as a ship requires ballast, to keep on a straight course."

There is a Russian expression: if you wake up feeling no pain, you know you're dead. While life is not only about pain, the experience of pain, which is particular in its intensity, is one of the surest signs of the life force. Schopenhauer said, "Imagine this race transported to a Utopia where everything grows of its own accord and turkeys fly around ready-roasted, where lovers find one another without any delay and keep one another without any difficulty: in such a place some men would die of boredom or hang themselves, some would fight and kill one another, and thus they would create for themselves more suffering than nature inflicts on them as it is . . . the polar opposite of suffering [is] boredom." I believe that pain needs to be transformed but not forgotten; gainsaid but not obliterated.

I am persuaded that some of the broadest figures for depression are based in reality. Though it is a mistake to confuse numbers with truth, these figures tell an alarming story. According to recent research, about 3 percent of Americans—some 19 million—suffer from chronic depression. More than 2 million of those are children. Manic-depressive illness, often called bipolar illness because the mood of its victims varies from mania to depression, afflicts about 2.3 million and is the second-leading killer of young women, the third of young men. Depression as described in *DSM-IV* is the leading cause of disability in the United States and abroad for persons over the age of five. Worldwide, including the developing world, depression accounts for more of the disease burden, as calculated by premature death plus healthy life-years lost to disability, than anything else but heart disease. Depression claims more years than war, cancer, and AIDS put together. Other illnesses, from alcoholism to heart disease, mask depression when it causes them; if one takes that into consideration, depression may be the biggest killer on earth.

Treatments for depression are proliferating now, but only half of Americans who have had major depression have ever sought help of any kind—even from a clergyman or a counselor. About 95 percent of that 50 percent go to primary-care physicians, who often don't know much about psychiatric complaints. An American adult with depression would have his illness recognized only about 40 percent of the time. Nonetheless, about 28 million Americans—one in every ten—are now on SSRIs (selective serotonin reuptake inhibitors—the class of drugs to which Prozac belongs), and a substantial number are on other medications. Less than half of those whose illness is recognized will get appropriate treatment. As definitions of depression have broadened to include more and more of the general population, it has become increasingly difficult to calculate an exact mortality figure. The statistic traditionally given is that 15 percent of depressed people will eventually commit suicide; this figure still holds for those with extreme illness. Recent studies that include milder depression show that 2 to 4 percent of depressives will die by their own hand as a direct consequence of the illness. This is still a staggering figure. Twenty years ago, about 1.5 percent of the population had depression that required treatment; now it's 5 percent; and as many as 10 percent of all Americans now living can expect to have a major depressive episode during their life. About 50 percent will experience some symptoms of depression. Clinical problems have increased;

treatments have increased vastly more. Diagnosis is on the up, but that does not explain the scale of this problem. Incidents of depression are increasing across the developed world, particularly in children. Depression is occurring in younger people, making its first appearance when its victims are about twenty-six, ten years younger than a generation ago; bipolar disorder, or manic-depressive illness, sets in even earlier. Things are getting worse.

There are few conditions at once as undertreated and as overtreated as depression. People who become totally dysfunctional are ultimately hospitalized and are likely to receive treatment, though sometimes their depression is confused with the physical ailments through which it is experienced. A world of people, however, are just barely holding on and continue, despite the great revolutions in psychiatric and psychopharmaceutical treatments, to suffer abject misery. More than half of those who do seek help—another 25 percent of the depressed population—receive no treatment. About half of those who do receive treatment—13 percent or so of the depressed population—receive unsuitable treatment, often tranquilizers or immaterial psychotherapies. Of those who are left, half—some 6 percent of the depressed population—receive inadequate dosage for an inadequate length of time. So that leaves about 6 percent of the total depressed population who are getting adequate treatment. But many of these ultimately go off their medications, usually because of side effects. "It's between 1 and 2 percent who get really optimal treatment," says John Greden, director of the Mental Health Research Institute at the University of Michigan, "for an illness that can usually be well-controlled with relatively inexpensive medications that have few serious side effects." Meanwhile, at the other end of the spectrum, people who suppose that bliss is their birthright pop cavalcades of pills in a futile bid to alleviate those mild discomforts that texture every life.

It has been fairly well established that the advent of the supermodel has damaged women's images of themselves by setting unrealistic expectations. The psychological supermodel of the twenty-first century is even more dangerous than the physical one. People are constantly examining their own minds and rejecting their own moods. "It's the Lourdes phenomenon," says William Potter, who ran the psychopharmacological division of the National Institute of Mental Health (NIMH) through the seventies and eighties, when the new drugs were being developed. "When you expose very large numbers of people to what they perceive and have reason to believe is positive, you get reports of miracles—and also, of course, of tragedy." Prozac is so easily tolerated that almost anyone can take it, and almost anyone does. It's been used on people with slight complaints who would not have been game for the discomforts of the older antidepressants, the monoamine oxidase inhibitors (MAOIs) or tricyclics. Even if you're not depressed, it might push back the edges of your sadness, and wouldn't that be nicer than living with pain?

We pathologize the curable, and what can easily be modified comes to be treated as illness, even if it was previously treated as personality or mood. As soon as we have a drug for violence, violence will be an illness. There are many grey states between full-blown depression and a mild ache unaccompanied by changes of sleep, appetite, energy, or interest; we have begun to class more and more of these as illness because we have found more and more ways to ameliorate them. But the cutoff point remains arbitrary. We have decided that an IQ of 69 constitutes retardation, but someone with an IQ of 72 is not in great shape, and someone with an IQ of 65 can still kind of manage; we have said that cholesterol should be kept under 220, but if your cholesterol is 221, you probably won't die from it, and if it's 219, you need to be careful: 69 and 220 are arbitrary numbers, and what we call illness is also really quite arbitrary; in the case of depression, it is also in perpetual flux.

Depressives use the phrase "over the edge" all the time to delineate the passage from pain to madness. This very physical description frequently entails falling "into the abyss." It's odd that so many people have such a consistent vocabulary, because the edge is really quite an abstracted metaphor. Few of us have ever fallen off the edge of anything, and certainly not into an abyss. The Grand Canyon? A Norwegian fjord? A South African diamond mine? It's difficult even to *find* an abyss to fall into. When asked, people describe the abyss pretty consistently. In the first place, it's dark. You are falling away from the sunlight toward a place where the shadows are black. Inside it, you cannot see, and the dangers are everywhere (it's neither soft-bottomed nor soft-sided, the abyss). While you are falling, you don't know how deep you can go, or whether you can in any way stop yourself. You hit invisible things over and over again until you are shredded, and yet your environment is too unstable for you to catch onto anything.

Fear of heights is the most common phobia in the world and must have served our ancestors well, since the ones who were not afraid probably found abysses and fell into them, so knocking their genetic material out of the race. If you stand on the edge of a cliff and look down, you feel dizzy. Your body does not work better than ever and allow you to move with immaculate precision back from the edge. You think you're going to fall, and if you look for long, you will fall. You're paralyzed. I remember going with friends to Victoria Falls, where great heights of rock drop down sheer to the Zambezi River. We were young and were sort of challenging one another by posing for photos as close to the edge as we dared to go. Each of us, upon going too close to the edge, felt sick and paralytic. I think depression is not usually going over the edge itself (which soon makes you die), but drawing too close to the edge, getting to that moment of fear when you have gone so far, when dizziness has deprived you so entirely of your capacity for balance. By Victoria Falls, we discovered that the unpassable thing was an invisible edge that lay well short of the place where the stone dropped away. Ten feet from the sheer drop, we all felt fine. Five feet from it, most of us quailed. At one point, a friend was taking a picture of me and wanted to get the bridge to Zambia into the shot. "Can you move an inch to the left?" she asked, and I obligingly took a step to the left—a foot to the left. I smiled, a nice smile that's preserved there in the photo, and she said, "You're getting a little bit close to the edge. C'mon back." I had been perfectly comfortable standing there, and then I suddenly looked down and saw that I had passed my edge. The blood drained from my face. "You're fine," my friend said, and walked nearer to me and held out her hand. The sheer cliff was ten inches away and yet I had to drop to my knees and lay myself flat along the ground to pull myself a few feet until I was on safe ground again. I know that I have an adequate sense of balance and that I can quite easily stand on an eighteen-inch-wide platform; I can even do a bit of amateur tap dancing, and I can do it reliably without falling over. I could not stand so close to the Zambezi.

Depression relies heavily on a paralyzing sense of imminence. What you can do at an elevation of six inches you cannot do when the ground drops away to reveal a drop of a thousand feet. Terror of the fall grips you even if that terror is what might make you fall. What is happening to you in depression is horrible, but it seems to be very much wrapped up in what is about to happen to you. Among other things, you feel you are about to die. The dying would not be so bad, but the living at the brink of dying, the not-quite-over-the-geographical-edge condition, is horrible. In a major depression, the hands that reach out to you are just out of reach. You cannot make it down onto your hands and knees because you feel that as soon as you lean, even away from the edge, you will lose your balance and plunge down. Oh, some of the abyss imagery fits: the darkness, the uncertainty, the loss of control. But if you were actually falling endlessly down an abyss, there would be no question of control. You would be out of control entirely. Here there is that horrifying sense that control has left you just when you most need it and by rights should have it. A terrible imminence overtakes entirely the present moment. Depression has gone too far when, despite a wide margin of safety, you cannot balance anymore. In depression, all that is happening in the present is the anticipation of pain in the future, and the present qua present no longer exists at all.

Depression is a condition that is almost unimaginable to anyone who has not known it. A sequence of metaphors—vines, trees, cliffs, etc.—is the only way to talk about the experience. It's not an easy diagnosis because it depends on metaphors, and the metaphors one patient chooses are different from those selected by another patient. Not so much has changed since Antonio in *The Merchant of Venice* complained:

> It wearies me, you say it wearies you;
> But how I caught it, found it, or came by it
> What stuff 'tis made of, whereof it is born
> I am to learn;
> And such a want-wit sadness makes of me,
> That I have much ado to know myself.

Let us make no bones about it: We do not really know what causes depression. We do not really know what constitutes depression. We do not really know why certain treatments may be effective for depression. We do not know how depression made it through the evolutionary process. We do not know why one person gets a depression from circumstances that do not trouble another. We do not know how will operates in this context.

People around depressives expect them to get themselves together: our society has little room in it for moping. Spouses, parents, children, and friends are all subject to being brought down themselves, and they do not want to be close to measureless pain. No one can do anything but beg for help (if he can do even that) at the lowest depths of a major depression, but once the help is provided, it must also be accepted. We would all like Prozac to do it for us, but in my experience, Prozac doesn't do it unless we help it along. Listen to the people who love you. Believe that they are worth living for even when you don't believe it. Seek out the memories depression takes away and project them into the future. Be brave; be strong; take your pills. Exercise because it's good for you even if every step weighs a thousand pounds. Eat when food itself disgusts you. Reason with yourself when you have lost your reason. These fortune-cookie admonitions sound pat, but the surest way out of depression is to dislike it and not to let yourself grow accustomed to it. Block out the terrible thoughts that invade your mind.

I will be in treatment for depression for a long time. I wish I could say how it happened. I have no idea how I fell so low, and little sense of how I bounced up or fell again, and again, and again. I treated the presence, the vine, in every conventional way I could find, then figured out how to repair the absence as laboriously yet intuitively as I learned to walk or talk. I had many slight lapses, then two serious breakdowns, then a rest, then a third breakdown, and then a few more lapses. After all that, I do what I have to do to avoid further disturbances. Every morning and every night, I look at the pills in my hand: white, pink, red, turquoise. Sometimes they seem like writing in my hand, hieroglyphics saying that the future may be all right and that I owe it to myself to live on and see. I feel sometimes as though I am swallowing my own funeral twice a day, since without these pills, I'd be long gone. I go to see my therapist once a week when I'm at home. I am sometimes bored by our sessions and sometimes interested in an entirely dissociative way and sometimes have a feeling of epiphany. In part, from the things this man said, I rebuilt myself enough to be able to keep swallowing my funeral instead of enacting it. A lot of talking was involved: I believe that words are strong, that they can overwhelm what we fear when fear seems more awful than life is good. I have turned, with an increasingly fine attention, to love. Love is the other way forward. They need to go together: by themselves pills are a weak poison, love a blunt knife, insight a rope that snaps under too much strain. With the lot of them, if you are lucky, you can save the tree from the vine.

I love this century. I would love to have the capacity for time travel because I would love to visit biblical Egypt, Renaissance Italy, Elizabethan England, to see the heyday of the Inca, to meet the inhabitants of Great Zimbabwe, to see what America was like when the indigenous peoples held the land. But there is no other time in which I would prefer to live. I love the comforts of modern life. I love the complexity of our philosophy. I love the sense of vast transformation that hangs on us at this new millennium, the feeling that we are at the brink of knowing more than people have ever known before. I like the relatively high level of social tolerance that exists in the countries where I live. I like being able to travel around the world over and over and over again. I like that people live longer than they have ever lived before, that time is a little more on our side than it was a thousand years ago.

We are, however, facing an unparalleled crisis in our physical environment. We are consuming the production of the earth at a frightening pace, sabotaging the land, sea, and sky. The rain forest is being destroyed; our oceans brim with industrial waste; the ozone layer is depleted. There are far more people in the world than there have ever been before, and next year there will be even more, and the year after that there will be many more again. We are creating problems that will trouble the next generation, and the next, and the next after that. Man has been changing the earth ever since the first flint knife was shaped from a stone and the first seed was sowed by an Anatolian farmer, but the pace of alteration is now getting severely out of hand. I am not an environmental alarmist. I do not believe that we are at the brink of apocalypse right now. But I am convinced that we must take steps to alter our current course if we are not to pilot ourselves into oblivion.

It is an indication of the resilience of humankind that we unearth new solutions to those problems. The world goes on and so does the species. Skin cancer is far more prevalent than it used to be because the atmosphere provides us far less protection from the sun. Summers, I wear lotions and creams with high SPF levels, and they help to keep me safe. I have from time to time gone to a dermatologist, who has snipped off an outsize freckle and sent it off to a lab to be checked. Children who once ran along the beach naked are now slathered in protective ointments. Men who once worked shirtless at noon now wear shirts and try to find the shade. We have the ability to cope with this aspect of this crisis. We invent new ways, which are well short of living in the dark. Sunblock or no sunblock, however, we must try not to destroy what's left. Right now, there's still a lot of ozone out there and it's still doing its job moderately well. It would be better for the environment if everyone stopped using cars, but that's not going to happen unless there's a tidal wave of utter crisis. Frankly, I think there will be men living on the moon before there will be a society free of automotive transport. Radical change is impossible and in many ways undesirable, but change is certainly required.

It appears that depression has been around as long as man has been capable of self-conscious thought. It may be that depression existed even before that time, that monkeys and rats and perhaps octopi were suffering the disease before those first humanoids found their way into their caves. Certainly the symptomatology of our time is more or less indistinguishable from what was described by Hippocrates some twenty-five hundred years ago. Neither depression nor skin cancer is a creation of the twenty-first century. Like skin cancer, depression is a bodily affliction that has escalated in recent times for fairly specific reasons. Let us not stand too long ignoring the clear message of burgeoning problems. Vulnerabilities that in a previous era would have remained undetectable now blossom into full-blown clinical illness. We must not only avail ourselves of the immediate solutions to our current problems, but also seek to contain those problems and to avoid their purloining all our minds. The climbing rates of depression are without question the consequence of modernity. The pace of life, the technological chaos of it, the alienation of

31

people from one another, the breakdown of traditional family structures, the loneliness that is endemic, the failure of systems of belief (religious, moral, political, social—anything that seemed once to give meaning and direction to life) have been catastrophic. Fortunately, we have developed systems for coping with the problem. We have medications that address the organic disturbances, and therapies that address the emotional upheavals of chronic disease. Depression is an increasing cost for our society, but it is not ruinous. We have the psychological equivalents of sunscreens and baseball hats and shade.

But do we have the equivalent of an environmental movement, a system to contain the damage we are doing to the social ozone layer? That there are treatments should not cause us to ignore the problem that is treated. We need to be terrified by the statistics. What is to be done? Sometimes it seems that the rate of illness and the number of cures are in a sort of competition to see which can outstrip the other. Few of us want to, or can, give up modernity of thought any more than we want to give up modernity of material existence. But we must start doing small things now to lower the level of socio-emotional pollution. We must look for faith (in anything: God or the self or other people or politics or beauty or just about anything else) and structure. We must help the disenfranchised whose suffering undermines so much of the world's joy—for the sake both of those huddled masses and of the privileged people who lack profound motivation in their own lives. We must practice the business of love, and we must teach it too. We must ameliorate the circumstances that conduce to our terrifyingly high levels of stress. We must hold out against violence, and perhaps against its representations. This is not a sentimental proposal; it is as urgent as the cry to save the rain forest.

At some point, a point we have not quite reached but will, I think, reach soon, the level of damage will begin to be more terrible than the advances we buy with that damage. There will be no revolution, but there will be the advent, perhaps, of different kinds of schools, different models of family and community, different processes of information. If we are to continue on earth, we will have to do so. We will balance treating illness with changing the circumstances that cause it. We will look to prevention as much as to cure. In the maturity of the new millennium, we will, I hope, save this earth's rain forests, the ozone layer, the rivers and streams, the oceans; and we will also save, I hope, the minds and hearts of the people who live here. Then we will curb our escalating fear of the demons of the noon—our anxiety and depression.

The people of Cambodia live in the compass of immemorial tragedy. During the 1970s, the revolutionary Pol Pot established a Maoist dictatorship in Cambodia in the name of what he called the Khmer Rouge. Years of bloody civil war followed, during which more than 20 percent of the population was slaughtered. The educated elite was obliterated, and the peasantry was regularly moved from one location to another, some of them taken into prison cells where they were mocked and tortured; the entire country lived in perpetual fear. It is hard to rank wars—recent atrocities in Rwanda have been particularly ravaging—but certainly the Pol Pot period was as awful as any time anywhere in recent history. What happens to your emotions when you have seen a quarter of your compatriots murdered, when you have lived yourself in the hardship of a brutal regime, when you are fighting against the odds to rebuild a devastated nation? I hoped to see what happens to feeling among the citizens of a nation when they have all endured such traumatic stress, are desperately poor, have virtually no resources, and have little chance for education or employment. I might have chosen other locations to find suffering, but I did not want to go into a country at war, since the despair psychology of wartime is usually frenzied, while the despair that follows devastation is more numb and all-encompassing. Cambodia is not a country in which faction fought brutally against faction; it is a country in which everyone was at war with everyone else, in which all the mechanisms of society were completely annihilated, in which there was no love left, no idealism, nothing good for anyone.

The Cambodians are in general affable, and they are friendly as can be to foreigners who visit them. Most of them are soft-spoken, gentle, and attractive. It's hard to believe that this lovely country is the one in which Pol Pot's atrocities took place. Everyone I met had a different explanation for how the Khmer Rouge could have happened there, but none of these explanations made sense, just as none of the explanations for the Cultural Revolution or for Stalinism or for Nazism makes sense. These things happen to societies, and in retrospect it is possible to understand why a nation was especially vulnerable to them; but where in the human imagination such behaviors originate is unknowable. The social fabric is always very thin, but it is impossible to know how it gets vaporized entirely as it did in these societies. The American ambassador there told me that the greatest problem for the Khmer people is that traditional Cambodian society has no peaceful mechanism to resolve conflict. "If they have differences," he said, "they have to deny them and suppress them totally, or they have to take out knives and fight." A Cambodian member of the current government said that the people had been too subservient to an absolute monarch for too many years and didn't think to fight against authority until it was too late. I heard at least a dozen other stories; I remain skeptical.

During interviews with people who had suffered atrocities at the hands of the Khmer Rouge, I found that most preferred to look forward. When I pressed them on personal history, however, they would slip into the mournful past tense. The stories I heard were inhuman and terrifying and repulsive. Every adult I met in Cambodia had suffered such external traumas as would have driven most of us to madness or suicide. What they had suffered within their own minds was at yet another level of horror. I went to Cambodia to be humbled by the pain of others, and I was humbled down to the ground.

Five days before I left the country, I met with Phaly Nuon, a sometime candidate for the Nobel Peace Prize, who has set up an orphanage and a center for depressed women in Phnom Penh. She has achieved astonishing success in resuscitating women whose mental afflictions are such that other doctors have left them for dead. Indeed her success has been so enormous that her orphanage is almost entirely staffed by the women she has helped, who have formed a community of generosity around Phaly Nuon. If you save the women, it has been said, they will in turn save the children, and so by tracing a chain of influence one can save the country.

We met in a small room in an old office building near the center of Phnom Penh. She sat on a chair on one side, and I sat on a small sofa opposite. Phaly Nuon's asymmetrical eyes seem to see through you at once and, nonetheless, to welcome you in. Like most Cambodians, she is relatively diminutive by Western standards. Her hair, streaked grey, was pulled back from her face and gave it a certain hardness of emphasis. She can be aggressive in making a point, but she is also shy, smiling and looking down whenever she is not speaking.

We started with her own story. In the early seventies, Phaly Nuon worked for the Cambodian Department of the Treasury and Chamber of Commerce as a typist and shorthand secretary. In 1975, when Phnom Penh fell to Pol Pot and the Khmer Rouge, she was taken from her house with her husband and her children. Her husband was sent off to a location unknown to her, and she had no idea whether he was executed or remained alive. She was put to work in the countryside as a field laborer with her twelve-year-old daughter, her three-year-old son, and her newborn baby. The conditions were terrible and food was scarce, but she worked beside her fellows, "never telling them anything, and never smiling, as none of us ever smiled, because we knew that at any moment we could be put to death." After a few months, she and her family were packed off to another location. During the transfer, a group of soldiers tied her to a tree and made her watch while her daughter was gang-raped and then murdered. A few days later it was Phaly Nuon's turn. She was brought with some fellow laborers to a field outside of town. Then they tied her hands behind her back and roped her legs together. After forcing her to her knees, they tied her to a rod of bamboo, and they made her lean forward over a mucky field, so that her legs had to be tensed or she would lose her balance. The idea was that when she finally dropped of exhaustion, she would fall forward into the mud and, unable to move, would drown in it. Her three-year-old son bellowed and cried beside her. The infant was tied to her so that he would drown in the mud when she fell: Phaly Nuon would be the murderer of her own baby.

Phaly Nuon told a lie. She said that she had, before the war, worked for one of the high-level members of the Khmer Rouge, that she had been his lover, that he would be angry if she were killed. Few people escaped the killing fields, but a captain who perhaps believed Phaly Nuon's story eventually said that he couldn't bear the sound of her children screaming and that bullets were too expensive to waste on killing her quickly, and he untied Phaly Nuon and told her to run. Her baby in one arm and the three-year-old in the other, she bolted deep into the jungle of northeastern Cambodia. She stayed in the jungle for three years, four months, and eighteen days. She never slept twice in the same place. As she wandered, she picked leaves and dug for roots to feed herself and her family, but food was hard to find and other, stronger foragers had often stripped the land bare. Severely malnourished, she began to waste away. Her breast milk soon ran dry, and the baby she could not feed died in her arms. She and her remaining child just barely held on to life and managed to get through the period of war.

By the time Phaly Nuon told me this, we had both moved to the floor between our seats, and she was weeping and rocking back and forth on the balls of her feet, while I sat with my knees under my chin and a hand on her shoulder in as much of an embrace as her trancelike state during her narrative would allow. She went on in a half-whisper. After the war was over, she found her husband. He had been severely beaten around the head and neck, resulting in significant mental deficit. She and her husband and her son were all placed in a border camp near Thailand, where thousands of people lived in temporary tented structures. They were physically and sexually abused by some of the workers at the camp, and helped by others. Phaly Nuon was one of the only educated people there, and, knowing languages, she could talk to the aid workers. She became an important part of the life of the camp, and she and her family were given a wooden hut that passed for comparative luxury. "I helped with certain aid tasks at that time," she recalls. "All the time while I went around, I saw women who were in very bad shape, many of them seeming paralyzed, not moving, not talking, not feeding or caring for their own children. I saw that though they had survived the war, they were now going to die from their depression, their utterly incapacitating post–traumatic stress." Phaly Nuon made a special request to the aid workers and set up her hut in the camp as a sort of psychotherapy center.

She used traditional Khmer medicine (made with varied proportions of more than a hundred herbs and leaves) as a first step. If that did not work or did not work sufficiently well, she would use occidental medicine if it was available, as it sometimes was. "I would hide away stashes of whatever antidepressants the aid workers could bring in," she said, "and try to have enough for the worst cases." She would take her patients to meditate, keeping in her house a Buddhist shrine with flowers in front of it. She would seduce the women into openness. First, she would take about three hours to get each woman to tell her story. Then she would make regular follow-up visits to try to get more of the story, until she finally got the full trust of the depressed woman. "I had to know the stories these women had to tell," she explained, "because I wanted to understand very specifically what each one had to vanquish."

Once this initiation was concluded, she would move on to a formulaic system. "I take it in three steps," she said. "First, I teach them to forget. We have exercises we do each day, so that each day they can forget a little more of the things they will never forget entirely. During this time, I try to distract them with music or with embroidery or weaving, with concerts, with an occasional hour of television, with whatever seems to work, whatever they tell me they like. Depression is under the skin, all the surface of the body has the depression just below it, and we cannot take it out; but we can try to forget the depression even though it is right there.

"When their minds are cleared of what they have forgotten, when they have learned forgetfulness well, I teach them to work. Whatever kind of work they want to do, I will find a way to teach it to them. Some of them train only to clean houses, or to take care of children. Others learn skills they can use with the orphans, and some begin toward a real profession. They must learn to do these things well and to have pride in them.

"And then when they have mastered work, at last, I teach them to love. I built a sort of lean-to and made it a steam bath, and now in Phnom Penh I have a similar one that I use, a little better built. I take them there so that they can become clean, and I teach them how to give one another manicures and pedicures and how to take care of their fingernails, because doing that makes them feel beautiful, and they want so much to feel beautiful. It also puts them in contact with the bodies of other people and makes them give up their bodies to the care of others. It rescues them from physical isolation, which is a usual affliction for them, and that leads to the breakdown of the emotional isolation. While they are together washing and putting on nail polish, they begin to talk together, and bit by bit they learn to trust one another, and by the end of it all, they have learned how to make friends, so that they will never have to be so lonely and so alone again. Their stories, which they have told to no one but me—they begin to tell those stories to one another."

Phaly Nuon later showed me the tools of her psychologist's trade, the little bottles of colored enamel, the steam room, the sticks for pushing back cuticles, the emery boards, the towels. Grooming is one of the primary forms of socialization among primates, and this return to grooming as a socializing force among human beings struck me as curiously organic. I told her that I thought it was difficult to teach ourselves or others how to forget, how to work, and how to love and be loved, but she said it was not so complicated if you could do those three things yourself. She told me about how the women she has treated have become a community, and about how well they do with the orphans of whom they take care.

"There is a final step," she said to me after a long pause. "At the end, I teach them the most important thing. I teach them that these three skills—forgetting, working, and loving—are not three separate skills, but part of one enormous whole, and that it is the practice of these things together, each as part of the others, that makes a difference. It is the hardest thing to convey"—she laughed—"but they all come to understand this, and when they do—why, then they are ready to go into the world again."

Depression now exists as a personal and as a social phenomenon. To treat depression, one must understand the experience of a breakdown, the mode of action of medication, and the most common forms of talking therapy (psychoanalytic, interpersonal, and cognitive). Experience is a good teacher and the mainstream treatments have been tried and tested; but many other treatments, from Saint-John's-wort to psychosurgery, hold out reasonable promise—though there is also more quackery here than in any other area of medicine. Intelligent treatment requires a close examination of specific populations: depression has noteworthy variants particular to children, to the elderly, and to each gender. Substance abusers form a large subcategory of their own. Suicide, in its many forms, is a complication of depression; it is critical to understand how a depression can become fatal.

These experiential matters lead to the epidemiological. It is fashionable to look at depression as a modern complaint, and this is a gross error, which a review of psychiatric history serves to clarify. It is also fashionable to think of the complaint as somehow middle-class and fairly consistent in its manifestations. This is not true. Looking at depression among the poor, we can see that taboos and prejudices are blocking us from helping a population that is singularly receptive to that help. The problem of depression among the poor leads naturally into specific politics. We legislate ideas of illness and treatment in and out of existence.

Biology is not destiny. There are ways to lead a good life with depression. Indeed, people who learn from their depression can develop a particular moral profundity from the experience, and this is the thing with feathers at the bottom of their box of miseries. There is a basic emotional spectrum from which we cannot and should not escape, and I believe that depression is in that spectrum, located near not only grief but also love. Indeed I believe that all the strong emotions stand together, and that every one of them is contingent on what we commonly think of as its opposite. I have for the moment managed to contain the disablement that depression causes, but the depression itself lives forever in the cipher of my brain. It is part of me. To wage war on depression is to fight against oneself, and it is important to know that in advance of the battles. I believe that depression can be eliminated only by undermining the emotional mechanisms that make us human. Science and philosophy must proceed by half-measures.

"Welcome this pain," Ovid once wrote, "for you will learn from it." It is possible (though for the time being unlikely) that, through chemical manipulation, we might locate, control, and eliminate the brain's circuitry of suffering. I hope we will never do it. To take it away would be to flatten out experience, to impinge on a complexity more valuable than any of its component parts are agonizing. If I could see the world in nine dimensions, I'd pay a high price to do it. I would live forever in the haze of sorrow rather than give up the capacity for pain. But pain is not acute depression; one loves and is loved in great pain, and one is alive in the experience of it. It is the walking-death quality of depression that I have tried to eliminate from my life; it is as artillery against that extinction that this book is written.

CHAPTER II

Breakdowns

I did not experience depression until after I had pretty much solved my problems. My mother had died three years earlier and I had begun to come to terms with that; I was publishing my first novel; I was getting along with my family; I had emerged intact from a powerful two-year relationship; I had bought a beautiful new house; I was writing for *The New Yorker*. It was when life was finally in order and all the excuses for despair had been used up that depression came slinking in on its little cat feet and spoiled everything, and I felt acutely that there was no excuse for it under the circumstances. To be depressed when you have experienced trauma or when your life is clearly a mess is one thing, but to sit around and be depressed when you are finally at a remove from trauma and your life is not a mess is awfully confusing and destabilizing. Of course you are aware of deep causes: the perennial existential crisis, the forgotten sorrows of a distant childhood, the slight wrongs done to people now dead, the loss of certain friendships through your own negligence, the truth that you are not Tolstoy, the absence in this world of perfect love, the impulses of greed and uncharity that lie too close to the heart—that sort of thing. But now, as I ran through this inventory, I believed my depression was both a rational state, and an incurable state.

I have not, in certain crucial material ways, had a difficult life. Most people would have been pretty happy with my cards at the start. I've been through some better times and some worse times, by my own standards, but the dips are not sufficient to explain what happened to me. If my life had been more difficult, I would understand my depression very differently. In fact, I had a reasonably happy childhood with two parents who loved me generously, and a younger brother whom they also loved and with whom I generally got on well. It was a family sufficiently intact that I never even imagined a divorce or a real battle between my parents, who loved each other very much indeed; and though they argued from time to time about this or that, they never questioned their absolute devotion to each other and to my brother and me. We always had enough to live comfortably. I was not popular in elementary school or in junior high, but by the end of high school I had a circle of friends with whom I was fairly happy. I always did well academically.

I had been somewhat shy as a child, fearful of rejection in highly exposed situations—but who is not? By the time I was in high school, I was aware of occasional unsettled moods which, again, seem not unusual for adolescence. At one period, in eleventh grade, I became convinced that the building in which I went to classes (which had been standing for almost a hundred years) was going to collapse, and I remember having to steel myself against that strange anxiety day after day. I knew it was peculiar and was relieved when, after about a month, it passed.

Then I went on to college, where I was blissfully happy, and where I met many of the people who are my closest friends to this day. I studied and played hard and woke up to both a range of new emotions and the scope of intellect. Sometimes when I was alone, I would suddenly feel isolated, and the feeling was not simply sorrow at being alone, but fear. I had many friends, and I'd go visit one of them, and I could usually be distracted out of my distress. This was an occasional and not crippling problem. I went on to do my MA in England, and when I finished my studies, I went relatively smoothly to a career as a writer. I stayed in London for a few years. I had a lot of friends, and some dalliance with love. In many ways, all of that has stayed more or less the same. I have had a good life so far, and I'm grateful for it.

When you start having major depression, you tend to look back for the roots of it. You wonder where it came from, whether it was always there, just under the surface, or whether it came on you as suddenly as food poisoning. Since the first breakdown, I've spent months on end cataloging early difficulties, such as they are. I was a breech birth, and some writers have linked breech birth to early trauma. I was dyslexic, though my mother, who identified the problem early, began teaching me ways to compensate for it when I was just two, and it has never been a serious impediment for me. As a small child, I was verbal and uncoordinated. When I asked my mother to identify my earliest trauma, she said that walking had not come easily to me, that while my speech seemed to have been no effort at all, my motor control and balance were late and imperfect. I am told that I fell and fell and fell, that only with great encouragement did I even attempt to stand upright. My subsequent unathleticism determined my unpopularity in elementary school. Of course not being condoned by my peers was disappointing to me, but I always had a few friends and I always liked adults, who also liked me.

I have many odd, unstructured memories from my early childhood, almost all of which are happy. A psychoanalyst I once saw told me that one faint sequence of early memories of which I could make little sense suggested to her that I had once been subject to juvenile sexual abuse. It is certainly possible, but I have never been able to construct a convincing memory of it or adduce other evidence. If something happened, it must have been fairly gentle, because I was a child much scrutinized, and any bruise or disruption would have been observed in me. I remember one episode at summer camp when I was six, when I was suddenly and unreasonably overcome with fear. I can see it vividly: the tennis court up above, the dining hall on my right, and some fifty feet away, the big oak tree under which we sat to hear stories. Suddenly, I couldn't move. I was overcome with the knowledge that something awful was going to happen to me, now or later, and that, as long as I was alive, I wouldn't be free. Life, which had until then seemed to be a solid surface upon which I stood, went suddenly soft and yielding, and I began to slip through it. If I stayed still, I might be all right, but as soon as I moved, I would be in danger again. It seemed to matter very much whether I went left or right or straight on, but I didn't know which direction would save me, at least for the moment. Fortunately a counselor came along and told me to hurry up, I was late for swimming, and the mood broke, but for a long time I remembered it and hoped it wouldn't come back.

I think these things are not unusual for small children. Existential angst among adults, painful though it may be, usually has a gaming self-consciousness to it; the first revelations of human frailty, the first intimations of mortality, are devastating and intemperate. I've seen them in my godchildren and in my nephew. It would be romantic and silly to say that in July of 1969, at Grant Lake Camp, I understood that I would someday die, but I did stumble, for no apparent reason, on my own vulnerability in general, on the fact that my parents did not control the world and all that happened in it, and that I would never be able to control it either. I have a poor memory, and after that episode at camp I became afraid of what is lost through time, and I would lie in bed at night trying to remember things from the day so that I could keep them—an incorporeal acquisitiveness. I particularly valued my parents' good-night kisses, and I used to sleep with my head on a tissue that would catch them if they fell off my face, so that I could put them away and save them forever.

Starting in high school, I was aware of a confused sense of sexuality, which I would say was my life's most impenetrable emotional challenge. I buried the issue behind sociability so as not to confront it, a basic defense that saw me through college. I had some years of uncertainty, a long history of being involved with men and with women; it complicated my relationship to my mother in particular. I have occasionally been prone to a mood of intense anxiety about nothing in particular, an odd mix of sadness and fear that springs from nowhere. It would come over me sometimes when I sat on the school bus as a small child. It would come over me sometimes on Friday nights in college, when the noise of forced festivity overwhelmed the privacy of the darkness. It would come over me sometimes when I was reading, and it would come over me sometimes during sex. It would come over me always when I left home, and it is still an accessory of departure. Even if I am just going away for the weekend, it rushes in as I lock the door behind me. And it would usually come also when I returned home. My mother, a girlfriend, even one of our dogs, would greet me and I would feel so sad, and that sadness frightened me. I dealt with it by interacting compulsively with people, which almost always distracted me. I had to keep whistling a happy tune to slide out of that sadness.

The summer after my senior year of college, I had a small breakdown, but at the time I had no idea what it was. I was traveling in Europe, having the summer I had always wanted, completely free. It had been a sort of graduation present from my parents. I spent a splendid month in Italy, then went to France, then visited a friend in Morocco. I became intimidated by Morocco. It was as though I had been set too free of too many accustomed restraints, and I felt nervous all the time, the way I used to feel backstage right before going on in a school play. I went back to Paris, met some more friends there, had a grand old time, and then went to Vienna, a city I'd always wanted to visit. I could not sleep in Vienna. I arrived, checked into a pension, and met some old friends who were also in Vienna. We made plans to travel together to Budapest. We had a congenial evening out and then I came back and stayed awake all night, terrified of some mistake I thought I'd made, though I didn't know what it was. The next day, I was too edgy to try breakfast in a room full of strangers, but when I went outside, I felt better and decided to see some art and thought I had probably just been overextending myself. My friends had to have dinner with someone else, and when they told me that, I felt stricken to the core, as though I had been told about a murder plot. They agreed to meet me for a drink after dinner. I did not eat dinner. I simply couldn't go into a strange restaurant and order alone (though I had done this many times before); nor could I strike up a conversation with anyone. When I finally met my friends, I was shaking. We went out and I drank much more than I ever drink, and I felt temporarily calm. That night, I stayed awake all night again with a splitting headache and a churning stomach, worrying obsessively about the boat schedule to Budapest. The next day I got through, and during the third night of not sleeping, I was so frightened that I was unable to get up to use the bathroom all night. I called my parents. "I need to come home," I said. They sounded more than a bit surprised, since before this trip I had negotiated every extra day and location, trying to extend my time abroad as much as I could. "Is anything wrong?" they asked, and I could only say that I didn't feel well and that it had all turned out to be less exciting than I had anticipated. My mother was sympathetic. "Traveling alone can be hard," she said. "I thought you were meeting friends there, but even so, it can be awfully tiring." My father said, "If you want to come home, go charge a ticket to my card and come home."

I bought the ticket, packed my bags, and came home that afternoon. My parents met me at the airport. "What happened?" they asked, but I could only say that I couldn't stay there anymore. In their hugs, I felt safe for the first time in weeks. I sobbed with relief. When we got back to the apartment where I'd grown up, I was depressed and felt completely stupid. I had blown my big travel summer; I had come back to New York, where I had nothing to do except old chores. I had never seen Budapest. I called a few friends, who were surprised to hear from me. I didn't even try to explain what had happened. I spent the rest of the summer living at home. I was bored, annoyed, and rather sullen, though we did have some good times together.

I more or less forgot about all that in the years that followed. After that summer, I went to graduate school in England. Starting at a new university in a new country, I hardly panicked at all. I settled right into the new way of life, made friends quickly, did well academically. I loved England, and nothing seemed to frighten me any longer. The anxious self that had gone off to college in America had given way to this robust, confident, easygoing fellow. When I had a party, everyone wanted to come. My closest friends (who are still among my closest friends) were people with whom I sat up all night, in a deep and rapid intimacy that was fantastically pleasurable. I called home once a week, and my parents observed that I sounded as happy as they'd ever heard me. I craved company whenever I was feeling unsettled, and I found it. For two years, I was happy most of the time, and unhappy only about bad weather, the difficulty of making everyone love me instantly, not having enough sleep, and beginning to lose my hair. The only depressive tendency that was always present in me was nostalgia: unlike Edith Piaf, I regret everything just because it is finished, and already when I was twelve, I lamented the time that had gone by. Even in the best of spirits, it's always been as though I wrestle with the present in a vain effort to stop its becoming the past.

I remember my early twenties as reasonably placid. I decided, almost on a whim, to become an adventurer and took to ignoring my anxiety even when it was connected to frightening situations. Eighteen months after I finished my graduate work, I started traveling back and forth to Soviet Moscow and lived part-time in an illegal squat with some artists I got to know there. When someone tried to mug me one night in Istanbul, I resisted successfully and he ran off without having got anything from me. I allowed myself to consider every kind of sexuality; I left most of my repressions and erotic fears behind. I let my hair get long; I cut it short. I performed with a rock band a few times; I went to the opera. I had developed a lust for experience, and I had as many experiences as I could in as many places as I could afford to visit. I fell in love and set up happy domestic arrangements.

And then in August 1989, when I was twenty-five, my mother was diagnosed with ovarian cancer and my irreproachable world began to crumble. If she had not fallen ill, my life would have been completely different; if that story had been a little bit less tragic, then perhaps I would have gone through life with depressive tendencies but no breakdown; or perhaps I would have had a breakdown later on as part of midlife crisis; or perhaps I would have had one just when and as I did. If the first part of an emotional biography is precursor experiences, the second part is triggering experiences. Most severe depressions have precursor smaller depressions that have passed largely unnoticed or simply unexplained. Of course many people who never develop depression have experiences that would retrospectively be defined as precursor episodes if they had led to anything, and that get dropped out of memory only because what they might have foreshadowed never materializes.

I will not detail how everything fell apart because to those who have known wasting sickness this will be clear and to those who have not it remains perhaps as inexplicable as it was to me when I was twenty-five. Suffice it to say that things were dreadful. In 1991, my mother died. She was fifty-eight. I was paralytically sad. Despite many tears and enormous sorrow, despite the disappearance of the person I had depended on so constantly and for so long, I did okay in the period after my mother's death. I was sad and I was angry, but I was not crazy.

That summer, I began psychoanalysis. I told the woman who would be my analyst that I needed one promise before I could begin, and that was that she would continue the analysis through until we had completed it, no matter what happened, unless she became seriously ill. She was in her late sixties. She agreed. She was a charming and wise woman who reminded me a little bit of my mother. I relied on our daily meetings to keep my grief contained.

In early 1992, I fell in love with someone who was brilliant, beautiful, generous, kind, and fantastically present in all our relations, but who was also incredibly difficult. We had a tumultuous though often happy relationship. She became pregnant in the autumn of 1992 and had an abortion, which gave me an unanticipated feeling of loss. In late 1993, the week before my thirtieth birthday, we broke up by mutual agreement and with much mutual pain. I slipped another ratchet down.

In March 1994, my analyst told me that she was retiring because the commute from her Princeton house into New York had become too burdensome. I had been feeling disconnected from our work together and had been considering terminating it; nonetheless, when she broke that news, I burst into uncontrollable sobs and cried for an hour. I don't usually cry much; I hadn't cried like that since my mother's death. I felt utterly, devastatingly lonely and entirely betrayed. We had a few months (she wasn't sure how many; it turned out to be more than a year) to work on closure before her retirement became effective.

Later that month, I complained to the selfsame analyst that a loss of feeling, a numbness, had infected all my human relations. I didn't care about love; about my work; about family; about friends. My writing slowed, then stopped. "I know nothing," the painter Gerhard Richter once wrote. "I can do nothing. I understand nothing. I know nothing. Nothing. And all this misery does not even make me particularly unhappy." So I too found all strong emotion gone, except for a certain nagging anxiety. I had always had a headstrong libido that had often led me into trouble; it seemed to have evaporated. I felt none of my habitual yearning for physical/emotional intimacy and was not attracted either to people in the streets or to those I knew and had loved; in erotic circumstances, my mind kept drifting off to shopping lists and work I needed to do. This gave me a feeling that I was losing my self, and that scared me. I made a point of scheduling pleasures into my life. During the spring of 1994, I went to parties and tried and failed to have fun; I saw friends and tried and failed to connect; I bought expensive things I'd wanted in the past and had no satisfaction from them; and I pushed on with previously untried extremes to reawaken my libido, attending pornographic films and in extremis soliciting prostitutes for their services. I was not particularly horrified by any of these new behaviors, but I was also unable to get any pleasure, or even release, from them. My analyst and I discussed the situation: I was depressed. We tried to get to the root of the problem while I felt the disconnect slowly but relentlessly increasing. I began to complain that I was overwhelmed by the messages on my answering machine and I fixated on that: I saw the calls, often from friends, as an impossible weight. Every time I returned the calls, more would come in. I had also become afraid of driving. When I drove at night, I couldn't see the road, and my eyes kept going dry. I constantly thought I was going to swerve into the barrier or into another car. I would be in the middle of the highway and suddenly I would realize that I didn't know how to drive. In consternation, I would pull over to the side of the road in a cold sweat. I began to spend weekends in the city to avoid having to drive. My analyst and I ran through the history of my anxious blues. It occurred to me that my relationship with my girlfriend had ended because of an earlier stage of depression, though I knew it was also possible that the end of that relationship had helped to cause the depression. As I worked on that knot, I kept redating the beginning of the depression: since the breakup; since my mother's death; since the beginning of my mother's two-year illness; since the end of a previous relationship; since puberty; since birth. Soon, I could not think of a time or a behavior that was not symptomatic. Still, what I was experiencing was only neurotic depression, characterized more by anxious sorrow than by madness. It appeared to be within my control; it was a sustained version of something I had suffered before, something familiar at one level or another to many healthy people. Depression dawns as gradually as adulthood.

In June 1994, I began to be constantly bored. My first novel was published in England, and yet its favorable reception did little for me. I read the reviews indifferently and felt tired all the time. In July, back home in New York, I found myself burdened by social events, even by conversation. It all seemed like more effort than it was worth. The subway proved intolerable. My analyst, who was not yet retired, said that I was suffering from a slight depression. We discussed reasons, as though to name the beast would be to tame it. I knew too many people and did too much; I thought I might try to cut back.

At the end of August, I had an attack of kidney stones, an ailment that had visited me once before. I called my doctor, who promised to notify the hospital and to expedite my passage through the emergency room. When I got to the hospital, however, no one seemed to have received any notice. The pain of kidney stones is excruciating, and as I sat waiting, it was as though someone, having dipped my central nervous column in acid, was now peeling the nerves to their raw core. Although I described the pain I was in several times to several attendants, no one did anything. And then something seemed to snap in me. Standing in the middle of my cubicle in the New York Hospital emergency room, I began to scream. They put a shot of morphine into my arm. The pain abated. Soon enough, it returned: I was in and out of the hospital for five days. I was catheterized four times; I was placed, ultimately, on the maximum allowed dose of morphine, which was supplemented with injections of Demerol every few hours. I was told that my stones did not visualize well and that I was not a candidate for lithotripsy, which would have eliminated them fast. Surgery was possible but it was painful and might be dangerous. I had not wanted to trouble my father, who was on holiday in Maine; now I wanted the contact with him, as he knew this hospital well from the days when my mother was always there, and could help with arrangements. He seemed unconcerned. "Kidney stones, those will pass, I'm sure you'll be fine, and I'll see you when I get home," he said. Meanwhile, I did not sleep more than three hours any night. I was working on an enormous assignment, an article about deaf politics, and in a haze I talked to fact-checkers and editors. I felt my control over my own life slipping. "If this pain doesn't stop," I said to a friend, "then I'm going to kill myself." I had never said that before.

When I left the hospital, I was afraid all the time. Either the pain or the painkillers had completely undermined my mind. I knew that the stones might still be moving around and that I could relapse. I was frightened of being alone. I went with a friend to my apartment, collected a few things, and moved out. It was a vagabond week; I migrated from friend to friend. These people mostly had to go to work during the day, and I would stay in their houses, avoiding the street, careful never to go too far from the phone. I was still taking prophylactic painkillers and I felt a little crazy. I was angry at my father, angry in an irrational, spoiled, foul way. My father apologized for what I called his uncaring behavior and tried to explain that he had only meant to communicate his relief that I had a nonfatal disease. He said he had believed my relative stoicism on the phone. I entered a hysteria of which I cannot now make any sense. I refused to speak to him or to tell him where I had gone. From time to time, I would call and leave a message on his machine: "I hate you and I wish you were dead" was how they usually began. Sleeping pills got me through the nights. I had one small relapse and went back up to the hospital; it was nothing serious, but it scared me to death. In retrospect, I can say that that was the week I went bananas.

At the end of the week, I headed up to Vermont for the wedding of some friends. It was a beautiful late-summer weekend. I had almost canceled the trip, but after getting details of a hospital near where the wedding was to take place, I decided to try to go. I arrived on Friday in time for dinner and square dancing (I did not do any square dancing), and I saw someone I had known very marginally in college ten years earlier. We talked, and I felt overcome with more emotion than I'd felt in years. I felt myself shining; I felt ecstatic and did not guess how nothing good was to come of that. I rode from emotion to emotion in a way that was almost absurd.

After the Vermont wedding, the slippage was steady. I worked less and less well. I canceled plans to go to England for another wedding, feeling that the trip was just more than I could handle, though I had, a year earlier, gone back and forth to London regularly without much trouble. I had begun to feel that no one could love me and that I would never be in a relationship again. I had no sexual feelings at all. I began eating irregularly because I seldom felt hungry. My analyst said that it was still depression, and I felt tired of that word and tired of the analyst. I said that I was not crazy but was afraid I could become crazy and did she think I was going to end up on antidepressants, and she told me that avoiding medication was courageous and that we could work everything through. That conversation was the last one I initiated; those were my last feelings for a long time.

Major depression has a number of defining factors—mostly having to do with withdrawal, though agitated or atypical depression may have an intense negativity rather than a flattened passivity—and is usually fairly easy to recognize; it deranges sleep, appetites, and energy. It tends to increase sensitivity to rejection, and it may be accompanied by a loss of self-confidence and self-regard. It seems to depend on both hypothalamic functions (which regulate sleep, appetites, and energy) and cortical functions (which translate experience into philosophy and worldview). The depression that occurs as a phase in manic-depressive (or bipolar) illness is much more strongly genetically determined (about 80 percent) than is standard depression (about 10 to 50 percent); though it is more broadly treatment-responsive, it is not easier to control, especially since antidepressant drugs may launch mania. The greatest danger with manic-depressive illness is that it sometimes bursts into what are called mixed states, where one is manically depressed—full of negative feeling and grandiose about them. That is a prime condition for suicide, and it too can be brought on by the use of antidepressant medications without the mood stabilizers that are necessary parts of bipolar medication. Depression can be enervating or atypical/agitated. In the first, you don't feel like doing anything; in the second, you feel like killing yourself. A breakdown is a crossover into madness. It is, to borrow a metaphor from physics, uncharacteristic behavior of matter that is determined by hidden variables. It is also a cumulative effect: whether you can see them or not, the factors leading to a depressive breakdown gather over the years, usually over a lifetime. There is no life that does not have the material for despair in it, but some people go too close to the edge and others manage to stay sometimes sad in a safe clearing far from the cliffs. Once you cross over, the rules all change. Everything that had been written in English is now in Chinese; everything that went fast is now slow; sleep is for clarity while wakefulness is a sequence of unconnected, senseless images. Your senses slowly abandon you in depression. "There's a sudden point when you can feel the chemistry going," Mark Weiss, a depressive friend, once said to me. "My breathing changes and my breath stinks. My piss smells disgusting. My face comes apart in the mirror. I know when it's there."

By the time I was three, I had decided I wanted to be a novelist. Ever since, I had been looking forward to publishing a novel. When I was thirty, my first novel was published, and I had scheduled a reading tour, and I was hating the idea. A good friend had volunteered to throw a book party for me on October 11. I love parties and I love books, and I knew I should have been ecstatic, but in fact I was too lackluster to invite many people, and too tired to stand up much during the party. Memory functions and emotional functions are distributed throughout the brain, but the frontal cortex and limbic systems are key to both, and when you affect the limbic system, which controls emotion, you also touch on memory. I remember that party only in ghostly outlines and washed-out colors: grey food, beige people, muddy light in the rooms. I do remember that I was sweating horribly during it, and that I was dying to leave. I tried to put it all down to stress. I was determined, at any cost, to keep up appearances, an impulse that was to serve me well. I did it: no one seemed to notice anything strange. I got through the evening.

When I got home that night, I began to feel frightened. I lay in bed, not sleeping, hugging my pillow for comfort. Over the next two and a half weeks things got worse and worse. Shortly before my thirty-first birthday, I went to pieces. My whole system seemed to be caving in. I was not going out with anyone at the time. My father had volunteered to organize a birthday party for me, but I couldn't bear the idea, and we had agreed instead to go to a favorite restaurant with four of my closest friends. On the day before my birthday, I left the house only once, to buy some groceries. On the way home from the store, I suddenly lost control of my lower intestine and soiled myself. I could feel the stain spreading as I hastened home. When I got in, I dropped the grocery bag, rushed to the bathroom, got undressed, and went to bed.

I did not sleep much that night, and I could not get up the following day. I knew I could not go to any restaurant. I wanted to call my friends and cancel, but I couldn't. I lay very still and thought about speaking, trying to figure out how to do it. I moved my tongue but there were no sounds. I had forgotten how to talk. Then I began to cry, but there were no tears, only a heaving incoherence. I was on my back. I wanted to turn over, but I couldn't remember how to do that either. I tried to think about it, but the task seemed colossal. I thought that perhaps I'd had a stroke, and then I cried again for a while. At about three o'clock that afternoon, I managed to get out of bed and go to the bathroom. I returned to bed shivering. Fortunately, my father called. I answered the phone. "You have to cancel tonight," I said, my voice shaky. "What's wrong?" he kept asking, but I didn't know.

There is a moment, if you trip or slip, before your hand shoots out to break your fall, when you feel the earth rushing up at you and you cannot help yourself, a passing, fraction-of-a-second terror. I felt that way hour after hour after hour. Being anxious at this extreme level is bizarre. You feel all the time that you want to do something, that there is some affect that is unavailable to you, that there's a physical need of impossible urgency and discomfort for which there is no relief, as though you were constantly vomiting from your stomach but had no mouth. With the depression, your vision narrows and begins to close down; it is like trying to watch TV through terrible static, where you can sort of see the picture but not really; where you cannot ever see people's faces, except almost if there is a close-up; where nothing has edges. The air seems thick and resistant, as though it were full of mushed-up bread. Becoming depressed is like going blind, the darkness at first gradual, then encompassing; it is like going deaf, hearing less and less until a terrible silence is all around you, until you cannot make any sound of your own to penetrate the quiet. It is like feeling your clothing slowly turning into wood on your body, a stiffness in the elbows and the knees progressing to a terrible weight and an isolating immobility that will atrophy you and in time destroy you.

My father came down to my apartment with a friend of mine, trailing my brother and his fiancée. Fortunately, my father had keys. I had had nothing to eat in almost two days, and they tried to get me to eat a little soup. Everyone thought that I must have some kind of terrible virus. I ate a few bites, then threw up all over myself. I couldn't stop crying. I hated my house but couldn't leave it. The next day, I managed, somehow, to get to my analyst's office. "I think I'm going to have to start taking medication," I said, diving deep for the words. "I'm sorry," she said, and called the psychopharmacologist, who agreed to see me in an hour. She did at last, however belatedly, see that we had to call in help. In the 1950s, in keeping with the thinking of his time, a psychoanalyst I know was told by his supervisor that if he wanted to start a patient on medication, he would have to stop the analysis. Perhaps it was something old-fashioned that had allowed my analyst to encourage me to avoid medication?

Or perhaps she too bought into the appearances I was struggling to keep up? I will never know.

The psychopharmacologist seemed to have come out of some movie about shrinks: his office had fading mustard-colored silk wallpaper and old-fashioned sconces on the walls and was piled high with books with titles such as *Addicted to Misery* and *Suicidal Behavior: The Search for Psychic Economy.* He was in his seventies, smoked cigars, had a Central European accent, and wore carpet slippers. He had elegant prewar manners and a kindly smile. He asked me a rapid string of specific questions—how did I feel in the morning versus the afternoon? How difficult was it for me to laugh about anything? Did I know what I was afraid of? Had my sleep patterns and appetites shifted?—and I did my best to answer him. "Well, well," he said calmly as I trotted out my horrors. "Very classic indeed. Don't you worry, we'll soon have you well." He wrote out a prescription for Xanax, then burrowed around to find a starter kit of Zoloft. He gave me detailed instructions on how to begin taking it. "You'll come back tomorrow," he said with a smile. "The Zoloft will not work for some time. The Xanax will alleviate your anxiety immediately. Do not worry about its addictive qualities and so on, as these are not your problems at the moment. Once we have lifted the anxiety somewhat, we will be able to see the depression more clearly and take care of that. Don't worry, you have a very normal group of symptoms."

My first day on medication, I moved into my father's apartment. My father was almost seventy at the time, and most men of that age cannot easily tolerate complete shifts in their lives. My father is to be praised not only for his generous devotion, but also for the flexibility of mind and spirit that allowed him to understand how he could be my mainstay through rough times, and for the courage that helped him to be that mainstay. He picked me up at the doctor's office and took me home with him. I had not brought clean clothes with me, but I didn't really need them since I was hardly to get out of bed for the next week. For the moment, the panic was my only sensation. The Xanax would relieve the panic if I took enough of it, but enough of it was enough to make me collapse completely into a thick, confusing, dream-heavy sleep. The days were like this: I would wake up, knowing that I was experiencing extreme panic. What I wanted was only to take enough panic medication to allow me to go back to sleep, and then I wanted to sleep until I got well. When I would wake up a few hours later, I wanted to take more sleeping pills. Killing myself, like dressing myself, was much too elaborate an agenda to enter my mind; I did *not* spend hours imagining how I would do such a thing. All I wanted was for "it" to stop; I could not have managed even to be so specific as to say what "it" was. I could not manage to say much; words, with which I have always been intimate, seemed suddenly very elaborate, difficult metaphors the use of which entailed much more energy than I could possibly muster. "Melancholia ends up in loss of meaning . . . I become silent and I die," Julia Kristeva once wrote. "Melancholy persons are foreigners in their mother tongue. The dead language they speak foreshadows their suicide." Depression, like love, trades in clichés, and it is difficult to speak of it without lapsing into the rhetoric of saccharine pop tunes; it is so vivid when it is experienced that the notion that others have known anything similar seems altogether implausible. Emily Dickinson wrote perhaps the most eloquent description of a breakdown ever committed to the page:

> I felt a Funeral, in my Brain,
> And Mourners to and fro
> Kept treading—treading—till it seemed
> That Sense was breaking through—
>
> And when they all were seated,
> A Service, like a Drum—
> Kept beating—beating—till I thought
> My Mind was going numb—
>
> And then I heard them lift a Box
> And creak across my Soul
> With those same Boots of Lead, again,
> Then Space—began to toll,
>
> As if the Heavens were a Bell,
> And Being, but an Ear,
> And I, and Silence, some strange Race
> Wrecked, solitary, here—
>
> And then a Plank in Reason, broke,
> And I dropped down, and down—
> And hit a World, at every plunge,
> And Finished knowing—then—

There has been relatively little written about the fact that breakdowns are preposterous; seeking dignity, and seeking to dignify the sufferings of others, one can easily overlook this fact. It is, however, real and true, and obvious when you are depressed. Depression minutes are like dog years, based on some artificial notion of time. I can remember lying frozen in bed, crying because I was too frightened to take a shower, and at the same time knowing that showers are not scary. I kept running through the individual steps in my mind: you turn and put your feet on the floor; you stand; you walk from here to the bathroom; you open the bathroom door; you walk to the edge of the tub; you turn on the water; you step under the water; you rub yourself with soap; you rinse; you step out; you dry yourself; you walk back to the bed. Twelve steps, which sounded to me then as onerous as a tour through the stations of the cross. But I knew, logically, that showers were easy, that for years I had taken a shower *every day* and that I had done it so quickly and so matter-of-factly that it had not even warranted comment. I knew that those twelve steps were really quite manageable. I knew that I could even get someone else to help me with some of them. I would have a few seconds of relief contemplating that thought. Someone else could open the bathroom door. I knew I could probably manage two or three steps, so with all the force in my body I would sit up; I would turn and put my feet on the floor; and then I would feel so incapacitated and so frightened that I would roll over and lie facedown, my feet still on the floor. I would sometimes start to cry again, weeping not only because of what I could not do, but because the fact that I could not do it seemed so idiotic to me. All over the world people were taking showers. Why, oh why, could I not be one of them? And then I would reflect that those people also had families and jobs and bank accounts and passports and dinner plans and problems, real problems, cancer and hunger and the death of their children and isolating loneliness and failure; and I had so few problems by comparison, except that I couldn't turn over again, until a few hours later, when my father or a friend would come in and help to hoist my feet back up onto the bed. By then, the idea of a shower would have come to seem foolish and unrealistic, and I would be relieved to have been able to get my feet back up, and I would lie in the safety of the bed and feel ridiculous. And sometimes in some quiet part of me there was a little bit of laughter at that ridiculousness, and my ability to see that, is, I think, what got me through. Always at the back of my mind there was a voice, calm and clear, that said, don't be so maudlin; don't do anything melodramatic. Take off your clothes, put on your pajamas, go to bed; in the morning, get up, get dressed, and do whatever it is that you're supposed to do. I heard that voice all the time, that voice like my mother's. There was a sadness and a terrible loneliness as I contemplated what was lost. "Did anyone—not just the red-hot cultural center, but anyone, even my dentist—care that I had withdrawn from the fray?" Daphne Merkin wrote in a confessional essay on her own depression. "Would people mourn me if I never returned, never took up my place again?"

By the time evening came around, I was able to get out of bed. Most depression is circadian, improving during the day and then descending again by morning. At dinner, I would feel unable to eat, but I could get up and sit in the dining room with my father, who canceled all other plans to be with me. I could also speak by then. I tried to explain what it was like. My father nodded, implacably assured me that it would pass, and tried to make me eat. He cut up my food. I told him not to feed me, that I wasn't five, but when I was defeated by the difficulty of getting a piece of lamb chop onto my fork, he would do it for me. All the while, he would remember feeding me when I was a tiny child, and he would make me promise, jesting, to cut up his lamb chops when he was old and had lost his teeth. He had been in touch with some of my friends, and some of my friends had called me anyway, and after dinner I would feel well enough to call some of them back. Sometimes, one would even come over after dinner. Against the odds, I could usually even have a shower before bed! And no drink after crossing the desert was ever lovelier than that triumph and the cleanliness. Before bed, Xanaxed out but not yet asleep, I would joke with my father and with friends about it, and that rare intimacy that surrounds illness would make itself felt in the room, and sometimes I would feel too much and begin to cry again, and then it was time to turn off the lights, so that I could go back to sleep. Sometimes close friends would sit with me until I drifted off. One friend used to hold my hand while she sang lullabies. Some evenings, my father read to me from the books he had read me when I was a child. I would stop him. "Two weeks ago, I was publishing my novel," I would say. "I used to work twelve hours and then go to four parties in an evening, some days. What's happened?" My father would assure me, sunnily, that I would be able to do it all again, soon. He could as well have told me that I would soon be able to build myself a helicopter out of cookie dough and fly on it to Neptune, so clear did it seem to me that my real life, the one I had lived before, was now definitively over. From time to time, the panic would lift for a little while. Then came the calm despair. The inexplicability of it all defied logic. It was hellishly embarrassing to tell people I was depressed, when my life seemed to have so much good and love and material comfort in it; for all but my close friends, I developed an "obscure tropical virus" that I "must have picked up last summer, traveling." The lamb-chop question became emblematic to me. A poet friend, Elizabeth Prince, wrote:

> The night
> was late and soggy: It was
> New York in July.

Breakdowns

I was in my room, hiding,
hating the need to swallow.

Later, I read in Leonard Woolf's diary his description of Virginia's depressions: "If left to herself, she would have eaten nothing at all and would have gradually starved to death. It was extraordinarily difficult ever to get her to eat enough to keep her strong and well. Pervading her insanity generally there was always a sense of some guilt, the origin and exact nature of which I could never discover; but it was attached in some peculiar way particularly to food and eating. In the early acute, suicidal stage of the depression, she would sit for hours overwhelmed with hopeless melancholia, silent, making no response to anything said to her. When the time for a meal came, she would pay no attention whatsoever to the plate of food put before her. I could usually induce her to eat a certain amount, but it was a terrible process. Every meal took an hour or two; I had to sit by her side, put a spoon or fork in her hand, and every now and again ask her very quietly to eat and at the same time touch her arm or hand. Every five minutes or so she might automatically eat a spoonful."

You are constantly told in depression that your judgment is compromised, but part of depression is that it touches cognition. That you are having a breakdown does not mean that your life isn't a mess. If there are issues you have successfully skirted or avoided for years, they come cropping back up and stare you full in the face, and one aspect of depression is a deep knowledge that the comforting doctors who assure you that your judgment is bad are wrong. You are in touch with the real terribleness of your life. You can accept rationally that later, after the medication sets in, you will be better able to deal with the terribleness, but you will not be free of it. When you are depressed, the past and future are absorbed entirely by the present moment, as in the world of a three-year-old. You cannot remember a time when you felt better, at least not clearly; and you certainly cannot imagine a future time when you will feel better. Being upset, even profoundly upset, is a temporal experience, while depression is atemporal. Breakdowns leave you with no point of view.

There's a lot going on during a depressive episode. There are changes in neurotransmitter function; changes in synaptic function; increased or decreased excitability between neurons; alterations of gene expression; hypometabolism in the frontal cortex (usually) or hypermetabolism in the same area; raised levels of thyroid releasing hormone (TRH); disruption of function in the amygdala and possibly the hypothalamus (areas within the brain); altered levels of melatonin (a hormone that the pineal gland makes from serotonin); increased prolactin (increased lactate in anxiety-prone individuals will bring on panic attacks); flattening of twenty-four-hour body temperature; distortion of twenty-four-hour cortisol secretion; disruption of the circuit that links the thalamus, basal ganglia, and frontal lobes (again, centers in the brain); increased blood flow to the frontal lobe of the dominant hemisphere; decreased blood flow to the occipital lobe (which controls vision); lowering of gastric secretions. It is difficult to know what to make of all of these phenomena. Which are causes of depression; which are symptoms; which are merely coincidental? You might think that the raised levels of TRH mean that TRH causes bad feelings, but in fact administering high doses of TRH may be a temporarily useful treatment of depression. As it turns out, the body begins producing TRH during depression for its antidepressant capacities. And TRH, which is not generally an antidepressant, can be utilized as an antidepressant immediately after a major depressive episode because the brain, though it is having a lot of problems in a depression, also becomes supersensitive to the things that can help to solve those problems. Brain cells change their functions readily, and during an episode, the ratio between the pathological changes (which cause depression) and the adaptive ones (which fight it) determines whether you stay sick or get better. If you have medications that exploit or aid the adaptive factors enough to put down the pathological ones once and for all, then you break free of the cycle and your brain can get on with its usual routines.

The more episodes you have, the more likely you are to have more episodes, and in general the episodes, over a lifetime, get worse and closer together. This acceleration is a clue to how the disease works. The initial onset of depression is usually connected either to kindling events or to tragedy; people with a genetic predisposition to develop depression are, as Kay Jamison—a charismatic psychologist whose texts, academic and popular, have done a great deal to change thinking about mood disorders—has observed, "like dry and brittle pyres, unshielded against the inevitable sparks thrown off by living." The recurrences at some point break free of circumstance. If you stimulate seizures in an animal every day, the seizures eventually become automatic; the animal will go on having them once a day even if you withdraw the stimulation. In much the same way, the brain that has gone into depression a few times will continue to return to depression over and over. This suggests that depression, even if it is occasioned by external tragedy, ultimately changes the structure, as well as the biochemistry, of the brain. "So it's not as benign an illness as we used to suppose," explains Robert Post, chief of the Biological Psychiatry Branch of the National Institute of Mental Health (NIMH). "It tends to be recurrent; it tends to run downhill; and so one should in the face of several episodes consider long-term preventative treatment to avoid all the horrible consequences." Kay Jamison thumps the table when she gets going on this subject. "It's not like depression's an innocuous thing. You know, in addition to being a miserable, awful, nonconstructive state, for the most part, it also kills people. Not only through suicide, but also through higher heart disease, lowered immune response, and so on." Frequently, patients who are medication-responsive cease to be responsive if they keep cycling on and off the medications; with each episode, there is an increased 10 percent risk that the depression will become chronic and inescapable. "It's sort of like a primary cancer that's very drug-responsive, but then once it metastasizes, it doesn't respond at all," Post explains. "If you have too many episodes, it changes your biochemistry for the bad, possibly permanently. At that point, many therapists are still looking in completely the wrong direction. If the episode now occurs on automatic, what good is it to worry about the stressor that kicked off the original process? It's just too late for that." That which is mended is but patched and can never be whole again.

Three separate events—decrease in serotonin receptors; rise in cortisol, a stress hormone; and depression—are coincident. Their sequence is unknown: it's a sort of chicken and chick and egg mystery. If you lesion the serotonin system in an animal brain, the levels of cortisol go up. If you raise levels of cortisol, serotonin seems to go down. If you stress a person, corticotropin releasing factor (CRF) goes up and causes the level of cortisol to go up. If you depress a person, levels of serotonin go down. What does this mean? The substance of the decade has been serotonin, and the treatments most frequently used for depression in the United States are ones that raise the functional level of serotonin in the brain. Every time you affect serotonin, you also modify the stress systems and change the level of cortisol in the brain. "I wouldn't say that cortisol causes depression," says Elizabeth Young, who works on this field at the University of Michigan, "but it may well exacerbate a minor condition and create a real syndrome." Cortisol, once it is produced, binds to glucocorticoid receptors in the brain. Antidepressants increase the number of these glucocorticoid receptors—which then absorb the excess cortisol that is floating around up there. This is extremely important for overall body regulation. The glucocorticoid receptors actually turn on and off some genes, and when you have relatively few receptors being swamped with a lot of cortisol, the system goes into overdrive. "It's like having a heating system," Young says. "If the temperature sensor for the thermostat is in a spot that's become drafty, the heat will never turn off even though the room is scalding. If you add a few more sensors located around the room, you can get the system back under control."

Under ordinary circumstances, cortisol levels stick to fairly straightforward rules. Cortisol's circadian pattern is to be up in the morning (it's what gets you out of bed) and then to go down during the day. In depressed patients, cortisol tends to remain elevated throughout the day. Something's wrong with the inhibitory circuits that should be turning off the production of cortisol as the day wears on, and this may be part of why the jolted feeling that is usual first thing in the morning continues so far into the day for depressed people. It may be possible to regulate depression by addressing the cortisol system directly, instead of working through the serotonin system. Building on basic research done at Michigan, investigators elsewhere have treated treatment-resistant depression patients with ketoconazole, a cortisol-reducing medication, and almost 70 percent of these patients showed marked improvement. At the moment, ketoconazole causes too many side effects to be attractive as an antidepressant, but several major pharmaceutical companies are investigating related medications that may not have these negative side effects. Such treatment must be carefully regulated, however, since cortisol is necessary for fight-or-flight responses; for that adrenal energy that helps one to struggle on in the face of difficulty; for anti-inflammatory action; for decision making and resolution; and most importantly, for knocking the immune system into action in the face of an infectious disease.

Cortisol patterning studies have recently been done on baboons and air traffic controllers. The baboons who had long-term high cortisol tended to be paranoid, unable to distinguish between a real threat and a mildly uncomfortable situation, likely to fight as desperately over a banana next to a tree heavy with ripe fruit as over their life. Among air traffic controllers, those who were psychologically healthy had an exact correlation between the extent to which they were overworked and their level of cortisol, while those who were in poor condition had their cortisol skyrocketing and peaking all over the place. Once the cortisol/stress correlation gets distorted, you can get hysterical about bananas; you will find that everything that happens to you is stressful. "And that is a form of depression, and then of course being depressed is itself stressful," observes Young. "A downward spiral."

Once you've had a stress sufficient to cause a protracted increase of your cortisol levels, your cortisol system is damaged, and in the future it will not readily turn off once it has been activated. Thereafter, the elevation of cortisol after a small trauma may not normalize as it would under ordinary circumstances. Like anything that has been broken once, the cortisol system is prone to break again and again, with less and less external pressure. People who have had myocardial infarction after great physical strain are subject to relapse even while sitting in an armchair—the heart is now a bit worn-out, and sometimes it just gives up even without much strain. The same thing can happen to the mind.

The fact that something is medical doesn't contravene its having psychosocial origins. "My wife is an endocrinologist," says Juan López, who works with Young, "and she sees kids with diabetes. Well, diabetes is clearly a disease of the pancreas, but external factors influence it. Not only what you eat, but also how stressed you are—kids in really bad homes get frantic and their blood sugar goes haywire. The fact that this happens doesn't make diabetes a psychological disease." In the field of depression, psychological stress transduces to biological change, and vice versa. If a person subjects himself to extreme stress, CRF is released and often helps bring about the biological reality of depression. The psychological techniques for preventing yourself from getting too stressed can help to keep down your levels of CRF, and so of cortisol. "You've got your genes," López says, "and there's nothing you can do about them. But you can sometimes control how they express themselves."

In his research work, López went back to the most straightforward animal models. "If you stress the hell out of a rat," he says, "that rat will have high levels of stress hormones. If you look at his serotonin receptors, they're clearly screwed up by stress. The brain of a highly stressed rat looks very much like the brain of a very depressed rat. If you give him serotonin-altering antidepressants, his cortisol eventually normalizes. It is likely that some depression is more seratonergic," López says, "and some is more tightly linked to cortisol, and most mixes these two sensitivities in some way. The cross talk between these two systems is part of the same pathophysiology." The rat experiments have been revealing, but the prefrontal cortex, that area of the brain that humans have and that makes us more developed than rats, also contains many cortisol receptors, and those are probably implicated in the complexities of human depression. The brains of human suicides show extremely high levels of CRF—"it's hyper, like they've been pumping this stuff." Their adrenal glands are larger than those of people who die from other causes because the high level of CRF has actually caused the expansion of the adrenal system. López's most recent work indicates that suicide victims actually show significant decrease in cortisol receptors in the prefrontal cortex (which means that the cortisol in that area is not mopped up as quickly as it should be). The next step, López says, is to look at the brains of people who can be subjected to huge amounts of stress and who can keep going despite it. "What is the biochemistry of their coping mechanism?" López asks. "How do they sustain such resilience? What are the patterns of CRF release in their brains? What do their receptors look like?"

John Greden, department chair for López and Young, focuses on the long-term effects of sustained stress and sustained depressive episodes. If you have too much stress and too high a level of cortisol for too long, you start destroying the very neurons that should regulate the feedback loop and turn down the cortisol level after the stress is resolved. Ultimately, this results in lesions to the hippocampus and the amygdala, a loss of neuronal networking tissue. The longer you remain in a depressed state, the more likely you are to have significant lesioning, which can lead to peripheral neuropathy: your vision starts to fade and all kinds of other things can go wrong. "This reflects the obvious fact that we need not only to treat depression when it occurs," says Greden, "but also to prevent it from recurring. Our public health approach at the moment is just wrong. People with recurrent depression must stay on medication permanently, not cycle on and off it, because beyond the unpleasantness of having to survive multiple painful depressive episodes, such people are actually ravaging their own neuronal tissue." Greden looks to a future in which our understanding of the physical consequences of depression may lead us to strategies to reverse them. "Maybe we'll be trying selective injection of neurotropic growth factors into certain regions of the brain to make some kind of tissue proliferate and grow. Maybe we'll be able to use other kinds of stimulation, magnetic or electric, to encourage growth in certain areas."

I hope so. Taking the pills is costly—not only financially but also psychically. It is humiliating to be reliant on them. It is inconvenient to have to keep track of them and to stock up on prescriptions. And it is toxic to know that without these perpetual interventions you are not yourself as you have understood yourself. I'm not sure why I feel this way—I wear contact lenses and without them am virtually blind, and I do not feel shamed by my lenses or by my need for them (though given my druthers, I'd choose perfect vision). The constant presence of the medications is for me a reminder of frailty and imperfection; and I am a perfectionist and would prefer to have things inviolate out of the hand of God.

Though the initial effects of antidepressants begin after about a week, it takes as much as six months to get the full benefits. Zoloft made me feel awful, and so my doctor switched me to Paxil after a few weeks. I was not wild about Paxil, but it did seem to work and it had fewer side effects for me. I did not learn until much later on that while more than 80 percent of depressed patients are responsive to medication, only 50 percent are responsive to their first medication—or, indeed, to any particular medication. In the meanwhile, there is a terrible cycle: the symptoms of depression cause depression. Loneliness is depressing, but depression also causes loneliness. If you cannot function, your life becomes as much of a mess as you had supposed it was; if you cannot speak and have no sexual urges, your romantic and social life disappear, and that is authentically depressing. I was, most of the time, too upset by everything to be upset by anything in particular; that is the only way I could tolerate the losses of affect, pleasure, and dignity that the illness brought my way. I also, inconveniently, had a reading tour to do immediately after my birthday. I had to go to a variety of bookstores and other venues and stand up in front of groups of strangers and read aloud from the novel I had written. It was a recipe for disaster, but I was determined to get through it. Before the first of these readings, in New York, I spent four hours taking a bath, and then a close friend who has had his own struggles with depression helped me to take a cold shower. He not only turned on the water, but also helped me to cope with exhausting difficulties such as buttons and fastenings, and stood in the bathroom so he could help me back out again. Then I went and read. I felt as though I had baby powder in my mouth, and I couldn't hear well, and I kept thinking I might faint, but I managed to do it. Then another friend helped to get me home, and I went back to bed for three days. I had stopped crying; and if I took enough Xanax, I could keep the tension under control. I still found mundane activities nearly impossible, and I woke up every day in a panic, early, and needed a few hours to conquer my fear well enough to get out of bed; but I could force myself out into public for an hour or two at a time.

Emergence is usually slow, and people stop at various stages of it. One mental health worker described her own constant struggle with depression: "It never really leaves me, but I battle with it every day. I'm on medication, and that helps, and I have just determined that I will not let myself give in to it. You see, I have a son who suffers from this disease, and I don't want him to think that it's a reason for not having a good life. I get up every single day, and I make breakfast for my kids. Some days I can keep going, and some days I have to go back to bed afterwards, but I get up every day. I come into this office at some point every day. Sometimes I miss a few hours, but I've never missed a whole day from depression." She had tears rolling down her face as we spoke, but her jaw was set and she went right on speaking. "One day last week I woke up and it was really bad. I managed to get out of bed, to walk to the kitchen, counting every step, to open the refrigerator. And then all the breakfast things were near the back of the refrigerator, and I just couldn't reach that far. When my kids came in, I was just standing there, staring into the refrigerator. I hate being like that, being like that in front of them." We talked about the day-to-day battle: "Someone like Kay Jamison, or someone like you, gets through this with so much support," she said. "My parents are both dead, and I'm divorced, and I don't find it easy to reach out."

Life events are often the triggers for depression. "One is much less likely to experience depression in a stable situation than in an unstable one," Melvin McGuinness of Johns Hopkins says. George Brown, of the University of London, is the founder of the field of life-events research and says, "Our view is that most depression is antisocial in origin; there is a disease entity as well, but most people are able to produce major depression given a particular set of circumstances. Level of vulnerability varies, of course, but I think at least two-thirds of the population has a sufficient level of vulnerability." According to the exhaustive research he has done over twenty-five years, severely threatening life events are responsible for triggering initial depression. These events typically involve loss—of a valued person, of a role, of an idea about yourself—and are at their worst when they involve humiliation or a sense of being trapped. Depression can also be caused by positive change. Having a baby, getting a promotion, or getting married are almost as likely to kindle depression as a death or loss.

Traditionally, a line has been drawn between the endogenous and reactive models of depression, the endogenous starting at random from within, while the reactive is an extreme response to a sad situation. The distinction has fallen apart in the last decade, as it has become clear that most depression mixes reactive and internal factors. Russell Goddard, of Yale University, told me the story of his battles with depression: "I took Asendin and it resulted in psychosis; my wife had to rush me to the hospital." He had better results with Dexedrine. His depression often escalated around family events. "I knew that my son's wedding would be emotional," he told me, "and that anything emotional, good or bad, sets me off. I wanted to be prepared. I'd always hated the idea of electroshock therapy, but I went and had it anyway. But it didn't do any good. By the time the wedding came, I couldn't even get out of bed. It broke my heart, but there was no way I could get there." This puts a terrible strain on family and on family relations. "My wife knew she couldn't do anything," Goddard explained. "She's learned to leave me alone, thank God." But family and friends are often unable to do that, and unable to understand. Some are almost too indulgent. If you treat someone as totally disabled, he will see himself as totally disabled, and that can cause him to be totally disabled, perhaps more totally disabled than he need be. The existence of medication has increased social intolerance. "You got a problem?" I once heard a woman say to her son in a hospital. "You get on that Prozac and get over it and then you give me a call." To set the correct level of tolerance is necessary not only for the patient but also for the family. "Families must guard themselves," Kay Jamison once said to me, "against the contagion of hopelessness."

What remains unclear is when depression triggers life events, and when life events trigger depression. Syndrome and symptom blur together and cause each other: bad marriages cause bad life events cause depression causes bad attachments, which are bad marriages. According to studies done in Pittsburgh, the first episode of major depression is usually closely tied to life events; the second, somewhat less; and by the fourth and fifth episodes life events seem to play no part at all. Brown agrees that beyond a certain point, depression "takes off on its own steam" and becomes random and endogenous, dissociated from life events. Though most people with depression have survived certain characteristic events, only about one in five who have experienced those events will develop depression. It is clear that stress drives up rates of depression. The biggest stress is humiliation; the second is loss. The best defense, for people with a biological vulnerability, is a "good enough" marriage, which absorbs external humiliations and minimizes them. "The psychosocial creates biological changes," Brown acknowledges. "The thing is that the vulnerability *must* initially be triggered by external events."

Just before my reading tour began, I started taking Navane, an antipsychotic with antianxiety effects, which, we hoped, would allow me to take the Xanax less often. My next engagements were out in California. I thought I could not go; I knew that I could not go alone. In the end, my father took me there; while I was in a Xanax haze, he got me on and off the plane, out of the airport, to the hotel. I was so drugged up that I was almost asleep, but in this state I could manage these changes, which would have been inconceivable to me a week earlier. I knew that the more I managed to do, the less I would want to die, so it seemed important to go. When we arrived in San Francisco, I went to bed and slept for about twelve hours. Then, during my first dinner there, I suddenly felt it lift. We sat in the big, cozy dining room of our hotel, and I chose my own food. I had been spending days on end with my father, but I had no idea what had been happening in his life, except me; we talked that night as though we were catching up after months apart. Upstairs, we sat talking further until late, and when I finally went to bed, I was almost ecstatic. I ate some chocolates from my minibar, wrote a letter, read a few pages of a novel I'd brought with me, cut my nails. I felt ready for the world.

The next morning, I felt just as bad as I had ever felt. My father helped me to get out of bed, turned on the shower. He tried to get me to eat, but I was too frightened to chew. I managed to drink some milk. I almost threw up several times, but not quite. I was afflicted with a sense of bleak misery, like what one would experience if one had just dropped and smashed a precious object. These days, a quarter milligram of Xanax will put me to sleep for twelve hours. That day, I took eight milligrams of Xanax and was still so tense I couldn't sit still. In the evening I felt better but not much. That's what a breakdown is like at that stage: one step forward, two steps back, two steps forward, one step back. A box step, if you will.

During the period that followed, the symptoms began to lift. I felt better earlier, and for longer, and more often. Soon, I could feed myself. It's hard to explain the quality of the disablement as it existed then, but it was a bit as I have imagined being very old. My great-aunt Beatrice was remarkable at age ninety-eight, because she was ninety-nine and yet every day, she got up and got dressed. If the weather was agreeable, she walked as much as eight blocks. She still cared about her clothes, and she liked to talk on the phone for hours. She remembered everyone's birthday and she occasionally went out to lunch. Emerging from a depression, you are at the point at which you get up and get dressed *every day.* If the weather is nice, you can go for a walk, and perhaps you can even have lunch. You talk on the phone. Aunt Bea was not gasping for breath at the end of one of her walks; she went a little slowly, but she had a nice time and was glad to have been out. So it is that when you are in the emerging stage of a depression, it is not the case that your being perfectly normal at lunch is like being all better, any more than Aunt Bea's ability to walk eight blocks meant that she was the all-night dancer she was at seventeen.

You don't get over breakdowns quickly or easily. Things go on being bumpy. Though certain depression symptoms seemed to be improving, I had an unfortunate, unusual cumulative adverse response to Navane. By the end of the third week on it, I had begun to lose the capacity to remain upright. I would walk for a few minutes and then I would *have* to lie down. I could no more control that need than I could the need to breathe. I would go off to do a reading and I would cling to the podium. Halfway through the reading, I would start skipping paragraphs so that I could just get through. When I was done, I would sit in a chair and hold on to the seat. As soon as I could leave the room, sometimes pretending I needed a bathroom, I would lie down again. I had no idea what was going on. I remember going out for a walk with a friend near the Berkeley campus, because she suggested that nature might do me good. We walked for a few minutes and then I began to feel tired. I forced myself on, thinking the weather and the air would help; I had been in bed for the previous fifty hours or so. Since I'd reduced my Xanax substantially, to stop sleeping fifty hours at a stretch, I was beginning to experience high anxiety again. If you have never experienced anxiety, think of it as the opposite of peace. All the peace—inward and outward—was stripped from my life at that moment.

Much depression incorporates anxiety symptoms. It's possible to read anxiety and depression separately, but according to James Ballenger of the Medical College of South Carolina, a leading expert in anxiety, "they're fraternal twins." George Brown said succinctly, "Depression is a response to past loss, and anxiety is a response to future loss." Thomas Aquinas proposed that fear is to sadness as hope is to pleasure; or, in other words, that anxiety is the precursor form of depression. I experienced so much anxiety when I was depressed, and felt so depressed when I was anxious, that I came to understand the withdrawal and the fear as inseparable. Anxiety is not paranoia; people with anxiety disorders assess their own position in the world much as do people without. What changes in anxiety is how one feels about that assessment. About half of patients with pure anxiety disorders develop major depression within five years. Insofar as depression and anxiety are genetically determined, they share a single set of genes (which are tied to the genes for alcoholism). Depression exacerbated by anxiety has a much higher suicide rate than depression alone, and it is much harder to recover from. "If you're having several panic attacks every day," says Ballenger, "it's gonna bring Hannibal to his knees. People are beaten into a pulp, into a fetal position in bed."

Between 10 and 15 percent of Americans suffer from some sort of anxiety disorder. In part, scientists think, because the locus coeruleus in the brain controls both norepinephrine production and the lower bowel, at least half of anxiety-disorder patients have irritable bowel syndrome as well; and anyone who has had really intense anxiety knows just how fast and furiously food can run through the digestive system. Both norepinephrine and serotonin are implicated in anxiety. "Two out of three times, life events are implicated, and it's always a loss of security," Ballenger says. About a third of panic attacks, endemic to some depression, occur during sleep, in deep, dreamless delta sleep. "In fact, panic disorders are kindled by things that make us all nervous," says Ballenger. "When we cure them, it's as though we've brought people to normal anxiety." The panic disorders are really disorders of scale. Walking in a crowd, for example, is somewhat distressing to most people even when they do not have an anxiety disorder; but if they do have an anxiety disorder, it may be unspeakably terrifying. We all exercise some care when we consider crossing a bridge—will it bear the weight? is it safe?—but for a person with an anxiety disorder, crossing a solid steel bridge that has borne a lot of traffic for decades may be as scary as crossing the Grand Canyon on a tightrope would be for the rest of us.

At my pitch of anxiety, my friend in Berkeley and I set out for a bit of exercise and we walked on and on and then I couldn't go farther. I lay down, fully dressed in perfectly nice clothes, in the mud. "Come on, get up on a log anyway," she said. I felt paralyzed. "Please let me stay here," I said, and I felt the crying start again. For an hour I lay in that mud, feeling the water seeping through, and then my friend pretty much carried me back to the car. Those same nerves that had been scraped raw at one point now seemed to be wrapped in lead. I knew it was a disaster, but that knowledge was meaningless. Sylvia Plath wrote in *The Bell Jar,* her wonderful evocation of her own breakdown: "I couldn't get myself to react. I felt very still and very empty, the way the eye of a tornado must feel, moving dully along in the middle of the surrounding hullabaloo." I felt as if my head had been encaged in Lucite, like one of those butterflies trapped forever in the thick transparency of a paperweight.

Doing those readings was the most difficult endeavor of my life: it was harder than any challenge I have faced before or since. The publicist who had organized my reading tour came with me herself for more than half of it and has since been a cherished friend. My father joined me for many of the trips; when we were apart, he called me every few hours. A few close friends took on responsibility for me, and I was never alone. I can tell you that I was not a fun companion; and that deep love and the knowledge of deep love were not by themselves the cure. I can also say that without deep love and the knowledge of deep love, I would not have found it in myself to go through with that tour. I would have found a place to lie down in the woods and I would have stayed there until I froze and died.

The terror lifted in December. Whether that was because the drugs had kicked in or because the reading tour was over, I do not know. In the end, I had canceled only one reading; between November 1 and December 15, I had managed to visit eleven cities. I had had a few random windows through the depression, like when the mist clears. Jane Kenyon, a poet who suffered severe depression through much of her life, has written about the emergence:

> . . . With the wonder
> and bitterness of someone pardoned
> for a crime she did not commit
> I come back to marriage and friends,
> to pink fringed hollyhocks; come back
> to my desk, books, and chair.

So on December 4, I walked into a friend's house on the Upper West Side, and I had an okay time there. For the next few weeks, I took pleasure not in the okay time I was having, but in the fact that I was having it. I made it through Christmas and New Year's and I was acting like some semblance of myself. I had lost about fifteen pounds, and now I began to put on weight again. My father and my friends all congratulated me on my astonishing progress. I thanked them. In my private self, however, I knew that what had gone away were only symptoms. I hated taking my pills every day. I hated that I had had a breakdown and lost my mind. I hated that unfashionable but relevant word *breakdown,* with its implication of the machinery giving in. I was relieved to have made it through the reading tour, but I was exhausted by all the things I had yet to make it through. I was overpowered being in the world, by other people and their lives I couldn't lead, their jobs I couldn't do—overpowered even by jobs I would never want or need to do. I was back to about where I had been in September, only now I understood how bad it could get. I was determined never again to go through such a thing.

This phase of half-recovery can last for a long time. It is the dangerous time. During the worst of my depression, when I could hardly cut up a lamb chop, I could not have done myself real harm. In this emerging period, I was feeling well enough for suicide. I could by now do pretty much all of what I had always been able to do, except that I was still in anhedonia, the inability to experience pleasure at all. I kept pushing myself for form's sake, but now that I had the energy to wonder why I was pushing myself, I could find no good reasons. I remember one evening in particular, when an acquaintance had convinced me that I should go out to the movies with him. I went along to prove my own gaiety and for several hours kept up every appearance of the fun the others were having, though I was pained by the episodes that they found funny. When I came home, I felt a return of panic, and a sadness of dinosaur proportions. I went into the bathroom and threw up repeatedly, as though my acute understanding of my loneliness were a virus in my system. I thought that I would die alone, and that there was no good reason to stay alive, and I thought that the normal and real world in which I had grown up, and in which I believed that other people lived, would never open itself up to receive me. And as these revelations burst into my head like shots, I retched on the bathroom floor, and the acid rode up the length of my esophagus, and when I tried to catch my breath, I inhaled my own bile. I had been eating big meals to try to put weight back on, and I felt as though all of them were coming back up, as though my stomach were going to turn itself inside out and hang limp in the toilet.

I lay on the bathroom floor for about twenty minutes, then crawled out and lay down on my bed. It was clear to my rational mind that I was going crazy again, and the awareness tired me further; but I knew that it was a bad plan to let the craziness run wild. I needed to hear another voice, even if only briefly, that could penetrate my fearful isolation. I did not want to call my father because I knew he would worry, and because I hoped the situation was temporary. I wanted to talk to someone sane and comforting (a poor impulse: crazy people are better friends when you are crazy; they know how crazy feels). I picked up the phone and dialed one of my oldest friends. We had talked previously about the medications, about the panic, and she had been smart and liberating in her responses.

I thought she could reignite my prelapsarian self. It was about two-thirty in the morning by then. Her husband answered the phone, then passed the receiver to her. "Hello?" she asked. "Hi," I said, and paused. "Has something happened?" she asked. It was immediately clear that I could not explain what had happened. I had nothing to say. My other line went; it was someone who had been at the movie with me, calling because he thought he had accidentally given me his key along with the change from our sodas. I checked my pocket and his key was there. "I've got to go," I said to my old friend, and got off the line. That night, I climbed up to the roof and realized as the sun came up that I was feeling absurdly melodramatic and that there was no point, if you lived in New York, attempting suicide from the top of a six-story building.

I did not want to sit on the roof, though I was also aware that if I didn't allow myself the relief of considering suicide, I would soon explode from within and commit suicide. I felt the fatal tentacles of this despair wrapping themselves around my arms and legs. Soon they would hold the fingers I would need to take the right pills or to pull the trigger, and when I had died, they would be the only motion left. I knew that the voice of reason ("For heaven's sake, just go downstairs!") was the voice of reason, but I also knew that by reason I would deny all the poison within me, and I felt already some strange despairing ecstasy at the thought of the end. If only I had been disposable like yesterday's paper! I would have thrown myself away so quietly then and been glad of the absence, glad in the grave if that was the only place that could allow some gladness.

My own awareness that depression is maudlin and laughable helped to get me off the roof. So did the thought of my father, who had tried so hard for me. I could not bring myself to believe in any love enough to imagine that the loss of me would be noticed, but I knew how sad it would be for him to have worked so hard at saving me and not to have succeeded. And I kept thinking about cutting up lamb chops for him someday, and I knew I had promised to do that, and I had always taken pride in breaking no promises, and my father had never broken a promise to me, and that, finally, was what led me downstairs. At about six in the morning, drenched with sweat and the remains of the dew and developing what would soon turn into a raging fever, I went back to my apartment. I didn't particularly want to die but I also didn't at all want to live.

The things that save you are as frequently trivial as monumental. One, certainly, is a sense of privacy; to kill yourself is to open your life's misery up to the world. A famous, astonishingly good-looking, brilliant, happily married man, posters of whom bedecked the walls of girls I knew in high school, told me that he had gone through a severe depression in his late twenties and had considered suicide quite seriously. "Only my vanity saved me," he said, quite in earnest. "I couldn't stand the idea of people afterwards saying that I couldn't succeed, or that I couldn't deal with success, or laughing at me." Famous and successful people seem particularly likely to suffer depression. Since the world is flawed, perfectionists tend to be depressed. Depression lowers self-esteem, but in many personalities, it does not eliminate pride, which is as good an engine for the fight as any I know. When you're so far down that love seems almost meaningless, vanity and a sense of obligation can save your life.

It was not until two days after the rooftop episode that I called back my old friend, who laid into me for waking her up and then disappearing. As she scolded, I felt the overpowering weirdness of the life I was living, which I knew I could not possibly explain. Dizzy with the fever and with terror, I said nothing. She never really spoke to me again. I would describe her as someone who cherished normality, and I had become much too peculiar. Depression is hard on friends. You make what by the standards of the world are unreasonable demands on them, and often they don't have the resilience or the flexibility or the knowledge or the inclination to cope. If you're lucky some people will surprise you with their adaptability. You communicate what you can and hope. Slowly, I've learned to take people for who they are. Some friends can process a severe depression right up front, and some can't. Most people don't like one another's unhappiness very much. Few can cope with the idea of a depression divorced from external reality; many would prefer to think that if you're suffering, it's with reason and subject to logical resolution.

A large proportion of my best friends are a little bit crazy. People have taken my frankness as an invitation to be frank themselves, and I have many friends with whom I have found a trust like that between schoolmates or former lovers, the ease of a vast mutual knowing. I try to be cautious with my friends who are too sane. Depression is itself destructive, and it breeds destructive impulses: I am easily disappointed in people who don't get it and sometimes make the mistake of telling off those who have frustrated me. After any given depression, there's the need for a lot of cleanup. I remember that I love friends I had thought of letting go. I try to rebuild what I have wasted. After any given depression comes the time to uncrack the eggs and to put the spilled milk back in the container.

In the spring of 1995, the late phase of my analysis was dragging on. My analyst was retiring gradually, and though I had not wanted to lose her, I found the bit-by-bit process agonizing, like ripping off scabs slowly. It was my mother's prolonged demise all over again. I finally ended it myself, walking in one day with a sudden burst of clarity and announcing that I would not be coming back.

In psychoanalysis, I had studied my own past in detail. I have since decided that my mother was also depressive. I can remember her once describing the sense of desolation she had felt as an only child. She was irritable as an adult. She used pragmatism as a force field permanently to shield her against uncontrolled sadness. It was, at best, only partially effective. I believe that she kept herself from ever experiencing a breakdown by regimenting and regulating her life; she was a woman of remarkable self-discipline. I believe now that her blessed rage for order was ordained by the pain she so fastidiously relegated to a place just below the surface. I ache for the pain she endured, which I mostly don't have to endure—what would her life, our lives, indeed, have been like if Prozac had existed when I was a child? I'd love to see better treatments with fewer side effects, but I am so grateful to live in this age of solutions rather than that age of ignorant struggle. So much of my mother's wisdom about how to live with one's difficulties turned out to be unnecessary for me, and if she had only lived a little bit longer, it would have been unnecessary for her. It seems poignant in retrospect. I have wondered, so often, what she would have said about my depressions, whether she would have recognized anything in them, whether we would have been drawn together in my collapse—but since it was her death that at least in part occasioned that collapse, I will never know. I didn't have the questions to ask until I had lost the person of whom I would have liked to ask them. Nonetheless, I had in my mother a model of someone in whom a certain sadness was always present.

When I stopped taking the drugs, I did it fast. I knew that this was dumb, but I just wanted desperately to be off medication. I thought I might be able to find out who I was again. It was not a good strategy. In the first place, I had never experienced anything like the withdrawal symptoms from the Xanax: I could not sleep properly, and I felt anxious and strangely tentative. I also felt the whole time as though I'd had several gallons of cheap cognac the night before. My eyes hurt and I had an upset stomach, which probably came from quitting the Paxil cold turkey. At night, when I was not really asleep, I had unrelenting terrifying nightmares, and I woke up with my heart pounding. The psychopharmacologist had told me over and over again that when I was ready to go off the drugs, I should do it gradually and under his supervision, but my determination had been sudden and I was afraid of losing it.

I felt a little bit like my old self, but the year had been so awful, had shaken me so deeply, that though I was now functioning again, I had also realized that I could not go on. This did not feel irrational, like the terror; it did not feel angry; it felt quite sensible. I had had enough of life, and I wanted to figure out how to end it with the least possible damage to the people around me. I needed something I believed in, something to show, so that everyone would understand how desperate I was. I had to give up the invisible impediment for a manifest one. There is little question in my mind that the particular behavior I chose was highly individual and related to neuroses of my own, but the decision to behave with such a hunger to be rid of the self was typical of agitated depression. All I had to do was to get sick, and that would give me permission. The wish for a more visible illness was, I would later learn, a commonplace among depressives, who often engage in forms of self-mutilation to bring the physical state in line with the mental. I knew that my suicide would be devastating for my family and sad for my friends, but I felt they would all understand that I had had no choice.

I could not figure out how to give myself cancer or MS or various other fatal diseases, but I knew just how to get AIDS, so I decided to do that. In a park in London, at a lonely hour well after midnight, a short, tubby man with thick tortoiseshell eyeglasses came up and offered himself to me. He pulled down his trousers and bent over. I went to work. I felt as though this were all happening to someone else; I heard his glasses fall off, and I thought only this: soon I will be dead, and so I will never become old and sad like this man. A voice in my head said that I had finally started this process and would soon die, and at the thought I felt such a sense of release and of gratitude. I tried to understand why this man had gone on living, why he got up and did things all day in order to come here at night. There was a half moon and it was springtime.

It was not my intention to die slowly of AIDS; it was my intention to kill myself with HIV as my excuse. At home, I had a burst of fear and called a good friend and told him what I had done. He talked me through it and I went to bed. When I woke up in the morning, I felt much as I had felt on the first day of college or summer camp or a new job. This was to be the next phase of my life. Having eaten of the forbidden fruit,

I decided to make applesauce. The end was at hand. I had a new sense of efficiency. That depression of purposelessness was gone. Over the next three months, I sought out other such experiences with strangers whom I assumed to be infected, taking ever greater and more direct risks. I was sorry that I could not seem to have any pleasure from these sexual encounters, but I was too preoccupied with my agenda to be jealous of those who did. I never got the names of these people, never went home with them or invited them home with me. I went once a week, often on Wednesdays, to a local spot where I could have an economical experience that would infect me.

In the meanwhile, I went through boringly typical symptoms of agitated depression. I had had anxiety, which is sheer terror; this was much more full of hatred, anguish, guilt, self-loathing. I have never in my life felt so temporary. I slept badly, and I was ferociously irritable. I stopped speaking to at least six people, including one with whom I had thought I might be in love. I took to slamming down the phone when someone said something I didn't like. I criticized everyone. It was hard to sleep because my mind was racing with tiny injustices from my past, which now seemed unforgivable. I could not really concentrate on anything: I am usually a voracious summer reader, but that summer I couldn't make it through a magazine. I started doing my laundry every night while I was awake, to keep busy and distracted. When I got a mosquito bite, I picked at it until it bled, then picked off the scabs; I bit my nails so far down that my fingers were always bleeding too; I had open wounds and scratches everywhere, though I never actually cut myself. My situation was so different from the vegetative symptoms that had constituted my breakdown that it did not occur to me that I was still in the grip of the same illness as before.

Then one day in early October, after one of my bouts of unpleasant unsafe sex, this one with a boy who had followed me to a hotel and made a beseeching move on the elevator, I realized that I might be infecting others—and that was not my agenda. I was suddenly terrified that I had given someone else the disease; I had wanted to kill myself, but not the rest of the world. I'd had four months to get infected; I'd had a total of about fifteen unsafe episodes; and it was time to stop before I began to spread disease everywhere. The knowledge that I would die had also lifted the depression I'd felt and had even in a strange way diminished the wish to die. I put that period of my life behind me. I became gentler again. At my thirty-second birthday, I looked around at the many friends who had come for my party, and I was able to smile, knowing that this was the last one, that I would never have a birthday again, that I would soon die. The celebrations were tiring; the gifts I left in their paper wrapping. I calculated how long I would have to wait. I wrote a note to myself of the date in March when six months would have elapsed from the last encounter, when I could get my test, my confirmation. And all the while, I acted fine.

I worked productively on some writing projects, organized both family Thanksgiving and Christmas, and was sentimental about my last holidays. Then a few weeks after New Year's, I reviewed the details of my encounters with a friend who was an expert on HIV, and he told me that I might well be fine. At first I was dismayed, but then the period of my agitated depression, whatever had driven me to that behavior, began to lift. I do not think that the HIV experiences were expiatory; time had just passed, curing the ill thinking that had driven me to such excess in the first place. Depression, which comes at you with the gale force of a breakdown, leaves gradually, quietly. My first breakdown was over.

The insistence on normality, the belief in an inner logic in the face of unmistakable abnormality, is endemic to depression. It is the everyman story of this book, one I have encountered time after time. The shape of each person's normality, however, is unique: normality is perhaps an even more private idea than weirdness. Bill Stein, a publisher I know, comes from a family in which both depression and trauma have run high. His father, born a Jew in Germany, left Bavaria on a business visa in early 1938. His grandparents were lined up outside the family house on Kristallnacht, in November of 1938, and though they were not arrested, they had to watch as many of their friends and neighbors were sent off to Dachau. The trauma of being a Jew in Nazi Germany was horrendous, and Bill's grandmother went into a six-week decline after Kristallnacht, which culminated with her suicide on Christmas Day. The following week, exit visas arrived for both Bill's grandparents. His father emigrated alone.

Bill's parents married in Stockholm in 1939 and moved to Brazil before settling in the United States. His father always refused to discuss this history; "that period in Germany," Bill recalls, "simply did not exist." They lived on an attractive street in a prosperous suburb in a bubble of unreality. In part perhaps because of his practice of denial, Bill's father suffered a severe breakdown at the age of fifty-seven and had repeated lapses straight through to his death more than thirty years later. His depressions followed the same patterns that his son would inherit. His first major breakdown occurred when his son was five years old; he continued to go to pieces periodically, with a particularly deep depression that lasted from the time Bill was in sixth grade until the time he finished junior high school.

Bill's mother came from a much wealthier and more privileged German Jewish family that had left Germany for Stockholm in 1919. A woman of strong character, she once slapped a Nazi captain in the face for being rude to her; "I'm a Swedish citizen," she told him, "and I won't be spoken to in that way."

By the age of nine, Bill Stein was experiencing lengthy periods of depression. For about two years, he was terrified of going to sleep and was traumatized when his parents went to bed. Then his dark feelings lifted for a few years. After some minor lapses, they returned when he got to college, spinning out of control in 1974, during the second term of his freshman year. "I had this sadistic roommate, and the academic pressure was intense. I was so anxious I was hyperventilating," he recalls. "I just couldn't take the pressure. So I went to the undergraduate health services and they gave me Valium."

The depression did not lift during the summer. "Often when I had deep depressions, the control of my bowels would go. I remember that summer was particularly severe in this way. I was dreading sophomore year. I couldn't face my exams or anything. When I got back to school and went through my first year and got straight As, I honestly thought someone had made a mistake. When it turned out that they hadn't, it gave me something of a high, and that pulled me out of the depression." If there are triggers for breakdowns, there are also triggers for turning around, and that was Stein's. "I came back down to normal again a day later, but I never truly sank again at school. I did, however, withdraw from my aspirations. If you had told me then what I would be doing now, the people I would be working with, I'd have been utterly shocked. I was ambitionless." Despite this acceptance of his lot, Stein worked slavishly hard. He continued to get straight As. "I don't know why I bothered," he says. "I didn't want to go to law school or anything. I just thought that somehow good grades would make me safe, would convince me that I was functional." When he graduated, Stein took a job teaching in a public high school in upstate New York. It was a disaster; he couldn't discipline a class and he lasted only one year. "I left a failure. I lost a lot of weight. I had another depression. And then the father of a friend said he could get me a job, and I took it to have something to do."

Bill Stein is a man of quiet, powerful intelligence and an entirely restrained ego. He is self-effacing almost to a fault. Bill suffered repeated depressions, each about six months long, somewhat seasonal, usually hitting a low point in April. The worst came in 1986, precipitated by turbulence at work, the loss of a good friend, and Bill's attempt to get off Xanax, which he had taken for just a month but to which he had become addicted. "I lost my apartment," Stein says. "I lost my job. I lost most of my friends. I couldn't stay in a house by myself. I was supposed to be moving from my old apartment I'd just sold to this new apartment that was being renovated, and I just couldn't. I crashed so quickly and the anxiety devastated me. I would wake up at three or four in the morning with these sort of rushes of anxiety that were so intense it would have been more pleasurable to jump out the window. When I was with other people, I always felt like I was going to faint from the stress. I'd been whizzing around the globe to Australia, *fine*, three months earlier, and now the world had been taken away from me. I was in New Orleans when it really hit and I suddenly knew I had to get home, but I couldn't board a plane. People took advantage of me; I was a wounded animal in an open meadow." He broke down completely. "When you're really bad, you have this sort of catatonic look on your face, as if you've been stunned. You act strangely because of your deficits; my short-term memory disappeared. And then it got even worse. I couldn't control my bowels and I would make in my pants. Then I was living in such terror of that that I couldn't leave my own apartment, and that was a further trauma. In the end, I moved back to my parents' house." But life at home was not ameliorative. Bill's father crumpled under the pressure of his son's illness and ended up in the hospital himself. Bill went to stay with his sister; then a school friend took him in for seven weeks. "It was horrendous," he says. "I thought, at that point, that I would be mentally ill for the rest of my life. The episode lasted for more than a year. It seemed better to float with the down than to fight it. I think you have to let go and understand that the world will be re-created and may never again resemble what you knew previously."

He went to the doors of a hospital several times but could not bring himself to register there. He finally signed in at Mt. Sinai Hospital in New York in September of 1986, and asked for electroconvulsive therapy. ECT had helped his father but failed to help him. "It was the most dehumanizing place I can imagine, to go from life on the outside to not being allowed to have your shaving kit or your nail clipper. Having to wear pajamas. Having to eat dinner at four-thirty. Being talked down to, as if you're retarded in addition to being depressed. Seeing other patients in padded cells. You can't have a telephone in your room because you might strangle yourself with the cord and because they want to control your access to the outside world. This is not like a normal hospitalization. You are deprived of your rights on the mental health ward. I don't think the hospital is a place for depressives unless they're totally helpless or desperately suicidal."

The physical process of the shock treatments was awful. "The man who administered them was a doctor who looked a lot like Herman Munster. The treatments were given in the basement of Mt. Sinai. All the patients who were going to get them went down there, into the depths of hell, and all of us wore bathrobes, and it felt like we were in a chain gang. Since I kept my composure pretty well, they made me the last, and I stood around there trying to comfort all the terrified people who were waiting around, while the janitorial staff came in and shoved past us to get to their lockers, which were also located down there. If I were only Dante, I'd be great explaining what it was like. I had wanted the treatments, but the room and the people—I felt like it was a barbaric Mengele scene of experimentation. If you're going to do this stuff, do it on the fucking eighth floor with light windows and bright colors! I wouldn't allow it now.

"I still mourn the loss of my memory," he says. "I had an exceptional memory, nearly photographic, and it has never come back. When I got out, I couldn't remember my locker combination, my conversations." At first, when he came out, he also couldn't even do filing at a volunteer job, but soon he began to function. He moved to Santa Fe for six months and stayed with friends. In the summer he returned to New York to live alone again. "Perhaps it is just as well that my memory was clearly suffering permanent deficits," he says. "It has helped me to blunt out some of the lows. I forget them as easily as I forget everything else." Recovery was gradual. "There is a lot of volition but you can't control the recovery. You can't figure out when it will happen, any more than you can predict when someone will die."

Stein took to visiting a synagogue, going weekly with a religious friend. "I was substantially assisted by faith. It somehow relieved the pressure on me to believe in something else," he says. "I had always been proud of being Jewish and drawn to things religious. After that big depression, I felt that if I believed hard enough, things might come about that would save the world. I had to sink so low there was nothing to believe in but God. I was slightly embarrassed to find myself drawn to religion; but it was right. It's right that no matter how bad the week, there's that service every Friday.

"But the thing that saved me was Prozac, which came along in 1988, just in time. It was a miracle. My head suddenly felt, after all these years, as if there wasn't a huge crack in it that was being pulled wider and wider. If you had told me in 1987 that a year later I'd be taking planes, working with governors and senators—well, I'd have laughed. I couldn't even cross the street." Bill Stein is now on Effexor and lithium. "My biggest fear in life was that I would not be able to handle my father's death. He died at the age of ninety, and when he died, I was almost euphoric to find that I could handle it. I was heartbroken and I cried, but I could do the normal things: play the son in the family, talk to the lawyers, write a eulogy. I handled it better than I would ever have thought possible.

"I still have to be careful. I always feel as though everyone wants a little piece of me. There's just so much I can give and then I'll get really really tense. I think, perhaps wrongly, that people will think less of me if I am completely open about my experiences. I still remember being avoided. Life is always on the edge of falling down again. I've learned to hide it, to make it so no one can tell when I'm on three drugs and about to collapse. I don't think I ever feel really happy. One can only expect that life not be miserable. When you're hugely self-conscious, it's hard to be fully happy. I love baseball. And when I see other guys at the stadium, swilling beer, seeming so unconscious of themselves and their relation to the world, I envy that. God, wouldn't it be great to be like that?

"I always think about those exit visas. If my grandmother had only waited. The story of her suicide taught me patience. There is no doubt that no matter how bad it gets again, I will get through it. But I would not be the person I am today without the wisdom I have gained from my experiences, the shedding of narcissism they've brought about."

Bill Stein's story has had considerable resonance for me. I have thought of those exit visas often since I first met Bill. I thought of the one that was never used and, also, of the one that was used. Getting through my first depression had involved holding on. A brief period of reasonable peace had followed. When I began to experience anxiety and major depression the second time around—while I was still in the shadow of my first depression and not yet clear where my flirtation with AIDS might have left me—I recognized what was happening. I became overwhelmed by the need to pause. Life itself seemed so alarmingly exigent, to require so much of the self. It was too difficult to remember and think and express and understand—all the things I needed to be able to do to talk. To keep my face animated at the same time was insult added to injury. It was like trying to cook and roller-skate and sing and type all at once. The Russian poet Daniil Kharms once described hunger: "Then begins the weakness. Then begins the boredom. Then comes the loss of the power of quick reason. Then comes the calmness. And then begins the horror." In just such logical and terrible stages did the second bout of depression begin—exacerbated by real fear of the HIV test I'd scheduled. I didn't want to go back on medication, and for a while I tried to ride it out. Then one day I realized that it wasn't going to work. I knew about three days ahead of time that I was heading for rock bottom. I started taking the Paxil I still had in my medicine chest. I called the psychopharmacologist. I warned my father. I tried to make the practical arrangements: losing your mind, like losing your car keys, is a real hassle. Out of the terror, I heard my voice holding on tight to irony when friends called. "I'm sorry, I'll have to cancel Tuesday," I said. "I'm afraid of lamb chops again." The symptoms came fast and ominously. In about a month, I lost a fifth of my body weight, some thirty-five pounds.

The psychopharmacologist thought that, since I had felt light-headed on Zoloft and highly strung on Paxil, it was worth trying something new, so he put me on Effexor and BuSpar, both of which I am still taking, six years later. In the throes of depression, one reaches a strange point at which it is impossible to see the line between one's own theatricality and the reality of madness. I discovered two conflicting qualities of character. I am melodramatic by nature; on the other hand, I can go out and "seem normal" under the most abnormal of circumstances. Antonin Artaud wrote on one of his drawings, "Never real and always true," and that is how depression feels. You know that it is not real, that you are someone else, and yet you know that it is absolutely true. It's very confusing.

By the week of the HIV test, I was taking twelve to sixteen milligrams of Xanax (I had squirreled away a small cache of the drug) every day, so that I could sleep all the time and not be anxious. On Thursday of that week, I got up and checked my messages. The nurse from my doctor's office said: "Your cholesterol is down, your cardiogram is normal, and your HIV test turned out fine." I called her immediately. It was true. I was HIV-negative after all. As Gatsby said, "I tried hard to die but have an enchanted life." I knew then that I wanted to live, and I was grateful for the news. But I went right on feeling terrible for two more months. I gritted my teeth against suicidality every day.

Then, in July, I decided to accept an invitation to go sailing with some friends in Turkey. It was cheaper for me to go there than it would have been for me to be hospitalized, and it was at least three times as effective: in the perfect Turkish sunshine, the depression evaporated. Things got steadily better after that. Late in the autumn, I suddenly found that I was lying awake at night, my body trembling, much as it had done at the lowest points of my depression, but I was awake this time with happiness. I climbed out of bed and wrote about it. Years had passed since I had felt happiness at all, and I had forgotten what it is like to want to live, to enjoy the day you are in and to long for the next one, to know that you are one of the lucky people for whom life is the living of it. As surely as the rainbow covenant that God gave to Noah, I felt I had proof that existence was and would always be worth it, though. I knew that episodes of pain might lie ahead, that depression is cyclical and returns to afflict its victims over and over. I felt safe from myself. I knew that eternal sadness, though very much within me, did not mitigate the happiness. I turned thirty-three shortly thereafter, and it was a truly happy birthday, at last.

That was all I heard from my depression for a long time. The poet Jane Kenyon wrote:

> We try a new drug, a new combination
> of drugs, and suddenly
> I fall into my life again
>
> like a vole picked up by a storm
> then dropped three valleys
> and two mountains away from home.
>
> I can find my way back. I know
> I will recognize the store
> where I used to buy milk and gas.
>
> I remember the house and barn,
> the rake, the blue cups and plates,
> the Russian novels I loved so much,
>
> and the black silk nightgown
> that he once thrust
> into the toe of my Christmas stocking.

And so it was for me that everything seemed to be returning, started strange, then went abruptly familiar, and I realized that a deep sadness had started when my mother got ill, had worsened when she died, had built beyond grief into despair, had disabled me, and was not disabling me anymore. I was still sad about the sad things, but I was myself again, as I used to be, as I always meant to go on being.

Since I am writing a book about depression, I am often asked in social situations to describe my own experiences, and I usually end by saying that I am on medication. "Still?" people ask. "But you seem fine!" To which I invariably reply that I seem fine because I am fine, and that I am fine in part because of medication. "So how long do you expect to go on taking this stuff?" people ask. When I say that I will be on medication indefinitely, people who have dealt calmly and sympathetically with the news of suicide attempts, catatonia, missed years of work, significant loss of body weight, and so on stare at me with alarm. "But it's really bad to be on medicine that way," they say. "Surely now you are strong enough to be able to phase out some of these drugs!" If you say to them that this is like phasing the carburetor out of your car or the buttresses out of Notre Dame, they laugh. "So maybe you'll stay on a really low maintenance dose?" they ask. You explain that the level of medication you take was chosen because it normalizes the systems that can go haywire, and that a low dose of medication would be like removing half of your carburetor. You add that you have experienced almost no side effects from the medication you are taking, and that there is no evidence of negative effects of long-term medication. You say that you really don't want to get sick again. But wellness is still, in this area, associated not with achieving control of your problem, but with discontinuation of medication: "Well, I sure hope you get off sometime soon," they say.

"I may not know the exact effects of long-term medication," says John Greden. "No one has yet taken Prozac for eighty years. But I certainly know the effects of nonmedication, or of going on and off medication, or of trying to reduce appropriate doses to inappropriate levels—and those effects are brain damage. You start to have consequences from chronicity. You have recurrences of increasing severity, levels of distress there is no reason for you ever to experience. We would never treat diabetes or hypertension in this on-again, off-again way; why do we do it with depression? Where has this weird social pressure come from? This illness has an eighty percent relapse rate within a year without medication, and an eighty percent wellness rate with medication." Robert Post, of the NIMH, concurs: "People worry about side effects from staying on medication for a lifetime, but the side effects of doing that appear to be insubstantial, very insubstantial compared to the lethality of undertreated depression. If you have a relative or a patient on digitalis, what would you think of suggesting he go off it, see if he has another bout of congestive heart failure, and have his heart get so flabby that it can never get back into shape again? It's not one iota different." The side effects of these drugs are for most people much healthier than the illness they address.

There is evidence of people having adverse reactions to everything: certainly plenty of people have had adverse responses to Prozac. A certain amount of caution is appropriate when you decide to consume anything, from wild mushrooms to cough syrup. One of my godchildren almost died through exposure to walnuts, to which he is allergic, at a London birthday party; it is a good thing that labeling law now requires products that may contain nuts to indicate as much on their labels. People who take Prozac should watch in the early stages for adverse responses. The drug can cause facial tics and stiffening of muscles. Antidepressant drugs bring up questions around addiction, which I address later on in this book. The lowered libido, weird dreams, and other effects mentioned on the labeling of the SSRIs can be miserable. I am troubled by reports that some antidepressants have been associated with suicide; I believe that this has to do with the enabling quality of the drugs, which may give someone the wherewithal to do what he was previously too debilitated to contemplate. I accept that we cannot definitively know the very long-term effect of the medications. It is most unfortunate, however, that some scientists have chosen to capitalize on these adverse reactions, spawning an industry of Prozac detractors who misrepresent the drug as a grave peril that is being foisted on an innocent public. In an ideal world, one would not take any drugs and one's body would regulate itself adequately; who wants to take drugs? But the ludicrous assertions made in such stridently foolish books as *Prozac Backlash* cannot be taken for more than pandering to the cheapest fears of an apprehensive audience. I deplore the cynics who keep suffering patients from the essentially benign cures that might give them back their lives.

Like childbirth, depression is a pain so severe as to be immemorial. I didn't develop it when a relationship ended badly during the winter of 1997. It was a breakthrough, I told someone, not to have a breakdown during my breakup. But you are never the same once you have acquired the knowledge that there is no self that will not crumble. We are told to learn self-reliance, but it's tricky if you have no self on which to rely. Others have helped me, and there is some chemistry that has wrought a readjustment, and I feel okay with all of that for the moment, but the recurring nightmares are no longer of the things that will happen *to* me, that happen from outside agency, but the things that happen *in* me. What if tomorrow I wake up and I am not myself but a manure beetle? Every morning starts off with that breathless uncertainty about who I am, with a check for the cancers of unseemly growth, with a momentary anxiety about whether nightmares might be true. It's as if my self turned around and spit at me and said, don't push it, don't count on me for much, I have problems of my own to take care of. But then who is it who resists the madness or is pained by it? Who is it who is spit at? I have done years of psychotherapy and lived and loved and lost, and I have, frankly, no idea. There is someone or something there stronger than chemistry or will, a me that got me through the revolt of my self, a unionist me that held on until the rebel chemicals and their consequent ideation had been brought back into line. Is that self a chemical matter? I am no spiritualist and I grew up without religion, but that ropy fiber that runs through the center of me, that holds fast even when the self has been stripped away from it: anyone who lives through this knows that it is never as simple as complicated chemistry.

One has the advantage during one's own breakdown of being *in* it, where one can see what's happening. From the outside, one can only guess; but since depression is cyclical, it can be fruitful to learn forbearance and recognition. Eve Kahn, an old friend, told me about the toll her father's depression took on her family: "My father had a hard time, starting early on. My grandfather died, and my grandmother banned religion from the house. She said, if God could take my husband and leave me with four children like this, there is no God. And so she began serving shrimp and ham on all the Jewish holidays! Platters of shrimp and ham! My father's six foot three, two hundred twenty pounds, was undefeated at handball and also a baseball and soccer player in college, the sort of guy you can't imagine being fragile. He became a psychologist. Then, I guess when he was thirty-eight or so—the chronology is all messed up because my mother doesn't want to talk about it and my father doesn't really remember it and I was a toddler when it started—one day somebody from the clinic where he was working calls my mother and says that my father has disappeared, has left the job, and they don't know where he is. And so my mother piles us all into the car and we drive around and drive around until we eventually find him leaning against a mailbox and crying. He had electroconvulsive therapy immediately thereafter, and when they were done with him, they told my mother to divorce him because he would never be the same. 'Your kids won't recognize him,' they said. Though she didn't really believe them, she sat in the car while driving him home from treatment and cried. When he woke up he was like a Xeroxed version of himself. A little fuzzy around the edges, memory not great, more careful with himself, less interested in us. Supposedly he'd been a really engaged father when we were tiny—came home early to see what we learned that day and brought us toys all the time. After the ECT, he was a little bit removed. And then it happened again four years later. They tried medications and more ECT. He had to give up work for a while. Most of the time he was down. His face wasn't recognizable; his chin had receded into his face. He would get out of bed and kind of helplessly go around the house with his hands shaking, these big hands just hanging there beside his body. You understand where theories of demon possession come in, because someone had taken over my father's body. I was five years old and I could see it. I remember it really well. He looked the same but there was nobody home.

"Then he seemed to get better and he had a high period for about two years, and then he crashed again. And then he stayed down and down and down. He got a little better eventually and then he crashed again, and then again. He crashed the car around that time, when I was about fifteen years old, because he was so woozy or because he was suicidal—who knows? It happened again my freshman year of college. I got the call; I had to miss an exam and go down to see him in the hospital. They had taken his belt and taken his tie, the whole thing. And then he was in again five years later. And then he just retired. And he restructured his life. He takes a lot of vitamins and he gets a lot of exercise and he doesn't work. And anytime anything stresses him out, he leaves the room. My baby daughter cries? He puts on his hat and goes home. But my mother stayed with him through all of this and when he was sane, he was a great husband to her. He had ten good years through the nineties, until a stroke sent him tumbling down again in early 2001."

Eve has been determined not to put her family through the same problems. "I've been through a couple of terrible episodes myself," she says. "By the time I was thirty or so, I had a pattern of working way too hard, taking on way too much, finishing it, and then staying in bed for a week totally unable to deal. I had been on nortriptyline at one point, which did nothing but make me gain weight. Then in September 1995, my husband got a job in Budapest and we had to move, and I went on Prozac to deal with the stress of moving. Over there, I just lost it completely. I was either in bed all day or irrational. The stress of being nowhere with no friends—and my husband had to work fifteen hours a day when we arrived because some deal had just kicked in. By the time that was finished, four months later, I was completely crazed. I came back to the U.S. to see doctors and I went on a huge cocktail: Klonopin, lithium, Prozac. It was impossible to have dreams or be creative and I had to carry around a gigantic pill case all the time, with pills marked morning, noon, afternoon, and evening because I couldn't remember what was going on. Eventually, I made a life over there, found some good friends, and got an okay job, so I lowered the meds until I was popping just a couple of pills a night. Then I got pregnant, went off all the drugs, and felt great. We moved back home, and then after I had the baby all those wonderful hormones wore off, and having an infant—I didn't have a decent night's sleep for a year—I began to fall apart again. I was determined not to put my daughter through that. I'm on Depakote, which I find less dulling and which is apparently a safe medication to take while breastfeeding. I will do whatever I have to do to give my daughter a stable environment, not to disappear on her, not to walk out all the time."

Two good years followed my second breakdown. I was content, and overjoyed to be content. Then in September 1999, I had a terrible experience of abandonment in love, by someone I had thought would be with me forever, and became sad—not depressed, just sad. And then a month later, I slipped on the stairs in my own house and dislocated my shoulder badly, ripping a great deal of muscle tissue. I headed up to the hospital. I attempted to explain to the staff of the ambulance and then to the staff of the emergency room that I was eager to thwart a recurrence of depression. I explained about the kidney stones and how they had triggered a previous episode. I promised to fill out every form in the book and to answer questions on every subject from the colonial history of Zanzibar on down if they would only alleviate a physical agony that I knew was far too powerful for my mind's peace. I explained that I had a history of severe breakdowns and asked that they look up my files. It took more than an hour to get any pain medication at all; and at that point I received a dose of IV morphine too small to alleviate my pain. A dislocated shoulder is a straightforward matter, but mine was not repositioned until eight hours after I had arrived in the hospital. I did finally have some meaningful pain relief, with Dilaudid, four hours and thirty minutes after my arrival—so the last three and a half hours were not quite so awful as what had gone before.

Attempting to remain calm during the early stages of all this, I requested a psychiatric consultation. The doctor who was supervising told me, "Dislocated shoulders are painful and it's going to be painful until we have it back in place, and you've just got to be patient with it and stop carrying on." She also said, "You are exercising no self-control, are getting angry, are hyperventilating, and I'm not going to do a thing for you until you pull yourself together." I was told that "we don't know you from Adam," that "we don't just give out strong pain medicine," and that I should "try breathing deeply and imagining yourself on a beach with the sound of water in your ears and the feeling of sand between your toes." One of the doctors told me, "Pull yourself together and stop feeling so sorry for yourself. There are people in this emergency room who are going through worse things than you are." And when I said that I knew I had to go through the pain but wanted to take the edge off it before we proceeded, that I didn't even mind this physical pain so much but was worried about psychiatric complications, I was told that I was being "childish" and "uncooperative." When I said that I had a history of mental illness, I was told that in that case I could not well expect anyone to take my views on these things seriously. "I'm a trained professional and I'm here to help you," the doctor said. When I said that I was an experienced patient and knew that what she was doing was in fact injurious to me, she told me that I had not been to medical school and would just have to proceed according to what she judged an appropriate protocol.

I repeated my requests for a psychiatric consult, but no such thing was offered. Psychiatric records are not available in emergency rooms, and so there was no way to check on my complaints, though the hospital where I found myself is the one with which all my primary-care physicians and my psychiatrist are associated. I believe that the emergency room policy in which saying "I have had severe psychotic depression exacerbated by extreme pain" is treated much the same as saying "I have to have a woolly teddy bear with me before you can use sutures" is unacceptable. The standard textbook on emergency room practice in the United States does not deal with the psychiatric aspects of somatic illness. No one in the emergency room was remotely equipped to deal with psychiatric complications. I was asking for steak at the fishmonger's.

Pain accumulates. Five hours of pain are at least six times as painful as one hour of pain. I remarked that physical trauma is among the primary triggers for psychiatric trauma, that to cure one in such a way that you generate the other is an act of medical stupidity. Of course the longer the pain went on, the more it wore me out; the more overstimulated my nerves became; the more serious the situation grew. The blood under the skin had pooled until my shoulder looked as if I'd borrowed it from a leopard. I was giddy by the time the Dilaudid came along. There were indeed people in that emergency room whose acute injuries were more serious than mine; why should any of us have endured gratuitous pain?

Within three days of my emergency room ordeal, I had acute suicidal feelings of a kind I had not experienced since my first severe episode; and if I had not been under twenty-four-hour watch by my family and friends, I would have arrived at levels of physical and psychic pain that were beyond unbearable and I would have sought immediate relief of the most extreme kind. It was the tree and the vine all over again. If you see a little shoot coming out of the ground and recognize it as the shoot of a heavy vine, you can pull it out of the ground with your thumb and forefinger and all will be well. If you wait until the vine has got a firm hold on the tree, you need to have saws and perhaps an ax and a shovel to get rid of the thing and dig out the roots. It is unlikely that you can remove the vine without breaking some of the branches of the tree. I am usually able to control suicidality in myself, but, as I pointed out to the hospital staff after the whole episode was finished, refusing to treat the psychiatric complaints of patients can take a relatively insignificant matter such as a dislocated shoulder and make it a fatal disease. If someone says that he is suffering, emergency room staff should respond accordingly. Suicides take place in this country because of the conservatism of doctors such as the ones I encountered in that emergency room, who deal with intolerance for extreme pain (physical and psychological) as a weakness of character.

The following week, I went to pieces again. I had had the problem of tears during previous episodes, but never in the way that I had them now. I cried all the time, like a stalactite. It was incredibly tiring to be synthesizing all those tears, so many of them that my face became chapped. It seemed to take the most colossal effort to do simple things. I remember bursting into tears because I had used up the cake of soap that was in the shower. I cried because one of the keys stuck for a second on my computer. I found everything excruciatingly difficult, and so, for example, the prospect of lifting the telephone receiver seemed to me like bench-pressing four hundred pounds. The reality that I had to put on not just one but *two* socks and then *two* shoes so overwhelmed me that I wanted to go back to bed. Though I did not have the acute anxiety that had characterized previous episodes, paranoia began to set in as well: I started to fear, every time my dog left the room, that it was because he wasn't interested in me.

There was an extra horror in this breakdown. My previous two breakdowns had taken place when I was not on medication. After the second one, I had accepted that I would have to be on medication permanently if I was to avoid further episodes. At considerable psychic cost, I had taken my medication every day for four years. Now I found myself having a total collapse despite the fact that I was on Effexor, BuSpar, and Wellbutrin. What could this mean? In working on this book, I had met some people who had had an episode or two, then gone on medication and been fine. I had also met people who got a year out of one medication, had a collapse, got a few months out of another one—people who could never put their depression into the safety of the past tense. I had believed myself to be in the first category. I now suddenly seemed to be in the second category. I had seen these lives in which mental health was never more than occasional. It was quite possible that I had outlived my capacity to be helped by Effexor—people do exhaust these drugs. If this were so, it was a terrible world I was joining. In my mind I saw a year on one thing, a year on another, until finally I had used up all the available options.

I now have procedures in place for breakdowns. I know which doctors to call and what to say. I know when it's time to put away the razor blades and keep walking the dog. I called around and said straight out that I was depressed. Some dear friends, recently married, moved into my house and stayed with me for two months, getting me through the difficult parts of the days, talking through my anxieties and fears, telling me stories, seeing to it that I was eating, mitigating the loneliness—they made themselves my soul mates for life. My brother flew in from California and surprised me on my doorstep just when I was at my lowest. My father snapped to attention. Here's what I knew that saved me: act fast; have a good doctor prepared to hear from you; know your own patterns really clearly; regulate sleep and eating no matter how odious the task may be; lift stresses at once; exercise; mobilize love.

I called my agent as soon as I could and said that I was doing badly and that I would be suspending work on this book. I said I had no idea what the course of my disaster would be. "Pretend I was hit by a car yesterday," I said, "and that I'm in the hospital in traction waiting for the results of the X rays. Who knows when I'll be typing again?" I took Xanax even when it made me feel spaced-out and groggy, because I knew that if I let the anxiety that was in my lungs and stomach run free, it would grow worse and I would be in trouble. I had not lost my mind, I explained to friends and family, but I had most certainly mislaid it. I felt like wartime Dresden, like a city that was being destroyed and could not shield itself from the bombs, that was simply caving in, leaving only the barest remnants of gold shimmering in the midst of rubble.

Weeping embarrassingly even in the elevator at the hospital where my psychopharmacologist keeps his office, I went to ask whether anything could be done. To my surprise, my psychopharmacologist didn't see the situation in nearly such dire terms as I did. He said he was not going to take me off Effexor—"it's been working for you for a long time and there's no reason for it to stop now." He put me on Zyprexa, an antipsychotic that has antianxiety effects as well. He increased the dose of Effexor because, he said, you should never ever switch away from the product that is helping you unless you absolutely have to do so. Effexor had done it before and maybe with a boost it would do it again? He lowered my dose of Wellbutrin because Wellbutrin is activating, and in the face of high anxiety I needed to be less activated. We left the BuSpar alone. My psychopharmacologist was adding things and subtracting things and reading my responses and my self-descriptions and constructing a somehow "true" version of me, perhaps just like the old one, perhaps a little bit different. I had a lot of expertise by now and read up on the products I took (though I avoided finding out about the side effects of anything until I'd been taking it for a while; knowing the side effects is more or less a guarantee of developing the side effects). Still, it was all a vague science of smells and flavors and blends. My therapist helped me to survive the experiments: he was a champion of continuity, calming me into a belief that the future would at the very least prove equal to the past.

The night after I started on Zyprexa, I was supposed to give a lecture on Virginia Woolf. I love Virginia Woolf. Giving a lecture on Virginia Woolf and reading aloud passages from her writing was for me comparable to giving a lecture on chocolate and eating my way through. I was giving this lecture at the home of friends, to a friendly group of perhaps fifty of their associates. It was a sort of charity function for a cause in which I believed. Under ordinary circumstances, it would have been wonderful fun and little effort, and I would have been able to bask in the spotlight—which is something I rather like doing when my mood is right. One might have expected that the lecture would exacerbate my problems, but actually I was so screaming meemies that the lecture was neither here nor there: it was nerve-racking being awake, and nothing could really make things worse. So I arrived and made a little bit of polite conversation during cocktails and then stood up with my notes and found myself calm, eerily calm, as though I were merely volunteering some ideas at the dinner table, and in a strange out-of-body sort of way I watched myself deliver a reasonably coherent lecture on Woolf from memory and the written text.

After the lecture, I went with a group of friends and the people who'd organized the event to dinner in a nearby restaurant. The evening included enough varied people so that some effort was required to muster the appearance of perfect politesse, but under ordinary circumstances it would have been a pleasure. As it was, it seemed as though the air around me was setting, the way glue sets, into a weird rigidity, so that people's voices all seemed to be breaking and cracking through the solid air, and that cracking noise made it hard to hear what they were saying. I had to break through just to lift my fork. I ordered the salmon and began to be aware that my odd situation was showing. I was slightly mortified but didn't know what to do about it. Those situations are embarrassing, no matter how many people you know who have taken Prozac, no matter how wonderfully at ease everyone is supposed to be with depression. Everyone at the table knew I was writing a book on the subject and most of them had read my articles. It didn't help. I mumbled and apologized my way through dinner like a Cold War diplomat. "So sorry if I seem a bit unfocused, but you know I've just been having another go-around with depression," I might have said, but then everyone would have felt obliged to ask about specific symptoms and causes and to attempt to reassure me, and those reassurances would in fact have exacerbated the depression. Or, "I'm afraid I can't actually follow what you're saying because I've been taking five milligrams of Xanax every day, though I'm of course not addicted, and have also just begun a new antipsychotic which I believe has strong sedating properties. Is your salad good?" On the other hand, I had a feeling that if I went on saying nothing, people were going to notice how peculiar I was being.

And then I found that the air was getting so hard and brittle that the words were coming through in stacatto noises that I couldn't quite string together. Perhaps you have had the experience of attending a lecture and realizing that in order to follow the main points you need to keep paying attention; but your mind wanders a bit and then you can't quite make sense of what is being said when you return to it. The logic is missing. So it was for me, but on a sentence-by-sentence basis. I felt the logic disappearing right out from under me. Someone had said something about

Breakdowns

China, but I wasn't sure what. I thought someone else had mentioned ivory, but I didn't know whether it was the same person who'd been talking about China, though I did remember that the Chinese had made ivory things. Someone was asking me something about a fish, perhaps my fish? Whether I'd ordered fish? Whether I liked fishing? Was there something about Chinese fish? I heard someone repeat a question (I recognized the sentence pattern from the time before), and then I felt my eyes close and I thought quietly, it is not polite to fall asleep when someone asks you a question for the second time. I must wake up. So I pulled my head up from my chest and smiled in what was meant to be an I-didn't-quite-catch-that way. I saw puzzled faces looking at me. "Are you okay?" someone asked again, and I said, "Possibly not," and some friends who were there took me by the arms and led me outside.

"So sorry," I kept saying, dimly aware that I had left everyone at the table thinking I was probably strung out on drugs, and wishing that I had simply said that I was depressed, hypermedicated, and unsure of how well I'd get through the evening. "So sorry," and everyone kept saying that there was nothing to be sorry about. And the friends who had saved me got me home and up to my bed. I took out my contact lenses and then tried to chat for a few minutes, to reassure myself. "So how are you?" I said, but when my friend started to answer me, he became rather faint, like the Cheshire cat, and then I passed out again and went into a cavernous sleep for seventeen hours and dreamed of a great war. My God, I had forgotten the *intensity* of depression. It cuts so deep, so far! We are determined by sets of norms that are quite beyond us. The norms to which I was brought up and which I established for myself are quite high by world standards; if I do not feel able to write books, I feel something is wrong with me. Some people's norms are much lower; those of other people are much higher. If George W. Bush wakes up one day feeling that he can't be the leader of the free world, something's wrong with him. But some people feel that they're okay as long as they can feed themselves and keep on living. Collapsing at dinner is well outside of the range I count okay.

I woke up feeling slightly less horrible than I had felt the day before, though I was also upset by my wander out of control. The idea of going outside still seemed shockingly difficult, but I knew that I could go downstairs (though I wasn't sure I wanted to do such a thing). I could send some E-mail. I made a bleary call to my psychopharmacologist, and he suggested that I cut back to half of a Zyprexa and lower the consumption of Xanax. I was frankly incredulous when my symptoms started to lift that afternoon. By the evening, I was nearly fine, like a hermit crab who had outgrown one shell and given it up, crawled vulnerable across the beach, and then found another shell elsewhere. Though I still had a ways to go, I was joyous at the knowledge that I was recovering.

So that was the third breakdown. It was a revelation. While the first and second breakdowns had been acute for periods of about six weeks each and had lasted in all about eight months each, the third break-down, which I call the mini-breakdown, was acute for six days and lasted about two months. I was lucky to have a very good response to the Zyprexa, but I also found that the research I had been doing for this book, whether it was to be of value to anyone else or not, was terrifically useful to me. I had been sad for a few months for a variety of reasons and was under considerable stress, coping with everything, but not easily. Because I had learned so much about depression, I recognized the crossover point immediately for what it was. I had found a psychophar-macologist who was capable of subtlety in modulating a drug cocktail. I believe that if I had gone on medication before my first breakdown had swept me all the way into the abyss, I would have been able to bring my first depression to heel before it got out of control, and that I might have avoided real breakdowns altogether. If I had not gone off the medication that helped me through that breakdown, I might never have had a second one. By the time I started heading for a third one, I was determined not to make a stupid mistake again.

Remission from mental illness requires maintenance: all of us period-ically encounter physical and psychological trauma, and chances are pretty good that those of us with a significant vulnerability will all have moments of relapse in the face of problems. A lifetime of relative freedom can unfold best with careful and responsible attention to medication, bal-anced with steadying, insight-producing talk. Most people with severe depression require a combination of drugs, sometimes at unorthodox doses. They also require an understanding of their shifting selves, one that a professional can facilitate. Among the people whose stories I have found achingly tragic are the many who have had depression, have sought help, and have been thrown some product that they have taken, often at the wrong dose, to half-help symptoms that could have been cured. Perhaps the most tragic among these are the ones who know they are getting poor treatment but whose health maintenance organi-zations (HMOs) and insurance make it impossible for them to do better.

There is an old fable that used to be told in my family about a poor family, a sage, and a goat. The poor family lived in misery and squalor, nine of them sharing one room, and no one had enough to eat and every-one's clothes were in rags and their life was one of utter, unrelenting mis-ery. Finally one day the man of the house set off to visit the sage and said to him, "Great sage, we are so miserable that we can barely stay alive.

The noise is terrible, and the filth is awful, and the lack of privacy could kill a person, and we never have enough to eat, and we are all beginning to hate one another, and it is just horrendous. What should we do?" To which the sage replied simply, "You must get a goat and have the goat live inside the house with you for one month. Then your problems will be solved." The man looked at the sage in astonishment. "A goat? To live with a goat?" But the sage insisted, and since he was a very wise sage, the man did as he had been told. For the next month, the hellish life of this man's family was beyond intolerable. The noise was worse; the filth was worse; there was nothing remotely resembling privacy; there was nothing to eat since the goat kept eating everything; and there were no clothes because the goat ate everyone's clothes as well. The rancor in the house became explosive. At the end of the month, the man returned to the sage in a fury. "We have lived for one month with a goat in our hut," he said. "It has been horrendous. How could you have given us such ludicrous advice?" The sage nodded sagely and said, "Now get rid of the goat and you will see how peaceful and sublime your lives are."

It's that way with depression. If you can knock out your depression, you can live in wonderful peace with the real-world problems you may have to confront, which always seem minimal by comparison. I called one of the people I was interviewing for this book and politely began the conversation by asking how he was. "Well," he said, "my back hurts; I've sprained an ankle; the children are mad at me; it's pouring rain; the cat died; and I'm facing bankruptcy. On the other hand, I'm psychologically asymptomatic at present, so I'd say all in all that things are fabulous." My third breakdown was a real goat of a breakdown; it came at a time when I was feeling discontent about a variety of things in my life that I knew, rationally, were ultimately fixable. When I pulled through it, I felt like throwing a small festival to celebrate the joyfulness of my messy life. And I felt surprisingly ready, indeed curiously happy, to return to this book, which I had pushed aside for the two months preceding. All of that being said, it was a breakdown and it had taken place while I was on medication, and I have never since then felt fully secure. During the late stages of writing this book I would get struck by paroxysms of fear and loneliness. They were not breakdown stuff, but sometimes I would type a page and then I'd have to go lie down for half an hour to recover from my own words. Sometimes I got weepy; sometimes I got anxious and spent a day or two in bed. I think those experiences accurately reflected the difficulty of this writing and a certain petrifying uncertainty about the rest of my life, but I do not feel free; I am not free.

I have done pretty well for side effects. My current psychopharmacologist is expert in side-effect management. I have had some sexual side effects from my medications—a slightly decreased libido and the universal problem of much-delayed orgasm. A few years ago, I added Wellbutrin to my regimen; it seemed to get my libido running again, though things have never come up to old standards. My psychopharmacologist has also given me Viagra, just in case I get that side effect, and has since added dexamphetamine, which is supposed to increase sexual drive. I think it does but it also make me twitchy. My body seems to go through shifts beyond my ability to discern, and what works just splendidly one night may be a bit tricky the next. Zyprexa is sedating and I mostly sleep too much, about ten hours a night, but I have Xanax around for the occasional night when I am assaulted by sensation and cannot get my eyes closed.

There is a curious intimacy that comes of swapping breakdown stories. Laura Anderson and I have communicated with each other almost daily for more than three years, and during my third breakdown, she was extraordinarily attentive. She came from nowhere into my life and we developed a friendship of strange and sudden intimacy: within a few months of her first letter to me, I felt as though I had known her forever, and though our contact—mostly by E-mail but sometimes by letter or postcard, very occasionally by phone, and once in person—remained separate from the rest of my life, it was nonetheless so habitual as to become, very soon, addictive. It took on the shape of a love story, running through discovery, ecstasy, tiredness, rebirth, habit, and profundity. At times Laura was too much too soon, and in the early stages of our contact I sometimes rebelled against her or tried to contain the contact between us—but soon I came to feel on the rare days when I didn't hear from Laura as though I'd missed a meal or a night's sleep. Though Laura Anderson is bipolar, her manic episodes are much less pronounced than her depressive ones, and they are more easily controlled—a condition that is with increasing frequency called bipolar two. She's one of the many people for whom, no matter how carefully medications and treatments and behaviors are regulated, depression always lies waiting— some days she's free of it and other days she's not, and there's nothing she can do to keep it at bay.

She sent me the first letter in January of 1998. It was a letter full of hope. She had read my magazine story about depression, and she felt that we knew each other. She gave me her home number and told me to call anytime at any hour whenever I wished, and she enclosed a list of albums that had helped her to get through bad times and one of the books she thought I would like that were on my wavelength. She was in Austin, Texas, because that was where her boyfriend lived, but she was somewhat isolated and bored there. She had been too depressed to work, though she was interested in government service and hoped to get a job in the Texas statehouse. She told me that she had taken Prozac, Paxil, Zoloft, Wellbutrin, Klonopin, BuSpar, Valium, Librium, Ativan, and "of course Xanax" and was now on several of these as well as Depakote and Ambien. She was having trouble with her supervising psychiatrist, "so—guess what—off to doctor number forty-nine." There was something in her letter that attracted me, and I wrote back as warmly as I could.

I next heard from her in February. "The Depakote is not proving itself," she wrote. "I am frustrated by memory loss and shaky hands and stuttering and forgetting the lighter when it's taken forty minutes to compile the cigarettes and the ashtray anyway. I am frustrated because these diseases seem to me so blatantly *multi*polar in many instances—it makes me wish Lévi-Strauss had never brought our attention to binary opposition. *Bicycle* is about as far as I'll go with the prefix. I am convinced there are forty different shades of black, and I don't like looking at this on a linear scale—I see it more as a circle and a cycle where the wheel is spinning too quickly and a desire for death can enter through any spoke. I thought of checking myself into the hospital this week, but I have been in there enough to know that I would not be allowed a stereo even with headphones, or scissors to make Valentine's Day cards, and that I would miss my dogs, and that I would be terrified without and would miss terribly Peter, my boyfriend, who loves me through all the vomit and anger and unrest and no sex and that I would have to sleep in the hall by the nurses' station or be locked in a room on suicide watch and so on—well, no thank you. I'm fairly confident that with the meds keeping me equatorial—between the two poles—I'll be okay."

As spring came her spirits lifted. In May, she became pregnant and was excited about having a baby. She learned, however, that Depakote has been associated with spina bifida and improper brain development; tried to go off it; worried that she had not gone off soon enough; began to destabilize; and soon wrote to me, "Here I sit in a postabortion blue stupor. I guess going back on the medication is my silver lining. I try not to get angry or resentful about all this, but sometimes it seems so unfair. It's a breezy, big blue-sky day here in Austin and I'm wondering why I feel so depleted. See? Anything—even a normal reaction to a crummy ordeal—sends me into a fit of worry over a possible imminent depression. I'm in a sort of lackluster, grumpy Valium haze, though: headachy and stressed from crying."

Ten days later, she wrote, "I have stabilized—perhaps going down a bit further than I'd like, but not into a worrisome range. I have changed doctors and medicine—from Depakote to Tegretol, with some Zyprexa thrown in to expedite the effects of the Tegretol. Zyprexa really slows me down. Physical side effects for mental illness seem such an insult! I think with all the stuff I've taken I now qualify for Advanced Depression. Still—I get this strange amnesia—it becomes impossible to remember, when an hour is an honest hour, just how dreadful depression is—eking one's way through endless minutes. I am so tired, so exhausted of trying to figure out who I am when I'm 'fine'—what is normal or acceptable for me."

A few days later she wrote, "The self-consciousness gets in the way of offering much depth of personality to people—as a result, most friends I've made in the past eight or nine years are fairly casual. This grows lonely, and leaves me feeling idiotic. I just called, for example, a very dear (and demanding) friend in West Virginia, who wants an explanation for my not coming to visit her and her new baby. What to say? That I would have loved to make the trip but was busy staying out of the mental hospital? It's so humiliating—so degrading. If I knew I wouldn't get caught, I'd love to lie about it—invent an acceptable cancer, that recurs and vanishes, that people could understand—that wouldn't make them frightened and uncomfortable."

Laura is constantly hindered; every part of her life is defined around her illness. "As for dating: I need people I date to be a little able to take care of themselves, because me taking care of me takes a lot of energy, and I can't be responsible for every little hurt feeling someone has. Isn't that a terrible way to feel about love? It's hard to manage professionally too—the short-lived jobs, the gaps in between them. Who wants to hear about your hopes for your new medication? How can you ask that anyone understand? Before I'd ever had this illness myself, I had a dear friend who was depressive. I listened to everything he said as if we understood the same language, when what I've realized since is that depression speaks, or teaches you, an entirely different one."

In the months that followed she seemed to be struggling against something she could feel in the wings. In the meanwhile, she and I set about the business of getting to know each other. I learned that she had been molested as a teenager and raped in her early twenties, and that each of these experiences had left deep marks. She had married at twenty-six and had had her first depression the following year. Her husband had seemed unable to cope with it, and she had coped by drinking too much. In the autumn, she had become slightly manic and gone to the doctor; he had told her that she was just tense and put her on Valium. "The mania was enveloping my mind but my body was gruesomely slowed down," she later told me. At the Christmas party she and her husband had held the next month, she had become furious and thrown a trout mousse at him. Then she had gone upstairs and swallowed the rest of the Valium. He had taken her to the emergency room and told the attending staff that he couldn't cope with her; she had been put in a mental health facility and had stayed there through Christmas. When she came home, heavily medicated, "the marriage was over. We sort of limped through the next year, but that following Christmas we went to Paris, and I looked at him over dinner and thought, 'I am no happier now than I was a year ago in the hospital.'" She moved out; met a new boyfriend fairly soon; and moved to Austin to be with him. The depression was fairly regular thereafter, at least once a year.

In September 1998, Laura wrote to tell me of a brief spate of "that terrible lethargic anxiety." By mid-October she was starting to sink and she knew it. "I am not yet in a full-blown depression, but am slowing down a little—I mean that I have to focus on each thing I do on more and more levels. I'm not completely depressed at this point, but I have entered a recession." She began taking Wellbutrin. "I just hate this feeling of distance from everything," she complained. Soon afterward, she started spending days in bed. The medications were failing her again. She cut herself off from extraneous people and focused on her dogs. "When my regular appetites are diminished by depression—my needs for laughter, sex, food—the dogs provide me with my only really numinous moments."

In early November she protested, "I only take baths now because the water beating down on me from the shower is too much to deal with in the morning and seems, these days, like a violent way to begin the day. Driving seems like such an effort. So does visiting the ATM, shopping—you name it." She rented *The Wizard of Oz* to distract herself, but "the sad parts made me cry." Her appetite was gone. "I tried some tuna today, but it made me throw up, so I just had a little rice when I made it for the dogs." She complained that even visits to the doctor made her feel bad. "It's hard to be honest with him about how I'm feeling because I don't want to let him down."

We kept up our daily correspondence; when I asked Laura whether she didn't find it difficult to keep writing, she said, "Giving attention to others is the simplest way to get attention *from* others. It is also the simplest way to keep a sense of perspective about yourself. I have a need to share my self-obsession. I am so aware of it in my life right now I wince every time I hit the 'I' key. (Ouch. Ouch.) The whole day thus far has been an exercise in FORCING myself to do the tiniest things and trying to evaluate how serious my situation is—Am I really depressed? Am I just lazy? Is this anxiety from too much coffee or from too much antidepressant? The self-assessment process itself made me start to weep. What bothers everyone is that they can't DO anything to help other than be present. I rely on E-mail to keep me sane! Exclamation points are little lies."

Later that week: "It is ten o'clock in the morning and I am already overwhelmed by the idea of today. I'm trying, I'm trying. I keep walking around on the verge of tears chanting, 'It's okay. It's okay,' and taking big breaths. My goal is to stay safely in between self-analysis and self-destruction. I just feel like I'm draining people right now, yourself included. There is only so much I can ask for while giving nothing back. I think if I wear something I like and pull my hair back and take the dogs with me, though, I will feel confident enough to go to the store and buy some orange juice."

Just before Thanksgiving she wrote, "I looked at old photos today, and they seem like they are snapshots of someone else's life. What a series of trade-offs medication mandates." But soon she was at least getting up. "Today I had a few good moments," she wrote at the end of the month. "More of those, please, from whoever doles them out. I was able to walk in a crowd and not feel self-conscious." The next day she had a little relapse. "I *was* feeling better and hoped it was the start of something wonderful, but today I have a lot of anxiety, of the falling-over-backward, drawstring-in-the-sternum variety. But I still have some hope, which helps." The next day, things were worse. "My mood continues to be grim. Morning terror and abject helplessness by late afternoon." She described going to the park with her boyfriend. "He bought a pamphlet identifying all the plants. By the description of one tree, it said, 'ALL PARTS DEADLY POISONOUS.' I thought maybe I could find the tree, chew on a leaf or two, and curl up under a rock ledge and drift off. I miss the Laura who would have loved to put on her bathing suit and lie in the sun today and look at the blue, blue sky! She has been plucked out of me by an evil witch and replaced by a horrid girl! Depression takes away whatever I really, really like about myself (which is not so much in the first place). Feeling hopeless and full of despair is just a slower way of being dead. I try to work through these large blocks of horror in the meantime. I can see why they call it 'mean.'"

But a week later she was getting distinctly better. Then suddenly, at a 7-Eleven store, she lost her temper when the man behind the counter started ringing up someone else's purchases ahead of hers. With a rage totally uncharacteristic of her, she yelled, "JESUS CHRIST! Is this a *convenience* store or a fucking hot dog stand?" and marched out without her soda. "It's just a jagged climb. I am so tired of talking about it, thinking about it." When her boyfriend said he loved her, she burst into tears. The next day she was feeling better and ate twice and bought herself a pair of socks. She went to the park and suddenly felt the urge to get on the swings. "While I have spent the last week with the falling-backward sensation looming large, it felt great to swing. You get the opposite feeling: a whooshy, light sensation in the middle of your chest, like when you go *just* fast enough over a hill in the car. It feels good just to do something so simple; I started to feel a little more myself, and a sense of being light and feeling smart and bright came back. I'm not going to hope for too much more time, but just that *feeling* of no abstract worries, no inexplicable weight or sadness, felt *so* rich and real and good that for once, I didn't feel like crying. I know the other feelings will come back, but I think I got a reprieve tonight, from God and the swingset, a reminder to be hopeful and patient, an augury of good things to come." In December she had an adverse reaction to lithium; it made her skin intolerably dry. She lowered her dose and went on Neurontin. It seemed to work. "Shifting back to the center, *a* center, known as ME feels good and real," she wrote.

The following October, we finally met. She was staying with her mother in Waterford, Virginia, a beautiful old town outside Washington, the place where she had grown up. I had become so fond of her by then that I couldn't believe we had never met. I took the train and she came to meet me at the station, bringing her friend Walt, whom I was also meeting for the first time. She was svelte, blond, and beautiful. But the time with her family was stirring too many memories and she was not doing well. She was desperately anxious, so anxious that she was having trouble speaking. In a hoarse whisper, she apologized for her condition. Her movements were clearly enormously effortful. She said she had been going down all week. I asked whether I was adding to the strain, and she assured me that I was not. We went out to lunch, and she ordered mussels. She seemed to be unable to eat them; her hands were shaking badly, and by the time she had tried to pry open a few shells, she was spattered with the sauce in which they had arrived. She was not able to talk and cope with the mussels at the same time, so Walt and I chatted. He described Laura's gradual descent during the week, and she made little sounds of acquiescence. She had given up on the mussels by now and was giving her full attention to a glass of white wine. I was really quite shocked; she had warned me that things were rough, but I was not prepared for her aura of futility.

We dropped Walt off and then I drove Laura's car since she was much too shaky to drive. When we got back to the house, her mother evinced concern. Laura and I had a conversation that drifted in and out of coherence; she seemed to be speaking from some faraway place. And then as we were looking at some photos, she suddenly got stuck. It was like nothing I'd ever seen or imagined. She was telling me who was who in the photos and she began repeating herself. "That's Geraldine," she said, and then she winced and began again, pointing, "That's Geraldine," and then again, "That's Geraldine," each time taking longer to pronounce the syllables. Her face was frozen and she seemed to be having trouble moving her lips. I called her mother and her brother, Michael. Michael put his hands on Laura's shoulders and said, "It's okay, Laura. It's okay." We eventually managed to get her upstairs; she was still saying over and over, "That's Geraldine." Her mother changed her out of the mussel-spattered clothes and put her in bed and sat and rubbed her hand. The meeting was hardly what I had anticipated.

As it turned out, some of her medications were having a bad interaction that had caused this seizure; indeed they were the reason for the strange stiffness in the afternoon, for the loss of speech, for the hyper-anxiety. By the end of the day, she had come through the worst, but "all the color had drained out of my soul, all the me of me I loved; I was a lit-tle doll-shell of what I had been." She was soon put on a new regimen. Not until Christmas did she began to feel like herself again; and then in March 2000, just as things were looking up, she had the seizures once more. "I am so frightened," she wrote to me. "And so humiliated. It's pretty pathetic when the best news you can share is that you're not convulsing." Six months later, they hit again. "I can't keep picking up my life again," she said to me. "I'm so afraid of the seizures that I get anxi-ety—today I left the house to go to work and I threw up on myself while I was driving. I had to go home and change my clothes so I could get to the office, and so I was late, and I told them I'd been having seizures but they just gave me a disciplinary notice. My doctor wants me to take Val-ium, but that makes me pass out. This is my life now. This will always be my life, these terrible plummeting descents into hell. The awful memo-ries. Can I stand to live this way?"

Can I stand to live the way I do? Well, can any of us stand to live with our own difficulties? In the end, most of us do. We march forward. The voices of past time come back like voices of the dead to sympathize about mutability and the passage of the years. When I am sad, I remem-ber too much, too well: always my mother and who I was when we sat in the kitchen and talked, from the time I was five until her death when I was twenty-seven; how my grandmother's Christmas cactus bloomed every year until she died when I was twenty-five; that time in Paris in the mideighties with my mother's friend Sandy, who wanted to give her green sun hat to Joan of Arc, Sandy who died two years later; my great-uncle Don and great-aunt Betty and the chocolates in their top drawer; my father's cousins Helen and Alan, my aunt Dorothy, and all the others who are gone. I hear the voices of the dead all the time. It is at night that these people and my own past selves come to visit me, and when I wake up and realize that they are not in the same world as I, I feel that strange despair, something beyond ordinary sadness and closely akin, for a moment, to the anguish of depression. And yet if I miss them and the past they made for and with me, the way to their absent love lies, I know, in living, in staying on. Is it depression when I think how I would prefer to go where they have gone, and to stop the maniacal struggle of staying alive? Or is it just a part of life, to keep living in all the ways we cannot stand?

I find the fact of the past, the reality of time's passage, incredibly difficult. My house is full of books I can't read and records to which I can't listen and photos at which I can't look because they are too strongly associated with the past. When I see friends from college, I try not to talk about college too much because I was so happy then—not necessarily happier than I am now, but with a happiness that was particular and specific in its moods and that will never come again. Those days of young splendor eat at me. I hit walls of past pleasure all the time, and for me past pleasure is much harder to process than past pain. To think of a terrible time that has gone: well, I know that post–traumatic stress is an acute affliction, but for me the traumas of the past are mercifully far away. The pleasures of the past, however, are tough. The memory of the good times with people who are no longer alive, or who are no longer the people they were: that is where I find the worst current pain. Don't make me remember, I say to the detritus of past pleasures. Depression can as easily be the consequence of too much that was joyful as of too much that was horrible. There is such a thing as post–joy stress too. The worst of depression lies in a present moment that cannot escape the past it idealizes or deplores.

CHAPTER III

Treatments

There are two major modalities of treatment for depression: talking therapies, which trade in words, and physical intervention, which includes both pharmacological care and electroshock or electroconvulsive therapy (ECT). Reconciling the psychosocial and the psychopharmacological understandings of depression is difficult but necessary. It is extremely dangerous that so many people see this as a one-or-the-other situation. Medication and therapy should not compete for a limited population of depressives; they should be complementary therapies that can be used together or separately depending on the situation of the patient. The biopsychosocial model of inclusive therapy continues to elude us. The consequences of this can hardly be overstated. It's fashionable for psychiatrists to tell you first the cause of your depression (lowered serotonin levels or early traumas are the most popular) and second, as if there were a logical link, the cure; but this is poppycock. "I do not believe that if the causes of your problems were psychosocial, they would require a psychosocial treatment; nor that if the causes were biological, they would require a biological treatment," Ellen Frank of the University of Pittsburgh has said. It is striking that patients who recover from depression by means of psychotherapy show the same biological changes—in, for example, sleep electroencephalogram (EEG)—as those who receive medication.

While traditional psychiatrists see depression as an integral part of the person who suffers from it and attempt to bring about change in that person's character structure, psychopharmacology in its purest form sees the illness as an externally determined imbalance that can be corrected without reference to the rest of a personality. The anthropologist T. M. Luhrmann has recently written about the dangers posed by this split in modern psychiatry: "Psychiatrists are supposed to understand these approaches as different tools in a common toolbox. Yet they are taught as different tools, based on different models, and used for different purposes." "Psychiatry," says William Normand, a practicing psychoanalyst who uses medications when he feels they are useful, "has gone from being brainless to being mindless"—practitioners who once neglected the physiological brain in favor of emotionality now neglect the emotional human mind in favor of brain chemistry. The conflict between psychodynamic therapy and medication is ultimately a conflict on moral grounds; we tend categorically to assume that if the problem is responsive to psychotherapeutic dialogue, it is a problem you should be able to overcome with simple rigor, while a problem responsive to the ingestion of chemicals is not your fault and requires no rigor of you. It is true both that very little depression is entirely the fault of the sufferer, and that almost all depression can be ameliorated with rigor. Antidepressants help those who help themselves. If you push yourself too hard, you will make yourself worse, but you must push hard enough if you really want to get out. Medication and therapy are tools to be used as necessary. Neither blame nor indulge yourself. Melvin McGuinness, a psychiatrist at Johns Hopkins Hospital, speaks of "volition, emotion, and cognition" running along in interlocked cycles, almost like biorhythms. Your emotion affects volition and cognition, but it doesn't take them over.

Talking therapies come out of psychoanalysis, which in turn comes out of the ritual disclosure of dangerous thoughts first formalized in the Church confessional. Psychoanalysis is a form of treatment in which specific techniques are used to unearth the early trauma that has occasioned neurosis. It usually requires a great deal of time—four to five hours a week is standard—and it focuses on bringing the content of the unconscious mind to light. It has become fashionable to bash Freud and the psychodynamic theories that have come down to us from him, but in fact the Freudian model, though flawed, is an excellent one. It contains, in Luhrmann's words, "a sense of human complexity, of depth, an exigent demand to struggle against one's own refusals, and a respect for the difficulty of human life." While people argue with one another about the specifics of Freud's work and blame him for the prejudices of his time, they overlook the fundamental truth of his writing, his grand humility: that we frequently do not know our own motivations in life and are prisoners to what we cannot understand. We can recognize only a small fragment of our own, and an even smaller fragment of anyone else's, impetus. If we take only that from Freud—and we can call this motive force "the unconscious" or "the disregulation of certain brain circuits"—we have some basis for the study of mental illness.

Psychoanalysis is good at explaining things, but it is not an efficient way to change them. The massive power of the psychoanalytic process appears to be misspent if the patient's goal is an immediate transformation of general mood; when I hear of psychoanalysis being used to ameliorate depression, I think of someone standing on a sandbar and firing a machine gun at the incoming tide. The psychodynamic therapies that have grown out of psychoanalysis, however, do have a crucial role to play. The unexamined life can seldom be repaired without some close examination, and the lesson of psychoanalysis is that such examination is almost always revealing. The schools of talking therapy that have the most currency are the ones in which a client talks to a doctor about his current feelings and experiences. For many years, talking about depression was considered the best cure for it. It is still a cure. "Take notes," wrote Virginia Woolf in *The Years*, "and the pain goes away." That is the underlying process of most psychotherapy. The role of the doctor is to listen closely and attentively while the client gets in touch with his true motivations, so that he can understand why he acts as he does. Most psychodynamic therapies are based on the principle that naming something is a good way to subdue it, and that knowing the source of a problem is useful in solving that problem. Such therapies do not, however, stop with knowledge: they teach strategies for harnessing knowledge to ameliorative use. The doctor may also make nonjudgmental responses that will allow the client sufficient insight to modify his behavior and so improve the quality of his life. Depression is often occasioned by isolation. A good therapist can help a depressed person to connect with the people around him and to set up structures of support that mitigate the severity of depression.

There are stalwarts to whom such emotional insight is meaningless. "Who cares about motives and origins?" asks Donald Klein of Columbia University, a leading psychopharmacologist. "No one's knocked out Freud because no one has any theory one bit better than all that internalized conflict. The point is that we can now treat it; philosophizing about where it comes from has not so far been of the slightest therapeutic usefulness."

It is true that medication has set us free, but we should all care about the origins of illness. Steven Hyman, director of the NIMH, says, "For coronary heart disease, we don't just write a prescription for drugs. We also ask people to limit their cholesterol and we give them an exercise regimen and dietary counseling and maybe stress management. Combinatorial process isn't unique to mental illnesses. The medication-versus-psychotherapy debate is ridiculous. Both are empirical questions. It's my philosophical prejudice that the two should work well together because the medication will make people more available for psychotherapy, will help to initiate an upwards spiral." Ellen Frank has conducted a number of studies showing that therapy is not nearly as effective as drugs for taking people out of depression, but that therapy has a protective effect against recurrence. Though the data in this field is complicated, it suggests that the combination of drugs and therapy works better than either one alone. "It's the treatment strategy for preventing the next episode of depression," she says. "It's not clear to me how much room there's going to be in the future of health care for an integrated view, and that's scary." Martin Keller, of Brown University's Department of Psychology, working with a multi-university team, found in a recent study of depressives that less than half experienced significant improvement with just medication; that less than half experienced significant improvement with cognitive behavioral analysis; and that more than 80 percent experienced significant improvement after being treated with both. The case for combination is pretty well incontrovertible. Exasperated, Robert Klitzman, of Columbia University, says, "Prozac should not *obviate* insight; it should *enable* insight." And Luhrmann writes, "Doctors feel that they have been trained to see and understand a grotesque misery, yet all they are allowed to do is hand out a biomedical lollipop to its prisoners and then turn their backs."

If real experience has triggered your descent into depression, you have a human yen to understand it even when you have ceased to experience it; the limiting of experience that is achieved with chemical pills is not tantamount to cure. Both the problem and the fact of the problem usually require urgent attention. It may be that more people will get treated in our pro-medication era; overall public health may go up. But it is terribly dangerous to put talking therapy on the back burner. Therapy allows a person to make sense of the new self he has attained on medication, and to accept the loss of self that occurred during a breakdown. You need to be reborn after a severe episode, and you need to learn the behaviors that may protect against relapse. You need to run your life differently from how you ran it before. "It's so hard to regulate your life, sleep, diet, exercise, under any circumstances," comments Norman Rosenthal of the NIMH. "Think how hard it is when you're depressed! You need a therapist as a sort of coach, to keep you at it. Depression is an illness, not a life choice, and you have to be helped through it." "Medicines treat depression," my therapist said to me. "I treat depressives." What calms you down? What exacerbates your symptoms? There is no particular difference, from the chemical standpoint, between the depression that has been triggered by the death of family members and the depression occasioned by the demise of a two-week affair. Though extreme responses seem more rational in the first instance than in the second, the clinical experience is nearly identical. As Sylvia Simpson, a clinician at Johns Hopkins, said, "If it looks like depression, treat it like depression."

When I started heading in for my second breakdown, I had terminated my psychoanalysis and was without a therapist. Everyone told me firmly that I should find a new one. Finding a new therapist when you are feeling up and communicative is burdensome and ghastly, but doing it when you are in the throes of a major depression is beyond the pale. It is important to shop around for a good therapist. I tried eleven therapists in six weeks. For each of my eleven, I rehearsed the litany of my woes, until it seemed that I was reciting a monologue from someone else's play. Some of the potential therapists seemed wise. Some of them were outlandish. One woman had covered all her furniture with Saran Wrap to protect it from her yapping dogs; she kept offering me bites of the moldy-looking gefilte fish she was eating from a plastic container. I left when one of the dogs peed on my shoe. One man gave me the wrong address for his office ("Oh, I used to have an office there!"), and one told me that I had no real problems and should lighten up a little bit. There was the woman who told me she didn't believe in emotion, and the man who seemed to believe in nothing else. There were the cognitivist, the Freudian who bit his nails for the length of our session, the Jungian, and the autodidact. One man kept interrupting me to tell me that I was *just* like him. Several seemed simply not to get it when I tried to explain to them who I was. I had long supposed that my well-adjusted friends must see good therapists. What I found out is that many well-adjusted people with straightforward relationships to their husbands or wives establish lunatic relationships with weirdo doctors for the sake, one can only presume, of balance. "We try to do studies of drugs versus therapy," Steven Hyman says. "Have we done longitudinal studies on bright therapists versus incompetent ones? We are really Lewis and Clark in this area."

I eventually made a choice with which I have been very happy since— someone whose mind seemed quick and in whom I saw glints of a real humanity. I chose him because he seemed intelligent and loyal. Given my bad experience with the analyst who had broken off our analysis and kept me from taking medication when I desperately needed it, I was guarded at first, and it took me a good three or four years to trust him. He has been steadfast through periods of turmoil and crisis. He has been entertaining during good times; I place high value on a sense of humor in anyone with whom I spend so much time. He has worked well with my psychopharmacologist. He has in the end persuaded me that he knows what he's doing and that he wants to help. It was worth trying ten other people first. Do not go to a therapist whom you dislike. People you dislike, no matter how skilled they are, cannot help you. If you think you are smarter than your doctor, you are probably right: a degree in psychiatry or psychology is no guarantee of genius. Use the utmost care in choosing a psychiatrist. It is mind-boggling how many people who would drive an extra twenty minutes to use a preferred dry cleaner and who complain to the manager when the supermarket runs out of their favorite brand of canned tomatoes seem to choose a psychiatrist as if he were a generic service-provider. Remember, you are at the very least placing your mind in the hands of this person. Remember, too, that you must tell the psychiatrist what you cannot show him. "It's so much harder," Laura Anderson wrote to me, "to trust someone when the problem is so nebulous that you can't tell whether they have understood you; it's harder for them to trust you too." I become incredibly controlled with psychiatrists even when I am feeling midnight miserable. I sit up straight and I don't cry. I represent myself with ironies and interject gallows humor in a peculiar effort to charm the ones who treat me, people who do not in fact wish to be charmed. Sometimes I wonder whether my psychiatrists believe me when I tell them how I've felt, because I can hear the detachment in my own voice. I imagine how they must deplore this thick social skin through which my real feelings penetrate so slightly. I often wish that I could emote fully in the psychiatrist's office. I have never managed to define the space of therapy as private. The way I can talk to my brother, for example, eludes me with my doctors. I suppose it must be too unsafe. Just occasionally, preciously, a glimmer of my reality makes it through in essence rather than via description.

One of the ways to judge a psychiatrist is to observe how well he seems to judge you. The art of an initial screening lies in asking the right questions. I did not sit in on confidential one-on-one psychiatric interviews, but I did sit in on a large number of hospital admissions, and I was amazed by how varied the approaches to depressed patients seemed to be. Most of the good psychiatrists I saw would begin by letting a patient tell his story and would then move briskly on to highly structured interviews in which they looked for particular information. The ability to conduct such an interview well is among a clinician's most important skills. Sylvia Simpson, a clinician at Johns Hopkins, established in the first ten minutes of an interview that an incoming patient fresh from a suicide attempt had bipolar illness. This woman's psychiatrist, with whom she had been in treatment for five years, had not established this extremely basic fact and had prescribed antidepressants without mood stabilizers—a regimen known to be inappropriate for bipolar patients, in whom it often causes mixed agitated states. When I asked Simpson about this later, she said, "It took years of steady work to arrive at those interview questions." Later, I sat in on interviews with recently homeless people conducted by Henry McCurtiss, chief of psychiatry at Harlem Hospital. He spent at least ten minutes of each twenty-minute interview taking incredibly detailed housing histories from his patients. When I finally asked him why he was pursuing this matter so arduously, he said, "Those who have lived in one place for long periods of time are temporarily homeless for circumstantial reasons but are capable of living well-regulated lives, and they require primarily a social intervention. Those who have moved around constantly, or who have been homeless repeatedly, or who can't remember where they've lived, probably have a severe underlying complaint and require primarily a psychiatric intervention." I am lucky to have good insurance that pays for me to make weekly visits to a therapist and monthly visits to a psychopharmacologist. Most HMOs are keen on medications, which are, comparatively speaking, cheap. They are not keen on talking therapies and hospitalizations, which take lots of time and cost plenty.

The two kinds of talking therapy that have the best record for the treatment of depression are cognitive-behavioral therapy (CBT) and interpersonal therapy (IPT). CBT is a form of psychodynamic therapy—based on emotional and mental responses to external events, in the present and in childhood—that is tightly focused on objectives. The system was developed by Aaron Beck of the University of Pennsylvania and is now in use throughout the United States and most of Western Europe. Beck proposes that one's thoughts about oneself are frequently destructive, and that by forcing the mind to think in certain ways one can actually change one's reality—it's a program that one of his collaborators has called "learned optimism." He believes depression is the consequence of false logic, and that by correcting negative reasoning one may achieve better mental health. CBT teaches objectivity.

The therapist begins by helping the patient make up a list of "life history data," the sequence of difficulties that have led him to his current position. The therapist then charts responses to these difficulties and attempts to identify characteristic patterns of overreaction. The patient learns why he finds certain events so depressing and tries to free himself of inappropriate responses. This macroscopic part of CBT is followed by the microscopic, in which the patient learns to neutralize his "automatic thoughts." Feelings are not direct responses to the world: what happens in the world affects our cognition, and cognition in turn affects feelings. If the patient can alter the cognition, then he can alter the concomitant mood states. A patient might, for example, learn to see her husband's preoccupation as his reasonable response to the demands of the workplace rather than as a rejection. She might then be able to see how her own

107

automatic thoughts (of being an unlovable jerk) turn into negative emotion (self-reproach) and identify how this negative emotion leads to depression. Once the cycle is broken, the patient can begin to achieve some self-control. The patient learns to distinguish between what actually happens and her ideas about what happens.

CBT functions according to specific rules. The therapist assigns lots of homework: lists of positive experiences and lists of negative experiences must be made, and sometimes they are put on graphs. The therapist presents an agenda for each session, continues in a structured fashion, and ends with a summary of what has been accomplished. Facts and advice are specifically excluded from the therapist's conversation. Pleasurable moments in the patient's day are identified, and the patient is instructed in the art of including emotional pleasure in his life. The patient should become alert to his cognition so that he can stop himself when he ventures toward a negative pattern and shift his processing to a less harmful system. All this activity is patterned into exercises. CBT teaches the art of self-awareness.

I have never been in CBT, but I have learned certain lessons from it. If you feel the giggles coming on in a conversation, you can sometimes stop yourself from laughing by forcing your mind to some sad subject. If you are in a situation in which you are expected to have sexual feelings you do not in fact have, you can push your mind into a world of fantasy quite remote from the reality you are experiencing, and your actions and the actions of your body can take place within that artifice rather than in the present reality. This is the underlying strategy of cognitive therapy. If you find yourself thinking that no one could ever love you and that life is meaningless, you reposition your mind and force yourself to think of some memory, no matter how narrow, of a better time. It's hard to wrestle with your own consciousness, because you have no tool in this battle except your consciousness itself. Just think lovely thoughts, lovely, wonderful thoughts, and they will sap the pain. Think what you do not feel like thinking. It may be fake and self-delusional in some ways, but it does work. Force out of your mind the people associated with your loss: forbid them entrance to your consciousness. The abandoning mother, the cruel lover, the hateful boss, the disloyal friend—lock them out. It helps. I know which thoughts and preoccupations can do me in and I exercise caution with regard to them. For example, I think of lovers I once loved and feel an aching physical absence and know that I have to pull back from those thoughts and preoccupations and I try not to conjure too many images of a happiness that existed between us and that is in its material form long over. Better to take a sleeping pill than to let my mind run free on sorry topics when I lie in bed waiting for sleep. Like a schizophrenic told not to listen to voices, I am always pushing these images away.

I once met a Holocaust survivor, a woman who had spent more than a year in Dachau and who had seen her entire family die in the camp. I asked her how she had managed, and she said she had understood right from the start that if she let herself think about what was going on, she would go crazy and die. "I decided," she told me, "that I would think only about my hair, and for the whole time that I was in that place that is all I thought about. I thought about when I could wash it. I thought about trying to comb it with my fingers. I thought about how to act with the guards to make sure they didn't shave my head entirely. I spent hours battling the lice that were all over the camp. This gave my mind a focus on something over which I could exercise some control, and it filled my mind so that I could close myself off from the reality of what was happening to me, and it got me through." This is how the principle of CBT might be carried to an extreme under extreme circumstances. If you can force your thoughts into certain patterns, that can save you.

When Janet Benshoof came to my house for the first time, she awed me. A brilliant lawyer, she has been a leading figure in the struggle for abortion rights. She is by any standards an impressive person—well read, articulate, attractive, funny, and unpretentious. She asks questions with the practiced eye of one who can read the truth fast. Utterly self-possessed, she spoke of depressions that laid her impossibly low. "My accomplishments are the whalebones in a corset that allows me to stand up; without them, I would be only a heap on the floor," she said. "Much of the time, I don't know who or what it is that they are supporting, but I know that they are my only protection." She has done considerable behavioral work with a therapist who has addressed her phobias. "Well, flying was a bad one," she explains. "So he took me on planes and monitored me. I was sure I would run into someone I hadn't seen since school and I'd be with this fat man in a shirt bursting open at the seams and I'd have to say, 'This is my behavioral therapist, and we're just practicing taking the shuttle.' But I must say that it worked. We went through exactly what I was thinking minute to minute and we changed it. Now I don't have anxiety attacks on planes anymore."

Cognitive-behavioral therapy is broadly used today, and it seems to show some significant effect on depression. There seem also to be extremely good results from interpersonal therapy, the treatment regimen formulated by Gerald Klerman, at Cornell, and his wife, Myrna Weissman, at Columbia. IPT focuses on the immediate reality of current day-to-day life. Rather than working out an overarching schema for an entire personal history, it fixes up things in the present. It is not about changing the patient into a deeper person, but rather about teaching the patient how to make the most of whoever he is. It is a short-term therapy with definite boundaries and limits. It assumes that many people who are depressed have had life stressors as the trigger or consequence of their depression, and that these can be cleaned up through well-advised interaction with others. Treatment is in two stages. In the first, the patient is taught to understand his depression as an external affliction and is informed about the prevalence of the disorder. His symptoms are sorted out and named. He takes on the role of the sick one and identifies a process of getting better. The patient makes up catalogs of all his current relationships, and with the therapist defines what he gets from each one and what he wants from each one. The therapist works with the patient to figure out what the best strategies are for eliciting what is needed in his life. Problems are sorted into four categories: grief; differences about role with close friends and family (what you give and what you expect in return, for example); states of stressful transition in personal or professional life (divorce or loss of job, for example); and isolation. The therapist and the patient then establish a few attainable goals and decide how long they will work toward them. IPT lays out your life in even, clear terms.

It is important not to suppress your feelings altogether when you are depressed. It is equally important to avoid terrible arguments or expressions of outrage. You should steer clear of emotionally damaging behavior. People forgive, but it is best not to stir things up to the point at which forgiveness is required. When you are depressed, you need the love of other people, and yet depression fosters actions that destroy that love. Depressed people often stick pins into their own life rafts. The conscious mind can intervene. One is not helpless. A fairly short time after I had snapped out of my third depression, I had dinner with my father and he said something that upset me, and I heard my voice go shrill and my words grow sharp and I was very much alarmed. I could see the trace of recoil in my father. I breathed deeply, and after a pregnant pause, I said, "I'm sorry. I promised not to yell at you and not to be manipulative about these things, and I'm sorry I did it." This sounds rather namby-pamby, but the ability to intervene consciously does in fact make an enormous difference. A snappy friend once said to me, "For two hundred dollars an hour, you'd think my psychiatrist could go change my family and leave me alone." Unfortunately, it doesn't work that way.

Though CBT and IPT have many specific strengths, any therapy is only as good as the practitioner. Your therapist matters more than your choice of therapeutic system. Someone to whom you connect profoundly can probably help you a lot just by chatting with you in an unstructured environment; someone to whom you do not connect will not really help you no matter how sophisticated his technique or how numerous his qualifications. The key things are intelligence and insight: the format in which that insight is communicated, and the type of insight that is used, are really secondary. In an important study done in 1979, researchers demonstrated that any form of therapy could be effective if certain criteria were met: that both the therapist and the patient were acting in good faith; that the client believed that the therapist understood the technique; and that the client liked and respected the therapist; and that the therapist had an ability to form understanding relationships. The experimenters chose English professors with this quality of human understanding and found that, on average, the English professors were able to help their patients as much as the professional therapists.

"Mind cannot exist without the brain, but mind can have influence on the brain. It's a pragmatic and metaphysical problem whose biology we do not understand," says Elliot Valenstein, professor emeritus of psychology and neuroscience at the University of Michigan. The experiential can be used to affect the physical. As James Ballenger of the Medical University of South Carolina says, "Psychotherapy changes biology. Behavior therapy changes the biology of the brain—probably in the same way the medicines do." Certain cognitive therapies that are effective for anxiety lower levels of brain metabolism while, in mirror image, pharmaceutical therapies lower levels of anxiety. This is the principle of antidepressant medication, which by modifying the levels of certain substances in the brain changes the way a patient feels and acts.

Most of the things that go on in the brain during a breakdown are still inaccessible to external manipulation. Research on medical cures for depression has focused tightly on affecting neurotransmitters, mostly because we are able to affect neurotransmitters. Since scientists know that lowering the levels of certain neurotransmitters can cause depression, they work on the assumption that raising levels of these same neurotransmitters can alleviate depression—and indeed drugs that raise levels of neurotransmitters are in many instances effective antidepressants. It is comforting to think that we know the relationship between neurotransmitters and mood, but we don't. It appears to be an indirect mechanism. People with lots of neurotransmitters bumping around in their heads are not happier than people with few neurotransmitters. Depressed people do not in general have low neurotransmitter levels in the first place. Putting extra serotonin in the brain does no immediate good at all; if you get people to eat more tryptophan (it is found in a number of foodstuffs, including turkey, bananas, and dates), which raises serotonin levels, that doesn't help immediately, though there is evidence that reducing dietary tryptophan may exacerbate depression. The current popular focus on serotonin is at best naive. As Steven Hyman, director of the National Institute of Mental Health, said rather dryly, "There's too much serotonin soup and not enough modern neuroscience. We're not organizing Serotonin Appreciation Day around here just yet." Under ordinary circumstances, serotonin is discharged by neurons and then reabsorbed to be discharged again. The SSRIs (selective serotonin reuptake inhibitors) block the reabsorption process, thus increasing the level of free-floating serotonin in the brain. Serotonin is one of nature's through lines in the development of species: it can be found in plants, in lower animals, and in human beings. It appears to serve multiple functions, which vary from one species to the next. In human beings, it is one of several mechanisms that control constriction and dilation of blood vessels. It helps form scabs, causing the clotting necessary to control bleeding. It is involved in inflammatory responses. It also affects digestion. It is immediately involved in regulation of sleep, depression, aggression, and suicide.

Antidepressants take a long time to cause palpable changes. Only after two to six weeks will the depressed patient experience any real result from his shifted neurotransmitter levels. This suggests that the improvement involves parts of the brain that respond to changed levels of neurotransmitters. Many theories are in circulation, none of which is definitive. The most fashionable until fairly recently was receptor theory. The brain has a number of receptors for each neurotransmitter. When there is more of the transmitter, the brain needs fewer receptors because the transmitter floods all the existing ones. When there is less of the transmitter, the brain needs more receptors to soak up every bit of available neurotransmitter. So increasing the amount of neurotransmitters would cause the number of receptors to go down and might allow the cells that had been acting as receptors to respecialize and take on other functions. Recent research reveals, however, that receptors do not take a long time to respecialize; in fact, they may alter within half an hour of a shift in neurotransmitter levels. So, receptor theory does not explain the time lag experienced with antidepressants. Still, many researchers hold to the notion that some kind of gradual change in brain structure accounts for the delayed response to antidepressants. The effect of the drugs is probably indirect. The human brain is stupefyingly plastic. Cells can respecialize and change after a trauma; they can "learn" entirely new functions. When you raise serotonin levels and cause certain serotonin receptors to close up shop, other things happen elsewhere in the brain, and those downstream things must correct the imbalance that caused you to feel bad in the first place. The mechanisms, however, are completely unknown. "There's the immediate action of the medication, which leads to some black box we don't know anything about, which leads to a cure," says Allan Frazer, chairman of the Department of Psychopharmacology at the University of Texas in San Antonio. "You get the same kind of results from raising serotonin that you get from raising norepinephrine. Do they lead into two different black boxes of function? Do they lead into the same black box? Does one thing lead to the other which leads to a black box?"

"It's like putting a grain of sand in an oyster," Steven Hyman says of antidepressant medication, "and it turns into a pearl. It's in the *adaptations* to altered neurotransmitters that slowly, over many weeks, the therapeutic effect occurs." Elliot Valenstein, at the University of Michigan, adds, "Antidepressants are pharmacologically specific, but not behaviorally specific. The chemistry of products is ever more specific, but God knows what's really happening in the brain." William Potter, who was running the psychopharmacological side of the NIMH through the seventies and eighties and has now gone to Eli Lilly to work on the development of new drugs, explains it this way: "There are multiple mechanisms that produce antidepressant effects; drugs with acutely different spectrums of biochemical activity actually have very similar effects. They converge in ways you would never have expected. You can get pretty much the same antidepressant effects through the serotonin or norepinephrine systems, and in some people, through dopamine. It's not simple; it's like a weather system. You do something somewhere that changes wind speeds or humidity, and you get a completely different kind of weather, but how which change will affect what, even the best meteorologists can't be sure." Does it matter that most antidepressants suppress REM sleep, or is that an irrelevant side effect? Is it important that antidepressants usually lower brain temperature, which, in depression, tends to go up at night? It has become clear that all the neurotransmitters interact and that each influences the others.

Animal models are imperfect, but useful information can be gained from animal studies. Monkeys separated from their mothers in infancy grow up psychotic; their brains become physiologically different and they develop much lower serotonin levels than do monkeys raised with their mothers. Repeated maternal separations in a range of animals give them excessive levels of cortisol. Prozac will reverse these effects. Put the dominant male from one colony of marsupials into another grouping in which he is not dominant, and he will go through weight loss, lowered sexual performance, disrupted sleep, and all the other characteristic symptoms of major depression. Raise his serotonin levels and he may well have a total remission of these symptoms. Animals with low serotonin tend to brutalize other animals; they take unnecessary and irrational risks and are confrontational without reason. Animal models of external factors and serotonin levels are extremely revealing. A monkey who rises through the dominance structure of his peer group will show higher levels of serotonin when his rank increases—and high serotonin is associated with lower levels of aggression or suicide. If such monkeys are isolated so that they do not have group status, their serotonin will fall by as much as 50 percent. On selective serotonin reuptake inhibitors (SSRIs), they become less aggressive and less prone to self-destructive activity.

Four classes of antidepressant medication are currently available. The most popular are the SSRIs, which bring about higher brain levels of serotonin. Prozac, Luvox, Paxil, Zoloft, and Celexa are all SSRIs. There are also two older kinds of antidepressants. The tricyclics, named for their chemical structure, affect serotonin and dopamine. Elavil, Anafranil, Norpramin, Tofranil, and Pamelor are all tricyclics. The monoamine oxidase inhibitors (MAOIs) inhibit the breakdown of serotonin, dopamine, and norepinephrine. Nardil and Parnate are both MAOIs. Another category, atypical antidepressants, includes drugs that operate on multiple neurotransmitter systems. Asendin, Wellbutrin, Serzone, and Effexor are all atypical antidepressants.

The choice of which medication to use is usually based, at least initially, on side effects. It is hoped that we will eventually find a way to test for responsiveness to specific drugs, but so far we are completely unable to do so. "There is little scientific basis for choosing a particular antidepressant for a particular patient, with a few exceptions," Richard A. Friedman of Cornell's Payne-Whitney Hospital says. "Prior response to a given drug is a good predictor of future response to the same drug. And if you have a special subtype of depression, atypical depression, where you overeat and oversleep, you'll do better on an MAOI than on a tricyclic, though most clinicians use the newer drugs in these patients anyway. Aside from that—you choose a drug that appears to have a low side-effect profile as the first line of action. You can decide on a more activating drug such as Wellbutrin for someone who is very withdrawn, or a deactivating drug for someone who is agitated, but beyond that—it's just trial and error with the individual patient. The labeling will tell you that one drug has more frequency of certain side effects than another, but in my clinical experience there really isn't much difference within a particular class in overall levels of side effect from drug to drug. The differences in response at the individual level, however, may be very pronounced." The great current popularity of the SSRIs—the Prozac revolution—is due not to superior efficacy but to their low side-effect profile and their safety. It's almost impossible to commit suicide with these drugs, and this is an important consideration in treating depressed people, who may, as they recover, become self-destructive. "Prozac is a very forgiving drug," says one scientist at Eli Lilly. Decreased side effects mean not only that people will more readily take the drug, but also that they will comply with their regimens better. It's the same as the principle that if your toothpaste tastes good, maybe you'll brush longer.

Some people experience upset stomach with the SSRIs, and there have been occasional reports of headaches, of feeling strung out, of insomnia, and of somnolence. Their major side effect, however, is their undermining of sexuality. "When I was on Prozac," Brian D'Amato, a depressive friend said to me, "Jennifer Lopez could have appeared at my bedside in a sarong and I'd have asked her whether she could help me with filing." The tricyclics and MAOIs also have negative sexual side effects; because those drugs, while they dominated the market until the late 1980s, tend to be used only for more severe depression, beside which sexual side effects seem insignificant, their diminishing of erotic pleasure has not been discussed so much and so broadly as that of the SSRIs has been. In studies at the time Prozac was launched, a limited number of patients reported that Prozac was having negative sexual effects. In subsequent studies, when patients were specifically asked about sexual problems, an overwhelming number of them reported difficulties. Anita Clayton, of the University of Virginia, divides sexual experience into four phases: desire, arousal, orgasm, and resolution. Antidepressants affect all four. Desire is compromised by decreased libido. Arousal is diminished by inhibited sexual excitement, diminished genital sensation, impotence, or lack of vaginal lubrication. Orgasm is delayed; some people become totally anorgasmic. Confusingly, these effects can be irregular: one day everything goes fine, and the next day there's crippling impotence, and you can't tell which way it's going to be until you're in the act itself. Resolution is of course rather undermined when there has been no desire or arousal or orgasm.

The sexual side effects are often brushed aside as insignificant compared to a severe depression, and by that standard they are insignificant. Nonetheless, they are unacceptable. One patient I interviewed said that he could not have an orgasm in intercourse at all and described the complicated process of going off medication for long enough to impregnate his wife. "If I didn't know how awful the consequences of being off medication might be," he said, "I'd have stayed off it. Oh, my sexual self—it was so nice to have it back for a few days. I wonder whether I'll ever have an orgasm with my wife again." When you're first recovering from a depressive episode, when you've got other things on your mind, sexual deficiency is not so bothersome, but then to get over unbearable pain at the cost of erotic pleasure—well, it sure struck me as a bum deal. It is also a motivation for noncompliance, which is probably the single biggest problem in the treatment of depression. Less than 25 percent of patients who take antidepressants continue the treatment for six months, and a large proportion of those who stop do so because of sexual and sleep-related side effects.

Once the sexual effects set in, sexual anxiety ensues, so that erotic encounters may become disturbing moments of failure; people afflicted with this burden may develop a psychological aversion to sexual interaction, which makes the symptoms worse. Most men who have impotence problems suffer from depression; lifting the impotence may be sufficient to reverse the depression. It is both important and difficult, as Clayton has observed, to tease out the sexual problems that are characteristic of the underlying psychology that may have made a person depressed; the sexual problems that are a result of the depression (99 percent of people with acute major depression report sexual dysfunction); and the sexual problems that are the result of antidepressant therapy. Clayton stresses the need for nonintrusive but rigorous scanning of patients for sexual problems.

Many substances are said to help contravene the sexual side effects of antidepressants: serotonin antagonists such as cyproheptadine and granisetron; alpha-2 antagonists such as yohimbine and trazodone; cholinergic agonists such as bethanechol; dopamine-enhancing drugs such as bupropion, amantadine, and bromocriptine; autoreceptor agonists such as buspirone and pindolol; stimulants such as amphetamine, methylphenidate, and ephedrine; and herbals such as ginkgo biloba and L-arginine. Taking brief holidays—usually about three days—from drugs achieves occasional positive results. Sometimes switching drugs helps improve libido. None of these have been proved to work particularly well; but they do have some effect, varying from person to person. One woman whose story is told in this book had an alarming experience when she was put on a constellation of these drugs including Dexedrine: she was having such acute libido overflow that she found it physically uncomfortable to sit through routine meetings in her office. Things got to the point that, contrary to her usual habit, she was having sex with strangers in elevators. "I could come three times between the eighth and fourteenth floors," she told me. "I stopped wearing underwear because it took too long to get it off. The guys thought they were doing something amazing—it was pretty uncomfortable for me, but I feel I really helped some male egos. But it just couldn't go on. I'm basically a highly repressed WASP. I'm not so young. I really wasn't up for all this." Some minor readjustments brought her back to a manageable level of sexual excitation. Unfortunately, the same drugs used on another patient I knew failed to do anything at all for her—"I couldn't have an orgasm if I got stuck in an elevator for four hours with the young Montgomery Clift," she sadly reported back to me.

Testosterone injections, administered to raise the level of free testosterone in the body, can have some useful effect, but they are difficult to administer and control and their effects are not entirely clear. The brightest ray of hope is Viagra. Because of its psychological and physical effects, it seems to affect three of Clayton's stages; it falls short only in that it does not stimulate libido. It may as a secondary step help to restore confidence in one's ability to interact sexually, and this helps one to relax, which in turn helps libido. It is to be hoped that dopamine boosters currently in development may take care of that, since dopamine appears to be strongly implicated in libido. Taken regularly, Viagra will also restore men's nighttime erections, which are often eliminated by antidepressants. This in turn has a positive effect on libido. It has been proposed that men who are on antidepressants should take Viagra every night as a therapeutic agent, even if they are not having sex each time they take it. It can in effect be a quick and effective antidepressant; high levels of sexual function lift mood like almost nothing else. The research of both Andrew Nierenberg of Harvard and Julia Warnock of the University of Oklahoma indicates that Viagra, while it is not officially approved for women, seems to have good effects on their sexual drive and may facilitate orgasm. This is in part because it helps the clitoris to enlarge with blood flow. Hormone therapies are also useful in women with sexual dysfunction. Keeping up levels of estrogen improves mood, and sudden declines in estrogen levels can be devastating. The 80 percent drop in estrogen that women experience during menopause has pronounced mood effects. Women with low levels of estrogen develop all kinds of complaints, and Warnock stresses that the estrogen levels need to be normalized before Viagra can have any useful effect. Though it is important not to raise testosterone levels too high in women, lest they become hairy and aggressive, testosterone is a necessary hormone for female libido, and it too needs to be kept at appropriate levels.

The tricyclic antidepressants work on several neurotransmitter systems, including acetylcholine, serotonin, norepinephrine, and dopamine. The tricyclics are particularly useful in severe or delusional depression. The acetylcholine inhibition carries a number of unpleasant side effects, including dry mouth and eyes and constipation. Tricyclics can also be somewhat sedating. Use of the tricyclics in people with bipolar illness can precipitate mania, so considerable care must be taken in prescribing them. The SSRIs and bupropion can also trigger mania, but are less likely to do so.

The MAOIs are particularly useful when depression carries acute physical symptoms such as pain, decreased energy, and interrupted sleep. These drugs block the enzyme that breaks down adrenaline and serotonin, thus increasing the level of these substances. MAOIs are excellent drugs but have many side effects. Patients taking them have to avoid a range of foodstuffs with which they have troubling interactions. They can also affect bodily function. One patient I interviewed got total urinary retention from MAOIs: "I pretty much needed to go to the hospital whenever I had to pee, which was not convenient."

The atypical antidepressants are just that: atypical. Each has its own novel mode of action. Effexor affects both serotonin and norepinephrine. Wellbutrin acts on dopamine and norepinephrine. Asendin and Serzone work on all the systems. It is popular at the moment to try for so-called clean drugs, drugs that have highly specific effects. Clean drugs are not necessarily more effective than dirty ones; specificity may to some degree be connected to the control of side effects, but it seems that the more things you muck around with in the human brain, the more effective the treatment is likely to be for depression. Clean drugs are developed by the pharmaceutical companies, which are enthusiastic about the tidiness of chemical sophistication; but such drugs are not particularly distinguished for therapeutic purposes.

The effects of antidepressants are unpredictable and cannot always be sustained. However, "I don't believe total poop-out happens nearly as often as they say," says Richard A. Friedman. "I believe that dosage may need to be readjusted, that the medication may need to be buffered. Psychopharmacology involves a lot of tinkering. And many of those who do have poop-out have it because they have lost a placebo response, which tends to be short-lived." Nonetheless, many patients do experience medication as only temporary relief. Sarah Gold, who had a history of depression for her entire adult life, had a total remission with Wellbutrin—for a year. She achieved the effect again briefly from Effexor, but that too wore off within eighteen months. "People noticed. I was sharing a house with a few other people, and one of them told me I had a black aura and she couldn't stand to be in the house when I was up in my room with the door closed." Gold went on a mix of lithium, Zoloft, and Ativan; now she is on Anafranet, Celexa, Risperdal, and Ativan and she is "less energetic, less secure, but able to cope." It may be that no current medications could give her the permanent remission that some people achieve, and for someone who will need to be on medication permanently, this darting from one solution to the next is intensely demoralizing.

A number of drugs, such as BuSpar, which acts on certain nerves sensitive to serotonin, are used for the long-term control of anxiety. There are also fast-acting drugs, the benzodiazepines—a category that includes Klonopin, Ativan, Valium, and Xanax. Halcion and Restoril, which are prescribed for insomnia, are also benzodiazepines. These drugs can be taken as needed to allay anxiety immediately. Fear of addiction, however, has led to gross underuse of the benzos. They are marvelous drugs for short-term use, and can make life tolerable during periods of acute anxiety. I have met people who were tortured with psychic anguish that could have been alleviated had their physicians been more permissive in the prescription of the benzos, and I always remember what my first psychopharmacologist told me: "If you get addicted, we'll get you unaddicted. Meanwhile, let's assuage your suffering." Most people who take benzodiazepines will develop tolerance and dependence, which means that they cannot stop them suddenly; but they will not take escalating doses to obtain therapeutic benefits. "With these drugs," says Friedman, "addiction is a problem mainly in people with a history of substance abuse. The addictive risk of the benzodiazepines is greatly overestimated."

In my case, Xanax made the horror disappear as a magician makes a rabbit vanish. While the antidepressants I have taken were slow as dawn, shedding light bit by bit on my personality and letting it come back into the known and patterned world, Xanax provided extraordinary instant relief from anxiety—"a finger in a dike at the crucial moment," as James Ballenger, an anxiety expert, says. For people who are not inclined toward abuse, benzos save lives. "What the general public knows," Ballenger says, "is largely incorrect. Sedation is a side effect; using the drugs as sleeping pills is an abuse. Using them for anxiety is not. Withdrawing quickly gives you symptoms, but that's true of many, many drugs." Though benzos can help anxiety, they do not, by themselves, alleviate depression. They can affect short-term memory. Over the long term, they can have depressant qualities, and long-term sustained use should be closely monitored.

Since that first visit to the first psychopharmacologist, seven years ago, I have been playing the medicine game. For the sake of my mental health, I have been on, in various combinations and at various doses, Zoloft, Paxil, Navane, Effexor, Wellbutrin, Serzone, BuSpar, Zyprexa, Dexedrine, Xanax, Valium, Ambien, and Viagra. I'm lucky; I responded well to drugs within the class with which I began. Nonetheless, I can attest to the hell of experimentation. Trying out different medications makes you feel like a dartboard. "Depression these days is curable," people told me. "You take antidepressants like people take aspirin for a headache." This is not true. Depression these days is treatable; you take antidepressants like you take radiation for cancer. They sometimes do miraculous things, but none of it is easy and results are inconsistent.

I have so far not gone in for a full hospitalization, but I know that I may need one someday. In a hospital, one is usually on medications and/or receiving ECT. Part of what can be curative, however, is the hospitalization itself, the close attention of staff, the systems to protect you from your destructive or suicidal impulses. Hospitalization should not be the very last resort of desperate people. It is a resource like any other and should be exploited when necessary—if only your insurance will allow it.

Researchers are working in four directions toward new treatments. The first is to shift as far as possible to preventative therapies: the sooner you catch mental problems of any kind, the better off you are. The second is increased specificity of drugs. The brain has at least fifteen different serotonin receptors. Evidence suggests that the antidepressant effects depend on only a few of these sites, and that many of the nasty side effects of SSRIs probably go with others. The third is faster drugs. The fourth is more specificity to symptom rather than to biological position, so that the experimentation to choose drugs can be abrogated. If we discover, for example, tags that would allow genetic subtypes of depression to be identified, it might be possible to find treatments specific to those subtypes. "The existing medications," says William Potter, formerly of the NIMH, "are just too indirect in the way they work for us ever to get much control over them." Thus this kind of specificity is likely to remain elusive. Mood disorders involve not a single signal from a single gene, but many genes, each one contributing a small increment of risk—which gets triggered by external circumstances to create a sum vulnerability.

The most successful physical treatment for depression is the least clean and specific one of all. Antidepressants are effective about 50 percent of the time, perhaps a bit more; ECT seems to have some significant impact between 75 and 90 percent of the time. About half of those who have improved on ECT still feel good a year after treatment, though others require repeated rounds of ECT or regular maintenance ECT. ECT works fast. Many patients feel substantially better within a few days of having an ECT treatment—a boon particularly striking in contrast to the long, slow process of medication response. ECT is particularly appropriate for the severely suicidal—for patients who repeatedly injure themselves and whose situation is therefore mortally urgent—because of its rapid action and high response rate, and it is used in pregnant women, the sick, and the elderly, because it does not have the systemic side effects or drug-interaction problems of most medications.

After some routine blood work, a cardiogram, often a chest X ray, and some anesthesia-related checks, patients who are deemed fit for ECT sign consent forms, which are also presented to their family. The night before the treatment, the patient fasts and has an IV put in place. In the morning, he is taken to the ECT room. After the patient has been hooked up to monitors, medical attendants put gel on his temples and then apply electrodes for either unilateral ECT to the nondominant side of the brain only—which is the preferred starting strategy, usually to right brain—or bilateral ECT. Unilateral ECT has fewer side effects, and recent research shows that high-dose unilateral ECT is as effective as bihemispheric treatment. The administering doctor also chooses between sine-wave stimulus, which gives more sustained stimulation, and brief-pulse square-wave stimulus, which induces seizures with fewer side effects. A short-acting IV general anesthetic is given, which will put the patient out completely for about ten minutes, and a muscle relaxant is also given to prevent physical spasms (the only movement during the treatment is a slight wiggling of the toes—unlike ECT of the 1950s, in which people thrashed around and injured themselves). The patient is connected to an EEG machine and an electrocardiogram (EKG) machine, so that a brain scan and a heart scan are running at all times. Then a one-second shock causes a temporal and vertex seizure in the brain that usually goes on for some thirty seconds—long enough to change brain chemistry, not long enough to fry up the grey matter. The shock is usually about two hundred joules, which is equivalent to the output of a hundred-watt bulb; most of this is absorbed by the soft tissue and skull, and only a tiny fraction of it reaches the brain. Within ten or fifteen minutes, the patient wakes up in the recovery room. Most people who receive ECT have ten or twelve treatments over about six weeks. ECT is being administered increasingly on an outpatient basis.

The writer Martha Manning has described her depression and ECT in a beautiful and surprisingly hilarious book called *Undercurrents*. She is now stabilized on Wellbutrin, a little lithium, some Depakote, Klonopin, and Zoloft—"It's like having the rainbow coalition in my hands when I look at 'em all," she jokes. "I'm a science project with no due date." She had intense and protracted experience with ECT when her depression was at its most severe. She took herself in for treatment the day she found the address for a gun shop to kill herself. "I didn't want to die because I hated myself; I wanted to die because I loved myself enough to want this pain to end. I had leaned against my daughter's bathroom door every day and listened to her singing—she was eleven, and always sang in the shower—and that was an invitation not to try for one more day. I just couldn't care enough, but suddenly I knew that if I did get and use a gun, I would stop that child's song. I would silence her. And that day, I checked myself in for ECT. It was like I finally said 'Uncle' to the one who'd wrestled me to the ground. I had treatment for weeks—waking up after each round feeling hungover, asking for a Diet Coke, knowing it's going to be a sort of Tylenol day."

ECT does result in disruption of short-term memory and can affect long-term memory. The disruptions are usually temporary, but some patients have had permanent memory deficits. One woman I met, who had been a practicing lawyer, came out of ECT minus any recollection of law school. She could not remember anything she'd studied, nor where she had studied, nor whom she had known during her studies. This is extreme and rare, but it does happen. ECT has also been associated with the death of about one in ten thousand patients, according to one study, usually because of cardiac problems after the treatment. Whether those deaths are coincident with ECT or caused by it is not entirely clear. Blood pressure does increase significantly during ECT. ECT does not appear to cause physiological damage; indeed, Richard Abrams, author of a seminal book on ECT, describes a patient who had received more than 1,250 bilateral ECT treatments and whose brain, when she died at the age of eighty-nine, was in perfectly good shape. "There is simply no evidence—and virtually no chance—that ECT as presently administered is capable of producing brain damage," he writes. Many of the short-term side effects—including grogginess and nausea—come from the anesthesia that is used with ECT, rather than from the ECT itself.

ECT is still the most stigma-loaded treatment. "You do feel like Frankenstein on the table there," says Manning. "And people don't want to hear about it; nobody brings you casseroles when you're in for ECT. It's very isolating for the family." It can be traumatizing conceptually for the patient as well. "I know it works," says one mental health worker. "I've seen it work. But the thought of losing precious memories of my kids and my family—you know, I don't have parents and I don't have a husband. Who *finds* those memories for you? Who tells you about them? Who'll remember the special recipe for pie that we made fifteen years ago? It would add to my depression to feel more dreamless. Memories are what helps me through the day, thoughts of love in the past."

On the other hand, ECT can be miraculously effective. "Before, I was aware of every swallow of water, that it was just too much work," Manning says. "Afterwards, I thought, do regular people feel this way all the time? It's like you've been not in on a great joke for the whole of your life." And the effects are usually rapid. "Vegetative symptoms went; then my body felt lighter; then I *really* wanted a Big Mac," says Manning. "I felt like I'd been hit by a truck for a while, but that was, comparatively speaking, not so bad." Manning is unusual. Many people who have electro-convulsive therapy are resistant to the idea that it is useful, especially if transient memory deficits have afflicted them, or if the reconstruction of their life has been gradual. Two people I know had ECT in early 2000. Both had been at rock bottom—unable to get out of bed or get dressed, eternally exhausted, direly negative about life, uninterested in food, incapable of work, and often suicidal. They had electroshock within a few months of each other. The first suffered severe manifest memory loss after the treatments—he had been an engineer and now couldn't remember how a circuit worked. The second came out as morose as she had gone in because she was still confronted with authentic life problems. The engineer's memory began to resurface about three months later, and by the end of the year, he was getting up, going out, had returned to a job, and was functioning well. He said it was "probably a coincidence." The second one went in for a second round of treatments despite her insistence that the first round had done her no good. After the second round, her personality began to return, and by the autumn she had not only a job but also a new apartment and a boyfriend. She continued to say that the ECT had been more upsetting than it was worth, until I finally suggested to her that what the ECT had wiped out was her memory of how she had been before it. When Manning's book was published, picket lines of people objecting to "electronic mind control" marched when she read. There have been laws against ECT in many states in the United States; the treatment methodology is subject to abuse and it's not for everyone and it should certainly not be used indiscriminately or without full patient consent—but it can be a wondrous thing.

Why does ECT work? We don't know. It seems to have a strong enhancing effect on dopamine and affects all the other neurotransmitters as well. It can also affect metabolism in the frontal cortex. High-frequency electricity seems to raise the metabolic level; low-frequency electricity can lower the metabolic level. Of course, it is not clear whether depression is one of many symptoms of hypometabolism, agitated depression a symptom of hypermetabolism, or whether both depression and these alterations of metabolism are functions of some other change in the brain. ECT temporarily lowers the blood-brain barrier. The effects of ECT are not limited to the frontal cortex; even the brain-stem functions are temporarily affected by the electric charge.

I've decided not to go off my medications. I'm not sure that I'm addicted, but I am dependent: without the drugs I would run the risk of emerging symptoms of illness. It's a fine line. I have gained an unbecoming amount of weight. I get weird hives for no apparent reason. I sweat more. My memory, never very good, is mildly impaired: I frequently forget what I am saying in the middle of a sentence. I get headaches a lot. I get occasional muscular cramps. My sex drive comes and goes and my sexual function is erratic: an orgasm is a special occasion nowadays. It's not ideal, but it seems to have put up a real wall between me and depression. The last two years are without question my best in a decade. Slowly, I will now catch up. When two friends died not long ago, both in freak accidents, I felt terribly sad, but I did not feel my self slipping out of my hands, and to feel just grief was almost (I know this sounds terrible, but in some selfish way it is true) a kind of satisfaction.

The question of what functions depression serves in the world we inhabit is not quite the same as the question of what function antidepressants are coming to serve. James Ballenger, anxiety expert, says, "We're eight inches taller than we were before the Second World War, and much healthier, and we're living longer. No one complains about the change. When you remove a disability, people go out in life and find more, both good and bad." And that, I think, is really the response to the question that I was asked by almost everyone to whom I mentioned this book. "Don't these drugs blank out your life?" No. What they do is to allow you to have your pain in more important places, in better places, for richer reasons.

"You've got twelve billion neurons," says Robert Post, chief of the Biological Psychiatry Branch of the National Institute of Mental Health. "Each one's got between one thousand and ten thousand synapses, all changing at rapid speed. Getting them all to run just right so that people are wonderfully happy all the time—we're a long, long way from that." James Ballenger says, "It's not been my impression that the suffering level in the universe has gone down much, with *all* our improvements, and I don't think we'll reach a tolerable level anytime soon. Mind control need not occupy us at present."

Normal is a word that haunts depressives. Is depression normal? I read of normal groups and depressive groups in studies; of medication that could "normalize" depression; of "normal" and "atypical" clusters of symptoms. One of the people I met during this research said to me, "At first when these symptoms began, I thought I was going crazy. It was a big relief to find out that it was just a clinical depression and that it was basically normal." It was, of course, basically the normal way to go crazy; depression is a mental illness, and when you are in its throes, you're crazy as a loon, a bit balmy, a few sandwiches short of a picnic, bats in the belfry.

At a cocktail party in London, I saw an acquaintance and mentioned that I was writing this book. "I had terrible depression," she said. I asked her what she had done about it. "I didn't like the idea of medication," she said. "I realized that my problem was stress-related. So I decided to eliminate all the causes of stress in my life." She counted off on her fingers: "I quit my job. I broke up with my boyfriend and never really looked for another one. I gave up my roommate and now I live alone. I stopped going to parties that run late. I moved to a smaller place. I dropped most of my friends. I gave up, pretty much, on makeup and clothes." I was looking at her with horror. "It sounds bad, but I'm really much happier, and much less afraid than before." And she looked proud. "And I did it without pills."

Someone who was standing in our group grabbed her by the arm. "That's completely crazy. That's the craziest thing I've ever heard. You must be crazy to be doing that to your life," he said. Is it crazy to avoid the behaviors that make you crazy? Or is it crazy to medicate so that you can sustain a life that makes you crazy? I could downgrade my life and do fewer things, travel less, know fewer people, and avoid writing books on depression—and perhaps if I made all those changes, I would not need medications. I might live my life within the bounds of what I can tolerate. It is not what I have opted primarily to do, but it is certainly a reasonable option. Living with depression is like trying to keep your balance while you dance with a goat—it is perfectly sane to prefer a partner with a better sense of balance. And yet the life I lead, full of adventure and complexity, affords me such enormous satisfaction that I would hate giving it up. I would hate that more than almost anything. I would sooner triple the number of pills I take than cut my circle of friends in half. The Unabomber—whose techniques of communicating his Luddite sensibilities were disastrous but whose insights into the perils of technology are sound—wrote in his manifesto, "Imagine a society that subjects people to conditions that make them terribly unhappy, then gives them the drugs to take away their unhappiness. Science fiction? It is already happening. . . . In effect, antidepressants are a means of modifying an individual's internal state in such a way as to enable him to tolerate social conditions that he would otherwise find intolerable."

The first time I ever saw clinical depression, I didn't recognize it; in fact, I didn't really even notice it. It was the summer after my freshman year in college, and a group of us were at a house where my family spends summers. My good friend Maggie Robbins was there, charming Maggie, always so lustrous with energy. Maggie had had a psychotic manic breakdown in the spring and had been in the hospital for two weeks.

Now she seemed to have recovered from that. She was no longer saying crazy things about finding secret information in the basement of the library and about having to stow away on a train to Ottawa, so we all presumed mental health; her long silences that summer weekend seemed ponderous and deep, as though she had learned to weigh the value of her words. It was strange that she hadn't brought a bathing suit—not until years later did she tell me she had felt that she couldn't be so naked and vulnerable and exposed as she would have been without all her clothes on. We were all splashing merrily, giddy and sophomoric. Maggie sat in a long-sleeved cotton dress on the diving board and watched the merriment and pulled her knees up under her chin. Seven of us were there, and the sun beat down, and only my mother said (in an aside to me) that Maggie seemed awfully withdrawn. I had no idea how hard Maggie was trying, not the slightest inkling of what she was pushing herself through. I didn't notice the dark circles she must have had under her eyes, the ones I have since learned to check for. I do remember that we all kept teasing her about not swimming, about missing the fun, until finally she stood up at the end of the diving board and took a dive, dress and all. I remember that leaden clothing clinging to her as she swam one length of the pool, then trudged damply back to the house to put on dry clothes, the water dripping off into the grass. It was a few hours before I found her inside, napping again. When she didn't eat much at dinner, I thought she didn't like steak or was watching her waistline. Curiously enough, I remember that as a happy weekend, and I was shocked when Maggie reported her experience as illness.

Fifteen years later, Maggie suffered the worst depression I have ever seen. With stunning incompetence, her doctor had told her that after fifteen years of doing well she might want to try going off lithium, as though curing had happened and her severe bipolar illness were rinsed out of her body. She had slowly lowered her dose. She had felt great. She had lost weight, and her hands had finally stopped shaking, and she had recovered some of that old Maggie energy, the energy she had had when she'd first told me that her lifelong goal was to be the most famous actress in the world. Then she began to feel inexplicably great all the time. We all asked her whether she wasn't worried that she was getting a teeny bit manic, but she assured us she had not felt so well in years. That should have told us all we needed to know: feeling so well was not a good thing. She was not so well. She was not so well at all. Within three months, she had concluded that God was directing her and she was on a mission to save the world. A friend took her in hand and, when he couldn't reach her psychiatrist, found another and got her back on medications. During the months that followed, she crashed into depression. The next autumn, she went to graduate school. "Graduate school gave me a lot; for one thing, it gave me the time and space and loans to have two more episodes," she joked. During her second term, she had a mild hypomania, then had a mild depression; at the end of her fourth term she skyrocketed into total mania, and then plunged into a depression so deep it seemed boundless. I remember Maggie at a friend's loft, curled up on the couch in a tight ball, wincing as though someone were putting slivers of bamboo under her fingernails. We didn't know what to do. She seemed to have lost speech altogether; when we finally got a few words out of her, they were barely audible. Fortunately, her parents had learned all about bipolar illness over the years, and that night we helped her move into their apartment. That was the last any of us was to see of her for two months as she lay in a corner there, not stirring for days at a time. I had been through depression, and I wanted to help, but she could not talk on the phone and she did not want visitors, and her parents knew enough to give her leeway for silence. I have felt more closely in touch with the dead. "I will *never* go through that ever again," she has said. "I know that I would do *anything* that I had to do to avoid that, that I absolutely *refuse*."

Now Maggie is doing well on Depakote and lithium and Wellbutrin, and though she keeps Xanax on hand, she has not needed it in a long time. She is off the Klonopin and Paxil she took at the beginning. She will be on medication permanently. "I needed to develop the humility to say, 'Wow, maybe some of the people who decided to go on medications are just like me and never meant to ever, ever, ever go on medications in their whole life for any reason. And then they did, and it has helped them.'" She writes and makes art; she works a day job as a copyeditor at a magazine. She doesn't want a more high-powered day job. She wants some security and some health insurance and a place where she needn't be brilliant all the time. When she gets pensive—or angry—she writes poetry about an alter ego she has created for herself, whom she calls Suzy. Some of her poetry is about being manic. Some of it is about being depressed:

> Someone's standing in the bathroom,
> staring into Suzy's eyes.
> Someone with the look of voices
> Suzy doesn't recognize.
> Someone living in the mirror
> Some fat face that cries and cries.
>
> Suzy's skull is packed and pounding.
> Suzy's teeth are shaking loose.
> Suzy's hands are slow and tremble

covering the glass with mousse.
Suzy studied knots one summer.
Suzy doesn't know a noose.

Suzy feels a veil get lifted.
Suzy hears a veil get torn.
Then the truth lies, pinned, before her—
stark and struggling, woken, worn.
Hunger pangs are all that's certain,
All we're given when we're born.

"I decided when I was eight years old," she told me, "that I was Maggie. I remember doing this in school, in a hallway, saying, 'You know, I'm Maggie. And I'm just always going to be me. This is the me, right now, that I'm going to be. I've been different because I can't even remember some of my life, but from right now on, it's going to be just me.' And it has been. And that's been my sense of identity. I'm that same person. I can look back and say, 'Oh, God, I can't believe I did that dumb thing when I was seventeen.' But it was me doing it. I don't have any discontinuity of self."

To have an immutable sense of self through the outrage of manic-depressive illness attests to a great strength. Maggie has reached stages of wanting to be released from this coherent self. In that horrifying, almost catatonic depression, she says, "I would lie in bed singing 'Where Have All the Flowers Gone' over and over to occupy my mind. I realize now that I could have had some other drugs, or that I could have asked someone to come and sleep in my room, but I was just too sick to think of that. I couldn't say what scared me so much, but I thought I would explode from the anxiety. I just went down and down and down and down. We kept changing medications and I just kept going further down. I believed my doctors; I always accepted that I would eventually come back to normal. But I couldn't wait; I couldn't even do the next minute. I was singing to blot out the things my mind said, which were: 'You are—you don't even deserve to live. You are worthless. You are never going to be anything. You're nobody.' And that was when I really started thinking about killing myself. I'd considered it before, but now I was really planning it. I had an almost constant imagining of my own funeral. While I was staying with my parents, I had this whole image of myself going up to the roof and over the edge in a nightgown. There was an alarm on the door to the roof and I would set off the alarm, but it wouldn't matter; I'd be over the edge before anyone else could get up there. I couldn't take any risk of it not working. I picked out what nightgown I would wear.

And then some vestige of my self-esteem kicked in and reminded me of how many people would be sad if I did that, and I couldn't bear the responsibility of causing that many man-hours of sadness. I had to acknowledge to myself the aggression of suicide against others.

"I think that I repressed a lot of the memory of it. I can't get at it; it's impossible to remember because it doesn't make sense. But I can remember certain parts of the apartment, and how bad I felt there. And I can remember the stage that came next, when I thought about money all the time. I would start to fall asleep and then wake up worried; I couldn't shake that. It wasn't very rational—I wasn't in trouble financially at the time. I'd think, what if I don't have very much money ten years from now? There's no relation whatsoever between feelings of fear and anxiety in my normal life and the kind of fear or anxiety I was having at that time. It's of a completely different quality, not just quantity. Man, those were terrible times. I finally had the good sense to switch doctors. And then I got the Xanax. I'd take a half milligram or so and I felt as if the heel of a giant hand came and settled itself on my hip and the rest of the hand pressed my side, the fingers on my shoulder. That whole hand just pushed me about two inches down into the bed. And then I would finally fall asleep. I was terrified that I'd get addicted, but the doctor assured me that I wouldn't—I wasn't taking anywhere near enough for that—and said that even if I did, he would get me off it when I was better able to handle life. So I thought, okay, I'm not going to think about it; I'm just going to do it.

"You don't think in depression that you've put on a grey veil and are seeing the world through the haze of a bad mood. You think that the veil has been taken away, the veil of happiness, and that now you're seeing truly. You try to pin the truth down and take it apart, and you think that truth is a fixed thing, but the truth is alive and it runs around. You can exorcise the demons of schizophrenics who perceive that there's something foreign inside them. But it's much harder with depressed people because we believe we are seeing the truth. But the truth lies. I look at myself and I think, 'I'm divorced,' and it seems like that is the most terrible thing. While I could be thinking, 'I'm divorced!' and feel great and free about it. Only one remark was really helpful through all of this. A friend said, 'It won't always be like this. See if you can just remember that. It's like this right now, and it won't always be like this.' The other thing she said, which also helped, was, 'That's the depression talking. It's talking through you.'"

Therapy and medication are the most accessible treatments for depression, but another system has helped many people to cope with their illness, and that is faith. Human consciousness may be seen bound by the sides of a triangle: the theological, the psychological, and the biological. It is enormously difficult to write about faith because it trades in the unknowable and the indescribable. Further, faith in the modern world tends to be highly personal. Nonetheless, religious belief is one of the primary ways that people accommodate depression. Religion provides answers to unanswerable questions. It cannot usually pull people out of depression; indeed, even the most religious people find that their faith thins or vanishes during the depths of depression. It can, however, defend against the complaint, and it can help people to survive depressive episodes. It gives reasons to live. Much religion allows us to see suffering as laudable. It grants us dignity and purpose in our helplessness. Many of the goals of cognitive and psychoanalytic therapy are accomplished by the systems of belief that underlie the world's primary religions—the refocusing of energy outside the self, the discovery of self-regard, the patience, the breadth of understanding. Faith is a great gift. It provides many of the advantages of intimacy without being contingent on the whim of a person, though God too is, of course, famous for his whims. There is a divinity that rough-hews our ends, shape them though we will. Hope is a great prophylactic, and faith in its essence offers hope.

You survive depression through a faith in life that is as abstract as any religious belief system. Depression is the most cynical thing in the world, but it is also the origin of a kind of belief. To endure it and emerge as yourself is to find that what you did not have the courage to hope may yet prove true. The discourse of faith, like that of romantic love, has the disadvantage that it carries the potential for disillusionment: depression is for many people an experience of being cast out by God or abandoned by Him, and many who have been depressed say they are unable to believe in a God who inflicts such cruelty so uselessly on the members of His flock. For most of the faithful, however, this rage against God lifts as the depression does. If belief is your norm, you return to it as you do to any other norm. Formal systems of religion lie outside my upbringing and experience, but I find it hard to stave off the sense of intervention that characterizes one's decline and one's rise. It is a matter too deeply felt to be a godless act.

Science resists the close study of religion and mental health mostly for methodological reasons. "When you get to things like meditation or prayer, what is the appropriate comparison standard for a double-blind test?" asks Steven Hyman, director of the National Institute of Mental Health. "Praying to the wrong God? It's the fundamental problem with testing the therapeutic richness of prayer." The prelate is, in addition to all else, the more acceptable face of the therapist. Indeed, Tristan Rhodes, a priest I know, said that he had for some years treated a psychotically depressed woman who refused psychotherapy but came to confession every week. She told him her stories; he then shared essential information with a psychiatrist friend; and then he reported back the views shared with him by the psychiatrist. She received in the most explicit terms the psychiatric support of the religious context.

For Maggie Robbins, faith and illness have coincided. She has become a High Church Episcopalian—at times a very devout one. She goes to church constantly: evening prayer most weekdays, sometimes two masses on Sundays (one for Communion and one just to listen), a Bible study class on Mondays, and a variety of parish activities the rest of the time. She is on the editorial board of the parish magazine and has taught Sunday school and painted backdrops for the Christmas pageant. She says, "You know, Fénelon wrote, 'Depress me or raise me up; I adore all your purposes.' Quietism may be heresy, but that idea is one of the central tenets of my faith. You don't have to understand what happens. I used to think that we had to make something of life even though it was meaningless. It is not meaningless. Depression makes you believe certain things: that you are worthless and should be dead. How can one respond to that other than with alternative beliefs?" All this being said, in the worst stages of depression, religion did little to help Maggie Robbins. "As I got better I remembered, 'Oh, yeah, religion—why didn't I use that to help me?' But it couldn't help me at the low points." Nothing could.

Evening prayer slows her down and helps to keep the chaos of depression at bay. "It's such a strong structure," she says. "You get up and say the same prayers every night. Someone has delineated what you're going to say to God and other people say it with you. I'm laying down these rituals to contain my experience. The liturgy is like the wooden slats of a box; the texts of the Bible and especially of the Psalter are considered to be an extremely good box for holding experience. Going to church is a set of attentional practices that move you forward spiritually." In some ways this seems pragmatic: it is not about belief but about scheduling and could be accomplished equally well with an aerobics class. Maggie admits that this is partly true, but denies the break between the spiritual and the utilitarian. "I'm sure one could achieve the same depth with some other religions and with some other things than religion. Christianity is just one model. It's just a model, and when I discuss my religious experience with my therapist, or my experience of therapy with my spiritual director, those models turn out to be quite similar. My spiritual director recently told me that the Holy Spirit uses my unconscious all the time! In therapy I learn to erect ego boundaries; in church, I learn to drop them and become one with the universe, or at least part of the body of Christ. I am learning to keep erecting them and dropping them until I can do it like that." And she snaps her fingers.

"According to Christian doctrine, you're not allowed to commit suicide because your life is not your own. You are the steward of your life and your body, but they are not yours to destroy. You don't end up battling everything out inside yourself; you think you're battling it out with these other characters, with Jesus Christ and God the Father and the Holy Spirit. The Church is an exoskeleton for those whose endoskeleton has been eaten away by mental illness. You pour yourself into it and adapt to its shape. You grow a spine within it. Individualism, this breaking of ourselves away from everything else, has denigrated modern life. The Church says we should act first within our communities, and then as members of the body of Christ, and then as members of the human race. It's so non-twenty-first-century American, but it's so important. I take from Einstein the idea that humans are laboring under an 'optical delusion' that each of them is separate from the others, and from the rest of the material world, and from the universe—when in fact we are all entirely interconnected parts of the universe. For me, Christianity is the study of what real love, useful love, consists of—and of what constitutes attention. People think that Christianity is against pleasure, as it sometimes is; but it's very, very pro-joy. You're aiming for joy that will never go away, no matter what kind of pain you're in. But of course you still go through the pain. I asked my priest, when I wanted to kill myself, 'What's the purpose of this suffering?' and he said, 'I hate sentences that have the word *suffering* and the word *purpose* in them. Suffering is just suffering. But I do think that God is with you in this, though I doubt you can sense him at all.' I asked how I could put something like this in God's hands, and he said, 'There's no "put," Maggie. That's just where it is.'"

Another friend, the poet Betsy de Lotbinière, has also struggled with faith from within depression, and she used belief as her primary conduit to recovery. In the low part of her depression, she says, "I hate the mistakes of myself, of course, and as I lose tolerance, I lose generosity and hate the world and the mistakes of those around me and end up wanting to scream because there are spills and stains and fallen leaves, parking fines and people who are late or don't return calls. None of this is good. Pretty soon the children will be crying, and if I ignore that, they'll end up very quiet and obedient, which is worse because the tears are now inside. Fear is in their eyes and they go silent. I stop hearing their secret hurts that are so easy to right when things are good. I hate myself like that. Depression takes me down and down."

She was brought up in a Catholic household and married a man of strong Catholic faith. Though she is not so regular a churchgoer as he, she turned to God and to prayer when she felt her grip on reality slipping, when she saw how her despair was destroying her pleasure in her children, and their pleasure in the world. But she did not stay entirely within Catholicism—in fact, she tried twelve-step programs, Buddhist meditation, firewalking, visiting Hindu temples, studying Kaballah, and pretty much anything else that seemed spiritual. "When you say a prayer at a moment of anxiety, of overstriving, it can be like pushing a button and letting out parachutes to stop you from crashing, full force, into a brick wall, or falling down so hard and so fast that all the bones in your emotional body will crush," she wrote to me in a rough time of my own. "Prayer can be your brake. Or, if your faith is big enough, prayer can be your accelerator, your amplifier in sending out into the universe a message about the direction you would like to go. Most religions of the world involve a form of stopping and accessing the inner being—so there is kneeling and there are lotus positions and there is lying flat on the floor. They also use movement to dislodge the everyday and reconnect with bigger ideas of Being—so there are music and ritual. You need both things to get out of a depression. People with a degree of faith before they reach the gutting darkness of the Abyss have a route out of there. Finding your balance in the dark is the key. This is where religions can be helpful. Religious leaders have practice in giving people some stability as they tread well-worn paths out of darkness. If you can get the hang of this balance outside you, then maybe you'll manage to achieve balance within. Then you are free again."

Most people cannot emerge from really serious depression just by fighting; a really serious depression has to be treated, or it has to pass. But while you are being treated or waiting for it to pass, you have to keep up the fighting. To take medication as part of the battle is to battle fiercely, and to refuse it would be as ludicrously self-destructive as entering a modern war on horseback. It is not weak to take medications; it does not mean that you can't cope with your personal life; it is courageous. Nor is it weak to seek help from a wise therapist. Faith in God and any form of faith in yourself are great. You must take your therapies, all kinds, with you into the struggle. You cannot wait to be cured. "Labour must be the cure, not sympathy—Labour is the only radical cure for rooted sorrow," wrote Charlotte Brontë; it is not the *whole* cure, but it is, still, the only one. Happiness itself can be a grand labor.

And yet we all know that labor on its own cannot bring about joy. Charlotte Brontë also wrote, in *Villette*, "No mockery in this world ever sounds to me so hollow as that of being told to *cultivate* happiness. What does such advice mean? Happiness is not a potato, to be planted in mould, and tilled with manure. Happiness is a glory shining far down upon us out of Heaven. She is a divine dew which the soul, on certain of its summer mornings, feels dropping upon it from the amaranth bloom and golden fruitage of Paradise. 'Cultivate happiness!' I said briefly to the doctor: 'do *you* cultivate happiness? How do you manage?'" Luck plays a significant role, bringing on us as if by chance those dews of happiness. Some people respond well to one treatment, some to another. Some people remit spontaneously after a brief struggle. Some who do not tolerate medication can in fact achieve much through talking therapies; some who have given over thousands of hours to psychoanalysis get better the minute they take a pill. Some people drag themselves out of one episode with one treatment only to descend into another that requires a different treatment. Some people have refractory depression that never lifts, no matter what they do. Some people have dismaying side effects from every form of treatment, and some people never encounter the slightest trouble from hideous-sounding therapies. There may come a time when we can analyze the brain and all its functions, when we will be able to explain not only the origins of depression but also the reasons for all these differences. I am not holding my breath. For the time being, we must accept that fate has given some of us a strong vulnerability to depression, and that among those who carry such a vulnerability, some have treatment-responsive brains and some have treatment-resistant brains. Those of us who can get substantially better in any way must count ourselves, no matter how dire our breakdowns may have been, among the lucky ones. We must, further, treat those for whom there can be no recovery with forbearance. Resilience is a frequent, but not a universal, gift, and no secret in this book or elsewhere can help the unluckiest ones of all.

CHAPTER IV

Alternatives

I f many remedies are prescribed for an illness," Anton Chekhov once wrote, "you may be certain that the illness has no cure." Many remedies are prescribed for depression—in addition to the standard measures, a stupefying number of alternatives. Some of these are wonderful and may be extremely helpful, most of them selectively. Others are perfectly ludicrous: the emperor has a whole new wardrobe in this business. Anecdotal marvels are everywhere, and people relate them with the ecstasy of the newly converted. Few of these alternative treatments are acutely harmful, except perhaps to the pocketbook; the only real danger comes when fairy-tale remedies are used in place of effective ones. The sheer quantity of alternative therapies reflects a persistent optimism in the face of the intractable problem of emotional pain.

In the wake of prior publications on depression, I have received hundreds of letters from people in nine different countries and most of the fifty states who, touchingly, have wanted to let me know about alternative treatments. One woman from Michigan wrote that after years of trying every medication, she had finally found the true solution, which was "doing things with yarn." When I wrote back to ask her what she did with yarn, she sent me a remarkable photograph of some eighty identical little bears she had made in rainbow colors and a self-published book about really, really easy weaving. A woman in Montana complained, "You might want to know that all the effects you describe come from chronic poisoning. Look around you. Did you have your house insecticided, your lawn herbicided? Are you living with particleboard subflooring? Until writers such as William Styron and yourself examine their surroundings for such exposures, and remove them, I have no patience with you and your depression narratives." I would not presume to speak on behalf of William Styron, whose floors may well be leaching Agent Orange, but I can say quite safely that my house, whose innards have been revealed to me during a decade of plumbing and wiring disasters, has only wood floors on a wood frame. Another of my readers thought I had mercury poisoning from the fillings in my teeth (but I don't have any fillings in my teeth). Someone wrote me an anonymous letter from Albuquerque saying that I had low blood sugar. Someone else volunteered to help me find a teacher if I wanted to try tap-dancing lessons. Someone in Massachusetts wanted to tell me all about biofeedback. A man in Munich asked whether I would like him to replace my RNA, an offer that I politely declined. My favorite came from a woman in Tucson who wrote simply, "Did you ever consider leaving Manhattan?"

My own (and William Styron's) situation notwithstanding, the effects of formaldehyde poisoning can in fact be similar to the symptoms of depressive illness. So too can the neurotoxicity of mercury poisoning from amalgam fillings in teeth. Low blood sugar is linked to depressed mood. I cannot testify to the therapeutic potential of tap-dancing lessons, but physical activity of any disciplined kind can be a mood elevator. Even the repeated soothing manual occupation of making things from yarn can probably serve a useful purpose under the right circumstances. Leaving Manhattan would most assuredly lower my stress level. My experience is that no one, no matter how lunatic he may seem at first glance, is completely off base. Many people achieve astonishingly good results with batty-sounding projects. Seth Roberts, in the psychology department at the University of California at Berkeley, has a theory that some depression is tied to waking up alone, and that the experience of having a talking head to look at for an hour as you begin the day may help. His patients have videotapes of the kind of talk shows that use a single camera so that the head on the screen stays about life-size. They watch these for the first hour of their day, and a convincing number of them feel miraculously much better. "I never knew that the TV could be my best friend," one of his patients said to me. The mitigation of loneliness, even in this hokey form, can have a most uplifting effect.

I had a blessed series of encounters with a man I took to calling "the incompetent mystic." The incompetent mystic wrote me about the energy therapies he practices, and after some considerable correspondence, I invited him to my house to demonstrate his work. He was extremely pleasant and clearly full of good intentions, and after a few minutes of discussion we set to work. He had me hold together the thumb and middle finger of my left hand to make an O and then make a similar O with my right hand. Then he had me link the two Os together. He then asked me to recite a number of sentences, claiming that when I spoke the truth, my fingers would hold firm against his attempts to pull them apart, but that when I lied, my fingers would grow weak. My gentle readers may perhaps imagine the self-consciousness I felt sitting in my own living room saying "I hate myself" while an earnest man in a light blue suit pulled at my hands. To describe the procedures that followed on this set of exercises would take pages and pages, but the high point came when he began a chant over me and forgot halfway through what it was he was supposed to be chanting. "Hold it for just a second," he said, and searched through his briefcase until he found, "You want to be happy. You will be happy." I decided that anyone who could not remember those two sentences was a big booby, and with some effort I got the incompetent mystic back out of my house. I have since been told by patients of their better experiences with energy therapy, and I must accept that some do reverse their "body polarity" and arrive at blissful self-love through the inspired practice of such methodologies. I, however, remain very much a skeptic—though I cannot doubt that some quacks are more gifted in their presentation than was mine.

Since depression is a cyclical illness that will go into temporary remission without any treatment, one might credit any sustained useless or useful activity with its eventual amelioration. It is my absolute belief that in the field of depression, there is no such thing as a placebo. If you have cancer and try an exotic treatment and then you think you are better, you may well be wrong. If you have depression and try an exotic treatment and think you are better, then you are better. Depression is a disease of thought processes and emotions, and if something changes your thought processes and emotions in the correct direction, that qualifies as a recovery. Frankly, I think that the best treatment for depression is belief, which is in itself far more essential than what you believe in. If you really truly believe that you can relieve your depression by standing on your head and spitting nickels for an hour every afternoon, it is likely that this incommodious activity will do you tremendous good.

Exercise and diet play an important role in the progress of affective illness, and I believe that some considerable control can be achieved through good regimes of fitness and nutrition. Among the more serious alternative treatments I count repeated transcranial magnetic stimulation (rTMS); the use of light boxes for people with seasonal affective disorder (SAD); eye movement desensitization and reprocessing (EMDR) therapy; massage treatments; survival courses; hypnosis; sleep deprivation therapy; the plant Saint-John's-wort; S-adenosylmethionine or SAMe; homeopathy; Chinese herbal medicine; group therapies; support groups; and psychosurgery. Only an infinite book could discuss every treatment that has ever given a reasonable result.

"Exercise is the first step for all my patients," Richard A. Friedman of

Payne-Whitney says. "It boosts everyone." I hate exercise, but as soon as I can drag myself out of bed, I do some calisthenics; or if I can manage it, I go to a gym. When I was emerging from depression, it didn't really matter what I did; StairMasters and treadmills were the easiest. It felt as though the exercise helped to clear the depression out of my blood, as though it helped me to get cleaner. "It's a very clear matter," says James Watson, president of Cold Spring Harbor Laboratory and one of the discoverers of DNA. "Exercise produces endorphins. Endorphins are endogenous morphine, and they make you feel great if you're feeling normal. They make you feel better if you're feeling awful. You have to get those endorphins up and running—after all, they're upstream of the neurotransmitters too, and so exercise is going to work to raise your neurotransmitter levels." Further, depression makes your body heavy and sluggish; and being heavy and sluggish exacerbates depression. If you keep making your body function, as much as you can, your mind will follow suit. A really serious workout is just about the most disgusting idea I can imagine when I'm depressed, and it's no fun doing it, but afterward I always feel a thousand times better. Exercise allays anxiety too: nervous energy gets used up by sit-ups, and this helps to contain irrational fear.

You are what you eat; you feel what you are. You cannot cause a depression to remit simply by choosing the right foods; but you can certainly bring on a depression by failing to eat the right foods, and you can to some extent protect against recurrence through careful monitoring of diet. Sugar and carbohydrates appear to raise the absorption of tryptophan in the brain, which in turn raises serotonin levels. Vitamin B_6, which is found in whole grains and shellfish, is important to serotonin synthesis; low levels of B_6 may precipitate a depression. Low cholesterol has been linked to depressive symptoms. The studies aren't in, but a good diet of lobster and chocolate mousse may do much toward improving one's state of mind. "The twentieth century's emphasis on a physically healthy diet," says Watson, "has probably given us a psychologically unhealthy one." Dopamine synthesis also relies on B vitamins, especially B_{12} (found in fish and dairy products) and folic acid (found in calf's liver and broccoli), and also on magnesium (found in cod, mackerel, and wheat germ). Depressed people often have low levels of zinc (which occurs in oysters, endive, asparagus, turkey, and radishes), vitamin B_3 (found in eggs, brewer's yeast, and poultry), and chromium; and these three have been used to treat depression. Low levels of zinc have been especially strongly associated with postpartum depression, since all reserves of zinc pass from the expectant mother to the baby at the very end of pregnancy. Increasing intake of zinc can elevate mood. One theory in circulation is that people in the Mediterranean have less depression because of the amount of fish oil—rich in B vitamins—they consume, which raises their level of omega-3 fatty acids. The evidence for beneficial mood effect from omega-3 fatty acids is the strongest of all.

While these foodstuffs may be effective in preventing depression, other foodstuffs may cause depression. "Many Europeans have wheat allergies, and many Americans have corn allergies," Vicki Edgson, author of *The Food Doctor*, explains. Food allergies can also trigger depression. "These common substances become brain toxins which precipitate all kinds of mental distress." Many people develop depressive symptoms as part of a syndrome of adrenal exhaustion, a consequence of excessive indulgence in sugars and carbohydrates. "If you've got a constantly fluctuating blood sugar level, with highs and lows throughout the day, quick fixes from sweets and junk food, this will cause sleep problems. It will limit not only the ability to cope throughout the day, but also patience and tolerance with other people. People with this syndrome are tired all the time; they lose their sex drive; they ache all over. The stress on their systems is ruinous." Some people develop celiac disease, which causes a general failure to thrive. "People who are depressed fool themselves into thinking that coffee is the one thing that provides energy," Edgson says, "but in fact it leaches energy and stimulates anxiety responses." Alcohol also, of course, takes a substantial toll on the body. "Sometimes," Edgson says, "the depression is your body's way of telling you to stop abusing it; it's evidence of how things are falling apart."

Robert Post at the NIMH has been working on repeated transcranial magnetic stimulation (rTMS), which uses magnetism to create metabolic stimulation much like that caused in ECT, but at lower levels. Modern technology allows magnetism to be focused and concentrated to provide intense stimulus to specific areas of the brain. While electric current has to be turned up quite high to get through the skull and scalp to the brain, magnetic fluxes travel through easily. So ECT causes a brain seizure, and rTMS doesn't. Post proposes that with the advance of neuro-imaging, it may ultimately be possible to pinpoint the areas of the brain that are depressed and to aim magnetic stimulations at those areas, customizing treatment to correspond to the specific form of illness. Also, rTMS offers the possibility of enormous specificity; the magnetic stimulation can be focused with precision. "Sometime," says Post, "we may use technology to put a hood, like an old-fashioned hairdryer, over your head. It would scan your brain and pick up the areas of depressed metabolism, and it would then focus stimulation on those areas. Half an hour later, you would leave with your brain rebalanced."

Norman Rosenthal discovered seasonal affective disorder (SAD) when he moved from South Africa to the United States and began getting rounds of the winter blues. Many people have seasonal changes of mood and develop recurrent winter depression; the changes of season—what one patient called "the crossfire between summer and winter"—are a difficult time for everyone. SAD is different from just not liking cold days. Rosenthal argues that human beings were made to respond to seasonal variation, which artificial light and the artificial constraints of modern life do not allow. When the days get shorter, many people go into withdrawal, and "asking them to perform in the face of their own biological shutdown is a formula for depression. How would a hibernating bear feel if you wanted it to enter the circus and stand up on its hind legs and dance all winter long?" Experiments have shown that SAD is affected by light, which influences the secretion of melatonin and so affects neurotransmitter systems. Light stimulates the hypothalamus, where many of the systems—sleeping, eating, temperature, sex drive—that depression deregulates are based. Light also influences serotonin synthesis in the retina. A sunny day offers about three hundred times as much light as the average household interior. The therapy generally prescribed for SAD sufferers is the use of a light box, which casts terrifyingly bright light at you. I find that light boxes make me a bit dizzy, and I feel as though they challenge my eyes, but I know people who love them. Some actually wear light visors, or head-mounted light boxes. A bright box, which is very much brighter than regular indoor lighting, has been shown to raise brain serotonin levels. "You see the SAD people beginning to go in the autumn," says Rosenthal. "It's like watching the leaves fall off the trees. And then we started treating them with intense light exposure, and it's like seeing the tulips come up."

Eye movement desensitization and reprocessing (EMDR) therapy originated in 1987 for the treatment of post–traumatic stress disorder. The technique is a bit kitschy. The therapist moves his hand at various rates across a field from your right-side peripheral vision to your left-side peripheral vision, so stimulating one eye and then the other. In a variant on the technique, you wear headphones that alternate sounds to stimulate one ear and then the other; or in a third possibility, you hold little vibrators, one in each hand, and they pulse alternatingly. While this is going on, you go through a psychodynamic process of remembering your trauma and reliving it, and at the end of the session you are free of it. While many therapies—psychoanalysis, for example—comprise beautiful theories and limited results, EMDR has silly theories and excellent results. Practitioners of the therapy speculate that it works by stimulating left and right brain in rapid alternation, so helping to transfer memories from one brain storage center to another. This seems unlikely. Something, however, about EMDR's oscillating stimulation does have a dramatic effect.

EMDR is increasingly being used for depression. Since the technique uses trauma memories, it is more often prescribed as a treatment for trauma-based depression than for more generalized depression. I tried all kinds of techniques in the course of researching this book, including EMDR. I was convinced that it was a cute but insignificant system and was very much surprised by the results. I had been told that the technique "speeds up processing," but that did not prepare me for the intensity of the experience. I put on the headphones and tried to think about my memories. I was flooded with incredibly powerful images from childhood, things I hadn't known were even in my brain. I could form associations in no time at all: my mind became speedier than it's ever been. It was an electrifying experience, and the EMDR therapist with whom I was working proficiently led me to all kinds of forgotten childhood difficulties. I am not sure that EMDR has much immediate effect on a depression that is not triggered by a single trauma, but it was so stimulating and so interesting that I kept it up for a twenty-session course.

David Grand, a trained psychoanalytic therapist who now uses EMDR with all his patients, says, "EMDR can help a person to do in six to twelve months what couldn't be done in five years of ordinary treatment. I'm not comparing in the abstract: I'm comparing my work with EMDR to my work without it. The activation bypasses the ego and activates deeply, quickly, and directly. EMDR is not an approach, like the cognitive or the psychoanalytic; it's a tool. You can't just be a generic EMDR therapist. You have to be a good therapist first and then figure out how to integrate EMDR. The oddity of it is a turnoff, but I have been doing it for eight years, and I could not go back to doing therapy without EMDR knowing what I know now. It would be such a regression, such a return to the primitive." I always came out of my EMDR therapist's office reeling (in a good way); and the things I learned have stayed with me and enriched my conscious mind. It's a powerful process. I recommend it.

In October 1999, I traveled to Sedona, Arizona, to have four days of New Age massage at a time when I was experiencing great stress. I am in general rather cynical about New Age treatments, and I greeted the "analyst" who would perform my first treatment with some suspicion as she laid out her crystals at the end of the room and told me about her dreams. I am not persuaded that deep inward tranquillity is an automatic result of being sprayed in sequence with oils from sacred Chaco Canyon and Tibet, and I don't know that the strand of rose quartz beads she draped like a rosary over my eyes was really connecting with my chakras; nor do I believe that the interpretive Sanskrit chants with which the room was filled were inscribing antidepressant virtues into my meridians. All that being said, four days of gentle handling by beautiful women in an opulent resort did a great deal for me, and I left high on peace. My final treatment—cranial-sacral massage—seemed to have particularly beneficial effects: a certain serenity descended on me and lasted for several days.

I believe that extensive massage, which reawakens the body that depression has cut off from the mind, can be a useful part of therapy. I don't think my Sedona experience could have done a thing for someone in the depths of major depression, but as a tune-up technique it was pretty terrific. The theorist Roger Callahan claims to mix applied kinesiology and traditional Chinese medicine. Callahan posits that we change on a cellular basis first, then a chemical, then neurophysiological, then cognitive. We have, he says, been working backward in treating the cognitive first and the neurophysiological second; he begins with the mystic realities of muscle responses. He has many followers. Though their practices seem hokey to me, the idea of starting from the physical seems rather intelligent. Depression is a bodily affliction, and the physical helps.

During the Second World War, many British soldiers had to spend extended periods adrift in the Atlantic after their ships had suffered disabling attacks. The soldiers who had the best rate of survival were not the most young and able but the most experienced, who often had a toughness of spirit that transcended the limits of their bodies. The educator Kurt Hahn observed that such toughness had to be learned, and he founded Outward Bound, which is now a large confederation of associations scattered around the globe. Through structured encounters with the wild, Outward Bound attempts to keep to Hahn's objectives: "I regard it as the foremost task of education to ensure survival of these qualities: an enterprising curiosity; an undefeatable spirit; tenacity in pursuit; readiness for sensible self-denial; and, above all, compassion."

In the summer of 2000, I went on an expedition with Outward Bound's Hurricane Island School. I could never have done Outward Bound from the seat of a depression, but doing it when I was not depressed seemed to strengthen the things in me that resist depression. The course was rigorous and sometimes quite punishing but also pleasurable, and it did make me feel that my life was tied to the organic processes of the larger world. That was a secure feeling: assuming one's place in the sweep of eternity is enormously comforting. We went sea kayaking, and our days were filled with muscular exertion. On a typical day, we might rise at about four in the morning, then run a mile, then go to a platform some twenty-eight feet above the sea and jump off it into the frigid Maine water. Then we'd strike camp and pack our supplies in our kayaks, then carry the kayaks—two-person boats some twenty-two feet long—down to the sea. We'd paddle perhaps five miles against the tide (going just over a mile an hour) until we reached a place where we could stop for breakfast, and we'd stretch and cook and eat there. Then we'd climb back in the boats and do another five miles of paddling, then arrive at our location for the night. We'd have lunch and then practice assisted rescues, turning our boats over and releasing ourselves underwater from the webbing that held us in, righting the kayaks in the sea, and reentering them. Then we'd be taken individually to separate spots for the night, which we would pass with a sleeping bag, a bottle of water, a plastic tarp, and a piece of string. Fortunately, the sun was shining during my trip; we would have stuck to the same agenda had there been sleet coming down on us. Our instructors were remarkable, people of the earth who seemed to be absolute survivors and strong and even sometimes wise. Through our close encounters with wilderness, and through their careful interventions, we gained some fragment of their intense competence.

At times I wished I had never come and felt that the final mark of my lunacy was that I had consented to let my life be stripped of its luxuries like this. But I also felt myself back in touch with something profound. It smacks of triumph to inhabit the unimproved world of nature, even if you do so in a fiberglass kayak. The rhythm of paddling helps, and so does the light, and the waves seem to pace the blood as it goes to the heart, and sadness ebbs. Outward Bound reminded me in many ways of psychoanalysis: it was a process of self-revelation that pushed out one's sense of limits. In this, it met the intention of its founder. "Without self-discovery," Hahn wrote, extending an idea of Nietzsche's, "a person may still have self-confidence, but it is a self-confidence built on ignorance and it melts in the face of heavy burdens. Self-discovery is the end product of a great challenge mastered, when the mind commands the body to do the seemingly impossible, when strength and courage are summoned to extraordinary limits for the sake of something outside the self—a principle, an onerous task, another human life." That is to say, one has to do things between bouts of depression that will build up the resilience so that you can survive despair when it comes knocking again—much as we do daily exercise to keep our bodies in shape. I would not suggest doing Outward Bound instead of therapy, but as a supplement to therapy, it can be powerful; and it is, in its entirety, gratifyingly beautiful. Depression cuts you off from your roots. Though it can feel leaden, depression is also a helium situation because nothing holds you to the earth. Outward Bound was my way into the rootedness of nature, and to have done what I did made me feel, finally, both proud and safe.

Hypnosis, like EMDR, is a tool that can be used in treatment rather than as a treatment itself. It is possible through hypnosis to take a patient back to his early experiences and help him to relive them in a way that brings about some resolution. In his book on the use of hypnosis in depression, Michael Yapko writes that hypnosis works best when the personal understanding of an experience seems to be the source of depression and can be changed to an alternative understanding that feels better. Hypnosis is also used to conjure in the patient's mind an image of a potential bright future, the anticipation of which may lift him out of current misery and so enable that bright future itself. At the least, a successful hypnosis is useful in breaking negative patterns of thought and behavior.

One of the primary symptoms of depression is a disruption in sleep patterns; really depressed people may have no deep sleep at all and may be spending lots of time in bed without ever getting rested. Does one sleep oddly only because of depression, or does one sink into depression in part because of sleeping oddly? "Grief, which leads to depression, disrupts your sleep one way; falling in love, which can lead to mania, disrupts your sleep another way," Thomas Wehr, at the NIMH, points out. Even people who do not suffer from depression have had the experience of waking up too early with a sensation of ominous dread; in fact, that fearful despairing state, which usually passes quickly, may be the closest that healthy people come to the experience of depression. Almost all people who suffer from depression feel worse in the morning and better as the day goes on. So Thomas Wehr has done a series of experiments that show that you can alleviate some symptoms of depression with controlled sleep deprivation. It's not a practical system for the long term, but it can be useful in people who are waiting for the effects of antidepressants to kick in. "By not letting someone go to sleep, you extend the day's improvement. Even though depressed people seek the oblivion of sleep, it is *in* sleep that the depression is maintained and intensified. What kind of horrible succubus visits during the night and brings about that transformation?" Wehr asks.

F. Scott Fitzgerald wrote in *The Crack-Up* that "at three o'clock in the morning, a forgotten package has the same importance as a death sentence, and the cure doesn't work—and in a real dark night of the soul it is always three o'clock in the morning, day after day." That demon of three o'clock has visited me.

When I am most depressed, I do feel a gradual lifting during the day, and though I become exhausted easily, the late, late night is my functional period—indeed, if I were to choose by mood states, I'd live my life at midnight. There has been limited research in this area because it is nonpatentable, but some studies indicate that the mechanisms are complicated and depend on when you sleep, what part of sleep you are in when you wake up, and a variety of other technical factors. Sleep is the primary determinant of circadian body patterns, and altering sleep disrupts the timing of neurotransmitter and endocrine release. But though we can identify much of what happens during sleep and can observe the emotional dip that sleep enables, we cannot yet draw direct correlations. Thyroid-releasing hormone goes down during sleep; is that what causes the emotional dip? Norepinephrine and serotonin go down; acetylcholine goes up. Some theorize that sleep deprivation increases dopamine levels; one series of experiments suggests that blinking causes dopamine release and that a long period of having your eyes shut therefore cuts down on dopamine.

You clearly can't deprive someone of sleep altogether, but you can keep people from going through the late stage of restless REM sleep by waking them up when it begins, and this can be an excellent way to keep a depression in check. I've tried it myself and it works. Napping, which I long to do during depressions, is counterproductive and can undo all the good achieved through being awake. Professor M. Berger of the University of Freiburg has practiced so-called sleep advancement, in which people are put to bed at five in the afternoon and woken up before midnight. This can have a beneficial effect, though no one seems to understand why. "These treatments sound kind of wacky," Thomas Wehr acknowledges. "But frankly, if you said to someone, 'I'd like to put some wires on your head and run electricity through your brain and induce a seizure because I think that might help your depression,' and if that were not a widely practiced and well-established treatment, it might be hard to get it going."

Michael Thase, of the University of Pittsburgh, has observed that many depressed people have substantially reduced sleep altogether, and that insomnia during depression is a predictor of suicidality. Even for those who can sleep, the quality of sleep is substantially altered during depression. Depressed people tend to have low sleep efficiency; they seldom or never enter the deep-wave sleep that is associated with feelings of being refreshed and well rested. They may have many brief episodes of REM sleep rather than the fewer and more protracted episodes typical of a healthy individual. Since REM sleep may be described as a minor awakening, this repetitive REM is exhausting rather than restful. Most antidepressants reduce REM sleep, though they don't necessarily improve the overall quality of sleep. Whether this is part of their mechanism of action is hard to know. Thase has observed that depressives with normal sleep may be more responsive to psychotherapy, and that those with abnormal sleep tend to require medication.

Though sleep during depression brings you down, chronic under-sleeping may be the thing that triggers depression. Since the invention of TV, the average night's sleep has gone down by two hours. Could society-wide increased depression be a result in part of decreased sleep? Of course we have a basic problem here: we not only don't know much about depression, but also don't know what sleep is for.

All the other body systems can be muddled in ways that appear to be productive. Cold exposure can have similar effects to sleep deprivation. Caribou who stand still through the relentless night of a northern winter before beginning to move again in the spring are in "arctic resignation," which can look a lot like human depression. Cold does, in some animals at least, cause a general slowdown.

Saint-John's-wort is an attractive shrub that blossoms around Saint John's Day (June 24). Its usefulness as a medicine has been established at least since Pliny the Elder, in the first century A.D., who took it for bladder troubles. In the thirteenth century, it was held to chase away the devil. In the United States at this time, Saint-John's-wort is sold in extracts; as a powder; in tea; as a tincture; and as an ingredient in everything from feel-good shakes to nutritional supplements. It is all the rage in northern Europe. Since there is no financial incentive to research naturally occurring substances that are not subject to patent, there have been relatively few controlled studies of Saint-John's-wort, though some government-sponsored research is underway at this time. Saint-John's-wort certainly appears to work, alleviating both anxiety and depression. What is not clear is how it works; in fact, it is not even clear which of the many biologically active substances in the plant does the working. The substance about which most is known is hypericum, which is usually about 0.3 percent of a given extract of the drug. Hypericum seems to be capable of inhibiting the reuptake of all three neurotransmitters. It is said to lower the production of interleukin-6, a protein involved in immune response, excessive quantities of which make people feel generally miserable.

The natural-medicine guru Andrew Weil claims that plant extracts are effective because they operate on multiple systems; his view is that many potent agents working in concert are better than overdesigned molecules, though how or whether these agents actually aid one another is pure conjecture. He celebrates the dirtiness of the plant remedies, the way they act in multiple ways on multiple systems of the body. His theories have limited scientific backing but a certain conceptual charm. Most people who choose to take Saint-John's-wort are not taking it for its therapeutic dirtiness. Rather, they have selected it because of a sentimental view that it is better to take a plant than to take a synthesized substance. The marketing of Saint-John's-wort exploits this prejudice. In an advertisement that ran for a while in the London Underground, a blonde woman with an expression of bliss on her face was identified as "Kira, sunshine girl," who was kept in high spirits by the "gently dried leaves" and "cheerful yellow flowers" of Saint-John's-wort. The implication of this ludicrous ad—as if the gentle drying or yellow color had anything at all to do with the efficacy of the treatment—reflects the sappy approach that has made Saint-John's-wort such a popular remedy. It is hardly "natural" to take Saint-John's-wort in a specified quantity regularly. That God put a certain configuration of molecule into a plant and left another configuration of molecule to be developed by human science hardly recommends the first arrangement over the second. There is nothing particularly attractive about "natural" illnesses such as pneumonia or "natural" substances such as arsenic or "natural" phenomena such as tooth decay. It should be remembered that many naturally occurring substances are extremely toxic.

I have noted that some people have adverse responses to the SSRIs. It is worth noting that Saint-John's-wort, for all that it grows wild in meadows, is not more innocent. Natural substances are sold in poorly controlled ways, so that you cannot be sure you are getting the same amount of the active ingredients from pill to pill, and they can certainly have dangerous interactions with other drugs. Saint-John's-wort can, for example, decrease the effectiveness of (among others) oral contraceptives, cholesterol-lowering statin drugs, beta blockers, calcium-channel blockers for high blood pressure and coronary heart disease, and protease inhibitors for HIV infection. My own view is that nothing is wrong with Saint-John's-wort, but nothing is particularly right about it either. It's less well regulated, less studied, and more fragile than the synthetic molecules, and it tends to be taken in a less consistent way than Prozac.

In the lusty search for "natural" remedies, researchers have dug up another curative substance, this one called S-adenosylmethionine, or

SAMe for short. While Saint-John's-wort has been a psychological panacea in northern Europe, SAMe has been the most popular treatment in southern Europe, with a particularly large following in Italy. Like Saint-John's-wort, it is unregulated, available from health food stores as a small white pill. SAMe does not come from a cheerful flower, as Saint-John's-wort does, but rather is found in the human body. The level of SAMe in individuals varies with age and gender. SAMe occurs all over the body and enables many chemical functions. Though depressed people do not have low levels of SAMe, studies of the substance's efficacy as an antidepressant have been encouraging. SAMe consistently beats placebos in the alleviation of depressive symptoms, and it seems to be at least as effective as the tricyclic antidepressants to which it has been compared. Many of the studies of the drug, however, were not well structured, and their results may not be entirely reliable. SAMe does not have a long catalog of side effects, but it can trigger mania in patients with bipolar disorder. No one seems to have any concrete idea what SAMe's mode of action is. It may be implicated in the metabolism of neurotransmitters; long-term use of SAMe in animals increases their brain neurotransmitter levels. It appears to enhance dopamine and serotonin in particular. A deficiency of SAMe may be linked to poor methylation, which would subject the body in general to stress. The elderly tend to have low levels of SAMe, and some researchers have proposed that this deficiency is linked to the lowered function of the aging brain. Many explanations for SAMe's apparent effectiveness have been proposed, with virtually no evidence to support any of them.

Homeopathy is occasionally used to counter depression: Practitioners administer tiny doses of various substances that might in larger doses give healthy people depressive symptoms. Many forms of non-Western medicine may be useful against depression. One woman who had battled depression all of her life, and who had had little help from antidepressants, found, at the age of sixty, that Qigong, a Chinese system of breathing and body exercises, could eliminate the problem altogether. Acupuncture, which has been gaining more and more adherents in the West—Americans now spend $500 million per year on it—has also had amazing effects for some people. The NIH acknowledges that acupuncture may change brain chemistry. Chinese herbal medicine seems less reliable, but some people have achieved great shifts in their consciousness through the use of herbal remedies.

Many people who use alternative therapies have tried conventional ones. Some prefer the alternative therapies, while others are seeking to supplement conventional treatments. Some are conceptually drawn to means of healing that are less intrusive than medication or ECT. Avoiding the talking therapies seems to be at best naive, but finding variant talking therapies, or using talking therapies with nontraditional forms of treatment, can be preferable for some people to visiting the pharmacologist and ingesting compounds about which we still know perilously little.

Among those I met who had danced any distance down the homeopathy highway, I hold Claudia Weaver in particularly high regard. Claudia Weaver is forcefully herself. Some people change with the situation and become reflections of the people with whom they are in dialogue, but Claudia Weaver has a particular mix of bluntness and eccentricity that knows no masters. It can be unsettling, but there is also something extremely satisfying about it. You know where you stand with Claudia Weaver—not that she isn't polite, because she in fact has impeccable manners, but because she is quite uninterested in disguising her essential self. Indeed she throws down her personality almost like a gauntlet: you can rise to the challenge and like her and she'll be pleased, or you can decide that it's a little bit too difficult, in which case you are welcome to go your merry way. As you get to know her, you find her idiosyncratic mind charming. With her deliberateness go loyalty and measureless integrity. She is a very moral person. "I certainly have my eccentricities, and I just became proud of them," she says, "because I couldn't understand how to live without them. I've always been very particular and opinionated."

When I first met Claudia Weaver, she was in her late twenties and was on homeopathic remedies as part of a whole-body treatment that was to control her allergies, her digestive problems, her eczema, and other aspects of her health. She was concurrently using meditation and had changed her diet. She carried with her some thirty-six vials of different substances at different potencies in tablet form (she had a further fifty at home), several oils, and an Ayurvedic tea. She was taking all this on a schedule of dazzling complexity, ingesting the tablets whole in some instances, grinding them up and dissolving them in others, and administering certain ointments topically. Six months earlier, she had put aside once and for all the medication on which she had relied on and off since age sixteen; she had had problems with drugs and was ready to try something else. As had happened on some other occasions when she had stopped, she experienced a temporary high and then began to slip down. A brief go with Saint-John's-wort had been ineffective for her. The homeopathic remedies had stopped her short of disaster and seemed to be fairly effective.

Her homeopathic practitioner, whom she had never met face-to-face, lived in Santa Fe, where he had treated a friend of hers with excellent results. She called him every day or two to discuss how she was feeling, and he asked her various questions—"Does your tongue feel coated?" or "Do your ears feel runny?" for example—on the basis of which he prescribed remedies, usually about six pills a day. The body, he maintains, is like an orchestra, and remedies are like tuning forks. Claudia is an enthusiast for rituals, and I think that she was somewhat persuaded by the very complexity of her regimen. She liked all the little bottles and the consultations and the protocol of the enterprise. She liked taking the elemental cures—sulfur, gold, arsenic—and the more exotic compounds and mixtures—belladonna, poison nut, squid's ink. The focus on treatment distracted her from the illness. Her practitioner could usually address an acute situation even if he couldn't alter the underlying arc of higher and lower spirits.

Claudia has had a lifetime of insight into and discipline concerning her depressions. "I have a lot of trouble remembering positive things when I'm depressed. I go over and over the negative things that people did to me, for which I have an elephant's memory, and times when I was wronged or shamed or embarrassed, and they escalate and become worse than they were in real life, I'm sure. And once I think of one of those things, I can think of ten and that leads to twenty more. In an alternative-spirituality group to which I belong, I was asked to write down negative things that have hindered my life, which I did for twenty pages; and then I was asked to write down positive things. I couldn't think of anything positive to say about myself. I also get fascinated with dark subjects, with Auschwitz or with a plane crash, and I can't stop imagining dying in such situations. My practitioner can usually figure out what to prescribe to alleviate my obsessive fear of disasters.

"I have quite a lot of experience with me. Next month it'll be twenty-nine years of experience with me. And I know that I can give you a linear story today and that tomorrow it will be a different linear story. My reality changes with my moods so much. One day I can tell you how terrible my depression is and how I've been racked with it all my life; and then if it seems to be more under control the next day, I can say that everything's just fine. I try to think of happy times. I try to do things to prevent me from introspection, which leads to depression fast. I feel ashamed of everything about myself when I am depressed. I can't take on board the idea that probably everyone else is also a human being and also going through various emotional states. I have humiliating dreams; even in my sleep I can't get away from this horrendous, weighty feeling of being oppressed, and life being hopeless. Hope is the first thing that goes."

Claudia Weaver felt oppressed by her parents' fixity: "What they wanted was for me to be happy in ways that were their ways." Already in childhood, "I felt very much in my own world. I felt I was different and apart. I felt small, and that I didn't count, and lost in my thoughts, and almost unaware of other people. If I was out in the backyard, I would just wander around there, not seeing anything." Her family was "very stiff upper lip" about the whole thing. In third grade, she began to withdraw physically. "I hated to be touched or hugged or kissed, even by my family. I was so tired all the time at school. I remember teachers saying to me, 'Claudia, pick your head up off that desk.' And nobody thought anything of it. I can remember getting to a gymnastics class and just falling asleep on the radiator. I hated my school and didn't feel like I had any friends. Anything other people said could hurt me, and did. I remember walking the halls by sixth or seventh grade and not being interested in anybody and not feeling like I cared about anything. I'm extremely bitter about my childhood, though at the time I was also strangely prideful of my difference from the rest of the world. The depression? It was always there; it just took a while to name it. I had a very loving family, but it never occurred to them—or to most parents of their generation—that their child could have a mood disorder."

Her one real pleasure was riding, at which she showed some talent. Her parents bought her a pony. "Riding gave me self-confidence, it gave me happiness, it gave me a window of hope that I didn't have anywhere else. I was good at it and I was recognized as being good at it and I loved that pony. We clicked together as a team and knew each other as partners. He seemed to know I needed him. It brought me out of my misery."

She went away to boarding school for tenth grade, and after a conflict in style with the riding instructor there, she gave up on the sport. She told her parents to sell her pony; she didn't have the energy to ride him. That first term at boarding school was a time of looking at what she now recognizes as "spiritual questions: Why am I really here? What is my purpose?" Her roommate, to whom she addressed some of these questions, promptly reported them to the school authorities, repeating fragments of conversation out of context. The authorities decided Claudia was suicidal and promptly sent her home. "It was so hugely embarrassing. I was very ashamed of it. And I just didn't feel like I wanted to be part of anything anymore. I had a tough time coping with that. Whether other people forgot about it quickly or not, I couldn't."

Later that year, very much shaken, she began cutting herself—suffering from what she calls the "totally unattractive alternative anorexia." Her trick was to make a slice and not have it bleed and then pull it apart so that it would bleed. The cuts were so fine that they did not scar. She knew four or five girls at school who were cutting themselves, "which seems like a significant number to be in the trenches." The cutting has continued very occasionally; she cut herself periodically in college, and in her late twenties she sliced parts of her left hand and her belly. "It is *not* a cry-for-help thing," she says. "You feel this emotional pain and you want to go away from it. And you happen to see a knife and you think, wow, that knife is sort of sharp-looking and it's very smooth and I wonder what it would be like if I just put pressure on it here . . . you become fascinated with the knife." Her roommate saw the cuts and once more reported her. "And they said I was *definitely* suicidal, and *that* put me off my rocker. My teeth were chattering, I was so nervous about it." She was sent home again with instructions to visit a psychiatrist. The psychiatrist she saw told her that she was really fairly normal and fine, and that her school and her roommate were nuts. "He recognized that I was not trying to commit suicide but was rather testing boundaries and who I was and where I was going." She returned to school a few days later, but by now she had no feeling of safety and she began to develop symptoms of acute depression. "I just got tireder and tireder and I slept more and more and I did less and less and I wanted to be alone more and more—I was extremely unhappy. And I didn't feel I could tell anyone."

Soon she was sleeping fourteen hours a day. "I would get up in the middle of the night and go into the bathroom and study, which everybody thought was extremely odd. People would knock on the door and wonder what I was doing in there. I'd say, 'I'm just studying.' They'd ask, 'Why are you studying in there?' and I'd say, 'I feel like it, you know?' And then they'd say, 'Why didn't you go to the common room?' But if I went in there, I might have had to interact with someone. That's what I was avoiding." By the end of the year, she had pretty much stopped eating ordinary food. "I would have seven or nine chocolate bars a day because that was enough so that I never had to go to the cafeteria. If I had gone to the cafeteria, people would have said, 'How are you?' and that was the last question I ever wanted to answer. I kept working and finished the year because I was more invisible if I just kept showing up; if I'd stayed in bed, the school would call my parents and I'd have had to explain, and I couldn't cope with the visibility, the vulnerability of that. I didn't even think of calling my parents and saying I wanted to go home; I thought I was trapped there. It's as though I was sort of hazy and couldn't see more than five feet away—and even my mother was six feet away. I was so ashamed of being depressed and I just felt everybody had only terrible things to say about me. Do you know it was embarrassing for me to go to the bathroom even when I was alone? I mean, certainly in a public place I would have a lot of trouble. But even alone, I just couldn't face me. I didn't feel worthy as a human being at all, even in that particular act. I felt like someone might know I was doing that and I was ashamed. It was incredibly painful."

The summer after tenth grade was rough. She developed eczema that was tension-related and that has continued to plague her. "Being around people was absolutely the most draining thing I could imagine. Just talking to someone. I avoided the world. I mostly stayed lying in bed, and I wanted my shades closed. The light hurt me then." As the summer progressed, she finally started on medication, taking imipramine. The people around her noticed a steady improvement, and "by the end of the summer I had worked up enough energy to go into New York City one day with my mother shopping, and go home again. That was the most exciting and energetic thing I did that summer." She also bonded with her therapist, who was to remain a close friend.

In the autumn, she switched schools. Her new school gave her a single room, which worked well for her. She liked the people there, and she had the medication buoying her spirits. She felt that during the summer her family had finally faced her mood states as a real issue, and that was a big help. She began working extremely hard and doing lots of extracurricular activities. She was made a proctor her senior year, and she was admitted to Princeton.

At Princeton, she put in place many of the coping strategies that would be with her for life. Though she was intensely private, she found it difficult to be alone, and to solve the isolation of the night she had six friends who would take turns putting her to bed. Often they stayed over in her bed—she was not yet active sexually and the friends respected these boundaries. They were there just for companionship. "Sleeping with people and that feeling of up-closeness snuggling became a very important antidepressant for me. In favor of snuggling, I would give up sex. I would give up food. I would give up going to the movies. I would give up work. I mean, I'd give up just about anything short of sleep and going to the bathroom to be in a safe, snuggling environment. I wonder if it stimulates chemical reactions in the brain, to be honest." It took her a little while to move on to the next step in physical intimacy. "I was always self-conscious about my naked body; I don't think I've ever tried on a bathing suit and not been traumatized by it. I was not the world's earliest person to have sex. People spent a lot of time trying to convince me that sex was an okay thing. I didn't think it really was. For years, I didn't think it was right for me at all. Just like 7UP—never had it, never will. But eventually I came round."

The winter of her freshman year, she went off medications for a while. "The imipramine I'd been on always gave me the side effects at just the wrong time. It was when I had to give a talk in front of a whole class of people that my mouth became so dry I couldn't move my tongue." She sank rapidly. "I couldn't go out to eat again," she explains, "so a friend of mine would cook me dinner every night and feed me. For eight weeks he did that. And it was always just in his room, so I wouldn't have to eat in front of other people.

"There's always the desire to keep going without the medication, and when you're in that mind-set, you don't realize how bad things are." Finally, friends convinced her to go back on the medications. That summer she went waterskiing, and a dolphin came up and swam beside her. "It was the closest thing to knowing God that I'd ever experienced. I was just like, I think I've got some company here." She felt so up that she went off the medications again.

She went on them again six months later.

At the end of her junior year, she started on Prozac, which worked well except that it killed certain parts of her inner self. She lived with that for about eight years. "I take medicine for a while and then I go off because I begin to think I'm fine and I don't really need it. Yeah, right. And then I go off it and I feel fine, fine, fine, and then a series of things will happen and I'll start feeling beaten down. Like I'm carrying too much weight. And then a couple of small things will happen—you know, it's really not so terrible that the toothpaste cap, for example, fell down the drain, but the fact that it did is the last straw and more upsetting than when my grandmother died. It takes me a while to see where I'm going; it's always down, up, down, up, down, up, and it's difficult to assess when the downs are further down than the ups are up." When a temporary setback caused her to miss a bridal shower—"I couldn't get out of my apartment and get on a bus to go there"—she felt she simply couldn't call. She went back on Prozac.

Eventually, she gave up the medications, so that she could reawaken sexual feeling, and began on the homeopathic remedies she was taking when I first got to know her. The homeopathic remedies seemed to work for quite a while; she feels they are effective at keeping her stable, but when circumstances drove her into a new depression, they could not bring her up out of it. There were some tough times, but she stuck out homeopathy through a long winter. When, once a month, she panicked that her depression was returning, she'd realize that it was just PMS. "I'm always so glad when I start bleeding; and I'd think, 'Oh! Well, that was that!'" Though the lack of medication did not cause any major regression, she did have a harder time with hard things. The overall treatment program seemed to be inconsistent for her physical ailments, the tension-related ailments in particular; her eczema got so bad at one point that her breasts bled through her shirt.

At about this time she gave up talking therapy and began writing what Julia Cameron calls "morning pages," twenty-minute written exercises in matinal stream of consciousness. She says that they help her to clarify her life; she has not missed a day in three years now. She also keeps on her bedroom wall a list of things to do when she is beginning to feel down or bored—a list that begins, "Read five kids' poems. Make a collage. Look at photographs. Eat some chocolate."

A few months after she started writing morning pages, she met the man who is now her husband. "I've come to realize I'm much happier in my life when I have someone in the next room working. Companionship is very important to me; it's very important to my emotional stability. I need comforting. I need small remembrances and attention. I can be in an imperfect relationship much better than I can be by myself." Her fiancé accepted that she had been depressed. "He knows that he has to be sort of poised and ready to help me when I come home from discussing my depression with you, for example," she said to me. "He knows he has to be ready all the time in case I relapse. When I have him around, I feel a lot better about myself and I'm much more able to do things." In fact, she felt so well after she met him that she decided to go off the homeopathic regimen she had been following. She spent the year in an up, happy place, designing with him the ceremonies to solemnize her marriage.

It was a beautiful summer wedding, planned with the same meticulous care as a homeopathic treatment program. Claudia looked beautiful, and it was one of those occasions at which you feel the great welling of affection from the many friends who are gathered. Each of us who knew Claudia was so happy for her: she had found love; she had transcended her lifetime of woes; and she was glowing. Claudia's family now live in Paris, but they have kept the house in which Claudia grew up, a seventeenth-century house in a prosperous town in Connecticut. We gathered there in the morning for a ceremony of intention at which the bride and groom invoked the four directions and the four winds. A luncheon followed at the home of a family friend across the road. The wedding ceremony took place in a beautiful garden at four in the afternoon, and then we had cocktails; Claudia and her husband opened a box of butterflies, which came out and flitted magically around us. There was an elegant dinner for 140 guests in the evening. I sat next to the priest, who maintained that he had never performed a wedding that was so carefully orchestrated; the ceremony, which Claudia had written with her husband, had had full directions "of operatic proportion," he said. Everything was exquisite. Our place cards were on handmade paper with a woodblock print that echoed the handmade paper and woodblock prints of the menus and of the order of service. The images had been drawn especially for the occasion. The groom had actually made the cake, a towering four-story affair, himself.

Change, even positive change, is stressful; and marriage is one of the most enormous changes you can make. Problems that had begun before the wedding worsened soon after it. Claudia believed the trouble was with her husband; it took quite a while for her to accept that her situation might be symptomatic. "He was actually more worried about me and my future than I was. During my wedding day, everyone remembers me happy. I look happy in the pictures. But I went through the whole day feeling I should be in love, I should really be in love if I'm doing this. And I felt like a lamb going to the slaughter. My wedding night, I was just exhausted. And our honeymoon was frankly disastrous. I had nothing nice to say to him the entire trip. I didn't want to be with him; I didn't want to look at him. We tried to have sex and it was painful for me and it just didn't work. I could see how in love he was. And I just thought: I can't believe this. I thought it would be different. And I felt miserable at the thought that I had ruined his life and broken his heart."

In late September, she returned to the homeopathic regimen. It had been stabilizing, but it couldn't lift her out of what had become a truly acute depression. "I'd be at work," she recalls, "and all of a sudden I'd feel like I was about to have a breakdown and cry. I was so worried I'd act in an unprofessional way that I could only just do my job. I'd have to just excuse myself and say I had a headache and had to leave the office for the day. I hated everything; I hated my life. I wanted a divorce or an annulment. I felt I had no friends; I felt I had no future. I had made this terrible mistake. I thought, my God, what are we going to talk about for the rest of our lives? We're going to have to have dinner together, and what are we going to say? I've nothing to say anymore. And he of course felt it was all his fault and had huge self-loathing and he didn't want to shave or go to work or anything. I was not nice to him and I know it. He was trying very hard and just had no idea what to do. Nothing he could have done would have been right to me, no matter what it was. But I didn't see that at the time. I would tell him to go away, that I wanted to be alone; and then what I really wanted was for him to insist on being with me. What really matters to me? I'd ask myself. I don't know. What would make me happy? I don't know. Well, what do I want? I just don't know. And that totally freaked me out. I had no clue. There was nothing I was looking forward to. I focused all that on him. I knew I was being horrible to him— I knew it in the moment and yet I felt powerless to stop it." In October, she had lunch with a friend who told her she had "that happy married glow" and she burst into tears.

It was her worst period since high school. Finally, in November, friends persuaded her to return to Western medicine. Her psychiatrist said she was crazy to have stuck it out on homeopathic treatments for so long and gave her forty-eight hours to get her system clean before he started her on Celexa. "It made an instant difference. I could still feel depressive moments and thoughts, and it does kill my sex drive, so that I feel like I have to try hard to do this for my husband—it's not just interest in sex that goes, but physical trouble, so that I can't even get wet! I have maybe two percent interest when I'm ovulating, and that's the high point of the month. But it's just all so much better. My husband is so sweet; he says, 'I didn't marry you for the sex, it doesn't matter.' I think he's just so relieved that I'm not the monster I was from the marriage on. Our lives feel restabilized. I can see the qualities in him that I wanted—the emotional security is back. The snuggling is back. I'm very needy and now he is filling those needs, and he loves the snuggling too. He has made me feel like I'm a good person. And I am happy to be with him again. He loves me and that is such a treasure now. At least eighty percent of our relationship is now wonderful.

"I feel slightly artificially up. When I was ten milligrams lower on my medication, the depressive moments would come in and they were very disturbing and disruptive and really painful and hard to get out of, although I could pull out of them and would. And I feel like I still need that to keep me up. I don't feel stable. I don't feel the same sense of smooth sailing that I had while I was planning the wedding. If I felt reasonably safe, I would go off the medicine; but I don't feel safe. I find it increasingly hard to draw a line between the depressive and the non-depressive me. I think a depressive tendency is much stronger in me even than the actual depressions. Depression is not the be-all and end-all of my life. You know, I'm not going to lie on my bed for the rest of my life and suffer. The people who succeed despite depression do three things. First, they seek an understanding of what's happening. Then they accept that this is a permanent situation. And then they have to somehow transcend their experience and grow from it and put themselves out into the world of real people. Once you've done the understanding and the growth, you realize that you can interact with the world and live your life and carry on your job. You stop being so crippled, and you feel such a sense of victory! A depressive person who can put aside navel gazing is not so insufferable as one who can't. At first, when I realized I would spend my life doing the mood dance, I was very, very bitter about it. But now I feel like I am *not* helpless. This has become a major focus of my life: How can I grow from this? Maybe this hurts me now, but how can I learn from it?" Claudia Weaver cocks her head to one side.

"I understood that. I'm lucky." It is her questing spirit as much as any experimental treatment that has allowed her to make it through with a life more or less intact, despite all the difficulties she has faced.

Of the group therapies I studied, the one that seemed to me most subtle and nurturing, the one that brought people closest to resolution, was based on the work of Bert Hellinger in Germany. Hellinger, a former priest who was once a missionary to the Zulu, has a large and devoted following for his Gestalt-style work. One of Hellinger's disciples, Reinhard Lier, came to the United States in 1998 and conducted an intensive treatment, in which I participated, my natural skepticism giving way to respect for the process as I became more richly enmeshed in it. Lier's treatment had some effect on me, and I saw that it had enormous effect on others in the group. Like EMDR, Hellinger-style work is probably most effective for people who are dealing with traumas; but for Lier's purposes, the traumatic thing can be a basic fact—"my mother hated me," for example—rather than a single event bounded by time.

A group of about twenty of us came together and established trust through some basic exercises. Then each of us was asked to construct a narrative of the thing that was most painful in his or her life. We shared our narratives in basic form and were asked to choose people from the group to represent the other figures in our narratives. Reinhard Lier then choreographed a kind of elaborate dance using these people as physical markers, placing one in front of the other, moving the subject around, and retelling the story toward a better resolution. He called these formations "family constellations." I chose to work on my mother's death as the point of origin of my depression. Someone played my mother, someone else my father, someone else my brother. Lier said he wanted my grandparents there as well, the one I had known and the three I had not known. As he shifted us around, I was asked to direct speech to these various figures. "What do you have to say to your mother's father, who died when your mother was still quite young?" he asked. Of all the work I did on depression, this was perhaps the treatment most contingent on a charismatic leader. Lier was able to arouse a great deal of force in each of us, and by the time I had done twenty minutes of his dance and of saying certain things, I did feel as though I were speaking to my own mother again, and I told her some things I thought or felt. Then the spell broke and I was in a seminar room in a conference center in New Jersey—but I left that day with a feeling of calm, as though something had been resolved. Maybe it was just the very fact of addressing words to these forces to which I never speak, these vanished grandparents and my lost mother, but I was moved by the process and thought it had something sacrosanct in it. It wouldn't cure depression, but it could bring some measure of peace.

The most compelling of our group was a man of German extraction who had found out that his parents had worked in a concentration camp. Unable to process this horror, he had become severely depressed. During his speeches to all the different members of his family, who were being physically positioned closer to him and farther away by Reinhard Lier, the man wept and wept and wept. "This is your mother," Lier said at one point. "She did terrible things. She also loved and protected you when you were a child. Tell her that she betrayed you, and then tell her that you will always love her. Do not try to forgive her." It sounds contrived, but it was in fact sweetly powerful.

It is hard to talk about depression during depression even with friends, and so the idea of depression support groups seems counterintuitive. Nonetheless, these groups have proliferated as incidents of depression have been more widely recognized, and as funding for therapy has dwindled. I did not go to support groups during my own depression—out of snobbery, apathy, ignorance, and a sense of privacy—but I began to go as I worked on this book. There are hundreds of organizations—mostly hospitals—running support groups across the United States and around the world. Depression and Related Affective Disorders Association (DRADA), at Johns Hopkins, runs sixty-two different support groups, has set up a one-on-one buddy system, and publishes a particularly good newsletter called *Smooth Sailing*. Mood Disorders Support Groups (MDSG), based in New York, is the largest support organization in the United States, running fourteen support groups every week and serving about seven thousand attendees per year; MDSG also sponsors ten lectures a year, each of which is attended by about one hundred fifty people. They publish a quarterly newsletter, which goes out to about six thousand people. MDSG meetings take place in several locations; I went mostly to the groups at Beth Israel Hospital in New York at seven-thirty every Friday night, when most depressed people are not having dates. To enter, you pay $4 in cash and are given a sticky label with your first name only, which you wear during meetings with about a dozen others and a facilitator. First, everyone introduces himself and explains what he wants from the meeting. Then a more general discussion opens up. People tell their stories and offer advice to one another, sometimes playing games of one-downsmanship. The sessions run two hours. They are terrifyingly, addictively heartbreaking, full of treatment-resistant and abandoned people who've had severe episodic histories. These groups try to fill in for the increasing impersonality of medical systems; a lot of the people at them have destroyed relationships in their illness and lost families and friends.

On a typical visit, I went into a room glaring with fluorescent light and found ten people waiting to tell their stories. Depressives are not great dressers, and they often find that bathing uses up too much energy. A lot of this crowd looked as ratty as they felt. I went seven Fridays. The last time I was there, John talked first, because he liked talking and was doing pretty well and had come almost every week for ten years and knew the ropes. John had kept his job, never missed a day of work. Didn't want to take medication but was experimenting with herbs and vitamins. Thought he was going to make it. Dana was too depressed to talk tonight. She pulled her knees up under her chin and promised she'd try to talk later. Anne hadn't been to MDSG in a while. She'd had a bad time: took Effexor for depression and it helped a lot. Then when her dose was raised, she'd gone paranoid, "flipped out." Believed the Mafia was out to get her and barricaded herself in her apartment. Eventually got hospitalized and had "every medication, every single one" and then when none of them helped, she got ECT. Couldn't remember much from that time; the ECT had wiped out a lot of the memories. She used to be an executive, white-collar. Now she fed people's cats for a living. Today she'd lost two clients, and rejection was tough. And humiliation. So she'd decided to come by tonight. Her eyes filled with tears. "You're all so nice, listening to one another," she said. "Out there, no one listens." We tried to help. "I had so many friends. They're all gone now. But I'm making it. Walking around to my different cats is good, it keeps up some movement, the walking helps."

Jaime had been forced to resign from his job with "a government agency" because he'd missed too many days. He'd been on disability leave for three years. The people he still knew, most of them wouldn't understand. He pretended still to have his job and didn't answer the phone during the day. He seemed well tonight, better than I'd seen him. "If I couldn't keep up appearances," he said, "I'd kill myself. That's all that keeps me going." Howie was next. He had been sitting all evening and hugging a big down coat to his chest. Howie came often and talked seldom. He looked around the room. He was forty years old and had never had a full-time job. Two weeks ago, he'd announced that he was about to take one, have a change in income, be like a normal person. He was on some good medications that seemed to be helping. But what if they stopped working? Could he get back his $85 per-month disability Supplemental Security Income (SSI)? We'd all told him to go for it, to try the job, but tonight he told us he'd turned it down; it was just too frightening to him. Anne asked whether his moods were constant, whether outside events had any effect, whether he felt different when he took a vacation. Howie looked at her blankly. "I've never had a vacation," he said. Everyone kept looking at him. He shuffled his feet on the floor. "I'm sorry. I mean, I guess I've never really had anything to take a vacation from."

Polly said, "I hear people talking about cycling, about going in and out of moods, and I feel really jealous. For me, it's never been like that. I've always been this way; I was a morbid, unhappy, anxious child. Is there any hope left for me?" She was on Nardil and had found that clonidine in microdoses saved her from the heavy sweating she experienced. She'd originally been on lithium, but it had caused her to gain about fifteen pounds a month, so she'd stopped. Someone thought she should try Depakote, which can be helpful with Nardil. The restricted eating with Nardil was a real pain. Jaime said that Paxil had made him sicker. Mags said she had had Paxil and it hadn't worked for her. Mags seemed to be speaking through the fog. "I can't decide," she said. "I can't decide anything." Mags was so apathetic she didn't get out of bed for weeks at a time. Her therapist had almost forced her to come to this group. "Before medication, I was this neurotic, miserable, suicidal person," she said. "Now I just don't care about anything." She looked around the room as if we were the jury at the Pearly Gates. "Which is better? Which person should I be?" John shook his head. "This is the problem, how the cure's worse than the disease," he said. And then it was Cheryl's turn. She looked around but you could tell that she wasn't seeing any of us. Her husband had brought her here hoping it would help and was waiting outside. "I feel," she said in a flat voice like a slowed-down old record-player, "as though I died a few weeks ago, but my body hasn't found out yet."

This sad gathering of shared pain was a singular release from isolation for many of the people there. I remembered from my own worst times those eager, questioning faces, or my father saying, "Are you doing any better?" and how disappointing I felt when I said, "No, not really." Some friends had been fantastic, but with others I had felt obliged to be tactful. And jokey. "I'd love to come, but I'm actually having a nervous breakdown right now, so could we do it another time?" It is easy to keep secrets by being honest in an ironic tone of voice. That basic feeling at the support group—I have my mind today, do you have yours?—spoke volumes, and almost in spite of myself, I began to relax into it. There is so much that cannot be said during depression, that can be intuited only by others who know. "If I were on crutches, they wouldn't ask me to dance," said one woman about her family's relentless efforts to get her to go out and have fun. There is so much pain in the world, and most of these people keep theirs secret, rolling through agonizing lives in invisible wheelchairs, dressed in invisible bodycasts. We held each other up with what we said. Sue, one night, in anguish, crying through her thick mascara, said, "I need to know if any of you have felt like this and made it. Someone tell me that, I came all this way to hear it, is it true, please tell me that it is." Another night someone said, "My soul hurts so much; I just need to interface with other people."

Practical purposes are also served at MDSG, especially for people who are not coddled by friends, family, and excellent health insurance. You don't want your employer to know, or your prospective employer; what can you say without lying about it? Unfortunately, the participants with whom I came in contact mostly seemed to give each other excellent support and terrible advice. If you've sprained your ankle, other people with sprained ankles may be able to give you useful pointers, but if you've got mental illness, you should not rely on people with mental illness to tell you what to do. I drew on my reading knowledge, horrified at what bad counsel a lot of these people had had, but it was hard to achieve much authority. Christian was clearly bipolar, unmedicated, and getting manic; I am sure he will have had a suicidal phase before this book is published. Natasha should not have been *thinking* of going off Paxil so soon. Claudia had been through what sounded like badly administered and excessive ECT, and then had been overmedicated into a zombie; Jaime might, with ECT, have been able to keep his real job, but he knew nothing about how it really worked, and what Claudia had to say did not reassure him.

One time, someone was talking about trying to explain things to friends. A longtime MDSG man, Stephen, asked the group, "Do you have friends outside?" Only one other person and I said that we did. Stephen said, "I try to make new friends, but I don't know how it works. I was such a recluse for so long. I took Prozac, and it worked for a year, and then it stopped. I think I did more that year, but I lost it." He looked at me curiously. He was sad and sweet-natured and intelligent—clearly a lovely person, as someone said to him that evening—but he was gone. "How do you meet people, besides here?" And before I could answer, he added, "And once you've met them, what do you talk about?"

Like all diseases, depression is a great equalizer, but I met no one with depression who seemed a less likely figure for it than Frank Rusakoff, twenty-nine, soft-spoken and polite and good-natured and good-looking and the sort of person who seems altogether normal, except that he suffers from horrendous depression. "You want inside my head?" he once wrote. "Welcome. Not exactly what you expected? It's not exactly what I expected either." A year or so after graduating from college, Frank

Rusakoff was at the movies when his first depression hit him. In the seven years that followed, he was hospitalized thirty times.

His first episode came on abruptly: "On the way home from a movie, I realized I was going to drive into a tree. I felt like there was a weight pushing my foot down, like someone was pulling my hands around. I knew I couldn't drive home because there were too many trees that way and they were getting harder and harder to resist, so I headed for the hospital." During the years that followed, Frank went through every medication in the book and got nowhere. "In the hospital, I actually tried to choke myself to death." He finally went in for ECT. That helped, but it also made him briefly manic. "I hallucinated, attacked another patient, had to go into the quiet room for a while," he recalls. For five years thereafter, Frank got booster ECT (one treatment, rather than a series) whenever the depression hit again, usually about once every six weeks. He was put on a combination of lithium, Wellbutrin, Ativan, doxepin, Cytomel, and Synthroid. "ECT works, but I hate it. It's totally safe and I would recommend it, but they're putting electricity into your head, and that's scary. I hate the memory problems. It gives me a headache. I'm always afraid they'll do something wrong, or I won't come out of it. I keep journals so I can remember what happened; otherwise, I'd never know."

Different people have different hierarchies of treatment in their heads, but surgery is the last resort for everyone. Lobotomies, first performed at the turn of the century, became popular in the 1930s and, especially, after World War II. Returning veterans with shell shock or neurosis were routinely given clumsy operations in which their frontal lobe (or other brain sections) was severed. In the heyday of lobotomies, about five thousand were performed annually in the United States, causing between 250 and 500 deaths a year. Psychosurgery lies under this shadow. "Sadly," says Elliot Valenstein, who has written a history of psychosurgery, "people still connect these surgeries with mind control and they run away from them." In California, where ECT was illegal for a while, psychosurgery is still illegal. "The figures on psychosurgery are significant," Valenstein says. "About seventy percent of the target population—people who have failed everything else—have at least some response; about thirty percent of these show really marked improvement. This procedure is done only for those people with severe and lasting psychiatric illness that has been unresponsive to pharmaceuticals and ECT, who've failed everything thrown at them, who remain severely disabled or ill: the most refractory cases. It is something of a last resort. We do only the gentlest procedure, and sometimes we have to do it two or three times, but we prefer that to the European model, which is to do more major surgery right away. With cingulotomy, we have found no permanent change in memory, or in cognitive or intellectual function."

When I first met Frank, he was just back from having a cingulotomy. In that procedure, the scalp is frozen locally and the surgeon drills a small hole in the front of the skull. He then puts an electrode directly onto the brain to destroy areas of tissue measuring about eight by eighteen millimeters. The procedure is performed under local anesthesia with sedation, using a stereotactic frame. This surgery is now done in only a few places, and the leading one is Massachusetts General Hospital, Boston, where Frank was seen by Reese Cosgrove, the leading psychosurgeon in the United States.

It is not easy to get into the cingulotomy protocol; you have to be reviewed by a screening committee and put through an endless barrage of tests and questions. The presurgery review takes at least twelve months. Mass General, the most active center, does only fifteen or twenty of them a year. As with antidepressants, the surgery usually has a delayed effect, often showing benefit after six or eight weeks, so it is probable that the benefit comes not from the elimination of certain cells but from what the elimination of those cells does to the functioning of other cells. "We don't understand the pathophysiology; we have no understanding of the mechanisms of why this works," says Cosgrove.

"I have hopes for the cingulotomy," Frank told me when we met. He described the procedure with an air of mild detachment. "I heard the drill going into my skull, like when you're at the dentist's office. They drilled two holes so that they could burn the lesions into my brain. The anesthesiologist had said if I wanted more medication I could have it, and I was lying there and listening to my skull opening up, so I said, 'This is kind of creepy; can you put me a little further under?' I hope it works; if it doesn't I have a plan, I've had a plan, for how to end it all, because I just can't keep going like this."

A few months later he was feeling marginally better and trying to reconstruct his life. "My future seems particularly clouded right now. I want to be writing, but my confidence is so low. I don't know what kind of writing I could do. I guess being depressed all the time was actually a relatively safe place to be. I didn't have the real-world worries that everyone else has because I knew that I simply couldn't function well enough to take care of myself. What do I do now? Trying to break the habits of years of depression is what I'm doing for the moment with my doctor."

Frank's surgery, in combination with Zyprexa, has been a success. During the year that followed, he had a few blips but was not hospitalized once. During this time he wrote to me about his progress and described being able to stay up all night to celebrate a friend's wedding. "Before," he wrote, "I couldn't do that because I was always afraid I'd affect my precarious mood." He was accepted in a graduate program at Johns Hopkins to learn science writing. With great trepidation, he decided to attend. He had a girlfriend with whom he was for the moment happy. "I'm kind of amazed when someone wants to tangle with the obvious problems that accompany me, but I'm really excited to have both companionship and romance. My girlfriend is something to look forward to."

He successfully completed his graduate work and got a job working for an Internet start-up. He wrote me in early 2000 about Christmas. "My dad gave me two presents: first, a motorized CD rack from The Sharper Image—it's totally unnecessary and extravagant but my dad knew I'd get a kick out of it. I opened this huge box and saw something I didn't need at all and knew my dad was celebrating the fact that I'm living on my own, have a job I seem to love, and can pay my own bills. The other present was a photo of my grandmother, who committed suicide. As I opened the present, I began to cry. She was beautiful. She is in profile, looking downward. Dad said it was probably from the early thirties: it's a black-and-white that he gave a soft blue matte and silver frame. My mom came over to the chair and asked if I was crying because of all the relatives I never knew and I said, 'She had the same disease I have.' I'm crying now—it's not that I'm so sad—I just get overwhelmed. Maybe it's that I could have killed myself but didn't because those around me convinced me to keep going—and I had the surgery. I'm alive and grateful to my parents and some doctors. We live in the right time, even if it doesn't always seem like it."

People travel from all over West Africa, some from even farther, for the mystic *ndeup* ceremonies for mental illness that are practiced by the Lebou (and some Sérèr) people of Senegal. I set off for Africa to explore. The head of the primary mental hospital in Dakar, Dr. Dou-dou Saar, who practices Western-style psychiatry, said that he believes that all of his patients have sought out traditional treatments. "They are sometimes embarrassed to tell me about these activities," he said. "But I believe that the traditional and modern healing, though they should be kept separate, must coexist; if I myself had a problem and foreign medicines did not cure me, I would go for traditional help." Even at his establishment, the Senegalese customs prevail. To enroll there, the one who is sick must come with a caretaker family member so that they can both stay at the hospital; the caretaker is given instruction and learns some basic psychiatric principles so that he can ensure the continuing mental health of the person who is being treated. The hospital itself is rather basic—private rooms are $9 per day, semiprivate $5, and large rooms with rows of beds $1.75. The whole place stinks, and those who have been declared dangerously insane are locked up behind iron doors; you can hear their wailing and banging at all times. But there is a pleasant garden where residents grow vegetables, and the presence of the many caretakers somewhat mitigates the aura of frightening weirdness that makes many Western hospitals so grim.

The *ndeup* is an animist ritual that probably antedates voodoo. Senegal is a Muslim country, but the local brand of Islam turns a blind eye to these ancient practices, which take place at once publicly and somewhat secretly; you may have an *ndeup* and everyone will congregate around you for it, but you do not speak about it much. The mother of a friend of the girlfriend of a friend who moved to Dakar some years ago knew a healer who could conduct the ceremony, and through this elaborate connection I arranged to undergo an *ndeup*. Late on a Saturday afternoon, some Senegalese friends and I took a taxi from Dakar to the town of Rufisque, through tiny alleyways and run-down houses, collecting people who would be involved, until at last we reached the house of Mareme Diouf, the old woman who would perform the ceremony. Mareme Diouf's grandmother had conducted the *ndeup* in this place and had taught Mareme; Mareme's grandmother had learned from *her* grandmother, and Mareme said the family lore and this chain went back as far as memory. Mareme Diouf came to meet us, barefoot, wearing a headdress and a long robe that was batiked with rather frightening images of eyes and trimmed in pea-green lace. She took us to the area behind her hut, where, under the spreading branches of a baobab, there were about twenty large clay pots and as many phallic wooden posts. She explained that the spirits she brought out of people were placed in the earth beneath, and that she fed them through these pots, which were all filled with water and roots. If those people who had been through the *ndeup* found themselves in trouble, they came to bathe in or drink the water.

After we had seen all this, we followed her into a small, rather dark room. Some considerable discussion about what to do ensued, and she said that it all depended on what the spirits wanted. She took my hand and looked at it closely, as though it had writing on it. Then she blew on my hand and had me place it on my forehead, and she began to feel around my skull. She asked me about my sleeping habits and wondered whether I had headaches, and then she declared that we would appease the spirits with one white chicken, one red cockerel, and one white ram. Then began the haggling about the price of the *ndeup*; we lowered the price (to about $150) by agreeing to acquire ourselves the ingredients she would require: seven kilos of millet, five kilos of sugar, one kilo of cola nuts, one calabash, seven meters of white cloth, two large pots, one reed mat, one threshing basket, one heavy club, the two chickens, and the ram. She told me that some of my spirits (in Senegal, one has spirits everywhere, some necessary to you, some neutral, some harmful—a little bit like microbes) were jealous of my sexual relations with my living partners and that this was the reason for my depression. "We must make a sacrifice," she declared, "to placate them, and then they will be quiet, and you will not suffer from this heaviness of depression. Your full appetites will be with you and you will sleep in peace without nightmares and the bad fear will be gone."

We made our second trip to Rufisque at dawn on Monday. Just outside the town we saw a shepherd and stopped to buy a ram. We had some difficulty getting it into the trunk of the taxi, where it made plaintive noises and relieved itself copiously; we drove another ten minutes and once more entered the labyrinth of little streets in the sprawl of Rufisque. We left the ram with Mareme and went to the market to get the other items, which one of my friends piled up on her head like the Tower of Pisa; then we returned by horse-drawn cart to the house of Mareme Diouf.

I was instructed to remove my shoes, and then I was taken to the place where the pots reside. Fresh sand had been spread, and five women had gathered, all in loose-fitting robes with huge necklaces of agate and belts made of cloth pouches like sausages (stuffed with iconic objects and prayers). One, in her late seventies, sported a pair of enormous Jackie Onassis sunglasses. I was made to sit on a mat with my legs straight out and my palms upturned for the divination. The women took quantities of millet and poured them into the threshing basket, then added an assortment of shamanistic power objects—short, fat sticks, someone's horn, a claw, a small bag tied up with a great deal of thread, a sort of round object made of red cloth with cowrie shells sewn onto it and a plume of horsehair. Then they put a white cloth over me and placed the threshing basket six times on my head, six times on each arm, and so on over my whole body. I was given the sticks to hold and let fall, and the women talked and consulted about the patterns. I did this six times with my hands and then six times with my feet. Several eagles came and perched in the baobab above us; this appeared to augur well. Then the women removed my shirt and put a string of agates around my neck. They rubbed my chest and back with the millet. They asked me to stand up and to remove my jeans and put on a loincloth, and they rubbed my arms and legs with the millet. Finally they collected the millet that had fallen all around and wrapped it up in a piece of newspaper and told me that I should sleep with it under my pillow for one night and give it to a beggar with good hearing and no deformities the next day. Because Africa is a continent of incongruities, the radio was playing the theme music from *Chariots of Fire* during this entire procedure.

Five drummers arrived about then and began to play the *tama* drums. About a dozen people had already been hanging around, and as the sound of the drums spread, more and more began to gather until there were perhaps two hundred, all come for the *ndeup*. They formed a circle around a grass mat. The ram's legs had been bound and he lay on his side, looking rather bemused by events. I was told that I must lie down behind him and hold him to me, as though we were spooning in bed. I was covered with a sheet, and then with perhaps two dozen blankets, so that I and the ram (which I had to hold down by the horns) were in total darkness and stifling heat. One of the blankets, which I saw afterward, had the words *Je t'aime* embroidered on it. The drums got louder and louder and the rhythms more inexorable, and I could hear the voices of the five women singing. Periodically, apparently at the end of a song, the drumming would stop; then one voice would begin and the drums would join and the other four voices would join and sometimes the voices of the hundreds of onlookers would also join. All the while the women were dancing around me in a tight circle, and I was embracing the ram, and they kept hitting us all over with what I later discovered was the red cockerel. I could hardly breathe and the smell of the ram was powerful (he had relieved himself again in our little bed), and the ground was shaking with the movement of the crowd and I could barely hold down the ram, which was squirming with increasing desperation.

At last the blankets were lifted and I was raised and led to dance to the drums, which kept increasing in pace. Mareme led the dancing, and everyone clapped as I imitated her stomping gestures and her swipes toward the drummers. Each of the other women in turn stepped forward and I had to imitate them, and then one at a time various women came from the crowd and I had to dance with them too. I was dizzy, and Mareme held out her arms to me and I nearly collapsed into them. One woman was suddenly possessed and danced hysterically, leaping about as though the ground were on fire, and then collapsed completely. I later learned that she had had her *ndeup* just a year earlier. When I was completely out of breath, the drums abruptly stopped, and I was told to remove my underwear as I would be wearing just the loincloth now. The ram was lying down and I had to step over him seven times from right to left and seven times from left to right, and then as I stood with one leg to each side of him, one of the men who had been drumming came and

168

placed the ram's head over a metal basin and slit the ram's throat. He wiped one side of his knife on my forehead and the other on the back of my neck. The blood poured out and soon it had half-filled the bowl. I was instructed to bathe my hands in the blood and to break apart the lumps as they began to congeal. Still dizzy, I did as I was told, as the man beheaded the cockerel and mixed its blood with the blood of the ram.

Then we left the crowd for the area near the pots, the place where I had been earlier that morning. There the women covered me with the blood. It had to be placed on every inch of my body; they rubbed it through my hair and across my face and over my genitals and on the bottoms of my feet. They rubbed it all over me, and it was warm and the semicoagulated parts smushed over me, and the experience was peculiarly pleasurable. When I was fully covered, one of them said it was midday and offered me a Coke, which I gladly took. She let me wash some of the blood off my hand and my mouth so that I could drink. Someone else brought me some bread. Someone with a wristwatch said we might as well relax until three o'clock. A sudden lightness entered into the proceedings, and one of the women tried to teach me the songs they had been singing around me during the morning when I lay under the blankets. My loincloth was soaked through, and thousands of flies began to settle all over me, drawn by the smell of the blood. The ram, meanwhile, had been hung in the baobab, and one of the men was skinning and butchering it. Another man had taken a long knife and was slowly digging three perfectly circular holes, each about eighteen inches deep, near the pots of water from previous *ndeup*s. I stood around trying to keep the flies out of my eyes and ears. At last when the holes were completed and it was three o'clock, I was told to sit down again, and the women fastened my arms and legs and chest with the intestines of the ram. I was told to drive seven sticks deep into each hole, making a prayer or wish with each one. Then we divided the ram's head into three parts and put one in each of the holes; they added some herbs and a small part of each section of the animal, then small pieces of the cockerel. Mareme and I took turns putting seven cakes of millet and sugar into each of the holes. Then she took out bags of seven different powders made from leaves and bark, and she sprinkled something from each one in each hole. Then we divided and poured the rest of the blood; I was untied; the intestines went into the holes; and Mareme put fresh leaves over everything and she and the man (who kept trying to pinch her bottom) filled the holes; and then I had to stamp on each one three times with my right foot. Then I repeated these words to my spirits: "Leave me be; give me peace; and let me do the work of my life. I will never forget you." Something about that incantation was particularly appealing to me. "I will never forget you"—as though one had to address the pride of the spirits, as though one wanted them to feel good about having been exorcised.

One of the women had glazed a clay pot with blood, and it was placed over the area we had just filled in. A club was driven into the ground, and a mixture of millet and milk and water was poured over all the inverted bowls from previous ceremonies and onto the top of the phallic clubs. Our bowl was filled with water and various herbal powders were added to it. By this time the blood on me had hardened and it was like being covered with an enormous scab, my skin utterly constricted. I was told that it was time for me to be washed. Laughing merrily, the women began peeling the blood off me. I stood up and they took mouthfuls of water and spit them over me, and in this fashion and with much rubbing the blood came off. At the end, I had to drink a pint or so of water full of the same leaf powders that Mareme had used earlier. When I was completely clean, and in a fresh white loincloth, the drumming began again and the crowd returned. This time the dancing was celebratory. "You are free of your spirits, they have left you," one of the women told me. She gave me a bottle of water mixed with leaf powder and told me to bathe myself with this curative potion if the spirits ever troubled me again. The drummers playfully increased rhythms and I had a sportive competition with one of them, who played more and more aggressively while I jumped higher and higher—and then he conceded that it was a match. Then everyone got a few cakes and a piece of the ram (we took a leg to barbecue that evening), and Mareme told me that now I was free. It was after six in the evening. The crowd followed our taxi as long as they could and then stood waving, and we came home with the buoyant feeling of having done something festive.

The *ndeup* impressed me more than many forms of group therapy currently practiced in the United States. It provided a way of thinking about the affliction of depression—as a thing external to and separate from the person who suffers. It jolted the system, which could certainly throw one's brain chemistry into overdrive—a kind of unplugged ECT. It entailed an intimate experience of community. It included close physical contact with others. It put one in mind of death and at the same time affirmed that one was oneself alive and warm and pulsating. It forced a great deal of physical movement on the sufferer. It introduced the comfort of a specific procedure to follow in the event of a recurrence. And it was bracingly energetic—an absolute tour de force of movement and sound. Finally, it was a ritual, and the effect of any ritual—being covered in the mixed blood of a ram and a cockerel or telling a professional what your mother did when you were small—is not to be underestimated. The mix of mystery and specificity is always enormously powerful.

How is one to choose among depression's thousand therapies? What is the optimum way to treat depression? And how can one combine these unorthodox treatments with more traditional ones? "I can tell you the answer that was correct in 1985," says Dorothy Arnsten, an interpersonal therapist who has studied myriad treatment systems. "I can tell you the answer that was correct in 1992; I can tell you the one that was correct in 1997; and I can tell you the one that's correct right now. But is there any point doing it? I can't tell you the one that will be correct in 2004, but I can tell you that it will definitely be different from the one that's correct right now." Psychiatry is as much subject to trend as is any other science, and one year's revelation is the next year's folly.

It is hard to know exactly what the future holds. We have made but small advances in our understanding of depression at the same time that we have made enormous advances in our treatment of depression. Whether treatment can continue to outstrip insight is hard to say, since that kind of development depends to some large extent on luck; and it will take a long time for knowledge to catch up with what we can already do. Of the drugs in late-stage trials now, the most promising is reboxetine, a selective norepinephrine reuptake inhibitor. Norepinephrine, which is boosted by tricyclic antidepressants, is implicated in depression along with serotonin and dopamine, and it seems likely that a norepinephrine booster might work well with SSRIs and perhaps with Wellbutrin, a combination that would attack all the neurotransmitters. Early studies show reboxetine as a good product for raising patients' energy and improving their social functioning, though it also seems to cause dry mouth, constipation, insomnia, increased perspiration, and accelerated heartbeat. Reboxetine is being produced by Pharmacia and Upjohn. In the meanwhile, Merck has been working on products targeted at another substance in the brain, substance P, which is involved in the pain response and which they believe is implicated in depression. The first substance P antagonist they have developed does not appear to be particularly successful in the treatment of depression, but they are investigating others.

Scientists working on the Brain Molecule Anatomy Project (BMAP) are trying to figure out what genes are involved in brain development and function. They also seek to know when those genes are active. Genetic manipulation will be greatly facilitated by the BMAP. "I'm placing my bets," Steven Hyman of the NIMH says. "One is on genes. I think once we have a few genes that are involved in mood regulation or in illness, all of a sudden we'll say, well, what pathway are these in? Might this pathway tell us about what happens in the brain? Therapeutic targets? When

171

in development are these genes on? Where are they in the brain? What's the difference in brain function between this version that creates vulnerability to illness and that version that doesn't? What are the genes that build this part of the brain when? Let's imagine that we find out that one particular subnucleus of the amygdala is critically involved in the control of negative affect, which is highly likely. What if we have before us every gene that is ever on in that structure through development? Well, then we have a tool kit for investigation. There is no such thing as a mood gene. It's just shorthand. Every gene that is involved in an illness probably has many other functions in the body or in the brain. The brain is a distributed processor."

If the human genome is made up of about thirty thousand genes—and that number seems to keep increasing as we discover more and more of them—and if each one has about ten important common varieties, that gives us $10^{30,000}$ candidates for human genetic vulnerability to all illnesses. How far is it from identifying some genes to trying to figure out what happens to those genes in different combinations at different stages in the face of different kinds of environmental stimuli? We need brute force of numbers to check out all the combinatorial possibilities. Then we need to see how they play out under various external circumstances. Rapid as our computers are, this knowledge is still an eternity away. Among all diseases, depression must ride near the top of the list for being overdetermined: I am no geneticist, but I would bet that there are at the very least a few hundred genes that may conduce to the development of depressive disorders. How such genes trigger depression would depend on how they interact with external stimuli and with one another. I would guess that most of those genes also serve useful functions, and that simply knocking them out would have significant deleterious effects. Genetic information may help us to control certain kinds of depression, but the chances of eliminating depression through genetic manipulation any time soon are, I believe, thinner than thin ice.

CHAPTER V

Populations

No two people have the same depression. Like snowflakes, depressions are always unique, each based on the same essential principles but each boasting an irreproducibly complex shape. Nonetheless, professionals love to group depressions: bipolar versus unipolar; acute versus mild; trauma-based versus endogenous; brief versus protracted—the list can be and has been drawn out endlessly, a process that has had disappointingly limited utility in diagnosis and treatment. There is something to be learned from the particular qualities of gender-specific depression and age-specific depression, as well as from the cultural determinants of the complaint. These raise a fundamental question: Are the distinctive qualities of such depressions determined by biological differences between men and women, between the very young and the very old, between Asians and Europeans, between gay or straight people, or are they determined by sociological differences, by patterns of expectation we impose on people according to the population they represent? The answer is that in every case, both are true. The monolithic problem of depression cannot be addressed with a monolithic response; depressions are contextual and must be interpreted within the contexts in which they occur.

For reasons variously attributed to chemistry and external conditions, about twice as many women as men seem to suffer depression. The distinction does not exist among depressed children but sets in during puberty. Women suffer several characteristic forms of depression—postpartum depression, premenstrual depression, and menopausal depression—as well as all the forms of depression that afflict men. Fluctuating rates of estrogen and progesterone clearly have mood effects, especially as they interact with the hypothalamic and pituitary hormone systems, but these are not predictable or consistent mood effects. Sudden lowering of estrogen levels will cause depressive symptoms, and high levels of estrogen promote a sense of well-being. Prior to menstruation, some women experience physical discomfort and some, because of bloating, perceive themselves to be less attractive; each of these experiences triggers low mood. Women who are pregnant or who have just given birth, though they are less likely than any others to kill themselves, are more likely than any others to suffer depression. Severe postpartum depression hits about one in ten procreative women. These new mothers tend to be weepy and are often anxious, irritable, and uninterested in their newborn children—perhaps in part because birthing drains estrogen reserves, which take some time to restore. The symptoms ordinarily abate within weeks. A milder version of the syndrome probably occurs in about a third of new mothers. Giving birth is a difficult, exhausting experience, and some of what now gets classed as postpartum depression is really the mild collapse that follows any extraordinary expenditure of effort. Women are likely to experience lower levels of depression around menopause, which strongly suggests a hormonal factor in women's depression—the period of most acute female depression is the childbearing years. It has been proposed that alterations in hormone levels might affect neurotransmitters, but no mechanism for such action has been located. More striking than the popular but vague focus on hormones is that men actually synthesize serotonin about 50 percent more rapidly than women do, which may well give men greater resilience. Women's slower replenishment of serotonin reserves may leave them prone to lagging depression.

Biology alone does not account for the high rate of women's depression. There are some biological differences between men's and women's depression; there are evident social differences between men's and women's positions of strength and power. Part of the reason women become depressed more often than men is that they are more frequently disenfranchised. Strikingly, the chances of postpartum depression in women under severe stress are particularly high; and women whose husbands take significant responsibility for the basics of child care have low levels of the baby blues. Feminists working on depression tend to prefer sociological to biological theories; they dislike the implication that women's bodies are somehow weaker than men's. Susan Nolen-Hoeksema, one of America's leading writers on women and depression, says, "It is dangerous to imply through the choice of the label that an aspect of women's reproductive biology is central to psychiatric illness." This kind of thinking has given much sociological work on women's depression a political agenda. Although it is an admirable agenda, its expression is not always true to experience, biology, or statistics. In fact, many theoretical approaches to women's depression exacerbate the troubles of those they seek to help. The overlap of some feminist theory's manipulation of scientific reality to achieve political goals, and most medical theory's insensitivity to social reality, has tied up the matter of gender and depression in a Gordian knot.

A recent study showed that on American college campuses, the rates of male and female depression are the same. Some pessimistic feminists have suggested that women who are prone to depression don't make it to college. Other more optimistic feminists have suggested that women are more entirely equal to men in college than in almost any other social context. I would throw into the mix the notion that men who are at college are probably more open to acknowledging their illness than are less educated or older men. The rate of female-to-male depression does not appear to vary in Western societies; it stays consistent overall at two to one. The world is dominated by men, and that makes things rough for women. Women are less well able physically to defend themselves. They are more likely to be poor. They are more likely to be the victims of abuse. They are less likely to be educated. They are more likely to suffer regular humiliations. They are more likely to lose social position through the visible signs of aging. They are likely to be subordinate to their husbands. Some feminists say that women develop depression because they do not have enough independent spheres in which to assert themselves and must rely on the triumphs of the home for all their feelings of self-worth. Others say that successful women have too many independent spheres in which to assert themselves and are always torn between their work and their home. That each of these situations is stressful is consistent with the finding that married housewives and working married women suffer from about the same rate of depression—which is much higher than that suffered by working married men. It is interesting to note that, across cultures, women have higher rates of not only depression but also panic disorders and eating disorders, while men have higher incidence of autism, attention deficit hyperactivity disorder, and alcoholism.

The English psychologist George Brown is one of the reigning experts on the sociological side of psychology. He has proposed that women's depression is linked to their concern for their children, a theory that has been borne out by other academics. If one discounts depression triggered by anxiety about offspring, the rate of depression for men and women appears to equalize; and in couples in which gender roles are less rigidly defined, rates of men's and women's depression tend to be closer— "Gender differences in rates of depression are, to a considerable extent, a consequence of role differences," Brown concludes. Myrna Weissman at Columbia has proposed that it makes evolutionary sense for women to be particularly acutely sensitive to loss since this would motivate them through childbearing and childrearing.

It is also the case that many women who are depressed suffered significant abuse as children. Little girls are far more likely to be sexually abused than are little boys, and victims of abuse are far more likely to be depressed than are others. Such women are also likely to suffer from anorexia, an illness that in recent years has been linked to depression. Malnutrition causes many symptoms of depression, so it may be that the depressive symptoms of anorexic women are the consequence of other symptoms; but many women who have experienced anorexia describe symptoms that persist even after they have achieved normal weight. Once more, it would appear that social constructs are implicated in causing both the painful obsession with self-control that is manifest in anorexia and the feelings of helplessness that characterize depression. Self-loathing may cause people to want to make themselves as small as possible until they nearly disappear. Certain key questions may be critical to diagnosis of a separate depressive complaint. It is often useful to ask anorexics whether they sleep badly even when they are not thinking about food or eating.

Mental illness has for a long time been defined by men. In 1905, Sigmund Freud maintained that his patient Dora was suffering hysteria when she rebuffed the unwelcome advances of a man three times her age. This kind of misprision is less common today than it was even fifty years ago. Nonetheless, women are often seen as depressed when they fail to show the vitality that their husbands expect or demand, and which the women have learned to expect or demand of themselves. This principle is, however, tricky: it is also argued that men undertreat women's depression because withdrawal is mistaken for feminine passivity. Women attempting to conform to ideals of femininity may *act* depressed out of conformism; or they may *become* depressed as a consequence of being unable to live within a stultifying definition of femininity. Women who complain of postpartum depression may in some instances be expressing only their shock and disappointment at failing to feel some kind of superemotion that the movies and popular TV have described as the essence of new motherhood. Told too often that maternal love is organic (which they take to mean effortless), they become depressed by the ambivalence that often accompanies infant care.

The feminist critic Dana Crowley Jack has systematized these ideas as components of women's loss of voice or loss of self. "As these women fail to hear themselves speak to their partners, they are unable to sustain the convictions and feelings of 'I' and slip, instead, into self-doubt about the legitimacy of their privately held experience." Jack's thesis is that women who cannot communicate effectively with their partner (most frequently, she suggests, because the partner is not willing to hear) lapse into silence.

They actually talk less frequently, and they undermine their own assertions with phrases such as "I don't know" or "I'm not sure anymore." To keep their fractured marriages or relationships from breaking up entirely, these women attempt to fit to an ideal of womanhood in which they say what they think their partner wants to hear—and so become false even in intimate interactions, simply dissolving as people. Jack states, "Women undertake massive self-negation as part of their search for intimacy." In fact, successful relationships are usually partnerships in which power can be passed back and forth between man and woman to suit the various circumstances that they encounter together and separately. It is true, however, that women frequently have less money or less financial control, and that in flawed relationships women accept abuse and battering more readily than do men. This is one more of depression's seemingly endless run of chicken-egg scenarios: depressed women are less able to defend themselves against abuse and are therefore abused more, becoming more depressed as a consequence of abuse, which makes them even less able to defend themselves.

Jack believes that the male power system scorns women's depression. In one of her moments of excess, Jack describes marriage itself as "the most persistent of myths imprisoning women," and elsewhere she writes that women are "easy targets for depression, a depression bound by patriarchy and robbed of its organic, mythic nature and consequently, its healing properties." This refrain is echoed in other radical feminist writing about women's depression. Another critic, Jill Astbury, suggests in her review of the subject that our notion of female depression is entirely a male construction: "The question about women's proneness to depression contains an assumption that is rarely made explicit. It has to do with seeing female rates of depression as pathological, too high and a problem. The only vantage point from which such a view is possible is that which assumes male rates of depression constitute a norm, are in themselves completely unproblematic and provide the only reasonable point of departure from which pathology in women can be measured. The pervasiveness of the androcentric approach can be appreciated if, instead of asking about the problem of women's depression, the rates of depression in men are positioned instead as problematic, perplexing and in need of clarification. Why, it could be asked but usually isn't, are male rates so abnormally low? Does testosterone interfere with the development of full humanity and emotional sensitivity?" and on and on and on. These recurring arguments made by reputable scholars in this field, usually in books published by major university houses (Jack is published by Harvard University Press; Astbury by Oxford), seem to focus on society's demonization of women's depression, as though that depression itself were innocuous. I would argue that if you do not experience personal distress over your symptoms, you don't have depression. If you do suffer personal distress, it is reasonable and perhaps even generous of the establishment to invest in finding solutions to your distress. Since the high rates of women's depression do not reflect a genetic predisposition that we can currently locate, we can say with some assurance that the rates of depression among women could be significantly reduced in a more equitable society. In the meanwhile, however, it is in general the depressed women who find their depression abnormal and who wish to do something about it. Abusive husbands, patriarchal oppressors that they are, tend to like depressed women and not to see those women's depression as symptomatic: it is empowered women who are most likely to recognize, name, and treat their depression. The idea that women are depressed because of the patriarchal conspiracy has some validity; the idea that we make women feel bad about their depression as part of the patriarchal conspiracy ignores women's own assertions of their experience of depression.

The literature makes much of the distinctive qualities of women's depression and says very little about any distinctive qualities of men's depression. Many depressed men are not diagnosed because they tend to deal with feelings of depression not by withdrawing into the silence of despondency, but by withdrawing into the noise of violence, substance abuse, or workaholism. Women report twice as much depression as men, but men are four times as likely to commit suicide as women. Single, divorced, or widowed men have a much higher rate of depression than married men. Depressed men may show what is somewhat euphemistically called "irritability"—they lash out at strangers, beat their wives, take drugs, and shoot people. The writer Andrew Sullivan recently wrote that injecting himself with testosterone, which he was doing as part of a regimen of HIV treatment, increased his tendency toward violence. In a series of interviews I did with wife batterers, I found consistent complaints of organic depression symptoms. "I get home and I feel all tired out the whole time," one man said, "and there is that woman asking me all these damn questions, and the noise of it just starts thumping in my head like hammers. I can't eat with it, I can't sleep with it, it's just she's there the whole time. I don't wanna hurt her but I gotta do something, I'm going crazy, you understand?" Someone else said that when he saw his wife he felt "so worthless on this earth I might never do nothing again if I don't fire out a punch or something."

Wife battering is obviously an inappropriate response to feelings of depression, but frequently the syndromes are closely tied. It seems likely that many other confrontational, injurious behaviors are manifestations of male depression. In most Western societies, admissions of weakness are held to be feminine. This has a negative effect on men, preventing them from crying, making them feel shame in the face of irrational fear and anxiety. The batterer who believes that hitting his wife is the only way for him to exist in the world manifestly buys into the idea that emotional pain is always a call to action, and that emotion without action negates him as a man. It is unfortunate that many men who—in the broadest sense—behave badly are not given antidepressant treatment. If women exacerbate their depression because they are not as happy as they think they should be, men exacerbate their depression because they are not as courageous as they think they should be. Most abuse is a form of cowardice, and some cowardice is a reasonable symptom of depression. I should know: I was once afraid of a lamb chop, and it's a very disempowering feeling.

I have had several episodes of violence since my first depression, and I have wondered whether these episodes, for which there was no precedent in my life, were connected to depression, were part of its aftermath, or were somehow to be associated with the antidepressants I have taken. As a child, I seldom hit anyone except my brother, and the last time I did that was when I was about twelve. And then one day when I was in my thirties, I became so irrationally angry that I began plotting murders in my mind; I eventually off-loaded that anger by smashing the glass on a series of pictures of myself that hung in a girlfriend's house, leaving the broken glass on the floor and the hammer in its midst. A year later, I had a serious falling-out with a man whom I had loved very much and by whom I felt profoundly and cruelly betrayed. I was already in a somewhat depressed state, and I became enraged. I attacked him with a ferocity unlike any I had experienced before, threw him against a wall, and socked him repeatedly, breaking both his jaw and his nose. He was later hospitalized for loss of blood. I will never forget the feeling of his face crumpling under my blows. I know that right after I hit him I had his neck in my hands for a moment and that it took a powerful summoning of my superego to save me from strangling him. When people expressed horror at my attack on him, I told them almost what the batterer told me: I felt as though I were disappearing, and somewhere deep in the most primitive part of my brain, I felt that violence was the only way I could keep my self and mind in the world. I was chagrined by what I had done; yet though one part of me regrets the suffering of my friend, another part of me does not rue what happened, because I sincerely believe that I would have gone irretrievably crazy if I had not done it—a view that this friend, to whom I am still close, has since come to accept. His emotional and my physical violence achieved a curious balance. Some of the feeling of paralytic fear and helplessness that afflicted me around that time was alleviated by the act of savagery. I do not accept the behavior of wife batterers and I certainly do not endorse what they do. Engaging in violent acts is not a good way to treat depression. It is, however, effective. To deny the inbred curative power of violence would be a terrible mistake. I came home that night covered with blood—mine and his—and with a feeling of both horror and exhilaration. I felt tremendous release.

I have never hit a woman, but about eight months after the jaw-breaking episode, I yelled at one of my closest friends and humiliated her terribly and publicly because she wanted to reschedule a dinner plan. I have learned that depression can easily erupt as rage. Since I've got out of the deepest trough of depression, those impulses are under control. I am capable of great anger, but it is usually tied to specific events, and my response to those events is usually in proportion to them. It is not usually physical. It is usually more considered and less totally impulsive. My attacks have been symptomatic. That does not relieve me of responsibility for violence, but it does help to make sense of it. I do not condone such behavior.

No woman I have met has described these feelings in quite this way; many depressed men I have met have had similar impulses toward destructiveness. Many have been able to avoid acting on them; many others have acted on them and felt release from irrational terror as a result of doing so. I do not think that depression in women is different from what it is in men, but I do think that women are different from men, and that their ways of handling depression are frequently different as well. Feminists who wish to avoid pathologizing the feminine and men who believe that they can deny their emotional state are looking for trouble. It is interesting that Jewish men, who are as a population particularly disinclined to violence, have a much higher rate of depression than non-Jewish men—in fact, studies show them having about the same rate of depression as Jewish women. Gender, then, plays an elaborate part not only in who gets depressed, but also in how that depression manifests itself and, consequently, how it may be contained.

Depressed mothers are usually not great mothers, though high-functioning depressives can sometimes mask their illness and fulfill their parenting roles. While some depressed mothers are easily upset by their children and behave erratically as a consequence, many depressed mothers simply fail to respond to their children: they are unaffectionate and withdrawn. They tend not to establish clear control or rules or boundaries. They have little love or nurturance to give. They feel helpless in the face of their children's demands. Their behavior is unregulated; they become angry for no apparent reason and then, in paroxysms of guilt, express extravagant affection for equally indistinct reasons. They cannot help a child to regulate his own problems. Their responses to their children are not contingent on what the children are doing or on displays of neediness. Their children are weepy, angry, and aggressive. Such children are often themselves incapable of caring behaviors; sometimes, however, they are too prone to caring behaviors and feel responsible for all the suffering of the world. Little girls are particularly likely to overempathize and so make themselves miserable; because they experience no lift in the mood of their mothers, they lose the capacity for elasticity of mood themselves.

The earliest manifestations of childhood depression, which are found in infants as young as three months, occur primarily in the offspring of depressed mothers. Such children do not smile and tend to turn their head away from all people, including parents; they may be at greater ease when they are not looking at anyone than when they look at their depressed mother. The brain-wave patterns of such children are distinctive; if you successfully treat the depression in the mothers, the brain-wave patterns of the children may improve. In older children, however, adjustment difficulties may not lift so readily; school-age children of a depressed mother were shown to be severely maladjusted even a year after their mother's symptoms had been alleviated. The children of parents who have been depressed are at a significant disadvantage. The more severe the depression of the mother, the more severe the depression of the child is likely to be, though some children seem to pick up on maternal depression more dramatically and empathetically than do others. In general, the children of a depressed mother not only reflect but also magnify their mother's state. Even ten years after an initial assessment, such children suffer significant social impairment and are at a threefold risk for depression and a fivefold risk for panic disorders and alcohol dependence.

To improve the mental health of children, it is sometimes more important to treat the mother than to treat the children directly; to try to change negative familial patterns to incorporate flexibility, hardiness, cohesion, and problem-solving ability. Parents can team up well for the circumvention of depression in their children even if their relationship to each other is highly flawed, though a single, clear front can be challenging to sustain. Children of depressed mothers have more difficulties in the world than do children of schizophrenic mothers: depression has a singularly immediate effect on the basic mechanisms of parenting. Children of depressed mothers may suffer not only depression but also attention deficit disorder, separation anxiety, and conduct disorder. They do badly in social and academic situations, even if they are intelligent and have some attractive qualities of personality. They have unusually high levels of physical complaints—allergies, asthma, frequent colds, severe headaches, stomachaches—and complain of feeling unsafe. They are often paranoid.

The University of Michigan's Arnold Sameroff is a developmental psychiatrist who believes everything in the world is a variable in every experiment; all events are overdetermined; nothing can be understood except by knowing all the mysteries of God's creation. Sameroff would suggest that though people have certain complaints in common, they have individual experiences, with individual constellations of complaints and individual networks of causes. "You know, there are these single-gene hypotheses," he says. "Either you have the gene or you don't, and those are very attractive to our quick-fix society. But it's never going to work." Sameroff has been looking at the children of people with major depression. He has found that these children, even if they start on a cognitive level with their peers, go downhill beginning around age two. By the age of four, they are distinctly "sadder, less interactive, withdrawn, and low-functioning." For this he proposes five primary possible explanations, all of which, he believes, come into play in various mosaics: genetics; empathetic mirroring, kids repeating back what they experience; learned helplessness, ceasing to attempt to connect because of lack of parental approval for emotional outreach; role-playing, as the child sees the advantages an ill parent gets from being too ill to do unpleasant things and decides to take on the illness role; and withdrawal, as a consequence of seeing no pleasure in communication between unhappy parents. Then there are all the subexplanations: depressed parents are more likely to be substance abusers than are other parents. What kind of treatment or trauma does a child experience at the hands of substance abusers? That would lead us right into stress.

A recent study has listed two hundred factors that may contribute to high blood pressure. "At a biological level," says Sameroff, "blood pressure is really pretty simple. If there are two hundred factors influencing it, think how many factors must influence a complex experience such as depression!" In Sameroff's view, the coincidence of a number of risk factors is the basis for depression. "Those people who get a group of risk factors all glommed together are the ones who have what we call a disorder," Sameroff says. "We found that in terms of depression, heredity was not nearly as strong a predictor as socioeconomic status. The interaction of heredity and socioeconomic status was the strongest predictor of all, but then what were the key components of low socioeconomic status that made small children get so depressed? Was it lack of parental education? Lack of money? Low social support? Number of kids in the family?" Sameroff made a list of ten such variables and then correlated them with degrees of depression. He found that any negative variable on its own was likely to contribute to low mood, but that any group of such variables was likely to produce significant clinical symptoms (as well as lowered IQ). Sameroff then did research that showed that the child of a seriously ill parent was likely to do better than the children of a moderately ill parent. "It turns out that if you're really, really ill, someone picks up the load. If there are two parents, the one who isn't ill knows he has to do the work. And the child has a way of understanding what's going on in the family; he grasps the principle that one of his parents is mentally ill and he isn't left with all the unanswered questions that afflict the children of the mildly mentally ill. So you see? It's not predictable according to a simple linear system. Every depression has its own story."

While poor parenting or depressed parenting may cause depression in children, good parenting may well help to allay or alleviate it. The old Freudian blame-your-mom principle has been discarded, but the world of children is still defined by their parents, and they can learn some degree of resilience or debility from their mother, father, and other caretakers. Indeed many treatment protocols now involve training parents in therapeutic interventions with their children. Those interventions must be based on *listening*. The young are a different population and cannot be treated as though they were just dwarfish adults. Firmness, love, consistency, and humility must come together in parental approaches to depressed children. A child who has watched a parent solve a problem gains enormous strength from that.

A distinct form of depression, called anaclitic depression, occurs in the second half of the first year for children who have been separated too much from their mother. In various combinations and degrees of severity, it mixes apprehension, sadness, weepiness, rejection of environment, withdrawal, retardation, stupor, lack of appetite, insomnia, and unhappy expressions. Anaclitic depression may develop into "failure to thrive" starting at four or five; children with this complaint don't have much affect and don't bond. By five or six, they may show extreme crankiness and irritability and poor sleeping and poor eating. They do not make friends and have inexplicably low self-esteem. Persistent bed-wetting points to anxiety. Some become withdrawn; others become steadily more cranky and destructive. Because children do not tend to consider their own future as adults do, and because they do not organize their memories lucidly, they are seldom preoccupied with the meaninglessness of life. Without the development of abstract feeling, children do not feel the hopelessness and despair characteristic of adult depression. But they can suffer persistent negativity.

Recent studies have been at such statistical odds as to be ludicrous: one of these definitively proved that depression affects about 1 percent of children; another demonstrated that about 60 percent of children experience major affective disorders. Attempts to assess children through self-reports are much more complicated than they are for adult populations. In the first place, questions must be put in such a way that they do not dictate apparently "desirable" answers; therapists must be brave enough to ask about suicide without proposing it as a feasible alternative. One therapist provided the formulation "Okay, if you hate all these things so much in your life, do you ever think about ways you could just make it so you'd never be around anymore?" Some kids will say, "What a stupid question!" and some will say "yes" and provide full details, and some will become quiet and thoughtful. The therapist needs to watch the child's body language. And the therapist has to persuade the child that he is prepared to listen to anything. Children with really serious depression talk about suicide under such circumstances. One depressed woman I met, who was striving to keep up a good front for her children, described the despair she felt when her son said, at age five, "You know, life's crummy and a lot of times I don't want to live." By age twelve, he had made a serious suicide attempt. "They'll talk about wanting to join someone, maybe a relative, who has died," says Paramjit T. Joshi, who heads the children's mental health division at Johns Hopkins Hospital. "They say they want to sleep forever; some five-year-olds will actually say, 'I want to die; I wish I was never born.' Then the behaviors set in. We see many kids who have jumped out of second-story windows. Some of them take five Tylenol and think it's enough to die. Others try to cut their wrists and arms, or to smother themselves, or to hang themselves. A lot of little children hang themselves with their belts in their closets. Some of them are already abused or neglected, but some of them are doing these things for no apparent reason. Thank goodness, they're seldom competent enough to succeed in suicide!" In fact, they can be surprisingly competent; suicides in the ten-to-fourteen age group increased by 120 percent between the early eighties and the midnineties, and the children who succeed are mostly using aggressive means: guns and hangings account for almost 85 percent of the deaths. The rate has been rising, as children, like their parents, experience escalating stress.

Children can be and increasingly are treated with liquid Prozac or liquid nortriptyline, carefully dripped into a glass of juice. Such medication appears to help. There are not, however, any adequate studies of how these medications work in children nor of whether they are safe or effective; "We have made children into therapeutic orphans," says Steven Hyman, director of the NIMH. Only a few of the antidepressants have been tested to show that they are safe for use with children, and almost none have been tested for efficacy in children. Anecdotal experience varies widely. One study showed, for example, that SSRIs work better with young children and with adults than they do with teenagers; another showed that MAOIs are the most effective for young children. One should not take the results of either study to be definitive, but they point to the distinct possibility that treating children may be different from treating adolescents, and that both may be different from treating adults.

Depressed children also require therapy. "You just have to show them that you are right there with them," says Deborah Christie, a charismatic child psychologist who is a consultant at University College London and Middlesex Hospital. "And you have to get them to be there with you too. I use a metaphor of mountain climbing a lot. We're thinking about climbing a mountain and we're sitting at base camp and just thinking about what kind of luggage we might need, and how many of us should go up together, and whether we should rope together. And we may decide to make the journey or we may decide we're not ready to make it yet, but maybe we can walk around the mountain so we can see which will be the easiest or best way up. And you have to acknowledge that they'll be doing some climbing, that you can't pick them up and carry them up there, but that you can stick by them every inch of the way. That's where you have to start: you have to stir up motivation in them. Kids who are really depressed don't know what to say or where to begin, but they know that they want change. I've never seen a depressed child who didn't want treatment if he could believe that there was a chance it would change things. One little girl was too depressed to speak to me, but she could write things down, so she'd write these words, randomly, on Post-its, and then she'd paste them on me, so that by the end of a session I was just a sea of the words she wanted to get through to me. And I took on her language and I started writing words on Post-its too, and putting them all over her, and that's how we broke through her wall of silence." There are many other techniques that have proven useful for helping children to recognize and improve their mood states.

"In children," says Sylvia Simpson, a psychiatrist at Johns Hopkins, "depression prevents personality development. All this energy goes into fighting depression; social development is retarded, which does not make life any less depressing later on. You find yourself in a world which expects you to be able to develop relationships, and you just don't know how to do it." Children with seasonal depression, for example, frequently spend years doing badly at school and having trouble; their complaint is not picked up because it appears to coincide with the school year. It's hard to know when and how aggressively to treat these disorders. "I work on the basis of family history," says Joshi. "It can be very confusing whether it's attention deficit hyperactivity disorder (ADHD) or real depression, or whether a child with ADHD has developed depression also; whether it's an abuse-related adjustment disorder or depressive illness." Many children with ADHD show extreme disruptive behaviors, and sometimes the natural response to these is to discipline the child; but the child is not necessarily able to control his actions if they are tied to deep cognitive and neurobiological problems. Of course the conduct disorders tend to make these children unpopular even with their own parents, and that exacerbates the depression—it's yet another of depression's novel downward spirals.

"I have to warn the parents of these children when they come in," Christie says, " 'Well, we'll be getting rid of this angry stuff, but you may then have a very sad child for a while.' Children never come by themselves. They are brought to therapy. You have to find out from them why they think they're there with you, and what they think is wrong. It's a very different situation from one in which people seek out psychological care on their own." One of the important elements in therapeutic work with young children is the creation of an alternative world of fantasy, a magical version of the safe space of psychodynamic therapies. Asking children to name their wishes will often reveal the exact nature of their deficits in self-esteem. It is important, as an opening gambit, to get silent children to transit into speech. Many of them cannot explain their feelings except to say that they feel okay or they feel not okay. They must be given a new vocabulary; and they must be taught, on the cognitive model, the difference between thoughts and feelings, so that they can learn to use thoughts to control feelings. One therapist described asking a ten-year-old girl to keep a diary of thoughts and feelings for two weeks and then bring it in. "You could say your thought is 'Mommy's angry at Daddy.' And your feeling could be 'I'm frightened.'" But the distinction was beyond this child's cognitive grasp because her depression had so disabled her cognitive functioning. When she brought the diary, she had written each day: "Thoughts: 'I'm sad'; Feelings: 'I'm sad.'" In her hierarchy, the world of thought and the world of feeling were simply inseparable. Later on, she was able to make a pie chart of her anxieties: this much of her anxiety was about school, this much about home, this much about people hating her, this much about being ugly, etc. Children who have worked with computers are often receptive to metaphors that work on the principle of technology; one therapist I met said he told such children that their minds have programs to process fear and sadness and that treatment would take the bugs out of those programs. Good child therapists inform and distract their patients at once; as Christie has observed, "There is nothing as unrelaxing to children as being told to relax."

Depression is also an acute problem for children who suffer physical illness or disability. "Kids come in with cancer and they are constantly being poked and prodded and having needles stuck in them, and they become accusatory and accuse their parents of punishing them with these treatments, and then the parents become anxious; and then everyone becomes depressed all together," Christie says. Illness breeds secrecy, and secrecy breeds depression. "I sat down with a mother and her very depressed son, and I said, 'So, tell me why you're here,' and the mother said, right in front of this little boy, in a loud stage whisper, 'He's got leukemia but he doesn't know it.' It was extraordinary. Then I asked to have some time alone with the little boy and I asked him why he had come to see me. He said it was because he had leukemia, but not to tell his mother because he didn't want her to know that he knew. So the depression was tied into huge issues around communication, and those were exacerbated and brought into play by the leukemia and the treatments that disease required."

It has now been established that depressed children usually go on to become depressed adults. Four percent of adolescents who have experienced childhood depression commit suicide. A huge number make suicide attempts, and they have high rates of almost every severe social-adjustment problem. Depression occurs among a good number of children before puberty, but it peaks in adolescence, with at least 5 percent of teenagers suffering clinical depression. By that stage, it is almost always combined with substance abuse or anxiety disorders. Parents underestimate the depth of the depression of their teenagers. Of course adolescent depression is confusing because normal adolescence is so much like depression anyway; it is a period of extreme emotions and disproportionate suffering. Over 50 percent of high school students have "thought about killing themselves." "At least twenty-five percent of teenagers in detention have depression," says Kay Jamison, a leading authority on manic-depressive illness. "It could be treated and they might become less obstructive. By the time they're adults, the depression level is high but the negative behavior has been ingrained into personality, and treating the depression isn't enough." Social interaction also plays a role; the onset of secondary sexual characteristics often leads to emotional confusion. Current research is directed at delaying the onset of depressive symptoms—the earlier your depression starts, the more likely it is to be resistant to treatment. One study says that those who experience depressive episodes in childhood or adolescence have seven times the rate of adult depression of the general population; another says that 70 percent of them will suffer recurrence. The need for early interventions and preventative therapies is absolutely clear. Parents should be on the lookout for early disengagement, disrupted appetites for food and sleep, and self-critical behavior; children who show these signs of depression should be taken in for professional assessment.

Teenagers in particular (and male teenagers most of all) fail to explain themselves clearly, and the industry of treatment pays too little attention to them. "I have teenagers who come in and sit in the corner and say, 'There's nothing wrong with me,'" one therapist explained. "I never contradict them. I say, 'Well, that's fantastic! How terrific that you're not depressed like so many kids your age and like so many of the kids who come in to see me. Tell me what it's like to feel totally okay. Tell me what it's like right this minute to be in this room feeling totally okay.' I try to give them opportunities to think and feel together with someone else."

It is unclear to what extent sexual abuse causes depression through direct organic processes, and to what extent the depression is reflective of the kind of fractured home environment in which sexual abuse tends to occur. Sexually abused children tend to have life patterns of self-destructive behavior, and they encounter high levels of adversity. They usually grow up in constant fear: their world is unsteady, and that unbalances their personalities. One therapist describes a young woman who had been sexually abused and couldn't believe that anyone could care for her and be reliable—"all she needed was for me to be consistent in my interactions with her" to break down the automatic mistrust with which she related to the world. Children deprived of early love and of encouragement toward cognitive development are often permanently disabled. One couple who adopted a child from a Russian orphanage said, "This was a kid who at five didn't seem to have any cause-and-effect thinking, who didn't know that plants were alive but furniture wasn't." They have been trying to compensate for that deficit ever since and now acknowledge that no full recovery will be possible.

For other children, though recovery seems impossible, accommodation is not. Christie describes treating a girl with horrible chronic headaches, "like banging hammers in my head," who had given up everything in her life because of the headaches. She couldn't go to school. She couldn't play. She couldn't interact with other people. When she met Christie for the first time, she announced, "You can't make my headache go away." Christie said, "No, you're right. I can't. But let's

think about ways to keep that headache all in one piece of your head a
see if you can't use another piece of your head even while the hammers
are hammering in there." Christie notes, "The first step is to believe what
the child says even if it's apparently untrue or implausible, to believe that
even if the child is using metaphoric language that doesn't make sense, it
must make sense to them." After extensive treatment, the girl in question
said she could go to school despite her headaches, and then she began
to have friends despite her headaches, and within another year, the
headaches themselves were gone.

The elderly depressed are chronically undertreated, in large part because
we as a society see old age as depressing. The assumption that it is logical for old people to be miserable prevents us from ministering to that
misery, leaving many people to live out their final days in unnecessary
extreme emotional pain. As early as 1910, Emil Kraepelin, father of
modern psychopharmacology, referenced depression among the elderly
as involutional melancholy. Since then, the breakdown of traditional
caretaking structures and the removal from old people of any sense of
importance have made things worse. Older people in nursing homes are
more than twice as likely to be depressed as those who live in the
world—in fact, it has been suggested that more than a third of those resident in facilities are significantly depressed. It is striking that the effects
of placebo treatment on elderly patients are substantially higher than the
norm. This would suggest that these people are experiencing some benefit from the circumstances around the taking of a placebo, beyond the
conventional psychosomatic benefits of believing that one is receiving
medication. The monitoring and close interviews that are a part of chart-
ing a study, the careful regulation and the focus for the mind, are having
a meaningful effect. Old people feel better when more attention is paid
to them. The elderly in our society must be horrifyingly lonely for this
small response to give them such a lift.
    While the social factors that lead to depression among the elderly are
powerful, it would appear that important organic shifts also affect mood.
Levels of all neurotransmitters are lower among old people. The level of
serotonin in people in their eighties is half of what it would have been in
the same people in their sixties. Of course the body is at this stage of life
going through many metabolic shifts and much chemical rebalancing, and
so diminishing neurotransmitter levels do not have the same immediate
effect (so far as we know) as they would in a younger person whose serotonin levels were suddenly reduced by half. The extent to which brains
change in plasticity and function with age is also reflected in the fact that
antidepressant treatment takes a particularly long time to kick in for old

people. The same SSRIs that in a midlife adult will begin to work within three weeks will in an elderly patient often take twelve weeks or longer to be effective. The rate of successful treatment, however, is not altered by age; the same proportion of people is treatment-responsive.

Electroconvulsive therapy is frequently indicated for the elderly for three reasons. The first is that, unlike medications, it acts rapidly; letting someone get more and more depressed for months before his meds begin to alleviate his despair is not constructive. Additionally, ECT does not have adverse interactions with other medications that elderly people may be taking—such interactions can in many cases limit the range of antidepressants that can be prescribed. Finally, depressed elderly people often have lapses in memory and may forget to take their medication or may forget that they have taken it and take too much. ECT is much easier to control in this regard. Short-term hospitalization is often the best way to care for older people who are experiencing severe depression.

Depression can be hard to spot in these populations. The libido issues that are important elements of depression among younger people do not play so significant a role among the elderly. They feel guilty less often than do younger depressives. Instead of getting sleepy, older depressed people tend to be insomniac, lying awake at night in the grip, often, of paranoia. They have wildly exaggerated catastrophic reactions to small events. They tend to somaticize a lot, and to complain of an enormous number of peculiar aches and pains and atmospheric discomforts: This chair isn't comfortable anymore. The pressure in my shower is down. My right arm hurts when I pick up a teacup. The lights in my room are too bright. The lights in my room are too dim. And so on, ad infinitum. They develop irritable characteristics and become grumpy, often showing a distressing emotional bluntness with or an emotional indifference to those around them and occasionally manifesting "emotional incontinence." These symptoms respond most frequently to the SSRIs. Their depression is often either a direct consequence of shifting organic systems (including lower blood supply to the brain) or a result of the pain and indignity of bodily decay. Elderly dementia and senility are often accompanied by depression, but the conditions, though they may occur together, are different. In dementia, the capacity for automatic mind functions goes down: basic memory, especially short-term, is compromised. In depressed patients, psychologically effortful processes are blocked: long-term complex memories become inaccessible, and processing of new information is impeded. But most elderly people are unaware of these distinctions, and they suppose the depression symptoms to be the quality of age and mild dementia, which is why they so often fail to take basic steps to ameliorate their situation.

One of my great-aunts fell in her apartment and broke her leg when she was in her late nineties. The leg was set, and she came home from the hospital with a team of nurses. She clearly found it hard to walk at first, and only with difficulty could she do the exercises set for her by her physiotherapist. A month later, her leg had healed remarkably well, but she was still afraid of walking and continued to struggle against locomotion. She had become accustomed to a commode, which could be brought to her bedside, and she refused to go the fifteen feet to get to the toilet. Her lifelong vanity was suddenly gone, and she refused to go to the hairdresser, whom she had visited twice every week for nearly a century. In fact, she refused to go out at all and kept postponing a visit to a podiatrist despite an ingrown nail that must have been painful. Weeks went by like this in her claustrophobic apartment. Meanwhile, her sleep was irregular and disturbed. She refused to talk to my cousins when they called her. She had always been meticulous about her personal affairs and somewhat secretive about details; now she asked me to open and pay her bills as they were too confusing for her. She couldn't assemble simple information—she'd ask me to repeat eight times my plans for the weekend, and this cognitive retardation seemed almost like senility. She grew repetitive, and though she was not sad, she was altogether diminished. Her GP insisted that she was just experiencing some trauma-related stress, but I saw that she was getting ready to die and believed that this was an inappropriate response to a broken leg, no matter how old she was.

I finally persuaded my psychopharmacologist to come to her apartment and talk to her, and he immediately diagnosed severe old-age depression and put her on Celexa. Three weeks later, we had an appointment with her podiatrist. I pressed her to come out in part because I thought her foot wanted attention, but mostly because I thought it was necessary for her to venture into the world again. She looked at me with anguish when I made her come outside and seemed to find the entire thing utterly debilitating. She was confused and frankly terrified. Two weeks later, we had an appointment with the doctor who had set her leg. I arrived at her apartment to find her in an attractive dress with her hair combed and some lipstick on, wearing a little pearl brooch that she had often sported in happier days. She came downstairs without complaining. She clearly found our outing stressful, and she was fractious in the doctor's office, and a bit paranoid, but when the surgeon came in, she was charming and quite articulate with him. At the end of her visit, her nurse and I wheeled her back toward the door of the building. She was pleased to learn that her leg had healed nicely and thanked everyone profusely. I was exultant at every sign of reawakening in her, but nothing had really prepared me for her to say, as we were leaving, "Darling, shall we go out to lunch?" And we went to a restaurant we used to like, and with my help she even walked a short distance in the restaurant, and we told little stories and laughed, and she complained that her coffee was not hot enough and sent it back, and she was *alive* again. I cannot say that she then returned to regular lunching, but thereafter she consented to go out once every few weeks, and her basic coherence and sense of humor gradually returned to her.

Six months later, she developed what turned out to be internal bleeding of minor significance, and had a three-day hospitalization. I was concerned about her, but was pleased that her mood was resilient enough so that she could cope with the hospital entry without becoming panicked or confused. A week after she came home, I visited her and checked to make sure she had sufficient supply of all her medications. I noticed that the Celexa bottle was about as full as it had been when I checked it previously. "Have you been taking these?" I asked her. "Oh, no," she said. "The doctor told me to stop taking them." I assumed that she must have misunderstood, but her nurse had been present when these instructions had been given and confirmed them. I was frankly astonished and horrified. Celexa has no gastroenterological side effects, and that it had been implicated in her bleeding seemed highly unlikely. There was no good reason for terminating it, and there could be no good reason for terminating it so abruptly; even someone young and fit should go off antidepressant medication gradually and according to a clear program. Someone who is receiving substantial benefit from medication should not be taken off it at all, but the gerontologist who treated my aunt had whimsically decided that it would be good for her to go off any "unnecessary" medications. I called that doctor and screamed holy hell down the line, wrote an outraged letter to the president of the hospital, and told my aunt to return to her medication. She is living rather happily and less than a month from her hundredth birthday as this book goes to press. We are going to the hairdresser in two weeks so that she'll look her best for the little party we're planning to throw. I go to visit her every Thursday, and our afternoons together, which were once a leaden burden, are now full of fun; when I gave her some good family news a few weeks ago, she clapped her hands and then started to sing. We talk about all kinds of things, and I have recently benefited from her wisdom, which came creeping back to her along with the gift of joy.

Depression is often a precursor state to severe impairment of the mind. It appears to predict, to some degree, senility and Alzheimer's disease; those diseases in turn may coexist with or kindle depression. Alzheimer's appears to lower serotonin rates even further than does aging. We have severely limited capacities to alter the confusion and cognitive decay that are the essence of senility or Alzheimer's, but we can alleviate the acute psychic pain that often accompanies those complaints. Many people are disoriented without being frightened or deeply sad, and this is, for the moment, a state we can achieve with these populations— but usually don't. Some experimentation has been done to gauge whether lowered levels of serotonin may be responsible for senility, but it seems more likely that dementia follows up on damage to various brain areas, including those responsible for serotonin synthesis. In other words, the senility and the lowered serotonin are separate consequences of a single cause. It appears that SSRIs do not have much influence on motor skills or intellectual skills that are damaged by senility; but better mood frequently allows older people to make better use of the capacities that are still organically present in them, and so there may be in practical terms a certain degree of cognitive improvement. Alzheimer's patients and other depressed elders also seem to respond to atypical medications such as tra-zodone, which are not usual first-line treatments for depression. They may also respond to benzodiazepines, but these tend to make them overly sedated. They respond well to ECT. The fact that they are incoherent need not consign them to misery. Among the patients who show sexual aggressivity in Alzheimer's—a not uncommon situation—hormone therapies may help; but this seems to me to be rather inhumane unless the sexual feelings are causing misery to those who experience them. Patients with dementia are not usually responsive to talking therapies.

Depression is also often a result of stroke. People in the first year after stroke are twice as likely to develop depression as are others. This may be the result of physiological damage to particular parts of the brain, and some research has suggested that strokes in the left frontal lobe are particularly likely to disregulate emotion. After initial recovery, many older people who have had strokes are given to terribly intense bouts of crying at slight matters negative or positive. One patient after a stroke burst into tears between twenty-five and a hundred times a day, each bout lasting between one and ten minutes, and this left him so exhausted he could hardly function. Treatment with an SSRI rapidly brought these crying fits under control; as soon as the patient went off the drug, however, the crying returned, and he is now permanently on medication. Another man who had had to give up work entirely for ten years because of depression that followed a stroke was given to fits of tears; treatment with an SSRI got him up and running again, and in his late sixties he returned to work. There is no question that strokes in certain areas of the brain have emotionally devastating consequences, but it appears that, in many instances, those consequences can be controlled.

Unlike gender or age in depression, ethnicity does not appear to harbor biological determinants. Cultural expectations around people do, however, cause them to manifest their illnesses in particular ways. In his remarkable book *Mad Travelers*, Ian Hacking describes a syndrome (physical travel while unconscious) that affected many people in the late nineteenth century and that disappeared after a few decades. No one now has the problem of making physical voyages without knowing he is doing so. Certain historical periods and social sectors have clearly been afflicted by certain mental symptoms. "By a 'transient mental illness,'" Hacking explains, "I mean an illness that appears at a time, in a place, and later fades away. It may be selective for social class or gender, preferring poor women or rich men. I do not mean that it comes and goes in this or that patient, but that this type of madness exists only at certain times and in certain places." Hacking expounds the theory set forth by Edward Shorter that the same person who would in the eighteenth century have suffered from fainting spells and convulsive cries, who would in the nineteenth century have had hysterical paralysis or contracture, is now likely to suffer depression, chronic fatigue, or anorexia.

The connections among ethnicity, education, and class, even among depressed Americans, are too tangled to catalog. Nonetheless, some broad generalities can be drawn. Juan López, of the University of Michigan, is a jolly fellow with a nice sense of humor and a warm, irreverent quality. "I'm a Cuban married to a Puerto Rican and we have a Mexican godchild," he says, "and I lived in Spain for a while. So for Latin culture, I've got the bases pretty well covered." López has worked extensively with the Michigan population of Hispanic migrant workers and with the priests who are their primary caretakers, and he has taken it upon himself to minister to their psychological needs. "The wonderful thing about the United States," he says, "is that you can have so many different cultural backgrounds interacting with the same disease." López has observed that Latin people are more likely to somaticize than to register their psychological problems. "You get these women, and I'm related to several of them, who come in saying, oh, my back hurts and my belly aches and my legs feel strange and so on. What I still want to know and can't find out is whether they just say this to avoid admitting to their psychological problems, or whether they are experiencing depression this way, without feeling the usual symptoms. If they get better, as many of them do, by listening to Walter Mercado, this Puerto Rican mystic who is like a cross between Jerry Falwell and Jeanne Dixon, then what has actually happened biologically inside of them?" Depression among more educated Latin populations is probably more closely akin to depression in a general population.

A Dominican friend of mine who is in his early forties had a surprising, sudden, overpowering breakdown when he and his second wife agreed to split up. She moved out, and he had increasing difficulty functioning in his job as a building superintendent. He was overwhelmed by simple tasks; he stopped eating; his sleep became irregular. He fell out of touch with his friends and even with his children. "I didn't think of it as depression," he later told me. "I thought I was probably dying and that maybe I had a physical disease. I guess I knew I was upset, but I didn't know what that had to do with anything. As a Dominican, I am very emotional but also I guess pretty macho, and so I have a lot of feelings but I don't feel that easy expressing them, and I wouldn't let myself cry." After spending two months sitting all day and night in the basement of the building where he worked—"I don't know how I kept my job, but fortunately no one's apartment had a serious leak or anything"—he finally took a trip home to the Dominican Republic, where he had lived for the first ten years of his life and where he still had a lot of family. "I was drinking. I sat on the plane and I got so drunk because I was so afraid of everything, of going home even. And I started crying on the plane and I cried all the length of the flight, and I stood there crying in the airport and I was still crying when I saw my uncle, who'd come to pick me up. That was bad. I was embarrassed and upset and scared. But at least I was out of that goddamned basement. Then at the beach a few days later I met this woman, this girlfriend, this pretty girl, who thought it was really glamorous that I came from the U.S. And somehow I got to seeing myself through her eyes and I began to feel better. I kept drinking, but I stopped crying because I couldn't cry in front of her, and maybe that was good for me. You know, for me as a Dominican, especially, the attention of women is a real necessity. Without it, who am I?" A few months later, he and his wife got back together, and though his feeling of sadness lingered, his anxiety evaporated. When I mentioned medications, he shook his head. "You know, it's not me," he said, "taking pills for feelings."

Depression among African-Americans comes with its own special set of difficulties. In her beautifully poignant book *Willow Weep for Me*, Meri Danquah describes the trouble: "Clinical depression simply did not exist within the realm of my possibilities, or, for that matter, in the realm of possibilities for any of the black women in my world. The illusion of strength has been and continues to be of major significance to me as a black woman. The one myth that I have had to endure my entire life is that of my supposed birthright to strength. Black women are *supposed* to be strong—caretakers, nurturers, healers of other people—any of the twelve dozen variations on Mammy. Emotional hardship is *supposed* to be built into the structure of our lives. It went along with the territory of being both black and female." Meri Danquah is, ordinarily, anything but depressed: a beautiful, stylish, dramatic woman with an aura of regal authority. Her stories of lost weeks and months from her life are shattering. She never forgets her blackness. "I am so glad," she said to me one day, "that I have a daughter and not a son. I hate to think about what life is like for black men these days, and what it would be like for a child with a family history of depression. I hate to think I might end up having that child grow up and go behind bars in the prison system. There's not much place for black women who get depressed, but there's no place for black men."

There is no typical story of black depression. Internalizing racism—self-doubt predicated on dominant social attitudes—often plays a strong role. Several of the people whose stories are included in this book are African-American; I have chosen not to identify people by race except where it seems particularly relevant to the details of their suffering. Among the many untypical stories I heard, I became especially intimate with the tale of Dièry Prudent, an African-American man of Haitian extraction, whose experiences of depression seem to have toughened his spirit and softened his interactions with other people, and who is deeply aware of the ways in which his blackness affects his emotional life. The youngest of nine children, he grew up in the impoverished Bedford-Stuyvesant area of Brooklyn and then in Ft. Lauderdale when his parents retired there. His mother worked part-time as a home health aide, his father as a carpenter. Both parents were sternly religious Seventh-Day Adventists who set high standards of comportment and rectitude, and Dièry had to reconcile these with some of the world's toughest streets. He made himself strong, physically and mentally, to survive the tension between his family's expectations and the daily challenges and battles imposed on him by the outside world. "I always had such a sense, even when I was a kid, of being an outsider, of being singled out for punishment and humiliation. There weren't many other Haitians in our neighborhood when I was growing up, and we were certainly the only Seventh-Day Adventists for miles around. I was teased for being different; the kids on my block called me 'coconut head.' We were one of the few families who weren't on welfare. And I was the darkest-skinned kid around, and I got singled out for that. In my family, somewhere between the cultural expectation that children be unquestioningly obedient and the religious doctrine of 'Honor thy father and thy mother,' I learned that it wasn't okay to be angry—or at least to show it. I learned early to keep a stone face and keep my feelings well hidden. In contrast, there was a lot of anger on the streets, a lot of violence in our neighborhood, and when I got attacked and picked on, I turned the other cheek like our church taught us to do, and people laughed at me. I lived in a state of fear. I developed a speech impediment for a while.

"Then when I was about twelve, I got tired of being slapped around, robbed, and beat up by bigger, tougher, more streetwise kids. I started working out and practicing martial arts. It felt good to endure the most punishing and grueling regimens I could make up. I had to make myself physically tough, but there was an emotional toughness too that I was looking for. I would have to fight my way through school, endure racism and police brutality—I'd started reading my brother's Black Panther magazines—avoid getting drugged out or locked up. Nine years younger than my next sibling, I knew I was going to end up attending a lot of funerals—starting with my parents, who were already old when I was born. I didn't think I had much to look forward to. My fear was combined with a deep hopelessness; I often felt sad, though I tried not to let it show. There was no release valve for the rage, so I worked out, took scaldingly hot baths for hours, read constantly to get away from my own feelings. By the time I was sixteen, my anger began bubbling to the surface. I cultivated this mystique of the kamikaze: 'You can do whatever you want to me, but if you fuck with me, I'm going to kill you.' The fighting became addictive, an adrenaline rush, and I felt like if I learn how to suffer, then no one can hurt me. I was trying so hard to cover up my feeling of helplessness."

Dièry survived the physical and the psychological pain of his adolescence and left the ghetto to attend the University of Massachusetts, where he majored in French literature. During a term abroad in Paris, he met the woman who is now his wife and decided to stay on an extra year. "Even though I was still a student," he recalls, "I had a life that appeared glamorous. I was modeling for ad campaigns and runway shows, hanging out in the jazz scene, traveling around Europe. But I wasn't prepared for the blatant racism of the French police." After being stopped, frisked, and detained in about a dozen random police checks in a year, he was publicly beaten and arrested for disorderly conduct when he objected to a particularly egregious incident with the Paris cops. Dièry's hidden rage blossomed into symptoms of acute depression. He continued to function, but there was "a heavy weight on me."

Dièry came back to the United States to finish his degree and in 1990 moved to New York to find a career. He landed a sequence of corporate public-relations jobs. But after five years, "I felt my professional options were very limited. I felt a lot of people I was associating with were more successful than I; others seemed to advance more quickly and have better prospects. Most importantly, I felt something was missing for me and my depression deepened."

In 1995, Dièry founded Prudent Fitness, his own boutique personal-training company, which has been very successful. It is with a sense of the redemptive power of exercise that he addresses his clients now, some of whom come for their sessions to the renovated Brooklyn brownstone where he lives with his wife and daughter. His treatment is holistic in spirit though disciplined in execution. His ability to bear difficulty becomes an inspiration to his clients. "I choose to engage with people at a pretty profound level, and I think my particular skill as a trainer is that I can take the most recalcitrant, resistant client and find a way to motivate him. It requires a lot of empathy, sensitivity, an adaptable style of communication. This work permits me to use all the best parts of myself to help other people, and I feel very good about that. I met a woman recently who is a social worker and who wants to combine fitness training with social work to empower the individual. I think it's a fabulous idea. You see, this work is about gaining control over the thing you can control: your own body."

Dièry suffers the difficulties of both the poorer world he comes from and the wealthier world where he lives. His gracefulness, which he wears in the most casual fashion, is hard-won, and he can hold his gravitas well because he turns a sharp eye on himself in a world that is constantly ready to turn a sharp eye on him. Dièry has had a hard time making his depression known to all the members of his family. He's not sure they would all be able to understand the disease from his perspective, even though his father and various other family members have exhibited its symptoms. It has been difficult at times for him to maintain the demeanor of the cheery younger brother, and he has not always been able to keep up the front. Fortunately, one of his sisters, a Ph.D. clinical psychologist with a private practice in Boston, helped him find a way forward when he first sought help. His wife was immediately sympathetic and was to be a staunch supporter, but for her too it was initially difficult to reconcile the masculinity and self-assurance of her husband with what she knew of depression.

Since his first therapy in Paris, he has been in talking treatment and intermittently on antidepressant medications much of the time. His most recent work has been a five-year therapy with a woman who "has given me a kind of validation. I came to realize how much difficulty I had processing anger. I was afraid of getting angry at anyone for fear that I would just explode and destroy them. Now I am free of that fear. Through my therapy, I've developed a whole set of new skills. I feel more balanced. I feel more self-aware. I have an easier time identifying my feelings instead of simply reacting with them." First his happy marriage and then the birth of his daughter have softened him. "My daughter's vulnerability is one of the most powerful things she has. It's her most powerful tool. It's changed the way I feel about vulnerability and fragility." Nonetheless, the depression returns. The fragility surfaces. The medication needs to be adjusted. "Suddenly one day a few bad things happen and I feel like I'm out of my depth in my own life. If I didn't have the love of my wife and daughter to help me ride it out, I'd have given up a long time ago. Through therapy, I'm learning to understand what triggers the depression. With the right care and support, I'm beginning to define the disease instead of letting it define me."

Dièry is the object of constant racism, which is exacerbated by his intimidating size and physique and, curiously enough, by his good looks. I have seen salespeople shy away from him in stores. I have been on street corners in New York with him when he was trying to hail a cab for fifteen minutes and none would stop for him; when I raised my hand, we had one in ten seconds flat. He was once arrested by the police three blocks from his house in Brooklyn, told that he fit the description of a suspect in a crime, and kept long hours in a holding cell, chained to a girder. His comportment and credentials made no difference to the authority figures who incarcerated him. The consistent indignities of racism and tokenism do not make depression easier to bear. The suspicion with which he is regarded on the streets and the presumptions of guilt are exhausting. It is isolating to be so misunderstood by so many people.

When Dièry is well, he is habituated to these constant assaults on his pride and he pays them relatively little heed, but "it just makes your day so much harder," he said to me once. "The depression itself is colorblind. I think when you're depressed, you could be brown or blue or white or red. When I'm down, I see happy people of every hue and every shape and size around me, and I feel like, God, I'm the only one on the planet who's this depressed. They have something going on and I don't.

"But then again the race card does come into play. You feel like the world is just hoping to pull you down. I'm a big, strong black man and no one is going to waste time feeling sorry for me. What would happen if you suddenly started crying on the subway? I think someone might very well ask you if there was something wrong. If I burst into tears on the subway, they'd assume I was on bad drugs. When someone reacts to me in a way that has nothing to do with who I am or what I'm really like, it's always a shock to me. It's always a shock, the discrepancy between my self-perception and how I am perceived in the world, between my internal vision of myself and the external circumstances of my life. When I'm down, it's a slap across the face. I've spent hours looking in the mirror, saying, 'You're a decent-looking guy; you're clean; you're properly groomed; you're polite and kindhearted. Why don't people just love you? Why are they always trying to beat you up and fuck with you? And putting you down and humiliating you? Why?' I just couldn't get it. So there are certain external difficulties that I face as a black man that are different from those faced by some other people. I hate to admit the fact that race plays a role for me—it's not in the symptoms but in the circumstances. You know—it's hard enough being me even if I weren't a black man! But I mean, it certainly is worth it. When I'm feeling okay, I'm really glad to be me and you know, it's hard to be you too, and you're not a black man. But that race problem is always there, always ticking me off, always tapping into my permanent anger, the permafrost inside me. It gets me so far down."

Dièry and I met through his wife, who is an old school friend of mine. We have been friends for about a decade and, in part because of our mutual experience of depression, have become extremely close. I am not good at exercising on my own, and for some time Dièry has also been my trainer—a position that breeds an intimacy in many ways as great as that, I experience with my psychiatrist. In addition to structuring an exercise program, he gets me up and keeps me going. Because he constantly tests my limits, he knows what those limits are. He knows when it makes sense to push me to my physical edge and when it is necessary to pull back short of my emotional one. He is one of the first people I call when I begin to dissolve—in part because I know that stepping up my exercise regimen will have a positive effect on my mood, and in part because he has a singular sweetness; in part because he knows whereof I speak, and in part because introspection has given him a capacity for genuine insight. I have had to trust him, and I do. He is the one who came to my house and helped me to shower and get dressed when I was at my lowest. He is among the heroes of my own depression story. And he is authentically generous, someone who chose his work because he believes he can make other people feel good, someone who can be gratified by his own kindness; he has turned the aggression of his self-torture into a productive discipline. This is a rare quality indeed in a world full of people who feel put-upon by the burden of others' suffering.

The panoply of national prejudices toward depression defies cataloging. Many East Asians, for example, avoid the subject to the point of abject denial. In this spirit, a recent feature on depression in a Singapore magazine described the full range of medications, then ended by saying definitively, "Seek professional help if you need it, but in the meantime, cheer up."

Anna Halberstadt, a New York–based psychiatrist who works exclusively with Russian immigrants disappointed by the United States, said, "You have to be able to hear in the Russian context what these people are saying. If a Soviet-born Russian person were to come to my office and not complain about anything, I'd have him hospitalized. If he complains about everything, I know he is fine. Only if he were to show signs of extreme paranoia or excruciating pain would I think he might be getting depressed. It's our cultural norm. 'How are you?' 'Not so good' is the standard answer for Russians. It's part of what confuses them about the U.S., this statement that seems ridiculous, really: 'Fine, thanks, and how are you?' And honestly it's difficult for me too, even now, to hear how people say this. 'Fine, thank you.' Who's fine?"

In Poland, the 1970s were a time of few pleasures and of limited freedom. In 1980, the first Solidarity movement began to make headway, and a consequent hope and exuberance ensued. It was possible to speak out boldly; people who had for a long time been burdened by an alien system of government began to feel the pleasure of individual expression, and media were born that reflected this new mood. But in 1981, martial law was imposed in Poland, and a huge number of arrests were made; most activists served sentences of about six months. "Being imprisoned was something they all accepted," recalls Agata Bielik-Robson, who was at that time going out with one of the leading activists and is a highly regarded political philosopher in her own right. "What they could not bear was the loss of hope." The public sphere in which they had expressed themselves simply ceased to exist. "That was the beginning of a kind of political depression, a time when these men lost their belief in communication of all kinds: if they could say nothing in a public context, they would not say anything in a private context either." The same men who had been organizing rallies and writing manifestos now lost or gave up jobs and sat at home, watching TV for hours on end and drinking. They became "morose, monosyllabic, disconnected, uncommunicative, closed." Their reality was not so very different from the reality of five years earlier, except that it now had the shadow of 1980 crossing it, and so what had once been an accepted reality came to smack of defeat.

"At this time, the only sphere in which there was any possibility of success was the domestic sphere," Bielik-Robson recalls. The women who had been involved in Solidarity, many of whom had abandoned home life for activism, withdrew into traditional women's roles and nursed their ailing men through the difficulties. "In this way we found a sense of purpose and had an agenda of our own. We got such satisfaction out of our role, which had turned out to be so essential! The early eighties was a period in which women were less depressed than at any other time in recent Polish history, and the men were more depressed than at any other time."

Among the groups most likely to suffer depression, gay people rank shockingly high. In a recent study, researchers looked at middle-aged twins of whom one was gay and one was straight. Among the straight people, about 4 percent had attempted suicide. Among the gay people, 15 percent had attempted suicide. In another study, of a random population sampling of almost four thousand men between the ages of seventeen and thirty-nine, 3.5 percent of heterosexuals had attempted suicide while almost 20 percent of those who had same-sex partners had attempted suicide. In yet another randomized study of about ten thousand men and women, those who had had sex with members of their own gender during the previous year had a significantly elevated rate of depression and panic disorder. A twenty-one-year longitudinal study conducted in New Zealand of some twelve hundred people showed that those who identified as gay, lesbian, or bisexual were at increased risk for major depression, generalized anxiety disorder, conduct disorder, nicotine dependence, suicidal ideation, and suicide attempts. A Dutch study conducted on six thousand people showed that homosexual men and women were likely to have substantially higher rates of major depression than heterosexuals. A study of forty thousand youth conducted in Minnesota indicated that gay males were seven times as likely as their counterparts to experience suicidal ideation. Yet another study of about thirty-five hundred students showed that homosexual males were almost seven times as likely to make a suicide attempt as heterosexual males. Another study showed that in a sample of about fifteen hundred students, gay people (of either gender) were more than seven times as likely to have made four or more suicide attempts as straight students. One study based in San Diego found, among male suicides, 10 percent are committed by gay men. If you're gay, your chances of being depressed are enormously, terribly increased.

Many explanations have been proposed for this, some more plausible than others. A few scientists have argued for a genetic link between homosexuality and depression (a proposal that I find not only disturbing but also untenable). Others have suggested that those people who expect their sexuality to prevent their having children may confront mortality earlier than most straight people. A number of other theories have circulated, but the most obvious explanation for the high rates of gay depression is homophobia. Gay people are more likely than a general population to have been rejected by their families. They are more likely to have had social adjustment problems. Because of those problems, they are more likely to have dropped out of school. They have a higher rate of sexually transmitted diseases. They are less likely to be in

stable couplings in their adult life. They are less likely to have committed caretakers in late life. They are more likely to be infected with HIV
in the first place; and even those who are not, once they become
depressed, are more likely to practice unsafe sex and contract the virus,
which, in turn, exacerbates the depression. Most of all, they are more
likely to have lived their lives furtively and to have experienced intense
segregation in consequence of this. In early 2001, I traveled to Utrecht
to meet with Theo Sandfort, who has done pioneering work on gay
depression. Unsurprisingly, Sandfort has found that the rate of depression is higher for closeted people than for uncloseted people, and is
higher for single people than for those in stable long-term relationships.
I would say that being uncloseted and being coupled are both factors
that allay a terrible loneliness that afflicts much of the gay population.
Overall, Sandfort found that the level of difficulty gay people experience in their day-to-day lives is extremely high in many subtle ways
and sometimes pass unnoticed even by those they affect; for example,
gay people are less likely to share information about their personal lives
with others in their workplace even if they are out of the closet with
those colleagues. "And this is in the Netherlands," Sandfort said,
"where we are more open to gayness than almost anywhere else in the
world. We feel that there is a lot of acceptance of homosexuality, but the
world is still straight, and the strain of being gay in a straight world is
substantial. Now, there are plenty of gay people with good lives; in fact,
there are people who, through dealing successfully with the complexities of being gay, have built up a really amazing psychological strength,
much greater than their straight counterparts. But the range of mental
health is broader in the gay community than in any other, from this
great strength to terrible incapacity." Sandfort knows whereof he
speaks. He had a very rough time coming out himself, suffering accusations from both parents. When he was twenty, he became depressed and
debilitated. He spent seven months in a psychiatric hospital, which
turned around his parents' attitudes, led him into a new intimacy with
them, and initiated a new kind of mental health he has since enjoyed.
"Since I fell apart and put myself back together," he said, "I know how I
am made, and in consequence know a little bit of how other gay men are
made too."

While researchers such as Sandfort have been conducting large, well-
structured studies to compile correlations and numbers, the meaning of
these statistics has had relatively little exposition. In two remarkable
papers, "Internalized Homophobia and the Negative Therapeutic
Reaction" and "Internal Homophobia and Gender-Valued Self-Esteem
in the Psychoanalysis of Gay Patients," Richard C. Friedman and Jen-

nifer Downey write movingly of the origins and mechanisms of internalized homophobia. At the center of their arguments is a notion of early trauma closely tied to the classic Freudian view that primary experiences shape us for life. Friedman and Downey, however, emphasize not early childhood, but late childhood, which they locate as the point of origin for the incorporation of homophobic attitudes. A recent study of socialization among gay men indicates that children who will be homosexual adults are usually brought up in heterosexist and homophobic contexts and at an early age begin to internalize the negative view of homosexuality expressed by their peers or parents. "In this situation," Friedman and Downey write, "the patient's developmental course was one in which early childhood was filled with self-hate, which was condensed into internalized homophobic narratives constructed during later childhood." Internalized homophobia often originates with early childhood abuse and neglect. "Before they become sexually active with others," Friedman and Downey write, "many children who will become gay men are labeled 'sissy' or 'fag.' They have been teased, threatened with physical violence, ostracized, and even assaulted by other boys." Indeed, a 1998 study found that a homosexual orientation was statistically connected to having one's property stolen or deliberately damaged in school. "These traumatic interactions may result in a feeling of masculine inadequacy. Isolation from male peers may result either from ostracism or anxious avoidance or both." These painful experiences can generate an almost intractable "global and tenacious self-hatred." This problem of internalized homophobia is similar in many ways to internalized racism and to all kinds of other internalized prejudice. I have always been struck by the very high suicide rates among Jews in Berlin in the teens and twenties, which suggest that people encountering prejudice are likely to doubt themselves, to undervalue their lives, and, ultimately, to despair in the face of odium. But there is hope. "We believe," Friedman and Downey write, "that many gay men and women truly leave the consequences of their childhood behind them, and integration into the gay subculture is instrumental in facilitating this felicitous pathway. Supportive relationships often have a therapeutic effect on trauma survivors, enhancing security, self-esteem, and buttressing the sense of identity. The complex processes involved in positive identity consolidation are fostered in the context of beneficent interpersonal interactions with other gay people."

Despite the wonderful and curative effects of the gay community, however, deep problems persist, and the most interesting part of Friedman and Downey's work looks at patients who seem similar in their "*manifest* behavior to those who appear to have put the worst consequences of trauma behind them," but who are in fact severely compromised by an enduring self-loathing. Often such people will express strong prejudice toward those whose homosexuality seems to them ostentatious in some way, including, for example, queeny or effeminate men, on whom they place the scorn they feel for their own feelings of unmasculinity. They may believe, consciously or unconsciously, that they are not truly esteemed in areas entirely separate from their erotic lives—in the workplace, for example—because they believe that those who perceive them to be gay believe them to be inferior. "A negative view of the self as inadequately masculine functions as an organizing unconscious fantasy," Friedman and Downey write. This fantasy is "an element in a complex internal narrative whose major theme is 'I am an unworthy, inadequate, unmasculine man.'" People afflicted with these attitudes may attribute all the problems of their lives to their sexuality. "Negative self-valuation may come to be attributed to homosexual desires; thus, although it may be rooted in phenomena that are quite different, the patient may consciously believe that he hates himself because he is homosexual."

I have always thought that the language of gay pride has dominated the gay establishment because it is in fact the opposite of what a large number of gay people experience. Gay shame is endemic. "Guilt and shame at being gay leads to self-hatred and to self-destructive behavior," Friedman and Downey write. This self-hatred is in part "a consequence of defensive partial identification with aggressors 'layered over' earlier occurring self-acceptance." Few people at the age of dawning sexual awareness would choose to be gay, and most people who are gay entertain for some stretch of time fantasies of conversion. These are made only more difficult by a gay pride movement that finds gay shame shameful. If you are gay and feel bad about it, pride-o-files will jeer at you for your embarrassment; homophobes will jeer at you for being gay; and you will be left genuinely bereft. We do indeed internalize our tormentors. Frequently, we repress the memories of how painful external homophobia was for us as we first experienced it. Gay patients will frequently discover, after extended therapy, profound beliefs such as, "My father (or mother) always hated me because I was homosexual." Sadly, they may be right. A New Yorker study asked a broad range of people, "Which would you prefer for your son or daughter: to be heterosexual, childless, and unmarried or somewhat unhappily married; or to be homosexual, involved in a stable, happy relationship, and have children?" More than a third of respondents chose "heterosexual, childless, and either unmarried or somewhat unhappily married." Indeed, many parents view homosexuality as a punishment visited on them for their own transgressions: it is not about the identity of their children, but about their own identity.

I had a rough time in connection with my sexuality and went through difficulties familiar to many gay men. There were no problems, to the best of my recollection, until I was seven years old. But in second grade, the tortures began. I was clumsy and unathletic; I wore glasses; I was not interested in spectator sports; I had my nose forever in a book; I formed friendships most easily with girls. I had an age-inappropriate fondness for opera. I was fascinated by glamour. I was shunned by many of my schoolmates. When I went to sleep-away camp the summer I was ten, I was teased and tormented and regularly called a faggot—a word that bewildered me as I had not formulated sexual desires of any kind to myself. By the time I was in seventh grade, the problem had become broader. At school, the watchful eye of a liberal faculty offered some protection, and I was just odd and unpopular: too academic, too uncoordinated, too artistic. On the school bus, however, brutality reigned. I can remember sitting rigidly still there, next to a blind girl with whom I'd made friends, while the entire bus chanted abuse at me, stomping their feet to the rhythm of their invective. I was an object not only of derision but also of an intense hatred that confused me as much as it pained me. This horrible period did not last very long; by the time I was in ninth grade, it had all abated, and I was not unpopular (at school or, indeed, on the bus) by my senior year. But I had learned too much about abhorrence and too much about fear, and I was never again to be free of them.

Within my family, I knew from the start that homosexuality was not going to be well tolerated. In fourth grade, I was taken to a psychiatrist, and years later my mother said she had asked him whether I was gay; he apparently said that I was not. The interest of the episode, for me, lies in my mother's having had intense concern already in my prepubescence about my possible sexual identification. I am sure that the benighted therapist would have received a commission in short order to straighten out the problem of my sexuality had he assessed it more accurately. I never told my family about the taunts at camp or at school; eventually someone told his mother about what happened on the school bus every day and his mother told my mother, who wanted to know why I hadn't said anything to her. How could I? As I began to experience piercing sexual desire, I kept it secret. When an adorably cute guy made a pass at me during a glee club trip, I thought he was just trying to get a rise out of me and that he would betray my ugly news to the world; and to my eternal sadness, I rebuffed his advances. I chose instead to lose my virginity to a stranger whose name I never learned in an unsavory public location. I hated myself then. During the years that followed, I was consumed by my terrible secret, and I bifurcated myself into the helpless person who did revolting things in basement lavatories and the bright student with lots of friends who was having a great time in college.

By the time I got into my first serious relationship, when I was twenty-four, I had incorporated bushels of unhappy experience into my sexual self. This relationship, which seems in retrospect to have been not only surprisingly affectionate but also astonishingly normative, marked my transition out of an accrued misery, and for the two years I lived with him, I felt that light had come to the dark part of my life. Later, I believed my sexuality was somehow implicated in my mother's suffering during her final illness; she hated what I was so much, and that hatred was a poison in her that seeped into me and corrupted my romantic pleasures. I cannot separate her homophobia from my own, but I know that they have both cost me dearly. Is it surprising that when I began to feel suicidal, I chose to court HIV? It was just a way to make the internal tragedy of my desires into a physical reality. I have supposed that my first breakdown was tied to the publication of a novel that alluded to my mother's illness and death; but it was also a book with explicit gay content, and surely that too was implicated in the breakdown. Perhaps, indeed, that was the dominant anguish: forcing myself to make public what I had so long immured in silence.

I can now recognize the elements of internalized homophobia, and I am less subject to them than I was in the past, and I have been in meaningful, longer relationships, one of which continued over many years. The road from knowledge to freedom is, however, a long and arduous one and I battle my way down it every day. I know that I have engaged in many activities referenced in this book in part as overcompensation for homophobic feelings of unmasculinity. I go skydiving, own a gun, did Outward Bound—all that helps to make up for the time I spend on my clothes, in the so-called feminine pursuit of art, and in the erotic and emotional embrace of men. I would like to think that by now I am free, but though I have a lot of positive emotion associated with my sexuality, I believe I will never escape fully from the abnegation. I have often described myself as bisexual, and have been in three long-term relationships with women and those have occasioned great delight, emotional and physical; but if matters had been reversed and I had had a great sexual interest in women and a minor interest in men, I would certainly not have tried the experiment of alternative sexual identity. I think it is likely that I entered into sexual relationships with women in good part so that I might further prove my own masculinity. Though this effort has led me to certain high joys, it has been an effort of sometimes devastating proportions. Even with men, I have sometimes tried to act out a dominance I didn't necessarily feel, attempting to redeem my masculinity still in the gay context—because, in fact, even liberated gay society homophobically looks down on yielding men. What if I hadn't spent so very, very much time and energy running away from what I perceive to be my unmasculine qualities? Would I perhaps have been able to avoid altogether my experiences of depression? Would I have been whole instead of fragmented? Perhaps. I think, at the very least, that I would have had years of happiness that are now forever lost.

To examine further the question of cultural difference in defining depression, I looked at the lives of the Inuit (Eskimo) peoples of Greenland—in part because depression is high in that culture, and in part because the culture's attitudes toward depression are particularly distinct. Depression affects as much as 80 percent of the population there. How can one organize a society in which depression plays such a central role? As a possession of Denmark, Greenland is currently integrating the ways of an ancient society with the realities of the modern world, and transitional societies—African tribal communities that are being folded into larger nations, nomadic cultures that are being urbanized, subsistence farmers who are being incorporated into larger-scale agricultural developments—almost always have high levels of depression. Even in the traditional context, however, depression has always run high among the Inuit, and the suicide rate has also been high—in some areas, about 0.35 percent of the population *per year* commit suicide. Some might say that this is God's way of indicating to people that they shouldn't live in such a forbidding place—and yet the Inuit peoples have not abandoned their icebound lives to migrate south. They have adapted to tolerate the difficulties of life above the Arctic Circle. I had assumed before I went that the issue in Greenland was primarily SAD, depression resulting from a three-month period when the sun never rises. I had expected that everyone dipped in the late autumn and began to improve in February. This is not the case. The prime suicide month in Greenland is May, and though foreigners who move to the northern part of Greenland get terribly depressed during the long periods of darkness, the Inuit have adapted over the years to the seasonal shifts in light and are generally able to preserve adequate mood during the season of darkness. Everyone likes springtime, and some find the darkness dreary; but SAD is really not the central problem of the Greenlandic people. "The richer, softer and more delectable nature becomes," the essayist A. Alvarez has written, "the deeper that internal winter seems, and the wider and more intolerable the abyss which separates the inner world from the outer." In Greenland, where the springtime shift is twice as dramatic as in a more temperate zone, these are the cruelest months.

Life is hard in Greenland, so the Danish government has instituted terrific programs of social support services, and there is universal free health care, education, even unemployment benefits. The hospitals are spotless, and the prison in the capital city looks more like a bed-and-breakfast than like an institution of punishment. But the climate and the forces of nature in Greenland are unfathomably harsh. One of the Inuit people I met, a man who had traveled to Europe, said, "We never made great art or built great buildings, the way that other civilizations did. But for thousands of years here, we survived." It struck me that this was quite possibly the greater achievement. The hunters and fishermen catch just enough to feed themselves and their dogs, and they sell the skins of the seals they eat to pay for the minor expenses of their lives and for the repair of sleds and boats. The people who live close to the old ways in settlements or villages are mostly warmhearted; they are story-tellers, especially about hunting escapades and near escapes from death; they are tolerant people. They have a wonderful sense of humor and they laugh a lot. Because of the climate in which they live, they have a high rate of trauma: of freezing, of starving, of injury, and of loss. Forty years ago, these people still lived in igloos; now they have Danish-style prefabricated houses with just two or three rooms. For three months every year, the sun goes away entirely. During this period of darkness, hunters dressed in trousers of polar-bear fur and coats of sealskin must run beside their dogsleds to forestall frostbite.

Inuit families are large. For months on end, families of perhaps twelve people stay unremittingly inside in their house, usually gathered in one room. It is simply too cold and too dark for anyone to go out except the father, who goes hunting or ice fishing once or twice a month to supplement the stock of dried fish from the summer. There are no trees in Greenland, so no jolly fires are burning inside; traditionally, in fact, there would have been only a small lamp burning seal fat inside an igloo where, as one Greenlander I met put it, "we all sat around together for months on end watching the walls melt." In these circumstances of enforced intimacy, there is no place for complaining or for talking about problems or for anger and accusations. The Inuit simply have a taboo against complaining. They are silent and brooding or they are story-tellers given to laughter, or they talk about the conditions outside and the hunt, but they almost never speak of themselves. Depressiveness, with concomitant hysteria and paranoia, is the price paid for the intense communality of Inuit lives.

The distinctive features of Greenlandic depression are not direct results of the temperature and light; they are the consequence of the taboo on talking of yourself. The extreme physical intimacy of this society necessitates emotional reserve. It is not unkindness; it is not coldness; it is simply another way. Poul Bisgaard, a gentle, large man with an air of bemused patience, is the first native Greenlander to become a psychiatrist. "Of course if someone is depressed within a family, we can see the symptoms," he says. "But we do not, traditionally, meddle with them. It would be an affront to someone's pride to say that you thought he looked depressed. The depressed man believes himself to be worthless and thinks that if he is worthless, there is no reason to bother anyone else. Those around him do not presume to interfere." Kirsten Peilman, a Danish psychologist who has lived in Greenland for more than a decade, says, "There is no sense of rules that include intruding on anyone else. No one tells anyone else to behave. You simply tolerate whatever people present and let them tolerate themselves."

I went in the season of light. Nothing could have prepared me for the beauty of Greenland in June, when the sun stays high overhead right through the night. We took a fisherman's small motorboat from the five-thousand-person town of Ilulissat, where I had landed in a small plane, southward toward one of the settlements I had selected in consultation with Greenland's head of public health. It is called Illiminaq, a place of hunters and fishermen with a total adult population of about eighty-five. There are no roads leading to Illiminaq, and there are no roads in Illiminaq. In the winter, the villagers travel across the frozen terrain by dogsled; in the summer, access can be gained only by boat. In the spring and autumn, people stay at home. At the time of year when I went, fantastical icebergs, some as large as office buildings, flow down the coast, grouping near the Kangerlussuaq ice fjord. We crossed the mouth of the fjord, navigating among the smooth, oblong shapes of older ice that had turned bottom up, and chunks of broken-off glacier, as big as apartment buildings, that were corrugated with age and curiously blue—our boat humble in the face of such natural majesty. As we progressed, we gently pushed aside the smaller icebergs, some of which were the size of refrigerators; others were like floating dinner plates, and they crowded the clear water so that if you let your sight line follow the remote horizon, you would have thought we were sailing through unbroken sheets of ice. The light was so clear that there seemed to be no depth of field, and I could not tell what was near and what was far away. We stayed near the shore, but I could not tell the land from the sea, and most of the time we were canyoned between mountains of ice. The water was so cold that when a piece of ice broke off the lip of an iceberg and fell in, the water dented as though it were custard, reclosing itself into smoothness only a measurable few seconds after it had split. From time to time, we'd see or hear a ringed seal plopping himself into the frigid water. Otherwise, we were alone with the light and the ice.

Illiminaq is built around a small natural harbor. There are some thirty houses, a school, a tiny church, and a store, which gets supplied about once a week. Each house has a team of dogs, who far outnumber the human residents of the place. The houses are painted in the bright, clear colors that the locals adore—Turkish blue, buttercup yellow, pale pink—but they hardly make an impression on the vast rocks that rise behind them, or on the white sea that stretches in front of them. It is hard to imagine a place more isolated than Illiminaq. The village does have a phone line, however, and the Danish government will pay for helicopters to airlift local people in a medical crisis if weather permits a landing. No one has running water or water-flow toilets, but there is a generator, and so some houses, and the school, have electricity, and several houses have televisions. Every house has an inconceivably beautiful view; at midnight, when the sun was high and the locals were asleep, I would walk among the silent houses and the sleeping dogs as if I were in a dream.

A notice had been posted outside the store a week before I came, asking for volunteers to discuss their mood states with me. My translator—a lively, educated, activist Inuit woman who was trusted in Illiminaq—had agreed, despite her misgivings, that she would try to help me persuade the reserved local people to talk about feelings. We were accosted, somewhat shyly, the day after we arrived. Yes, they had some stories to tell. Yes, they had decided to tell them to me. Yes, it was easier to talk about these things with a foreigner. Yes, I must talk to the three sage women—the ones who had started this whole business of talking about emotions. The Inuit are in my experience kind people, and they wanted to help, even when that help involved a loquaciousness somewhat alien to their usual way. Because of the recommendations that had been sent ahead for me, and because of the fisherman who had brought me in his boat, and because of my translator, they made me part of their intimate community while granting me the courtesies due a guest.

"Ask no open questions" was the advice of the Danish doctor in charge of the district that included Illiminaq. "If you ask them how they feel, they won't be able to tell you anything." Nevertheless, the villagers knew what I wanted to know. They did not usually give answers of more than a few words, and the questions had to be as concrete as possible, but even if the emotions were not available to them linguistically, they were clearly present conceptually. Trauma is a regular part of the lives of Greenlandic people; anxiety after trauma was not uncommon; neither was a descent into dark feelings and self-doubt. Old fishermen at the docks told me stories of their sleds going under (a well-trained dog team will pull you out, if the ice doesn't break further, if you don't drown first, if the reins don't break) and of having to go miles in subzero temperatures in wet clothes; they talked about hunting when the ice was moving and the thunder of sound made it impossible for one man to hear another, and you felt yourself rising up as a chunk of glacier shifted position, not knowing whether it would soon turn over and plunge you into the sea. And they talked about how, after such experiences, it had been difficult to keep going, to wrest the next day's food from the ice and the darkness.

We went to see the three woman elders. Each of them had suffered terribly. Amalia Joelson, the midwife, was the closest there was to a doctor in town. She had had a stillborn child one year; the next year, she gave birth to a child that died the night after it was born. Her husband, mad with grief, accused her of killing the child. She herself could hardly bear at that time to know she could deliver the children of her neighbors but could have none herself. Karen Johansen, the wife of a fisherman, had left her native town to come to Illiminaq. Shortly afterward, in rapid sequence her mother, her grandfather, and her older sister died, all independently. Then her brother's wife became pregnant with twins. The first twin was stillborn at five months. The second was born healthy but died of sudden infant death syndrome at three months. Her brother had one child left, a six-year-old daughter, and when she drowned, he hanged himself. Amelia Lange was the minister in the church. She had married young, a tall hunter, and she had borne him eight children in rapid succession. Then he had a hunting accident: a bullet ricocheted off a rock and his right arm was split halfway between the elbow and the wrist. The bone never healed, and the break line would bend like an extra joint if you took his hand. He lost the use of his right arm. A few years later, he was just outside the house during a storm and was blown over by a strong wind. Without his arm to break his fall, he broke his neck and has since been largely paralyzed from the head down. His wife has had to care for him and move his wheelchair around the house, bring up the children, and hunt for food. "I would do my work outdoors and cry the whole time while I did it," she recalled. When I asked whether others had not come to her when they saw her weeping at her work, she said, "They did not interfere so long as I could do the work." Her husband felt he was such a burden to her that he stopped eating, hoping to starve himself to death, but she saw what he was doing, and seeing it broke down her silence, and she pleaded with him to live.

"Yes, it is true," Karen Johansen said. "We Greenlanders are too close to be intimate. And we all have so many burdens here, and none of us wants to add our burdens to the burdens of others." Danish explorers of the early and middle twentieth century found three primary mental illnesses among the Inuit, described by the Inuit themselves time out of mind. These have now largely died out except in very remote locations. "Polar hysteria" was described by one man who had suffered it as "a rising of the sap, of young blood nourished by the blood of walruses, seals, and whales—sadness takes hold of you. At first you are agitated. It is to be sick of life." A modified form of it exists to this day as what we might call activated depression or a mixed state; it is closely related to the Malaysian idea of "running amok." "Mountain wanderer syndrome" affected those who turned their back on the community and left—in earlier times, they were never allowed to return and had to fend for themselves in absolute solitude until they died. "Kayak anxiety," the belief contra reality that water is in your boat and you will sink and drown, was the most common form of paranoia. Though these terms are now primarily used historically, they still evoke some of the conflicts of Inuit life. In Umanaaq, according to René Birger Christiansen, head of public health for Greenland, there was recently a spate of complaints from people who believed they had water under their skin. The French explorer Jean Malaurie wrote in the 1950s, "There is an often dramatic contradiction between the Eskimo's basically individualistic temperament and his conscious belief that solitude is synonymous with unhappiness. Abandoned by his fellowmen, he is overcome by the depression that always lies in wait for him. Is the communal life too much to bear? A network of obligations link one person to another and make a voluntary prisoner of the Eskimo."

The women elders of Illiminaq had each borne her pain in silence for a long time. Karen Johansen said, "At first, I tried to tell other women how I felt, but they just ignored me. They did not want to talk about bad things. And they did not know how to have such a conversation; they had never heard anyone talk about her problems. Until my brother died, I was proud also not to be a cloud in the sky for other people. But after this shock of his suicide, I had to talk. People did not like it. In our way, it is rude to say to someone, even a friend, 'I am sorry for your troubles.'" She describes her husband as a "man of silence" with whom she negotiated a way to weep while he listened, without either of them having to use the words that were so alien to him.

These three women were drawn to one another's difficulties, and after many years, they spoke together about the depth of their anguish, about their loneliness, about all the feelings that were in them. Amalia Joelson had gone to the hospital in Ilulissat for training in midwifery, and there she had become aware of talking therapies. She found comfort in her conversation with these other two women, and she proposed an idea to them. It was a new idea for that society. In church one Sunday, Amelia Lange announced that they had formed a group and that they wanted to invite anyone who wished to talk about problems to come and see them, individually or together. She proposed that they use the consulting room at Amalia Joelson's place. Lange promised that such meetings would remain entirely confidential. She said, "None of us needs be alone."

In the following year, all the women of the village, one at a time, each unaware of how many others had taken up the offer, came to see them. Women who had never told their husbands or their children what was in their hearts came and wept in the midwife's delivery room. And so this new tradition began, of openness. A few men came, though the men's idea of toughness kept many of them away, at least at the beginning. I spent long hours in the houses of each of these three women. Amelia Lange said it had been a great insight for her to see how people were "released" after talking to her. Karen Johansen invited me in with her family and gave me a bowl of fresh whale soup, which she had said was often the best answer to one's problems, and told me that she had found the real cure for sadness, which was to hear of the sadness of others. "I am not doing this only for the people who speak to me," she said, "but also for myself." In their homes and in their intimacies, the people of Illiminaq do not talk about each other. But they go to their three elders and draw strength from them. "I know that I have prevented many suicides," Karen Johansen said. "I'm glad I could talk to them in time." The matter of confidentiality was of the utmost importance; there are many hierarchies in a small settlement, and these cannot be disrupted without making problems far greater than the problem of silence. "I see the people outside who have told me their problems, and I never bring up those problems or ask in a different way about someone's health," Amalia Joelson said. "Only if, when I say politely, 'How are you?' they begin to cry, then I will bring them back with me to the house."

The idea of talking therapies is frequently discussed in the West as though it had been made up by psychoanalysts. Depression is a disease of loneliness, and anyone who has suffered it acutely knows that it imposes a dread isolation, even for people surrounded by love—in this case, an isolation caused by crowding. The three women elders of Illiminaq had discovered the wonder of unburdening themselves and of helping others to do the same. Different cultures express pain in different ways, and members of different cultures experience different kinds of pain, but the quality of loneliness is infinitely plastic.

Those three women elders asked me about my depression too, and sitting in their houses and eating dried cod wrapped in seal blubber, I felt them reaching from their experience to mine. When we left the town, my translator said this had been the most exhausting experience of her life, but she said it with incandescent pride. "We are strong people, the Inuit," she said. "If we did not solve all our problems, we would die here. So we have found our way to solve this problem, this depression, too." Sara Lynge, a Greenlandic woman who has set up a suicide hot line in a large town, said, "First, people must see how easy it is to talk to someone, then how good it is. They don't know that. We who have discovered that must do our best to spread the news."

Confronted with worlds in which adversity is the norm, one sees shifting boundaries between the accurate reckoning of life's difficulty and the state of depression. Inuit life is hard—not morally demeaning in the way of concentration camps, and not emotionally vacant in the mode of modern cities, but unrelentingly arduous and without the quotidian material luxuries that most Westerners take for granted. Until quite recently, the Inuit could not afford even the luxury of speaking their problems: they had to suppress all negative emotion lest it sweep away their entire society. The families I visited in Illiminaq made their way through tribulation by observing a pact of silence. It was an effective system for its purpose, and it saw many people through many cold, long winters. Our modern Western belief is that problems are best solved when they are pulled out of darkness, and the story of what has happened in Illiminaq bears out that theory; but the articulation is limited in scope and location. Let us remember that none of the depressed people in the village talked about their problems with the objects of those problems, and that they did not discuss their difficulties regularly even with the three women elders. It is often said that depression is a thing to which a leisured class falls prey in a developed society; in fact, it is a thing that a certain class has the luxury of articulating and addressing. For the Inuit, depression is so minor in the scale of things and so evident a part of everyone's life that, except in severe cases of vegetative illness, they simply ignore it. Between their silence and our intensely verbalized self-awareness lie a multitude of ways of speaking of psychic pain, of knowing that pain. Context, race, gender, tradition, nation—all conspire to determine what is to be said and what is to be left unsaid—and to some extent they thereby determine what is to be alleviated, what exacerbated, what endured, what forsworn. The depression—its urgency, its symptoms, and the ways out of it—is all determined by forces quite outside of our individual biochemistry, by who we are, where we were born, what we believe, and how we live.

CHAPTER VI

Addiction

Depression and substance abuse form a cycle. People who are depressed abuse substances in a bid to free themselves of their depression. People who abuse substances disrupt their lives to the point that they become depressed by the damage. Do people who are "genetically inclined" to alcoholism become drinkers and then experience depression as a consequence of consuming a substance; or do people who are genetically inclined to depression use drink as a form of self-medication? The answer to both questions is yes. Falling serotonin appears to play a significant role in reinforcing alcoholism, so that an escalating depression might cause organic escalation of alcoholism. In fact there is an inverse relationship between serotonin levels in the nervous system and alcohol consumption. Self-medication with illicit drugs is frequently counterproductive: while licit antidepressant meds start off with side effects and build up to desirable effects, the substances of abuse usually start with desirable effects and build up to side effects. The decision to take Prozac instead of cocaine is a version of the strategy of deferred gratification, and the decision to take cocaine instead of antidepressants is predicated on a yearning for immediate gratification.

All substances of abuse—nicotine, alcohol, marijuana, cocaine, heroin, and about twenty others currently known—have major effects on the dopamine system. Some people have a genetic predisposition to use these substances. Substances of abuse act on the brain in three stages. The first stage is in the forebrain and affects cognition; this in turn excites fibers leading to the most primitive areas of the brain—the ones we have in common with reptiles—and these, finally, send tingling messages to many other parts of the brain, frequently affecting the dopamine system. Cocaine, for example, seems to block dopamine uptake, so that more dopamine is floating around in the brain; morphine causes the release of dopamine. Other neurotransmitters are also involved; alcohol affects sero-

217

tonin, and several substances seem to raise levels of enkephalin. The brain, however, is self-regulating and tends to sustain constant levels of stimulation; if you keep flooding it with dopamine, it will develop resistance so that it will require more and more dopamine to trigger a response. It either increases the number of dopamine receptors or decreases the sensitivity of existing dopamine receptors. This is why addicts need escalating quantities of their substance of abuse; it is also why people in recovery, who are no longer stimulating the excessive release of dopamine through substances, usually feel flat and greyed out and depressed: their natural dopamine levels are, by the standards of their adapted brains, extremely low. When the brain adjusts itself anew, withdrawal is complete.

Most people, if they take enough of an abusable substance for long enough, will become addicted to it. A third of all people who ever smoke a cigarette go on to develop a nicotine addiction; about a quarter of those who try heroin become dependent on it; about a sixth of those who try alcohol become dependent on that. The speed with which substances cross the blood-brain barrier and so intoxicate the user is often determined by the way the substance is ingested, with injection being fastest, inhalation next, and oral consumption slowest. Of course the speed also varies from substance to substance and will determine how rapidly reinforcing the substance is. "The question of who tries a substance once is pretty random," David McDowell, director of the Substance Treatment and Research Service of Columbia University, says. "It has to do with where someone is and what his social climate is. But the follow-up is anything but random. Some people who try a substance go on with their lives and never give it another thought; some get hooked almost immediately." For substance abusers as for depressives, a genetic predisposition interacts with external experience; people are born with a capacity to become substance abusers and, once they have abused a given substance for long enough, will become addicted to it. Depressed people who tend toward alcoholism will usually begin chronic heavy drinking about five years after the first major depressive episode; those who tend toward cocaine will on average start abusing it chronically about seven years after such an episode. No test exists at present to show who can use what substances with what levels of risk, though attempts to formulate such tests, mostly on the basis of certain enzyme levels in the bloodstream, are under way. It is not yet possible to see whether a physiological transformation in depressed people makes them more vulnerable to substance abuse, or whether the increased vulnerability is primarily psychological.

Most depressed substance abusers have two linked illnesses running concurrently, each of which requires treatment and each of which exacerbates the other. These illnesses interact within the dopamine system. The popular idea that you have to get a person off substances before you pay attention to his depression is faintly ludicrous: you are asking someone who tamps down his misery to let that misery blossom before you do anything about it. The idea that you can ignore addiction and treat depression as the primary illness, helping someone feel so good that he won't want substances anymore, overlooks the reality of physical dependence. "If there's anything we've learned in the addiction field," says Herbert Kleber, who was for some years deputy drug czar for the United States and who now heads Columbia University's Center for Addiction and Substance Abuse, "it's that once you get addicted—it doesn't matter how you got there—you have a disease with a life of its own. If you treat a depressed alcoholic with an antidepressant, you produce a nondepressed alcoholic." Taking away the original motivation for abusing substances does not free someone who has developed a pattern of substance abuse.

Theoreticians are keen to separate mood state and substance dependency. Some straightforward measures—family history of depression, for example—can identify a primary depression, and a family history of substance abuse may point to a primary substance problem. Beyond this, the terms get vague. Alcoholism causes the symptoms of depression. The mainstream therapeutic philosophy at present holds that substance abuse should be treated first, and that after a person has been "clean" or "sober" for about a month, his emotional condition should be assessed. If the person is feeling good, the addiction was probably the cause of the depression, and so lifting the addiction has lifted the depression. This is all well and good in principle, but in fact the upheaval caused by withdrawal is enormous. Someone who feels great at the end of a month off substances is probably suffused with pride at his self-control and is experiencing adjusted levels of all kinds of hormones, neurotransmitters, peptides, enzymes, and so on; such a person is not necessarily free of either his alcoholism or his depression. Someone who is depressed at the end of a month off substances may be depressed for life-related reasons that reflect neither the emotional state that first led him into substance abuse nor an underlying emotional state now laid bare. The notion that someone can be restored to a condition of purity, this idea that substances mask an abuser's true self, is perfectly ludicrous. Furthermore, withdrawal-related mood problems may make their first appearance only after a sober month or two. It takes many months for the body to achieve optimal recovery from long-term substance abuse; some brain alteration "appears to be permanent," according to Kleber, and some has a life of at least a year or two. Positron-emission tomography (PET) scans show the effects of various substances of abuse on the brain, and they show limited recovery even at the three-month point. There are persisting lesions, and chronic abusers of substances often suffer permanent memory damage.

If it is sadistic to begin by taking depressed substance abusers off their substances, then does it make sense to begin by giving them medication? The use of antidepressants on depressed alcoholics will cause some alleviation of their desire for drink if depression is a primary motive for their alcoholism. This mode of testing—to begin by alleviating the depression—is more generous than the stripping away of substances to reveal a person with or without a "real depression." Antidepressant treatment is undeniably useful in reducing substance abuse; recent studies have shown that putting alcoholics on SSRIs increases the chances that they will be able to come off alcohol. Clearly, depression can be significantly ameliorated with psychodynamic therapy, or just with attention—and the close attention paid to people who participate in studies can have a beneficial effect on substance use quite apart from the protocol of the study. Depressed alcoholics tend to be terribly isolated, and interrupting that isolation often alleviates some depressive symptoms.

"There's a certain judgmental quality in trying to get technical about what illness is primary and what is secondary, trying to apportion blame to self-indulgence or mental illness," says Elinore McCance-Katz of Albert Einstein College of Medicine. "As someone who treats people with addiction problems and mental health problems, however, I do want to know because it may be predictive of how they're going to do in the future; it's going to be helpful to me in terms of how I educate and work with them; it's going to be helpful to me in terms of what medications I may treat them with and for how long. But the bottom line is that if they have both disorders, both disorders have to be treated." It is sometimes the case that self-medicators are using substances to control agitated depression that might, unchecked, include suicidal wishes or acts. If you get such a person off the alcohol without making plans to control the depression in some better way, you run a severe risk of creating a suicide. "When depression is not diagnosed because of the lack of abstinence," David McDowell of Columbia says, "maintaining abstinence may hinge upon treating the depression." In other words, if you're depressed, you may not be able to cope with the stress of detoxifying.

Correlations are manipulated to try to construct a system of diagnosis in a field where knowing the origin of the illness is only a small piece of knowing how to treat it. One recent study, for example, looked at sleep patterns and determined that shortened latency for rapid eye movement (REM) sleep (the length of time before one enters the first REM stage after falling asleep) indicated that depression was the primary illness, while a protracted latency for REM sleep indicated that alcoholism was the primary illness. Some clinicians claim that early-onset alcoholism is more likely to be the consequence of depression than is later-onset alcoholism. Some tests measure metabolites of serotonin, or levels of cortisol and other hormones, and hope to demonstrate through these measurements the presence of a "real" depression—but since much real depression does not manifest itself in such metabolites, the tests are of limited utility. An incredibly broad range of statistics is available, but it seems that about a third of all substance abusers suffer from some kind of depressive disorder; and it is evident that a high number of depressives abuse substances. Substance abuse frequently begins in early adolescence, at a stage at which people with a predisposition for depression may not yet have developed the complaint. Abuse may begin as a defense against a developing depressive tendency. Sometimes, depression makes someone who has been a user of an addictive substance into an addict. "People who are taking things because they're anxious or because they're depressed are much more likely to develop a real dependence," Kleber says. People who have recovered from substance abuse are far more likely to relapse when they're depressed than otherwise. R. E. Meyer has proposed five possible relationships between substance abuse and depression. Depression may be the cause of substance abuse; depression may be the result of substance abuse; depression may alter or exaggerate substance abuse; depression may coexist with substance abuse without affecting it; depression and substance abuse may be two symptoms of a single problem.

It is extremely confusing that substance use, withdrawal from substance use, and depression have overlapping symptoms. Depressants such as alcohol and heroin relieve anxiety and aggravate depression; stimulants such as cocaine relieve depression and aggravate anxiety. Patients with depression who abuse stimulants may have behavior that appears schizophrenic, though that behavior will remit with *either* a discontinuation of substance use or a successful treatment of the depression. In other words, the symptoms of the combination are worse than the combined symptoms of the two component diseases. In dual-diagnosis cases, the alcoholism is often more severe than average alcoholism, and the depression is also often more severely symptomatic than average depression. Fortunately, people with dual diagnosis are more likely to seek help than those with either problem alone. They are also, however, more likely to relapse. Though substance abuse and depression may be separate problems, unquestionably each of them has physiological consequences in the brain that may severely exacerbate the others. Some substances (cocaine, sedatives, hypnotics, and anxiolytics) that do not cause depression when they are being used do affect the brain in such a way that they cause depression during withdrawal; some substances (amphetamines, opioids, hallucinogens) cause depression as part of their immediate intoxicating effect. Some (cocaine, ecstasy) cause a high and then a compensatory low. This is not a tidy matter. All of these substances, and alcohol in particular, will exacerbate suicidality. All of them blur minds enough to disrupt compliance with prescription regimens, which can create real chaos for people ostensibly on sustained antidepressant treatment.

All of this being said, depression remits more or less permanently in some people after they detoxify themselves, and the correct treatment for such people is abstinence. Other people's interest in drugs and alcohol simply peters out when their depression is brought under control, and the correct treatment for such people is antidepressant medication and therapy. Most substance abusers, like most depressives, require psychosocial intervention, but this is not invariably the case. Unfortunately, clinicians still have inadequate understanding of how many antidepressant medications may interact with substances of abuse. Alcohol accelerates the absorption of medications, and this rapid absorption significantly raises the side effects of drugs. Tricyclic antidepressants, an older form of treatment, may in combination with cocaine cause significant stress to the heart. It is important, when prescribing antidepressants to a substance abuser who has gone sober, to assume that that person could return to his substance of choice, and to exercise caution in prescribing drugs that may in combination with substances cause significant harm. In some instances, psychodynamic therapy may be the safest way initially to address depression in substance abusers.

The language of addiction has become vague over the last twenty years, so that one can now be addicted to work, to sunshine, to foot massage. Some people are addicted to eating. Some are addicted to money—both getting and spending. One anorexic girl I met had been diagnosed with an addiction to cucumbers, a complaint about which, one cannot help feeling, Dr. Freud would have much to say. Howard Shaffer, director of the division on addictions at Harvard Medical School, has studied compulsive gambling, and he believes that the addiction pathways are in the brain and that the object of the compulsion is not really significant; for him, addiction to behaviors does not differ significantly from addiction to substances. It is the helpless need to keep repeating something damaging that drives dependence, rather than the physiological response to the thing repeated. "You don't talk about addictive dice," he says.

Bertha Madras, however, from Harvard's department of psychiatry, says that the most frequently abused substances tap into pathways that exist in the brain, enabled by their similarity to substances that more naturally occur there. "The chemical structure of drugs happens to resemble the chemical structure of the brain's own neurotransmitters," she says. "I call them 'the great brain impostors.' They target the same communications systems as the brain's natural messages. But the complex communication and control systems in the brain are geared for the natural message, not the impostor. As a result, the brain adapts to, and compensates for, the abnormal signals generated by the drug. Here is where the addictive process begins. Brain adaptation is central to addiction. In the case of drugs that produce physical or psychological withdrawal, there is a compulsion to restore the brain to the status it had when it was awash with drugs." Addictive dice notwithstanding, physical addiction involves the activation of addiction pathways in the brain, and many of those pathways lead to physiological alterations that may in turn cause depression.

People with family histories of alcoholism tend to have lower levels of endorphins—the endogenous morphine that is responsible for many of our pleasure responses—than do people genetically disinclined to alcoholism. Alcohol will slightly raise the endorphin level of people without the genetic basis for alcoholism; it will dramatically raise the endorphin level of people with that genetic basis. Specialists spend a lot of time formulating exotic hypotheses to account for substance abuse. Most people who abuse substances do so because it feels good. There are, the experts point out, strong motivations for avoiding drugs; but there are also strong motivations for taking them. People who claim not to understand why anyone would get addicted to drugs are usually people who haven't tried them or who are genetically fairly invulnerable to them.

"People are very poor judges of their own susceptibility," Herbert Kleber of Columbia says. "No one wants to be an addict. The problem in treatment is that the goal of the therapist—abstinence—and the goal of the patient—control—are not the same. All the crack addict wants is to be able to take an occasional hit off the pipe. And one of the problems is that they were once able to do that. Every addict had a honeymoon, during which they could control use. For an alcoholic, that might have been five or ten years; for the crack addict it may have been as little as six months." Feeling the wish to repeat something because it is pleasurable is not quite the same as feeling the need to repeat something because being without it is intolerable. Frequently, the determinant of need is an external circumstance such as depression; a depressed individual is likely, therefore, to become addicted much more rapidly than is a nondepressed person. If you're depressed, the ability to get gratification from ordinary life is diminished. Substance abusers may be classed as precontemplative—which means they're not even thinking of giving up their drug of choice—or contemplative, or externally motivated, or internally motivated. Most have to go through these four stages before they can achieve freedom from dependency.

The medical literature claims that addiction comes from problems with "(1) affects, (2) self-esteem, (3) self-other relationships, and (4) self-care." I would propose that what is extraordinary, really, is how many of us manage to avoid addiction. We are motivated in part by the knowledge of just how harmful and unpleasant addiction can be, by fear of losing relationships, and by pleasure in self-control. Nonetheless, it is the physical side effects of substance abuse that make the biggest difference of all. If there were no such thing as a hangover, there would be a lot more alcoholics and cocaine addicts around. Drugs reward and punish, and the border between the level of use in which the rewards are greater than the punishments, and the level of use in which the punishments overtake the rewards, is fuzzy. The depressant effects of a drink help people to unwind and deal with social situations without crippling anxiety, and this kind of use is socially sanctioned in most non-Muslim societies. The stimulant effects of occasional cocaine use are to depression what alcohol is to anxiety, though the illegality of cocaine reflects our social discomfort with it. The most common addictions by far are caffeine and nicotine. A doctor who specializes in addiction described to me visiting friends abroad and having a paralytic hangover and a terribly depressed feeling for a full two days before he realized that his friends had only herbal tea in the house and that he was going through not an alcohol-based dehydration problem, but caffeine withdrawal symptoms. A few cups of full-strength coffee later and he was back on his feet. "I'd never even thought about it, but coffee was not simply an acquired taste: it was an addiction and any messing around with it was going to entail withdrawal." As a society, we don't object to addictions that are not disabling; we do object to the use of certain addictive substances even when that use is occasional and nonaddictive in nature. The debates over the legalization of marijuana and the illegalization of tobacco point to our split views on this subject.

Genes are not destiny. Ireland has an extremely high rate of alcoholism; it also has an extremely high rate of teetotalism. Israel has an extremely low rate of alcoholism but almost no teetotalers. In a society in which people are prone to alcoholism, they may also be prone to exercising great self-control in the face of substances. "Alcoholism," Kleber says, "is not a disease of the elbow. It's not muscular spasms that bring the glass to your mouth. An alcoholic does have choices. The ability to exercise those choices, however, is influenced by many variables, one of which may be a mood disorder." If you take drugs, you do it deliberately. You know when you're doing it. It involves volition. And yet do we have choice? If one knows that there is ready relief for immediate pain, what does it mean to deny oneself? T. S. Eliot wrote in "Gerontion," "After such knowledge, what forgiveness?" In the dark night of the soul, is it best not to know what cocaine can do for you?

Part of what is most horrendous about depression, and particularly about anxiety and panic, is that it does not involve volition: feelings happen to you for absolutely no reason at all. One writer has said that substance abuse is the substitution of "comfortable and comprehensible pain" for "uncomfortable and incomprehensible pain," eliminating "uncontrollable suffering which the user does not understand" in favor of "a drug-induced dysphoria which the user does understand." In Nepal, when an elephant has a splinter or spike in his foot, his drivers put chili in one of his eyes, and the elephant becomes so preoccupied with the pain of the chili that he stops paying attention to the pain in his foot, and people can remove the spike without being trampled to death (and in a fairly short time, the chili washes out of his eye). For many depressives, alcohol or cocaine or heroin is the chili, the intolerable thing the horror of which distracts from the more intolerable depression.

Caffeine, nicotine, and alcohol are the primary legal addictive substances incorporated to varying degrees into the norms of our society and advertised to consumers. Caffeine, we largely ignore. Nicotine, though highly reinforcing, is not an intoxicant and is therefore relatively untroubling to daily life; it is the effects of the tar that accompanies the usual intake of nicotine that is worrying to the leaders of the antismoking movement. The delayed negative side effects of smoking make nicotine an easy drug to abuse: if people got horrendous hangovers every time they smoked cigarettes, they would smoke a lot fewer of them. Since the adverse effects—most notably emphysema and lung cancer—are the ultimate result of long-term smoking, they are more easily ignored or denied. The high rate of smoking among depressed people seems to reflect not any particular attribute of nicotine, but a general self-destructiveness among people for whom the future is only bleak. The lower oxygenation of the blood that occurs as part of smoking may also have an active depressant effect. Smoking appears to lower serotonin levels, though it is possible that low serotonin levels in fact cause people to be attracted to nicotine and to take up smoking.

Of the significantly disabling substances of abuse, the most common is alcohol, which can do an excellent job of drowning out pain. While drinking during depression is not unusual, some people drink less when they are depressed, often because they recognize that alcohol is a depressant and that excessive drinking during a depression can severely exacerbate the depression. My experience is that alcohol is not particularly tempting when you are experiencing pure depression, but that it is very tempting when you are experiencing anxiety. The problem is that the same alcohol that takes the edge off anxiety tends to exacerbate depression, so that you go from feeling tense and frightened to feeling desolate and worthless. This is not an improvement. I've gone for the bottle under these circumstances and have survived to tell the truth: it doesn't help.

Having lived with various norms of alcohol consumption, I believe that what constitutes an addiction is highly socially determined. I grew up in a household in which wine was served with dinner, and I had two sips in my glass starting when I was about six. When I got to college, I found that I was a pretty good drinker: I could handle liquor well. On the other hand, drinking was more or less discouraged at my school, and people who drank too much were thought of as "troubled." I conformed to the standards. At the university I subsequently attended in England, drinking was all the rage, and people who held back were thought of as "stiff" and "unamusing." I do not like to consider myself a sheep, but I conformed perfectly to this new system. A few months after I began my graduate work in England, I was initiated into a dining society, and as part of a rather stupid ritual I was made to drink a half gallon of gin. It was something of a breakthrough for me and broke down an incipient fear of drunkenness that had previously afflicted me. At that stage of my life, I did not suffer from depression to any great extent, but I was an anxious person given to paroxysms of trepidation. A few months later I went to a dinner and was seated next to a girl with whom I was infatuated, and believing that alcohol would take the edge off the intense self-consciousness she caused me, I agreeably downed about two and a half bottles of wine during dinner. Apparently self-conscious as well, she drank nearly as much, and we both woke up on a pile of coats in the small hours of the morning. No particular shame was attached to this. If you were willing to pay out in headaches and could get the reading done for your next essay, you were most welcome to drink yourself into a stupor every night of the week. It never occurred to me or my friends that I was in danger of becoming an alcoholic.

When I was twenty-five, I started working on my first book, which was about vanguard Soviet artists. While my English drinking had been sporadic and intense, my Russian drinking was steady. It was not, however, depressive: the society in which I lived in Russia was one of alcoholic exhilaration. Moscow water was almost undrinkable, and I can remember saying that I thought the real miracle would be for someone to turn my wine to water, not the other way around. I spent the summer of 1989 living in a squat with a group of artists on the outskirts of Moscow, and I would guess that I drank a quart of vodka a day. By the end of a month, I didn't notice how much I was drinking; I was accustomed to stumbling out of bed at noon and finding a circle of friends smoking cigarettes, boiling water for tea on a little electric burner, and drinking vodka out of dirty glasses. I thought the tea was disgusting—like warm water with bits of mud floating in it—and so I would have the morning vodka and the day would go on, getting softer with the steady consumption of alcohol. This sustained drinking never made me feel drunk, and I can say in retrospect that it did a lot for me. I had grown up in a rather protected way in the United States, and my feeling of camaraderie with my Russian friends was very much enabled by the combination of communal living and persistent drinking. Of course, a few people among us drank too much even by the standards of the society we inhabited. One man would drink himself into a stupor, wander around incoherent, then pass out every night. He snored like the percussion section of a heavy-metal band. The great trick was to make sure he didn't pass out in your room and especially on your bed. I can remember standing with six other men and heaving the enormous bulk of this unconscious character onto the floor; once we hauled him down three flights of stairs without his ever waking up. To have stuck to my U.S. drinking standards would have been not only rude but also peculiar in these circles. Perhaps more significantly, the drinking liberated my Moscow friends from their social diet of boredom and dread. They were leading marginal lives in an oppressive society at a confusing moment in history, and to express ourselves freely and to dance and laugh in the way we did, to achieve a certain exaggerated intimacy, we had to keep drinking. "In Sweden," one of my Russian friends said after he had visited that country, "people drink to avoid intimacy. In Russia, we drink because we love one another so much."

Drinking is not a simple matter: it has divergent motivations and effects on various people in disparate places. Raising the taxes on alcoholic beverages in Scandinavian countries is believed to keep a lid on suicide rates. I have read many studies that say that being an alcoholic is depressing, but I do not believe that all alcoholics are depressed. The relationship between depression and alcohol is a matter of temperament and context, two highly variable attributes. I definitely drink more when I am anxious—in ordinary anxiety-producing social interactions or when a little bit of depression-style anxiety comes sweeping across me—and I have found myself disturbingly reliant on alcohol during rough times. My tolerance goes up and down and my response is inconsistent; I have taken alcohol and felt the tension lift, but I have also had a bit to drink and felt perilously suicidal, and overwhelmed, and weak, and afraid. I know that I shouldn't drink when I'm feeling depressed, and if I stay at home, I don't drink; but in social situations it's hard to say no, and harder yet to tread that line between alleviating fretfullness and inviting despondency. I often get it wrong.

Acute drinking will of course lead to headaches and feelings of inefficiency or incompetence, as well as indigestion. Serious alcoholism over a protracted time may lead to cognitive impairment or even to psychosis, as well as to severe physical ailments such as cirrhosis; alcoholics tend to die younger than nondrinkers. Withdrawal from chronic alcohol use may include delirium tremens, which can be fatal. Ninety percent of Americans now living have consumed alcohol at some stage during their life. In the United States, about 10 percent of men and 5 percent of women develop physiological alcohol addiction—which means that they will experience elevated heart rate, delirium tremens, and agitation if they attempt to give up drinking. The physiological mechanism of alcohol in the brain is not fully understood; nor is the physiological basis for consumption, though serotonin seems to affect one's ability to resist the temptation to drink. It appears that alcohol at high doses has an adverse effect on neurotransmitters, possibly via certain GABA receptors, which are also the target for Valium. Continued drinking seriously affects memory and appears to cause permanent damage to the ability to order new experiences, incorporating them into a through line of recollection. This means that one loses the essential shape of one's own history; life is remembered in spots and episodes rather than as a coherent narrative.

There are many models for treating alcoholism apart from depression, but when the two conditions exist together, psychodynamic therapies appear to be most effective. Alcoholics Anonymous and other twelve-step programs provide supportive settings in which people can share both their experiences of alcoholism and their experiences of depression. Other group therapies and even short-term institutionalization are also highly productive at addressing alcoholism and depression as if they spring from a single cause. For many people, this works whether there is a single cause or not. Practitioners at Columbia University use an individual cognitive-behavioral therapy in the interests of relapse prevention. The program is written down and can be practiced in the same way by any clinician. "It is very much a 'here and now' form of therapy," David McDowell explains. The typical treatment course begins with a week or two to address the person's cravings and then goes on to elucidate an individual's triggers for relapse and to figure out how to deal with them.

Alcoholism has more recently been treated with Antabuse, a drug that alters alcohol metabolism and diminishes tolerance for alcohol. It is a sort of self-discipline extender. People who wake up full of determination but find their will weakening at noonday often take Antabuse to enforce their decision not to drink. People in detox are usually highly ambivalent, and Antabuse helps them to seize on the desire for freedom rather than the desire for an addictive substance. One doctor who works with high-powered substance abusers, mostly doctors and lawyers, has them write and sign and give to him letters of resignation to their licensing board; if they relapse, he mails the letters. Some of those who work on addiction have been using drugs that block the effects of substances of abuse, thus destroying motivation for abuse. Naltrexone, for example, is a narcotic antagonist that blocks the effects of heroin. It also prevents alcohol from exerting an influence on endorphins, so destroying the most common motives for drinking. If you're on Naltrexone, you aren't going to get any form of pleasure out of the substances you abuse. The drug has been successful in helping people to break the patterns of addiction because it undermines motivational desire.

The earliest written reference to marijuana is in a Chinese text on herbal remedies of the fifteenth century B.C., but the stuff did not become common in the West until Napoleon's army brought it back from Egypt. Like alcohol, marijuana interferes with REM sleep. The brain has a specific receptor that responds to at least one of the many chemicals contained in marijuana smoke, which taps into the pleasure-reward circuitry of the brain. Marijuana is antimotivational and in this mimics symptoms of depression. Withdrawal is unpleasant but not agonizing (as with heroin), nor potentially life-threatening (as with alcohol), nor protracted (as with cocaine), and so the drug is often described as nonaddictive. Marijuana slows you down and may be used as an antianxiety drug; agitated depression may in fact be helped by marijuana. Since marijuana is not legally available, it is hard to control quantities and proportions ingested; and because the smoked or pyrolyzed dry leaf has about four hundred identifiable compounds, the effects of most of which are unknown, the effects are not pure. Occasional use of marijuana by a nonaddicted person to take the edge off a highly agitated depression is not an unreasonable mode of self-treatment. Though much work is now being done on medical uses for marijuana, these studies have not, so far, focused on its use for psychiatric complaints. Regular marijuana use becomes antimotivational and "has real neuro-cognitive changes which might as well be physiologically permanent if you're high all the time," McDowell says. Marijuana also, of course, carries all the toxicity of cigarettes, causing significant damage to the lungs.

Hard drugs are those that cause high morbidity: caffeine is a stimulant and so is crack, but crack is classed as a hard drug because it is much more addictive and because it has a more sudden effect on the brain. Hard drugs are the most likely to become depressing—in part because they are super-illegal and acquiring them can mess up your life, in part because they are expensive, in part because they are usually impure, in part because people who abuse them tend to abuse alcohol too, in part because of the way they operate on your central nervous system. The relatives of people who abuse stimulants have high rates of depression. This would seem to indicate that a genetic predisposition toward depression may precede use of cocaine and other stimulants. Only about 15 percent of people who try cocaine become addicted to it, but for those who are prone, cocaine is the most addictive drug there is. Some lab rats will consistently choose cocaine-type stimulants over food or sex and, if they are given unlimited access, will use these stimulants until they die of exhaustion.

Cocaine is an expensive antidepressant that causes an intense crash, which usually hits rock bottom about forty-eight to seventy-two hours after the high. "It's a dirty drug that affects everything," David McDowell says. "And it's constantly depleting your neurotransmitter stores, so that you come crashing down." The crash is characterized by intense feelings of agitation, depression, and fatigue. It would appear that the rush of dopamine that is released when one is experiencing the amphetamine or cocaine high actually depletes stores of dopamine, resulting in reduced dopamine levels in the brain. Herbert Kleber of Columbia says, "If the crash were bad enough, no one would use cocaine; and if the crash were mild enough, it wouldn't matter that people use it. It's that particular cocaine crash that does all the negative reinforcing, that gets people desperate." The more addicted you get, the less pleasure you experience, and the more pain follows on the heels of pleasure. Cocaine and amphetamines seem to adversely affect many neurotransmitter systems, not only dopamine but also norepinephrine and serotonin. In some people, nonetheless, acute craving for the drugs can last for decades after giving them up.

Continued use of cocaine exacerbates depressive symptoms. A ten-week course of antidepressants will often get someone who wants to get off cocaine through the extended aftermath of the drug crash, but depending on underlying conditions and neurological damage, depression may require permanent treatment. Regular use of cocaine or amphetamines may do permanent damage to the dopamine systems of the brain, giving one a permanent physiological depressed baseline. Cocaine is one of a number of drugs that might be called long-term depression augmenters. It seems to alter the functioning of the anxiety mechanisms of the brain by altering levels of corticotropin releasing factor (CRF). Whether, or when, the brain has enough plasticity to recover from such changes is not clear. Some brains seem to be able to compensate better than others. A brain on antidepressants, a brain that has a capacity to sink into severe depression, is a delicately balanced organ. Parts of the brain that are involved in addiction and drugs of abuse are also involved in the regulation of moods, and they are germane to affective disorder. Depleting the dopamine reserves and mucking around with CRF in such a brain is inviting disaster. If you have any inclination whatsoever toward depression, don't use cocaine: no matter how good you may feel during the initial rush, you will feel terrible afterward, much more terrible than can possibly be worth it.

I had taken cocaine and found it charmless when I was in college. I tried it again a decade later and it was a totally different experience—perhaps because of aging; perhaps because of a brain more vulnerable in the aftermath of my depression; perhaps because of the antidepressants I take. It gives me a kind of blissful energy and a sexual exuberance and a feeling of superhero power that are quite fantastic. I get to the point of being unable to string together a sentence and I don't care if I never string together a sentence again. I realize that the solutions to everything are simple and straightforward. Being high on cocaine breaks up your memory enough so that the past can't haunt the future. The chemical happiness of a good hit of cocaine feels completely uncircumstantial. I can remember sitting around with a numb nose, thinking that if I could freeze life in that second, I would do so and stay there forever. I almost never use the drug, but the idea that I would never want it is ridiculous. I fell in love with cocaine in those first minutes of rush. The specter of imbalancing my brain and the devastating hangover are all that keep me away from the cocaine high.

Opiates, another class of much abused substances, are extremely dangerous in part because of how they are consumed; and they are depressants, which means that they do not do great things for depression. On the other hand, they don't lead to the kind of desperate crash that cocaine will bring about. A quarter to half of opiate abusers are depressive. Opiates, including opium, heroin, and prescription drugs such as Demerol, are to the mind what the fetal position is to the body. Opiates blot out time, so that you cannot remember where your thoughts come from, cannot tell whether they are new or old, cannot get them to interact with one another. The world closes in around you. Your eyes can process only one object at a time, and your mind can hold just one thought at a time, and you don't really care what you do because the present has become unfocused and piecemeal the way memories are usually unfocused and piecemeal. The opiate high lasts for hours. It is an experience of perfect not-wanting. I have never taken heroin, but I have smoked opium, and only on opium have I ever felt that I simply don't want anything: to scratch my head, to eat, to sleep, to get up, to lie down, to make plans, to be truly great, to remember friends. It is a nonintimate drug; it kills my sex drive and cuts me off from other people, so that I lie shallow-eyed, staring off into diagonal space. It provokes a happy listlessness, an idleness that driven people can't experience any other way. It also entails a kind of short-term absence of memory (Did I say anything to that person? Do I know which one that is?) that, when it's brief, constitutes a high—and, were it further protracted, would be suggestive of Alzheimer's disease. Writing this, I can recall how opium set my brain free and made me balloon man, floating serenely through the air. Opiates are classed as depressants, but their effect is not simple suppression of feelings; it is a species of joy that comes of having your feelings suppressed. On opiates, you can give anxious depression the slip. An opiate high feels like the prelapsarian version of life, when doing nothing at all was quite sufficient.

People who have come off heroin and other opiates and are being maintained either drug-free or on methadone suffer a high rate of depression. Neurologists say this is because of organic damage to the brain. Psychologists say this is because these people were depressive in the first place and depression led them to addiction. Either way, your mood prognosis after extended abuse of opiates is not good. The opiate withdrawal period is particularly gruesome; the cravings are strong, and depression weakens will, making it much harder to withdraw. On the other hand, heroin is not as highly addictive as the "war on drugs" rhetoric would suggest. During the Vietnam War, most of the ground troops used heroin, and there was fear that upon their return, the United States would have to fight a terrible battle with the drug. In fact, studies indicate that most veterans of Vietnam have used heroin at least once since their return, but only a small proportion of them have a continuing addiction.

Hallucinogens and the "club drugs" (ecstasy/MDMA, Special K/ketamine, GHB) make up another class of substances of abuse. Perhaps my personal favorite (and least favorite) drug of all is ecstasy, which I have taken only four times. I saved one relationship that was in trouble when

I took E and said a lot of things I felt but hadn't been able to say. I got another year out of that relationship, and I wonder whether with another dose of E every six months I might have ended up in a happy marriage. I'm kind of a passionate idealist under the best of circumstances, and when I have taken E, I realize that I can save the world and I get excited about doing it. I begin by communicating enormous love to everyone within reach. The solutions to all my problems become clear. Unfortunately, the solutions I devise usually turn out, when I come back down, to be rather unsatisfactory. It would not solve all my problems (or theirs) for me to marry into the British royal family, nor would there be any expedient way of accomplishing that objective. It would not be a good idea to title this book *Poems from the Dark Side* or *The Little Golden Book of Depression*. I do not have the qualifications to become a professional ski instructor in Argentina or anywhere else. But though the lucidity is false, the feeling of lucidity is lovely. Ecstasy also gives me an unbelievable three-day hangover during which my jaw aches, my mouth is dry, and my head feels like the French Revolution. I don't tend to get bad hangovers from alcohol or any other drugs, but my down stretch after ecstasy was enough to keep me from using it regularly.

Reading the clinical pharmacology of ecstasy makes my stomach turn. The idea that I ever allowed such a substance to enter my body appalls me. At the doses used for recreational purposes (between a hundred and a hundred fifty milligrams), ecstasy damages brain serotonin axons—the part of the nerve cell that reaches out to other cells—in monkeys and other mammals. The evidence strongly suggests that it does the same thing in humans. The drug essentially causes an explosion of serotonin and dopamine, releasing big stores of these substances and then damaging the cells where they were stored. Furthermore, it prevents the synthesis of more serotonin. Regular users of ecstasy have lower serotonin levels than other people, sometimes as much as 35 percent lower. Researchers have reported a number of episodes of a single dose of ecstasy triggering permanent psychiatric illness—sometimes immediately, and sometimes years later. Depressed people are in no position to be lowering their serotonin levels and should therefore give this drug the widest possible berth. "If you take a lot of it over an extended time, you may destroy your capacity to feel happiness; it can cause in the long term the adverse effects that cocaine causes in the short term," David McDowell of Columbia says of the drug. "Freshmen love it; sophomores like it; juniors worry about it; and seniors are afraid of it. Alcohol can become your best friend, but ecstasy can't. My real fear is that a lot of people who have used a lot of ecstasy in the past two decades are going to think they're fine, and then when they turn fifty, they're going to plummet. Depressed patients who use the drug? I say to them, 'In twenty years, do you want to be on three medications or on ten?'"

The benzodiazepines (or benzos)—Valium, Xanax, Klonopin—and their cousins (Ambien and Sonata) are perhaps the most confusing drugs of all: they are addictive and they are useful for psychiatric complaints. They are very effective against anxiety, but because there is a lot of cross-tolerance between them and barbiturates or alcohol, they should not usually be prescribed for people likely to abuse those substances. The benzos are a valid short-term way of dealing with something that needs both an immediate and a long-term solution. The idea is to get on other medications that will allow you to taper off the benzos and then to use them only for regulatory purposes, to help on days when one particularly requires help. To take the benzos daily long-term is ill-advised and dangerous. The benzos that are most often sold on the street are short-acting ones, roofies, called the "date-rape drug" because they induce a temporary miasma in which someone cannot necessarily assert or defend herself. In general, however, the benzos are abused by people for whom they have been prescribed. You should always think twice before you take a benzo, and if you find yourself needing escalating doses, you should figure out why. Covering up symptoms with benzos is like taking antacids for stomach cancer.

I am a huge fan of the benzos because I believe that Xanax saved my life when it alleviated my insane anxiety. I have used Xanax and Valium for sleep when I am in agitated periods. I have gone through miniature benzo withdrawal a good dozen times. It is important to use the benzos only for their primary purpose, which is to allay anxiety; this they will do fairly consistently at fairly consistent levels. When my anxiety is high, I need more of the benzos; when it is moderate, I need less. Nonetheless, I am aware of the dangers of these drugs. I have made little forays into substance abuse, but I had never been addicted to anything until Xanax was prescribed for me. I stopped taking drugs abruptly at the end of my first go-around with depression. It was not a good strategy. The withdrawal symptoms from Xanax—which I had been taking on doctor's advice for several months at a rate of, on average, two milligrams a day—were horrible. For at least three weeks after I stopped taking Xanax, I could not sleep properly, and I felt anxious and strangely tentative. I also felt the whole time as though I'd had several gallons of cheap cognac the night before. My eyes hurt and I had an upset stomach. At night, when I was not really asleep, I had unrelenting, terrifying half-waking nightmares, and I kept sitting up with my heart pounding.

I went off Zyprexa, the drug that saved me from my mini-breakdown, a few weeks after I finished a draft of this book, and I had another round of acute withdrawal. I put myself through it because Zyprexa had caused me to gain seventeen pounds in eight months, but while I was getting off the drug, I felt unspeakably awful. My dopamine system was dysregulated, and I was anxious, withdrawn, and overwhelmed. There was a knot in the pit of my abdomen that seemed to tighten like an internal noose around my stomach. If I had not had hopes for improvement, I would have contemplated suicide. The horrendous strung-out feeling was worse than I could have remembered. I kept poking at my little potbelly and asking myself why I was so vain. I wondered whether I could control my weight while on Zyprexa by doing a thousand sit-ups every day, but I knew that when I was on Zyprexa, I didn't have the wherewithal to do a hundred sit-ups every day. Going off Zyprexa just turned up all my energies—it grated in the same way that a perfectly nice piece of music will suddenly turn painful and distorted if you shoot the volume way up to the top of your stereo's range. It was hell. I put up with this for three long weeks; and though I did not have a breakdown, I felt so low by the end of the third week that I lost interest in seeing whether my body could bring my dopamine system back into line. I chose fat and functional over slender and miserable. I forced myself to give up the sweets I always loved and to do ninety minutes of exercise every morning, and I stabilized at a weight that didn't please me. I gradually cut my dose in half. I soon lost ten pounds. To get my energy up and going while on the Zyprexa, my psychopharmacologist added in Dexedrine. *Another* pill? What the hell—I take it only when I'm at my worst.

I no longer take Xanax regularly, but am I addicted to the little cocktail of antidepressants—Effexor, Wellbutrin, BuSpar, and Zyprexa—that allowed me to write this book? Am I dependent on them? The most acute version of this question is whether the drugs I have been taking will all remain legal. Heroin was originally developed by the Bayer aspirin people as a cough medicine, and ecstasy was patented by pharmacologists in Germany before the First World War. Drugs regularly move from the world of medicine to the world of abuse and back. We seem currently to endorse any drug that does not essentially impair functioning. I think about the effect that Zyprexa had in my most recent round of battles with depression. What is Zyprexa really doing inside my brain? If going off Zyprexa gave me all those fidgety, anxious symptoms of withdrawal, then was it a drug on which I was reliant? How would I react if someone told me that in the wake of recent discoveries, Zyprexa had been positioned among the enemies in the war against drugs?

Michael Pollan has argued in the *New York Times Magazine* that there is in fact no truly consistent basis for declaring substances legal or illegal and writes, "The media are filled with gauzy pharmaceutical ads promising not just relief from pain but also pleasure and even fulfillment; at the same time, Madison Avenue is working equally hard to demonize other substances on behalf of a 'drug-free America.' The more we spend on our worship of the good drugs (twenty billion dollars on psychoactive prescription drugs last year), the more we spend warring the evil ones (seventeen billion dollars the same year). We hate drugs. We love drugs. Or could it be that we hate the fact that we love drugs?" In principle, addictive, illicit drug taking crowds out all other activities, while antidepressant drugs make you function better than you would without them and do not cause long-term harm. William Potter, who formerly ran the psychopharmacological division of the NIMH, comments, "We've made a judgment that drugs that prevent you from experiencing appropriate emotional response are not acceptable. That's why cocaine is illegal. There are too many problems when you cease to detect warning signs and threats. You pay a price for an excessive high. That's not moralizing; that's just my observation." In contrast, "No one gets an intense Zoloft craving," says Steven Hyman. "No one would ever kill to get a Zoloft." They also do not produce either euphoria or supersize relaxation. One does not speak of a diabetic as being addicted to insulin. Perhaps our society's emphasis on deferred gratification is so intense that we simply prefer those drugs that make you feel bad (side effects) and then good (mood effects) to drugs that make you feel good (high) and then bad (hungover)? Still, are new-generation antidepressants anabolic steroids for the brain? The psychiatrist Peter Kramer, in his famous book *Listening to Prozac*, wondered whether people who take these drugs have an unfair advantage, thus creating pressure for others to take them. Will they reproduce the effect of modernization, which has been not to give people free time but to raise expectations and speed up life? Are we at the brink of making a breed of Supermans?

It is certainly true that antidepressant drugs are hard to give up; I have in two years tried three times to get off Zyprexa and failed every time. Getting people off the SSRIs can be very difficult. The drugs are not intoxicants, but they make you feel better and they do have a lot of adverse side effects—mostly adverse for the individual rather than for the society, but distinctly adverse nonetheless. I feel some concern for my overall state of mental health, and I exercise considerable care around readjusting my brain chemistry: I am terrified of plummeting back into the abyss, and no high could be worth that. I'm too mistrustful of recreational drugs to get much pleasure out of them these days. But on the rare occasions when I have taken them and had a high, I have had to contrast that heady feeling with the effect of the prescribed medications on which

I am now reliant. I wonder whether the permanent repitching of my personality just a notch higher is not somewhat akin to the heady high. I actually write pretty well in altered states: I have come up with good prose at the end of a night of drinking, and I have spun out some ideas when I was flying on cocaine. I certainly wouldn't want to be in either state all the time, but I wonder just where I would pitch my personality if anything were possible. I'd definitely bring it up a few levels from where it is now. I'd like to have the boundless energy, the quick precision, and the apparent resilience of, say, Wayne Gretzky. If I found a drug that would give me those properties, would it necessarily be an illicit one? Much is made of the fact that antidepressant medications do not provide immediate relief, while substances of abuse mostly give you a desired high really fast. Is it simply that speed of effect that so disturbs us, that eerie bewitched-before-your-very-eyes phenomenon? If someone made up a powder that didn't deplete neurotransmitters and that didn't bring about a crash and that instead allowed me to function like Wayne Gretzky so long as I inhaled it every five hours, would that necessarily have to be illegal?

To my mind, I am no longer independent. The medications are expensive, though they are at least regularly and conveniently supplied. I don't mind the idea that I am reliant on them, nor the idea that reliance is a cousin of addiction. So long as they work, I'm pleased to take them. I carry pills around in my pocket all the time every day, so that I will have them in case I can't for some reason get home one night. I take bottles of pills on airplanes because I have always thought that if I were hijacked and held prisoner, I'd try to keep the medication secreted about my person. Janet Benshoof recalls being put in prison in Guam and calling her psychiatrist from jail. "He was frantic about my having a depression in prison, not to mention withdrawal, and he was vigorously trying to get antidepressants through the security system for me. It was hysterical; I was hysterical too."

I pop about twelve pills a day to keep myself from getting too down. Frankly, if I could accomplish the same effect with two good drinks (and I know people who can), that would be a perfectly satisfactory alternative, so long as it didn't turn into three drinks or four drinks or eight drinks—which, if you are fighting depression, it usually does. A dependence on alcohol may be fully socially acceptable even if it interferes with REM sleep. I was charmed by someone I used to know who would at six o'clock sharp cry out, as he decanted his whiskey, "Every fiber of my being cries out for alcohol." He had built a life that accommodated his evening vagaries, and I think it was a happy life, though when he once visited a Mormon household in which alcohol was unavailable, he hardly made it through the evening. It would be stupid to put such a man on

Prozac instead. For other substances, the law often creates trouble instead of controlling it—or as Keith Richards put it, "I don't have a drug problem; I have a police problem." I have known people who used marijuana and even cocaine in truly controlled and disciplined ways that improved their states of mind and being. Ann Marlowe's book *how to stop time: heroin from A to Z* convincingly describes reasonable controlled manipulation of mood with heroin. She took heroin on and off for many years without ever becoming addicted to it.

The big problem with self-medication, far worse than the selection of inappropriate substances, is that it is so often inept and ill-informed. "I deal with bad cocaine abusers," says David McDowell of Columbia. "People who are using a hundred fifty dollars' worth of cocaine a day at least twenty-two days a month. And they don't like the idea of medication and think it sounds unnatural. Unlike what they get from Billy the dealer! These substances are unregulated, and utterly unreliable."

Many of the people quoted in this book have had substantial problems with substance abuse, and many of them have blamed substances for their depression. Tina Sonego is unusually frank about the interaction of the two kinds of trouble. She is a woman with unusual vitality, a rich sense of humor, and staying power. Over a span of three years, fifty letters, and dozens of E-mails, she created an intimacy with me purely by supposing it. She took to "freebasing my dark moods on paper," as she described it, and the result was a remarkable set of documents of rising and falling moods. Her struggles with self-destructiveness and addiction and depression are so tightly bound together that it is nearly impossible to see where one breaks off and another begins.

Tina Sonego is a flight attendant for an international charter airline flying the U.S. military to engagements and flying customers for cruises and group holidays. She calls herself a "people pleaser" who has spent a lifetime trying to be nice enough to people so they'd like her. "I am funny," she says, "and loud, and cute, and sexy—I'm everything you'd want a stewardess to be. I form completely happy emotional attachments to my passengers, for eight hours, and then they're gone." She is in her mid-forties, and her upbeat manner belies a lifelong struggle with depression and alcoholism. She has a quick mind, but "intelligence was not a thing in my family; no one ever even thought of it," and since she suffers from dyslexia, she never got past high school. Her grandmother was a maid who was expected to provide sexual services to her employer in Morocco; her grandfather was a furniture maker who grew hash there for export. She was born of first-generation immigrants on both sides and grew up in a Moroccan enclave in California, speaking a mix of French, Spanish, and Arabic at home. Mental illness had no place in this world. "I was asking questions that didn't have any place in our house. So I learned to perform, and I had an outside persona so that no one would ever see the sad, self-loathing woman inside me. I was split in half. And depression was what happened when the halves hit." Tina's father was moody, perhaps depressive, a man who had to be sheltered from anything upsetting; her mother "needs TLC but does not give it. She told me years ago, 'Honey, I can't make myself more sensitive just to understand you.'" Her sister was the same. "I was watching TV with her a few years ago, and I said, 'Who's that character?' and she told me everything that had happened in the character's life for the past twenty years. And she doesn't even know what guy I'm going out with. I grew up thinking I was damaged goods." After Tina's father died, her mother remarried. Tina adores her stepfather and gives him much credit for her relative good health today.

Tina had her first full-fledged breakdown when she was nineteen, traveling in Israel and planning to write a book about kibbutzim. Her sister had to come and rescue her and bring her home. A few years later, she decided to move to Rome to be with a man she loved, and when she arrived, "the relationship turned metallic, sex was beyond impossible, and I had nothing to say." She had sunk into another depression. Like many depressives who abuse substances, she suffered from particularly acute self-loathing and was drawn to criminal people who would treat her violently. A few years after the Rome episode, she married a Dane and moved to Copenhagen. That lasted less than two years; after the murder of her husband's mistress, both she and her husband were questioned at length. Though they were both released, the marriage had been destroyed; he threw her out, and she had another breakdown. Her work at the time was flying soldiers to Desert Storm. She was on a layover in Rome and suddenly found she could not go on. "I still remember the moment. I ordered a chicken salad and it tasted like chalk. I knew I was depressed. And I went downhill so fast. That's when I really started drinking. I just did everything to fuck myself up to the bitter end. I would just black out and drink and black out and drink and black out and drink. I always left suicide notes: if I don't wake up, call my mother. I was using alcohol to kill myself. It was the easiest drug I knew; it was cheap; it was accessible. And it is respectable."

She entered a psychiatric hospital in South Carolina, which was "like a holding area, where they were supposed to try to fix you, and the depressed people never got any attention because we didn't make noise like the other crazies. I felt like Chicken Little, like the sky was falling. Oh, the anxiety! Anxiety in depression is this feeling like you have a terrible secret, and everyone's going to find out, and you don't even know what the secret is." She went on antidepressants and some other prescription drugs and mixed them with alcohol in an attempt to overcome anxiety. She had two grand mal convulsions as a result and ended up unconscious for three days in another hospital.

For Tina, depression was not numbness but pain. "I felt like a sponge that was waterlogged with passion, heavy and bloated. I was not silent in my pain. I would stay up all night writing letters to God in the dark. I was not born to be happy, joyous, free. If my body had its druthers, I'd be depressed all the time. When I was a little girl, my mother used to tell me, 'Be happy or go to your room with that sour face.' I wasn't being deliberately like that. It's just that that's who I am." Interaction with other people is often acutely painful for Tina Sonego. "Dating, to me, was the most excruciating thing that God ever made. I used to throw up in the bathroom. I got married to escape the pain—it hurts me to death, wondering why no one asks me out." Tina Sonego soon married her second husband, a Malaysian living in the United States who got in trouble with the law and returned home. She followed him to his mother's traditional Islamic household. The constraints were simply beyond her. "My breakdown spiraled fast when I was there; I flew home sicker than I had ever been in twenty years."

Back in the United States, she continued drinking; it was the only way she could find to control crippling anxiety. Periodically she would go to rehab and recover partway for a short time—she has now been through full-scale rehab four times. Her insurance didn't cover treatment for addiction, but she was able to use the mental health diagnosis to get expenses covered. "The rehab program? It's the last stop before Lourdes," she says.

Tina Sonego went to her first AA meeting about a decade ago, and the program has been her lifesaver. She describes it as the only place she has ever been able to be honest with people. The program has not freed her of depression, but it has given her a different methodology for dealing with it. "Without the alcohol in your body trying to blot out the bad emotions, they all come out like firecrackers. But thank God I was at least a drunk, and there was something I could do about it. I went to a meeting of Emotions Anonymous, and I felt so bad for all those people because they had nothing to remove, nothing they could see to fix. Drunks are such hard-core people. There's nothing like a drunk saying, 'Well, did you take a drink over it?' I can talk to them about depression, like I own it. It's like getting a college degree, and then you have the right to talk about some things and not feel weird about them. That's all us drunks really want, is someone to tell our story to, someone we know will listen."

When she first began to be sober, Tina Sonego despaired. "That was the worst depression I ever had. That was when I secluded myself in my apartment, and since I couldn't make decisions, I just ate turkey and bologna sandwiches for a month. Depression is a search for invalidation. And you can always find as much as you want. When you're depressed, you keep seeking to prove that you're unworthy. We had this discussion at AA: Who are our judges? And I realized that if one judge wasn't giving me the negative response I needed, I'd just find another one. Even now, as I catch on to a rising star, I hear my sister saying, 'Oh, you're trying to be bigger than you are.'

"I've now been through my fifth, sixth, seventh episodes and it's like 'It's back! I know what's happening!' It reminds me of when you've been absorbed in a movie and suddenly the credits start to roll and you fall back into your own life. That's how it feels. Like the movie is over. I still can't do a thing about it. But you do get to the point where you realize it's not going to last forever, where you can finally be able to just wait."

She has continued going to AA meetings for five years now—"it's like summer camp for your brain," she says. "I'm tired of trying to find out why. Why did I have breakdowns, become a drunk? It would be interesting to know, but why waste the time: knowing isn't going to make me feel any better. Sobriety is like a pyramid, and every time we go up a step we feel like we're getting somewhere, and yet there's always another step to go. When we look down, we can't really see the steps we've taken and so we feel desperate, but if we look up, we'll see God's finger piercing the sky and know we're going the right way."

Tina Sonego describes the moment when she felt the drinking and the worst of the depression had lifted. "I was in Japan, and they had these beautiful flowers in the middle of a department store. And I just stopped there and touched these flowers, and I said, 'I have a relationship with you.' I looked at those beautiful flowers and said, 'I've got a relationship with you right now.' It doesn't mean it has to last forever; it doesn't mean I have to carry you with me. It's just, I have a relationship with you right now. And so, to this day, I still remember those flowers. I still remember the joy they gave me for that one moment." A few years later "I had an epiphany at the Frankfurt airport. I walked around, drank coffee, smoked cigarettes, and just wondered what the hell was going on in my life, because something felt different. And I didn't know what it was. And then I did. I finally had a voice. I didn't know what to do with it yet, but I knew I had a voice."

It is a hard-won voice, but it is a clarion one. Tina Sonego is capable of being amazingly upbeat; she is a trained tap dancer who will go up to the roof of the hotel where she is staying to practice dancing and breathe the night air.

"I miss the hungry years. God, I miss the hungry years. I miss the therapists who just got down on their hands and knees and tried to make me well. And I miss the amount of emotion, even if it was bad emotion. I'll never again have that amount of emotion unless I crash again. Life will always be an experiment for me after depression, the big Ds. But I have realized the fruits of depression—though I would have slapped the face of anyone who mentioned that idea to me when I was sick. I have this dream, of getting together with a bunch of survivors of serious depression and addiction and spending a night all together dancing and laughing about the big Ds. That's my idea of heaven."

I have a fairly nonaddictive personality. I have had withdrawal from certain substances, but I have never had a compulsion to consume anything. A drink does not particularly make me want another drink. A good feeling that I know to be dangerous does not overwhelm me to the point at which I want another good feeling. I had never been very sympathetic with addiction until I started taking Zyprexa. It was not the addiction to Zyprexa that made the difference. No, it was that Zyprexa destroyed the set point of my appetite. Nowadays, I can eat a perfectly normal meal and still be famished, and that hunger can be so extreme as to drive me out of my house in the middle of the night to get food. I sit with my hunger and think about how ugly a paunch can be; I remember hours of exercise that burned only a few calories. Then I feel that if I don't eat, I'll die, and I break down, and I go and stuff myself. Then I hate having done it. I don't make myself throw up because I don't want to get into a pattern of doing so; and besides, I have an iron stomach and almost nothing makes me throw up. Zyprexa addicted me to food, and at one point I had gained twenty-five pounds because of it. If you could find something that did for libido what Zyprexa does for appetite, you'd be spinning out the Don Juans. I have learned what it is like to have an overpowering, compelling drive toward a self-destructive consuming. Within the normal fluctuations of my moods, a good mood gives me self-discipline and I stave off the chocolate cupcakes; but a depressed mood saps me of that strength. Depression enables addiction. Resisting desires takes so much energy and will, and when you are depressed, it is too hard just to say no—to food, to alcohol, to drugs. It's really simple. Depression weakens you. Weakness is the surest path to addiction. Why should you say no when no will lead you only to more intolerable misery?

CHAPTER VII

Suicide

Many depressives never become suicidal. Many suicides are committed by people who are not depressed. The two subjects are not parts of a single lucid equation, one occasioning the other. They are separate entities that frequently coexist, each influencing the other. "Suicidality" is one of the nine symptoms of a depressive episode listed in *DSM-IV,* but many depressed people are no more inclined to end their lives than are people with appalling arthritis: the human capacity to bear pain is shockingly strong. Only if one decides that suicidality is a sufficient condition for a diagnosis of depression can one say that the suicidal are always depressed.

Suicidality has been treated as a *symptom* of depression when it may in fact be a problem that coexists with depression. We no longer treat alcoholism as a side effect of depression: we treat it as a problem that occurs simultaneously with depression. Suicidality is at least as independent of the depressions with which it often coincides as is substance abuse. George Howe Colt, author of *The Enigma of Suicide,* says, "Many clinicians believe that if they successfully [treat depression], they've treated the suicidal patient, as if suicidality were simply a nasty side effect of the underlying illness. Yet some suicidal patients have no diagnosable underlying illness, and patients often kill themselves shortly after coming out of a depression—or long after a depression has lifted." A clinician treating someone who is depressed and suicidal will in general focus on curing the depression. While curing the depression may help to forestall the suicide, it will not necessarily do so. Almost half of all suicides in the United States are committed by people who have been in the care of a psychiatrist, and yet most come as a great surprise. There is something wrong with our thinking. One should not assume that suicidality can be lumped in with symptoms such as disrupted sleep; nor should one stop treating suicidality simply because the depression with which it has been associated seems to have lifted. Suicidality is an associated problem that requires its own treatment. Why is it not classed as a diagnosis of its own, related to and overlapping with depression, but essentially distinct from it?

Attempts to define suicidal depression have been singularly fruitless. No strong correlation exists between the severity of depression and the likelihood of suicide: some suicides seem to occur during mild disorders, while some people with desperate situations cleave to life. Some people in the inner cities have lost all of their children to gang violence, are physically disabled, are starving to death, have never known a minute of love of any kind, and yet cling to life with every ounce of energy in them. Some people with every bright promise in their life commit suicide. Suicide is not the culmination of a difficult life; it comes in from some hidden location beyond the mind and beyond consciousness. I can look back now at my own little para-suicidal period: the logic that seemed so abundantly reasonable to me at that time now seems as alien as the bacteria that gave me pneumonia a few years earlier. It is like a powerful germ that entered the body and took over. I had been hijacked by strangeness.

There are fine but important distinctions between wanting to be dead, wanting to die, and wanting to kill yourself. Most people have from time to time wished to be dead, null, beyond sorrow. In depression, many want to die, to undertake the active change from where they are, to be freed from the affliction of consciousness. To want to kill yourself, however, requires a whole extra level of passion and a certain directed violence. Suicide is not the result of passivity; it is the result of an action taken. It requires a great deal of energy and a strong will in addition to a belief in the permanence of the present bad moment and at least a touch of impulsivity.

Suicides fall into four groups. The first group commit suicide without thinking through what they are doing; it is as dire and unavoidable to them as breathing. These people are the most impulsive, and the most likely to be spurred to suicide by a specific external event; their suicides tend to be sudden. They make, as the essayist A. Alvarez has written in his brilliant meditation on suicide, *The Savage God*, "an attempt at exorcism" of the pain that life can blunt only gradually. The second group, half in love with easeful death, commit suicide as revenge, as though the act were not irreversible. Of this group Alvarez writes, "Here's the difficulty about suicide: it is an act of ambition that can be committed only when one has passed beyond ambition." These people are not so much running away from life as running toward death, wanting not the end of existence but the presence of obliteration. The third group commit suicide through a faulty logic in which death seems to be the only escape from intolerable problems. They consider options and plan their suicides, write notes, and address the pragmatics as though they were organizing a holiday in outer space. They usually believe not only that death will improve their condition, but also that it will remove a burden from the people who love them (in fact the opposite is usually true). The last group commit suicide through a reasonable logic. These people—because of physical illness, mental instability, or a change in life circumstance—do not wish to experience the painfulness of life and believe that the payoff they might receive in pleasure is insufficient to requite current pain. These people may or may not be accurate in their predictions of the future, but they are not deluded, and no amount of antidepressant medication or treatment will change their mind.

To be or not to be? There is no other subject about which so much has been written and about which so little has been said. Hamlet proposes that the decision may rest on that "undiscover'd country from whose bourn no traveler returns." And yet men who do not fear the unknown, who gladly venture into territories of strange experience, do not so gladly leave this world of slings and arrows for a state of which nothing can be known, much can be feared, and all can be hoped. In fact, "conscience does make cowards of us all; and thus the native hue of resolution is sicklied o'er with the pale cast of thought." This is the real question of being and not being: conscience here is consciousness, resisting annihilation not only through cowardice but also through some underlying will to exist, to seize control, to act as it is necessary to act. Moreover, the mind that recognizes itself cannot derecognize itself, and it is contrary to introspective life to destroy itself. The "pale cast of thought" is that within us that keeps us from suicide; those who kill themselves have perhaps felt not only despair, but also the momentary loss of self-consciousness. Even if the choice is simply between being and nothingness—if one believes that there is nothing at all beyond death and that the human spirit is no more than a temporary chemical arrangement—being cannot conceive of not being: it can conceive of the absence of experience but not of absence itself. If I think, I am. My own view when I am healthy is that there may be glory, peace, horror, or nothing on the other side of death, and as long as we don't know, we should hedge our bets and make the most of the world we inhabit. "There is but one truly serious philosophical problem, and that is suicide," Albert Camus wrote. Indeed, a large number of French people devoted their lives to this problem in the middle part of the twentieth century, taking up in the name of existentialism the questions religion had once sufficed to answer.

Schopenhauer unpacks the question. "Suicide may be regarded as an experiment," he writes, "a question which man puts to Nature, trying to force her to answer. The question is this: What change will death produce in man's existence and in his insight into the nature of things? It is a clumsy experiment to make, for it involves the destruction of the very consciousness which puts the question and awaits its answer." It is impossible to know the consequences of suicide until one has undertaken it. To travel to the other side of death on a return ticket is an attractive idea: I have often wanted to kill myself for a month. One shrinks from the apparent finality of death, from the irretrievability of suicide. Consciousness makes us human, and there seems to be general agreement that consciousness as we know it is unlikely to exist beyond death, that the curiosity we would satisfy will not exist by the time it is answered. When I have wished not to be alive and wondered what it would be like to be dead, I have also recognized that to be dead would defeat the wondering. It is that wondering that keeps one going: I could give up the externalities of my life, but not the puzzling.

Though brute instinct plays the lead part, the rationale for living is, in a secular society, extremely difficult. "That life is worth living is the most necessary of assumptions," George Santayana wrote, "and were it not assumed, the most impossible of conclusions." The many afflictions that assail us must be considered, but perhaps more urgent is the fact of mortality. Death is so alarming and its inevitability such a disappointment that some people feel they might as well get it done with. The idea of an ultimate nothingness seems to negate the value of a current somethingness. In fact, life denies suicide by obscuring, most of the time, the reality of one's own mortality. If death is not proud, that is because it is so generally disregarded.

I do not believe that you have to be insane to kill yourself, though I think many insane people do kill themselves and that many other people kill themselves for insane reasons. It is obvious that the analysis of the suicidal personality has to be undertaken either retrospectively or after a failed suicide attempt. Freud himself said that "we have no adequate means of approaching" the problem of suicide. One must appreciate his deference to this subject; if psychoanalysis is the impossible profession, suicide is the impossible subject. Is it crazy to want to die? The question is ultimately a religious rather than a medical one, since it depends not only on what lies on the far side of death, but also on how highly we value life. Camus suggested that what is really crazy is the lengths to which most of us go to postpone inevitable death by a few decades. Is life only an absurd deferral of death? I believe that most people, on balance, experience more pain than pleasure in a lifetime, but we hunger for the pleasure and for the cumulative joy it breeds. Ironically, most of the religious faiths that posit eternal life have prohibitions against suicide, prohibitions that prevent the fervent from leaping off cliffs to join the choirs of angels (though religions can celebrate giving up life for the cause, as in Christian martyrdoms or Islamic holy wars).

The power to commit suicide has been lauded by many men who cherished life, from Pliny, who said, "In all miseries of our earthly life, to be able to compass one's own death is the best of God's gifts to man"; to John Donne, who wrote in *Biathanatos* in 1621, "Whensoever any affliction assails me, methinks I have the keys of my prison in mine own hand and no remedy presents itself so soon to my heart as mine own sword"; to Camus. "It will generally be found," Schopenhauer has declared, "that as soon as the terrors of life reach the point at which they outweigh the terrors of death, a man will put an end to his life." I have myself experienced in depression a terror of life that was utterly overpowering, and at that time I was dangerously inured to the fear of dying. I believed, however, that my terror was temporary, and that mitigated it enough to make it bearable. Rational suicide in my view cannot be a present-tense operation; it must be contingent on an accurate assessment of the longer term. I am a believer in rational suicide, which responds to futility rather than to hopelessness. The problem is that it is frequently difficult to see which suicides are rational, and it is, I believe, better to save too many people than to let too many people go. Suicide is famously a permanent solution to an often temporary problem. The right to suicide should be a basic civil liberty: no one should be forced to live against his will. On the other hand, suicidality is often temporary, and vast legions of people are glad to have been pulled back from suicide attempts or constrained from making them. If I ever attempt suicide, I'd like someone to save me, unless I have reached a point at which I accurately believe that the amount of joy left in my life cannot exceed the amount of sorrow or pain.

Thomas Szasz, an influential critic of the mental health establishment who has favored limiting the power of psychiatrists, says, "Suicide is a fundamental human right. This does not mean that it is desirable. It only means that society does not have the moral right to interfere, by force, with a person's decision to commit this act." Szasz believes that by intervening forcibly with the suicidal, one deprives them of the legitimacy of their selves and actions. "The result is a far-reaching infantilization and dehumanization of the suicidal person." A Harvard study gave doctors edited case histories of suicides and asked them for diagnoses; while the doctors diagnosed mental illness in only 22 percent of the group if they were not told that the patients had committed suicide, the figure was 90 percent when the suicide was included in the patient profile. Clearly, suicidality creates a smooth diagnosis, and it is likely that some degree of infantilization—or at least paternalism—occurs. Szasz's position has some basis in reality, but making clinical decisions on the basis of it can be extremely dangerous. The psychologist Edwin Shneidman, who began the suicide prevention movement, represents the other extreme. For him, self-murder is a mad act. "There is at least a touch of insanity in every suicide in the sense that, in suicide, there is some disconnection between thought and feelings," he writes. "This results in an inability to label emotions, or to differentiate them into more subtle shades of meaning, and communicate them to others. It is this abnormal 'split' between what we think and what we feel. There lies the illusion of control; there lies madness." This tautological view gives a basis for depriving people of their right to suicide. "Suicide is not a 'right,'" Shneidman has written in pungent opposition to Szasz, "any more than is the 'right to belch.' If the individual feels forced to do it, he will do it." One does, it seems worth noting, have control over belching some of the time, and one does restrain oneself as much as possible in public situations, in deference to others.

Suicide is astonishingly common and is disguised and trumped up more even than depression. It is, indeed, a vast public health crisis that makes us so uncomfortable that we divert our eyes from it. Every seventeen minutes, someone in the United States commits suicide. Suicide ranks number three among causes of death for Americans under the age of twenty-one, and it is number two for college students. In 1995 (for example), more young people died of suicide than of AIDS, cancer, stroke, pneumonia, influenza, birth defects, and heart disease combined. From 1987 to 1996, more men under the age of thirty-five died of suicide than of AIDS. Nearly half a million Americans are taken to hospitals every year because of suicide attempts. Suicide was, according to the World Health Organization, responsible for almost 2 percent of deaths worldwide in 1998, which puts it ahead of war and way ahead of homicide. And the rate of suicide is climbing steadily. One recent study conducted in Sweden showed the likelihood that a young man in the study's catchment area would commit suicide has increased by 260 percent since the 1950s. Half of those with manic-depression will make a suicide attempt; one in five people with major depression will do the same. Someone in a first depressive episode is particularly likely to attempt suicide; a person who has lived through a few cycles has in general learned to live through cycles. Previous attempts at suicide are the strongest factor in predicting suicide: about a third of the people who kill themselves have tried before; 1 percent of those attempting suicide will complete a suicide within a year; 10 percent will kill themselves within ten years. There are approximately sixteen suicide attempts to every completed suicide.

I have seen in a single document both the assertion that depressed people are five hundred times as likely to commit suicide as their nondepressed counterparts and the statistic that depressed patients have a suicide rate twenty-five times the societal norm. I have read, elsewhere, that depression increases the likelihood of suicide twofold. Who knows? Such rates depend in large part on how one defines that slippery demon depression. For what appear to be public health reasons, the National Institute of Mental Health grandly if unscientifically averred for a long time that "almost all people who kill themselves have a diagnosable mental or substance abuse disorder"; they recently downgraded the "almost all" to "90 percent." This notion helps people who have made unsuccessful suicide attempts, and those left grieved by the suicide of someone to whom they were close, to expel some of the guilt that might otherwise fetter them. Comforting though this is, and useful though it may be in drawing attention to the high level of illness-associated suicide, it is a gross exaggeration, not corroborated by anyone I've met who has treated suicidal patients.

Suicide statistics are even more chaotic than depression statistics. People most often commit suicides on Mondays; suicides are most prevalent between later morning and noon; the preferred season for suicide is springtime. Women have a high rate of suicide during the first and last weeks of the menstrual cycle (a phenomenon for which there may be hormonal explanations) and a low rate during pregnancy and in the first year after birth (a phenomenon that makes obvious evolutionary sense, but for which we have so far no definitive chemical explanation). One school of suicide researchers loves comparative statistics and uses them as though correlation implied causality. Some of these correlations come close to absurdity: one can calculate the average body weight of those who commit suicide, or the average length of their hair, but what exactly would that prove and what use would it be?

Émile Durkheim, the great nineteenth-century sociologist, pulled suicide out of the realm of morality and placed it in the more rational domain of social science. Suicides are subject to categorization, and Durkheim argued that there are four significant types. Egoistic suicide is committed by people who are inadequately integrated into the society they inhabit. Apathy and indifference motivate them to sever permanently their relationship to the world. Altruistic suicide comes of being overly integrated into one's society; Durkheim's category would include, for example, Patrick Henry's devotion to the idea "Give me liberty or give me death!" Those who commit altruistic suicide are energetic, passionate, and determined. Anomic suicide is the consequence of irritation and disgust. "In modern societies," Durkheim writes, "social existence is no longer ruled by custom and tradition, and individuals are increasingly placed into circumstances of competition with one another. As they come to demand more from life, not specifically more of something but simply more than they have at any given time, so they are more inclined to suffer from a disproportion between their aspirations and their satisfactions, and the resultant dissatisfaction is conducive to the growth of the suicidal impulse." As Charles Bukowski once wrote, "We demand more of life than there is"—and our inevitable disappointment may be occasion enough to end life. Or as de Tocqueville wrote of American idealism in particular, "the incomplete joys of this world will never satisfy the human heart." Fatalistic suicide is committed by people whose lives are genuinely miserable in a way beyond change—the suicide of a slave, for example, would be fatalistic in Durkheim's taxonomy.

Durkheim's categories are no longer used for clinical purposes, but they have defined much modern thinking about suicide. Contrary to beliefs of his time, Durkheim proposed that though suicide is an individual act, its sources are societal. Any single suicide is the result of psychopathology, but the relatively consistent appearance of psychopathological suicidality seems to be tied to social constructs. In each society there is a different context for the act, but it may be the case that a certain percentage of the population in every society kill themselves. The values and customs of a society determine which causes will lead to the act in which place. People who believe that they are operating on the basis of unique trauma are often, in fact, simply manifesting a tendency in their society that drives people to death.

Though many meaningless statistics clutter suicide studies, some tendencies can usefully be identified. Members of families in which there has been a suicide are far more likely than others to kill themselves. This is in part simply because family suicides make the unthinkable thinkable. It is also because the pain of living when someone you love has annihilated himself can be almost intolerable. A mother whose son had hanged himself said to me, "I feel as though my fingers are being caught in a slamming door and I've been stopped permanently in midscream." It is also because, at a presumably genetic level, suicide runs in families. Adoption studies show that biological relatives of a suicidal person are more frequently suicidal than are that person's adoptive relatives. Identical twins tend to share suicidality, even if they are separated at birth and have no knowledge of one another; nonidentical twins do not. It cannot be a selective advantage to have single-function "suicide genes," but the combination of genes that cause depression and violence and impulsivity and aggression may provide a genetic map that is both somewhat predictive of suicidal behavior and advantageous in particular situations.

Suicide breeds suicide in social communities as well. The contagion of suicide is incontrovertible. If one person commits suicide, a group of friends or peers will frequently follow; this is especially true among teenagers. Locations for suicide are used over and over again, carrying the curse of those who have died: the Golden Gate Bridge in San Francisco, Mount Mihara in Japan, particular stretches of railway lines, the Empire State Building. Suicide epidemics have recently occurred in Plano, Texas; Leominster, Massachusetts; Bucks County, Pennsylvania; Fairfax County, Virginia; and in a number of other apparently "normal" communities in the United States. Public accounts of suicides also inspire suicidal behavior. When Goethe's *The Sorrows of Young Werther* was published in the early nineteenth century, copycat suicides in the mode of Goethe's protagonist's were committed across Europe. Whenever a major suicide story breaks in the media, the suicide rate goes up. In the period immediately following Marilyn Monroe's suicide, for example, the rate of suicide in the United States increased 12 percent. If you are hungry and see a restaurant, you're likely to go in. If you're suicidal and read about a suicide, you're likely to take the final step. It seems clear that a reduction in reporting on suicide would lower the suicide rate. At the moment, evidence suggests that even the best-intentioned suicide-prevention programs often introduce the idea of suicide to a vulnerable population; it seems possible that they actually increase the suicide rate. They are helpful, however, insofar as they make people aware that suicide is often the result of mental illness and that mental illness is treatable.

Contrary to popular myth, those who talk about suicide are the most likely to kill themselves. Those who attempt tend to attempt again; in fact, the best predictor of an actual suicide is an attempt. No one makes much use of this fact. Maria Oquendo's 1999 study of treatments points out that though "a history of attempting suicide could be used by clinicians as a marker of a propensity for future attempts, patients with such a history were not treated more intensely than those without. It remains unclear whether those patients at substantial risk for suicide in association with major depression because of their history of suicidal acts are either not being recognized as at risk or are not receiving adequate somatic treatment despite the clinician's recognition of their heightened vulnerability."

Though sweeping existential arguments are engaging, the reality of suicide is not fine and pure and philosophical, but messy and appalling and physical. I have heard it said that severe depression is "a living death anyway." A living death is not pretty, but unlike a dead death, it offers scope for amelioration. Suicide's finality makes it a problem beyond any other discussed in this book, and the capacity of antidepressants to avert suicide needs urgently to be measured so that the appropriate medications can be deployed. Industry researchers find suicidality hard

251

to monitor, especially as culminating self-abnegation does not ordinarily take place during the twelve-week span of a "long-term" controlled study. None of the SSRIs, the most popular class of antidepressant drugs in the world, have been monitored for their capacity to prevent suicide. Among other drugs, lithium has been most rigorously tested—the rate of suicide among bipolar patients who discontinue lithium treatment increases sixteenfold. Some drugs that alleviate depression may increase the motivation for suicide because they augment motivation in general; drugs can set off mechanisms of self-destruction as they mitigate depression's torpor. It is important to distinguish between this enabling and actual causality. I do not believe that people commit suicide as a direct result of medication unless the suicidality has been strong in them for some time. Careful interviews should be conducted with patients before they are prescribed activating antidepressants. ECT can immediately allay urgent or delusional suicidal impulses. One study shows the suicide rate nine times higher for patients with severe illness on medications than for similarly ill patients treated with ECT.

Freud, at about the same time as Durkheim, proposed that suicide is frequently a murderous impulse toward someone else that is carried out on oneself. The psychologist Edwin Shneidman has more recently said that suicide is "murder in the one hundred eightieth degree." Freud posited that a "death instinct" is always in uncertain balance with the life instinct. This fascination does clearly exist and is certainly responsible for suicides. "The two basic instincts operate against each other or combine with each other," Freud wrote. "Thus the act of eating is a destruction of the object with the final aim of incorporating it, and the sexual act is an act of aggression with the purpose of the most intimate union. The concurrent and mutually opposing action of the two basic instincts gives rise to the whole variation of the phenomena of life." Suicide, here, is the necessary counterpoint to the will to live. Karl Menninger, who has written extensively on suicide, said that suicide requires the coincidence of "the wish to kill, the wish to be killed, and the wish to die." G. K. Chesterton, following in this mode, wrote:

> The man who kills a man kills a man
> The man who kills himself kills all men.
> As far as he is concerned, he wipes out the world.

As we confront chronic stresses for which we are ill equipped, we rely on and overuse neurotransmitters. The rush of neurotransmitters we induce in sudden stress cannot be kept up during more sustained stress.

For this reason, people who experience chronic stress tend to sap their transmitters. Suicidal depression appears to have some distinguishing neurobiological characteristics, which may cause suicidal behavior or may simply reflect suicidal tendencies. Actual suicide attempts are usually brought on by external stresses, which frequently include use of alcohol, acute medical illness, and negative life events. How prone someone is to suicide is determined by personality, genetics, childhood and rearing, alcoholism or substance abuse, chronic illness, and cholesterol level. Most of our information on the suicidal brain comes from postmortem studies. Suicides have low levels of serotonin at certain key locations in the brain. They have excessive numbers of serotonin receptors, which may reflect the brain's attempt to make up for the low levels of serotonin. The level of serotonin seems to be especially low in the areas associated with inhibition, and this deficiency appears to create a powerful freedom to act impulsively on emotion. People given to unbridled aggression often have low serotonin in the same area. Impulsive murderers and arsonists have lower serotonin levels than do most people— lower than those of nonimpulsive murderers or other criminals. Animal experiments show that primates with low serotonin are more likely to take risks and be aggressive than are their counterparts. Stress can cause both leaching of neurotransmitters and excess production of enzymes that destroy them. Levels of noradrenaline and norepinephrine appear to be reduced in postmortem suicidal brains, though the results are less consistent than the serotonin results. Enzymes that break down norepinephrine appear to be present in excessive quantities, and chemicals necessary for adrenaline to function are present in low quantities. What all of this means in functional terms is that people with low levels of essential neurotransmitters in key areas are at a high risk for suicide. This is the result consistently found by John Mann, a leading suicide researcher now working at Columbia University. He has used three different measures of serotonin levels in suicidal patients. Marie Åsberg, at the Karolinska Hospital in Sweden, has extrapolated clinical implications from such material. In a pioneering study, she kept track of patients who had previous suicide attempts and whose levels of serotonin appeared to be low; 22 percent of them had killed themselves within a year. Subsequent work has confirmed that while only 15 percent of depressives kill themselves, 22 percent of low-serotonin depressives will commit suicide.

Given that stress leaches serotonin and low serotonin increases aggressivity and high aggressivity leads to suicide, it is no surprise that stressed depression is the sort most likely to lead to suicide. Stress leads to aggressivity because aggressivity is frequently the best way to deal with short-term threats that induce stress. Aggressivity, however, is nonspecific, and though useful in combating an attacker, it may likewise be turned against oneself. It seems likely that aggression is a basic instinct, while depression and suicidality are more sophisticated cognitive impulses that developed later on. In evolutionary terms, the desirable trait of learning self-protective behavior is inextricably mingled with the undesirable trait of learning self-destructive behavior. The capacity for suicide is a burden that comes with the consciousness that distinguishes us from other animals.

Genetics may determine low levels of serotonin, and the gene that sets levels of the enzyme tryptophan hydroxylase is now clearly associated with high rates of suicide. Genes not only for mental disease but also for impulsivity, aggression, and violence may open them up to heavy risk. Animal experiments on monkeys brought up without mothers show that a deprived upbringing lowers serotonin levels in specific areas. It seems likely that early abuse may permanently lower serotonin levels and so increase the likelihood of suicide (quite apart from the problem of cognitive depression caused by that abuse). Substance abuse may further lower serotonin levels—and so, interestingly, does low cholesterol. Neurological damage to the fetus, caused by alcohol or cocaine use, may predispose children to mood disorders that lead to suicide; lack of maternal attention may deprive them of early developmental stability; diet may work adversely on their brain. Men have lower serotonin levels than women. So a stressed male with a genetic predisposition to low serotonin who has had a deprived upbringing, abuses substances, and has low cholesterol would fit the profile of a likely suicide. Drugs that increase serotonin levels in such individuals would be good agents to prevent suicide. Brain scans to detect levels of serotonin activity in the relevant parts of the brain—technology that does not exist now but may exist soon— might be used to estimate the likelihood of someone's attempting suicide. Better brain-imaging techniques may eventually allow us to check out the brains of depressed people and assess who is likely to attempt suicide. We have a long way to go. "For scientists to minimize the complexity of the chemical interactions within the brain or at the synapses," Kay Jamison writes in her masterful book on suicide, "would be a damning mistake, a late-twentieth-century equivalent of earlier, primitive views that deranged minds were caused by satanic spells or an excess of vapors."

There is evidence that the rate of suicide can be contained by external factors: where guns and barbiturates are hard to get, suicide rates are distinctly lower than elsewhere. Modern technology has made suicide easier and less painful than it has ever been before, and this is extremely dangerous. When England switched its gas services from lethal coke gas to less toxic natural gas, the suicide rate dropped by one-third, with annual gas-related suicides dropping from 2,368 to 11. If suicidality may be expressed impulsively, reducing immediate availability of means to kill oneself would allow the impulse to pass without being realized. The United States is the only country in the world where the primary means of suicide is guns. More Americans kill themselves with guns than are murdered with them every year in the United States. The ten states with the weakest gun-control laws have a suicide rate twice that of the ten states with the strongest laws. In 1910, at a meeting of the Vienna Psychoanalytic Society, David Oppenheim said, "A loaded pistol positively urges the idea of suicide on its owner." In 1997, about eighteen thousand Americans killed themselves with guns, responding to that urge. Technique may vary by location, age, and situation. In China, huge numbers of women commit suicide by eating toxic pesticides and fertilizers because those substances are so readily available. In Punjab in India, more than half of suicides are committed by leaping in front of trains.

Suicide is often the manifestation of the depressive end of a manic-depressive mood spectrum, and this is the reason usually given for the high rate of suicide among people who are highly successful. It is also the case that people who are successful tend to set high standards for themselves and are often disappointed even in their greatest achievements. Self-examination and rumination may lead to suicide, which occurs frequently among artists and other creative people. But the rate is also high among successful businessmen: it would appear that some of the qualities that make for success also make for suicidality. Scientists, composers, and high-level businessmen are five times more likely to kill themselves than the general population; writers, especially poets, have an even higher rate of suicide.

Approximately one-third of all completed suicides and one-quarter of all attempts are committed by alcoholics. Those suicide attempters who are drunk or on drugs at the time of their attempts are much more likely to succeed in killing themselves than are those who are sober. Fifteen percent of serious alcoholics take their own lives. Karl Menninger has called alcoholism "a form of self-destruction used to avert a greater self-destruction." For some, it is the self-destructiveness that enables self-destruction.

Advance detection is tricky. When I was deeply depressed, I visited a psychiatrist with whom I hoped to do therapy, who told me that he would take me on as a patient so long as I promised not to commit suicide while under his care. This was, I thought, a bit like having a specialist in infectious diseases agree to treat your tuberculosis so long as you never coughed again. I don't think that this was simply naïveté. On an airplane on my way home from a conference on brain imaging, I was drawn into conversation by someone who had observed that I was thumbing through a book about depression. "I'm kind of interested in what you're reading," he said. "I've had depression myself." I closed my book and listened as he described his psychiatric history. He had been hospitalized twice for severe depression. He had been on medication for a while but had been feeling good for more than a year and had therefore stopped taking his medication. He'd also given up his therapy because he'd worked through the problems that had afflicted him in the past. He had been arrested twice for possession of cocaine and had served a brief prison sentence. He was not in touch with his parents much, and his girl-friend didn't know he'd ever been depressed. It was about ten-thirty in the morning and he ordered a whiskey on ice from the stewardess.

"Do you often tell strangers a lot about yourself?" I asked as gently as I could.

"Well, sometimes I do," he conceded. "Sometimes I find it easier to talk to strangers than to people I really know. Y'know? Less judgment and all that. But not just any stranger—you know, it's like I get a real feeling for people and I just know they're good people to talk to. Like I had that feeling sitting here next to you."

Impulsivity. Recklessness. "Do you ever get speeding tickets?" I asked him.

"Wow," he said. "Are you a psychic or something? I get a lot of speed-ing tickets all the time; actually I had my license suspended for a year."

If I had been fresh from a conference on cardiology and were sitting next to a three-hundred-pound man who was smoking like a chimney and eating sticks of butter, and who complained of chest pain that radiated down his left arm, I might have felt that it was appropriate to warn him that he was in real and current danger. To tell someone that he is at risk for suicide is much more difficult. I hinted around the subject, advised my new friend to go back on medications, told him it was good to be in touch with a psychiatrist just in case he ever had a recurrence. Some sense of social convention made it impossible for me to say, "You may feel fine right now, but you're heading toward suicide and must immediately take preventative measures."

Animal models for suicide are imperfect since animals presumably do not understand their mortality per se and are unable to seek out their own death. You cannot long for what you do not understand: suicide is a price humans pay for self-consciousness, and it does not exist in com-

parable form among other species. Members of such species can, however, hurt themselves deliberately, and they frequently do so if subjected to excessive vicissitudes. Rats kept crowded together will chew off
their own tails. Rhesus monkeys reared without mothers begin self-
injuring actions at about five months; this behavior continues throughout
life even when the monkeys are placed in a social group. These monkeys
appear to have lower than normal levels of serotonin in crucial areas of
the brain; the biological is once more correlated with the sociological. I
was fascinated to hear of the suicide of an octopus, trained for a circus,
that had been accustomed to do tricks for rewards of food. When the circus was disbanded, the octopus was kept in a tank and no one paid any
attention to his tricks. He gradually lost color (octopuses' states of mind
are expressed in their shifting hues) and finally went through his tricks a
last time, failed to be rewarded, and used his beak to stab himself so
badly that he died.

Recent research with human models has uncovered a close connection between suicide and parental death. One study suggests that three-
quarters of completed suicides are committed by people who have been
traumatized in childhood by the death of someone to whom they were
close, most often a parent. Inability to process this loss early in life leads
to an inability to process loss generally. Young people who lose a parent
often internalize blame, foreclosing their sense of self-worth. They may
also surrender their sense of object constancy: If the parent on whom
one so depends can simply disappear from one day to the next, then
how can one trust anything? The statistics may be exaggerated, but
clearly, the more a person loses, the more likely he is to destroy himself,
other matters being equal.

Suicide early in life is widespread. About five thousand people
between eighteen and twenty-four kill themselves in the United States
each year; at least eighty thousand make suicide attempts. One in every
six thousand Americans between the ages of twenty and twenty-four
kills himself. Suicide is showing up more and more often in younger
people. Suicide is number three among causes of death for Americans fifteen to twenty-four years old. There is no consensus on why suicide is
on the upswing in this group. George Howe Colt has remarked, "To
account for this 'epidemic' of youth suicide, a host of explanations has
been proposed: the unraveling of America's moral fiber, the breakdown
of the nuclear family, school pressure, peer pressure, parental pressure,
parental lassitude, child abuse, drugs, alcohol, low blood sugar, TV,
MTV, popular music (rock, punk, or Heavy Metal, depending on the
decade), promiscuity, lagging church attendance, increased violence,
racism, the Vietnam War, the threat of nuclear war, the media, rootless-

ness, increased affluence, unemployment, capitalism, excessive freedom, boredom, narcissism, Watergate, disillusionment with government, lack of heroes, movies about suicide, too much discussion of suicide, too little discussion of suicide." Adolescents with high academic expectations of themselves may kill themselves if their performance does not live up to their own or their parents' expectations: suicide is more common among high-achieving adolescents than among their less ambitious peers. The hormonal disruptions of puberty and the years immediately following are also strong predeterminants of adolescent suicide.

Adolescents who commit suicide have often been protected from a bleak view of death. Many seem to believe that death is not a total cessation of consciousness. In a school with a suicide epidemic, one student who killed himself had said that he found it strange that he should be alive and his friend dead. A small Greenlandic city that I visited in 1999 had seen a bizarre sequence of deaths: one student had killed himself, and soon a dozen others followed. One of those follower suicides had said the day before he took his life that he missed his absent friend, and it seemed almost as though he were killing himself as a means to pass into the place where his friend had gone. Younger people are also more likely to believe that a suicide attempt will not lead to death. These people may use a suicide attempt to punish others; as my mother used to say to me, caricaturing my attitudes, when I was a child, "I'll eat worms and then I'll die and you'll be sorry you were mean to I." Such acts, no matter how manipulative, are at the very least a loud cry for help. Young people who survive a suicide attempt deserve our gentle attention; their problems are indeed grave, and even if we do not understand why, we must accept the seriousness of the matter.

Though there is a dramatic suicide peak among adolescents, the highest rate of suicide is among men over the age of sixty-five; the subgroup of white men over the age of eighty-five has a suicide rate of one in two thousand. There is a sorry tendency to think the suicides of the elderly less pitiful than the suicides of the young. Despair to the point of death is devastating no matter whom it affects. That every day of life brings us closer to death is evident; but that every day of life makes one's self-destruction more acceptable is a bizarre variation on this theme. We tend to suppose that elderly suicide is rational, but in fact it is frequently the consequence of untreated mental disturbances. Furthermore, the elderly have in general a rich understanding of death. While adolescents turn to suicide to escape life for a different experience, the elderly tend to see death as a final state. And they know what they are doing: unsuccessful suicide attempts are much less frequent in this population than they are among younger people. The elderly employ particularly lethal methods for their suicides and are less likely than any others to have communicated their intent in advance. Divorced or widowed men have the highest suicide rate of all. They seldom seek professional help for depression and often accept that their negative feelings are simply the true reflection of their diminished lives.

In addition to explicit suicide, many of the elderly engage in chronic suicidal behaviors: they choose not to feed themselves, not to take care of themselves, to let go before their bodies fully fail them. After retirement, they allow their rate of activity to lag and in many instances give up on their recreational activities because of poverty and low social status. They isolate themselves. As they develop particularly exacerbated forms of depression—motor problems, hypochondria, and paranoia—people suffer considerable physical decay. At least half of depressed elderly people have partially delusional physical complaints, which, in the period prior to suicide, they often believe to be more disabling and more intractable than they actually are.

Suicide is chronically underreported, in part because some suicides disguise their actions and in part because those left behind do not wish to recognize the reality of a suicide. Greece has one of the lowest reported suicide rates in the world; this reflects not only the sunny climate and relaxed culture of the country, but also that, per the Greek church, suicides cannot be buried in holy ground. This is a specific reason for not reporting a suicide in Greece. Societies where the level of shame is higher have fewer reported suicides. Then there are plenty of what one might call unconscious suicides, in which someone lives carelessly and dies of the incaution—perhaps through mild suicidality and perhaps through simple boldness. The line between self-destructiveness and suicide can be blurry. People who push their own decay without obvious recompense are proto-suicidal. Some religions differentiate active and passive self-destruction; ceasing to nourish yourself in the late stages of a terminal illness may be blameless, while taking an overdose of pills is a sin. One way and another, there is *much* more suicide in the world than you think, whatever you think.

The means of suicide are fascinatingly various. Kay Jamison catalogs some exotic techniques in *Night Falls Fast*, such as drinking boiling water; pushing broom handles down the throat; thrusting darning needles into the abdomen; gulping down leather and iron; jumping into volcanoes; thrusting turkey rumps down the throat; swallowing dynamite, hot coals, underwear, or bedclothes; strangling oneself with one's own hair; using electric drills to bore holes in the brain; walking into the snow with no protective clothing; placing the neck in a vise; arranging for self-

decapitation; injecting peanut butter or mayonnaise into the bloodstream; flying bomber planes into mountains; applying black widow
spiders to the skin; drowning in vats of vinegar; suffocating in refrigerators; drinking acid; swallowing firecrackers; applying leeches to the
body; and strangling on a rosary. In the United States, the most common
methods are the obvious ones: guns, drugs, hanging, and jumping.

I am not given to overpowering suicidal fantasy. I think about suicide
often, and at my most depressed the idea is never far from my mind; but
it tends to stay in my mind, glossed with the irreality with which children
imagine old age. I know when things are getting worse because the
kinds of suicide I imagine become more various and to some extent
more violent. My fantasies leave behind the pills in my medicine chest and
even the gun in my safe and extend to figuring out whether the blades of
a Gillette sensor razor could be used to slit my wrists, or whether I would
be better off using an X-Acto knife. I have gone so far as to try a beam just
to see if it would be strong enough to support a noose. I have worked on
figuring out timing: when I would be alone in the house, at what hour I
could carry things through. Driving when I am in such a mood, I think a
lot about cliffs, but then I think about air bags and the possibility of hurting other people, and that way usually feels too messy for me. These are
all very real imaginings and can be very painful, but they have so far
remained in my imagination. I have engaged in some reckless behavior
that could be called para-suicidal, and I have often wanted to die; at low
points, I have toyed with the idea, much as I have at high points in my life
toyed with the idea of learning to play the piano; but it never flew out of
control in me or turned into much of an accessible reality. I wanted out of
life, but I had no impulse to drain my being out of existence.
  If my depressions had been either worse or longer, I can imagine that
I would have become more actively suicidal, but I don't think I could
have killed myself without hard evidence that my situation was irreversible. Though suicide assuages present suffering, in most instances it
is undertaken to avoid future suffering. I was born with a strong optimism from my father's side of the family, and for reasons that may well
be purely biochemical, my negative feelings, though sometimes intolerable, have never felt conclusively immutable to me. What I can remember is the curious sense of futurelessness that came to me at low points
in my depression—feeling inappropriately relaxed during the takeoff of
a small plane because I genuinely didn't care whether it crashed and
killed me or flew and delivered me to my destination. I took foolish risks
when they presented themselves to me. I was game to eat poison; I was
just not particularly inclined to find or brew it. One of my interviewees,

who has survived multiple suicide attempts, told me that if I'd never even slit my wrists, I'd never *really* been depressed. I chose not to enter that particular competition, but I have certainly met people who have suffered enormously but have never made attempts on themselves.

In the spring of 1997, I went skydiving for the first time, in Arizona. Skydiving is often discussed as a para-suicidal activity, and if I had in fact died while I was doing it, I imagine that it would have been tied in the imagination of my family and friends to my mood states. And yet—and I believe this is often the case for para-suicidal action—it felt not like a suicidal impulse but like a vital one. I did it because I felt so good that I was capable of it. At the same time, having entertained the idea of suicide, I had broken down certain barriers that had stood between me and self-obliteration. I did not want to die when I jumped out of an airplane, but I didn't fear dying in the way I had feared it before my depression, and so I didn't need so rigorously to avoid it. I've gone skydiving several times since then, and the pleasure I've had from my boldness, after so much time lived in reasonless fear, is incalculable. Every time at the door of the plane, I feel the adrenal rush of real fear, which, like real grief, is precious to me for its simple authenticity. It reminds me what those emotions are actually about. Then comes the free fall, and the view over virgin country, and the overwhelming powerlessness and beauty and speed. And then the glorious discovery that the parachute is there after all. When the canopy opens, the updrafts in the wind suddenly reverse the fall, and I rise up and up away from the earth, as though an angel has suddenly come to my rescue to carry me to the sun. And then when I start to sink again, I do it so slowly and live in a world of silence in multiple dimensions. It is wonderful to discover that the fate you have trusted has warranted that trust. What joy it has been to find that the world can support my most rash experiments, to feel, even while falling, that I am held tightly by the world itself.

I first became acutely aware of suicide when I was about nine years old. The father of a classmate of my brother's killed himself, and the topic had to be addressed at home. The man in question had stood up in front of his family, made some extraordinary remark, and then leapt through the open window, leaving his wife and children to look down at a body condensed into lifelessness several stories below. "Some people just have problems they can't solve and they get to the point at which they can't stand to live anymore," my mother explained. "You've got to be strong to get through life. You've got to be one of the survivors." Somehow I didn't understand the horror of what had happened; it had an exotic and fascinating, almost pornographic quality.

When I was a sophomore in high school, one of my favorite teachers

261

shot himself in the head. He was found in his car, with a Bible open beside him. The police shut the Bible without noting the page. I remember discussing that at the dinner table. I had not yet lost anyone who was really close to me, so the fact that his death was a *suicide* did not stand out as much as it does in retrospect; I was confronting for the first time the fact of death. We talked about how no one would ever know to which page that Bible was open, and something literary in me suffered more about that foiled closure of the life than about the loss of it.

My freshman year of college, the ex-girlfriend of my girlfriend's ex-boyfriend jumped off a building at school. I didn't know her, but I knew that I was implicated in a chain of rejection that included her, and I felt guilty about the death of this stranger.

A few years after college, an acquaintance killed himself. He drank a bottle of vodka; slit his wrists; and apparently discontent with the slow progress of his blood, went to the roof of his New York apartment building and jumped off. This time I was shocked. He was a sweet-natured, intelligent, good-looking man, someone of whom I had occasionally been jealous. I wrote at that time for the local paper. He used to pick up his copy early from an all-night newsagent, and every time I published something he would be the first one to call and congratulate me. We were not close, but I will always remember those calls, and the tone of slightly inappropriate awe he brought to his praise. He would reflect a bit sadly on how he was not sure about his career and how he perceived me to know what I was doing. That was the only melancholic thing I ever observed in him. Otherwise, I think of him still as a cheerful person. He had fun at parties; in fact, he gave good parties. He knew interesting people. Why would such a person slit his wrists and jump off the roof? His psychiatrist, who had seen him the day before, was not able to shed light on the question. Was there a why to answer? When it happened, I still thought that suicide had a logic, albeit a defective one.

But suicide is not logical. "Why," wrote Laura Anderson, who has battled such acute depression, "do they always have to come up with a 'reason'?" The reason given is seldom sufficient to the event; it is the task of analysts and kind friends to search for clues, causes, and categories. I have since learned that from the catalogs of suicide I have read. The lists are as long and painful as those on the Vietnam Veterans Memorial (and more young men committed suicide during the Vietnam War than died in action). Everyone had some acute trauma proximate to his suicide: a husband insulted one, a lover abandoned another, someone hurt himself badly, someone lost his true love to illness, someone went bankrupt, someone totaled her car. Someone simply woke up one day and didn't want to be awake. Someone hated Friday nights. If they killed themselves, they did it because they were suicidal, and not because it was the obvious outcome of such reasoning. While the medical establishment insists that there is always a connection between mental illness and suicide, a sensationalist media often suggests that mental illness plays no real part in suicides. It makes us feel safe to locate causes for suicide. This is a more extreme version of the logic according to which acute depression is the consequence of whatever triggers it. There are no clean lines here. How suicidal do you have to feel to *attempt* suicide, and then how suicidal do you have to feel to *commit* suicide, and where does one intention become the other? Suicide may indeed be (as per the WHO) a "suicidal act with a fatal outcome," but what are the conscious and unconscious motives underlying that outcome? High-risk actions—from deliberately exposing oneself to HIV to provoking someone to homicidal rage to staying outside in an ice storm—are frequently parasuicidal. Suicide attempts range from the conscious, focused, utterly deliberate, and purely objective-oriented to the most slightly self-destructive action. "Ambivalence," Kay Jamison writes, "saturates the suicidal act." A. Alvarez writes, "A suicide's excuses are mostly by the way. At best they assuage the guilt of the survivors, soothe the tidy-minded, and encourage the sociologists in their endless search for convincing categories and theories. They are like a trivial border incident which triggers a major war. The real motives which impel a man to take his own life are elsewhere; they belong to the internal world, devious, contradictory, labyrinthine, and mostly out of sight." "Newspapers often speak of the 'personal sorrows' or 'incurable illnesses,'" Camus wrote. "These explanations are plausible. But one would have to know whether a friend of the desperate man had not that very day addressed him indifferently. He is the guilty one. For that is enough to precipitate all the rancors and all the boredom still in suspension." And the critical theorist Julia Kristeva describes the profound randomness of timing: "A betrayal, a fatal illness, some accident or handicap that abruptly wrests me away from what seemed to me the normal category of normal people or else falls on a loved one with the same radical effect, or yet . . . What more could I mention? An infinite number of misfortunes weigh us down every day."

In 1952, Edwin Shneidman opened the first suicide-prevention center, in Los Angeles, and tried to come up with useful (rather than theoretical) structures for thought about suicide. He proposed that suicide is the result of thwarted love, shattered control, assaulted self-image, grief, and rage. "It is almost as though the suicidal drama were autonomously writing itself, as though the play had a mind of its own. It has to sober us to realize that as long as people, consciously or unconsciously, can successfully dissemble, no suicide prevention program can be a hundred percent successful." Kay Jamison refers to this dissembling when she laments that "the privacy of the mind is an impermeable barrier."

A few years ago, another of my college classmates killed himself. This one had always been peculiar, and in some ways his suicide was easier to explain away. I'd had a message from him some weeks before he died and had been meaning to call back and make a plan for lunch. I was out with mutual friends when I heard. "Anyone speak to so-and-so lately?" I asked when a topic reminded me of him. "Haven't you heard?" answered one of my friends. "He hanged himself a month ago." For some reason, that image is the worst for me. I can imagine the friend with the slit wrists in the air, and I can imagine his body disintegrated after a jump. The image of this friend swaying from a beam like a pendulum: well, I never got my mind around it. I know that my phone call and lunch invitation would not have saved him from himself, but suicide inspires guilt all around it, and I cannot shake from my mind the idea that I would have received a clue if I'd seen him, and that I would have done something with that clue.

Then the son of a business associate of my father's killed himself. And then the son of a friend of my father's killed himself. Then two other people I knew killed themselves. And friends of friends killed themselves too, and since I was writing this book, I heard from people who had lost their brothers, children, lovers, parents. It is possible to understand the paths that have led someone toward suicide, but the mentality of that actual moment, of the leap required to undertake the final action—that is incomprehensible and terrifying and so strange that it makes one feel as though one had never really known the person who did it.

While writing this book, I heard about many suicides, in part because of the worlds with which I had been thrown in contact and in part because people looked to me, with all my research, for some kind of wisdom or insight of which I was in fact entirely incapable. A nineteen-year-old friend, Chrissie Schmidt, called me in shock when one of her Andover classmates hanged himself in the stairwell behind his dorm room. The boy in question had been elected class president. After being caught drinking (aged seventeen), he had been removed from office. He had delivered a resignation speech that had received a standing ovation, then had taken his own life. Chrissie had known the boy only in passing, but he had seemed to occupy an enchanted world of popularity from which she sometimes felt excluded at Andover. "After fifteen minutes or so of disbelief," Chrissie wrote in an E-mail, "I dissolved into tears. I think I felt many things at the same time—inexpressible sadness at the life cut short, voluntarily, so soon; anger at the school, a place smothered by its own mediocrity, for making such a huge deal about drinking and being so hard on the boy; and perhaps above all fear that I, at some point, might have felt capable of hanging myself in the stairwell of my dorm. Why didn't I know this boy when I was there? Why did I feel that I was the only one who was so out of sorts, so miserable, when the most popular boy in school might have been feeling so many of the same things? Why the hell didn't someone notice that he was carrying such a burden around with him? All those times, lying in my dorm room sophomore year, feeling desperately sad and baffled by the world around me and the life I was living . . . well, here I am. And I know I wouldn't have taken that final step. I really do. But I came pretty close to feeling it was at least in the realm of possibility. What is it—bravery? pathology? solitude?—that can push someone over that final, fatal edge, when life is something we're willing to lose?" And the next day she added, "His death stirs up and throws into relief all these unanswered questions—that I must ask these questions and that I will never get my answer is unbearably sad to me right now." That, in essence, is the catastrophe of suicide for those who survive: not only the loss of someone, but the loss of the chance to persuade that person to act differently, the loss of the chance to connect. There is no one to whom one so yearns to connect as a person who has committed suicide. "If we had only known" is the plea of the parents of a suicide, people who rack their minds trying to figure out what failing of their love could have allowed such a thing to come and surprise them, trying to think what they should have said.

But there is nothing to say, nothing that can assuage the loneliness of self-annihilation. Kay Jamison tells the painful story of her own suicide attempt at a time when her thought was as disrupted as her mood: "No amount of love from other people—and there was a lot—could help. No advantage of a caring family and fabulous job could be enough to overcome the pain and hopelessness I felt; no passionate or romantic love, however strong, could make a difference. Nothing alive and warm could make its way in through my carapace. I knew my life to be a shambles and I believed—incontestably—that my family, friends, and patients would be better off without me. There wasn't much of me left anymore, anyway, and I thought my death would free up the wasted energies and well-meant efforts that were being sent on a fool's errand." It is not unusual to believe that one is a burden to others. One man who committed suicide wrote in his final note, "I have pondered it and have decided I would hurt friends and relatives less dead than alive."

Great misery does not make me suicidal, but occasionally in a depression something small will overwhelm me and I get a ridiculous feeling. There are too many dirty dishes in this kitchen, and I don't have the stamina to clean them. Perhaps I will just kill myself. Or—look, the train is coming and I could just jump. Should I? But it's in the station before I make up my mind. These thoughts are like waking dreams and I can see their absurdity, but I know that they are there. I do not want to die in these thoughts, and I do not want violence, but in some ludicrous fashion, suicide seems to simplify things. If I killed myself, I wouldn't have to fix the roof or mow the lawn or take another shower. Oh, imagine that luxury of never having to comb my hair again. My conversations with the acutely suicidal have led me to believe that this feeling is closer to the one that most often leads to a suicide attempt than is the feeling of total despair that I had during darkest depression. It is a sudden perception of a way out. It is not exactly a melancholy feeling, though it may occur in an unhappy context. I also know the feeling of wanting to kill the depression and of being unable to do so except by killing the self it afflicts. The poet Edna St. Vincent Millay wrote:

> And must I then, indeed, Pain, live with you
> All through my life?—sharing my fire, my bed,
> Sharing—oh, worst of all things!—the same head?—
> And, when I feed myself, feeding you, too?

Nourishing your own misery can grow too wearisome to bear, and that tedium of helplessness, that failure of detachment, can lead you to the point at which killing the pain matters more than saving yourself.

I talked to a large number of suicide survivors while I was working on this book, and one particularly frightened me. I met him in a hospital the day after his attempt. He was successful and attractive and fairly happily married, living in a nice suburb of an American coastal city, and working as a chef in a popular restaurant. He had suffered from periodic depression but had gone off his medication about two months earlier, believing that he would be fine without it. He had not told anyone that he was going to stop the medication, but he had appropriately lowered his dose over a few weeks before entirely discontinuing treatment. He had felt fine for a few days but had then begun to develop repetitive and explicit suicidal thoughts that were independent of other depression symptoms. He continued to go to work, but his mind drifted regularly to the idea of self-extermination. Eventually he had decided, with what he believed to be good reason, that the world would be better off without him. He tidied up a few loose ends in his life and made arrangements for things to continue after he was gone. Then one afternoon when he had decided it was time, he swallowed two bottles of Tylenol. About halfway through, he called his wife at her office to say good-bye, quite certain that she would see his logic and would not oppose his decision. She was not sure at first whether this was some kind of joke, but she soon realized that he was serious. Unbeknownst to her, he was taking pills by the handful even as they spoke on the telephone. Eventually, he got annoyed with her for arguing against his plan, said good-bye, and hung up the phone. He took the rest of the pills.

Within a half hour, the police arrived. The man, who realized his plans were going to be foiled, stepped outside to chat with them. He explained that his wife was a bit nutty, that she did this sort of thing to cause him grief, and that there was really no reason for them to be there. He knew that if he could stall them for a further hour or so, the Tylenol would destroy his liver function (he'd done some careful research), and he hoped that if he couldn't make them leave, he could at least distract them. He invited them in for a cup of tea and set the water to boil. He was so calm and convincing that the policemen believed his story. He did get some delay out of them; but they said that they really had to follow up a possible suicide attempt and would regretfully have to compel him to accompany them to the emergency room. His stomach was pumped in the nick of time.

When I talked to him, he described the whole thing the way that I sometimes describe dreams, events in which I appear to have played a bewilderingly active role whose meaning I cannot distinguish. He was recovering from the stomach pumping and was very shaken, but he was quite coherent. "I don't know why I wanted to die," he said to me, "but I can tell you that yesterday it made perfect sense to me." We went over the details. "I decided the world would be a better place with me not in it," he said. "I thought it all through and I saw how it would free my wife, how it would be better for the restaurant, how it would be a relief to me. That's what's so strange, that it seemed like such an obviously good idea, so sensible."

He was enormously relieved to have been saved from that good idea. I would not describe him as happy that day in the hospital; he was as terrified by his brush with death as the survivor of a plane crash might be. His wife had been with him most of the day. He said that he loved her and that he knew she loved him. He enjoyed his work. Perhaps something unconscious in him led him to the telephone when he was ready to kill himself, causing him to call his wife rather than to write a note. If there was, it was little comfort to him because it had so entirely failed to register with his conscious mind. I asked his doctor how long the patient would remain hospitalized, and the doctor said it would make sense to keep him until his flawed logic could be better explored and his blood levels of medication could be set. "He seems healthy enough to go home today," said the doctor, "but he would have seemed healthy enough not to be here the day before yesterday." I asked the man whether he thought he would make another suicide attempt. It was as though I had asked him to predict someone else's future. He shook his head and looked at me with a pale, bewildered expression. "How can I know?" he asked me.

His bewilderment, his emotional defeat, are commonplaces of the suicidal mind. Joel P. Smith, a man in Wisconsin who has survived multiple suicide attempts, wrote to me, "I am alone. A large proportion of depressed people I know are more or less alone, having lost their jobs and used up their families and friends. I become suicidal. My ultimate guardian—namely myself—has not just gone off duty, but, so much more dangerously, has become the advocate, the agent of destruction."

On the day it took place, when I was twenty-seven, I understood and believed in the reasons for my mother's suicide. She was in the late stages of terminal cancer. In fact, with my father and brother, I helped my mother kill herself and, in doing so, experienced a great intimacy with her. We all believed in what she did. Unfortunately, many who believe in rational decision making—including Derek Humphry, author of *Final Exit*, and Jack Kevorkian—seem to think that *rational* means "straightforward." It was not easy to arrive at this rational decision. It was a slow, tangled, peculiar process whose convolutions were as madly individual as those experiences of love that can lead to marriage. My mother's suicide is the cataclysm of my life, though I admire her for it and believe in it. It so distresses me that I mostly draw up shy of thinking and talking about its details. The simple fact of it is now a fact of my life and I will gamely share that with anyone who asks. The reality of what happened, however, is like something sharp that is embedded in me, that cuts whenever I move.

Activists draw an obsessively careful distinction between "rational" and all other suicides. In fact a suicide is a suicide—overdetermined, sad, toxic in some measure to everyone it touches. The worst and the best kind lie at either end of a continuum; they differ more in degree than in essential quality. Rational suicide has always been a popular and frightening idea. The narrator of Dostoyevsky's *The Possessed* asks whether people kill themselves from reason. "Lots," Kirilov replies. "But for prejudice there would be more; many more; all." When we speak of a rational suicide and distinguish it from an irrational one, we are sketching out the details of our own or our society's prejudices. Someone who killed himself because he didn't like his arthritis would seem suicidal;

someone who killed herself because she couldn't bear the prospect of a painful and undignified death from cancer seems perhaps quite rational. A British court recently awarded a hospital permission to force-feed a diabetic anorexic and to inject her with insulin against her will. She was extremely wily and had contrived to substitute a mix of milk and water for the insulin that she was supposed to be injecting, and she soon reached a nearly comatose state. "Well, is that anorexia?" asked the therapist who was treating her. "Is that suicidal behavior? Is that para-suicidal? I think it's obviously a very depressed and very angry thing to do." What about people with miserable but not immediately fatal ill-nesses? Is it reasonable to kill oneself in the face of Alzheimer's or Lou Gehrig's disease? Is there such a thing as a terminal mental state, in which someone who has received lots of treatment and remains unhappy may commit rational suicide even if he is not ill? What is rational for one person is irrational for another, and all suicide is calamitous.

In a hospital in Pennsylvania, I met a man in his late teens whose wish to die I would be particularly inclined to honor. He was born in Korea and abandoned as an infant; when he was found, half-starved, he was put into a Seoul orphanage from which he was adopted when he was six by an American alcoholic couple who abused him. By the time he was twelve, he had been made a ward of the state and sent to live in the mental hos-pital where I encountered him. He suffers from cerebral palsy, which has crippled his lower body into uselessness, and speech is painful and labo-rious for him. In the five years he has lived full-time at the hospital, he has received every medication and treatment known to mankind, including a full spectrum of antidepressant treatment and electroconvulsive therapy, but he has remained bitter and anguished. He has made innumerable sui-cide attempts since late childhood, but because he is in a care facility, he has always been saved; and since he is confined to a wheelchair on a locked ward, he can seldom make his way to a situation private enough for his attempts to stand a chance. Desperate, he tried to starve himself to death; when he hit unconsciousness, he was fed intravenously.

Though his physical disability makes speech a struggle for him, he is perfectly capable of rational conversation. "I'm sorry to be alive," he said to me. "I didn't want to be here in this form. I just don't want to be here on earth. I have had no life. There are no things I like or that give me joy. This is my life: upstairs in building number nine of this hospital and then back here to building number one, which is no better than building number nine. My legs are painful. My body hurts me. I try not to talk to the people in here. They basically all talk to themselves anyway. I've taken a lot of medication for my depression. I don't think the medicine works for me. I lift weights upstairs with my arms, and I use the computer. That keeps my mind occupied and it distracts from what I have. But it is not enough. This will never change. I will never not feel like killing myself. It feels good to cut my wrists. I like seeing my own blood. Then I fall asleep. When I wake up, I say to myself, 'Damn it, I woke up.'" Plenty of people with cerebral palsy lead rich and satisfying lives. This young man, however, is so psychologically bruised and so violently hostile that he will probably not encounter much love and would perhaps be unable to appreciate it if it were offered to him. He is moving to me and to some of the people who help to take care of him, but no heroic person who wants to give up a life to helping him has materialized; there are not enough selfless people on earth to devote themselves to all the people like him who fight against their own life every minute on this planet. His life is physical pain and mental pain and physical incompetence and mental shadows. To me, his depression and his wish to die seem untreatable, and I am glad that I do not have responsibility for ensuring that he wakes up every time he manages to cut his wrists, that I am not the one who inserts the feeding tube when he has deliberately stopped eating.

In another hospital, I encountered an eighty-five-year-old man in good health who, with his wife, took mortal doses of barbiturates when she began to develop liver cancer. They had been married sixty-one years and had a suicide pact. She died. He was revived. "I was sent in to cure this guy's depression," a young psychiatrist said to me. "Give him some pills and therapy so he won't be depressed because he's old, sick, in constant pain, his wife dead, suicide didn't work. It's been six months, he's still in the same state, he could live ten years. I treat depression. What he's got, it's not that kind of depression."

Tennyson's poem "Tithonus" tells the story of such late-life despair. Tithonus was the lover of Eos, the dawn; she asked Zeus to give him eternal life. Zeus granted her request; but she had forgotten to ask for eternal youth. Unable to kill himself, Tithonus lives forever growing infinitely old and infinitely more old. He longs to die, saying to his former lover:

> Coldly thy rosy shadows bathe me, cold
> Are all thy lights, and cold my wrinkled feet
> Upon thy glimmering thresholds, when the steam
> Floats up from those dim fields about the homes
> Of happy men that have the power to die,
> And grassy barrows of the happier dead.

Petronius' story of the Cumaean Sibyl, who was doomed also to immortality without eternal youth, was to form the despairing epigraph to T. S. Eliot's *The Waste Land*: "When asked, 'Sibyl, what do you want?'

she would reply, 'I want to die.'" And even Emily Dickinson, living quietly in New England, came to a similar conclusion about the gradual descent into loss:

> The Heart asks Pleasure—first—
> And then—Excuse from Pain—
> And then—those little Anodynes
> That deaden suffering—
> And then—to go to sleep—
> And then—if it should be
> The will of its Inquisitor
> The privilege to die—

In our family, discussions about euthanasia began long before my mother developed ovarian cancer. We all signed living wills in the early eighties and talked at that time—entirely in the abstract—about how uncivilized it was that the euthanasia options famously available in the Netherlands were not available to Americans. "I hate pain," my mother said casually. "If I reach the point at which I'm in nothing but pain, I hope one of you will shoot me." We all, laughingly, agreed. We all hated pain, all thought that a quiet death was the best kind—in your sleep, at home, when you were very old. Young and optimistic, I assumed that we would all die that way at some point in the remote future.

In August 1989, my mother was diagnosed with ovarian cancer. During her first week in the hospital, she announced that she was going to kill herself. We all tried to shrug off this declaration, and she didn't particularly insist on it. She was not at that time speaking of a considered agenda of terminating her symptoms—she had scarcely any symptoms—but was rather expressing a sense of outrage at the indignity of what lay ahead and a profound fear of being out of control of her life. She spoke of suicide, then, as people disappointed in love may speak of it, as a swift and easy alternative to the painful, slow process of recovery. It was as though she wanted vengeance for the snub she had received from nature; if her life could not be as exquisite as it had been, she would have no more of it.

The subject lay low as my mother went through an excruciating, humiliating bout of chemotherapy. When, ten months later, she went in for exploratory surgery to assess the chemotherapy's efficacy, we discovered that the regimen had not been as effective as we'd hoped, and a second round was prescribed. After her surgery, my mother lingered for a long time in a resistance to consciousness forged out of rage. When she finally began to speak again, a flood of anger came out of her, and this time when she said she was going to kill herself, it was a threat. Our protests were thrown back in our faces. "I'm already dead," she said as she lay in her hospital bed. "What's here for you to love?" Or else she instructed, "If you loved me, you'd help me out of this misery." Whatever meager faith she had had in chemotherapy had vanished, and she laid down as a condition of her accepting another round of punishing treatments that she would do it if someone would get her "those pills," so that she could stop whenever she was ready.

One tends to accommodate the very, very sick. There was no answer to my mother's rage and despair after her surgery but to say yes to whatever she demanded. I was living in London at that time: I came home every other week to see her. My brother was in law school in New Haven and spent long days on the train. My father neglected his office to be at home. We were all clinging to my mother—who had always been the center of our close family—and we wavered between the light but meaningful tone that had always been our mien and a terrifying solemnity. Still, when she had relaxed into a facsimile of her usual self, the idea of her suicide, though it had gained resonance, once more receded. My mother's second round of chemotherapy seemed to be working, and my father had researched a half dozen more treatment options. My mother made her dark remarks about suicide on occasion, but we continued to tell her that there was a long time before such measures could be relevant.

At four o'clock on a blustery September afternoon in 1990, I called to check on some test results that were due that day. When my father answered, I knew at once what had happened. We would continue, he told me, with this therapy for the moment while we explored other options. I had no doubt what other options my mother would be exploring. So I should not have been surprised when she told me, in October, over lunch, that the technical details had been taken care of, and that she now had the pills. In the early stages of her illness, my mother, stripped of disguises, had suffered the loss of her looks as a side effect of her treatments, a ravagement so obvious that only my father could contrive to be blind to it. My mother had previously been beautiful, and she found the physical losses of chemotherapy intensely painful—her hair was gone, her skin too allergic for any makeup, her body emaciated, her eyes ringed with exhaustion and constantly drooping. By the time of that October lunch, however, she had begun to take on a new kind of pale, illuminated, ethereal beauty, completely different in its effect from the 1950s all-American appearance she had had during my childhood. The moment that my mother actually sought the pills was also the moment at which she accepted (perhaps prematurely, perhaps not) that she was dying, and this acceptance afforded her a radiance, both physical and profound, that seemed to me, at last, more powerful than her decay. When I remember that lunch, I remember, among other things, how beautiful my mother had become again.

I protested, as we ate, that she might still have lots of time, and she said that she had always believed in planning things carefully, and that now that she had the pills, she could relax and enjoy whatever was left without worrying about the end. Euthanasia is a deadline matter, and I asked my mother what her cutoff would be. "As long as there is even a remote chance of my getting well," she said, "I'll go on with treatments. When they say that they are keeping me alive but without any chance of recovery, then I'll stop. When it's time, we'll all know. Don't worry. I won't take them before then. Meanwhile, I plan to enjoy whatever time there is left."

Everything that had been intolerable to my mother was made tolerable when she got those pills, by the sure knowledge that when it became really intolerable, it would stop. I would have to say that the eight months that followed, though they led inexorably toward her death, were the happiest months of her illness; that in some obscure way, despite or perhaps because of the suffering in them, they were among the happiest months of our lives. Once we had all settled the future, we could live fully in the present, something that none of us had really done before. I should emphasize that the vomiting, malaise, hair loss, adhesions, were all relentless, that my mother's mouth was one great sore that never seemed to heal, that she would have to save up strength for days to have an afternoon out, that she could eat almost nothing, was a mess of allergies, shook so badly that on some days she couldn't use a fork and knife—and yet the excruciating business of the continuing chemotherapy seemed suddenly unimportant because these symptoms were permanent only until she decided she could take no more, and so the disease was no longer in control of her. My mother was an adoring woman, and in those months she gave herself over to love as I have never seen anyone else do. In *A Short History of Decay*, E. M. Cioran writes, "Consolation by a possible suicide widens into infinite space this realm where we are suffering. . . . What greater wealth than the suicide each of us bears within himself?"

I have since then read and been particularly moved by Virginia Woolf's suicide note, so similar in spirit to the terms of my mother's departure. Woolf wrote to her husband:

Dearest:
I want to tell you that you have given me complete happiness. No one could have done more than you have done. Please believe that.
But I know that I shall never get over this: and I am wasting your life. It is this madness. Nothing anyone says can persuade

273

me. You can work, and you will be much better off without me. You see, I can't write this even, which shows I am right. All I want to say is that until this disease came on we were perfectly happy. It was all due to you. No one could have been so good as you have been, from the very first day till now. Everyone knows that.

V.

Will you destroy all my papers?

It is an unusually sympathetic note precisely because it is dispassionate and so clear about illness. There are people who kill themselves because they have not yet found, or perhaps because they have not yet sought, an existing cure. Then there are those who kill themselves because their illness is genuinely refractory. If I had truly believed when I was ill that my situation was permanent, I would have killed myself. Even if I had believed that it was cyclical, as Virginia Woolf knew her complaint to be, I would have killed myself if the cycles seemed too much weighted toward despair. Woolf knew that whatever pain she was feeling would pass, but she didn't want to live through it and wait for it to pass; she'd had enough of waiting and time and it was time to go. She wrote:

> Oh, its beginning is coming—the horror—physically like a painful wave swelling about the heart—tossing me up. I'm unhappy, unhappy! Down—God, I wish I were dead. Pause. But why am I feeling this? Let me watch the wave rise. I watch. Failure. Yes; I detect that. Failure, failure. (The wave rises.) Wave crashes. I wish I were dead! I've only a few years to live I hope. I can't face this horror any more—(this is the wave spreading out over me).
>
> This goes on; several times, with varieties of horror. Then, at the crisis, instead of the pain remaining intense, it becomes rather vague. I doze. I wake with a start. The wave again! The irrational pain: the sense of failure; generally some specific incident.
>
> At last I say, watching as dispassionately as I can, Now take a pull of yourself. No more of this. I reason. I take a census of happy people & unhappy. I brace myself to shove to throw to batter down. I begin to march blindly forward. I feel obstacles go down. I say it doesn't matter. Nothing matters. I become rigid & straight, & sleep again, & half wake & feel the wave beginning & watch the light whitening & wonder how this time, breakfast & daylight will overcome it. Does everyone go through this state? Why have I so little control? It is not creditable, nor lovable. It is the cause of much waste & pain in my life.

I wrote to my brother during my third bout of depression, before I knew how fast that one would pass, "I can't spend every other year this way. In the meanwhile, I'm trying my best to hold on. I'd bought a gun which I had around the house, and I gave it to a friend to take care of because I didn't want to end up using it in a moment of impulsiveness. Isn't that ridiculous? To be afraid you'll end up using your own gun yourself? To have to put it someplace else and instruct someone not to give it back to you?" Suicide is really more of an anxiety response than a depression solution: it is not the action of a null mind but of a tortured one. The physical symptoms of anxiety are so acute that they seem to demand a physical response: not simply the mental suicide of silence and sleep, but the physical one of self-slaughter.

My mother had worked out the details, and my father, given to careful planning, went over the whole thing as though a dress rehearsal would exhaust in advance some of the pain of the event itself. We planned how my brother and I would come to the house, how my mother would take the antiemetics, what time of day would be best for this exercise; we discussed every detail down to the funeral home. We agreed to hold the funeral two days after the death. We planned it together much as we had on previous occasions planned parties, family vacations, Christmas. We discovered, there as elsewhere, an etiquette within which a great deal would be determined or communicated. My mother quietly set about making her emotions completely clear to all of us, intending in the course of a few months to resolve every family difference into transparency. She talked about how much she loved us all and unearthed the shape and structure of that love; she resolved old ambivalences and articulated a new clarity of acceptance. She set aside individual days with each of her friends—and she had many friends—to say good-bye; though few of them knew her actual agenda, she made sure that each knew the large place she occupied in her affections. She laughed often in that period; her sense of humor, warm and encompassing, seemed to spread to include even the doctors who poisoned her monthly and the nurses who witnessed her gradual demise. She recruited me one afternoon to help buy my ninety-year-old great-aunt a handbag, and though the expedition left her exhausted to the point of collapse for three days, it also renewed us both. She read everything I wrote with a mixture of acuity and generosity that I have not encountered elsewhere, a new quality in her, softer than the insight she had previously brought to my work. She gave little things away to people and made order of larger things that were not for giving away yet. She set about having all our furniture reupholstered so that she would leave the house in reasonable order, and she selected a design for her tombstone.

Bit by bit, that her suicide plans would become a reality seemed to settle on us. Later she was to say that she had considered doing the whole thing on her own, but that she had thought that the shock would be worse than the memories of having been with her for this experience. As for us—we wanted to be there. My mother's life was of other people, and we all hated the idea of her dying alone. It was important, in my mother's last months on earth, that we all feel very connected, that we none of us be left with a sense of secrets kept and agendas hidden. Our conspiracy brought us closer together, closer than we had ever been.

If you have never tried it yourself or helped someone else through it, you cannot begin to imagine how difficult it is to kill yourself. If death were a passive thing, which occurred to those who couldn't be bothered to resist it, and if life were an active thing, which continued only by virtue of a daily commitment to it, then the world's problem would be depopulation and not overpopulation. An awful lot of people lead lives of quiet desperation and don't kill themselves because they cannot muster the wherewithal to do it.

My mother decided to kill herself on June 19, 1991, age fifty-eight, because if she had waited longer, she would have been too weak to take her life, and suicide requires strength and a kind of privacy that does not exist in hospitals. That afternoon, my mother went to see a gastroenterologist, who told her that large tumors were blocking her intestine. Without immediate surgery, she would be unable to digest food. She said that she would be in touch to schedule the surgery, then rejoined my father in the waiting room. When they got home, she called me and called my brother. "It was bad news," she said calmly. I knew what that meant, but I couldn't quite bring myself to say it. "I think it's time," she said. "You'd better come up here." It was all very much as we had planned it.

I headed uptown, stopping to collect my brother from his office on the way. It was pouring, and the traffic was slow. My mother's absolutely calm voice—she used the logical tone she had always used for things she had planned, as though we were coming up to the apartment for dinner—had made the whole thing seem straightforward, and when we arrived at the apartment, we found her lucid and relaxed, wearing a nightgown with pink roses on it and a long bathrobe. "You're supposed to try to have a light snack," my father said. "It helps to keep the pills down." So we went into the kitchen and my mother made English muffins and tea. At dinner a few nights earlier, my mother and my brother had pulled a wishbone, and my mother had won. "What did you wish?" my brother now asked my mother, and she smiled. "I wished for this to be over as quickly and as painlessly as possible," she said. "And I got my wish." She looked down at her English muffin. "I got my wishes so often." My brother put out a box of cookies just then, and my mother, with that tone of fond irony that was so much her own, said, "David. For the last time. Would you put the cookies on a plate." Then she reminded me to collect some dried flowers she'd had arranged for the front hall in the country. These matters of form had become intimacies. I think that there is a certain natural drama to death from natural causes: there are sudden symptoms and seizures, or in their absence the shock of surprises of interruption. What was so curious about this experience was that there was nothing sudden or unanticipated about it. The drama lay in the absence of drama, in the choking experience of no one's acting out of character in any regard.

Back in her bedroom, my mother apologized again for involving us all. "But at least you three should be together afterwards," she added. My mother—who always believed in having an adequate supply of everything—actually had by then twice as much Seconal as she needed. She sat up in bed and dumped forty pills on the blanket in front of her. "I'm so tired of taking pills," she said wryly. "That's one thing I won't miss." And she began taking them with a sort of expert's finesse, as though the thousands of pills she had had to take during two years of cancer had been practice for this moment—as I have since learned to take antidepressants in handfuls. "I think that should do it," she said when the heap had vanished. She tried to down a glass of vodka, but she said it was making her nauseated. "Surely this is better than your seeing me screaming in a hospital bed?" And of course it was better, except that that image was still only fantasy and this one had become reality. Reality in these instances is actually worse than anything.

Then we had about forty-five minutes, while she said all the last things she had to say, and we said all the last things we had to say. Bit by bit her voice slurred, but it was clear to me that what she was saying had also been thought through. And it was then that the drama of her death came, because as she became hazier she also became even clearer, and it seemed to me that she was saying even more than she could have planned. "You were the most beloved children," she said, looking at us. "Until you were born, I had no idea that I could feel anything like what I felt then. Suddenly, there you were. I had read books all my life about mothers who bravely said that they would die for their children, and that was just how I felt. I would have died for you. I hated for you to be unhappy. I felt so deeply for you whenever you were unhappy. I wanted to wrap you in my love, to protect you from all the terrible things in the world. I wanted my love to make the world a happy and joyful and safe place for you." David and I were sitting on my parents' bed, where my mother was lying in her accustomed place. She held my hand for a second, then David's. "I want you to feel that my love is always there, that it will go on wrapping you up even after I am gone. My greatest hope is that the love I've given you will stay with you for your whole life."

Her voice was steady at that point, as though time were not against her. She turned to my father. "I would gladly have given decades of my life to be the one who went first," she said. "I can't imagine what I would have done if you had died before me, Howard. You are my life. For thirty years you have been my life." She looked at my brother and me. "And then you were born, Andrew. And then you, David. Two more came along, and then there were three people who all really loved me. And I loved you all. I was so overwhelmed, so overpowered by it." She looked at me—I was crying, though she was not—and she took on a tone of gentle reprimand. "Don't think you're paying me some kind of great tribute if you let my death become the great event of your life," she said to me. "The best tribute you can pay to me as a mother is to go on and have a good and fulfilling life. Enjoy what you have."

Then her voice became dreamily torpid. "I'm sad today. I'm sad to be going. But even with this death, I wouldn't want to change my life for any other life in the world. I have loved completely, and I have been completely loved, and I've had such a good time." She closed her eyes for what we thought was the last time, then opened them again and looked at each of us in turn, her eyes settling on my father. "I've looked for so many things in this life," she said, her voice slow as a record played at the wrong speed. "So many things. And all the time, paradise was in this room with the three of you." My brother had been rubbing her shoulders. "Thanks for the back rub, David," she said, and then she closed her eyes for good. "Carolyn!" my father said, but she didn't move again. I have seen one other death—someone shot by a gun—and I remember feeling that that death did not belong to the person who died: it belonged to the gun and the moment. This death was my mother's own.

The contemporary American philosopher Ronald Dworkin has written, "Death has dominion because it is not only the start of nothing but the end of everything, and how we think and talk about dying—the emphasis we put on dying with 'dignity'—shows how important it is that life ends *appropriately*, that death keeps faith with the way we have lived." If I can say nothing else of my mother's death, I can say that it was in keeping with her life. What I would not have anticipated was how it would tempt me toward suicide. In his "Requiem," Rilke wrote, "We need, in love, to practice only this: letting each other go. For holding on comes easily; we do not need to learn it." If I had been able to absorb that lesson, I would perhaps not have fallen into depression; for it was this extraordinary death that precipitated my first episode. I do not know what my level of vulnerability was, or whether I would have had a breakdown if I had not been through such a desolating experience. My attachment to my mother was so strong, our sense of family so impermeable, that perhaps I was always being set up to be incompetent to tolerate loss.

Assisted suicide is a legitimate way to die; at its best it is full of dignity, but it is still suicide, and suicide is in general the saddest thing in the world. Insofar as you assist in it, it is still a kind of murder, and murder is not easy to live with. It will out, and not always in savory ways. I have not read anything about euthanasia, written by those who have taken part, that was not at some profound level an apologia: writing or speaking about your involvement in euthanasia is, inevitably, a plea for absolution. After my mother's death, I was the one who took on the cleaning up of my parents' apartment, sorting through my mother's clothes, her personal papers, and so on. The bathroom was thick with the debris of terminal illness, including instruments for the care of wigs, salves and lotions for allergic reactions, and bottles and bottles and bottles of pills. Back in the corner of the medicine chest, behind the vitamins, the painkillers, the drugs to calm her stomach, the ones to rebalance certain hormones, the various combinations of sleeping pills she had taken when the disease and fear conspired to keep her awake—behind all of them I found, like the last gift out of Pandora's box, the rest of the Seconal. I was busy throwing away bottle after bottle, but when I got to those pills, I stopped. Fearful myself of both illness and despair, I pocketed the bottle and hid it in the farthest corner of my own medicine chest. I remembered the October day my mother had said to me, "I have the pills. When the time comes, I'll be able to do it."

Ten days after I finished clearing out my mother's bathroom, my father called in a rage. "What happened to the rest of the Seconal?" he asked, and I said that I had thrown away all the pills in the house that were in my mother's name. I added that he seemed depressed and that it disturbed me to think of his having ready access to the drug. "Those pills," he said, his voice breaking, "you had no right to throw away." After a long pause, he said, "I was saving them for myself, in case someday I was ill also. So I wouldn't have to go through that whole process to get them." I think that for each of us it was as though my mother lived on in those red pills, as though whoever possessed the poison by which she had died retained also some strange access to her life. It was as though by planning to take the remaining pills we were somehow reattached to my mother, as though we could join her by dying as she had died. I understood then what suicide epidemics were all about. Our one comfort in the face of our loss of my mother was to plan to repeat her departure on ourselves.

Not until some years later could we reverse that formulation, by making a better story for ourselves. My recovery from depression was for my father a triumph of his love and of intelligence and will: he had tried to save one member of the family and failed, but he was able to save another. We had participated in one suicide and averted another. I am not intensely suicidal so long as my situation, psychological or otherwise, seems to me or to those around me to allow of improvement. But the terms of my own suicide, should matters change too far, are entirely clear to me. I am relieved and even proud not to have bowed down to ending my life when I felt low. I plan to stand up to adversity again as necessary. Psychologically, I will not have to seek far if I decide to kill myself, because in my mind and my heart I am more ready for this than for the unplanned daily tribulations that mark off the mornings and afternoons. In the meanwhile, I have got the gun back, and I have checked out sources for more Seconal. Having witnessed the comfort my mother found in her final dominion, I can understand how, when the misery seems great and recovery impossible, the logic of euthanasia becomes incontrovertible. It is not savory, in political terms, to conflate suicide in the face of psychiatric illness with suicide in the face of physical illness, but I think there are surprising similarities. It would have been dreadful if the paper had announced the day after her death that a breakthrough discovery could cure ovarian cancer. If your sole complaint is suicidality, or depression, then to kill yourself before you have tried every expedient is tragic. But when you get to the psychic breaking point and know, and have the agreement of others, that your life is too awful—suicide becomes a right. Then (and it is such a fragile, difficult moment), it becomes an obligation for those who are living to accept the will of those who do not and will not wish to live.

The question of suicide as control has not been sufficiently well explored. An attachment to control motivated my mother's death, and that motivation exists for many people who kill themselves under very different circumstances. Alvarez writes, "Suicide is, after all, the result of a choice. However impulsive the action and confused the motives, at the moment when a man finally decides to take his own life he achieves a certain temporary clarity. Suicide may be a declaration of bankruptcy which passes judgment on a life as one long history of failure. But it is a decision which, by its very finality, is not wholly a failure. There is, I believe, a whole class of suicides who take their own lives not in order to die but to escape confusion, to clear their heads. They deliberately use suicide to create an unencumbered reality for themselves or to break through the patterns of obsession and necessity which they have unwittingly imposed on their lives."

Nadezhda Mandelstam, wife of the great Russian poet Osip Mandelstam, once wrote, "In war, in the camps and during the periods of terror, people think much less about death (let alone suicide) than when they are living normal lives. Whenever at some point on earth mortal terror and the pressure of utterly insoluble problems are present in a particularly intense form, general questions about the nature of being recede into the background. How could we stand in awe before the forces of nature and eternal laws of existence if terror of a mundane kind was felt so tangibly in everyday life? Perhaps it is better to talk in more concrete terms of the fullness or intensity of existence, and in this sense there may have been something more deeply satisfying in our desperate clinging to life than what people generally strive for." When I mentioned this to a friend who was a survivor of the Soviet punitive system, he confirmed it. "We opposed those who wanted to make our lives bitter," he said. "To take our lives was to be defeated, and almost all of us were determined not to give that satisfaction to the oppressors. It was the ones who were strongest who could live, and our lives were opposition—that is what fueled them. The people who wanted to take our lives were the enemy, and our hatred for and resistance to them kept us alive. Our desire became stronger in the face of our suffering. It was not while we were there that we wanted to die, even if beforehand we had been somewhat moody people. After we came out, it was another matter; it was not uncommon for survivors of the camps to kill themselves when they returned to the society they'd left behind. Then, when there was nothing to oppose, our reasons for living out our lives had to come from within our selves, and in many cases our selves had been ruined."

Writing of Nazi camps rather than of Soviet ones, Primo Levi observed, "In the majority of cases, the hour of liberation was neither joyful nor lighthearted. For most it occurred against a background of destruction, slaughter, and suffering. Just as they felt they were again becoming men, that is, responsible, the sorrows of men returned: the sorrow of the dispersed or lost family; the universal suffering all around; their own exhaustion, which seemed definitive, past cure; the problems of a life to begin all over again amid the rubble, often alone." Like the monkeys and rats that disfigure themselves when they are subjected to inappropriate separations, overcrowding, and other appalling conditions, people have in themselves an organic form for and expression of despair. There are things you can do to a person to make him suicidal, and those things were done in concentration camps. Once you have crossed that boundary, it is hard to sustain good spirits. Concentration camp survivors have a high rate of suicide, and some people express surprise that you could survive the camps and then end your life. I do not think that is surprising. Many explanations have been given for Primo Levi's suicide. Many people have said that his medications must be to blame since he had manifested so much hope and light in the later years of his life. I think that his suicide was always brewing in him, that there had never been an ecstasy of being saved, never been anything comparable to the horror he had known. Perhaps the pills or the weather or something else loosed in him the same impulse that would cause a rat to chew off its tail, but I think that the essential caprice was always there after the horror of the camp. Experiences can easily trump genetics and do this to a person.

Homicide is more common than suicide among the disenfranchised, while suicide is higher than homicide among the powerful. Contrary to popular belief, suicide is not the last resort of the depressive mind. It is not the last moment of mental decay. The chances of suicide are actually higher among people recently returned from a hospital stay than they are among people at a hospital, and not simply because the restraints of the hospital setting have been lifted. Suicide is the mind's rebellion against itself, a double disillusionment of a complexity that the perfectly depressed mind cannot compass. It is a willful act to liberate oneself of oneself. The meekness of depression could hardly imagine suicide; it takes the brilliance of self-recognition to destroy the object of that recognition. However misguided the impulse, it is at least an impulse. If there is no other comfort in a suicide not avoided, at least there is this persistent thought, that it was an act of misplaced courage and unfortunate strength rather than an act of utter weakness or of cowardice.

My mother took Prozac, then a brand-new drug, for a month during her fight with cancer. She said it numbed her too much—and it made her jittery, which, in combination with the side effects of her chemo, was too much to bear. "I was walking down the street today," she said, "and I thought, I am probably dying. And then I thought, should we have cherries or pears at lunch? And the two things felt too much the same." She had a sufficient external reason to be depressed, and she was a great believer in authenticity. As I have said, I think she had suffered from mild depression for years; if I have depression genes, I suspect they came from her. My mother believed in order and in structure. I cannot remember—and in psychoanalysis I sought hard—a single time that my mother broke a promise she had made. I cannot remember her ever being late for an appointment. I believe now that she kept this martial law over her life not only out of regard for others, but also because it circumscribed a wistfulness that was always in her. My greatest happiness when I was a little boy came from making my mother happy. I was good at it, and it was not easy to do. I think, in retrospect, that she always needed to be distracted from sadness. She hated to be alone. Once she told me that it was because she had been an only child. I think a reservoir of loneliness was in her, something that went far deeper than being an only child. For the sake of her surpassing love for her family, she held it in check, and she was fortunate to have the capacity to do that. Nonetheless, the depression was there. And I think that this is why she was so well prepared for the rigor of killing herself.

I would say of suicide not that it is always a tragedy for the person who dies, but that it always comes too soon and too suddenly for those left behind. Those who condemn the right to die are committing a grave disservice. We all want more control over life than we have, and dictating the terms of other people's lives makes us feel safe. That is no reason to forbid people their most primitive freedom. Nonetheless, I believe that those who, in supporting the right to die, distinguish some suicides absolutely from others are telling a lie to accomplish a political objective. It is up to each man to set limits on his own tortures. Fortunately, the limits most people set for themselves are high. Nietzsche once said that the thought of suicide keeps many men alive in the darkest part of the night, and I would say that the more fully one comes to terms with the idea of rational suicide, the safer one will be from irrational suicide. Knowing that if I get through this minute I could always kill myself in the next one makes it possible to get through this minute without being utterly overwhelmed. Suicidality may be a symptom of depression; it is also a mitigating factor. The thought of suicide makes it possible to get through depression. I expect that I'll go on living so long as I can give or receive anything better than pain, but I do not promise that I will never kill myself. Nothing horrifies me more than the thought that I might at some stage lose the capacity for suicide.

CHAPTER VIII

History

The history of depression in the West is closely tied to the history of Western thought and may be divided into five principal stages. The ancient world's view of depression was startlingly similar to our own. Hippocrates declared that depression was essentially an illness of the brain that should be treated with oral remedies, and the primary question among the doctors who followed him was about the humoral nature of the brain and the correct formulation of these oral remedies. In the Dark and Middle Ages, depression was seen as a manifestation of God's disfavor, an indication that the sufferer was excluded from the blissful knowledge of divine salvation. It was at this time that the illness was stigmatized; in extreme episodes, those who suffered from it were treated as infidels. The Renaissance romanticized depression and gave us the melancholic genius, born under the sign of Saturn, whose dejection was insight and whose fragility was the price of artistic vision and complexity of soul. The seventeenth to nineteenth centuries were the era of science, when experiment sought to determine the composition and function of the brain and to elaborate biological and social strategies for reining in the mind gone out of control. The modern age began in the early twentieth century with Sigmund Freud and Karl Abraham, whose psychoanalytic ideas of the mind and self gave us much of the vocabulary still in use to describe depression and its sources; and with the publications of Emil Kraepelin, who proposed a modern biology of mental illness as an affliction separable from or superadded to a normal mind.

Disruptions long called melancholia are now signified by the strangely causal word *depression*, which was first used in English to describe low spirits in 1660, and which came into common usage in the mid–nineteenth century. I use *depression* here to describe states for which we would now use that term. It is fashionable to look at depression as a modern complaint, and this is a gross error. As Samuel Beckett once observed, "The tears of the world are a constant quantity." The shape and detail of depression have gone through a thousand cartwheels, and the treatment of depression has alternated between the ridiculous and the sublime, but the excessive sleeping, inadequate eating, suicidality, withdrawal from social interaction, and relentless despair are all as old as the hill tribes, if not as old as the hills. In the years since man achieved the capacity for self-reference, shame has come and gone; treatments for bodily complaints have alternated and crossed with treatments for spiritual ones; pleas to external gods have echoed pleas to internal demons. To understand the history of depression is to understand the invention of the human being as we now know and are him. Our Prozac-popping, cognitively focused, semi-alienated postmodernity is only a stage in the ongoing understanding and control of mood and character.

The Greeks, who celebrated the idea of a sound mind in a sound body, shared the modernist idea that an unsound mind reflects an unsound body, that all illness of the mind is connected in some fashion to corporeal dysfunction. Greek medical practice was based on humoral theory, which viewed character as the consequence of the four bodily fluids: phlegm, yellow bile, blood, and black bile. Empedocles described melancholy as the consequence of an excess of black bile, and Hippocrates, astonishingly modernist, had imagined a physical cure by the end of the fifth century B.C., at a time when the idea of illness and doctors was itself just emerging. Hippocrates located the seat of emotion, thought, and mental illness in the brain: "It is the brain which makes us mad or delirious, inspires us with dread and fear, whether by night or by day, brings sleeplessness, inopportune mistakes, aimless anxieties, absentmindedness, and acts that are contrary to habit. These things that we suffer all come from the brain when it is not healthy, but becomes abnormally hot, cold, moist, or dry." Hippocrates thought that melancholy mixed internal and environmental factors, that "a long labor of the soul can produce melancholy"; and he distinguished illness that arose in the wake of terrible events from illness without apparent cause. He classified both as versions of a single illness precipitated when excess of black bile—cold and dry—unbalanced ideal equilibrium with the other three humors. Such an imbalance, he said, might have a uterine origin—one might be born with a tendency toward it—or might be induced by trauma. The Greek words for black bile are *melaina chole*, and the symptoms of its malign ascendancy, which Hippocrates associated with the autumn, included "sadness, anxiety, moral dejection, tendency to suicide," and "aversion to food, despondency, sleeplessness, irritability, and restlessness" accompanied by "prolonged fear." To rebalance the humors, Hippocrates proposed changes in diet and the oral administration of mandrake and hellebores, cathartic and emetic herbs thought to eliminate excess black and yellow bile. He also believed in the curative properties of advice and action; he cured the melancholy of King Perdiccas II by analyzing his character and persuading him to marry the woman he loved.

Theories about the temperature, location, and other details of black bile became increasingly complex during the next fifteen hundred years, which is curious because there actually is no such thing as black bile. Yellow bile, produced in the gallbladder, may turn quite brownish, but it is never black, and it seems unlikely that discolored yellow bile was the stuff described as *melaina chole*. Black bile, hypothetical or otherwise, was nasty; it was said to cause not only depression but also epilepsy, hemorrhoids, stomachache, dysentery, and skin eruptions. Some scholars have suggested that the word *chole*, meaning bile, was often used in association with the word *cholos*, which means anger, and that the notion of black bile may have come from a belief in anger's darkness. Others have proposed that the association of darkness with negativity or pain is an inbuilt human mechanism, that depression has been represented cross-culturally in black, and that the notion of a black mood is amply established in Homer, who describes "a black cloud of distress," such as afflicted the depressive Bellerophon, "But the day soon came / When even Bellerophon was hated by all gods. / Across the Alean plain he wandered, all alone, / Eating his heart out, a fugitive on the run / From the beaten tracks of men."

The divide between the medical view and the philosophical/religious view of depression was strong in ancient Athens. Hippocrates denounced the practitioners of "sacred medicine," who invoked the gods to effect cures, as "swindlers and charlatans"; and he said that "all that philosophers have written on natural science no more pertains to medicine than to painting." Socrates and Plato were resistant to Hippocrates' organic theories and claimed that though mild impairments might be treated by physicians, deep disorders were the province of philosophers. They formulated notions of the self that have exerted a powerful influence in modern psychiatry. Plato originated the developmental model that suggests that a man's childhood may determine the quality of his adult character; he speaks of the family's power to determine for good or ill a man's lifelong political and social attitudes. His tripartite model of the adult psyche—the rational, the libidinal, and the spiritual—is uncannily like Freud's. Hippocrates is, in effect, the grandfather of Prozac; Plato is the grandfather of psychodynamic therapy. During the span of two and half millennia between them and the present, every variation on their two themes has been introduced, and genius and folly seem to have alternated like pistons.

Doctors soon began to propose oral remedies for melancholy. In the post-Hippocratic ancient world, Philotimus, for example, having noticed that many depressives complained of "a light head, arid, as though nothing existed," put a lead helmet on his patients so that they might be made fully aware that they had heads. Chrysippus of Cnidus believed that the answer to depression was the consumption of more cauliflower, and he cautioned against basil, which he claimed could cause madness. Philistion and Plistonicus, opposing Chrysippus, proposed that basil was the best treatment for patients who had lost all feelings of vitality. Philagrius believed that many symptoms of depression came from the loss of too much sperm in wet dreams, and he prescribed a mixture of ginger, pepper, epithem, and honey to control them. Anti-Philagrians of the period thought depression was the organic result of abstinence from sex and sent their patients back to the bedroom.

Within seventy years of the death of Hippocrates, the School of Aristotle began to exert powerful influence on how we think about thinking. Aristotle accepted neither Hippocrates' diminution of the importance of the soul and its philosophers, nor Plato's dismissal of the doctor as a mere artisan. Aristotle proposed instead a theory of a united self in which "a disturbance of the body affects the soul; the diseases of the soul come from the body, except those that are born in the soul itself. Passion changes the body." His wisdom on human nature is not matched by any particular knack for anatomy. Saying that "the brain is a residue lacking any sensitive faculty," Aristotle proposed that the heart had a regulatory mechanism that controlled the balance of the four humors, and that either heat or cold could disrupt this balance. Aristotle's view of depression, unlike that of Hippocrates, was not entirely negative. Aristotle took from Plato the notion of divine madness and medicalized it by associating it with melancholia. Though Aristotle sought ways to understand and alleviate the ailment, he also felt that a certain amount of cold black bile was necessary to genius: "All those who have attained excellence in philosophy, in poetry, in art, and in politics, even Socrates and Plato, had a melancholic habitus; indeed some suffered even from melancholic disease." Aristotle wrote, "We are often in the condition of feeling grief without being able to ascribe any cause to it; such feelings occur to a slight degree in everyone, but those who are thoroughly possessed by them acquire them as a permanent part of their nature. Those who possess an atrabilious temperament in slight degree are ordinary, but those who have much of it are quite unlike the majority of people. For, if their condition is quite complete, they are very depressed; but if they possess a mixed temperament, they are men of genius." Heracles was the most famous of the classical geniuses afflicted with the black bile complaints, and they also touched Ajax ("the flashing eyes of Ajax raging, and his mind weighted down," as it is written in *The Sack of Troy*). This notion of inspired melancholia was carried forward by Seneca, who said that "there has never been great talent without some touch of madness"; it resurfaced in the Renaissance and has reared up regularly ever since.

In the fourth to first centuries B.C., medical science and philosophy developed along closely associated lines, describing psychiatry in an increasingly unified way. Melancholy was seen in this period to be a universal destiny in one form or another; the fourth-century poet Menander wrote, "I am a man, and that is reason enough for being miserable." The Skeptics believed that it was important to study the visible world and therefore looked to symptoms without theorizing about the origins of those symptoms or their deep meaning. Uninterested in the big, difficult questions of the nature of the physical and cerebral self that had preoccupied Hippocrates and Aristotle, they tried to categorize symptoms to delineate disease.

In the third century B.C., Erasistratus of Juli separated the brain and the cerebellum, determining that intelligence resided in the brain and that motor ability was based in the cerebellum; and Herophilus of Calcedonius then determined that from the brain "motive power goes toward the nerves," so establishing the idea of a controlling organ supervising a nervous system. Menodotus of Nicomedia, who lived in the first century A.D., combined all previous wisdom, incorporating the thoughts of the symptom-oriented empiricists with those of the grand philosophers and the early doctors. He recommended for depression the same hellebores that Hippocrates had discovered, and the same self-examination that had come from Aristotle, and introduced also the use of gymnastics, travel, massage, and mineral water to help the depressive. Such a total program is just what we strive for today.

Rufus of Ephesus, Menodotus' contemporary, isolated melancholy delusion from the rest of the mind and spoke of melancholy as a discrete aberration that occurred in otherwise stalwart minds. He cataloged the delusions of some depressive patients: Rufus treated at various stages a man who believed himself to be an earthenware pot; another who believed that his skin had desiccated and was peeling off his body; and one who thought that he had no head. Rufus noted the physical symptoms of what we now recognize to be hypothyroidism, a hormonal imbalance whose symptoms are similar to depression's. He believed that the primary causes of melancholy were heavy meats, inadequate exercise, too much red wine, and inordinate intellectual toil, and he noted that a genius might be particularly prone to the complaint. Some melancholiacs "are that way by nature, by virtue of their congenital temperament," while others "become that way." He also spoke of degrees and types of melancholy: one in which black bile infected all the blood, one in which it affected only the head, and one in which it affected "the hypochondria." Rufus found that his melancholy patients also suffered the buildup of unreleased sexual fluids, whose putrefaction infected the brain.

Rufus was in favor of routing out depressive illness before it became ingrained. He proposed bloodletting, and a "purge with dodder of thyme and aloe, because these two substances, taken daily in a small dose, bring about a moderate and soothing opening of the bowels." This might be supplemented with black hellebore. Regular walking was suggested, and so was travel, and so was washing before meals. Rufus also formulated his "sacred remedy," the Prozac of its day, which remained widely popular at least through the Renaissance and was used on occasion even later. This was a liquid compounded of colocynth, yellow bugle, germander, cassia, agaric, asafetida, wild parsley, aristolochia, white pepper, cinnamon, spikenard, saffron, and myrrh, mixed all with honey and given in four-dram doses in hydromel and salt water. Other physicians of the time proposed everything from chains and punishments, to placing a dripping water pipe near the melancholic to lure him to sleep, to putting him in a hammock, to giving him a diet of light-colored, moist foods such as fish, poultry, diluted wine, and human breast milk.

The late Roman period was a time of considerable learning on these matters. Aretaeus of Capidoccia studied mania and depression, as associated and as separate complaints, during the second century A.D. He believed in a physical soul that traveled around in the body, bursting forth in heat among angry men (whose faces therefore turned red) and withdrawing in fearful ones (whose faces therefore went pale). He proposed that among melancholiacs the level of black bile "may be stirred by dismay and immoderate anger," and that the humors had a circular relationship with the emotions, so that a cooling of the soul's vital energy might lead to severe depression, while depression served to cool the bile. Aretaeus was the first to give a convincing portrait of what we now call agitated depression—a complaint for which recent popular philosophy misguidedly tends to blame postindustrial life. It is as organic and eternal as sadness. Aretaeus wrote, "The melancholic isolates himself; he is afraid of being persecuted and imprisoned; he torments himself with superstitious ideas; he is terror-stricken; he mistakes his fantasies for the truth; he complains of imaginary diseases; he curses life and wishes for death. He wakes up suddenly and is seized by a great tiredness. In certain cases, depression seems to be a sort of demi-mania: the patients are always obsessed with the same idea and can be depressed and energetic at the same time." Aretaeus emphasized that severe depression often occurred in people already inclined toward sadness, especially those who were old, obese, weak, or alone; and he suggested that "the physician Love" was the most powerful in curing the complaint. His oral remedy of choice was the regular consumption of blackberries and leeks; he also encouraged the psychodynamic practice of articulating symptoms and claimed he could help patients to release fears by describing them.

Claudius Galen, born in the second century A.D., personal physician to Marcus Aurelius, likely the most important doctor after Hippocrates, tried to arrive at a neurological and psychological synthesis of the work of all his forebears. He described melancholic delusions—one of his patients believed that Atlas would get tired and drop the world, while another thought he was a fragile-shelled snail—and identified beneath them a mixture of fear and despondency. He saw "tremors in the hearts of healthy young people and adolescents weak and thin from anxiety and depression." Galen's patients experienced "scarce, turbulent, and interrupted sleep, palpitations, vertigo . . . sadness, anxiety, diffidence, and the belief of being persecuted, of being possessed by a demon, hated by the gods." Galen also shared Rufus' belief in the disastrous consequences of deficient sexual release. He treated one of his female patients, whose brain, he believed, was troubled by the noxious fumes of her rotting unreleased sexual fluids, "with a manual stimulation of the vagina and of the clitoris and the patient took great pleasure from this, much liquid came out, and she was cured." Galen also had his own patent recipes, many of which included Rufus' ingredients, though he recommended an antidote made of plantains, mandrake, linden flowers, opium, and arugula for the treatment of combined anxiety and depression. Interestingly, while Galen was formulating his cordial, a continent away the Aztecs began the use of strong hallucinogenic drugs to prevent depression among prisoners, which they believed was a bad omen. Captives who were to be sacrificed were given a special brew to keep them from despairing so that they would not offend the gods.

Galen believed in a physical soul, what we might call a psyche, located in the brain; this soul was subject to the rule of a self as masterful in the body as God is in the world. Mixing the idea of the four humors with notions about temperature and moisture, Galen formulated the idea of nine temperaments, each a type of soul. One was dominated by a melancholia conceived not as pathology but as part of the self: "There are people who are by nature anxious, depressed, anguished, always pensive; for them the doctor can do but little." Galen noted that melancholia could be the result of a lesion to the brain; or it could follow on external elements that altered the functioning of an intact brain. In the event of humoral imbalance, black bile could go to the brain, drying it; and this would

291

damage the self. "The humor, like a darkness, invades the seat of the soul, where reason is situated. As children who fear the darkness, so adults become when they are the prey of the black bile, which supports fear; they have in their brain a continual night, are in uncessant fear. For this reason the melancholiacs are afraid of death and wish for it at the same time. They avoid light and love darkness." The soul could in effect be dimmed. "The black bile envelops reason as the crystalline lens of the eye, if it is limpid, allows a clear view, but if it becomes ill and opaque, does not allow a distinct view. In the same way the qualities of animal spirits may become heavy and opaque." Galen, preferring psychobiology to philosophy, was sharply critical of those who attributed melancholy to emotional, abstract factors; but he believed such factors could exacerbate symptomatology of a mind already skewed by humoral imbalance.

The next stage of medical history traces its roots back to the Stoic philosophers. Their belief that external agency caused mental illness was dominant in the Dark Ages that followed the fall of Rome. The rise of Christianity was highly disadvantageous for depressives. Though Galen was the medical authority of the Middle Ages, his notion of psychopharmaceutical treatments conflicted with the paradigm of the Church. His treatments, in philosophical exile, were used less and less.

Saint Augustine had declared that what separated men from beasts was the gift of reason; and so the loss of reason reduced man to a beast. From this position, it was easy to conclude that the loss of reason was a mark of God's disfavor, His punishment for a sinning soul. Melancholy was a particularly noxious complaint, since the melancholic's despair suggested that he was not suffused with joy at the certain knowledge of God's divine love and mercy. Melancholia was, in this view, a turning away from all that was holy. Furthermore, deep depression was often evidence of possession; a miserable fool contained within himself a devil, and if that devil could not be exorcised from him, why then he himself must go. Clerics soon found support for this idea in the Bible. Judas had committed suicide, and so, the reasoning ran, he must have been melancholic; and so all melancholiacs must be Judas-like in their carnality. The description of Nebuchadnezzar in Daniel 4:33 was taken to demonstrate that God sent insanity to punish the sinful. In the fifth century, Cassian writes of the "sixth combat" with "weariness and distress of the heart," saying that "this is 'the noonday demon' spoken of in the Ninetieth Psalm," which "produces dislike of the place where one is, disgust, disdain, and contempt for other men, and sluggishness." The section in question occurs in Psalms and would be literally translated from the Vulgate: "His truth shall compass thee with a shield: thou shalt not be afraid of the terror of the night. / Of the arrow that flieth in the day, of the business that walketh about in the dark: of invasion, or of the noonday demon"—"*ab incrusus, et daemonio meridiano.*" Cassian presumed that "the terror of the night" refers to evil; "the arrow that flies in the day" to the onslaught of human enemies; "the business that walketh in the dark" to fiends that come in sleep; "invasion" to possession; and "the noonday demon" to melancholia, the thing that you can see clearly in the brightest part of the day but that nonetheless comes to wrench your soul away from God.

Other sins might waste the night, but this bold one consumes day and night. What can one say in favor of a man unprotected by the shield of God's truth? Punishment might be effective in redeeming such a hopeless case: Cassian insisted that the melancholy man be set to manual labor, and that all his brethren should withdraw from and abandon him. Evagrius, using the same phrase, said that melancholic dejection was a "noonday demon" that attacked and tempted the ascetic; he listed it as one of the eight main temptations we must resist on earth. I have taken the phrase as the title of this book because it describes so exactly what one experiences in depression. The image serves to conjure the terrible feeling of invasion that attends the depressive's plight. There is something brazen about depression. Most demons—most forms of anguish—rely on the cover of night; to see them clearly is to defeat them. Depression stands in the full glare of the sun, unchallenged by recognition. You can know all the why and the wherefore and suffer just as much as if you were shrouded by ignorance. There is almost no other mental state of which the same can be said.

By the time of the Inquisition, in the thirteenth century, some depressives were fined or imprisoned for their sin. In this period, Thomas Aquinas, whose theory of body and soul placed the soul hierarchically above the body, could conclude that the soul was not subject to bodily illness. Since the soul was, however, below the divine, it was subject to intervention by God or Satan. Within this context, an illness had to be of the body *or* the soul, and melancholia was assigned to the soul. The medieval Church defined nine deadly sins (they were subsequently compacted to seven). Among these was *acedia* (translated as "sloth" in the thirteenth century). The word seems to have been used almost as broadly as the word *depression* is in modern times, and it described symptoms familiar to anyone who has seen or felt depression—symptoms that had not previously been counted as vice. Chaucer's Parson describes it as a thing that "deprives the sinner of the quest for all goodness. *Acedia* is man's enemy because it is hostile to industry of any kind, and it is also a great enemy to the livelihood of the body, for it makes no provision for temporal necessities and even wastes, spoils, ruins, all earthly goods by negligence. It makes living men [be] like those who already suffer the pains of Hell. It makes a man peevish and encumbered." The passage goes on and on, becoming more disagreeable and judgmental with each phrase. *Acedia* is a compound sin whose elements the Parson enumerates. "It is so tender and delicate, as Solomon says, that it will suffer no hardship or penance. The shirking makes man fear even to begin to perform any good work. Despair, loss of hope in the mercy of God, springs from unreasonable remorse and sometimes from excessive fear, which makes the sinner imagine that he has sinned so much that it will do him no good to repent. If it persists to a man's last moment, it is numbered among the sins against the Holy Ghost. Then comes the sluggish sleepiness that makes a man dull and indolent of body and soul. Last comes the sin of World Weariness, called sadness, which produces the death of soul and body alike. Because of it, a man becomes annoyed with his own life. So the life of man is often ended before, by way of nature, his time has really come."

Monks were particularly likely to develop *acedia*, which among them manifested itself in exhaustion, listlessness, sadness or dejection, restlessness, aversion to the cell and the ascetic life, and yearning for family and former life. *Acedia* was distinguished from the sadness *(tristia)* that leads a man back to God and to repentance. Medieval sources are not clear about the role volition plays in this. Was it a sin to let oneself develop *acedia*? Or was *acedia* a punishment meted out to those who had committed some other sin? Its most passionate opponents equate it with original sin; the eloquent nun Hildegard von Bingen wrote, "At the moment when Adam disobeyed the divine law, at that exact instant, melancholy coagulated in his blood."

Order was somewhat precarious in the Middle Ages, and disorder of the mind was therefore particularly frightening to the medieval sensibility. Once reason was impaired, the whole of the human mechanism would fall apart; and then the social order would disintegrate. Folly was a sin; mental disease was a far more serious one. Reason is necessary to allow a man to choose virtue. Without it, he has not enough self-control for such a choice. The psyche, as understood by classical thinkers, could not be detached from the body; the soul, as understood by medieval Christians, was barely coincident with the body.

It is from this tradition that the stigma still attached to depression today has grown. The soul, being a divine gift, should be perfect; we should strive to sustain its perfection; and its imperfections are the primary source of shame in modern society. Dishonesty, cruelty, greed, egotism, and lapses of judgment are all shortcomings of the soul, and so we automatically attempt to suppress them. So long as depression is grouped with these "afflictions of the soul," it seems to us to be abhorrent. There are many stories of how the association cast depression in the worst possible light. The fifteenth-century painter Hugo van der Goes, for example, entered a monastery in the 1480s, but continued, by virtue of great talent, to have regular interaction with the outer world. Returning one night from a journey, Hugo is recorded as having been "struck by a strange disorder of his imagination. He cried out incessantly that he was doomed and condemned to eternal damnation. He would even have injured himself, phantasmagorias clouding his diseased mind." According to his fellow brothers, who attempted treatment with music therapy, "his condition did not improve; he continued to talk unreasonably, and to consider himself a child of perdition." The monks considered whether Hugo had artistic frenzy or was possessed by an evil spirit, and decided that he had both complaints, perhaps exacerbated by consumption of red wine. Hugo was terrified of the work he had agreed to do and could not imagine that he could finish his commissions. With time, and with great rituals of religious repentance, he eventually recovered his equanimity for some time; but he had a subsequent relapse and died in a bad state.

If the Middle Ages moralized depression, the Renaissance glamorized it. Reaching back to classical philosophers (more than to classical doctors), Renaissance thinkers posited that depression indicated profundity. Humanist philosophy presented an increasingly strong challenge to Christian doctrine (though, in other cases, it strengthened Christian beliefs and tenets). The irrational pain that in the Middle Ages had been described as a sin and curse was now an illness (increasingly called melancholia) and the defining quality of a personality (increasingly called melancholy). Among all Renaissance writers who discussed depression—and they were legion—Marsilio Ficino was its greatest philosopher in the Renaissance. He believed that melancholy, present in every man, is the manifestation of our yearning for the great and the eternal. He wrote of those for whom melancholia is a default state: "It is astonishing that whenever we are at leisure, we fall into grief like exiles, though we do not know, or certainly do not think of, the cause of our grief . . . in the midst of the plays of pleasure we sigh at times, and when the plays are over, we depart even more sorrowful." The melancholy here described is what is revealed beneath the busyness of daily life, a constant quality of the soul. Ficino reverts to the Aristotelian idea of divinely mad sadness and goes on to say that the philosopher, the deep thinker, or the artist will of necessity be more in touch with his melancholy than the common man, that the very profundity of his experience of melancholy will reflect his success in raising his mind above the distractions of ordinary life. For Ficino, the tortured mind is the more worthy, as it is catapulted up toward the melancholy inadequacy of its knowledge of God. This becomes a holy credo as he explains the nature of divine melancholy: "As long as we are representatives of God on earth, we are continually troubled by nostalgia for the celestial fatherland." The state of knowledge is dissatisfaction, and the consequence of dissatisfaction is melancholy. Melancholy divorces soul from world and so propels the soul toward purity. The mind "increases in perfection the more it goes away from the body, and so the mind will be most perfect at the time when it flies away entirely." Ficino's description of the divinity of melancholy acknowledges that the state is very near death.

Ficino subsequently proposed that artistic creation relied on a muse who descended during temporary insanity: melancholia was a prerequisite to inspiration. Nonetheless, Ficino recognized that depression was a terrible complaint and recommended treatments for it, including exercises, alterations of diet, and music. Ficino himself was a depressive, who, when feeling low, could not conjure all these attractive arguments in favor of depression; when his friends came to see him, they often had to make his own arguments to him. Ficino's philosophy, like much post-Renaissance thought on the subject of melancholy, is autobiography—and so he speaks of steering the course between nonmelancholic phlegm on the one hand and desperate melancholic illness on the other, titling the sixth chapter of his first book "How Black Bile Makes People Intelligent."

The Renaissance attempted to reconcile its understandings of classical thought with certain accepted "knowledge" that came from the Middle Ages. In bringing together the classical idea of the temperaments with the medieval fascination with horoscopes, Ficino described Saturn as the weighty, isolated, ambivalent planet that reigned over melancholy. Saturn is "himself the author of mysterious contemplation," according to the alchemist and cabalist Agrippa, "not given to public dealing, the highest of the planets, who first recalls the soul from outer offices to its core, then has it ascend from lower matters, leading it to the highest, and granting it the sciences." These views are borne out in the writings of Giorgio Vasari on the great artists of this time.

The English Renaissance held more closely to medieval views about melancholy than did the Italian, but the southern influence began to creep up in the late fifteenth century. So, for example, the English continued to believe that melancholy came from "the intercourse or meddling of euill angels," but accepted that those afflicted with such intervention were not responsible for it. For the English Renaissance thinker, the sense of sin experienced by the melancholic is a dangerous misfortune rather than a sign of the absence of God's love and is not to be confused with the true sense of sin experienced by the true sinner. Of course it was not always easy to distinguish between the delusional and the real. One student of "melancholick Constitution, distracted with grief," claimed that he had actually felt an "evil Spirit enter by his fundament with wind, and so did creep up his body until it possessed the head." Though he was ultimately cured of the devil's presence, others were not so lucky. George Gifford wondered, "What manner of persons are fittest for the devill to make his instruments in witchcraft and sorceries" and found for his answer that the devil seeks "ungodly persons which are blind, full of infidelity, and overwhelmed and drowned in dark ignorance. If there be above all these a melancholike constitution of body, his impressions print the deeper in the minde."

The northern idea of a relationship between witches and melancholy gives the southern idea of a relationship between genius and melancholy a good run for its money. The Dutch court doctor Jan Wier (whose *De praestigiis daemonum* was listed by Freud as one of the ten greatest books of all time) was a great defender of witches as the victims of their own melancholia; his assertion that these unfortunate ladies were sick in the head saved a number of them from execution. He argued his position by showing that the victims of witches were usually delusional, focusing on the large number of men in northern Europe who accused witches of stealing their penises. Wier insisted other men could usually spot the stolen organs physically present right where they had always resided and proposed that men were seldom abandoned by their "needles." If the men who were the "victims" of witches suffered from delusions, then surely the ones who supposed that they were witches were only the more delusional. This model was taken up by the Englishman Reginald Scot, who in his 1584 book on witchcraft proposed that witches were all merely depressed and foolish old women, prodded by evil as though it were a mosquito, who ineptly took on themselves blame for the problems they saw around them. In their "drousie minds the divell hath goten a fine seat; so as, what mischeefe, mischance, calamitie, or slaughter is brought to passe, they are easilie persuaded the same is doone by themselves." This view, that what had been held to be religious truth was all merely delusion and connected to melancholic mental illness, had strong opponents who continued to champion the medieval position; though Scot's book was broadly read in Elizabethan England, King James commanded that all copies of it be burned—as though the books themselves were witches.

Illness gradually overtook possession. In a French case of this period, physicians perceived in a witch "some rumbling under her short ribs on the left side, proper to those that are subject to the Spleene," and this led to the 1583 synod command that priests "inquire diligently into the life of the possessed" before an exorcism, "for oftentimes those that are Melancholike, Lunatike, and Bewitched by Magicall Artes . . . have more neede of Phisitians Remedie, than of the Exorcists Ministrie." Renaissance rationalism triumphed over medieval superstition.

The French were the first to treat effectively symptoms that could reflect either primary disease or affliction of imagination. Montaigne, something of a melancholic himself, was a great believer in philosophy as physic, and he created an antimelancholic theater of illusion. He tells, for example, of a woman who was in terror because she believed she had swallowed a needle; so he made her throw up and put a needle in her vomit, and she was cured.

Andreas Du Laurens's *Discourse of Melancholike Diseases* was published in English in 1599. Du Laurens stated that melancholy was "a cold and drie distemperature of the brain" that could proceed "not of the disposition of the bodie," but of patients' "manner of living, and of such studies as they bee most addicted unto." Du Laurens divided up the mind into three parts: reason, imagination, and memory. Concluding that melancholia was an illness of imagination, he left to the melancholic an intact reason, which meant that in the eyes of the Church the melancholic was not deprived of his humanity (his "immortal rational soul") and was therefore not cursed by God. He took on board the idea that melancholy can come in degrees, separating "melancholike constitutions which keep within the bounds and limits of health" from the ones that did not keep within those bounds. Like most other writers on the subject, his book is full of anecdotal descriptions of individuals, including "one Sienois a Gentleman, who had resolved with himselfe not to pisse, but to dye rather, and that because he imagined that when he first pissed, all his towne would be drowned." The man was apparently paralyzed with a depressive anxiety and a sense of his own destructiveness and was causing trauma to his bladder; eventually, his physicians built a fire next door, persuaded the man that the town was burning down and that only by his relieving himself could he save it, and so brought him through this particular anxiety.

Du Laurens is perhaps best known for his complicated idea that people see backward: that their eyes roll inward and look at their brain. He fails to make clear what rainbow spectacular the cheery individual might find when he looks backward into his brain, but he does stipulate that, since the brain of the melancholic is suffused with black bile, the eyes of the melancholic, when they roll backward, see darkness everywhere. "The spirits and blacke vapours continually passe by the sinews, veines and arteries, from the braine unto the eye, which causeth it to see many shadows and untrue apparitions in the aire, whereupon from the eye the

formes thereof are conveyed unto the imagination." Then the unpleasantness really gets going, these black visions continuing to flash on the
eye even when it is directed at the outside world, and the melancholic
sees "many bodies flying, like to Ants, flyes, and long haires, the same
also does such as are readie to vomit."

It began to be a commonplace, at this time, that one might divide
normative grief from melancholy by assessing the appropriate proportions of loss to sorrow, and measuring how some people exceeded those
proportions—a principle Freud would develop three centuries later, and
which continues to be used in the diagnosis of depression today. One
doctor of the early seventeenth century wrote that a patient had gone so
far as to "take no joy of anything" following a death; another was "troubled by melancholy, how to live for the death of her mother that died a
quarter of a year since. Will weep and cry and wander and can follow no
business." Another doctor wrote that ordinary discontent or sorrow
"makes more way for the greatest enemy of nature, *viz.*, melancholy."
Melancholy, then, becomes an ordinary thing carried too far as well as an
abnormal thing; this dual definition rapidly became a standard one.

By the end of the sixteenth century and throughout the seventeenth,
the "ordinary" melancholy had become a common affliction that could
be as pleasurable as it was unpleasant. The arguments of Ficino and of
his counterparts in England were increasingly echoed all across the
Continent. Levinus Lemnius in Holland, Huarte and Luis Mercado in
Spain, Joannes Baptista Silvaticus in Milan, and Andreas Du Laurens in
France each wrote of the melancholy that makes a man better and more
inspired than his nonmelancholic counterparts. Romantic Aristotelian
conceptions of melancholy seemed to sweep Europe, and melancholy
came into fashion. In Italy, where Ficino had definitively identified
melancholy with genius, all those who believed themselves to be
geniuses expected themselves to be melancholy. While men of real brilliance might suffer, those who hoped to be mistaken for brilliant men
acted out suffering. Around Ficino, there assembled in Florence a group
of cosmopolitan Saturnist intellectuals. Englishmen who traveled to
Italy and saw this milieu would go home boasting a sophistication that
was manifest in their melancholic attributes upon their return, and since
only the wealthy could afford to travel, melancholy soon became, in the
eyes of the English, an illness of the aristocracy. The upper-class mal-
content—dark-eyed, sorrowful, taciturn, disheveled, irritable, surly,
austere—becomes by the late sixteenth century a social prototype,
described and caricatured in literature of the time, most brilliantly in the
figure of "the melancholy Jacques" in *As You Like It*.

Shakespeare's mastery of melancholia—which is most transparently his subject in the character of Hamlet—was to change forever the under-standing of the subject. By no other author was the matter described so sympathetically or with such complexity, woven so intimately into cheer and sadness, shown to be so essential to wisdom and so much the basis of folly, given the attributes of both cunning and self-destruction. Previous to Shakespeare, the melancholy of a man had been a discrete entity; after Shakespeare, it was no more easily separable from the rest of self than are the indigo rays from the rest of the white-light spectrum. What a prism might reveal for an instant cannot alter the everyday reality of the sun.

By the time *Hamlet* was performed, melancholy was almost as much of a privilege as a disease. A morose hairdresser in a play of the mid–seventeenth century complains that he feels melancholy and meets with a stern reprimand. "Melancholy? Marry, gup, is *melancholy* a word for a barber's mouth? Thou shouldst say heavy, dull, and doltish: melan-choly is the crest of the courtier's arms!" According to the notes of a physician of the period, 40 percent of his melancholy patients had titles—despite the fact that much of his practice was devoted to caring for farmers and their wives. Two-thirds of the aristocrats who came to him complained of melancholy humors; and these men and women were well informed, speaking not simply of waves of sadness but com-plaining quite specifically on the basis of the scientific knowledge and fashion of the time. One such patient was "desirous to have something to avoid the fumes arising from the spleen." Concoctions based on helle-bores were still the favorites; the doctor who treated this man prescribed *hiera logadii*, lapis lazuli, hellebore, cloves, licorice powder, *diambra,* and *pulvis sancti,* all of them to be dissolved in white wine, and borage. Astro-logical charts were consulted (for independent information and to deter-mine the timing of treatment); the possibility of bloodletting was also considered. And of course religious counseling was also usually held to be a good idea.

Just as in the early Prozac days, everyone and his uncle Bob seemed to be getting depressed and battling depression and talking about battling depression, so in the early seventeenth century the nonmelancholic man began to focus on the idea of melancholy. In both the 1630s and the 1990s the meaning of the disease-associated word—*melancholy* or *depression*—grew confused. When *acedia* was a sin, only those who were so ill that they could not function, or who suffered delusional anxiety, would admit to their complaint. Now that the word *melancholia* was used also to signify great depth, soulfulness, complexity, and even genius, people took on the behaviors of a depressive without medical cause; they soon discovered that, though real depression might be painful, depressive behavior could be pleasurable. They took to lounging for hours on long sofas, staring at the moon, asking existential questions, professing fear of whatever was difficult, failing to respond to questions put to them, and altogether carrying on in just the way that the prohibition against *acedia* had been meant to prevent. Yet it was the same basic structure of complaint, the same as what we now call depression. This melancholia was a praiseworthy ailment that one was constantly analyzing. Those who were truly ill with severe melancholia had sympathy and respect heaped on them, and these, with various medical advances, gave them a better time of it than they would have enjoyed in any period since Galen's Rome. The state of mind so elegized was what might be called white melancholy, something more shimmering than shadowy. Milton's "Il Penseroso" describes the seventeenth-century idea exquisitely:

> . . . hail thou Goddess, sage and holy,
> Hail, divinest Melancholy,
> whose saintly visage is too bright
> To hit the sense of human sight

until in a celebration of monastic isolation and gloom and old age, Milton waxes grand:

> Find out the peaceful hermitage,
> The hairy gown and mossy cell,
>
> . . . .
>
> Till old experience do attain
> To something like prophetic strain.
> These pleasures, Melancholy, give,
> And I with thee will choose to live.

The seventeenth century found history's greatest champion of the melancholy cause. Robert Burton mixed a millennium of thought and a steady supply of scattered personal intuitions in *The Anatomy of Melancholy,* the volume to which he devoted his entire life. The most often-quoted book on the subject prior to Freud's *Mourning and Melancholia* is a subtle, self-contradictory, badly organized, hugely wise volume that synthesizes and attempts to reconcile the philosophies of Aristotle and Ficino, the sense of character of Shakespeare, the medical insights of Hippocrates and Galen, the religious impulses of the medieval and Renaissance Church, and personal experiences of illness and introspection. Burton's ability to locate real ties between philosophy and medicine, and between science and metaphysics, started us on the path to a unifying theory of mind and matter. And yet one cannot credit Burton so much with reconciling conflicting views as with tolerating their contradictions; he is quite capable of giving six discrepant explanations for a single phenomenon without ever suggesting that the phenomenon might be overdetermined. To the modern reader, this sometimes seems bizarre; but the same reader, examining texts recently issued by the National Institute of Mental Health, will find that the complexity of depressive complaints lies precisely in that they are usually overdetermined—that depression is the common destination to which many pathways lead, and that in any individual, a certain set of symptoms may be the result of one or any several of these pathways.

Burton comes up with a physical explanation for melancholy: "our body is like a Clocke, if one wheele be amisse, all the rest are disordered, the whole Fabricke suffers." He acknowledges that "as the Philosophers make eight degrees of heat and cold: we may make 88 of Melancholy, as the parties affected are diversely seized with it, or have been plunged more or lesse into this infernall gulfe." Later he says, "Proteus himself is not so diverse; you may as well make the *Moon* a new coat, as a true character of a melancholy man; as soon find the motion of a brin in the air as the heart of a melancholy man." Burton makes a general distinction among brain-based "head melancholy," "whole body melancholy," and that which comes from the "Bowels, Liver, Spleene, or Membrane," which he calls "windie melancholy." These he then divides and subdivides, creating a map of distress.

Burton distinguishes melancholy from simply being "dull, sad, sowre, lumpish, ill disposed, solitary, any way moved, or displeased." Such qualities, he says, are within the scope of any man alive and should not by themselves be taken as evidence of the complaint. "Man that is borne of a woman," he says, quoting the *Book of Common Prayer,* "is of short continuance and full of trouble." This does not mean that we are all melancholiacs. Indeed Burton says, "These miseries encompasse our life. And 'tis most absurd and ridiculous for any mortall man to looke for a perpetuall tenor of happinesse in this life. Nothing so preposterous, and he that knowes not this, and is not armed to indure it, is not fit to live in this world. Get thee hence, if thou canst not brook it, there is no way to avoid it, but to arme thy self with magnamitie, to oppose thyself unto it, to suffer affliction, constantly to bear it."

You cannot live in the world unless you can tolerate misfortune, and misfortune comes to us all; but misfortune easily runs out of control. While a simple cough is tolerable, "continual and inveterate causeth a consumption of the lungs; so doe these our Melancholy provocations." And Burton identifies the very modern principle that everyone has a different level of tolerance for trauma, and that it is the interaction of the quantity of trauma and the level of tolerance that determines illness. "For that which is but a flea-biting to one, causeth insufferable torment to another, & which one by his singular moderation, & well composed carriage can happily overcome, a second is no whit able to sustaine, but upon every small occasion of misconceived abuse, injurie, griefe, disgrace, losse, crosse, rumor, &c. yeelds so farre to passion, that his complexion is altered, his digestion hindered, his sleepe gone, his spirits obscured, and his heart heavy . . . and he himselfe overcome with *Melancholy*. And as it is with a man imprisoned for debt, if once in the gaole, every Creditor will bring his action against him, and there likely to hold him: If any discon- tent sease upon a patient, in an instant all other perturbations will set upon him, and then like a lame dogge or broken winged goose hee droopes and pines away, and is brought at last to that malady of melancholy it selfe." Burton recapitulates the experience of anxiety as well, correctly includ- ing it in his description of depression: "In the daytime they are affrighted still by some terrible object, and torne in pieces with suspicion, feare, sor- row, discountents, cares, shames, anguish, &c., as so many wild horses, that they cannot be quiet an houre, a minute of the time."

Burton describes melancholiacs variously as "distrustful, envious, malicious," "covetous," "repining, discontent," and "prone to revenge." The selfsame Burton writes that "melancholy men of all others are most witty, and [their melancholic disposition] causeth many times divine rav- ishment, and a kind of *enthusiasmus* . . . which causeth them to be excellent Philosophers, Poets, Prophets, &c." He defers to the censors of his time by addressing the religious issues around the illness in a tactful fashion— but he also asserts that excessive religious enthusiasm can be a sign of melancholy or can engender mad despair; and he affirms that sad people who receive from God scary commands to which they feel inadequate are probably experiencing melancholy delusions. And he says, finally, that melancholy is really an illness of both body and soul, but then, like Du Laurens, avoids suggesting any loss of reason (which render his subjects inhuman and therefore animal) by saying that illness is a "default of the Imagination" rather than of reason itself.

Burton classifies the then current treatments for depression. There were the illegal ones "from the Divel, Magicians, Witches, &c., by charmes, spels, incantations, Images, &c.," and the legal ones, "immedi- ately from God *a Jove principium*, metiatelly by Nature, which concernes & works by 1. *Physician*; 2. *Patient*; 3. *Physicke*." Though he rambles through dozens of categories of treatment, he does in the end say that the "chiefest" consists in trying to address directly the "passions and per- turbations of the mind," and he commends "opening up" to friends and seeking out "mirth, music, and merry company." He recommends his own catalog of treatments: marigold, dandelion, ash, willow, tamarisk, roses, violets, sweet apples, wine, tobacco, syrup of poppy, featherfew, Saint-John's-wort if "gathered on a Friday in the hour of Jupiter," and the wearing of a ring made from the right forefoot of an ass.

Burton tackles also the difficult problem of suicide. While melancholy was voguish in the late sixteenth century, suicide was forbidden by law and by Church, the prohibition strengthened by economic sanctions. If a man in England at this time committed suicide, his family had to give up all his chattel, including plows, rakes, merchandise, and other material necessary for any kind of economic life. A miller from a small town in England lamented on his deathbed, after having given himself a fatal wound, "I have forfeited my estate to the king, beggared my wife and children." Careful once more of the censors of his own day, Burton discusses the religious implications of suicide, but acknowledging how intolerable acute anxiety is, he wonders "whether it be lawful, in this case of melancholy, for a man to offer violence to himself." He later writes, "In the midst of these squalid, ugly, and such irksome days, they seek at last, finding no comfort, no remedy in this wretched life, to be eased of all by death . . . to be their own butchers, and execute themselves." This is striking because, until Burton, the matter of depression had been quite separate from the crime against God of self-annihilation; and in fact the word *suicide* appears to have been coined shortly after the publication of Burton's magnum opus. The book includes stories of those who ended their lives for political or moral reasons, who made the choice out of aggrieved prudence rather than out of illness. It then proceeds to the suicides of people who are not rational, and so brings together these two matters, previously held to be anathema, to make suicide into a single topic of discussion.

Burton describes a winning sequence of melancholy delusions—a man who thought he was a shellfish, some who believe "that they are all glasses, and therefore will suffer no man to come neere them; that they are all corke, as light as feathers, others as heavy as lead, som are afraid their heads will fall off their shoulders, that they have frogs in their bellies, &c. Another dares not goe over a bridge, come neere a poole, rock, steep hill, lye in a chamber where crosse beames are, for feare he be tempted to hang, drowne, or praecipitate himselfe." These delusions were characteristic of melancholy at this time, and accounts of them abound in the medical and common literature. The Dutch writer Caspar Barlaeus at various stages of his life believed himself to be made of glass and to be made of straw, which might at any moment catch fire. Cervantes wrote a novella, *The Glass Licentiate*, about a man who believed himself to be made of glass. Indeed such a misapprehension was so common that it is referred to by some doctors of the time simply as "the glass delusion." It occurs as a phenomenon in the popular literature of every Western country at about this time. A number of Dutchmen were persuaded that they had glass buttocks and were at great pains to avoid sitting down lest they break; one insisted that he could travel only when packed in a box with straw. Ludovicus a Casanova wrote a long description of a baker who believed himself to be made of butter and was terrified of melting, who insisted on being always completely naked and covered with leaves to keep him cool.

These delusions generated systems of melancholic behavior—they caused people to dread ordinary circumstances, to live in constant fear, and to resist any human embrace. Those who suffered from them seem invariably to have suffered from the usual symptoms—unwarrantable sadness, constant exhaustion, lack of appetites, and so on—that we associate with depression today. This tendency to delusion, which had existed to some extent in earlier periods (Pope Pius II recounts that Charles VI of France, called "the Foolish," had believed already in the fourteenth century that he was made of glass and had iron ribs sewn into his clothing so that he would not break if he fell; along these lines ancient delusions had been recorded by Rufus) and which reached its apex in the seventeenth century, is not unknown today. There are recent reports of a depressed Dutch woman who believed that her arms were made of glass and would not get dressed lest she break them, and patients with schizo-affective conditions frequently hear voices and see visions; obsessive-compulsives are driven to equally irrational fears, such as a terror of uncleanliness. However, the delusional nature of depression has tended, with the advance of modernity, to be less specific. All of these seventeenth-century delusionals are really manifesting paranoias and conspiracy fears and the sense that the ordinary demands of life are beyond their scope, and those sensations are absolutely characteristic of modern depression.

I can remember, in my own depression, being unable to do ordinary things. "I can't sit in a movie theater," I said at one stage when someone tried to cheer me up by inviting me out to a film. "I can't go outside," I said later. I didn't have a specific rationale for these feelings, didn't expect to melt at the movies or to be turned to stone by the breeze outside, and I knew in principle that there was no reason why I couldn't go outside; but I knew that I couldn't do it as surely as I now know that I can't leap tall buildings in a single bound. I could (and did) blame my serotonin. I do not think that there has been any convincing account of why the delusions of depression took on such concrete form in the seventeenth century, but it would seem that until scientific explanations and treatments for depression began to emerge, people devised explanatory armatures for their fears. Only in a more mature society could one be afraid to be touched or to stand or to sit without concretizing the fear as being predicated on having a glass skeleton; and only in a sophisticated context might one experience an irrational fear of heat without actually describing a fear of melting. These delusions, which can seem puzzling to modern practitioners, are more easily grasped if they are contextualized.

The great transformer of seventeenth-century medicine, at least from the philosophical standpoint, was René Descartes. Though his mechanistic model of consciousness was not so far removed from the Augustinian tradition of dividing soul and body, it had specific ramifications for medicine, and especially for the treatment of mental illnesses. Descartes placed considerable emphasis on mind's influence on body and vice versa, and described in *The Passions of the Soul* how the state of the mind may immediately affect the body, but his followers tended to work on the assumption of a total mind-body split. In effect, a Cartesian biology came to dominate thinking; and that biology was largely wrong. Cartesian biology caused considerable reversal in the fate of the depressed. The endless hairsplitting about what is body and what is mind—whether depression is "a chemical imbalance" or "a human weakness"—is our legacy from Descartes. Only in recent years have we begun to resolve this confusion. But how did Cartesian biology take on such power? As a psychologist at the University of London put it, "In my experience, no body, no mind, no problem."

Thomas Willis, working to prove the bodily susceptibility of the mind, published in midcentury *Two Discourses Concerning the Soul of Brutes*, the first coherent chemical theory of melancholy, one that was not contingent on ancient humoral theories of black bile, spleen, or liver. Willis believed that an "inkindled flame" in the blood was supported by "sulfureous food" and "nitreous air" and that the brain and nerves focused the resulting spirits to guide sensation and motion. For Willis, the soul is a physical phenomenon, the "shadowy hag" of the visible body that "depends upon the temperament of the bloody mass." Willis thought that a variety of circumstances could turn the blood salty and so limit its flame, which would cut down the illumination in the brain and give rise to the brain darkness of melancholy. Willis believed that this salination of the blood could be caused by all kinds of external circumstances including the weather, excessive thinking, and insufficient exercise. The brain of the melancholic fixates on its sights of darkness and incorporates them into character. "Hence, when that the vital flame is so small and languishing, that it shakes and trembles at every motion, it is no wonder if that the

Melancholick person is as it were with a sinking and half overthrown mind always sad and fearful." The effect of this kind of problem if sustained would be an organic transformation of the brain. The melancholic blood can "cut new Porosites in the neighboring bodies"; the "Acetous disposition of the Spirits" and "*Melancholik* foulnesses" alter "the conformation of the brain itself." Then the spirits "observe not their former tracts and ways of their expansion, but they thickly make for themselves new and unwonted spaces." Though the origins of this principle are confused, the reality indicated is confirmed by modern science; persistent depression does indeed alter the brain, carving out "unwonted spaces."

The end of the seventeenth and the beginning of the eighteenth centuries saw enormous strides in science. Accounts of melancholy underwent significant shifts as a consequence of new theories of the body, which brought with them a series of new theories about the biology of the mind and its dysfunctions. Nicholas Robinson proposed a fibrous model of the body and, in 1729, said that depression was caused by failure of the elasticity of fibers. About what we would now call talking therapies, Robinson was not confident. "You may as soon attempt to counsel a Man out of the most violent Fever," he wrote, "as endeavour to work any Alteriation in their Faculties by the Impressions of Sound, tho' never so eloquently apply'd." Here begins the total abandonment of the melancholic as an individual whose ability to explain himself might be considered in his cure.

In 1742, Hermann Boerhaave pursued this idea and came up with the so-called iatromechanical model, according to which all the functions of the body could be explained through a theory of hydraulics; he treated the body "as a living and animated Machine." Boerhaave posited that the brain is a gland, and that nervous juices from this gland travel around in the blood. Blood is made of many different substances mixed together, and when the balance is confused, he held, problems ensue. Depression occurs when the oily and fatty stuffs of the blood accumulate and the nervous juices are in short supply. Under these circumstances, the blood stops circulating in the appropriate places. Boerhaave argued that the reason for this was often that one had used up too much of the nervous juice in thinking (which was taxing); the solution was to think less and act more, so producing a better balance of the components of the blood. Like Willis, Boerhaave was onto something: reduced blood supply to certain areas of the brain may result in depression or in delusion; and the onset of depression in the senile elderly is often based on the failure of blood to circulate correctly in the brain, where certain areas have become thick (as though coagulated) and do not absorb the blood's nourishments.

All this theory served the dehumanization of the human. Julien Offray

307

de La Mettrie, one of Boerhaave's great champions, scandalized the godly when he published his *L'Homme Machine* in 1747; he was cast out of the French court and went to Leiden, only to be cast out of Leiden and die at the age of forty-two in remote Berlin. He suggested that man was nothing more than a consortium of chemical substances engaged in mechanical actions—the theory of pure science as it has come down to us. De La Mettrie maintained that living substance was by nature irritable, and that from its irritation all action derived. "Irritability is the source of all our feeling, of all our pleasure, of all our passion, and of all our thoughts." The view depended on a concept of human nature that was, above all, orderly; disorders such as depression amounted to malfunctions of the wondrous machine, a departure from, rather than an element of, its function.

From here it was a short step to conceive of melancholy as an aspect of the general problem of mental illness. Friedrich Hoffman was the first to suggest coherently and forcefully what would come to be genetic theory. "Madness is an hereditary disease," he wrote, "and continues often during life; it has sometimes long intermissions, in which the patient appears perfectly in his senses; and returns at regular periods." Hoffman proposed some rather conventional cures for melancholy, then endearingly said that "of madness in young women from love, the most effectual remedy is marriage."

Scientific explanations of the body and of the mind developed at a vastly accelerated pace throughout the eighteenth century. But in an Age of Reason, those without reason were at a severe social disadvantage, and while science made great leaps forward, the social position of the depressed made great leaps backward. Spinoza had said at the end of the seventeenth century, foreshadowing the triumph of Reason, that "an emotion comes more under our control, and the mind is less passive in respect to it, in proportion as it is more known to us," and that "everyone has the power of clearly and distinctly understanding himself and his emotions, and of bringing it about that he should become less subject to them." So the melancholic would be now not a demonic but a self-indulgent figure, refusing the accessible self-discipline of mental health. Apart from the time of the Inquisition, the eighteenth century was probably the worst time in history to suffer from a rough mental disorder. While Boerhaave and de La Mettrie were theorizing, the severely mentally ill, once they were so categorized by their relatives, were treated half as though they were lab specimens and half as though they were wild animals fresh from the jungle and in need of taming. Obsessed with the manners and mores, hostile to those who did not comply with them, and titillated by alien peoples brought back from colonial territories, the eighteenth century imposed severe punishment on those whose erratic behavior seemed to threaten convention, no matter what their class or nationality. Segregated from their society, they were placed in the all-lunatic world of Bedlam (in England) or in the horror hospital of Bicêtre (in France), places that would drive the most implacably rational to insanity. Though such institutions had long existed—Bedlam was founded in 1247 and was a home for pauper lunatics by 1547—they came into their own in the eighteenth century. The concept of "reason" implies natural concord among human beings and is essentially a conformist notion; "reason" is defined by consensus. The idea of incorporating extremes into the social order is antithetical to such reason. By the standards of the Age of Reason, extremes of mental condition are not remote points on a logic continuum; they are points wholly outside of a defined coherence. In the eighteenth century, the mentally ill were outsiders without rights or position. So societally constricted were the delusional and the depressed that William Blake complained, "Ghosts are not lawful."

Among the mentally ill, the depressed had the advantage of being relatively docile and were therefore abused in just slightly less atrocious ways than were the maniacal and the schizophrenic. Filth, squalor, torture, and misery were the lot of the melancholic through the Age of Reason and the Regency. Society squashed the notion that those with severe psychological complaints might recover from them; once you had shown yourself to be barmy, you went into the mental hospital and you stayed there, for you were no more likely to emerge into human reason than was a captive rhinoceros. The chief physician of Bedlam, Dr. John Monro, said that melancholy was intractable and that "the cure of the disorder depends on *management* as much as on medicine." Those who suffered from the most severe forms of melancholy were often subjected to the most horrifying treatments. Boerhaave himself had proposed causing great physical pain in patients to distract them from the pain within their minds. Virtually drowning depressives was not uncommon, and mechanical devices of Boschian complexity were produced to make melancholiacs swoon and vomit by turns.

Those with milder (but still severe) depression often found themselves living nearly clandestine lives in consequence of that complaint. James Boswell wrote at length, to his friends, about his experiences with depression; and so, after him, did the poet William Cowper. Their accounts give a feeling for the grievous suffering attached to depression throughout this period. In 1763, Boswell wrote: "Expect not in this letter to hear of anything but the misery of your poor friend. I have been melancholy to the most shocking and most tormenting degree. I sunk altogether. My mind was filled with the blackest ideas, and all my powers of reason forsook me. Would you believe it? I ran frantic up and down the streets, crying out, bursting into tears, and groaning from my innermost heart. O good GOD! what have I endured! O my friend, how much was I to be pitied! What could I do? I had no inclination for anything. All things appeared good for nothing, all dreary." Later that year he added, writing to another friend, "A deep melancholy seized upon me. I thought myself old and wretched and forlorn. All the horrid ideas you can imagine, recurred upon me. I took general speculative views of things; all seemed full of darkness and woe." Boswell undertook the writing of ten lines a day addressed to himself and found that by describing what he was going through as he went through it, he could keep some measure of sanity, though he filled his lines with ellipses. So we find entries such as "You was direfully melancholy and had the last and most dreadful thoughts. You came home and prayed . . ." and a few days later, "Yesterday you was very bad after dinner, and shuddered with dire ideas. You was incertain and confused and lay, talked of going to bed, and could scarcely read Greek . . ."

Samuel Johnson, whose life Boswell recorded, was also given to severe depression, and indeed, their mutual experience of depression for some time bound the two men. Johnson maintained that Burton's *The Anatomy of Melancholy* was the only book that got him up "two hours sooner than he wished to rise." Johnson was always aware of mortality and terrified of wasting time (though in his blackest depressions he lay unproductive for long stretches). "The black Dog," wrote Johnson, "I hope always to resist, and in time to drive though I am deprived of almost all those that used to help me. When I rise my breakfast is solitary, the black dog waits to share it, from breakfast to dinner he continues barking." And as Boswell once said to him, playing on Dryden's line, "Melancholy, like 'great wit,' may be near allied to madness; but there is, in my opinion, a distinct separation between them."

William Cowper poeticized his sorrow, but it was perhaps even more desperate than Boswell's. To a cousin Cowper wrote in 1772, "I will endeavour not to repay you in notes of sorrow and despondence, though all my sprightly chords seem broken." The following year he had a severe breakdown and was utterly incapacitated for some time. During that time he wrote a horrifying series of poems, including one that ends, "I, fed with judgement, in a fleshly tomb, am / Buried above ground." Cowper did not find much salvation in writing; ten lines a day were not likely to mitigate his desperation. Indeed, though he knew himself to be a great poet, he felt that his ability with words was almost irrelevant to his experience with depression. In 1780, he wrote to John Newman, "I am trusted with the terrible Secret Myself but not with the power to Communicate it to any purpose. I carry a load no Shoulders Could Sustain, unless underpropped as mine are, by a heart Singularly & preternaturally hardened." Edward Young, writing roughly contemporaneously, spoke of "the stranger within thee" and described the bleakness of the world: "Such is the earth's melancholy map! But far / More sad! this earth is a true map of man!" And Tobias Smollett wrote, "I have had a hospital these fourteen years within myself and studied my own case with the most painful attention."

The lot of women was particularly hard. The Marquise du Deffand wrote to a friend in England, "You cannot possibly have any conception of what it is like to think and yet to have no occupation. Add to that a taste that is not easily satisfied and a great love of truth and I maintain that it would be better never to have been born." In another letter, she wrote in disgust with herself, "Tell me why, detesting life, I still fear death."

The Protestant ascetics of the later eighteenth century attributed depression to society's decadence and pointed to high rates of the complaint among an aristocracy nostalgic for its past. What had once been a mark of aristocratic sophistication was now the mark of moral decay and weakness, and the solution was to eviscerate complacency. Samuel Johnson said that hardship prevents spleen and observed that "in *Scotland,* where the inhabitants in general are neither opulent nor luxurious, Insanity, as I am informed, is very rare." John Brown held that "our effeminate and unmanly Life, working along with our Island-Climate, hath notoriously produced an Increase of *low Spirits* and *nervous Disorders.*" Edmund Burke argued that "melancholy, dejection, despair, and often self-murder, is the consequence of the gloomy view we take of things in this relaxed state of body. The best remedy for all these evils is exercise or *labour.*" Voltaire's Candide struggles even after his troubles have come to an end; finally his depressed mistress asks, "I should like to know which is the worst, to be ravished a hundred times by Negro pirates, to have one buttock cut off, to run the gauntlet of a Bulgar regiment, to be whipped and hanged at an auto-da-fé, to be dissected, to row in the galleys—in fact to experience all the miseries through which we have passed—or just to stay here with nothing to do?" The problem is solved when she and Candide apply themselves to tending the kitchen garden; tilling the soil has a most propitious effect on mood. And yet the contrarian idea, that a high life might lift the spirits and work weigh them down, was also in circulation; Horace Walpole wrote a friend a prescription, "*Rx CCCLXV days of London,*" to lift the weight of an illness no country cordial had been able to heal.

By the end of the eighteenth century, the spirit of romanticism was starting to stir, and disillusion with the dryness of pure reason set in.

Minds began to turn to the sublime, at once magnificent and heartrending. Depression was let in once more, better loved than it had been since Ficino. Thomas Gray captured the mood of an age that would once more look on depression as the source of knowledge rather than as a folly removed from it. His "Elegy Written in a Country Churchyard" became a standard text of wisdom achieved through a sadness proximate to truth, through which one learns that "the paths of glory lead but to the grave." Looking out at the playing fields of Eton, he saw:

> To each his suff'rings: all are men,
> Condemn'd alike to groan,
> The tender for another's pain,
> The unfeeling for his own.
>
> . . . .
>
> No more; where ignorance is bliss,
> 'Tis folly to be wise.

S. T. Coleridge wrote in 1794 that his will was palsied by "The Joy of Grief! A mysterious Pleasure broods with dusky Wing over the tumultuous Mind." Immanuel Kant held that "melancholy separation from the bustle of the world due to a legitimate weariness is noble" and that "genuine virtue based on principles has something about it which seems to harmonize most with the melancholy frame of mind." This was the mood in which the nineteenth century was to greet depression.

Before leaving the eighteenth century, it is worth looking at what was happening in the colonies in North America, where the moral force of Protestantism was even stronger than in Europe. The problem of melancholy had much vexed the settlers, and a school of American thought on the subject had evolved shortly after they had arrived in Massachusetts. Of course the settlers tended to be conservative in comparison to their counterparts in Europe; and since they often represented extreme religious views of one kind or another, they favored religious explanations of depression. At the same time, they had a lot of depression to cope with. Their lives were extremely hard; their societies maintained certain formal rigidities; the mortality rates were extremely high; and their feeling of isolation was particularly intense. Horace Walpole's prescriptions were unavailable to them; there was not much by way of glamour or fun to lift melancholic spirits. The focus on salvation and its mysteries also drove people to the point of distraction, since the sole focus of their lives was something definitionally uncertain.

Melancholiacs in these societies were almost always held to be the subjects of the devil's interference, prey through their own weakness or their inattention to the redeeming God. Cotton Mather was the first to comment at length on these problems. Though in his earlier life he was inclined toward extreme moral judgment, his position softened and changed somewhat when his wife, Lydia, developed a depression "little short of a Proper Satanical Possession." In the years that followed, Mather gave considerable time and attention to the problem of melancholy, and began to hatch a theory in which the divine and the biological, the natural and the supernatural, acted in complex synchrony.

In 1724, Mather published *The Angel of Bethesda*, the first book written in America to address depression. He focused more on treatments than on the diabolical causes of the complaint. "Lett not the Friends of these poor *Melancholicks*, be too soon *Weary* of the *Tiresome Things*, which they must now *Bear with Patience*, Their *Nonsense* and *Folly* must be *born with Patience, We that are Strong must bear the Infirmities of the Weak*; and with a patient, prudent, Manly Generosity, pitty them, and Humour them like *Children*, and give none but *Good Looks* and *Good Words* unto them. And if they utter Speeches that are very *Grievous* (and like *Daggers*) to us, We must not Resent them as uttered by these Persons; tis not *They* that speak; Tis their *Distemper!* They still are *Just what they were before.*" The treatments Mather suggested are an odd mix of the exorcistic, the biologically effective ("the Decoction of Purple-flowered *Pimpernel;* as also the Tops of *St. Johns Wort;* as a Specific for *Madness*") and the rather dubious (the application of "living swallows, cut in two, and laid hott reeking unto the shaved Head" and "the *Syrup of Steel,* four Ounces, a Spoonful to be taken twice a day in a Convenient Vehicle").

Henry Rose, publishing in Philadelphia in 1794, attributed to the passions the ability to "increase or diminish the power of the vital and natural functions." He maintained that as "they exceed their order and limits, the passions become dissolute and ought to be avoided; not because they disturb the tranquility of the mind alone, but as they injure the temperament of the body." In the best Puritan tradition, he recommended dispassion—the quelling of strong feeling and eros—as the best means to protect oneself from going right over the edge. This Puritanical notion was to keep its hold over the American popular imagination long after it had faded elsewhere. Even in the middle of the nineteenth century, America boasted religious revivals closely associated with illness. The United States was the location for "evangelical anorexia nervosa," in which people who believed themselves unworthy of God deprived themselves of food (and often sleep) until they starved themselves to illness or even death; those who suffered accordingly were called "starving perfectionists" by their contemporaries.

If the Age of Reason was a particularly bad one for depression, the Romantic period, which went from the end of the eighteenth century to the flowering of Victorianism, was a particularly good one. Now melancholy was thought of not as a condition for insight, but as insight itself. The truths of the world were not happy; God was manifest in nature but his precise status was in some doubt; and the stirrings of industry bred the first strains of modernist alienation, distancing man from his own production. Kant held that the sublime was always "accompanied by some terror or melancholia." In essence, this was the time when an unqualified positivism was denounced as naive rather than holy. Clearly, in the past, the rather distant past at that, man had been closer to nature, and the loss of that immediate relationship to wilderness amounted to the loss of some irretrievable joy. People in this period explicitly mourned the passage of time—not simply growing old, not simply the loss of young energy, but that time could not be held in check. This is the era of Goethe's Faust, who said to the moment, "Stay! Thou art fair!" and for that sold his soul into eternal damnation. Childhood recapitulated innocence and joy; its passing led into a postlapsarian adulthood of shadows and pain. As Wordsworth said, "We Poets in our youth begin in gladness; / But thereof come in the end despondency and madness."

John Keats wrote, "I have been half in love with easeful death"—for the very exercise of life was too exquisitely painful to bear. In his paradigmatic "Ode on Melancholy" and in the "Ode on a Grecian Urn," he speaks with unbearable sadness of a temporality which makes the most cherished thing the most sad, so that there is in the end no separation between joy and sorrow. Of melancholy itself he says:

> She dwells with Beauty—Beauty that must die;
> And Joy, whose hand is ever at his lips
> Bidding adieu; and aching Pleasure nigh,
> Turning to Poison while the bee-mouth sips:
> Aye, in the very temple of Delight
> Veil'd Melancholy has her sovran shrine.

So Shelley also conjures the mutability of experience, the quickness of time, the sense that a respite from sorrow is followed only by greater sorrow:

> The flower that smiles today
> Tomorrow dies;
> All that we wish to stay,

Tempts and then flies.

. . . .

Whilst yet the calm hours creep,
Dream thou—and from thy sleep
Then wake to weep.

In Italy, Giacomo Leopardi echoed the sentiment, writing, "Fate has bequeathed unto our race / no gift except to die." This is a far cry from the moodiness of Thomas Gray pondering beauty in a country churchyard; it is the earliest nihilism, a vision of utter futility, more like Ecclesiastes ("Vanity of vanities: all is vanity") than like *Paradise Lost.* In Germany, the feeling would acquire a name beyond that of melancholy: *Weltschmerz,* or world-sadness. It would become a lens through which all other feeling would have to be perceived. Goethe, the greatest exponent of *Weltschmerz,* did perhaps more than any other author to delineate the stormy, tragic nature of existence. In *The Sorrows of Young Werther,* he narrates the impossibility of entry into the true sublime: "In those days I yearned in happy ignorance to get out into the unfamiliar world, where I hoped to find so much nourishment, so much enjoyment for my heart, wherewith to fill and to satisfy my aspiring, yearning bosom. Now I am returning from the wide world—O my friend, with how many disappointed hopes, with how many ruined plans? . . . Does not man lack force at the very point where he needs it most? And when he soars upward in joy, or sinks down in suffering, is he not checked in both, is he not returned again to the dull, cold sphere of awareness, just when he was longing to lose himself in the fullness of the infinite?" Depression, here, is truth. Charles Baudelaire introduced the word *spleen* and its concomitant emotion to French romanticism. His dank world of sorry evil could no more manage to transcend melancholy than could Goethe's striving after the sublime:

When the low heavy sky weighs like a lid
Upon the spirit aching for the light
And all the wide horizon's line is hid
By a black day sadder than any night

. . . .

And hearses without drum or instrument,
File slowly through my soul; crushed, sorrowful,
Weeps Hope, and Grief, fierce and omnipotent,
Plants his black banner on my drooping skull.

Beside this poetic line runs a philosophical one that reaches back beyond Kant's romantic rationalism, Voltaire's optimism, and Descartes's relative dispassion to a fearful impotence and helplessness rooted in the character of Hamlet or even to *De Contempli Mundi.* Hegel, in the early nineteenth century, gave us, "History is not the soil in which happiness grows. The periods of happiness in it are the blank pages of history. There are certain moments of satisfaction in the history of the world, but this satisfaction is not to be equated with happiness." This dismissal of happiness as a natural state to which civilizations might reasonably aspire initiates modern cynicism. To our ears, it seems almost obvious, but in its time it was a heretical position of gloom: the *truth* is that we are born into misery and will miserably go on, and that those who understand misery and live intimately with it are the ones who best know history past and future. And yet glum Hegel states elsewhere that to give in to despair is to be lost.

Among philosophers, Søren Kierkegaard is depression's poster boy. Free of Hegel's commitment to resisting despair, Kierkegaard followed every truth to its illogical final point, striving to eschew compromise. He took curious comfort from his pain because he believed in its honesty and reality. "My sorrow is my castle," he wrote. "In my great melancholy, I loved life, for I loved my melancholy." It is as though Kierkegaard believed that happiness would enfeeble him. Incapable of loving the people around him, he turned to faith as an expression of something so remote as to be beyond despair. "Here I stand," he wrote, "like an archer whose bow is stretched to the uttermost limit and who is asked to shoot at a target five paces ahead of him. This I cannot do, says the archer, but put the target two or three hundred paces further away and you will see!" While earlier philosophers and poets had spoken of the melancholic man, Kierkegaard saw mankind as melancholic. "What is rare," he wrote, "is not that someone should be in despair; no, what is rare, the great rarity, is that one should truly not be in despair."

Arthur Schopenhauer was an even greater pessimist than Kierkegaard because he did not believe that pain is ennobling in any way; and yet he was also an ironist and an epigrammatist for whom the continuity of life and history was more absurd than tragic. "Life is a business whose returns are far from covering the cost," he wrote. "Let us merely look at it; this world of constantly needy creatures who continue for a time merely by devouring one another, pass their existence in anxiety and want, and often endure terrible affliction, until they fall at last into the arms of death." The depressive, in Schopenhauer's view, lives simply because he has a basic instinct to do so "which is first and unconditioned, the premise of all premises." He answered Aristotle's age-old suggestion that men of genius are melancholy by saying that a man who has any real intelligence will recognize "the wretchedness of his condition." Like

Swift and Voltaire, Schopenhauer believed in work—not because work breeds cheer so much as because it distracts men from their essential depression. "If the world were a paradise of luxury and ease," he wrote, "men would either die of boredom or kill themselves." Even the bodily pleasure that should remove one from despair is only a necessary distraction introduced by nature to keep the race alive. "If children were brought into the world by an act of pure reason alone, would the human race continue to exist? Would not a man rather have so much sympathy with the coming generation as to spare it the burden of existence?"

It was Friedrich Nietzsche who actually attempted to bring these views back to the specific question of illness and insight. "I have asked myself if all the supreme values of previous philosophy, morality, and religion could not be compared to the values of the weakened, the *mentally ill,* and neurasthenics: in a milder form, they represent the same ills. Health and sickness are not essentially different, as the ancient physicians and some practitioners even today suppose. In fact, there are only differences in degree between these two kinds of existence: the exaggeration, the disproportion, the nonharmony of the normal phenomena constitute the pathological state."

The mentally troubled and the mentally ill turned back into people in the nineteenth century. Having spent the previous hundred years like animals, they were now to be imitators of middle-class propriety—whether they wished it or not. Philippe Pinel was among the earliest reformers of treatment for the mentally ill, publishing his *Treatise* in 1806. He introduced the notion of "the moral treatment of insanity," which, given that "the anatomy and pathology of the brain are yet involved in extreme obscurity," seemed to him the only way forward. Pinel set up his hospital to conform to high standards. He persuaded his chief of staff to "exercise towards all that were placed under his protection, the vigilance of a kind and affectionate parent. He never lost sight of the principles of a most genuine philanthropy. He paid great attention to the diet of the house, and left no opportunity for murmur or discontent on the part of the most fastidious. He exercised a strict discipline over the conduct of the domestics, and punished, with severity, every instance of ill treatment, and every act of violence, of which they were guilty towards those whom it was merely their duty to serve."

The chief achievement of the nineteenth century was the establishment of the asylum system for residential care of the mentally ill. Samuel Tuke, who managed one such institution, said, "In regard to melancholiacs, conversation on the subject of their despondency is found to be highly injudicious. The very opposite method is pursued. Every means is taken to seduce the mind from its favorite but unhappy musings, by bodily exercise, walks, conversation, reading, and other innocent recreations." The effect of this kind of program (as opposed to the punishing shackles and bizarre "taming" techniques of the previous century) was, according to the master of another asylum, that "melancholia, not deepened by the want of all ordinary consolations, loses the exaggerated character in which it was formerly beheld."

Asylums pullulated like toadstools after a rainstorm. In 1807, 2.26 persons in every ten thousand of England's general population were judged to be insane (a category that would have included the severely depressed); in 1844, the number was 12.66, and by 1890, it was 29.63. That there were thirteen times as many nutters in the late Victorian period as there were at the dawn of the century can be explained only in small part by the actual increase of mental illness; in fact, in the sixteen years between Parliament's two Lunatics Acts (of 1845 and 1862), the number of identified poor mentally ill people doubled. This was occasioned in part by the increasing willingness of people to identify their relatives as crazy, in part by more rigorous standards of sanity, and in part by the depredations of Victorian industrialism. The same depressive, not sufficiently ill for Bedlam, who would once have skulked silently around the kitchen was now removed from the jolly family circle of Dickensian Britain and placed out of reach, where he did not interrupt social interaction. The asylum gave him a community in which to operate, but it also cut him off from the company of those who had any natural cause to love him. The growth of the asylum was also intimately connected to the growth in rates of "cure"—if some people's illness could actually be ameliorated through time in an asylum, then it was very nearly a duty to place anyone who might be at the brink of a lifetime of misery somewhere where he might be saved.

The principle of the asylum was to go through a long sequence of refinements. It was already a topic of debate in parliamentary select committees in 1807. The first Lunatics Act passed by Parliament required that every county provide asylum for the poor insane, including the severely depressed; and the 1862 Act to Amend the Law Relating to Lunatics opened up the possibility of voluntary confinement, so that those experiencing symptoms might, with the approval of medical authorities, put themselves into asylums. This provision demonstrates quite clearly how far the asylum had come; you would have had to be far more than crazy to check yourself into one of the eighteenth century's hospitals for the insane. By this time, county asylums were being run with public funds; private asylums run for profit; and registered hospitals (such as Bedlam, which in 1850 housed some four hundred patients) for the more acutely ill supported with a mix of public funds and private charitable contributions.

The nineteenth century was a time of classifications. Everyone debated the nature of illness and its parameters, and everyone redefined what had previously been simply identified as melancholy into categories and subcategories. Great theoreticians of classification and cure succeeded one another rapidly, each determined that some minor adjustment of his predecessor's theory would improve treatment by leaps and bounds. Thomas Beddoes wondered already in the first year of the century "whether it be not necessary either to confine insanity to one species, or to divide it into almost as many as there are cases."

Benjamin Rush, in America, believed that all insanity was a fever that had become chronic. This condition, however, was subject to external influence. "Certain occupations predispose to madness more than others. Poets, painters, sculptors, and musicians, are most subject to it. The studies of the former exercise the imagination, and the passions." Delusional depression was strong among Rush's patients. One, for example, was a sea captain who believed absolutely that he had a wolf in his liver. Another believed himself to be a plant. The plant man was persuaded that he needed to be watered, and one of his friends, a bit of a prankster, took to urinating on his head, so enraging the patient as to effect a cure. Though Rush, unlike others, did not rise to Pinel's level of sympathy for patients, he did, unlike his predecessors, believe in listening to them. "However erroneous a patient's opinion of his case may be, his disease is a real one. It will be necessary, therefore, for a physician to listen with attention to his tedious and uninteresting details of its symptoms and causes."

W. Griesinger, working in Germany, reached back to Hippocrates and declared once and for all that "mental diseases are brain diseases." Though he was not able to identify the origin of these brain diseases, he firmly insisted that there was one; and that the fault in the brain should be located and then treated, either preventatively or curatively. He accepted the movement of one mental illness into another, what we might call dual diagnosis, as part of *Einheitspsychose*—the principle that all mental illness is a single disease and that once your brain goes wonky, anything can happen in it. This principle led to the acceptance of manic-depression, the understanding that patients who fluctuated between extreme states might have a single disease rather than two in fateful alternation. On the basis of this work, brain autopsies became common, especially in instances of suicide.

Griesinger was the first to present the idea that some mental disease is only treatable, while other mental illness is curable, and on the basis of his work most asylums began to divide their patients, separating those who stood a chance of recovery and of return to functional life from the more desperate cases. Though the lives of the truly insane remained horrible, the lives of the other patients began to take on a greater semblance of normality. Treating depressed people once more *as people* kept them from descending into total dependence Meanwhile, research along the lines of Griesinger's began to usurp religion; the change in social standards that began in the late Victorian period may in some ways be linked to the rise of the medical model of the brain.

In Griesinger's hands, depression came to be fully medicalized. In the twentieth century's most influential history of mental illness, Michel Foucault has suggested that this was part of a grand scheme of social control related to colonialism and the entrenchment of ruling wealth over a trampled underclass. By classing those who found life too difficult as "ill" and by removing them from society, the ruling class could impose levels of genuine social strain and difficulty that were in fact inhuman, and against which a less contained class of miserable people might have rebelled. If the proletariat of the industrial revolution were to be effectively oppressed, those among their number who were truly at the brink of self-destruction had to be removed, lest they serve as warnings to those around them and foment revolution.

Foucault makes good reading, but the influence he has had is much crazier than the people who are his subject. Depressed people cannot lead a revolution because depressed people can barely manage to get out of bed and put on their shoes and socks. I could no more have joined a revolutionary movement during my own depression than I could have had myself crowned king of Spain. The truly depressed were not made invisible by asylums; they had *always* been largely invisible because their very disease causes them to sever human contacts and allegiances. The general reaction of other members of the proletariat (or, indeed, of any other class) to people who are severely depressed is revulsion and discomfort. Those who are not themselves afflicted with the complaint dislike seeing it because the sight fills them with insecurity and provokes anxiety. To say that the severely ill were "taken away" from their natural context is to deny the reality, which is that the natural context rejected them, as it had always done insofar as it could. No conservative parliamentarians came into the streets of the cities soliciting patients for the asylums; the asylums overflowed with people being checked in by their own families. The attempt to define the social conspirators continues like an interminable Agatha Christie novel in which everyone has actually died of natural causes.

Busy asylums were in part a consequence of the general alienation of late Victorianism, which was articulated in one form or another by everyone from the pillars of the social order (Alfred Lord Tennyson, for example, or Thomas Carlyle), to the ardent reformists (Charles Dickens or Victor Hugo), to those at the decadent fringe of society (Oscar Wilde or Joris-Karl Huysmans). Carlyle's *Sartor Resartus* chronicles alienation from an overcrowded world, a kind of universal depression, foreshadowing Brecht and Camus. "To me the Universe was all voice of Life, of Purpose, of Volition, even of Hostility: it was one huge, dead, immeasurable Steam-engine, rolling on, in its dead indifference, to grind me limb from limb." And later, "I lived in a continual, indefinite, pining fear; tremulous, pusillanimous, apprehensive of I knew not what: it seemed as if all things in the Heavens above and the Earth beneath would hurt me; as if the Heavens and the Earth were but boundless jaws of a devouring monster, wherein I, palpitating, waited to be devoured."

How to endure life, itself so burdensome in this sorrowful time? The American philosopher William James most directly addressed these problems and correctly identified the apparent source of early modernist alienation as the breakdown of unquestioning faith in a supreme God benevolently disposed toward his creation. Though James himself ardently believed in a personal creed, he was also a sharp reader of the process of disbelief. "We of the nineteenth century," he wrote, "with our evolutionary theories and our mechanical philosophies, already know nature too impartially and too well to worship unreservedly any God of whose character she can be an adequate expression. To such a harlot, we owe no allegiance." Addressing a group of Harvard students, he said, "Many of you are students of philosophy and have already felt in your own persons the skepticism and unreality that too much grubbing in the abstract roots of things will breed." And of the triumph of science, he wrote, "The physical order of nature, taken simply as science knows it, cannot be held to reveal any one harmonious spiritual intent. It is mere *weather.*" This is the essence of Victorian melancholy. Periods of greater and lesser faith had alternated through human history, but this relinquishing of the notion of God and of meaning opened the way to agonies that have endured since, far more plangent than the sorrow of those who thought that an omnipotent God had forsaken them. To believe oneself to be the object of intense hatred is painful, but to find oneself the object of indifference from a great nothingness is to be alone in a way that was in some sense inconceivable to the imagination of earlier eras. Matthew Arnold gave voice to this despair:

> The world, which seems
> To lie before us like a land of dreams,

So various, so beautiful, so new,
Hath really neither joy, nor love, nor light,
Nor certitude, nor peace, nor help for pain;
And we are here as on a darkling plain
Swept with confused alarms of struggle and flight,
Where ignorant armies clash by night.

This is the form that modern depression takes; the crisis of losing God is far more common than the crisis of being cursed by Him.

If William James defined the philosophical gap between what had been thought to be true and what philosophy had revealed, then the eminent doctor Henry Maudsley defined the consequent medical gap. It was Maudsley who first described a melancholy that recognizes but cannot resolve itself. "It is not unnatural to weep," Maudsley commented, "but it is not natural to burst into tears because a fly settles on the forehead, as I have known a melancholic man to do. [It is] as if a veil were let down between him and [objects]. And truly no thicker veil could well be interposed between him and them than that of paralyzed interest. His state is to himself bewildering and inexplicable. The promises of religion and the consolations of philosophy, so inspiring when not needed and so helpless to help when their help is most needed, are no better than meaningless words to him. There is no real derangement of the mind; there is only a profound pain of mind paralyzing its functions. Nevertheless, they are attended with worse suffering than actual madness is, because the mind being whole enough to feel and perceive its abject state, they are more likely to end in suicide."

George H. Savage, who wrote about insanity and neurosis, spoke of the need, at last, to bridge definitively the gap between philosophy and medicine. "It may be convenient," he wrote, "but it is not philosophical to treat the body apart from the mind, and the physical symptoms separately from the mental. Melancholia is a state of mental depression, in which misery is unreasonable either in relation to its apparent cause, or in the peculiar form it assumes, the mental pain depending on physical and bodily changes and not directly on the environment. A saturated solution of grief," he wrote, "causes a delusion to crystallize and take a definite form."

The twentieth century saw two major movements in the treatment and understanding of depression. One was the psychoanalytic, which has in recent years spawned all kinds of social science theories of mind. The other, the psychobiological, has been the basis for more absolutist categorizations. Each has at times seemed to have a more convincing claim on truth; each has at times seemed positively ludicrous. Each has taken a certain quantity of real insight and extrapolated absurdities from it; and each has undertaken an almost para-religious self-mystification that, had it occurred in anthropology or cardiology or paleontology, would have been laughed out of town. The reality doubtless incorporates elements from both schools of thought, though the combination of the two is hardly the sum total of the truth; but it is the competitive gleam with which each school has viewed the other that has been the basis for excessive statements that are in many instances less accurate than Robert Burton's seventeenth-century *Anatomy.*

The modern period for thought about depression really began with Freud's publication, in 1895, of the "Fliess Papers." The unconscious, as formulated by Freud, replaced the common notion of a soul and established a new locus and cause of melancholia. At the same time, Emil Kraepelin published his classifications of mental illness, which defined the category of depression as we now know it. These two men, representing the psychological and biochemical explanations of illness, established the rift that the field of mental health is now trying to close. While the separation between these two versions of depression has been damaging to modern thinking about depression, the independent ideas themselves have considerable significance, and without their parallel development we could not have begun to pursue a synthetic wisdom.

The imaginative framework for psychoanalysis had been in place for years, albeit in a distorted form. Psychoanalysis has much in common with the bloodletting that had been popular some time before. In each instance, there is the assumption that something within is preventing the normal functioning of mind. Bloodletting was to remove malign humors by drawing them physically from the body; psychodynamic therapies are to disempower forgotten or repressed traumas by drawing them from the unconscious. Freud stated that melancholy is a form of mourning and that it rises from a feeling of loss of libido, of desire for food, or for sex. "Whereas potent individuals easily acquire anxiety neuroses," Freud wrote, "impotent ones incline to melancholia." He called depression "the effect of suction on the adjoining excitation," which creates "an internal hemorrhage," "a wound."

The first coherent psychoanalytic description of melancholy came not from Freud but from Karl Abraham, whose 1911 essay on the subject remains authoritative. Abraham began by stating categorically that anxiety and depression were "related to each other in the same way as are fear and grief. We fear a coming evil; we grieve over one that has occurred." So anxiety is distress over what will happen, and melancholy is distress over what has happened. For Abraham, one condition entailed the other; to locate neurotic distress exclusively in the past or future was impossible. Abraham said that anxiety occurs when you want something you know you shouldn't have and therefore don't attempt to get, while depression occurs if you want something and try to get it and fail. Depression, Abraham says, occurs when hate interferes with the individual's capacity to love. People whose love is rejected perceive, paranoiacally, that the world has turned against them and so they hate the world. Not wishing to acknowledge such hatred to themselves, they develop an "imperfectly repressed sadism."

"Where there is a great deal of repressed sadism," according to Abraham, "there will be a corresponding severity in the depressive affect." The patient, often without realizing it, gets a certain pleasure from his depression as a result of his sadistic attitudes. Abraham undertook the psychoanalysis of a number of depressed patients and reported substantial improvements in them, though whether these patients were redeemed by true insight or comforted by the idea of knowledge is unclear. In the end, Abraham admitted that the kind of trauma that leads to depression can also lead to other symptoms, and "we have not the least idea why at this point one group of individuals should take one path and the other group another." This, in his words, is "the *impasse* of therapeutic nihilism."

Six years later, Freud wrote his brief, seminal essay "Mourning and Melancholia," which has probably had more effect on contemporary understanding of depression than any other single piece of written material. Freud questioned the coherence of what is called melancholia; the definition of depression "fluctuates even in descriptive psychology." And what, asked Freud, are we to make of the fact that many of the symptoms of melancholia, which we are so anxious to alleviate, occur also in grief? "It never occurs to us to regard it as a morbid condition and hand the mourner over to medical treatment. . . . We look upon any interference with it as inadvisable or even harmful. . . . It is really only because we know so well how to explain it that this attitude does not seem to us pathological." (This is not necessarily still the case; *The New England Journal of Medicine* recently published a paper that suggested that "since normal bereavement can lead to major depression, grieving patients who have symptoms of depression lasting longer than two months should be offered antidepressant therapy.") Depressives, however, compromise their self-esteem. "In grief," Freud wrote, "the world becomes poor and empty; in melancholia, it is the ego itself [which becomes poor and empty]." The mourner is distressed by an actual death; the melancholiac, by the ambivalent experience of imperfect love.

No man willingly gives up the object of his desire. A loss of self-esteem must result from an unwilling loss, which Freud assumed is also unconscious—as the pain of conscious loss is usually ameliorated by time. Freud suggested that the accusations the melancholiac makes against himself are really his complaints against the world, and that the self has been divided in two: into an accusing self that threatens and an accused one that cowers. Freud saw this conflict in the melancholic symptoms: the accused ego wishes to sleep, for example, but the threatening ego punishes it with sleeplessness. Depression here is really a breakdown of the coherent human being or ego. Angry at the ambivalence of his love object, the melancholic undertakes revenge. He turns his anger inward to avoid punishing the loved one. "It is this sadism," Freud wrote, "and only this that solves the riddle." Even suicidality is a sadistic impulse against another that has been redirected at the self. The splitting of the ego is a way of internalizing the loved one. If you reproach yourself, the object of your feeling is always present; if you need to reproach someone else, who may die or leave, you are left with no object for your feelings. "By taking flight into the ego," Freud wrote, "love escapes annihilation." Self-accusatory narcissism is the result of intolerable loss and betrayal, and it causes the symptoms of depression.

Abraham, responding to "Mourning and Melancholia," proposed that depression has two phases: the loss of the love-object, and the resuscitation of the love-object through internalization. He describes the disorder as the result of a hereditary factor, a fixation of the libido on that lost breast of the mother, an early injury to self-love because of a real or perceived rejection by the mother, and a pattern of repetition of that primary disappointment. "An attack of melancholic depression is ushered in by a disappointment in love," he wrote; and the melancholiac becomes "insatiable" for attention.

It is easy enough to apply the insights of Freud and Abraham, albeit in somewhat reductive terms, to one's own life. At the time of my first breakdown, I was devastated by my mother's death, and in dreams and visions and writing I most certainly incorporated her into myself. The pain of losing her made me furious. I also regretted all the pain I had ever caused my mother and regretted the complex mixed feelings that persisted in me; full closure in this relationship was forestalled by her death. I believe that internal systems of conflict and self-reproach played a large part in my falling apart—and they centered on my publication of my novel. I regretted the sabotaging privacy that I had developed because my mother so highly prioritized reticence. I decided to publish anyway, and this gave me some feeling of being freed of my demons. But it also made me feel that I was acting in defiance of my mother, and I felt guilty about that. When it came time to read aloud from the book, to declare publicly what I was doing, my self-reproach began to eat into me;

and the more I tried not to think about my mother in this situation, the more the "internalized love-object" of my mother obtruded. A secondary cause of my first breakdown was a disappointment in romantic love; my third breakdown was triggered by the failure of a relationship in which I had invested all my faith and hope. This time there were not so many complicating factors. While friends told me I should be furious, what I felt was despair and self-doubt. I accused myself endlessly as a means of accusing the other. My own attention was fixed on the person whose attention I truly wanted, who was absent, and yet alive within me. My anxiety seemed to follow only too closely the patterns of my childhood and the story of the loss of my mother. Oh, there was no shortage of internalized sadism there!

The great exponents of psychoanalysis have each offered some further refinement on these subjects. Melanie Klein proposed that every child must undergo the sad experience of losing the breast that feeds it. The clarion certainty of that infant wish for milk and the total satisfaction of having it answered are Edenic. Anyone who has ever listened to a baby screaming for nourishment will know that the absence of that milk at the moment when it is desired can result in catastrophic rage. Watching my nephew, born while I was writing this book, in his first month of life, I saw (or projected) struggles and satisfactions that were very much like my own moods and found an approximation of depression settling on him even in the seconds it might take his mother to lift him to her breast. Nor, as I draw close to finishing this book, does he appear pleased about giving up the breast as he is weaned. "In my view," Klein wrote, "the infantile depressive position is the central position in the child's development. The normal development of the child and its capacity for love would seem to rest largely on how the ego works through this nodal position."

The French analysts go one step further. For Jacques Hassoun, who brought the notion of depression to Jacques Lacan's cryptic deconstruction of the human being, depression was a third passion, as powerful and as urgent as the love or hatred that might trigger it. There was no such thing as autonomy without anxiety for Hassoun. In depression, Hassoun said, we are not properly separated from the other and perceive ourselves to be contiguous with the world. It is the nature of libido to desire the other; and since we cannot perceive a separate other in depression, we have no basis for desire. We are depressed not because we are so far removed from what we want, but because we are merged with it.

Sigmund Freud is the father of psychoanalysis; Emil Kraepelin is the father of psychobiology. Kraepelin separated acquired mental diseases from hereditary ones. He believed that all mental illness had an internal biochemical basis. He said that some illness was permanent, and some was degenerative. Kraepelin introduced order to the chaotic world of mental illness, maintaining that there were specific, easily defined, discrete diseases, and that each of these had distinctive characteristics and, most importantly, a predictable outcome that could be understood in relation to time. This basic assertion is probably untrue, but it was extremely useful in giving psychiatrists some basis for approaching complaints as they manifested.

Depression he sorted into three categories, allowing a relationship among them. In the mildest, he wrote, "there appears gradually a sort of mental sluggishness; thought becomes difficult; the patients find difficulty in coming to a decision and in expressing themselves. It is hard for them to follow the thought in reading or ordinary conversation. They fail to find the usual interest in their surroundings. The process of association of ideas is remarkably retarded; they have nothing to say; there is a dearth of ideas and a poverty of thought. They appear dull and sluggish, and explain they really feel tired and exhausted. The patient sees only the dark side of life" and so on and so forth. Kraepelin concluded, "This form of depression runs a rather uniform course with few variations. The improvement is gradual. The duration varies from a few months to over a year." The second form includes poor digestion, skin without luster, numbness of the head, anxious dreams, and so on. "The course of this form shows variations with partial remissions and very gradual improvement. The duration extends from six to eighteen months." The third form includes "incoherent and dreamlike delusions and hallucinations." It is frequently a permanent state.

Overall, Kraepelin suggested, "the prognosis is not favorable, considering that only one-third of the cases recover, the remaining two-thirds undergoing mental deterioration." He prescribed a "rest cure," "the use of opium or morphine in increasing doses," and various dietary restrictions. He cataloged depression's causes: "defective heredity is the most prominent, occurring in from 70 to 80 percent of cases," he wrote, concluding that "of external causes, beside gestation, alcoholic excesses are perhaps the most prominent; others are mental shock, deprivation, and acute diseases." There is little room here for such tangled principles as the divided ego or oral fixation on the breast. Kraepelin brought utter clarity to diagnosis, what one of his contemporaries called "a logical and aesthetic necessity." Comforting though this clarity was, it was often wrong, and in 1920 even Kraepelin had to admit that his assumptions had to be dealt with in limited terms. He began to give way to the increasingly strong wisdom that disease was always complex. The Canadian physician Sir William Osler summed up a newer way of thinking when he wrote, "Don't tell me what type of disease the patient has; tell me what type of patient has the disease!"

Adolf Meyer, a Swiss immigrant to the United States, much influenced by American philosophers such as William James and John Dewey, took a pragmatic approach and, impatient with both Kraepelin and Freud, reconciled what had become opposite views of the mind and brain. His principles, once articulated, were so rational that they seem almost commonplace. Of Kraepelin, Meyer was ultimately to say, "To try and explain a hysterical fit or a delusion system out of hypothetical cell alterations which we cannot reach or prove is at the present stage of histophysiology a gratuitous performance." He characterized the false precision of such science as "neurologizing tautology." On the other hand, he also felt that the cultic tendencies of psychoanalysis were belabored and foolish; "any attempt at inventing too many new names meets a prompt revenge," he said, adding, "My common sense does not permit me to subscribe uncritically to whole systems of theories of what the human being must be like and should work like." Observing that "steering clear of useless puzzles liberates a mass of new energy," he asked finally, "Why should we have to insist so on the 'physical disease,' if it is a mere formula of some vague obstacles, while the functional difficulties give a plain and controllable set of facts to work with?" This is the beginning of psychiatry as a dynamic therapy. Meyer believed that man had infinite adaptive capacities, embodied in the plasticity of thought. He did not believe that each new patient's experience would lead to absolute definitions and grand insights; he believed that treatment had to work on the basis of understanding this *specific* patient, and he told his pupils that each patient was an "experiment in nature." Patients might well have hereditary predispositions, but that something was inherited did not mean that it was immutable. Meyer became head of psychiatry at Johns Hopkins, the greatest medical school in America in his time, and trained a whole generation of American psychiatrists; his wife, Mary Brooks Meyer, became the world's first psychiatric social worker.

Meyer worked with Freud's idea that infantile experience was destiny, and with Kraepelin's idea that genetics was destiny, and came up with the idea of behavioral control, which was distinctly American. Meyer's greatest contribution was that he believed people were capable of change—not only that they could be liberated from misconceptions and medicated away from biological predetermination, but that they could learn to live their lives in a way that would leave them less prone to mental illness. He was very much interested in social environment. This strange new country, America, where people arrived and reinvented themselves, was thrilling to him, and he introduced an enthusiasm about self-transformation that was half Statue of Liberty and half new frontier. He called the surgeon a "hand-worker" and the physician the "user of physic" and then called the psychiatrist "the user of biography." Near the end of his life he said, "The goal of medicine is peculiarly the goal of making itself unnecessary: of influencing life so that what is medicine today becomes mere commonsense tomorrow." This is what Meyer did. Reading his many essays, one finds in them a defining of the human experience that is the medical realization of an ideal whose political exponents were Thomas Jefferson and Abraham Lincoln, and whose artistic champions included Nathaniel Hawthorne and Walt Whitman. It is an ideal of equality and simplicity, in which external embellishment is stripped away to reveal the essential humanity of each individual.

The revelations of psychoanalytic and biochemical truth about depression, mixed with the theory of evolution, left mankind newly isolated and alienated. Meyer's work with American patients was highly productive, but in Europe his ideas did not find such ready acceptance. Instead, the continent spawned the new desolation-based philosophies of the middle part of this century, especially the existentialist thought of Camus, Sartre, and Beckett. While Camus portrays an absurdity that gives neither reason to continue life nor reason to terminate it, Sartre plunges into a more desperate realm. In his first book about the onset of existential despair, he describes many of the symptoms typical of modern depression. "Something has happened to me," the hero of *Nausea* says. "I can't doubt it anymore. It came as an illness does, not like an ordinary certainty, not like anything evident. It came cunningly, little by little; I felt a little strange, a little put out, that's all. Once established it never moved, it stayed quiet, and I was able to persuade myself that nothing was the matter with me, that it was a false alarm. And now it's blossoming." A bit later, he continues, "Now I knew: things are entirely what they appear to be— and behind them, there is nothing. I exist—the world exists—and I know that the world exists. That's all. It makes no difference to me. It's strange that everything makes so little difference to me: it frightens me." And finally: "A pale reflection of myself wavers in my consciousness . . . and suddenly the 'I' pales, pales, and fades out." This is an end to meaning, to one's meaning anything else. What better way to explain the diminution of the self than to say that the "I" disappears? *Nausea* paints an absolutely cheery picture in comparison with Samuel Beckett's seminal texts, in which neither work nor anything else can offer even temporary redemption. For Beckett, feeling is anathema. In one of his novels, he writes, "But what matter whether I was born or not, have lived or not, am

dead or merely dying. I shall go on doing as I have always done, not knowing what it is I do, nor who I am, nor where I am, nor if I am." In
another, he describes how, "The tears stream down my cheeks from my
unblinking eyes. What makes me weep so? From time to time. There is
nothing saddening here. Perhaps it is liquified brain. Past happiness in any
case has clean gone from my memory, assuming it was ever there. If I
accomplish other natural functions it is unawares." How much more bleak
can one get?

In the middle decades of the twentieth century, two questions troubled
the neuroscience of depression. One was whether mood states traveled
through the brain in electrical or in chemical impulses. The initial
assumption had been that if there were chemical reactions in the brain,
they were subsidiary to electrical ones, but no evidence supported this.
The second was whether there was a difference between endogenous
neurotic depression, which came from within, and exogenous reactive
depression, which came from without. Endogenous depressions all
seemed to have precipitating external factors; reactive depressions usually followed on a lifetime of troubled reactions to circumstance that suggested an internal predisposition. Various experiments "showed" that one
kind of depression was responsive to one kind of treatment, another to
another. The idea that all depression involves a gene-environment interaction was not even entertained until the last quarter of the century.

Though this is in part because of the divided nature of modern thought
on the matter, it is also because of a much older problem. Patients suffering from depression dislike the idea that they have fallen apart in the
face of difficulties someone else might endure. There is a social interest in
saying that depression is caused by internal chemical processes that are
somehow beyond the control of the afflicted. In the same way that those
who lived during the medieval period tended to hide their complaint
behind a wall of shame, so did those who lived in the second half of the
twentieth century—unless they could claim endogenous depression,
something that had descended for no external reason, that was simply the
unfolding of a genetic plan on which no regimen of ideas could have the
slightest effect. It is in this context that antidepressants are so very popular. Because their function is internal and relatively incomprehensible,
they must affect some mechanism that one could never possibly control
with the conscious mind. They are as opulent and luxurious as having a
chauffeur; you simply sit, relaxed, in the backseat and let someone or
something else face the challenges of traffic signs, policemen, bad weather,
rules, and detours.

Antidepressants were discovered in the early 1950s. The most charming version of the story is that a group of patients isolated with tuberculosis and put on iproniazid, a new compound that was supposed to help their lungs, became curiously exultant. Before long the substance was being used for nontubercular patients (it did little for TB), and so its discovery preceded the discovery of its mode of action. In fact, whether the big insights came first from Nathan Kline (who, in the United States, discovered iproniazid, an MAO inhibitor) or from Lurie and Salzer (who, also in the United States, showed early good results with isoniazid, again without knowing its mechanism) or from Roland Kuhn (who, working in Germany, discovered imipramine, a tricyclic) has been the subject of extensive nationalist, ego-driven debate. Since iproniazid caused jaundice, its manufacturer withdrew it relatively soon after it went into distribution. Isoniazid was never widely distributed. Imipramine, on the other hand, is today the official antidepressant of the World Health Organization, and until Prozac it was the world's first-line antidepressant medication. Kuhn's interest in these drugs was classification-based; he thought they could be used in the cataloging that had obsessed German psychiatric researchers since Kraepelin. Kline, on the other hand, had started from psychoanalysis and discovered his drug while he was attempting to prove a theory about the location of ego energy. Lurie and Salzer were pragmatists. Though Kuhn's drug became the most successful, his agenda failed: there was no apparent logic governing responsiveness to his drug, and so it did not define categories of depression. Kline, on the other hand, who had wanted to help patients cope with their past traumas, was surprised to find that many of them ceased to care about their past traumas. Lurie and Salzer, who just wanted to make depressed people less depressed, came close to their goal.

Discovering antidepressants was exciting, but figuring out how or why they worked was an entirely different matter. Neurotransmitter theory had been introduced in 1905; acetylcholine was isolated in 1914; and in 1921 the function of acetylcholine was demonstrated. In 1933, serotonin was isolated, and in 1954, researchers proposed that brain serotonin might be linked to emotional functions. In 1955, an article published in *Science* stated that behavior was in some instances the immediate result of biology. Drugs that apparently *lowered* the level of serotonin in the brain caused animals to be sedated or to spasm. Later that year, another researcher found that the same drug caused levels of another neurotransmitter, norepinephrine, to drop as well. Attempts to boost norepinephrine appeared to normalize the animals' behavior—but had no effect on norepinephrine, which remained depleted. It turned out that the boosting drug was acting on dopamine, yet another transmitter. Norepinephrine, epinephrine, dopamine, and serotonin are all chemical "monoamines" (so called because they have a single amine ring as part of their chemical structure), and the new drugs beginning to come into use were monoamine oxidase inhibitors (MAO inhibitors), which effectively raised the levels of the monoamines in the bloodstream (oxidation breaks down the monoamines; MAOIs prevent oxidation).

The tricyclics, whose efficacy had been demonstrated, should have performed the same function; but tests showed that they *lowered* the level of norepinephrine in the bloodstream. Further experimentation showed that norepinephrine, though not flowing freely in the bloodstream, was still present in the body, and eventually Julius Axelrod, a U.S. scientist working at the newly formed National Institute of Mental Health, proposed the idea of reuptake. The norepinephrine got released; it did something in a no-man's-land called the "synaptic cleft" (some of it even fell out of the cleft and got metabolized); and it was then reabsorbed into the same nerve through which it had been released. Axelrod, who won a Nobel Prize in 1970, later said that if he'd known more, he would never have arrived at such a far-fetched hypothesis. And yet it worked. It was soon demonstrated that the tricyclics blocked the reuptake mechanism, increasing norepinephrine in the synaptic cleft without raising the overall body and bloodstream level of it.

Over the next twenty years, scientists debated which neurotransmitters were the really important ones. The original idea that serotonin mattered the most was replaced by new insight showing that mood was strongly affected by norepinephrine. Joseph Schildkraut's 1965 article in *The American Journal of Psychiatry* put together all this information and proposed a coherent theory: that emotion was regulated by norepinephrine, epinephrine, and dopamine (a group collectively called the catecholamines); that the MAO inhibitors prevented the breakdown of these substances and so raised the quantity of them in the brain and, therefore, in the synaptic cleft; and that the tricyclics, by inhibiting reuptake, also increased the catecholamines in the synaptic cleft.

The publication of this theory marked the definitive split between psychoanalysts and neurobiologists. Though the synaptic-cleft theories were actually not totally incompatible with the ego-sublimation ones, they were so different that it seemed to most people who were close to either of them that they could not both be true. Recent scholarship persuasively questions most of our assumptions about the action of antidepressant medications and looks at the holes in Schildkraut's influential argument. Many new arguments are elaborate and technical, but the gist of them is that though it is true that some compounds affect catecholamine levels and are effective antidepressants, it is not clear how these two facts are linked; and more extensive study shows that many substances that affect the level of catecholamine in the brain do *not* have antidepressant effects.

The direct derivative of Schildkraut's thought is the serotonin theory, which is much the same but with a different neurotransmitter. Reuptake theories about the amount of transmitter in the synaptic cleft spawned receptor theories, which are about the transmitters' destination rather than about the transmitters themselves. These theories suggest that if the receptor is not functioning correctly, the brain may act as though it has depleted neurotransmitters even when it has an ample supply. It has since turned out that high levels of neurotransmitters can cause receptors to desensitize. First articulated by a group of Scottish scientists in 1972, receptor theories have almost as many holes as the reuptake theories did: some substances that bond with receptors have no antidepressant qualities, and some drugs that are highly effective antidepressants (mianserin and iprindole, for example) do not bond with receptors or affect transmitter levels. Further, receptors are not steady entities, ports to which vessels return time and time again. They are constantly changing, and the number of them in the brain can be altered easily. Within half an hour of taking a medication, you can alter both the level of neurotransmitters in the synaptic clefts and the number and location of receptors.

A theory published in 1976 held that the delay in response to early antidepressants was due to one group of receptors, the beta-adrenergic receptors, which were desensitized by most antidepressants after a few weeks. This is another theory that has been neither proved nor disproved; it has, in fact, been mostly ignored since the advent of the SSRIs and the attempt to redefine depression as a problem in the serotonin system. As early as 1969, Arvid Carlsson suggested that the effectiveness of the existing antidepressants might be due to their peripheral effects on serotonin, rather than their primary effects on norepinephrine, epinephrine, and dopamine. He took that idea to Geigy, one of the major manufacturers of antidepressants, but they said that the idea of an antidepressant that targeted the serotonin system was uninteresting to them. Meanwhile, in Sweden, a group of scientists began to experiment with altering the structure of the existing antidepressants, and they developed the first serotonin drug in 1971. After nine years of testing, it was released in Europe in 1980. Unfortunately, like several promising drugs before it, it had serious side effects, and despite clinical successes, it was soon taken off the market. Carlsson was working with Danish researchers, and they released citalopram (Celexa), the first usable serotonin drug and still the most popular one in Europe, in 1986. While more theories about the mode of action of these drugs went in and out of circulation, the American scientist David Wong, working at Eli Lilly, had in 1972 developed another serotonin drug, called fluoxetine. Lilly wanted to use this drug as an antihypertensive, but it was not particularly effective, and in the early 1980s they began looking at its possibilities as an antidepressant. In 1987, it was launched as Prozac. Other SSRIs followed fast. Fluvoxamine (Luvox/Faverin) was already out in Europe and soon became available in the United States. Sertraline (Zoloft/Lustral), paroxetine (Paxil/Seroxat), and venlafaxine (Effexor/Efexor) were all launched within ten years. These compounds, all of which block the reuptake of serotonin, are structurally diverse and are all multifunctional.

The latest science on depression echoes Hippocrates' suggestion that depression is an illness of the brain that may be treated with oral remedies; scientists of the twenty-first century A.D. are better at formulating the remedies than were those of the fifth century B.C., but the basic perceptions have in essence come full circle. Social theories, in the meanwhile, conform to an Aristotelian mode of thought, though the development of specific kinds of psychotherapy is more sophisticated than its distant antecedents. What is most distressing is that these two kinds of insight are still being argued as though truth lay elsewhere than between them.

CHAPTER IX

Poverty

Depression cuts across class boundaries, but depression treatments do not. This means that most people who are poor and depressed stay poor and depressed; in fact, the longer they stay poor and depressed, the more poor and depressed they become. Poverty is depressing and depression is impoverishing, leading as it does to dysfunction and isolation. Poverty's humility is a passive relationship to fate, a condition that in people of greater ostensible empowerment would require immediate treatment. The poor depressed perceive themselves to be supremely helpless, so helpless that they neither seek nor embrace support. The rest of the world dissociates from the poor depressed, and they dissociate themselves: they lose that most human quality of free will.

When depression hits someone in the middle classes, it's relatively easy to recognize. You're going about your essentially okay life and suddenly you begin feeling bad all the time. You can't function at a high level; you don't have the will to get to work; you have no sense of control over your life; it seems to you that you will never accomplish anything and that experience itself is without meaning. As you become increasingly withdrawn, as you approach catatonia, you begin to attract the notice of friends and coworkers and family, who cannot understand why you are giving up on so much of what has always given you pleasure. Your depression is inconsistent with your private reality and inexplicable in your public reality.

If you're way down at the bottom of the social ladder, however, the signs may be less immediately visible. For the miserable and oppressed poor, life has always been lousy and they've never felt great about it; they've never been able to get or hold a decent job; they've never expected to accomplish anything much; and they've certainly never entertained the idea that they have control over what happens to them. The normal condition of such people has a great deal in common with depression, and so there's an attribution problem with their symptoms. What is symptomatic? What is rational and not symptomatic? There is a vast difference between simply having a difficult life and having a mood disorder, and though it is common to assume that depression is the natural result of such a life, the reality is frequently just the other way around. Afflicted by disabling depression, you fail to make anything of your life and remain stranded at the lowest echelon, overwhelmed by the very thought of helping yourself. Treating the depression of the depressed indigent often allows them to discover within themselves ambition, competence, and pleasure.

Depression is a big field full of subcategories, many of which have been studied at length: depression among women; depression among artists; depression among athletes; depression among alcoholics. The list goes on and on. And yet—indicatively—little work has been done on depression among the poor. This is curious, because depression occurs more often among people living below the poverty line than in an average population; indeed, welfare recipients have a rate of depression approximately three times as high as the general population. It has been fashionable to talk about depression in isolation from life events. In fact, most of the poor depressed fit several profiles for initial onset of depression. Their economic hardship is only the beginning of their problems. They are often in bad relationships with parents, children, boyfriends, girlfriends, husbands, or wives. They are not well educated. They do not have easy distractions from their sorrow or suffering, such as satisfying jobs or interesting travel. They do not have the fundamental expectation of good feelings. In our rage to medicalize depression, we have tended to suggest that "real" depression occurs without reference to external materiality. This is simply not true. Lots of poor people in America suffer from depression—not just the hangdog, low-down feeling of being at the bottom, but the clinical illness whose symptoms include social withdrawal, inability to get out of bed, disruptions of appetite, excessive fear or anxiety, intense irritability, erratic aggression, and inability to care for the self or others. Virtually all of America's indigent are, for obvious reasons, displeased with their situation; but many of them are, additionally, paralyzed by it, physiologically unable to conceive of or undertake measures to improve their lot. In this era of welfare reform, we are asking that the poor pull themselves up by their bootstraps, but the indigent who suffer from major depression have no bootstraps and cannot pull themselves up. Once they have become symptomatic, neither reeducation programs nor civic citizenship initiatives can help them. What they require is psychiatric intervention with medication and with therapy. It is being amply demonstrated in several independent studies across the country that such intervention is relatively inexpensive and highly effective, and that most of the indigent depressed, liberated from their depression, are keen to better themselves.

Indigence is a good trigger for depression; relief of indigence is a good trigger for recovery. The focus of liberal politics has been on ameliorating the external horrors of indigent lives, with the assumption that this will make people happier. That goal should never be discounted. It is sometimes more feasible, however, to relieve the depression than to fix the indigence. Popular wisdom holds that unemployment must be remedied before the fancy business of the mental health of the unemployed is addressed. This is poor reasoning; fixing the mental health problem may well be the most reliable way to return people to the workforce. In the meanwhile, some advocates for the disenfranchised have worried that Prozac will be added to the tap water to help the miserable tolerate the intolerable. Unfortunately, Prozac neither makes nor keeps the miserable happy, and so the paternalistic totalitarian scenario sketched by social alarmists has no basis in reality. Treating the consequences of social problems will never substitute for solving them. Indigent people who have received appropriate treatment may, however, be able to work in concert with liberal politics to change their own lives, and those changes can cause a shift in the society as a whole.

Humanitarian arguments for treating depression among the indigent are sound; the economic arguments are at least equally sound. Depressed people are an enormous strain on society: 85 to 95 percent of people in the United States with serious mental illness are unemployed. Though many of them struggle to lead socially acceptable lives, others are given to substance abuse and self-destructive behaviors. They are sometimes violent. They pass these problems on to their children, who are likely to be mentally slow and emotionally dysfunctional. When a poor depressed mother is not treated, her children tend to head into the welfare and prison systems: the sons of mothers with untreated depression are far more likely to become juvenile delinquents than are other children. Daughters of depressed mothers will go through puberty earlier than other girls, and this is almost always associated with promiscuity, early pregnancy, and emotional instability. The dollar cost of treating depression in this community is modest when compared to the dollar cost of not treating depression.

It is extremely difficult to find any poor people who have had sustained treatment for depression, because there are no coherent programs in the United States for locating or treating depression in this population. Medicaid recipients qualify for extensive care but have to claim it, and depressed people seldom exercise rights or claim what should be theirs, even if they have the sophistication to recognize their condition. Aggressive outreach programs—which seek out people who may need treatment and bring that treatment to them, even if such people are disinclined to pursue help—are morally justified, because those seduced into treatment are almost always glad to have received such attention; here more than elsewhere, the resistance is a symptom of the illness. Many states promise more or less adequate treatment programs for those among the indigent depressed who are able to visit the appropriate offices, fill in the appropriate forms, wait in the right lines, provide three kinds of photo identification, research and enroll in programs, and so on. Few indigent depressed people have these capacities. The social status and serious problems of the indigent depressed make it virtually impossible for them to function at this level. This population can be treated only by addressing illness before addressing the passivity with which they tend to experience that illness. Speaking of mental health intervention programs, Steven Hyman, director of the NIMH, says, "It's not like the KGB rolling up in a bread truck and pulling you in. But you need to pursue these people. You could do this in the workfare programs. If you want to have the most effective transition from welfare to work, that is a good place to start. It is probably an unprecedented experience in these people's lives to have somebody really interested in them." Most people are initially uncomfortable with unprecedented experiences. Desperate people who dislike help are usually unable to believe that help will set them free. They can be saved only through muscular exhortation of missionary zeal.

It is hard to make specific numerical estimates of the costs associated with serving this population, but 13.7 percent of Americans are below the poverty line, and according to one recent study, about 42 percent of heads of households receiving Aid to Families with Dependent Children (AFDC) meet the criteria for clinical depression—more than twice the national average. A staggering 53 percent of pregnant welfare mothers meet the same criteria. From the other side, those with psychiatric disorders are 38 percent more likely to receive welfare than are those without. Our failure to identify and treat the indigent depressed is not only cruel but also expensive. Mathematica Policy Research, Inc., an organization that compiles social-issue statistics, confirms that "a substantial proportion of the welfare population . . . have undiagnosed and/or untreated mental health conditions," and that offering services to these individuals would "enhance their employability." State and federal governments spend roughly $20 billion per year on cash transfers to poor nonelderly adults and their children. We spend roughly the same amount for food stamps for such families. If one makes the conservative estimate that 25 percent of people on welfare are depressed, that half of them could be treated successfully, and that of that percentage two-thirds could return to productive work, at least part-time, factoring in treatment costs, that could still reduce welfare costs by as much as 8 percent—a savings of roughly $3.5 billion per year. Because the U.S. government also provides health care and other services to such families, the true savings could be substantially higher. At the moment, welfare officers do no systematic screening for depression; welfare programs are essentially run by administrators who do little social work. What tends to be described in welfare reports as apparently willful noncompliance is in many instances motivated by psychiatric trouble. While liberal politicians tend to emphasize that a class of miserable poor people is the inevitable consequence of a laissez-faire economy (and is therefore not subject to rectification through mental health interventions), right-wingers tend to see the problem as one of laziness (which is therefore not subject to rectification through mental health interventions). In fact, for many of the poor, the problem is neither the absence of employment opportunities nor the absence of motivation toward employment, but rather severe mental health handicaps that make employment impossible.

Some pilot studies are under way on depression among the indigent. A number of doctors who work in public health settings are accustomed to addressing this population, and they have shown that the problems of the indigent depressed are manageable. Jeanne Miranda, a psychologist at Georgetown University, has for twenty years been advocating sound mental health care for inner-city residents. She recently completed a treatment study of women in Prince George's County, Maryland, a poverty-stricken district outside Washington, D.C. Since the services of family planning clinics are the only medical care available to the indigent population in Maryland, Miranda selected one for random screenings for depression. She then enrolled those whom she judged to be depressed in a treatment protocol to address their mental health needs. Emily Hauenstein, of the University of Virginia, has recently conducted a treatment study of depression among rural women. She began researching troubled children and moved on to treating their mothers. She based her work in Buckingham County in rural Virginia—where most jobs are at prisons or in a few factories, where a good part of the population is illiterate, where a quarter of the population has no access to a telephone, where many people live in substandard housing with no insulation, no indoor toilet, frequently not even running water. Both Miranda and Hauenstein screened substance abusers out of their protocols, referring them to rehabilitation programs. Glenn Treisman, of the Johns Hopkins University Hospital, has for decades been studying and treating depression among indigent HIV-positive and AIDS populations in Baltimore, most of whom are also substance abusers. He has become both a treating clinician and an outspoken advocate for this population. Each of these doctors uses techniques of tenacious care. In all of this work, the per patient per year cost is well under $1,000.

The results of these studies are surprisingly consistent. I was given full access to patients in all of these studies, and to my surprise, everyone I met believed that his or her life had improved at least a bit during treatment. All those who had recovered from severe depression, no matter how dreadful their circumstances, had begun the slow climb toward functioning. They *felt* better about their lives and also lived better. They had been introduced to agency and had begun to exercise it; even when they were up against nearly insurmountable obstacles, they progressed—often fast, and sometimes far. The horrible stories of their lives were way beyond anything I had anticipated, so much so that I repeatedly checked the stories with their treating doctors, asking whether they could really be accurate. So too were their Cinderella-like stories of recovery, as lovely as the one with the pumpkin coach and the glass slipper. Over and over again, as I met poor people who were being treated for depression, I heard tones of astonishment and wonder: How, after so many things had gone wrong, had they been swept up by this help that had changed their entire life? "I asked the Lord to send me an angel," said one woman, "and he answered my prayers."

When Lolly Washington—who was part of Jeanne Miranda's study—was six, a disabled friend of her alcoholic grandmother's began abusing her sexually. In seventh grade, "I felt there was no reason to go on. I did my schoolwork and everything, but I was not happy in any way." Lolly began to withdraw. "I would just stay to myself. Everyone thought I couldn't talk for a while, because for a few years there I wouldn't say anything to no one." Like many victims of abuse, Lolly believed herself to be ugly and unfit. Her first boyfriend was physically and verbally brutal, and after the birth of her first child, when she was seventeen, she managed to "escape from him, I don't know how." A few months later she was out with her sister and her cousin and her cousin's child and an old family friend "who was always just a friend, a really good friend. We were in his house, all of us, and I knew his mom kept pretty flower arrangements on her dresser. So I went to look at them because I loved flowers. And then suddenly, somehow everybody in the house was gone, and I didn't know. He raped me, violent, and I was screaming and hollering and no one answered. Then we went downstairs and we got into the car with my sister. I couldn't speak, I was so afraid, and bleeding."

Lolly became pregnant with and bore the rape baby. Soon after, she met another man and under family pressure married him even though he too was abusive. "My whole wedding day was not right," she told me. "It was like going to a funeral. But he was the best option I had." She had three more children by him in the next two and a half years. "He was abusing the children too, even though he was the one who wanted them, cursing and yelling all the time, and the spankings, I couldn't take that, over any little thing, and I couldn't protect them from it."

Lolly began to experience major depression. "I'd had a job but I had to quit because I just couldn't do it. I didn't want to get out of bed and I felt like there was no reason to do anything. I'm already small and I was losing more and more weight. I wouldn't get up to eat or anything. I just didn't care. Sometimes I would sit and just cry, cry, cry. Over nothing. Just cry. I just wanted to be by myself. My mom helped with the kids, even after she got her leg amputated, which her best friend accidentally shot off around then. I had nothing to say to my own children. After they left the house, I would get in bed with the door locked. I feared when they came home, three o'clock, and it just came so fast. My husband was telling me I was stupid, I was dumb, I was ugly. My sister has a problem with crack cocaine, and she has six kids, and I had to deal with the two little ones, one of them was born sick from the drugs. I was tired. I was just so tired." Lolly began to take pills, mostly painkillers. "It could be Tylenol or anything for pain, a lot of it though, or anything I could get to put me to sleep."

Finally one day, in an unusual show of energy, Lolly went to the family planning clinic to get a tubal ligation. At twenty-eight, she was responsible for eleven children, and the thought of another one petrified her. She happened to go in when Jeanne Miranda was screening for study subjects. "She was definitely depressed, about as depressed as anyone I'd ever seen," recalls Miranda, who swiftly put Lolly into group therapy. "They told me I was 'depressed,' and that was a relief, to know there was something specific wrong," Lolly says. "They asked me to come to a meeting, and that was so hard. I didn't talk when I went there, but I just cried the whole time." Psychiatric wisdom holds that you can help only those who want to be helped and will keep their appointments themselves, but this is ostentatiously untrue in these populations. "Then they kept calling, telling me to come, pestering and insisting, like they wouldn't let go. They even came and got me at my house once. I didn't like the first meetings. But I listened to the other women and realized that they had the same problems I was having, and I began to tell them things, I'd never told anyone those things. And the therapist asked us all these questions to change how we thought. And I just felt myself changing, and I began to get stronger. Everyone began to notice I was coming in with a different attitude."

Two months later, Lolly told her husband that she was leaving. She tried to get her sister into rehab, and when she refused, Lolly cut her off. "I had to get rid of them two who were pulling me down. There was no arguing because I just didn't argue back. My husband was trying to get me out of the group because he didn't like the change in me. I just told him, 'I'm gone.' I was so strong, I was so happy. I went outside to walk, for the first time in so long, just making time for my happiness." It took two more months for Lolly to find a job, working in child care for the U.S. Navy. With her new salary, she set up in a new apartment with the children for whom she is responsible, who ranged in age from two to fifteen. "My kids are so much happier. They want to do things all the time now. We talk hours every day, and they are my best friends. As soon as I come in the door, I put my jacket down, purse, and we just get out books and read, doing homework all together and everything. We joke around. We all talk about careers, and before they didn't even think careers. My eldest wants to go to the air force. One wants to be a firefighter, one a preacher, and one of the girls is gonna be a lawyer! I talk to them about drugs, and they've seen my sister, and they keep clean now. They don't cry like they used to and they don't fight like they did. I let them know, they can talk to me about anything, I don't care what it is. I took in my sister's kids, and the one with the drug problem, he's getting over it. The doctor said he never expected that boy could be talking so soon, trying to get to the potty, he's way ahead of where they thought he'd be.

"There's one room in the new place for the boys and one for the girls and one for me, but they all just like to get up on my bed with me and we're all sitting around there at night. That's all I need now, is my kids. I never thought I would get this far. It feels good to be happy. I don't know how long it's gonna last, but I sure hope it's forever. And things keep on changing: the way I dress. The way I look. The way I act. The way I feel. I'm not afraid anymore. I can walk out the door not being afraid. I don't think those bad feelings are coming back." Lolly smiled and then shook her head in wonder. "And if it weren't for Dr. Miranda and that, I'd still be at home in bed, if I was still alive at all."

The treatments Lolly received did not include psychopharmaceutical intervention and were not closely based on cognitive models. What was it that enabled this metamorphosis? In part, it was simply the steady glow of affectionate attention from the doctors with whom she worked. As Phaly Nuon in Cambodia observed, love and trust can be great justifiers, and the knowledge that someone else cares what happens to you is by itself sufficient to affect profoundly what you do. I was struck by Lolly's statement that the naming of her complaint as *depression* had brought her relief. Miranda described Lolly as "clearly" having depression, but this had not been clear to Lolly even when she had suffered extreme symptoms. The labeling of her complaint was an essential step toward her recovery from it. What can be named and described can be contained: the word *depression* separated Lolly's illness from her personality. If all the things she disliked in herself could be grouped together as aspects of a disease, that left her good qualities as the "real" Lolly, and it was much easier for her to like this real Lolly, and to turn this real Lolly against the problems that afflicted her. To be given the idea of depression is to master a socially powerful linguistic tool that segregates and empowers the better self to which suffering people aspire. Though the problem of articulation is a universal, it is particularly acute for the indigent, who are starved for this vocabulary—which is why basic tools such as group therapy can be so utterly transforming for them.

Because the poor have limited access to the language of mental illness, their depression is not usually manifest cognitively. They are unlikely to experience intense guilt and to articulate to themselves the perception of personal failure that plays so large a role in middle-class depression. Their complaint is often evident in physical symptoms: sleeplessness and exhaustion, sickness, terror, an inability to relate to others. These in turn make them vulnerable to physical illness; and being ill is often the straw that breaks a camel's wide back and makes someone with mild depression go over the edge. Insofar as the indigent depressed do get to hospitals, they tend to get there for physical ailments, many of which are symptoms of their mental anguish. "If a poor Latin woman seems depressed," says Juan López of the University of Michigan, who has done extensive mental health work among poor, depressed Spanish-speaking populations, "I try her on antidepressants. We talk about them as tonics for her general complaints, and when they work, she is delighted. She herself does not experience her condition as psychological." Lolly too was experiencing her symptoms outside the realm of what she would have perceived to be craziness, and craziness (acute hallucinatory psychosis) was her only model for mental illness. The idea of a debilitating mental illness that was not rendering her incoherent was outside her lexicon.

Ruth Ann Janesson was born in a trailer in rural Virginia and grew up fat with glasses. At seventeen, she got pregnant by a nearly illiterate man who had dropped out of her school, and she cut off her own education to marry him. They had a disastrous marriage; she worked and made ends meet for a while, but after the birth of their second child, she left him. A few years later she married a laborer who operates machinery in a construction yard. She had managed to get a truck-driving license, but within six months her husband had told her that her place was at home taking care of the family and taking care of him. They had had two children. Ruth Ann was trying to make ends meet, "which is hard for a family of six on two hundred dollars a week, even with the food stamps."

She soon began to drift downward, and by the third year of her second marriage she was losing all signs of vitality. "I had just decided, well, I'm here, I'm existing, and that's it. I was married, I had children, but I had no life and I was feeling bad basically all the time." When Ruth Ann's father died, she "lost it completely," she said. "That was the bottom. My daddy never beat us, it wasn't the physical, it was the mental. Even if you'd done good, you never got praise, but you were criticized all the time. I guess I felt that if I couldn't please him, I couldn't do anything else. And I felt I'd never managed to please him well enough, and now I wasn't ever gonna have the chance." Recounting this period of her life to me, Ruth Ann began to cry, and by the time she finished her story, she had used up an entire box of Kleenex.

Ruth Ann went to bed and mostly stayed there. "I knew something was wrong, but I didn't put a medical term to it. I had no energy whatsoever. I began gaining more and more weight. I was going through the motions inside our trailer, but I never went out and I stopped communicating totally. Then I realized that I was neglecting my own children. Something had to be done." Ruth Ann has Crohn's disease, and even though she was doing barely anything, she began to get what appeared to be stress-related symptoms. Her doctor, who knew about Emily Hauenstein's study, recommended her for it. Ruth Ann began taking Paxil and started seeing Marian Kyner, a therapist who worked full-time with the women in Emily Hauenstein's study. "If it wasn't for Marian, I probably would've just stayed sitting in that same hole I was in until I just stopped living, stopped existing. If it wasn't for her, I wouldn't be here today," Ruth Ann told me, and once more burst into tears. "Marian made me reach inside me, she wanted me to get all the way down to my toes. I found out who I am. I didn't like it, didn't like me."

Ruth Ann calmed herself. "And then the changes began," she said to me. "They tell me I have a big heart. I didn't think I had a heart at all, but now I know that it's there somewhere and eventually I'm gonna find it completely." Ruth Ann started working again, as a part-time temp for At Work Personnel Service. She soon became office manager and at that point phased out her antidepressants. In January 1998, she and a friend bought out the business, which is a franchise under license from a national company. Ruth Ann began taking night courses in accounting so that she could keep the books well, and she soon recorded an ad for cable TV. "We work with the unemployment office," she told me, "getting jobs for people who are out of work, placing them in private industry. We train them in our own office, where they help us, and then we send them out with good skills. We're now covering seventeen counties." At her heaviest, she weighed 210 pounds. Now she goes to a gym regularly and with intensive dieting is down to 135.

She left her husband, who wanted her to be in the kitchen waiting for him, depressed or not, but she is giving him time to adjust to her new self and when I last saw her was still hoping for a reconciliation. She glowed. "Sometimes a new feeling will hit me," she said, "and it scares me. It takes me a few days to figure out what it is. But at least I know now that my feelings are there, that they exist." Ruth Ann had a profoundly new relationship with her children. "I help them with schoolwork at night, and my oldest son decided computers were awesome, and now he's teaching me how to use them. That's really helped his confidence. We've got him working in the firm this summer, and he's great. It's not so long ago that he was complaining of being tired, that he was missing school most days. Until now, the only thing that seemed to motivate him was watching TV and laying on the couch." Days, she would leave the younger kids with her mother, who is disabled but sufficiently mobile for child care. Ruth Ann soon got a mortgage on a new house. "I am a business owner and a property holder," she said, smiling. As our interview drew to a close, Ruth Ann produced something from her pocket. "Oh, for heaven's sake," she heaved, pressing the buttons on her beeper. "Sixteen calls while I've been sitting here!" I wished her luck as she sprinted across the yard to her car. "We made it, you know," she called just before she got in. "All the way down to my toes, and back again!" She revved the engine, and she was gone.

While depression is a terrible burden on its own, it is even more traumatic for those with multiple physical and psychological illnesses. Most of the indigent depressed suffer physical symptoms and are prone to attacks on their exhausted immune systems. If it is difficult to help someone who is depressed to believe that a miserable life and the depression are separable, it is even more difficult to convince someone with the burden of mortal illness that his despondency can be treated. In fact, distress over pain, distress over bleak life circumstances, and a distress without object can be disentangled, and an improvement in one arena in turn eases the others.

When Sheila Hernandez arrived at Johns Hopkins, she was, according to her physician, "virtually dead." She had HIV, endocarditis, and pneumonia. Constant use of heroin and cocaine had so affected her circulation that she couldn't use her legs. Doctors gave her a Hickman catheter, hoping through IV feeding to build up enough physical strength so that she could withstand treatment for her infections. "I told them to take this out of me, I'm not gonna stay," she recounted to me when we met. "I said, 'I'll leave with this thing in me if I have to and I'll use it to put the drugs in.'" At that point, Glenn Treisman came to see her. She told him she didn't want to talk to him since she was dying soon and leaving the hospital sooner. "Oh no you're not," Treisman said. "You're not heading out of this place to go and die a stupid, useless death out on the streets. That's a crazy idea you have. That's the nuttiest thing I ever heard. You're going to stay here and get off those drugs and get over all these infections of yours, and if the only way I can keep you in here is to declare you dangerously insane, then that's what I'll do."

Sheila stayed. "I went into the hospital on April fifteenth, 1994," she told me, cackling ironically, crisply. "I didn't even see myself as a human being then. Even as a child I remember feeling really alone. The drugs came into play as far as me trying to get rid of that inner pain. My mother gave me away when I was three to some strangers, a man and a lady, and the man molested me when I was around fourteen. A lot of painful things happened to me, and I just wanted to forget. I would wake up in the mornings and just be angry that I woke up. I felt like there wasn't any help for me, 'cause I was just on this earth wasting space. I lived to use drugs and used drugs to live, and since the drugs made me even more depressed, I just wanted to be dead."

Sheila Hernandez was in the hospital for thirty-two days and went through physical rehabilitation and treatments for her addiction. She was put on antidepressants. "It turned out that all what I felt before I went in, I found it was wrong. These doctors told me I had this to offer and that to offer, I was worth something after all. It was like being born all over again." Sheila dropped her voice. "I'm not a religious person, never was, but it was a resurrection, like what happened to Jesus Christ. I came alive for the first time. The day I left, I heard birds singing, and do you know I'd never heard them before? I didn't know until that day that birds sang. For the first time I smelled the grass and the flowers and—even the sky was new. I had never paid any attention to the clouds, you know."

Sheila's younger daughter, who was sixteen and already had her first baby, had dropped out of school a few years earlier. "I saw her going on a painful road I knew," Sheila says. "I saved her from that, at least. She got her GED, and now she's a sophomore in college, and she's also a certified nursing assistant working at Churchill Hospital. It wasn't as easy with the older one, she was already twenty, but finally she's in college now too." Sheila Hernandez never took drugs again. Within a few months, she returned to Hopkins—as a hospital administrator. She did advocacy work during a clinical study of tuberculosis, and she secured permanent housing for the study's participants. "My life is so different. I do these things to help other people all the time, and you know I really *enjoy* that." Sheila's physical health was now excellent. Though she was still HIV-positive, her T cells had doubled and her viral load was undetectable. She had residual emphysema, but after a year on oxygen, she managed on her own. "I don't feel like anything is wrong with me," she announced cheerily. "I'm forty-six, and I'm planning on being around here for a good long time. Life's life, but I would say that, most of the time at least, I'm happy, and every day I thank God and Dr. Treisman that I'm living."

After I met Sheila Hernandez, I went upstairs with Glenn Treisman to see his notes on her original admission: "Multiple disorders, traumatized, self-destructive, suicidal, depression or bipolar illness, physically a complete wreck. Unlikely to live long; extreme rooted problems may prevent response to existing treatment strategies." What he had written seemed utterly incommensurate with the woman I'd met. "It looked pretty hopeless then," he said, "but I thought it was necessary to try."

Despite the extended debates in the last decade about depression's causes, it seems fairly clear that it is usually the consequence of a genetic vulnerability activated by external stress. Checking for depression among the indigent is like checking for emphysema among coal miners. "The traumas in this whole culture are so terrible and so frequent," Jeanne Miranda explains, "that even the most mild vulnerability is likely to get triggered. These people experience frequent intrusive, unexpected, sudden violence, and they have very limited resources for dealing with it. What is surprising when you examine lives so full of psychosocial risk factors is that at least a quarter of the population is *not* depressed." *The New England Journal of Medicine* has acknowledged a connection between "sustained economic hardship" and depression; and the depression rate among the indigent is the highest of any class in the United States. And people who are without resources are less able to rebound from adverse life events. "Depression is highly related to social opposition," says George Brown, who has worked on the social factors that determine mental states. "Deprivation and poverty will do you in." Depression is so common in indigent communities that many people don't notice or question it. "If this is how all your friends are," says Miranda, "it has a certain terrible normality to it. And you attribute your pain to external things, and believing that these externals can't change, you assume that nothing internal can change." Like all other people, the poor develop, with repeated episodes, an organic dysfunction that runs by its own rules on its own course. Treatment without attention to the actual lives of this population is unlikely to be successful; drawing someone through the biological chaos that has stemmed from repeated traumas does little good if that person is going to be retraumatized constantly for the rest of his life. While people who are not depressed are sometimes able to muster their meager resources to change their position and escape some of the difficulty that characterizes their life, people who are depressed have a hard time maintaining their place in the social order, much less improving it. So the poor require novel approaches.

Trauma among the American indigent is not in general directly connected to the absence of cash. Relatively few of the American poor are starving, but many suffer from learned helplessness, a precursor state of depression. Learned helplessness, studied in the animal world, occurs when an animal is subjected to a painful stimulus in a situation in which neither fight nor flight is possible. The animal will enter a docile state that greatly resembles human depression. The same thing happens to people with little volition; the most troubling condition of American poverty is passivity. As director of inpatient services at Georgetown University Hospital, Joyce Chung worked closely with Miranda. Chung was already seeing a difficult population. "The people whom I generally treat can at least make an appointment and follow through. They understand that they need help, and seek it. The women in our study would never get into my office on their own." Chung and I were discussing this phenomenon in the elevator at the clinic in Prince George's County where treatment is given. We got downstairs and found one of Chung's patients standing inside the glass doors of the clinic, waiting for the taxi that had been called for her three hours earlier. It had not occurred to her that the cab wasn't coming; it had not occurred to her to try to call the cab company; it had not occurred to her to be mad or frustrated. Chung and I gave her a ride home. "She lives with the father who repeatedly raped her," says Chung, "because she needs to do that in order to make ends meet. You lose the will to fight for some kinds of change when you're up against realities like that. We can't do anything to get her other housing; we can't do anything about the realities of her life. It's a lot to handle."

The simplest practicalities are also enormously difficult for the indigent population. Emily Hauenstein said, "One woman explained that when she has to come to the clinic on Monday, she asks her cousin

Sadie, who asks her brother to come and get her to bring her in, while her sister-in-law's sister takes care of the kids, except if she gets a job that week, in which case her aunt can cover if she's in town. Then the patient has to have someone else to come and pick her up, because Sadie's brother goes to work just after he drops her off. Then if we meet on a Thursday, there's a whole other cast of characters involved. Either way, they have to cancel about seventy-five percent of the time, leaving her to make last-minute arrangements." This is just as true in the cities. Lolly Washington missed one appointment the day of a rainstorm because, after arranging child care for the eleven children and clearing her schedule and figuring out everything else, she discovered that she didn't have an umbrella. She walked five blocks in the pouring rain, waited about ten minutes for a bus, and when she began to shiver from being drenched, turned around and went back home. Miranda and her therapists sometimes drove to the homes of their patients and took them in to group therapy; Marian Kyner arranged to see the women in their homes to save them the difficulty of coming to her. "Sometimes you can't tell whether it's resistance to treatment, like you'd assume with a middle-class patient," Kyner said, "or just too much of a challenge in their life to get it together and keep appointments."

Joyce Chung said that one of her patients "was so relieved to be called when I did some phone therapy with her. And yet when I asked whether she'd have called me, she said, 'No.' Reaching her, having her return my calls—that is *so* hard, and I've been ready to give up more than once. She runs out of medication and she does nothing about it. I have to go by her house and give her the refills for her prescriptions. It took a long time for me to understand that her conduct didn't mean that she didn't want to come. Her passivity is actually characterological, and not untypical of a person who's suffered repeated abuse as a child."

The patient in question, Carlita Lewis, is someone injured all the way to the core. It appears that, in her thirties, she cannot substantially change her life; treatment has really changed only how she feels about her life, but the effect of that change of feeling on the people around her is substantial. As a child and into adolescence, she had a terrible time with her father, until she was big enough to fight back. She dropped out of school when she got pregnant; her daughter, Jasmine, was born with sickle-cell anemia. Carlita has probably had a mood disorder from childhood. "The littlest things would be just *irritating* me, and I'd fly off the handle," she told me. "I'd pick fights. Sometimes, I was just crying and crying and crying until I got a headache, and then that headache would get so bad I wanted to kill myself." Her moods easily turned violent; at dinner once, she stabbed one of her brothers in the head with a fork and nearly killed him. She took overdoses of pills on several occasions. Later in life, her best friend found her after a suicide attempt and said, "You know how much your daughter cares about you. Jasmine don't have her father in her life, and now she ain't gonna have her mother. How do you think she will be? She's gonna be the same way you are if you kill yourself."

Jeanne Miranda thought Carlita's problems went well beyond the situational, and she put her on Paxil. Since beginning the medication, Carlita has talked with her sister about what their father did to them, which neither knew the other had experienced. "My sister don't have anything to do with my father forever," explained Carlita, who never lets her daughter stay in the house alone with her grandfather. "I couldn't see my daughter before, sometimes for days, for fear I was gonna take out my moods on her," Carlita said. "I didn't want no one to hit her ever, least of all me, and I was always ready to hit her then."

When sadness hits, Carlita can cope with it. "'What's wrong, Mama?' Jasmine asks, and I'm like, 'Nothing's wrong, I'm just tired.' She tries to push it out of you, but then she says, 'Momma, everything's gonna be all right, don't you worry 'bout it,' and she'll hold me and kiss me and pat me on my back about it. We have so much love going on between us all the time now." Given that Jasmine appears to have a natural disposition similar to Carlita's, this ability to be nurturing without anger signals a great leap forward. "Jasmine says, 'I'm gonna be just like my mommy,' and I just say, 'I hope you don't,' and I guess she's gonna be fine."

The mechanisms by which one achieves positive change in life are incredibly basic, and most of us learn them in infancy in maternal interactions that demonstrate a link between cause and effect. I have been watching my five godchildren, ages three weeks to nine years. The youngest cries to get attention and food. The two-year-old breaks rules to find out what he can and can't do. The five-year-old has been told she may paint her room green if she can keep it neat for six months. The seven-year-old has been collecting car magazines and has learned encyclopedically about automobiles. The nine-year-old announced that he did not want to go away to school as his father had done, appealed to parental sentiment and reason, and is now enrolled in a local school instead. Each of them has volition and will grow up with a sense of power. These successful early assertions of power will have far more effect than the relative affluence and intelligence of these children. The absence of a person who can respond to such assertions, even negatively, is cataclysmic. Marian Kyner says, "We had to give some patients lists of feelings and help them understand what a feeling is, so they could know rather than simply repress their emotional life. Then we had to convince them they could change those feelings. Then we went on to setting goals. For some of these people, the idea even of figuring out what you want and stating it to yourself is revolutionary." I thought of Phaly Nuon then, who had worked in Cambodia to teach people how to feel after the paralysis of the Khmer Rouge period. I thought of the difficulty of unrecognized feelings. I thought of that mission to attune people to their own minds.

"I sometimes have the feeling that we're doing sixties consciousness-raising groups in the new millennium," says Miranda, who herself grew up among the "working poor" in rural Idaho but did not have the "long-term demoralization" she now encounters daily among people who are "unemployed and without pride."

Danquille Stetson is part of a hard, criminal culture of the rural South. She is African-American amidst racial prejudice and violence, and she feels threat from every side. She carries a handgun. She is a functional illiterate. Danquille's place, where we talked, is an old, run-down trailer, with the windows blocked shut and every stick of furniture redolent of decay. The only light when I was there came from the TV, which was playing *Planet of the Apes* throughout our conversation. Still, the place was tidy and not unpleasant.

"It's like a hurt," she said, first thing as I came in, skipping any introductions. "It's just like they raking your heart out your body, and it won't stop, it's just like somebody's taking a knife and keep stabbing you all the time." Danquille was sexually abused by her paternal grandfather when she was a child, and she told her parents. "They really didn't care, they just swept it right under the rug," she said, and the abuse went on for years.

It was often difficult to tell what, in Danquille's mind, was the work of Marian Kyner, what was the work of Paxil, and what was the work of the Lord. "By me getting close to the Lord," she told me, "He brought me into the depression and out of there too. I done prayed to the Lord for help and He sent me Dr. Marian, and she told me to think more positive and take these pills and I could be saved." Controlling negative thinking as a way to bring about behavioral change is the essence of cognitive therapy. "I don't know why my husband, he always hitting me," Danquille said, pummeling her own arm as she said it, "but after him I just running from man to man looking for love in all the wrong places."

Danquille's children are now twenty-four, nineteen, and thirteen. Her biggest revelation in treatment was quite a fundamental one. "I done realized that the things parents do affects the kids. You know? I ain't been knowing that. And I been doing a lot of things wrong. I put my son through hell, my own boy. If I had of been more understanding—but at the time, I didn't know. So now I sat down my kids and I say to them, 'If anybody come to you and say your mama did this and your mama did this, I'm telling you now it's true. Don't do what I done.' And I told them, 'Ain't nothing that bad you can't come talk to me about.' And it's because if I had somebody that would have listened at me and reassured me everything's gonna be okay, it would've been a big difference, I see that now. Your parents don't realize a lot of your problems come from them, *they* responsible when you begin looking for love in all the wrong places. I know my good friend, I posted his bail when he went shooting his nephew—saw his mother with different men, they made love in the car right there in front of him, and that influenced his life. His mama don't know that right today. Whatever you do in the dark come to the light in a matter of time."

Danquille has now become a sort of community resource, teaching friends and strangers her methods for depression control. "A whole lot of people keep asking me, 'How did you change?' Since I think positive, I laugh all the time, smile all the time. Now, I had this happen to me, that the Lord started sending people for me to help. I said, 'Lord, will you give me what they need to hear and help me listening?'" Danquille listens to her children now, and she listens to the people she knows at her church. When someone there was suicidal, "I told him, 'You not by yourself. I was like that.' And I said, 'I made it. Ain't nothing that bad you can't get through.' I said, 'You start thinking positive and I promise you that girl what is leaving you now, she gonna call.' He told me yesterday, 'If it wasn't for you, I would've been dead.'" Danquille has taken a new place in her family. "I'm breaking a pattern more or less. My nieces, they come to me instead of to their parents, and the pattern of not listening be broken. They say to me, since I been talking to you, I want to live. And I say to everyone, you got a problem, you get help. That's what God put them doctors here for, to help you. I say that loud with these people, they just dogs eating dog. And anyone can be saved. I had one woman, she drank, smoke, had been with my husband, right with him, no saying she was sorry either, and then with my new friend, but when she come round, I gonna help her, 'cause in order for her to get better she gotta have someone to help her."

The poverty-stricken depressed are not represented in the statistics on depression because the research those statistics reflect is based primarily on work with people within existing health plans, who are already a middle-class—or at least a working—population. Raising expectations among disadvantaged populations is a tangled issue, and it is true that planting false goals in people's minds can be dangerous. "I'll never stop seeing Dr. Chung," one woman told me confidently, though the actual parameters of the study had been explained to her over and over. It is heartbreaking that if she were to have another collapse later in life, she will perhaps be unable to get the kind of help that has pulled her through— though all the therapists involved in these studies feel an ethical obligation to provide, paid or not, ongoing basic services to their patients. "To withhold treatment to people who are suffering acutely because it's going to raise expectations," says Hauenstein, "well, that's ignoring the large ethical issue for the sake of the small one. We try our best to give people a set of skills they can use themselves in another situation—to do all we can do to help them stay afloat." The cost of ongoing medication is an enormous problem. The problem is partly resolved by industry-based programs that distribute antidepressants to the poor, but these barely begin to meet needs. One feisty Pennsylvania doctor I met told me that she got "truckfuls of samples" from pharmaceutical salesmen to give to her indigent patients. "I tell 'em that I'll use their product as my first-line treatment on patients who can pay and who are likely to renew over a lifetime," she said. "In exchange, I tell 'em I'll need a more or less unlimited supply of product so that I can medicate my low-income patients for free. I write a hell of a lot of prescriptions. The smart salesmen always say yes."

Schizophrenia occurs twice as often among low-income populations as in the middle class. Researchers initially assumed that difficulty triggered schizophrenia in some way; but more recent research shows that schizophrenia leads to difficulty: mental illness is expensive and confusing, and a chronic illness that impairs productivity and occurs in youth tends to pull a person's entire family down a rung or two on the social ladder. This "downward drift hypothesis" appears to hold true for depression as well. Glenn Treisman says of the indigent HIV population, "Many of these people have never had a success in their whole lives. They can't have a relationship, or a long-term commitment to a job." People think of depression as being a consequence of HIV, but it is often in fact an antecedent. "If you have a mood disorder, you're much more careless about sex and about needles," Treisman says. "Very few people get HIV from a broken condom. Many people get HIV when they can't muster the energy to care anymore. These are people who are utterly demoralized by life and don't see any point in it. If we had treatments more broadly available for depression, I would guess from my clinical experience that the rate of HIV infection in this country would be cut in half at least, with enormous consequent public health savings." The public health costs of an illness that enables HIV infection and then disables people from taking appropriate care of themselves (and others) is absolutely gigantic. "HIV takes away all your money and assets and often your friends and family too. Society disenfranchises you. So these people sink to the very bottom." The researchers I met all stressed the need for treatment, but they also talked about the need for *good* treatment. "There's a really small number of people that I would trust the care of these people with," says Hauenstein. The standards of mental health care for those few indigent people who are sick enough to get treatment—outside these studies—are terribly low.

The only depressed indigent men I have interviewed are HIV-positive. They are among the few who have been forced up against the reality of their depression—because indigent men's depression manifests in ways that put them in jail or the morgue more often than in depression treatment protocols. Men are certainly much more resistant than women to being drawn into depression therapy when their mood disorders are noted. I asked the women I interviewed whether their husbands or boyfriends might be depressed, and many said yes; and they all told me about their depressed sons. One of the women in Miranda's study said that her boyfriend, who had given her some rosy bruises, had confided he wanted to find a group to attend himself—but he found the idea of following through "too embarrassing."

I was taken aback when Fred Wilson came in to talk to me one afternoon at Hopkins. He was six foot six and wore gold rings, a big gold medallion, and a pair of sunglasses; he had an almost shaved head; he had impressive muscles; and he seemed to take up about five times as much room as I did. He was just the kind of person I cross the street to avoid, and as we talked, I realized that this was a good policy. He had had a heavy drug habit, and to keep it going he had mugged people, broken into stores and homes, knocked down old women for their handbags. He had been homeless for a while and he was tough. Though he provoked righteous indignation, this scary man had an air of despair and loneliness.

Fred's therapeutic breakthrough had occurred when he recognized that he had a mood disorder that had probably started him on drugs, that he wasn't "just messed up by smack." He was, when I saw him, seeking an antidepressant that would help him. Fred had charisma and a hard-knocks grin; he had known what it was to be on top of the world. "I always had the ability to get whatever I wanted. And when you got that ability, you just don't really work or nothing, you just go get it. I didn't know what it was like to be patient. There weren't no limits," he said. "There were no precautions, you know what I'm saying? Just getting what I wanted and getting high. Getting high, you know? With that I kind of had some acceptance. It helped me get past the blame and the shame." Fred took the HIV test after he got "incarcerated off the street" and soon thereafter found out that his mother was also positive. Since her death from AIDS, "it never seemed like nothing mattered, because the end result of life always gonna be death. I achieve some goals, man, I be looking at other things I've gotta do, you know? But anyways, I just start disliking myself even more. Then one of them times when I got arrested, when I was living out on the street, I realized I was living like I was living because of the choices I was making. I changed to face that, you know what I'm saying? Because I was all alone at that time. And ain't nobody gonna give you the drugs when you're needing 'em unless you got the money to pay."

Fred has been given a regimen of meds for HIV, but he stopped taking them some time ago because they weren't making him feel good. His side effects were slight, and the inconvenience of the drugs was also slight, but "before I go, I may as well enjoy myself," he said to me. His HIV doctors, disappointed, persuaded him to stick with antidepressants; they hope these medications will waken in him the wish to stay alive, to take the protease inhibitors.

Strength of will is often the best bulwark against depression, and in this population, the will to go on, the tolerance of trauma, is often quite extraordinary. Many among the indigent depressed have personalities so passive that they are free of aspirations, and such people may be the most difficult to help. Others retain a zest for life even during their depression.

Theresa Morgan, one of Emily Hauenstein's and Marian Kyner's patients, is a sweet-natured woman whose life has been dotted with a surreal helping of horror. She lives in a house about the size of a double-wide trailer, right in the middle of Buckingham County, Virginia, five miles south of the Highway of Faith Congregation and five miles north of Gold Mine Baptist Church. When we met, she told me her story with an air of great specificity, as though she had been taking notes her whole life.

Theresa's mother became pregnant at fifteen, gave birth to Theresa at sixteen, and was seventeen when Theresa's father beat her so badly she had to crawl out of the house. Theresa's grandfather told her mother to go away and hide herself, that if she was ever seen in the county again, if she ever tried to contact Theresa, he'd get her put in jail. "My daddy was twenty-two then, so he's the big jerk—but they used to tell me that she was a slut, that I was gonna be a slut like her. And my daddy used to tell me that I ruined his life just by being born," Theresa told me.

Early on, Theresa was diagnosed with an inoperable benign tumor, a hemangioma, located between her rectum and her vagina. She was sexually abused by close relatives every night from her fifth birthday until she was nine, when one of the perpetrators married and left the house. Her grandmother told her that men lead the family, and that she should keep her mouth shut. Theresa went to church and to school, and that was the circumference of her life. Her grandmother believed in strict discipline, which meant daily attacks with whatever household objects came to hand: whippings with extension cords, beatings with broom handles and frying pans. Her grandfather was an exterminator, and starting when she was seven, Theresa spent a lot of time under houses trying to catch blacksnakes. In eighth grade, Theresa took an overdose of her grandmother's heart medication. Doctors at the hospital pumped her stomach and advised therapy, but her grandfather said none of his family needed help.

In eleventh grade Theresa went out on her first date, with a guy called Lester, who had "kinda touched my soul, because we could honestly talk to each other." As Lester was dropping her off at home, her father came in and went berserk. He was just five foot one, but he weighed over three hundred pounds, and he sat on top of Theresa (who is four foot nine and at that time weighed one hundred five pounds) and banged her head on the ground for hours, until the blood flowed through his fingers. Theresa's forehead and scalp are still covered with scars so extensive it looks as if they came from burns. He also broke two of her ribs, her jaw, right arm, and four toes that night.

As Theresa told me this story, her nine-year-old daughter, Leslie, was playing with a pet dachshund. These many details seemed to be as familiar to her as the Passion is to a churchgoer. But they did register: Leslie would become aggressive with the dog at the mention of any real horror. She never cried, however, and she never interrupted.

After the big beating, Lester invited Theresa to move in with him and his family, "and for three years it was great. But then he really wanted me to be like his mother, not work, not even drive, just stay at home and wash the treadmarks out of his underwear. I didn't want that." Theresa became pregnant and they married. Lester proved his independence by "running around" while Theresa took care of the baby. "Lester had liked me because I had a mind," Theresa said. "He'd liked it when I'd told him things. I'd gotten him to listen to good jazz, away from all that Lynyrd Skynyrd stuff. I'd talked to him about art and poetry. And now he wanted me at home, and with his mother because it was her home."

A year later, just after Leslie was born, Lester had a massive stroke that destroyed most of the left side of his brain. He was twenty-two, a heavy-equipment operator for roadwork, now half-paralyzed and unable to speak. Over the following months, before the doctors discovered his underlying complaint—a form of lupus that causes blood clots—another blockage destroyed his leg, which was subsequently amputated; other clots damaged his lungs. "I could've left," said Theresa.

Leslie stopped playing and looked up at her, a blank, curious stare.

"But Lester was the love of my life, even if we'd been having some rough times, and I don't give up on things too easy. I went to see him at the hospital, and he had one eye closed and one open. His face had started to swell and his features had dropped on one side. They'd taken the bone off the left side of his head because the swelling was so bad, just sawed off his skull. But he was tickled to see me." Theresa went and stayed at the hospital, teaching him to use a bedpan, helping him to pee, beginning to learn the gestures with which they now communicate.

Theresa paused in her account of this. Leslie came and handed me a photo. "That's your second birthday, isn't it, honey?" Theresa said to her gently. In the picture, a giant, good-looking man, bandaged like a mummy, hooked up to monitors, was hugging a tiny little girl to him. "That was four months after the stroke," Theresa said, and Leslie solemnly took the photo away again.

Lester came home at the end of six months. Theresa got a job working full-time in a factory, cutting out children's clothes. She had to work close to home so she could go back and forth every few hours to check on Lester. The day she got her driver's license, she showed it to Lester, and he wept. "Now you can leave me," he gestured. Theresa laughed, recounting this. "But he found out otherwise."

Lester's personality fractured. He would stay awake all night, calling Theresa once an hour to help him defecate. "I would come home and make dinner and do the dishes and wash a couple of loads of clothes and clean the house up, and then I'd fall asleep, sometimes just collapse right there in the kitchen. Lester would call his mom on the phone, and when she heard his breathing on the line, she'd call back and the phone would wake me up. He'd have refused to eat dinner, and now he'd want me to make him a sandwich. I was trying to be all sunny and perky the whole time, not to make him feel bad." Lester and Leslie fought a lot over Theresa's attention; they'd scratch each other and pull each other's hair. "I began to lose it," Theresa said. "Lester wouldn't even try to do his exercises, and he lost more and more mobility and he got enormous, fat. I guess I was in a selfish period and I couldn't sympathize with him like I should've done."

The stress caused Theresa's hemangioma, which she had managed to ignore for some time, to expand, and it started bleeding heavily through her rectum. Theresa had become foreman, but her job still involved eight to ten hours of standing every day. "That, and the bleeding, and taking care of Lester and Leslie—well, I guess I should be able to deal with pressure, but I kind of wigged out. We've got a Remington twenty-two-inch pistol with a nine-inch barrel. I sat on the bedroom floor and I spun the barrel and I put it in my mouth and clicked. Then I did it again.

It felt so good to have that gun in my mouth. Then Leslie knocked on the door and said, 'Mama, please don't leave me. Please.' I laid the gun down then, and I promised I'd never go anywhere without her."

"I was four," Leslie said proudly. "After that, I came and slept with you every night."

Theresa called a suicide hot line and talked for four hours on the phone. "I just bawled. Lester was having a staph infection. Then I had kidney stones. That was so physically painful I told the doctor I was gonna rip off his face if he didn't help. When your body really goes, your mind wants the time off too. I couldn't eat; I hadn't slept in like a month, I was so wired, so hurting, and bleeding so I was totally anemic on top of it. I was walking around hateful." Her doctor took her to meet Marian Kyner. "Marian saved my life, no question. She taught me how to think again." Theresa started on Paxil and Xanax.

Kyner told Theresa that there was no power forcing her to do all the stuff she did, that it had to be worth it to her. One night shortly thereafter, when things with Lester got out of hand, Theresa calmly put down her frying pan. "Come on, Leslie," she said. "Get a couple of your clothes, let's go." Lester suddenly remembered that Theresa had the power to abandon him, and he fell on the floor weeping, begging. Theresa took Leslie out and they drove around for three hours, "just to teach Daddy a lesson." When they got back, he was penitent, and their new lives began. She arranged for him to get Prozac. And she explained the toll their life was taking on her. The doctors told Theresa that to prevent further bleeding from her hemangioma, she was not to walk or exercise or move unnecessarily. "I still lift Lester out of the car, and I still lift his wheelchair. I still clean the house. But Lester had to learn independence pretty fast." For health reasons, Theresa had to give up her job.

Lester now has a job folding aprons in a laundry. He gets picked up by a special bus for the disabled and he goes in every day. He washes the dishes at home, and sometimes he can even help vacuum. With disability, he brings in $250 a week, on which they live.

"I never abandoned him," Theresa said. Pride suddenly came back to her. "They told me I was gonna burn out, but we're going so strong now. We can talk about anything. He was a redneck from hell, and now he's turned liberal. I've cleaned out some of that prejudice and hatred he grew up with." Lester has learned to urinate by himself, and he can almost get dressed with one hand. "We talk every day and every night," Theresa said. "And you know what? He is the one true love of my life, and even if I regret a lot of what happened, I wouldn't want to give up anything about us and this family. But if it wasn't for Marian, I'd have waited until I could bleed to death and that would have been it."

At this statement, Leslie climbed up into Theresa's lap. Theresa rocked her back and forth. "And this year," Theresa said, suddenly elated, "I found my mama. I looked up her last name in the phone book, and after about fifty calls I found some cousin and did some detective work, and when she answered the phone, she said she'd been waiting for me all these years, hoping I'd call. Now she's like my best friend. We see her all the time."

"We love Grandma," Leslie announced.

"Yeah, we do," Theresa confirmed. "She and I got the same rough treatment out of my daddy and his family, so we got a lot in common." Theresa said it was unlikely she'd be able to stand and do factory labor again. "Someday, when Leslie can take care of Lester in the evenings, and if they let me move around a little more, if they manage to contain the hemangioma, I'm going to finish high school doing night classes. I learned about art and poems and music from a black lady teacher, Miss Wilson, at my high school. I'm gonna go back and learn more about the writers I love most, Keats, Byron, Edgar Allan Poe. I read Leslie 'The Raven' and 'Annabel Lee' last week, didn't I, honey, when we got that book from the library." I looked at the prints up on her walls. "I love Renoir," she said. "Don't think I'm pretentious, but I really love that, and that one of the horse, by an English artist. And I love music too, I like to listen to Pavarotti when he's on.

"You know what I wanted when I was a little girl in that horrible house? I wanted to be an archaeologist and go to Egypt and Greece. Talking to Marian helped me stop wigging out and all and it also got me *thinking* again. I'd missed using my mind so much! Marian's so smart, and after years with only Leslie and a husband who never finished ninth grade and can't talk . . ." She drifted off for a minute. "Boy, there are these beautiful things waiting out there. We're gonna find them, Leslie, aren't we gonna find them all? Like we found those poems." I began to recite "Annabel Lee," and Theresa joined in. Leslie looked up attentively as her mother and I drummed through the first few of those American lines. " 'But we loved with a love that was more than love,'" Theresa said, as though describing a journey of her own.

Part of the difficulty in getting better services to these people is the blockade of disbelief. I wrote an early version of this chapter as a feature for a wide-circulation newsmagazine, and they told me that I had to rewrite it for two reasons. First, the lives I described were implausibly horrendous. "It becomes comical," one editor said to me. "I mean, no one can have all this stuff happening to them, and if they do, it's no surprise they're depressed." The other problem was that the recovery was too quick and too dramatic. "This whole thing about suicidal homeless women becoming virtually hedge-fund managers," the editor said somewhat acidly, "comes off as pretty ludicrous." I tried to explain that this was in fact the strength of the story, that people in authentically desperate situations had had their lives changed beyond recognition, but I got nowhere. The truth I had discovered was intolerably stranger than fiction.

When scientists first observed the Antarctic hole in the ozone layer, they presumed their observational equipment was flawed because the hole was so enormous as to be unbelievable. It turned out that the hole was real. The hole of indigent depression in the United States is also real and gigantic, but unlike the hole in the ozone layer, this one can be filled. I cannot imagine what it was like for Lolly Washington, Ruth Ann Janesson, Sheila Hernandez, Carlita Lewis, Danquille Stetson, Fred Wilson, Theresa Morgan, and the tens of other people I interviewed at length among the indigent depressed. But I do know this: we have been trying to solve the problem of poverty by material intervention at least since biblical times and have in the last decade tired of such intervention, realizing that money is not a sufficient antidote. We have now over-hauled welfare with the cheery thought that if we don't support the poor, they'll work harder. Is it not worthwhile giving them the support, medical and therapeutic, that would allow them to function, that could free them to make good on their lives? It is not so easy to find the social workers who can transform the lives of this population; but without pro-grams of raised consciousness and allocated funding, those who have the gifts and the devotion to work with such people have scant means to do so, and the terrible, wasteful, lonely suffering goes on and on and on.

CHAPTER X

Politics

Politics plays as big a role as science in current descriptions of depression. Who researches depression; what is done about it; who is treated; who is not; who is blamed; who is coddled; what is paid for; what is ignored: all these questions are determined in the sancta of power. Politics also determines fashions in treatment: Should people be placed in institutions? Should they be treated in the community? Should the treatment of the depressed remain in the hands of doctors, or should it be assumed by social workers? What kind of diagnosis is necessary to warrant a government-funded intervention? The vocabulary of depression, which can be enormously empowering to marginal people who have no way to describe or understand their experiences, is endlessly manipulable. Those more advantaged members of a society experience their illness through that vocabulary, which is nonconspiratorially spun by Congress, by the American Medical Association, and by the pharmaceutical industry.

Definitions of depression strongly influence the policy decisions that in turn affect the sufferers. If depression is a "simple organic disease," then it must be treated as we treat other simple organic diseases—insurance companies must provide coverage for severe depression as they provide coverage for cancer treatment. If depression is rooted in character, then it is the fault of those who suffer from it and receives no more protection than does stupidity. If it can afflict anyone at any time, then prevention needs to be taken into consideration; if it is something that will hit only poor, uneducated, or politically underrepresented people, the emphasis on prevention is in our inequable society much lower. If depressed people injure others, their condition must be controlled for the good of society; if they simply stay home or disappear, their invisibility makes them easy to ignore.

U.S. government policy on depression has changed in the last decade and continues to do so; substantial shifts have occurred in many other countries as well. Four principal factors influence the perception of depression—and thus implementation of policy relating to it—at the governmental level. The first is medicalization. It is deeply ingrained in the American psyche that we need not treat an illness that someone has brought on himself or has developed through weakness of character, though cirrhosis and lung cancer at least are covered by insurance. A general public perception persists that visiting a psychiatrist is a self-indulgence, that it's more like visiting a hairdresser than like visiting an oncologist. Treating a mood disorder as a medical illness contravenes this folly, takes away responsibility from the person who has that illness, and makes it easier to "justify" treatment. The second factor to shape perception is vast oversimplification (curiously out of keeping with twenty-five hundred years of not much clarity about what depression is). In particular, the popular supposition that depression is the result of low serotonin the same way that diabetes is the result of low insulin—an idea that has been substantially reinforced by both the pharmaceutical industry and the FDA. The third factor is imaging. If you show a picture of a depressed brain (colorized to indicate rate of metabolism) next to a picture of a normal brain (similarly colorized), the effect is striking: depressed people have grey brains and happy people have Technicolor brains. The difference is both heartrending and scientific-looking, and though it is utterly artificial (the colors reflect imaging techniques rather than actual tints and hues), such a picture is worth ten thousand words and tends to convince people of the need for immediate treatment. The fourth factor is the weak mental health lobby. "Depressed people don't nag enough," Representative Lynn Rivers (Democrat, Michigan) says. Attention for particular illnesses is usually the result of the concerted efforts of lobbying groups to raise awareness of those illnesses: the terrific response to HIV/AIDS was spurred by the dramatic tactics of the population that had the illness or was at risk for it. Unfortunately, depressed people tend to find everyday life overwhelming, and they are therefore incompetent lobbyists. Moreover, many of those who have been depressed, even if they are doing better, don't want to talk about it: depression is a dirty secret, and it's hard to lobby about your dirty secrets without revealing them. "We get blown away when people come to their representatives to proclaim the severity of a particular illness," says Representative John Porter (Republican, Illinois), who, as the chair of the Labor, Health and Human Services Appropriations Subcommittee, dominates House discussions of budgets for mental illness. "I have to fight off amendments brought to the floor to reflect someone's excitement about a story he's been told, earmarking a particular disease for a particular sum. Members of Congress often try to do that—but seldom for mental illness." However, several mental health lobbying groups in the United States do champion the cause of the depressed, the most noteworthy being the National Alliance for the Mentally Ill (NAMI) and the National Depressive and Manic-Depressive Association (NDMDA).

The greatest block to progress is still probably social stigma, which clings to depression as it clings to no other disease, and which Steven Hyman, director of the National Institute of Mental Health, has described as a "public health disaster." Many of the people with whom I spoke while I was writing this book asked me not to use their names, not to reveal their identities. I asked them what exactly they thought would happen if people found out that they'd been depressed. "People would know I am weak," said one man whose record of fantastic career success despite terrible illness seemed to me to be an indication of terrific strength. People who had "come out of the closet" and spoken publicly about being gay, being alcoholics, being victims of sexually transmitted diseases, in one instance being a child abuser, were still too embarrassed to talk on record about being depressed. It took considerable effort to find the people whose stories feature in this book—not because depression is rare, but because those who will be frank about it with themselves and the outside world are exceptional. "No one would trust me," said a depressed lawyer who had taken some time off the year before "to make plans about the future." He had invented an entire history for himself to fill in the months he'd missed and used considerable energy (including some trumped-up holiday pictures) to win credence for his tales. Waiting for the elevator in the large office building where I had just interviewed him, I was accosted by one of the junior staff. My alibi was that I'd had to see a lawyer about a contract, and the young staffer asked me what I did. I said that I was working on this book. "Oh!" he said, and named the man I had just interviewed. "Now there's a guy," he volunteered, "who went through a real, total breakdown. Depression, psychosis, you name it. Completely bonkers for a while. He's actually still kind of weird; he has these bizarre beach photos sitting out in his office and he sort of makes up these stories about himself? In a kind of bananas way? But he's back at work, and professionally speaking, he's batting a thousand. You should really meet him and find out about it if you can." In this instance, the lawyer seemed to enjoy more prestige for his skill in battling depression than stigma for the disease itself; and his dissembling was an unsuccessful dishonesty on a par with a poor hair transplant—a far more ridiculous fact than anything nature could have manufactured. But the secrecy is ubiquitous. After my *New Yorker* article was published, I had letters signed "From One Who Knows" and "Sincerely, Name Withheld" and "A Teacher."

I have never in my life worked on a subject that invited so many confidences as this one; people told me the most amazing stories at dinner parties and on trains and anywhere else where I admitted to my subject, but almost all of them said, "But please don't tell anyone." One person I'd interviewed called and said that her mother had threatened to stop speaking to her if she let her name be included in this book. The natural state of minds is closed, and deep feelings are usually kept secret. We know people only by what they tell us. None of us can break through the barrier of another's fathomless silence. "I never mention this," someone once told me in relation to his struggle, "because I don't see the use in it." We are blind to the epidemic proportions of depression because the reality is so seldom uttered; and the reality is so seldom spoken in part because we do not realize how common it is.

I had an extraordinary experience during a house-party weekend in England. I had been asked what I was doing and had dutifully admitted that I was writing a book about depression. After dinner, a rather beautiful woman with long blond hair tied up in a tight coil behind her head approached me in the garden. Gently placing a hand on my arm, she asked whether she might speak to me for a moment, and for the next hour we paced the garden as she told me of her terrible unhappiness and her battles with depression. She was on medication and it was helping somewhat, but she still felt unable to cope with many situations, and she feared that her state of mind would ultimately destroy her marriage. "Please," she said as we finished our talk, "don't tell anyone any of this. Especially not my husband. He mustn't know. He wouldn't understand it and couldn't tolerate it." I gave my word. It was a good weekend of bright sunshine and cozy fires in the evenings, and the group of people, including the woman who had confided in me, kept up a totally delightful banter. On Sunday, after lunch, I went riding with the husband of the depressed woman. Halfway back to the stables, he suddenly turned to me and said awkwardly, "I don't say this much." And then he stopped both his sentence and his horse. I thought he was going to ask me something about his wife, with whom he had seen me talking on various occasions. "I don't think most blokes would really understand." He coughed. I smiled encouragingly. "It's depression," he finally said. "You're writing about depression, eh?" I answered in the affirmative and waited another moment. "What brought someone like you to that kind of topic?" he asked. I said that I'd had a depression of my own and began my usual explanation, but he cut me off. "You did? You had a depression and now you're writing about it? Because here's the thing, and I don't like to say this much, but it's the truth. I've been having an awful time. Can't think why. Good life, good marriage, good kids, all that, very close to everyone, but I've actually had to go and see a psychiatrist, and he's put me on these bloody pills. So now I'm feeling a bit more like myself, but you know, am I actually myself? If you see what I mean? I wouldn't ever tell my wife or my children because they just wouldn't get it, wouldn't think me much of a paterfamilias and all that. I'm going to stop taking them soon, but you know, who am I here?" At the end of our little talk, he swore me to secrecy.

I did not tell the man that his wife was on the same medication as he; nor did I tell the wife that her husband would have been able to understand her situation only too well. I didn't tell either of them that living with secrets is taxing, and that their depression was probably exacerbated by shame. I didn't say that a marriage in which basic information is not exchanged is weak. I did, however, tell each of them that depression is often hereditary and that they should look to their children. I commended openness as an obligation to the next generation.

Recent dramatic statements by a broad range of celebrities have certainly helped to destigmatize depression. If Tipper Gore and Mike Wallace and William Styron can all talk about being depressed, then perhaps less visible people too can talk about it. With the publication of this book, I forsake an expedient privacy. I would have to say, however, that talking about my depression has made it easier to bear the illness and easier to forestall its return. I'd recommend coming out about depression. Having secrets is burdensome and exhausting, and deciding exactly when to convey the information you've kept in check is really troublesome.

It is also astonishing but true that no matter what you say about your depression, people don't really believe you unless you seem acutely depressed as they look at and talk to you. I am good at masking my mood states; as a psychiatrist once said to me, I am "painfully over-socialized." Nonetheless, I was startled when a social acquaintance of mine called me to say that he was going through AA and wanted to make restitution to me for his sometime coldness, which was, he said, the consequence not of snobbery but of a deep jealously of my "perfect-seeming" life. I did not go into my life's innumerable imperfections, but I did ask him how he could say he envied me my *New Yorker* article, express interest in the progress of this book, and still think my life seemed perfect. "I know you were depressed at one point," he said, "but it doesn't seem to have had any effect on you." I proposed that it had in fact changed and determined the whole rest of my life, but I could tell my words were not getting through. He had never seen me cowering in bed and he couldn't make any sense of the image. My privacy was bewilderingly inviolate. An editor from the *New Yorker* recently told me that I'd never really been depressed. I protested that people who have never been depressed don't tend to pretend about it, but he was not to be persuaded. "C'mon," he said. "What the hell do you have to be depressed about?" I was swallowed up by my recovery. My history and my ongoing intermittent episodes seemed quite irrelevant; and that I had publicly stated that I was on antidepressants seemed not to faze him. This is the strange flip side of stigma. "I don't buy into this whole depression business," he said to me. It was as though I and the people I wrote about were conspiring to wrest more than our share of sympathy from the world. I've run into this paranoia again and again, and it still astonishes me. No one ever told my grandmother that she didn't really have heart disease. No one says that increasing rates of skin cancer are in the public imagination. But depression is so scary and unpleasant that many people would just as soon deny the disease and repudiate its sufferers.

Still, there is a fine line between being open and being tiresome. It's a downer to talk about depression, and nothing is more boring than a person who talks about his own suffering all the time. When you are depressed, you sort of can't control yourself and your depression is all that's happening to you; but that doesn't mean that depression has to be your primary topic of conversation for the rest of your life. I have often heard people say, "It took years for me to be able to tell my psychiatrist that . . ." and have thought that it is madness to repeat at cocktails the things you tell your psychiatrist.

Prejudice, rooted largely in insecurity, still exists. Driving with some acquaintances recently, I passed a well-known hospital. "Oh, look," said one of them. "That's where Isabel got herself electrocuted." And he moved his left index finger around his ear in a sign for crazy. All my activist impulses rising toward the surface, I asked what exactly had happened to Isabel and found, as I'd anticipated, that she had received ECT at the hospital in question. "She must have had a hard time," I said, attempting to defend the poor girl without being too earnest. "Think how shocking having shock must be." He burst out laughing. "I nearly gave myself electroshock treatments the other day when I was trying to fix my wife's hair dryer," he said. I am a great believer in a sense of humor and I was not really offended, but I did try—and fail—to imagine our going past a hospital at which Isabel might have had chemotherapy and making similar jokes.

ADA (the Americans with Disabilities Act), the congressional fiat that granted significant accommodation to the handicapped, requires that employers not stigmatize the mentally ill. This brings up tough questions, many of which have been under public consideration since *Listening to Prozac*. Should your boss be able to require that you take antidepressants if you are not performing up to speed? If you become withdrawn, should he be able to fire you for not doing what is appropriate to the situation? It is true that people with illness under control should not be prevented from doing such work as they can. On the other hand, the ugly truth is that paraplegics cannot work as baggage handlers and fat girls can't be supermodels. If I employed someone who regularly lapsed into depression, I'd be more than a little bit frustrated. The prejudice and the pragmatics interact to the disadvantage of those with depression, blatantly in some areas and less blatantly in others. The Federal Aviation Administration does not permit people suffering from depression to pilot commercially; if a pilot goes on an antidepressant, he must retire. The effect of this is probably to cause large numbers of depressed pilots to avoid treatment, and I would guess that passengers are a lot less safe than they would be with pilots on Prozac. That being said, one can pull through most acute crises; medication has given much strength; but there are boundaries on resilience. I would not vote for a fragile president. I wish this weren't so. It would be nice to see the world run by someone who would understand through personal experience what I and others like me have been through. I couldn't be president, and it would be a disaster for the world if I were to try. The few exceptions to this rule—Abraham Lincoln, or Winston Churchill, each of whom suffered from depression—use their anxiety and their concern as the basis for their leadership, but that requires a truly remarkable personality and a particular brand of depression that is not disabling at crucial times.

On the other hand, depression does not make someone useless. When Paul Bailey Mason and I first made contact, he had been suffering from depression for most of his life; in fact, it was the fiftieth anniversary of his first round of ECT. He had led a traumatized life; his mother, when he presented "disciplinary problems" in adolescence, had got some friendly Klansmen to attack him. Later, he was involuntarily committed to an asylum and while there was nearly beaten to death; he finally managed to escape during a riot by patients. He has been on full-scale social security disability payments for almost twenty years. During that time, he has earned two master's degrees. In his late sixties, afflicted with the twin burdens of his age and his medical history, he sought help finding work and was told by officials at every level that there was no work for someone like him and that he shouldn't bother. I know how productive a worker Mason was because I read the long stream of letters he sent to rehabilitative services in South Carolina, where he lives, and to the governor's office, and to just about anyone else he could think of, all of which he copied to me. On medication, he seemed to function well most of the time. The sheer number of words was overwhelming. Mason was told that the jobs available to people in his situation were all manual labor, and that if he wanted a job using his mind, he was on his own. Taking occasional teaching jobs, most of which involved horrendous commutes from his home, he managed to keep body and soul together while he wrote hundreds and hundreds of pages arguing his case, explaining himself, calling out for help—all of which earned him a handful of form letters. Reading them, I doubt that Paul's letters were ever even passed up to someone who might have been able to help him. "Depression creates its own prison," he wrote to me. "I sit here in an apartment I can barely cope with and fight for help finding a job. When I can't bear to be alone, as on Christmas Day last year, I go and ride the subway around Atlanta. It's the closest I can come to other people under present circumstances." His sentiments were echoed by many others I met. One woman who felt socially isolated by her professional failures wrote, "I am finally suffocating under the weight of not being employed."

Richard Baron is a sometime board member of the International Association of Psychosocial Rehabilitation Services (IAPSRS), the organization for nonmedical psychiatric workers, which currently has a membership of nearly two thousand. Depressed people themselves, he writes, "have begun to voice deep concerns about the emptiness of their lives in the community without the ego-building, social-binding, and income-producing benefits of a job, demonstrating how solidly work persists as a fundamental part of the recovery process." An analysis of current aid programs reveals a terrible problem with them. Those depressed people who can get themselves classed as disabled in the United States are eligible for Social Security Disability Insurance (SSDI) and Supplemental Security Income (SSI); they also qualify, in general, for Medicaid, which pays for what tend to be expensive ongoing treatments. People who receive SSDI and SSI are afraid of taking a job lest they lose them; indeed, less than half a percent of those who receive SSDI or SSI give them up to reenter the workforce. "The subculture of serious mental illness has no 'folk wisdom,' " writes Baron, "as unshakable (and thoroughly wrong) as the notion that people who return to work will immediately lose all their SSI benefits and never be able to regain them. The mental health system acknowledges the importance of employment as a goal, but remains paralyzed in its ability to fund rehabilitation services."

Though the most immediately applicable research in mental health has been done within the pharmaceutical industry, in the United States the brain's most primitive mechanisms are revealed at the National Institute of Mental Health (NIMH), located on a vast, sprawling campus in

Bethesda, Maryland. It is one of twenty-three line items within the budget of the National Institutes of Health (NIH); another line item is for the Substance Abuse and Mental Health Services Administration (SAMHSA), which does some depression-related work but is not part of the NIMH. At both the NIMH and SAMHSA, the instant benefit of applied research is subsidiary to an increase in human knowledge through basic research. "If you can unlock the secrets of the disease," says Representative John Porter pragmatically, "you can do a great deal to prevent the disease. If you put money into research, you can ultimately save lives and curtail misery. People are beginning to see that the benefits are very large compared to the investment being made."

In the early nineties, the U.S. Congress asked six prominent Nobel Prize winners in the sciences each to nominate two subjects for major research. Five of the six chose the brain. Congress declared the span from 1990 to 2000 the "Decade of the Brain" and devoted vast resources to brain research. "This will be remembered as one of the single most important edicts Congress passed to advance human knowledge about itself," says Representative Bob Wise (Democrat, West Virginia). During the decade of the brain, mental illness funding increased enormously, and "people started to understand that mental illness is an illness like other illnesses," Porter says. "People used to see mental illness as a bottomless pit that devoured money, requiring interminable psychiatric treatment, the meter always running, the progress in doubt. The new medicines changed all that. Now, however, I worry that we begin to look away from people who are not helped by or cannot be helped by the drugs."

Within the U.S. government, Senator Paul Wellstone (Democrat, Minnesota) and Senator Pete Domenici (Republican, New Mexico) have been the most outspoken advocates of improvements in mental health law. For the moment, the political struggle at center stage concerns insurance parity. Even Americans who have comprehensive health coverage often have limited provisions for mental health; in fact, over 75 percent of health plans in the United States offer less coverage for mental health complaints than for other illnesses. At both the lifetime and the annual level, your mental health insurance may be capped at less than 5 percent of the cap for "regular" illnesses. Since the beginning of 1998, it has not been legal for U.S. companies with more than fifty employees that offer health plans to have reduced caps on mental health coverage, but those companies can still have a higher copay (the amount the patient has to pay as opposed to what the insurer pays) for mental illness than for other complaints, so that the diseases are still, in effect, not comparably covered. "That most policies would not provide coverage for my daughter with depression on the same basis as if she had epilepsy is simply incredible," says Laurie Flynn, who heads the National Alliance for the Mentally Ill, the country's leading advocacy group. "I have a favorable copayment for rheumatoid arthritis because that's a 'real' illness, and my daughter's illness isn't? Mental health is very hard to define; few people have perfect mental health. Our society has no obligation, and cannot afford, to offer me insurance coverage for my personal happiness. But mental illness is much more straightforward. It's joining the train of disenfranchised groups that are rising up and claiming their fair share." The Americans with Disabilities Act (ADA) protects those with "mental and physical disabilities," but mental illness is still a severe barrier to employment, and heavy with stigma. "There's still a sense that if you were a really strong person," says Flynn, "this wouldn't have happened to you. If you were a really clean-living, well-raised, properly motivated person, it wouldn't happen."

Like all political movements, this one depends on oversimplification. "It's a chemical imbalance just like the kidney or liver," says Flynn. In fact there's a certain wanting to have it both ways: wanting to be treated and wanting to be protected. "We've developed a five-year campaign to end discrimination by making these illnesses understood to be brain disorders and nothing more." Which is tricky, since they are brain disorders *and* something more. Robert Boorstin is bipolar and is among the most prominent openly mentally ill people in the country. He has become a public spokesman on the subject of mental illness. "There are people in the 'movement,'" he says, "who literally go nuts when they see the word *crazy* used incorrectly."

Health maintenance organizations (HMOs) are not good news for the depressed. Sylvia Simpson, who regularly confronts HMOs in her work as a clinician at Johns Hopkins, has only horror stories to tell. "I spend more and more time on the phone with representatives of managed care companies, trying to justify patients' staying here. When patients are still very, very ill, if they're not acutely suicidal that day, I get told to let them out. I'll say they need to be here and they just say, 'I'm denying it.' I tell family members to get on the phone, to call lawyers, to struggle. The patients are obviously too sick to do it. We feel we have to keep people here until it's safe for them to go someplace else. So the family ends up getting the bill; if they can't pay it, we write it off. We can't sustain the policy, and besides, it makes the insurance companies take advantage. It also makes people more depressed; it's just terrible." At hospitals less wealthy, with less determined leadership, such absorbing of patient debt is often not possible; and depressed people are in no shape to argue their own cases with their insurers. "We know of numerous cases," avers Flynn, "of people being discharged because of an HMO mandate, when they were not ready, who have committed suicide. There are deaths being caused by these policies." "If you have the gun to your head," says Jeanne Miranda, "you can perhaps get your treatment covered. Put it down, and you're back out on your own."

Depression is one hell of an expensive illness. My first breakdown cost me and my insurance five months of work; $4,000 worth of visits to the psychopharmacologist; $10,000 of talking therapy; $3,500 for medications. I of course saved a lot since I didn't talk on the telephone, go to restaurants, or buy or wear clothes; and living at my dad's place lowered my home electric bill. But the economics are not easy. "Let's say your insurance policy covers fifty percent of twenty visits a year to a psychiatrist," says Robert Boorstin. "Plus, after a thousand dollars it covers eighty percent of drugs. And that's considered a good policy. Who can afford that? When I was admitted for my second hospitalization, my insurers said I was capped out and my brother had to put eighteen thousand dollars on his American Express card to get me *admitted* to the hospital." Boorstin subsequently sued his insurer and won a settlement, but the resources to undertake such suits are few and far between. "I now spend about twenty thousand dollars per year on maintaining my mental health, without hospitalization. Even the simplest depression has to run at least two thousand or twenty-five hundred dollars per year, and a three-week hospitalization starts at fourteen thousand dollars."

In fact, the *Journal of the American Medical Association* recently estimated the annual cost of depression in the United States at $43 billion: $12 billion in direct costs and $31 billion in indirect costs. Of that amount, $8 billion is lost because of the premature death of potentially productive members of the workforce; $23 billion is lost through absence from or loss of productivity in the workplace. This means that the average employer loses about $6,000 per year per depressed employee. "The model used in this study," writes *JAMA*, "underestimates the true cost to society because it does not include the adverse effects of pain and suffering and other quality-of-life issues. Moreover, these estimates are conservative because the study did not take into account other important costs such as additional out-of-pocket expenses for families, excessive hospitalization for nonpsychiatric conditions due to depression, and excessive diagnostic tests looking for general medical diagnoses when depression is the cause of a patient's symptoms."

Since he first introduced mental health legislation in 1996, Senator Wellstone has led the battle to make such discrimination between mental and physical illness illegal. While parity legislation is pending, the notion that there *is* a separation between physical and mental diseases is breaking down, and it is politically expedient, perhaps even necessary, to

371

cleave to the biological view, to let chemistry alleviate personal responsibility, giving mental illness symmetry with major physical illness. "It would be interesting to bring a lawsuit sometime against an insurer who refused parity, and say, on grounds of equal protection, that mental disorders *are* physical disorders and that you can't exclude mental illness if you purport to cover all physical ailments defined and described by doctors," Senator Domenici says. Initial parity legislation recently passed, but it is "a can of spaghetti it has so many loopholes," as Representative Marcy Kaptur (Democrat, Ohio) put it. It does not apply to businesses with few employees; allows overall dollar limits on health care; allows insurers to place strict limits on hospital stays or outpatient services for the mentally ill; and allows insurers to require higher copayments and set higher deductibles for mental than for physical illnesses. While the spirit of the law is cheering, it does little to alter the status quo. Wellstone and Domenici hope to introduce a more rigorous bill.

It is hard to find anyone in Congress who is opposed on principle to healing the mentally ill; "the opposition is competition," says Representative Porter. While declarations about the tragic nature of suicide and the danger of psychiatric complaints accumulate on the *Congressional Record*, legislation pertinent to these statistics does not pass easily. When the extent of coverage is increased, the cost of coverage goes up, and in the current U.S. system that means that fewer people have medical coverage. Four hundred thousand people fall off the insurance registers for every 1 percent increase in the cost of insurance. So if mental health parity were to increase the cost of medical care by 2.5 percent, a million more Americans would go uninsured. Experiments with parity demonstrate that in fact it does not necessarily raise costs by more than 1 percent; people who receive adequate mental health care are much better able to regulate their diet and exercise and to visit doctors in time for preventative medicine to be effective, and so mental health insurance largely pays for itself. Furthermore, with increasing evidence that people with serious depression are much more subject to a variety of illnesses (including infection, cancer, and heart disease) than are the general population, mental health care becomes part of an economically and socially well-balanced program for physical health. In those places where parity has been introduced, the overall added cost in the first year is less than 1 percent for family insurance. The insurance lobby, however, is always fearful that costs will spiral out of control, and arguments on the floor of the Senate show that in the minds of many people, the economics of mental health care are still highly problematical.

"Postponement of intervention because of insurance restrictions does *not* result in savings," Representative Marge Roukema (Republican,

New Jersey) says emphatically. "You're really building in greater costs." The House has formed the Working Committee on Mental Health (after it was decided that a Working Committee on Mental Illness sounded dire), which is chaired by Representative Roukema and Representative Kaptur. Discussions in the Senate have been about parity as a civil rights issue. "I'm actually a marketplace guy myself," says Senator Domenici. "But I think we're violating civil rights when we take a large group like this and just say, 'Well, struggle along.' We can't treat the mentally ill like they're some kind of freaks." Senator Harry Reid (Democrat, Nevada) says, "Now I see a young lady who has problems with her menstruation and we get her to a doctor right away; or a young man who has asthma gets taken care of real quick. But if that young lady and that young man are not talking to anyone, weigh two hundred ninety pounds at five feet tall, you know, so what? 'Mr. Chairman,' I recently said, 'I think we should do a hearing on suicide.' We spend lots and lots of money making sure that people drive safely. We do so much to make sure airplanes are safe. But what do we do about those thirty-one thousand lives a year that go to suicide?"

In the House, the focus has been on the idea that the mentally ill are dangerous. Various episodes of illness-related violence have become iconic: the shooting of Ronald Reagan by John Hinckley; the Unabomber; the gunning down of two policemen on Capitol Hill by Russell Weston Jr.; the episode in which a diagnosed schizophrenic, Andrew Goldstein, pushed a woman under a New York subway train; the shootings in post offices, and, most of all, the terrible shootings in schools: in Littleton and Atlanta, in Kentucky and Mississippi and Oregon, in Denver and in Alberta. According to recent press releases, over one thousand homicides were attributed in 1998 to people with mental illnesses. Depression is implicated much less frequently than manic-depression or schizophrenia, but agitated depression does lead people to violent acts. The focus on mentally ill people who are dangerous increases stigma and reinforces negative public perception of people suffering from mental illness. It is, however, extremely effective for fund-raising; many people who will not pay to help strangers will gladly pay to protect themselves, and using the "people like that kill people like us" argument enables political action. A recent British study showed that though only 3 percent of the mentally ill are considered dangerous to others, nearly 50 percent of all press coverage of the mentally ill is focused on their dangerousness. "Very intelligent members of Congress are willing to develop a bunker mentality rather than try to understand the conditions that motivate horrendous acts," Representative Kaptur has said, "and so they want to build barbed-wire fences and increase policing to avoid problems that should be addressed by increasing mental health funding. We're spending billions of dollars on defending ourselves against these people when for much less we could be helping them." President Clinton, who had a strong record on defending the rights of the mentally ill and who backed Tipper Gore's White House Conference on Mental Illness, said to me, "Well, we can only hope that people will sit up and pay attention to the urgency of this problem after the tragedy in Littleton, after Atlanta, after the shooting of those policemen on Capitol Hill. Major legislative change in this area— it takes tragedy after tragedy."

"People around here, nice or otherwise, don't make decisions just because they are right in some abstract moral sense," Representative Lynn Rivers points out. "You have to bring it home to a general population that this is in *their* best interest." She is a strong supporter of the bill proposed by Roukema and Kaptur and, like those two representatives, is apologetic about the phrasing of the bill. It does not use the moral language of ethical responsibility. Proposed in the wake of the Weston shooting at the Capitol, it talks about self-protection. "*Of course* we want to help nonviolent mentally ill people just as much as we want to control violent ones," Roukema said to me. "But we're the ones on the inside track. To draw any kind of substantial support, we have to show people that it serves their *urgent* self-interest to do something about this. We have to talk about preventing atrocious crimes that could be visited on them or their constituents at any moment. We can't talk simply about a better and more prosperous and more humane state." The economic arguments have relatively seldom been used, and the idea of getting people off social assistance and into the capitalist system is still obscure for Congress—though a recent study at MIT showed that when people have major depression their ability to do work falls dramatically but returns to base level with antidepressant treatment. Two other studies show that supported employment for the mentally ill is the most economically beneficial way of dealing with them.

Recent research linking depression to other illnesses is beginning to carry weight with lawmakers and even with HMOs. If untreated depression does makes you more prone to infection, cancer, and heart disease, then it's an expensive illness to ignore. Through an irony of politics, the more expensive untreated depression is, the more money will be made available to treat the illness. John Wilson, a onetime candidate for mayor of Washington, D.C., who committed suicide, once said, "I believe that more people are dying of depression than are dying of AIDS, heart trouble, high blood pressure, anything else, simply because I believe depression brings on all these diseases."

While arguments about insurance parity rage, there is no discussion of what to do about depression among the uninsured. Medicare and Medicaid supply various levels of service in various states, but they do not provide for outreach programs, and most of the indigent depressed are not able to get themselves together to seek out assistance. The arguments in favor of treatment for the indigent depressed seem to me to be overwhelming, and so I went to Capitol Hill to share the experiences related in the last chapter. I was there in a strange capacity, an accidental activist as well as a journalist. I wanted to know what was being done, but I also wanted to persuade the American government to press forward with reforms that would serve the interests of the nation and of the people by whose stories I had been so deeply moved. I wanted to share my insider's knowledge. Senator Reid had a real grasp of the situation: "A few years ago, I dressed myself up in disguise, like I was homeless, baseball hat and old bum clothes, and I spent an afternoon and a night in a homeless shelter in Las Vegas and then the next day did the same in Reno. You can write all the articles you want about Prozac and about all the modern miracle drugs that stop depression. That doesn't help this group of people." Reid himself grew up in poverty and his father killed himself. "I have learned that had my dad had someone to talk to, and some medication, he probably wouldn't have killed himself. But we're not legislating for that at present."

When I met with Senator Domenici, joint sponsor of the Mental Health Parity Act, I laid out for him the anecdotal and statistical information I had collated, and then I proposed fully documenting the tendencies that seemed so obviously implied by these stories. "Suppose," I said, "that we could put together incontrovertible data, and that the questions of bias, inadequate information, and partisanship could all be fully resolved. Suppose we could say that sound mental health treatment for the severely depressed indigent population served the advantage of the U.S. economy, of the bureau of Veterans Affairs, of the social good—of the taxpayers who now pay cripplingly high prices for the consequences of untreated depression, and of the recipients of that investment, who live at the brink of despair. What, then, would be the path to reform?"

"If you're asking whether we can expect much change simply because that change would serve everyone's advantage in both economic and human terms," said Domenici, "I regret to tell you that the answer is no." Four factors block the development of federal programs to achieve care for the indigent. The first, and perhaps the most formidable, is simply the structure of the national budget. "We are now niched with programs and program costs," Domenici said. "The question we must confront is whether the program you're describing is going to grow and require new funds, not whether there'll be some overall savings for the Treasury of the United States." You can't immediately reduce other costs: you can't in one year take the money out of the prison system and out of welfare to pay for a new mental health outreach service, because the economic advantages of that service are slow to accrue. "Our evaluation of medical delivery systems is simply not outcome-oriented," Domenici confirmed. Second is that the Republican leadership of the U.S. Congress does not like to give directives to the health care industry. "It would be a mandate," Domenici said. "There are people who would support this kind of legislation at every level but who are ideologically opposed to mandating states, mandating insurance companies, mandating anyone." Federal law, the McCarran-Ferguson Act, makes the administration of health insurance a states' issue. Third is that it is difficult to get people elected for limited terms to focus on long-range improvement of the social infrastructure rather than on the quick spectacle of immediately visible effects on the lives of voters. And fourth is that, in the sad and ironic words of Senator Wellstone, "This is a representative democracy we're living in. People defend the causes their voters care about. Indigent, depressed people are at home in bed on Election Day with the covers over their heads—and that means they don't have much representation up here. The indigent depressed are not what you'd call an empowered group."

It is always strange to go from intense experiences with an utterly disenfranchised population to intense experiences with a powerful one. I was as much stirred by my conversations with members of Congress as I had been by my conversations with the indigent depressed. The subject of mental health parity cuts straight across party lines; Republicans and Democrats are, in Domenici's words, "in a bidding war to see who loves the NIMH more." Congress consistently votes more money to the NIMH than is provided in the budget; in 1999, President Clinton allowed $810 million; Congress, led by Representative John Porter, the extremely capable chairman of the subcommittee on appropriations, who is in his eleventh consecutive term in Congress and who is a big fan of basic scientific research, raised that figure to $861 million. For calendar year 2000, Congress increased funding for the Community Health Services Block Grant by 24 percent, bringing it to $359 million. The president asked his personnel office to make concessions to people with mental illness who are seeking employment. "If we're going to be compassionate conservatives," Roukema said, "we might as well start here." Every significant mental health bill has had Democratic and Republican sponsorship.

Most of the people who battle for the mentally ill in Congress have stories of their own that have brought them to this arena. Senator Reid's father killed himself; Senator Domenici has a schizophrenic daughter who is very ill; Senator Wellstone has a schizophrenic brother; Representative Rivers has a severe bipolar disorder; Representative Roukema has been married now for almost fifty years to a psychiatrist; Representative Bob Wise was swayed to enter public service by a college summer spent working in a psychiatric ward, where he developed relationships with mentally ill patients. "It shouldn't be this way," Wellstone said. "I wish I'd gained my understanding of this subject solely through research and ethical inquiry. But for many people, the problems of mental illness are still utterly abstract, and their urgency becomes apparent only through intense involuntary immersion in them. We need an education initiative to pave the way for a legislative one." When the 1996 parity act was heard on the Senate floor, Wellstone, who speaks of the mentally ill as compassionately as though he were related to all of them, stood before Congress and, in a breathtakingly eloquent speech, described his own experiences. Domenici, who is by no means a sentimental man, gave a shorter exposition of his experience, and then a few other senators came down to the floor and told stories of their own friends and relatives. That day in the Senate was more like EST than a political debate. "People came up to me before the vote," Wellstone recalled, "and said, 'This really really matters to you, doesn't it?' I said to them, 'Yes, it matters more than anything.' That's how we got the votes." It was from the start more a symbolic act than one that could bring about major change, because it left the decision on whether to increase overall cost of treatment in the hands of the insurers. It did not improve the quality of care for patients.

Community health programs, most of which retrenched with cuts in the late nineties, are regularly blamed for the violent actions of those who are supposed to be under their care; if they could keep everyone quiet, they would, by the standards of much of the world, be doing their job. Their inadequacies in protecting the healthy from the ill win them excoriation in the press. The question of whether they are serving the interest of the well is often examined; whether they are helping their target community seldom comes up. "Huge numbers of federal tax dollars are going to these programs," Representative Roukema said, "and there is strong evidence that the money is being diverted into all kinds of irrelevant local projects." Representative Wise described the Clinton health care debate of 1993 as "a depressing experience in and of itself" and said that the NIH is not providing the concrete information that would show local chambers of commerce why universal parity would be to their advantage. Community mental health clinics, where they do exist, tend to focus on relatively uncomplicated conditions such as divorce. "They should be for giving out medication and for follow-through and for verbal counseling for a full range of complaints," Representative Kaptur said.

Institutionalization is a point of contention between a legal community that supports civil liberties and a social-work and legislative community that sees people who are crazy and suffering and feels that it is criminal not to intervene. "Civil libertarians who take extreme views on this matter are both incompetent and inconsequential," Roukema said. "Under the guise of civil liberties, they're inflicting cruel and unusual punishment on people despite the fact that society has science that can make a better way. It's cruelty; if we were doing that to animals, the ASPCA would be after us. If people don't take their medication and follow through with their treatment, maybe it should be mandated that they be reinstitutionalized." There are precedents for such policies. The treatment of tuberculosis is one such example. If someone has TB and is not disciplined enough to take the right medications at the right times, in some states a nurse will actually go out and find him and give him his isoniazid every day. Of course TB is communicable and, uncontained, can mutate and cause a public health crisis; but if mental illness is dangerous to society, intervention may be rationalized on the TB model.

Involuntary-commitment laws were the great issue of the 1970s, during the heyday of the institution. These days, most people who want treatment have trouble getting it; large institutions are closing down; and short-term-care facilities push out people who are not yet ready to face the world on their own. "The reality," the *New York Times Magazine* said in the spring of 1999, "is that hospitals can't get rid of [patients] fast enough." While all this is happening, however, there are also people who are being incarcerated against their will. It is better, where possible, to seduce people into treatment than to force them into it. Further, it is important to come up with universal standards on the basis of which force may be used. The worst abuses have occurred when unqualified or malignant individuals have assigned themselves the power to judge who is ill and who is not and have incarcerated people without due process.

You can be hospitalized in an institution with open doors. Most of the patients at long-term-care facilities are free to walk down the driveway and off to the streets; only a limited number are on twenty-four-hour supervision or in forensic units. The contract between a care facility and its denizens is voluntary. Legal scholars tend to favor letting people run their own lives even if they run themselves into destruction, while psychiatric social workers and anyone else who has actually dealt closely with the mentally ill tend to be interventionist. Who is to decide when to give someone the liberty of his mind and when to deny it? Broadly sketched, the view of the right is that crazy people must be locked away so that they don't drag down the society—even if they don't pose an active threat. The view of the left is that no one should have his civil liberties infringed on by people who are acting outside of primary power structures. The view of the center is that some people do need to be brought into treatment while others do not. Because resistance to diagnosis and despair about a cure are among the symptoms of mental illness, involuntary commitment continues to be a necessary part of treatment.

"You need to treat these people as people, to respect their individuality, but to connect them up to the mainstream," Representative Kaptur explains. The American Civil Liberties Union (ACLU) takes the moderate position. It has published a statement that "the freedom to be wandering the streets, psychotic, ill, deteriorating, and untreated, when there is a reasonable prospect of effective treatment, is not freedom; it is abandonment." The problem is that the choice is too often between total commitment and total abandonment: the present system is predicated on categorical psychosis and grossly lacks the intermediary-care solutions most depressives require. We must check out the people who gibber on our streets, assess the fluctuations of their suicidality, determine their potential danger to others—and then attempt to predict who, after resisting a cure, will upon recovery be grateful that the cure was thrust upon him.

No one really wants to be depressed, but some people do not want to be made well as I would define *well*. What options should they have? Should we let them withdraw into their illness? Should we pay the social expense of such withdrawal? Through what due process should we determine these matters? The potential for bureaucracy is terrifying, and the delicate negotiation of who needs what will never be well resolved. If one accepts that perfect balance will be impossible, one must assume that we have two options: to imprison some people who should be free, or to free some people who will destroy themselves. The question, really, is not so much *whether* treatment should be foisted on people as *when* it should be foisted on them and by *whom*. I cannot look at this problem and turn away from Sheila Hernandez, the poor HIV-positive woman who fought against her imprisonment at Hopkins, who wanted to be left free to die—and who is now delighted to be alive and has her cell phone ringing every minute. But I am reminded also of the Korean boy with cerebral palsy, a patient with acute multiple disorders, including physical disabilities that prevent him from committing suicide, who is forced into a life in which there will be no happiness and from which he is not permitted to escape. Despite much pondering and consideration, I cannot find the right answer to this question.

The problem of aggression has spawned defensive laws; though few depressives are violent, they are in the purview of schizophrenia's legalities. The mentally ill are a diverse body, and the monolithic approach to mental illness laws causes intense suffering. Since the landmark 1972 action against Willowbrook, an institution for the mentally retarded that was, among other things, doing experiments on uninformed patients, the policy of providing the "least restrictive placement" possible has held sway. While the mentally ill may be deprived of rights because of their aggressive behaviors, they also lose out on rights because the state assumes *parens patriae* power, taking a protective position, much as it does toward minors. The ACLU does not believe that *parens patriae* should be extended, and certainly the idea of *parens patriae* was abused in places such as the Soviet Union; it is a phrase too much associated with paternalistic police power. But how much suffering should be supported in defense of such a legal principle?

The Treatment Advocacy Center (TAC), based in Washington, D.C., is the most conservative body on treatment, and its position is that people should be incarcerated even if they do not pose a clear and present danger. Jonathan Stanley, the assistant director of the center, complains that it is only the criminal element that is receiving treatment. "People will pay a whole lot more attention to a one-in-two-million chance that they'll be pushed under a subway than they will to a one hundred percent chance that they'll run into twenty psychotics on a given day in Central Park." For Stanley, deinstitutionalization was the unfortunate result of civil libertarians' defending the "wrong" people while the government went wild about cutting costs. Deinstitutionalization was supposed to translate into a diverse range of care in the community, but nothing of the sort has occurred. The consequence of deinstitutionalization has been the disappearance of a multitiered system of treatment in which people are gently shoehorned back into their communities: far too often, patients are in for total incarceration or they're out on their own. The idea of providing a full social-work force to ease people from despair to high levels of functioning has not yet caught on in government circles. The TAC has strongly backed legislation such as Kendra's Law, a New York act that allows suits to be brought against mentally ill people who fail to take their medications, criminalizing the ill. Depressed people are taken to court, fined, and then are released again into the streets to fend for themselves, since there is no room or budget for providing more extensive treatment. If they cause too much trouble, they are incarcerated as criminals: the result of deinstitutionalization has in many instances been to shift people from hospitals to prisons. And in the prisons, where they receive inadequate and inappropriate treatment, they cause a terrific amount of trouble. "No one else," Stanley maintains, "wants a good mental health system so much as a jailer does."

The Bazelon Center in Washington, D.C., at the liberal end of the spectrum, believes that commitment should always be voluntary and defines mental illness as interpretive. "Supposed lack of insight on the part of the individual," they have said, "is often no more than disagreement with the treating professional." Sometimes it is; but not always.

The Veterans Administration, still persuaded that psychiatric complaints are unbecoming to strong military men, spends less than 12 percent of its research budget on psychiatry. In fact, psychiatric disturbances may be the most frequently occurring problem for veterans, who have a high rate of post–traumatic stress disorder, homelessness, and substance abuse. Given that a large part of the taxpayers' money has already been spent training these men and women, the relative negligence of them is particularly troubling and reveals further the political naïveté of mental health policy. Depressed veterans, particularly those who fought in the Vietnam War, make up a large part of the American homeless population. These people have undergone two traumas in a row. The first is war itself, the horror of killing people, of seeing the desolation all around, and of sustaining oneself in a situation of great danger. The other is enforced intimacy and group dynamics; many veterans become almost addicted to army standards of structure and get lost when they are thrown back on their own resources and have to shape their own activities. The Veterans Committee has estimated that about 25 percent of veterans who arrive at hospitals have a primary diagnosis of mental illness. Given that more than half the doctors in the United States have received some form of training in veterans' hospitals, prejudice in such institutions spreads its contagion into civilian hospitals and emergency rooms.

Representative Kaptur tells the story of going to a Veterans Administration hospital near Chicago. She was in the emergency room when the police brought in a man in bad shape, and the social worker who was on duty said, "Oh, it's one of my regulars." Kaptur asked her what she meant, and she explained that this was this man's seventeenth admission for mental health problems. "We get him in here; clean him up; get him on his medication; let him go; and within a few months he comes back here." What can be said of a mental health system in which such things happen? "Seventeen admissions for emergency care," says Kaptur. "Do you know how much money we'd have to help other people if we avoided seventeen admissions by providing adequate community care? The cost of improper treatment is so much higher than the cost of good treatment."

We seem to be moving back toward involuntary commitment, to have come full circle. We have gone from a monolithic and malign mental health system for the depressed to a shattered, limited one. "Things are better than the old system, which left these people locked in a room to rot," says Beth Haroules of the New York Civil Liberties Union, "but given how much we now know about the origins and treatment of mental illness, the public system is even farther behind than it was twenty years ago." The reality is that some people are not capable of making their own decisions and do require involuntary commitment; others, though ill, do not require such commitment. It would be best to provide a graduated system of care that can offer extensive services at various levels and that incorporates aggressive outreach for outpatients who are likely to diverge from their treatment regimens. It is necessary to set up guidelines for due process and put all those who require commitment through the same examinations, into which we must incorporate checks and balances. That due process must take account of both the threat that an ill person may pose to society and the pain that an ill person experiences unnecessarily. Standards must be established by which people will be put into prison, into involuntary psychiatric commitment, into involuntary psychiatric treatment, or into voluntary psychiatric treatment. Space must be made for those people who, with full information and at no significant cost to others, wish to eschew treatment. An efficient and disinterested system must be established to oversee these matters.

Lynn Rivers is the only member of the U.S. Congress who has come out of the closet about her own struggles with mental illness. Married while she was pregnant at eighteen, she worked at first in food preparation and as a Tupperware lady to support her family. She began to develop symptoms shortly after the birth of her first daughter. When her illness escalated, she went to see a doctor. Her husband, an autoworker, had a joint Blue Cross/Blue Shield plan. "I believe it covered six visits to a psychiatrist," she said to me sarcastically. For the next decade, half of her and her husband's take-home pay went to psychiatric bills. By the time she was twenty-one, she was having difficulty working and was afraid to answer the telephone. "It was horrible. Long. The depressive episodes would go on for months. I spent months in bed. I'd sleep twenty-two hours a day. People here often think of depression as being sad: no matter what I tell other legislators, they don't know. They don't understand how it is emptiness, how it is a vast nothing."

Faced with the costs of treatment, Rivers's husband worked two full-time jobs and much of the time a third one part-time, holding his place in a car factory, working at the university, and delivering pizzas at night. He had a paper route for a while and he worked at a toy store. "I don't know where he found the strength," Rivers says. "We just did what we had to do. I can't imagine what it would be like to go through a severe mental illness without familial support. It was so horrible anyway, and if the family, if anger—" Rivers paused. "I don't know how anybody could survive. He took care of me too. We had two little kids. I could do a bit with them, but not much. We somehow rose above reality and made it work." Rivers still carries guilt about the children, "though if I had broken my back in a car accident, I would not have been more disabled, and I would have felt justified in needing so much healing time. But as it was, every time my kids had trouble in school or ran into any problem, I would think, it's because of me and it's because I wasn't there and I wasn't this and I wasn't that. Guilt was my constant companion, guilt about things I couldn't control."

She finally found "the perfect mix" of medications in the early nineties; she now takes lithium (her dose has gone as high as 2,200 mg per day, though it is now stable at 900), desipramine, and BuSpar. As soon as she was well enough to do it, she launched a career in public service. "I am a walking, talking advertisement for mental health research. I prove it. If you will invest in me, I will pay you back. And that's true of most people suffering with this disorder: they just want a chance to be productive." Rivers earned a college degree by studying part-time while caring for her family; graduated with distinction; and went on to complete law school. She was elected, when she was in her late twenties and having relatively controlled illness, to the Board of Education in Ann Arbor. Two years later, for unrelated reasons, she had a hysterectomy, and because she developed anemia, she missed six months of work. When she decided to run for Congress, "my opponent found out that I had had mental illness and tried to indicate that I'd missed that time at work because I'd had a nervous breakdown." Rivers was doing a call-in radio interview, and a planted caller asked whether it was true that she had had a problem with depression. Rivers immediately acknowledged that she had and that it had taken her ten years to stabilize. After the interview she went to a meeting of a local Democratic board. When she walked in, a local party bigwig said, "Lynn, I heard you on the radio. What were you doing, are you nuts?" And she said calmly, "Of course, that's what the radio show was about." Her serene, composed approach to the issue made it a nonissue. She won the election.

Several other members of the House have told Rivers of their depressive illness but are afraid to tell their voters. "One colleague said that he wanted to tell people but that he felt he couldn't. I don't know his electorate. Perhaps he can't. Most people who have depression don't make these judgments very accurately because they're mired in guilt. It's a very lonely disease. But in the same way my gay friends say that being out of the closet relieves them of a great burden, I have been liberated: my depression is just not an issue anymore." Representative Bob Wise calls mental illness "the family secret everyone has."

"You have to self-refer," Lynn Rivers says. "You have to find your community's mental health services. Let the record show that I sneered when you mentioned 'community mental health.' Listen, if you're waiting for an autoworker to go across the shop floor to find his union steward and say, 'My son has schizophrenia, my wife has manic-depressive disease, my daughter is going through psychotic episodes'—it ain't gonna happen." This country," she avers, "hasn't moved forward enough for us to claim the kind of care we need. Furthermore, prescribing is frequently done by doctors who don't know enough; and in an effort to save money, HMOs give them a formulary that limits the number of medications they can prescribe. "If your idiosyncratic response can't be negotiated with that list of medications, that's it for you!" Rivers says. "Even when the illness is stabilized, you have to replace the coping mechanisms that made sense in the context of the illness and that do not make sense in the context of health." She is appalled by cuts in funding for ongoing psychodynamic support, which she believes will increase across-the-board social costs. "It's a mess," she said.

Joe Rogers, executive director of the Mental Health Association of Southeastern Pennsylvania, is a genial spread of a man, with easy manners, a curious air of disheveled authority, and a fluent, engaging way of speaking. He can be garrulous and philosophical, but he is also shrewd and pragmatic, with an eye that never for a moment shifts from its goal. When we first met, for lunch at a Philadelphia hotel, he was wearing a blue suit and a striped tie, and he had a briefcase that seemed to spill executive habit from its guts. While I looked over the menu, he said that he had lived in New York for a while. "Oh, where'd you live?" I asked. "Washington Square," he said. He took a roll from the bread basket on the table. "I live around Washington Square myself," I replied, closing my menu. "It's a great neighborhood. Where were you?" He smiled a bit wanly and said, "Washington Square. *In* it. On a bench. For nine months. One stretch when I was homeless."

Joe Rogers, like Lynn Rivers, has gone from the "consumer" end of the mental health network to the "supplier" end. One of four children, he grew up in Florida with an alcoholic mother and a gun-toting father who was usually absent and intermittently suicidal. Though his parents came from backgrounds of relative comfort, their dysfunction led them into real destitution. "We lived in a house that was falling apart and there were cockroaches running around everywhere," Rogers recalls. "There were times when the grocery money would disappear, and later I found out that my father was pretty addicted to gambling, so we didn't see even whatever salary he was earning. We weren't starving, but in relation to where my parents had come from, we were really in poverty." Rogers dropped out of school at age thirteen. His father would habitually take out a Luger and tell his son that he was ready to kill himself, and Rogers developed some finesse at dealing with the situation. "When I was twelve, I'd learned to take the gun away from him and hide it." In the meanwhile, his mother's alcoholism got worse and worse, and she went through frequent hospitalizations; she too made suicide attempts, though Rogers describes them as rather halfhearted. Rogers's father had died by the time Rogers was sixteen; his mother died when he was twenty.

"Looking back on it, I think my father would have responded to treatment," Rogers says. "I don't know about my mother." Rogers himself was largely inactive from thirteen to eighteen, but at eighteen he began working toward a GED; he met a woman he liked and he began to try to build a life for himself. He went to a Quaker meeting where he met a psychologist who tried to give him some help. Eventually he hit a crisis and found himself one day in his car at a stop sign, unable to decide whether to go forward or backward or left or right. "I was just sitting there, with a total sense of loss." Soon after that he became acutely suicidal. His Quaker friend helped him to get into a hospital, where he was diagnosed and put on lithium. It was 1971, and Rogers had no place to go. His girlfriend left; his parents were dead; he was living on social security.

Rogers went through repeated hospitalizations. Antidepressant therapy was primitive at that time, and Rogers lived on sedating psychotropics, "which made me feel dead." He hated the hospital. "I started acting better because I wanted to get the heck out of there." Rogers still cannot speak of state hospitals without a shiver of horror. "I spent six months in one and—just the smell. They spend a hundred twenty-five thousand dollars per patient per year, and they could at least have a decent physical plant. You're sharing a room with two or three other people. You're locked up with them in a small area. There isn't much by way of staffing and the staff aren't well trained, and they won't listen to anything you say. They are often abusive. And very authoritarian, which sits badly with my rebellious streak. Those places are prisons. As long as the funding is in place, no one thinks about discharge—no one has the job of trying to get people out of the red tape they've been wrapped in. It destroys you as a person to be in one of those places for long." In hospitals, he was put on strong sedation that made him "manageable" though it frequently failed to address his problems in any substantive way; sedated anxiety and irritability without antidepressant treatment is simply a withdrawal into a haze of misery. Rogers does not believe in forcing people into treatment on grounds that afterward they'll be glad you did. "If you went into a bar and grabbed someone who was drinking too much and put him into a detox center and counseled his wife, he might be glad you did, but it would be kind of a violation of our social norms and his civil liberties," he says.

I found the experience of visiting state mental hospitals shocking. To be completely mad in a world of relative sanity is disorienting and unpleasant, but to be walled off in a place where madness is the norm is absolutely ghastly. I dug up all kinds of stories of abuse in the state system. In a brilliant and courageous piece of undercover research, the journalist Kevin Heldman checked himself into the psychiatric unit at Brooklyn's Woodhull Hospital, claiming that he was suicidal. "The overall environment was custodial rather than therapeutic," he writes, then quotes Darby Penney, special assistant to the commissioner for the New York State Office of Mental Health, who said, "From my own experience, the last place I'd want to be if I was in an emotionally distraught state is in an inpatient [psychiatric] unit [at a state hospital]." Not one of the state's meaningful official policies on mental health care was observed at Woodhull. Patients were given no opportunity to converse or interact with psychiatrists; they were given no structure for their days and simply watched TV for ten hours at a stretch; their rooms were filthy; they could not find out what medications they were being given. They were subjected to totally unnecessary involuntary sedation and restraint. The one nurse with whom Heldman had a meaningful interaction told him that having a baby might help his depression. For these services, the state of New York paid $1,400 per day.

My interest as I considered institutions was more in the quality of a good hospital than in the misery of a bad one. My aim was not to seek out abuses so much as to see whether the very model of the state facility was misguided. The question of institutionalization is terribly difficult, and I have not found a solution. Short-term facilities for the mentally ill can be good or bad; I spent some considerable time on the wards of such places, and I would not hesitate to check myself into, for example, Johns Hopkins if I needed such care. But long-term public facilities, where people come to stay for years or forever, are utterly, devastatingly different. I spent several long stretches visiting Norristown Hospital near Philadelphia, an institution run by people who are strongly committed to helping their patients. I was favorably impressed by the doctors I met, by the social workers who interact daily with residents, and by the superintendent of the place. I liked a number of the patients I met. Despite all that, Norristown put my teeth on edge and made my skin crawl, and visiting it was one of the most upsetting and difficult tasks I undertook in my research. I'd *much* rather engage with every manner of private despair than spend a protracted time at Norristown. Institutionalization may be the best we have at present, and the problems posed by Norristown may not be fully resolvable, but they must be acknowledged if we are to develop the missing link in interventionist law.

Norristown Hospital has a campus that looks at first like a second-tier East Coast college. It is set atop a verdant hill and commands a panoramic view. Big, full trees cast their shade on well-kept lawns; red-brick buildings in a neo-Federal style are covered in vines; the gates to the place are open during the day. Aesthetically speaking, patients are mostly better off in the hospital than out of it. The reality of the place, however, is hellishly like the classic TV series *The Prisoner,* or like a charmless version of Alice's Wonderland, where the appearance of an inaccessible logic belies the breakdown of logic altogether. The place has a vocabulary entirely its own, which I learned slowly. "Oh, she's not doing so good," one patient would tell me confidingly about another. "She's gonna end up back in building fifty if she don't watch it." To ask someone what happened at "building fifty" was unproductive: in the eyes of patients, building fifty—emergency services—was fearfully anathema. When I eventually went into building fifty, it was really not as bad as the threat of it had been, but building thirty, on the other hand, was really quite awful. Most of the people in it were under physical restraint and constant supervision to prevent them from injuring themselves. Some of them were in nets so that they could be kept from active suicide attempts. I did not see much inappropriate intervention; the people so treated mostly required the treatments, but they were awful to behold nonetheless, and they were worse for being grouped together like the waxworks of criminals in the basement of Madame Tussaud's. The hierarchy of buildings and numbers, and fear, and embargo of liberty, all whispered around the campus, could not but exacerbate the condition of someone already suffering from depression.

I hated being there. It hit too close to home. If I had been poor and alone and if my illness had been untreated, would I have ended up in such a place? The very possibility made me want to run screaming out the nice gates and back to my safe bed. These people didn't have any place left outside that would constitute home. Even when there were full complements of doctors and social workers present, the mentally ill were superior in number, and I developed an awful us-and-them feeling. Since affective disorders are the second most common diagnosis in state mental hospitals I could not figure out whether I was more a part of "us" or of "them." We live our lives by the norms of consensus and hold on to reason because it is affirmed over and over again. If you went to a place where everything was filled with helium, you might cease to believe in gravity because there would be so little evidence for it. At Norristown, I found my grip on reality growing tenuous. In such a location, you have no certainties at all, and sanity becomes as peculiar to the context as insanity is to the outside world. Every time I went to Norristown, I felt my psyche go weightless and begin to disintegrate.

My first visit there, arranged through the administration, was on a lovely spring day. I sat down with a depressed woman who had volunteered to talk to me. We were in a sort of gazebo on a pretty knoll, and we drank undrinkable coffee out of plastic cups that were half-melted from the lukewarm beverage. The woman I was interviewing was articulate and "presentable," but I was ill at ease, and it was not just the plastic-flavored coffee. As we started talking, people never versed in social convention came and positioned themselves between the two of us or interrupted to ask me who I was and what I was doing, or, in one instance, came over and patted my neck as if I were a Bedlington terrier. A woman I had never seen before stood about ten feet away from us staring for a while, then burst into tears and wept on and on despite my attempts to calm her. "Oh, she's just a screamer," someone else explained to me comfortingly. People who weren't crazy before they arrived in this place would have had to be crazy by the time they left. The population of Norristown is much reduced from what it was in the heyday of the mental-hospital-cum warehouse, and so more than half of the buildings on the campus are deserted. Those empty edifices, many of them built in the sixties in the utilitarian, modernist vocabulary of inner-city schools, exude a ghoulish threat; chained shut, empty for years on end, they suggest a greenish excess of festering life between their beams and in their vacant silence.

Schizophrenic patients stand around Norristown Hospital talking to Martians the rest of us can't see. An angry young man pounded on the wall with his fists, while patients at the brink of catatonia stared with blind, glazed faces, motionless, depressed or sedated. The you-can't-hurt-yourself-on-them furnishings were battered and worn, as tired as the people using them. Faded construction-paper decorations made for bygone holidays festooned in a lobby as though they had been there since the patients were in kindergarten. No one had remembered to grant these people adulthood. Each of the dozen or so times I went to Norristown, someone who insisted I was her mother bombarded me with questions to which I could not possibly know the answers, and someone who seemed anxious and highly irritable told me to leave, right away, to just scram before there was trouble. A man with a severe facial deformity had appointed himself my friend and told me that I shouldn't pay any attention, shouldn't leave; everyone would get used to me by the end of a month. "You're not so bad, you're not so ugly, stay around, you'll get used to it," he said abstractedly, in a kind of monotonous monologue to which I was hardly even an accessory. An obscenely fat woman demanded money and kept grabbing at my shoulders for emphasis. At no time was I able to escape the *basso continuo* of nonverbal clamor at Norristown that sounded constantly under the harangue of words: people banging things, people screaming, people snoring loudly, people gibbering, people weeping, people making strange strangled noises or farting shamelessly, the racking coughs of men and women whose only pleasure is smoking. There is no love lost in these places; arguing and arguing and arguing seeps out of the walls and floors. There isn't enough room at Norristown, despite the closed buildings and the grassy acres. Patients there are pinioned by misery. Forty percent of patients in such facilities are in for depression; they have gone, to recover, to some of the most depressing places on earth.

And yet Norristown was the best public long-term care facility I visited, and the people who ran it impressed me as not only committed but also intelligent and kind. The patients were mostly in the best health they could achieve. The place was hardly Bedlam; everyone was well fed and on appropriate medication, and an expert staff was keeping paternalistic beneficent watch over everyone. People seldom get hurt at Norristown. Everyone is clean and neatly dressed. People can in general name their illnesses and tell you why they are there. The staff, heroically, lavish a surprising degree of love on their wards, and though the place feels lunatic, it also feels safe. Patients are protected there both from the outside world and from their frightening inner selves. The flaws of the place are only those endemic to long-term care.

After a few years in the hospital, Joe Rogers was shifted out of his long-term-care facility to a halfway house in Florida, where he got better treatment and some decent medications. "But I began to understand myself differently—I began to see myself as a mental patient. They told me that I was incurable, and they didn't see any point to my going to school. I was in my midtwenties. They said I should just get on social security and stay there. I ended up getting very sick and I totally lost my sense of self." When Rogers left, he took to the streets, where he lived for the better part of a year. "The more I tried to put it together, the more it would fall apart. I tried a geographical cure. It was time to get away from my habits and my relationships. I decided it would be great to be in New York City. I had no idea what I was doing there. I ended up finding a park bench which was not too bad—there weren't so many homeless then in New York and I was a kind of nice-looking young white kid. I was disheveled, but not grungy, and people took an interest in me."

Rogers would tell his story to strangers who offered a dime, but he withheld any information that might send him back to the hospital. "I thought that if I went back, I'd never get out. I thought they were going to take me in. I had abandoned all hope, but I was too afraid of pain to kill myself." It was 1973; "I remember all this noise once, all these people celebrating, and when I asked them why, they told me the war in Vietnam had ended. And I said, 'Oh, that's neat.' But I couldn't understand what it was or what was happening, though I remembered that I'd once marched to oppose that war." Then it began to get colder and colder, and Rogers had no coat. He was sleeping on the big piers on the Hudson River. "By that time, I believed that I had become so alienated from the rest of humanity that if I approached someone, he'd be horrified. I hadn't bathed or changed my clothes in a long time. I probably was pretty disgusting. These people from a church came and I knew they'd seen me toddling around, and they told me they'd get me to the YMCA in East Orange. If they had said they were taking me to a hospital, I would have run a hundred miles to get away and they would never have seen me again. But they didn't do that; they kept an eye on me and waited until I was ready, and then offered me something I could do. I had nothing to lose."

It was in this way that Rogers first experienced outreach, which was to become the cornerstone of his social policy. "People who are isolated and lost are usually desperate for a little human connection," Rogers says. "Outreach can work. You have to be willing to go out and engage them and reengage them until they're ready to come with you." Joe Rogers was depressed; but depression is an illness that sits squelchingly on top of personality, and Rogers's underlying personality was very insistent. "A sense of humor was perhaps the thing that was most crucial," he says now. "At my craziest and my most depressed, I could still find something to joke about." Rogers moved to the East Orange YMCA for a few months, and he got a job in a car wash. Later, he moved to the Montclair YMCA, where he met his wife. Marriage was "a huge stabilizing influence." Rogers decided to go to college. "We sort of took turns. She'd go through periods of acting depressed and I'd take care of her, and then we'd reverse roles." Rogers began doing voluntary work in the mental health field—"the only area I knew anything about at that point"—when he was twenty-six. Though he disliked state hospitals intensely, "people in serious need of help needed something, and I thought we could just reform hospitals and make them better places. I tried for years, but I found that the system could not be reformed."

The Mental Health Association of Southeastern Pennsylvania is a nonprofit organization that Rogers founded. It is dedicated to increasing the power of the mentally ill. Rogers has helped to make Pennsylvania one of the most progressive states in the nation for mental health, has personally overseen the closing of state hospitals, and has proposed remarkably good community mental health initiatives, which currently operate on an annual budget of about $1.4 billion. If you're going to go completely to pieces, Pennsylvania is a pretty good place to do it, and in fact many people from neighboring states make their way into Pennsylvania so they can take advantage of the systems there. Homelessness has traditionally been a big problem in Philadelphia, and when the current mayor was elected, he favored reopening the mental hospitals that had closed down and filling the ones that were still up and running. Rogers persuaded him to close institutions in favor of other care systems.

The guiding principle of Pennsylvania's current system is that people should not be immersed in hospitals where madness is the given rule, but should rather live in the larger community, exposed constantly to the salutary effects of sanity. Pennsylvania patients with serious illness stay in long-term structured residential services. These are small places, with perhaps fifteen beds each, which offer intensive support, rigorous care, and an ongoing emphasis on integration. They support intensive case management, which allows a psychiatric social worker to establish a one-on-one relationship with a patient. "It's someone who sort of follows you around and finds out what's going on and butts in a little bit," Rogers says. "It needs to be an aggressive program. One person I worked with early in my career threatened to get a restraining order against me. I wouldn't take no for an answer; I'd push my way in, and if I'd had to, I would have kicked his door down." These places also offer programs of psychosocial rehabilitation, which aim to help people with the pragmatics of "normal" life. About 80 percent of patients hospitalized for depression in Pennsylvania appear to do better under these circumstances. Full-scale intervention—up to and including forced shelter and treatment—is undertaken when someone is a danger to others or a danger to himself, as when he is outside in extreme cold. The only people who are consistently resistant to treatment of this kind are mentally ill abusers of drugs, especially heroin; such patients must detox before the state mental health system will offer them care.

Rogers also has created a chain of what he calls "drop-in centers," street-level storefronts, usually staffed by people themselves recovering from mental illnesses. This creates employment for the people who are just beginning to cope with a structured environment, and it gives people who are in bad shape a place to go, hang out, and receive structured advice. Once they are introduced to such places, homeless people terrified of more active intervention will return to them again and again. Drop-in centers provide a transition zone between mental isolation and companionship. Pennsylvania has now established a massive tracking system that smacks of the police state, but it does prevent people from falling off the edge and disappearing. A database includes all treatment through state systems, including every emergency-room visit every patient has ever made. "I typed my name in," says Rogers, "and I was shocked by what came out." If a patient in the Pennsylvania system goes AWOL, social workers will seek him out and continue to check on him regularly. It's impossible to escape such attention except by recovering.

The problem with this whole program is its fragility. At the most pragmatic level, it's fiscally unstable: big mental hospitals are elephantine things with established costs, while noninstitutional programs can easily be pared down during times of budgetary crisis. Then the insertion of mentally ill people into a community requires tolerance, even in open-minded, prosperous areas. "Everybody's a liberal for deinstitutional-ization until they get the first homeless person on their front porch," says Representative Bob Wise. The greatest problem is that for some mentally ill people, all this independence and immersion in the community is too much. Some cannot function outside a totally insular environment such as a hospital. Such people are regularly expelled into a world whose functioning overwhelms them, and this is not helpful to them or to those who encounter and help to care for them.

None of this is discouraging to Rogers. He has forced the closing of hospitals by using the carrot-and-stick approach, ingratiating himself with highly placed government officials and also suing them in class action suits that cite the Americans with Disabilities Act. Rogers has modeled his efforts on Cesar Chavez's United Farm Workers movement; he has, in effect, attempted to unionize the mentally ill, giving that extremely diffuse body of disenfranchised people a collective voice. In the 1950s, during the heyday of institutionalization, about fifteen thousand patients were warehoused in facilities around Philadelphia. Rogers has closed down two of these, and Norristown, the last one standing, numbers its patients in the hundreds. The primary opposition to Rogers's class action lawsuits has come from the unionized workers (mostly in maintenance) at the hospitals. The closing of the hospitals has been achieved by moving people out as they achieve sufficient health to enter long-term community-care facilities. "We close them down gradually and through attrition," Rogers says.

If major hospitals have been sites of abuse, the chances are that community-based programs will become sites of comparable or worse abuse. The checks and balances within these programs are hard to maintain. Large numbers of officials and mental health workers rule over tiny principalities of care, each with its own internal workings. How can the operations of such centers be fully visible to those who in principle oversee them, people who usually come through only for occasional, quick visits? Is it possible to sustain high standards of vigilance when authority has undergone devolution?

The question of what constitutes mental illness and who should be treated rides very much on the back of public perceptions about sanity. There is such a thing as sanity and there is such a thing as madness, and the difference is both categorical and dimensional, of kind and of degree. Ultimately there is a politics of what one asks of one's own brain and of the brains of others. There is nothing wrong with this politics. It is an essential part of our self-definition, a cornerstone of the social order. It is wrong to spot collusion behind it; unless one believes that consensus on complex subjects can emerge uncorrupted, one must work with that curious mix of personal opinion and public history that determines all our ways as social animals. The problem is not so much the politics of depression as our failure to recognize that there *is* a politics of depression. There is no freedom from this politics. For those without money there is less freedom than for those who have the prerogatives of financial wherewithal; the politics of depression echoes the rest of life. For those whose disease is mild there is more freedom than for those who are vastly ill; and this is probably as it should be. In the late 1970s, Thomas Szasz, most famous for his defense of the right to suicide, put forward arguments against the use of medications, claiming that there was no natural law according to which the psychiatrist was entitled to intervene in the personal life of the patient with prescriptions. It's interesting to learn that one has a right to be depressed. It's just as well to know that under the right rational circumstances one can decide not to take medication. Szasz, however, exceeded his mandate and enabled the belief among his patients that they were being powerfully self-realizing in giving up their medications. Is it a political act to do this? Some of Szasz's patients believed that it was. Our definitions of "responsible behavior" from psychiatrists are also political. As a society, we take exception to Szasz's viewpoint, and he had to pay $650,000 to the widow of one of his patients after that patient killed himself in a particularly brutal and distressing way.

Is it more important to protect someone from his death or to allow him the civil liberty to avoid treatment? The problem has been much debated. A particularly disturbing recent op-ed article in the *New York*

Times, written by a psychiatrist at a conservative think tank in Washington in response to the new Surgeon General's Report on Mental Health, proposed that helping the mildly ill would deprive the seriously ill, as though mental health care were a finite mineral resource. She stated categorically that it was not possible to get unsupervised people to take their medications and proposed that those mentally ill ("with debilitating illnesses like schizophrenia and bipolar disorder") who end up in prison probably need to be there. At the same time, she proposed that the 20 percent of the U.S. citizenry who carry the burden of some kind of mental illness (including, apparently, all those who have major depression) in many instances do not need therapy and therefore should not get it. The key word here is *need*—because the question of need turns on quality of life rather than on existence of life. It is true that many people can stay alive with crippling depression, but they can also stay alive, for example, with no teeth. That one could manage okay on yogurt and bananas for the rest of one's life is not a reason to leave modern people toothless. A person can also live with a clubfoot, but these days it's not unusual to take measures to reconstruct one. The argument in effect comes down to the same one that is heard over and over again from outside the world of mental illness, which is that the only people who *must* be treated are those who pose an immediate expense or threat to others.

Doctors, especially those who are not attached to teaching hospitals, often learn about advances in medicine from pharmaceutical salesmen. This is a mixed blessing. It ensures that doctors do get continuing education, and that they learn about the merits of new products as those products become available. It is not an adequate form of continuing education. The industry focuses on drugs over other therapies. "This has helped to prejudice us toward medications," says Elliot Valenstein, professor emeritus of psychology and neuroscience at the University of Michigan. "The medications are excellent and we are grateful to the companies for making them, but it's a shame that the educational process isn't balanced better." Further, because industry funds many of the largest and most comprehensive studies, there are better studies of patentable substances than there are of nonpatentable ones such as Saint-John's-wort; there are more studies of new drug therapies than of other new treatments such as EMDR (eye movement desensitization and reprocessing). We have no national programs sufficient to balance against the work sponsored by the pharmaceutical companies. In a recent article in *The Lancet*, a leading medical journal, Professor Jonathan Rees proposed a complete reconception of the patent process to put a profit motive into therapies that are currently nonpatentable, including what he calls "genomics and informatics." For the time being, however, little financial incentive exists in this area.

Members of the pharmaceutical industry know that in the free market-place the best cures are likely to be the most successful. Their pursuit of good treatments is of course entwined with their pursuit of lucre; but I believe, contrary to some grandstanding politicians, that pharmaceutical executives are less wantonly exploitative of their society than are people in most other industries. Many of the discoveries that distinguish modern medicine have been possible only because of the huge research and development programs of the pharmaceutical trade, which spends about seven times as much on developing new products as do other industries. These programs are predicated on profit; but it is perhaps nobler to make a profit by inventing cures for the ill than by inventing powerful armaments or producing pandering magazines. "It had to be in industry," said David Chow, one of the three scientists at Eli Lilly who invented Prozac. William Potter, also now at Lilly after departing from the NIMH, said, "It was the lab scientists here who drove the development of Prozac. The important research is funded by industry. Society has made that choice and given us this system of great progress." I tremble to think where I would be if industry had not developed the medications that have saved my life.

For all the good that the industry has done, however, it *is* an industry, afflicted with all the bizarre trappings of modern capitalism. I have attended any number of educational sessions staged by companies torn between research and material seduction. At one of these, held at the Baltimore Aquarium, a choice was offered between a lecture on "Neurobiology and Treatment of Bipolar Disorder" and a "Stingray Feeding and Presentation for Special Guests and Their Families." I eventually attended the U.S. launch of one of the major antidepressants, a product that was quickly to capture a significant market share. Though the launch operated under the constraints of a tight regulatory body—the Food and Drug Administration (FDA)—which governed what could be said about the product, it was something of a circus at which emotions were tuned with a deliberateness that no flying Wallendas could ever achieve. It was, further, an incongruously wild fiesta, replete with disco parties, barbecues, and hatching romances. It was the epitome of corporate America high on its commodities. This is how salesmen for any product are motivated to sell in the intensely competitive promotional U.S. marketplace, and the glitz was, I think, harmless; but it was somewhat anomalous for the promotion of a product for people suffering from a terrible affliction.

For the keynote addresses, the salespeople assembled in a hulking conference center. The size of the audience—more than two thousand people—was overwhelming. When we all were seated, there rose out of the stage, like the cats in *Cats,* an entire orchestra, playing "Forget Your Troubles, C'mon Get Happy" and then Tears for Fears's "Everybody Wants to Rule the World." Against this backdrop, a Wizard of Oz voice welcomed us to the launch of a fantastic new product. Gigantic photos of the Grand Canyon and a sylvan stream were projected onto twenty-foot screens, and the lights went up to reveal a set built to resemble a construction site. The orchestra began playing selections from Pink Floyd's *The Wall.* A wall of gigantic bricks slowly rose at the back of the stage, and on it the names of competitive products appeared. While a chorus of kick dancers wearing mining helmets and carrying pickaxes performed athletic contortions on an electronically controlled scaffold, a rainbow of lasers in the form of the product logo shot from a stagecraft spaceship at the back of the room and knocked out the other antidepressants. The dancers kicked up their workboots and did an incongruous Irish jig as the bricks, apparently made of stage plaster, crashed down in thuds of dust. The head of the sales force stepped over the ruins to crow gleefully as numbers appeared on a screen; he enthused about future profits as though he had just won on *Family Feud.*

The extravagance made me very uncomfortable. It did, however, seem to rev everyone up. Cheerleading squads at halftime have seldom provoked more enthusiasm from spectators. By the time this burlesque was done, the crowd was all set to punch misery in the nose. After the opening ceremonies came a serious plea to the humanity of the sales force. The room dimmed for a short film made specifically for the occasion, which showed people who had actually taken the product during Phase III studies. These real people had emerged from terrible suffering; some had found in this product relief from refractory depression that had disabled them for half a lifetime. The images were in Vaseline focus that went with the other aspects of the launch, but they were real, and I saw representatives deeply moved by the horror people had authentically endured. The sense of mission with which people left the outsize auditorium was heartfelt. Over the next few days, the contradictory tenor of the launch was sustained; the salesmen's aggression and empathy were encouraged in tandem. At the end, however, everyone was showered with products: I came home with a T-shirt, a polo shirt, a windbreaker, a notepad, a baseball cap, an airplane carry-on, twenty pens, and a range of other goods that had the product's logo displayed as boldly as a Gucci label.

David Healey, former secretary of the British Association for Psychopharmacology, has questioned the approval process for depression treatments. In his view, the industry has used the term *selective serotonin reuptake inhibitors* (SSRIs) to suggest a false simplicity of function. Healey writes, "Drugs that block serotonin reuptake may be antidepressant, as may compounds that selectively block catecholamine reuptake. Indeed, there is a strong suggestion that in severe cases of depression, some of the older compounds that act on multiple systems may be more effective than the newer compounds. ECT is almost certainly the treatment that is least specific to a particular neurotransmitter system, but it is believed by many clinicians to be the fastest and most effective of current treatments. What this suggests about depression is not that it is a disorder of one neurotransmitter or a particular receptor, but rather that in depressive disorders a number of physiological systems are compromised or shut down or desynchronized in some way." This suggests that the very traits that many pharmaceutical companies advertise for their drugs are in fact not particularly useful to consumers of those drugs. Based on a bacterial model of illness, the federal system of regulation that was put in place in the 1960s supposes that every illness has a specific antidote and that every antidote works on a specific illness. Unquestionably, current rhetoric, on the part of the FDA, the U.S. Congress, pharmaceutical companies, and the general public, reflects the notions that depression invades a person and proper treatment can expel it. Does the category "antidepressant," which presupposes the illness "depression," make sense?

If depression is an illness that affects as much as 25 percent of the people in the world, can it in fact be an illness? Is it something that supersedes the "real" personality of people afflicted with it? I could have done this book in double time if I could function on four hours of sleep a night. I am significantly disabled by my need for sleep. I could not be secretary of state, because that job requires more activity than can be packed into fifteen-hour days. One of the reasons I chose to become a writer is that I can regulate my schedule, and anyone with whom I have worked knows that I do not do morning meetings except under duress. I have occasionally taken an over-the-counter drug—it's called coffee—to help me get by on less sleep than I would need without it. It's an imperfect drug; it's quite effective for short-term treatment of my disorder, but taken over the long term as a substitute for sleep, it brings on anxiety, nausea, dizziness, and reduced efficiency. Because of this, it does not work well enough for me to be able to take up a schedule like that of the secretary of state. It seems likely that if the World Health Organization were to do a study and figure out how many useful manhours are lost each year to people who require more than six hours of sleep per night, the toll taken by sleepiness would quite possibly be even greater than that taken by depression.

I have met people who need to sleep fourteen hours every night, and they, like people with major depression, face difficulties functioning in the social and professional world of our times. They suffer a terrific disadvantage. What is the edge of disease? And who, if a better drug than caffeine comes along, would be classed as ill? Would we invent an ideal of the secretary of state's sleep schedule and start recommending medication to everyone who sleeps more than four hours a night? Would it be bad to do that? What would happen to people who refused drug therapy and slept their natural hours? They would be unable to keep up; the rapid pace of modern life would be much more rapid if most people could now avail themselves of this hypothetical medication.

"During the 1970s," writes Healey, "the major psychiatric disorders became defined as disorders of single neurotransmitter systems and their receptors. The evidence to support any of these proposals was never there, but this language powerfully supported psychiatry's transition from a discipline that understood itself in dimensional terms to one that concerned itself with categorical ones." Indeed, this is perhaps the most alarming thing about current wisdom on depression: it dismisses the idea of a continuum and posits that a patient either has or doesn't have depression, is or is not depressed, as though to be a little bit depressed were the same as being a little bit pregnant. The categorical models are appealing. In an era in which we are increasingly alienated from our feelings, we might be comforted by the idea that a doctor could take a blood test or a brain scan and tell us whether we had depression and what kind we had. But depression is an emotion that exists in all people, fluctuating in and out of control; depression the illness is an excess of something common, not the introduction of something exotic. It is different from one person to the next. What makes people depressed? You might as well ask what makes people content.

A doctor may help facilitate dosage choices, but it may someday be as easy to put oneself on one of the SSRIs as it is to go on antioxidant vitamins, whose long-term benefits are obvious, and whose side effects are minimal, nonlethal, and easily controlled. These SSRIs help mental health, which is fragile; they keep the mind fit. Taking the wrong dosages or taking the drugs inconsistently will prevent them from functioning as they should, but as Healey points out, people take nonprescription drugs with reasonable care. We do not usually overdose on them. We undertake trial and error on ourselves in figuring out how much to take (which is more or less what prescribing doctors do with the SSRIs). The SSRIs are not fatal or dangerous even in extreme overdose. Healey believes that the glamorization of drugs through their prescription status is particularly striking with the antidepressants, which have relatively few side effects and which are used to treat a disease that for the moment exists only in the patient's explanation of it, a disease that cannot be tested in any medical terms other than the patient's self-reports. There is no way to determine whether an antidepressant drug is necessary or not except by asking the patient—and that asking is most frequently done by GPs who have no more information about the pills than does a well-read layman.

My drug regimen is now elaborately and specifically balanced, and I would not have had the expertise to get through my last breakdown without the close consultation of a capable expert. But many of the people I know who are on Prozac simply went to a doctor and requested it. They had already performed a self-diagnosis, and the doctor saw no reason to doubt their insight into their own mind. Taking Prozac unnecessarily doesn't appear to have any particular effect, and those for whom it is unhelpful probably stop taking it. Why shouldn't people be free to make these decisions entirely on their own?

Many of the people I have interviewed take antidepressants for "mild depression," and they lead happier and better lives because of it. I'd do the same. Perhaps what they want to change is really personality, as Peter Kramer suggested in *Listening to Prozac*. The news that depression is a chemical or biological problem is a public relations stunt; we could, at least in theory, find the brain chemistry for violence and monkey around with that if we were so inclined. The notion that all depression is invasive illness rests either on a vast expansion of the word *illness* to include all kinds of qualities (from sleepiness to obnoxiousness to stupidity) or on a convenient modern fiction. Severe depression, nonetheless, is a devastating condition that is now treatable, and it must be treated as vigorously as possible, for the sake of a just society in which people live rich, healthy lives. It should be covered by insurers, protected by acts of Congress, addressed by great researchers as a matter of the utmost importance. There is an apparent paradox here that points to existential questions about what constitutes the person and what constitute his afflictions. Our rights to life and liberty are comparatively straightforward; our right to the pursuit of happiness becomes more puzzling every day.

An older friend of mine once said to me that sex had been destroyed by its public existence. When she was young, she said, she and her first lovers discovered a new thing with only their roughest instincts to guide them. They had no specific expectations of one another, no standards. "You have read so many articles about who should have how many orgasms when and how," she said to me. "You have been told what to do and in which positions and how to feel. You have been told the right way and the wrong way of everything. What chance of discovery do you have now?"

Dysfunction of the brain too was once a private affair, the history recounted in this volume notwithstanding. One came to it with no expectations, and how things went wrong was largely individual. How those around you dealt with it was also individual. Now we enter into psychic pain within guidelines. We thrive on artificial categorizations and reductive formulae. When depression tumbled out of the collective closet, it became an externally ordered sequence. That is where politics meets depression. This book itself is helplessly enmeshed in the politics of the disease. If you read these pages closely, you can learn how to be depressed: what to feel, what to think, what to do. Nonetheless, the individuality of every person's struggle is unbreachable. Depression, like sex, retains an unquenchable aura of mystery. It is new every time.

CHAPTER XI

Evolution

A great deal has been said about the who and what and when and where of depression. Evolutionists have turned their attention to the why. The interest in the why begins with the historical: evolutionary biology explains how things came to be the way they are. Why would such an obviously unpleasant and essentially unproductive condition occur in so large a part of the population? What advantages could it ever have served? Could it be simply a defect in humanity? Why was it not selected out a long time ago? Why do particular symptoms tend to cluster? What is the relation between the social and the biological evolution of the disorder? It is impossible to answer without looking at the questions that precede the matter of depression. Why, in evolutionary terms, do we have moods at all? Why indeed do we have emotions? What exactly caused nature to select for despair and frustration and irritability, and to select for, relatively speaking, so little joy? To look at the evolutionary questions about depression is to look at what it means to be human.

It is evident that mood disorders are not simple, singular, discrete conditions. Michael McGuire and Alfonso Troisi, in their book *Darwinian Psychiatry*, point out that depression "can occur with and without known precipitants, can sometimes run in families and sometimes not, can show different concordance rates among monozygotic twins, can sometimes last a lifetime and at other times remit spontaneously." Further, depression is obviously the common outcome of many causes; "some persons with depression grow up and live in adverse social environments while others do not; some come from families in which depression is common while others do not; and significant individual differences in depression-causing physiological systems (e.g., norepinephrine, serotonin) have been reported. What is more, some respond to one type of antidepressant medication but not to another; some do not respond to any type of medication but do respond to electroconvulsive treatment; and some do not respond to any known intervention."

The suggestion is that what we call depression seems to be a peculiar assortment of conditions for which there are no evident boundaries. It is as though we had a condition called "cough" that included some cough that responds to antibiotics (tuberculosis) and some cough that responds to changes in humidity (emphysema) and some that responds to psychological treatments (cough may be a neurotic behavior) and some that requires chemotherapy (lung cancer) and some that appears to be intractable. Some cough is fatal if untreated and some is chronic and some is temporary and some is seasonal. Some goes away on its own. Some is related to viral infection. What is cough? We have decided to define cough as a symptom of various illnesses rather than as an illness of its own, though we can also look at what might be called the consequent symptoms of cough itself: sore throat, poor sleep, difficulty with speech, irritating tickly feelings, troubled breathing, and so on. Depression is not a rational disease category; like cough, it is a symptom with symptoms. If we didn't know about the range of illnesses that cause coughs, we would have no basis for understanding the "refractory cough" and we would come up with all kinds of explanations for why some cough seems to resist treatment. We do not at this time have a clear system for sorting out the different types of depression and their different implications. It is unlikely that such an illness has a single explanation. If it occurs for a whole catalog of reasons, one must use multiple systems for examining it. There is something inherently sloppy about the current modes, which take a pinch of psychoanalytic thinking and a little bit of biology and a few external circumstances and throw them together into a crazy salad. We need to disentangle depression and grief and personality and illness before we can make real sense of depressed mental states.

The most basic animal response is sensation. The experience of hunger is unpleasant and the feeling of satiety is pleasant for all living creatures, which is why we make the effort to feed ourselves. If hunger were not a disagreeable sensation, we would starve. We have instincts that lead us to food, and when those instincts are foiled—by the unavailability of food, for example—we experience extreme hunger, a condition we will do almost anything to alleviate. Sensations tend to trigger emotions: when I am unhappy about being hungry, I am having an emotional response to a sensation. It appears that insects and many invertebrates have sensation and response to sensation, and it is difficult to say where in the animal hierarchy emotion begins. Emotion is not a characteristic exclusively of the highest mammals; but it is also not an appropriate word to use in describing the behavior of an amoeba. We are afflicted with the pathetic fallacy and have an anthropomorphic tendency to say, for example, that an underwatered plant is unhappy when it droops—or, indeed, that the car is being grumpy when it keeps stalling. It is not easy to distinguish between such projections and true emotion. Is a swarm of bees angry? Is a salmon going upstream resolute? The highly regarded biologist Charles Sherrington wrote in the late forties, when he looked through a microscope at a flea biting, that "the act whether reflex or not, seemed charged with the most violent emotion. Its Lilliput scale aside, the scene compared with that of the prowling lion in *Salambo*. It was a glimpse suggesting a vast ocean of 'affect' pervading the insect world." What Sherrington describes is how action appears to the human eye to reflect emotion.

If emotion is a more sophisticated matter than sensation, mood is a yet more sophisticated idea. The evolutionary biologist C. U. M. Smith describes emotion as weather (whether it's raining out right now) and mood as climate (whether it's a damp, rainy part of the world). Mood is a sustained emotional state that colors responses to sensation. It is made up of emotion that has acquired a life of its own quite outside of its immediate precipitants. One can be unhappy because of hunger and get into an irritable mood that will not necessarily be alleviated by eating something. Mood exists across species; in general, the more developed the species, the more powerfully mood occurs independent of immediate external circumstance. This is most true in people. Even those who do not suffer from depression have blue moods sometimes, when little things seem to be full of reminders of mortality, when those who are gone or those times that are gone are missed suddenly and profoundly, when the simple fact that we exist in a transient world seems paralyzingly sad. Sometimes people are sad for no apparent reason at all. And even those who are frequently depressed sometimes experience high moods when the sun seems extra bright and everything tastes delicious and the world is explosively full of possibilities, when the past seems like just a little overture to the splendor of the present and the future. Why this should be so is both a biochemical and an evolutionary puzzle. The selective advantages of emotion are much easier to see than the species' need for mood.

Is depression a derangement, like cancer, or can it be defensive, like nausea? Evolutionists argue that it occurs much too often to be a simple dysfunction. It seems likely that the capacity for depression entails mechanisms that at some stage served a reproductive advantage. Four possibilities can be adduced from this. Each is at least partially true. The first is that depression served a purpose in evolution's prehuman times that it no longer serves. The second is that the stresses of modern life are incompatible with the brains we have evolved, and that depression is the consequence of our doing what we did not evolve to do. The third is that depression serves a useful function unto itself in human societies, that it's sometimes a good thing for people to be depressed. The last is that the genes and consequent biological structures that are implicated in depression are also implicated in other, more useful behaviors or feelings—that depression is a secondary result of a useful variant in brain physiology.

The idea that depression at one time served a useful function that it no longer serves—that it is in effect a relic—is borne out by our many vestigial emotional responses. As the psychologist Jack Kahn has pointed out, "People do not have a natural fear of real dangers like cars and light sockets, but waste their time and energy being afraid of harmless spiders and snakes"—animals it would have been useful to fear in a different time at a different stage of our development as a species. Following this pattern, depression often clusters around what seem to be utterly unimportant matters. Anthony Stevens and John Price have proposed that some form of depression is necessary for the formation of primitive rank societies. Though lower organisms and some higher mammals, such as the orangutan, are loners, most advanced animals form social groupings, which furnish better defense against predators, better access to resources, greater and more accessible reproductive opportunities, and the prospect of cooperative hunting. There is no doubt that natural selection has favored collectivity. The impulse toward collectivity is extremely strong in human beings. We inhabit societies and most of us rely heavily on the sense of belonging. Being well liked is one of life's great pleasures; being excluded, ignored, or in some other way unpopular is one of the worst experiences we can have.

Someone is always top dog; a society without a leader is chaotic and soon dissolves. Usually the positions of individuals within a group are subject to change over time, and the leader has to keep defending his position against challengers until he is ultimately defeated. Depression is critical to the resolution of conflict about dominance in such societies. If a lower-ranking animal challenges the leader and doesn't get discouraged, he will keep challenging the leader and there will be no peace and the group will not be able to function as a group. If, upon losing, such an animal stops being self-assertive and withdraws into a somewhat depressed state (one characterized more by passivity than by existential crisis), he thereby acknowledges the winner's triumph, and he accepts perforce the dominance structure. This subdominant figure, by yielding to authority, frees the winner from the obligation to kill him or to expel him from the group. So through the appropriate occurrence of mild to moderate depression, social consonance can be achieved in a rank-based society. That those who have suffered depression frequently relapse may indicate that those who have fought and lost ought to avoid fighting again, so minimizing damage to themselves. The evolutionist J. Birtchnell has said that brain centers are constantly monitoring one's status in relation to others, and that we all function according to internalized notions of rank. The result of a fight will determine how most animals rank themselves; depression can be useful in preventing such animals from challenging their rank when they have no real chance of improvement. Often, even if not engaged in improving social position, people suffer the criticism and attack of others. Depression pulls them out of the territory in which they are subject to such criticism; they disengage so that they do not get put down (this theory seems to me to have a bit of a sledgehammer-to-mosquito problem). The anxiety element of depression is then tied to the fear of being the object of such vigorous attack as to be excluded from the group, a development that in animal societies and in human hunter-gatherer times would have had fatal consequences.

This particular argument for the evolutionary structures of depression is not highly relevant to depression as we now experience it in societies that have enormous numbers of external structuring principles. In pack-animal societies, group structure is determined by physical strength expressed through fights in which one party triumphs over the other by diminishing or defeating it. Russell Gardner, for many years the head of the Across-Species Comparisons and Psychopathology (ASCAP) Society, has looked at how human depression is linked to animal models. He proposes that, in humans, success is less contingent on putting down others than on doing things oneself. People are not successful solely on the basis of their preventing anyone else from being a success; they succeed because of their own achievements. This is not to say that one is entirely free of the business of competition and of doing injury to others, but the competition that characterizes most human social systems is more constructive than destructive. In animal societies, the essential subject of success is "I'm stronger than you," while in human societies it is to a greater degree "I'm fantastically good."

Gardner proposes that while actual testable strength determines the animal social order, with those who are weak developing depressionlike states, in human societies, public opinion determines the social order. So while a baboon might act depressed because each of the other baboons can (and does) beat him up, a human being might become depressed because nobody thinks well of him. Still, the basic rank hypothesis is borne out by contemporary experience—people who lose rank do become depressed, and that can sometimes make them more accepting of a lower rank in society. It should be noted, nonetheless, that even those who refuse to accept lower rank are not usually thrown out of contemporary societies—some of them, indeed, become respectable revolutionaries.

Depression is an agitated cousin of hibernation, a silence and withdrawal that conserves energy, a slowing down of all systems—which seems to support the idea that depression is a relic. That depressed people long for their own bed and don't want to leave the house evokes hibernation: an animal should hibernate not in the middle of a field but in the relative safety of its cozy den. According to one hypothesis, depression is a natural form of withdrawal that must take place in a secure context. "It may be that depression is associated with sleep," Thomas Wehr, the sleep man at the NIMH, has suggested, "because it's really associated with a place where sleep occurs, with being at home." Depression may also be accompanied by altered levels of prolactin, the hormone that causes birds to sit for weeks on end on their eggs. That's also a form of withdrawal and quiescence. Of milder depression, Wehr says, "The members of the species who were too anxious to deal with crowds, didn't go to high places, didn't enter tunnels, didn't single themselves out, shied away from strangers, went home when they sensed danger—they probably lived long and had lots of babies."

It is important to bear in mind evolution's putative singularity of purpose. Natural selection does not wipe out disorders or move toward perfection. Natural selection favors the expression of certain genes over other genes. Our brains evolve less rapidly than our way of life. McGuire and Troisi call this the "genome-lag hypothesis." There is no question that modern life carries burdens incompatible with the brains we have evolved. Depression may, then, well be a consequence of our doing what we did not evolve to do. "I think, in a species that's designed to live in groups of fifty to seventy," says Randolph Nesse, a leader in evolutionary psychology, "living in a group of several billion is just hard on everyone. But who knows? Maybe it's diet, maybe exercise rates, maybe changes in family structure, maybe changes in mating patterns and sexual access, maybe sleep, maybe having to confront death itself as a conscious idea, maybe none of these." James Ballenger of the Medical University of South Carolina adds, "The stimuli for anxiety just weren't there in the past. You stayed within easy distance of home, and most people can learn to deal with one place. Modern society is anxiety-provoking." Evolution invented a paradigm in which a particular response was useful in particular circumstances; modern life provokes that response, that constellation of symptoms, under many circumstances in which they are not useful. Rates of depression tend to be low in hunter-gatherer or purely agricultural societies; higher in industrial societies; and highest in societies in transition. This supports McGuire and Troisi's hypothesis. There are a thousand difficulties in modern societies that more traditional societies did not have to face. Adjusting to them without having time to learn coping strategies is nearly impossible. Of these difficulties, the worst is probably chronic stress. In the wild, animals tend to have a momentary awful situation and then to resolve it by surviving or dying. Except for persistent hunger, there is no chronic stress. Wild animals do not take on jobs that they regret; do not force themselves to interact calmly, year after year, with those they dislike; do not have child custody battles.

Perhaps the primary source of the extremely high level of stress in our society is not these evident afflictions but the freedom offered us in the form of an overwhelming number of uninformed choices. The Dutch psychologist J. H. van den Berg, who published his *The Changing Nature of Man* in 1961, argues that different societies have different systems of motivation and that each era requires a new round of theory—so that what Freud wrote may well have been true of human beings of the late nineteenth and early twentieth centuries in Vienna and London, but was no longer necessarily true of human beings in the mid–twentieth century, nor was it ever strictly true of people in Peking. Van den Berg suggests that there is no such thing as informed choice about way of life in modern culture. He speaks of the invisibility of the professions, whose continuing diversification has resulted in an array of possibilities that is beyond comprehension. In preindustrial societies, a child could walk through his village and see the adults at work. He tended to choose (where choice was operative at all) his own job on the basis of a fairly thorough understanding of what each of the available options entailed— what it was to be a blacksmith, a miller, or a baker. Perhaps the details of the life of the priest were unclear, but the way of life of the priest was fully visible. This is simply not true in postindustrial society. Few people have understood since childhood what exactly a hedge-fund manager or a health-care administrator or an associate professor actually does, or what it is like for him to do it.

The realm of the personal is the same. Up until the nineteenth century, one's social options were limited. With the exception of a few adventurers and heretics, people grew up and died in the same place. They were held in rigid class structures. A tenant farmer in Shropshire had few options about whom to marry: he chose among the women who were of the right age and class in his locale. Perhaps the one he truly loved proved unavailable and he had to settle for someone else, but at least he'd reviewed the options, knew what he might have done, and knew what he was doing. Members of the upper classes occupied a world that was somewhat less geographically constricted but was numerically small. They too tended to know all the people whom they might have the opportunity to marry and to be aware of the full range of their options. This is not to say that cross-class marriages did not take place, or that people did not move from one spot to another, but such gestures were infrequent and reflected a conscious disavowal of convention. Highly structured societies that do not present unlimited opportunity may engender acceptance of one's lot in life, at least in a relatively large percentage of the population—though of course a full acceptance of one's situation achieved through introspection is rare in any society in any time. With the development of better transportation, the growth of cities, and the advent of class mobility, the range of possible mates suddenly swelled to immeasurable proportions. The people who in the mid–eighteenth century could say that they had reviewed all available members of the opposite sex and chosen the fairest have been forced in more recent times to settle for the less comforting assurance that they have chosen the best of those with whom they happen to have come in contact so far. Most of us will meet thousands of other people in our lifetimes. So loss of the basic assurance—of feeling one knows whether one had chosen the right profession and of feeling that one knows whether one had chosen the right spouse—has left us bereft. We cannot accept that we simply don't know what to do; we cling to the idea that one should make choices on the basis of knowledge.

In political terms, freedom is often burdensome, which is why transitions out of dictatorship often cause depression. In personal terms, slavery and excessive freedom are both oppressive realities, and while some part of the world is paralyzed by the narrow despair of inescapable poverty, the more developed nations are paralyzed by the very mobility of their populations, by the twenty-first-century nomadism of constantly pulling up roots and resettling to accommodate jobs and relationships and even fancy. A writer addressing this problem tells the story of a boy whose family had moved five times in a short period, who hanged himself from an oak in the backyard, leaving a note pinned to the tree that said, "This is the only thing around here that has any roots." The feeling of perpetual disruption holds for the jetting executive who visits thirty countries in an average year, and the middle-class city dweller whose job keeps getting redescribed as his company is bought out time and again and who does not know from year to year who will work for him or for whom he will work, or for the person who lives alone and encounters different checkout staff every time he goes grocery shopping. In 1957, an average American supermarket had sixty-five items in the produce section: shoppers knew what all the fruits and vegetables were and had had each of them before. In 1997, an average American super-market had over three hundred items in the produce section, with many markets pushing a thousand. You are in the realm of uncertainty even when you select your own dinner. This kind of escalation of choices is not convenient; it is dizzying. When similar choices present themselves in every area—where you live, what you do, what you buy, whom you marry—the result is a collective uneasiness that explains much, in my view, about the rising rates of depression in the industrialized world.

Further, we live in an era of dazzling, bewildering technologies, and we have no concrete grasp of how most of the things around us work. How does a microwave function? What is a silicon chip? How do you genet-ically engineer corn? How does my voice travel when I use a cell phone as opposed to a regular phone? Is it real money that a bank machine in Kuwait deducts from my account in New York? One can research any of these particular questions, but to learn the answers to all the small sci-ence questions of our lives is an overwhelming task. Even for someone who understands how the motor of a car works and where electricity comes from, the actual mechanics of daily life have become increas-ingly obscure.

There are many specific stresses for which we are ill prepared. The breakdown of the family is certainly one, and the advent of the solitary life is another. The loss of contact, and sometimes intimacy, between working mothers and their children is another. Living a working life that entails no physical movement or exercise is another. Living in artificial light is another. Loss of the comforts of religion is yet another. Incorpo-rating the explosion of information in our age is yet another. The list can be expanded almost indefinitely. How could our brains be prepared to process and tolerate all this? Why wouldn't it be a strain for them?

Many scientists have subscribed to the idea that depression serves a use-ful function in our society as it exists today. Evolutionists would want to see that the presence of depression favors the reproduction of certain genes—but if one looks at the reproductive rates of depressives, one finds that depression in fact decreases reproduction. Like physical pain, depression is intended to warn us off certain dangerous activities or behaviors by making them too unpleasant to tolerate so it is the *capacity* for depression that is most obviously useful. Paul J. Watson and Paul Andrews, evolutionary psychiatrists, have proposed that depression is actually a means of communication and have modeled evolutionary sce-narios according to which depression is a social disease, one that exists for its interpersonal role. Mild depression, in their view, causes intense intro-spection and self-examination, on the basis of which it is possible to make sophisticated decisions about how to effect changes in one's life so that it better suits one's character. Such depression can be and often is kept secret, and its function is private. Anxiety—distress in advance of an event—is often a component of depression and can be useful in preventing trouble. Mild depression—low mood that has taken on a life separate from the triggering circumstance—can motivate a return to what had been foolishly cast off, valued only after its loss. It can cause one to regret true mistakes, and to avoid making them again. Life decisions often follow the old rule of investments: high-risk decisions may bring high rewards, but at a cost that is potentially too high for most people. A situation in which a person cannot disengage from a truly hopeless goal may be resolved through depression, which forces disengagement. People who pursue their goals with excessive tenacity and cannot relinquish attachments that are evidently unwise are especially subject to depression. "They're trying to do something interpersonally that's not going to succeed, but they can't give up because they are so emotionally over-invested," Randolph Nesse says. Low mood serves to delimit persistence.

Depression can certainly interdict behaviors that have negative effects we might otherwise tolerate. Excessive levels of stress, for example, cause depression, and the depression may cause us to avoid the stress. Too little sleep may lead to depression, and depression can throw us back to more sleep. Among the primary functions of depression is changing nonproductive behaviors. Depression is often a sign that resources are being poorly invested and need to be refocused. Practical examples of this abound in modern life. I heard of a woman who had been trying to make her way in the world as a professional violinist, despite the discouragements of her teachers and colleagues, and who suffered from an acute depression that was only minimally responsive to medication and other therapies. When she gave up music and switched her energies to an area to which her abilities were better suited, her depression lifted. Paralyzing though it feels, depression can be a motivator.

More serious depression may arouse the attention and support of others. Watson and Andrews suggest that pretending one needs help from others does not necessarily secure that help: others are too smart to be deluded by phony neediness. Depression is a convenient mechanism because it supplies the convincing reality: if you're depressed, then you really are helpless, and if you really are helpless, you may be able to extort assistance from others. Depression is a costly form of communication, but it is all the more compelling because it is so costly. It is the sincere horror of it that gets others motivated, so say Watson and Andrews; the dysfunction caused by the onset of depression may serve a useful function in that it is "a device for the elicitation of altruism." It may also convince those who are responsible for causing you difficulties to leave you alone.

My depression brought out all kinds of helping behaviors in my family and friends. I received a much higher level of attention than I might otherwise have expected, and those around me took measures to relieve certain burdens—financial, emotional, and behavioral. I was freed of all kinds of obligations to friends because I was simply too sick to come through for them. I stopped working: I had no choice about that. I even used my illness to get permission to delay payment of my bills, and various pesky folk were obliged to stop bothering me. Indeed, when I had my third depressive episode, I took an extension on the completion of this book and did so with absolute certainty; fragile though I may have felt, I was able to state categorically that no, I could not just go on working anyway, and that my situation would have to be accommodated.

The evolutionary psychologist Edward Hagen sees depression as a power play: it involves the withdrawal of one's services to others until they accommodate one's needs. I disagree. The depressed make lots of demands on people around them, but then—if they weren't depressed, they wouldn't need to make all those demands. The chances of those demands being fully met are relatively slender. Depression can be a useful blackmail, but it is generally too unpleasant for the blackmailer and too inconsistent in its results to be a well-selected way of achieving specific ends. Though it can be gratifying to get support when you are feeling dreadful, can indeed help to build a depth of love that would otherwise be unimaginable, it is much better not to feel so dreadful and not to need so much support. No—I believe that low mood serves the function of physical pain in causing one to avoid certain behaviors because of unpleasant consequences, but the voguish idea that depression is a means to accomplish *social* goals makes little sense to me. If major depression is nature's strategy for making independent beings seek help, it's a risky strategy at best. The fact is that most people are appalled by depression. Though some respond to a display of depression with increased sympathy and altruism, more respond with revulsion and disgust. It is not unusual to discover in a depression that people you had believed were reliable are actually unreliable—a valuable piece of information you might have preferred not to have. My depressions have sorted the wheat from the chaff among my friends, but at how high a cost? And is it worth forsaking other relationships that give me pleasure simply because they were not reliable in a terrible time? What kind of a friend should I be to such people? How much of friendship is about being reliable anyway? How does being reliable in a crisis relate to being kind or generous or good?

The idea that depression is the misfiring of mechanisms that also serve useful functions is perhaps the most convincing of all the evolutionary theories. Depression most frequently stems from, and represents an aberrant form of, grief. It is not possible to understand melancholia apart from mourning: the basic pattern of depression exists in sorrow. Depression may be a useful mechanism that gets stuck. We have a range of heart rates to allow us to function in varying circumstances and climates. Real depression is, like a heart that doesn't pump blood to the fingers and toes, an extreme in which there is virtually no inherent advantage.

Grief is profoundly important to the human condition. I believe that its most important function is in the formation of attachment. If we did not suffer enough loss to fear it, we could not love intensely. The experience of love incorporates sadness into its intensity and range. One's wish not to injure those whom one loves—indeed, to help them—also serves the preservation of the species. Love keeps us alive when we recognize the difficulties of the world. If we had developed self-consciousness and not developed love as well, we would not long tolerate the slings and arrows of life. I've never seen a controlled study, but I believe that people with the greatest capacity to love are more likely to cleave to life, to remain alive, than those without it; they are more likely also to be loved, and that too keeps them alive. "A lot of people would see heaven as a place where there would be infinite intensity and variety," Kay Jamison has said. "Not a place that is trouble-free. You would want to eliminate some extremes, but not to cut the spectrum in half. There's a very fine line between saying that you want people to suffer and saying you don't want people to be denied emotional range." To love is to be vulnerable; to reject or decry vulnerability is to refuse love.

Crucially, love prevents us from abandoning our attachments too readily. We are made to agonize if we walk out on the people whom we truly love. Perhaps the anticipation of grief is critical to the formation of emotional attachments. It is the contemplation of loss that makes one hold tight to what one has. If there were no despair after the loss of someone, one would spend time and emotional energy on that person only as long as it was pleasurable to do so, and not one minute longer. "Evolutionary theory," says Nesse, "is generally thought to be a cynical practice. Evolutionary biologists interpret all the complexity of moral behavior as though it were simply a system for the selfish benefit of one's own genes. Of course much of one's behavior is explicitly for that purpose. But often one's actions lie outside of these parameters." Nesse's field of study is commitment. "Animals cannot make complex contingent promises about the future to one another. They cannot bargain and say, 'If you will do this for me in the future, then I will do this for you.' A commitment is a promise in the present to do something in the future that may not be in your best interests at that time. Most of us live by such commitments. Hobbes saw this. He understood that our capacity for such commitments is what makes us human."

The capacity to make commitments is to the evolutionary advantage of one's genes; it is the basis of the stable family unit that provides the ideal environment for the young. But once we have that capacity, which serves an evolutionary advantage, we can use it in any way we choose; and in these choices lies the moral compass of the human animal. "People's reductive notions of science have caused us to see relationships mostly as mutual manipulations and mutual exploitations," says Nesse, "but in fact feelings of love and hate often extend to the impractical. They don't fit with our rationalistic system at all. The capacity for love may serve an evolutionary advantage, but how we act in the face of love is a process of our own. The superego pushes us to do things that give benefit to others at the cost of our own pleasure." It invites us into the realm of moral alternatives, a realm that loses its meaning if we try to eliminate grief and its milder sad cousin, regret.

Some insects are born from untended egg sacs with a lifetime food supply intact; they need sexual impulse, but not love. The precursors of attachment, however, exist even in the world of reptiles and birds. The instinct to sit on an egg and keep it warm—in contrast to laying an egg and then sauntering off and leaving it to get cold, be crushed, or be devoured by passing animals—clearly enhances reproductivity. In most postreptilian species, mothers who feed their young, as good birds do, have more young who survive, and this enhances their success in producing little chicks who will grow into big birds and procreate. The first emotion, and one for which selection would most significantly occur, is a version of what we call love between a mother and her young. It seems likely that love emerged among the first mammals and that it motivated these creatures to care for the relatively helpless young born without an eggshell into the threatening world. A mother who associates strongly with her offspring, who protects them from marauders and who readily nurses and feeds them, has a much better chance of passing on her genetic material than does a mother who leaves her young to be attacked and eaten up by predators. The offspring of protective mothers stand a far greater chance of reaching maturity than do the offspring of indifferent mothers. Selection would favor the loving mother.

Various other emotions serve various specific advantages. The male who harbors anger and hatred will compete more effectively against other males; he will attempt to destroy them and will therefore advantage his own reproductive tendencies. The male who is protective of his mate will also have an advantage; and the male who keeps other males away from his mate will maintain the chances for his genes to be passed along every time the female becomes fertile. The best shot at promoting genetic material, for animals who produce few young, is to combine a loving and attentive mother and a jealous and protective father (or vice versa). Passionate animals stand a good chance of reproducing more frequently. Animals who are energized by rage are likely to win in competitive circumstances. Love—eros, agape, friendship, filiality, maternity, and all the other forms of that ill-contained emotion—functions on a rewards and punishments model. We express love because the gratification of love is enormous, and we continue to express love and to act protectively because the loss of love is traumatic. If we did not experience pain on the demise of those we love, if we had the pleasure of love but felt nothing when the object of our love was destroyed, we would be considerably less protective than we are. Grief makes love self-protective: we will take care of those we love to avoid intolerable pain to ourselves.

This argument seems the most plausible to me: that depression itself serves little useful function, but that emotional range is invaluable enough to justify all the extremes we know.

The social evolution of depression and the biochemical evolution of it are linked but are not the same. Our genetic mapping is not sufficiently specific at this time for us to know the exact functions of the genes that may lead to depression, but it appears that the condition is linked to emotional sensitivity, which is a useful trait. It may also be that the very structure of consciousness opens the pathway to depression. Contemporary evolutionists work with the idea of the triune (or three-layer) brain. The innermost part of the brain, the reptilian, which is similar to that found in lower animals, is the seat of instinct. The middle layer, the limbic, which exists in more advanced animals, is the seat of emotion. The top layer, found only in higher mammals such as primates and people, is the cognitive and is involved in reasoning and advanced forms of thought, as well as in language. Most human acts involve all three layers of the brain. Depression, in the view of the prominent evolutionist Paul Mac-Lean, is a distinctly human concern. It is the result of disjunctions of processing at these three levels: it is the inevitable consequence of having instinct, emotion, and cognition all going on simultaneously at all times. The triune brain sometimes fails to coordinate its response to social adversity. Ideally, when one feels instinctive withdrawal, one should experience emotional negativity and cognitive readjustment. If those three are in sync, one may experience a normal and nondepressive withdrawal from the activity or circumstance that is causing the deactivation

414

of the instinctive brain. But sometimes the higher levels of the brain fight against the instinctive. One may, for example, have withdrawal at the instinctive level but feel emotionally activated and angry. This causes an agitated depression. Or one may feel withdrawn at the instinctive level but make a conscious decision to go on fighting for what one wants, so subjecting oneself to terrible stress. This kind of conflict is experientially familiar to us all and does indeed seem to result in depression or other disruptions. MacLean's theory fits neatly with the idea that our brain is doing more than it evolved to do.

Timothy Crow at Oxford has moved beyond the principle of the tri-une brain. His theories are very much his own; whether they are true or not, they are calisthenically refreshing to minds worn out by the some-times improbable claims made by mainstream evolutionary theorists of mind. He proposes a linguistic-evolutionary model in which speech is the origin of self-consciousness, and self-consciousness the origin of mental illness. Crow starts by rejecting modern classification systems and places the mental illnesses on a continuous spectrum. For him, the differences between ordinary unhappiness, depression, bipolar illness, and schizophrenia are all really differences of degree rather than of kind—dimensional differences rather than categorical ones. In his view, all mental illness springs from common causes.

Crow believes (while physiologists battle about it) that the primate brain is symmetrical, and that what makes humans human—the specia-tion point—is the asymmetrical brain (which, he proposes, on the basis of some rather complex genetic arguments, came about through a muta-tion of the X chromosome in males). While brain size was increasing rel-ative to body size—in the evolution of the primates and then of man—a mutation allowed the two halves of the brain to develop with some meas-ure of independence. So while the primate cannot, as it were, look from one part of his brain to the other, the human being can. This opened the way to self-consciousness, to an awareness of one's own self as a self. A number of evolutionists have said that this could have been a simple mutation—one related to growth factors for each side of the brain—that over the course of evolution became a meaningful asymmetry.

The asymmetry of the brain is in turn the basis for language, which is the left-brain expression or processing of right-brain concepts and per-ceptions. This notion that language is located in the two sides of the brain seems to be borne out by evidence from stroke victims. Patients who have had limited strokes in the left brain can understand concepts and perceive objects, but they cannot name anything and they do not have access to language or to linguistic memory. This is not simply a vocal matter. Deaf people with left-hemisphere strokes can use emotional gesture and gesticulation (as all people and primates do), but they cannot use sign language nor understand the deep grammar we all use to assemble words into sentences and sentences into paragraphs. Patients with right-brain strokes, on the other hand, preserve intellectual abilities but lose the concepts and feelings those abilities may ordinarily express. They cannot process complex abstractions and their emotional capacities are very much compromised.

What are the anatomical structures that make us prone to mood disorders? Crow has proposed that schizophrenic and affective disorders may be the price we pay for an asymmetrical brain—the same neurological development he credits with human sophistication, cognition, and language. He then proposes that all mental illness is the consequence of a disruption of normal interaction between the two halves of the brain. "It can be too much communication between them or too little; if what the hemispheres are doing is not in concert, the result will be a mental illness," he explains. Crow suggests that asymmetry provides "increased flexibility of interaction" and "enhanced capacity for learning" and "an escalating capacity to communicate with members of the same species." These developments, however, slow brain maturation, which takes longer in human beings than in other species. Human beings appear to retain greater brain plasticity as adults than do most other species—you can't easily teach an old dog new tricks, but old men can learn whole new systems of motor activity as they accommodate later-life disabilities.

Our flexibility allows us to reach new insights and new understandings. It also means, however, that we can bend too far. For Crow, the same elasticity causes us to vary outside the normal range of personality and into psychosis. The change may well be triggered by external events. What evolution would have selected for, in this model, is not the particular expressions of the plasticity, but the plasticity itself.

The study of brain asymmetry is a hot topic at the moment, and the most impressive work in the United States is being done by the neuroscientist Richard J. Davidson at the University of Wisconsin at Madison. Davidson's work has been made possible by increasingly good brain-scanning equipment. Scientists can now see all kinds of things in the brain that they couldn't see five years ago, and it seems likely that in five years, they'll be able to see a lot more. Using a combination of PET (positron-emission tomography) and MRI (magnetic resonance imaging), brain-imaging specialists can get a three-dimensional snapshot of the entire brain approximately every two and a half seconds, with spatial information accurate only to within about three and a half millimeters. MRI has better time and spatial resolution; PET does a better job of mapping neurochemical reactions in the brain.

Davidson has begun by mapping neural and chemical activity in the brain in response to "normal" stimulus—what areas do what when a subject sees an erotic photograph or hears a scary noise. "We want to look at the parameters of emotional reactivity," he says. Once you've figured out where in the brain the reaction to a particular kind of image takes place, you can measure how long the brain remains activated, and it turns out that this varies from person to person. Some people, exposed to a gruesome photo, will have a neurochemical rush that dies down fast; others will have the same chemical rush and it will take a long time to come back down. This matter is consistent for any given patient: some of us have snappy brains in this regard and some of us have slow ones. Davidson believes that people with a slow recovery time are much more vulnerable to mental illness than are those with a brisk recovery. Davidson's group at Wisconsin have shown detectable changes in the speed of recovery in individual brains after six weeks of treatment with antidepressant medication.

These changes seem to be in the prefrontal cortex and they are not symmetrical—when someone is recovering from a depression, speed of activation and deactivation increases on the left side of the prefrontal cortex. It is known that antidepressants alter levels of neurotransmitters. It is possible that neurotransmitters control blood flow to various areas of the brain. Whatever the mechanisms, Davidson explains, "activation asymmetries"—differences in left-side and right-side activity—"in the prefrontal cortex are related to disposition, mood, and the symptoms of anxiety and depression. People with more right-side activation are more likely to have depression and anxiety." And Davidson, like Crow, ultimately questions the categorical purity of depression as a condition. "One of the things that distinguishes human behavior from the behavior of other species is that we have a greater capacity to regulate our emotions. We also have the flip side, a greater capacity to disregulate our emotions. I think both mechanisms will prove to be very much associated with activity in the prefrontal cortex." In other words, our troubles are a consequence of our strengths.

This kind of work, in addition to showing how the genetics of mood disorder may have developed, has enormous practical implications. If researchers can locate the exact area of altered activity in a depressed brain, they can develop the apparatus to stimulate or inhibit that area. Recent work suggests that abnormalities in serotonin metabolism occur in the prefrontal cortex in patients with depression. Asymmetrical stimulation of the brain may result from this; or there may be physical asymmetry—of capillary distribution and hence of blood flow, for example—in some brains.

Certain patterns of brain activity are set up early in life. Others change. We have now found that brain cells can and do reproduce in adult humans. It may be that we are gaining cells in some areas or depleting cells in others when we go through depression. New technologies may ultimately allow us to stimulate growth of or to lesion certain areas of the brain. Some early studies show that rTMS (repeated transcranial magnetic stimulation), which uses tightly focused magnetism to increase activity in a particular location, may, when directed at the left prefrontal cortex, cause amelioration of the symptoms of depression. It may be possible, through external intervention or through measured work oneself, to learn to activate the left brain. Resilience itself can be learned, especially in young people. It may be possible to scan brains and catch deactivated left frontal cortexes early and take preventative measures—"which might include meditation, for example," Davidson says—to help people avoid falling into the pit of depression in the first place.

Some people have more highly activated left prefrontal cortexes and some people have more highly activated right prefrontal cortexes. (This has nothing to do with the question of hemispheric dominance that determines whether you are right-handed or left-handed, which occurs in other areas of the brain.) The majority of people have higher left-side activation. People with higher right-side activation tend to experience more negative emotion than people with higher left-side activation. Right-side activation also predicts how easily someone's immune system will become depressed. The right-brain activation is also correlated with high baseline levels of cortisol, the stress hormone. Though the settled patterns of activation do not stabilize until adulthood, babies with greater right-side activation will become frantic when their mothers leave a room; babies with strong left-side activation will be more likely to explore the room without apparent distress. In babies, however, the balance is subject to change. "The likelihood," Davidson says, "is that there's more plasticity in the system in the early years of life, more opportunity for the environment to sculpt this circuitry."

There are enormously interesting ideas to be adduced from putting together this thinking with some of Crow's ideas about language. "One of the first things that you see when toddlers begin giving out single-word utterances is that they point," Davidson says. "The utterance is a label for an object. And they point almost invariably, at first, with the right hand. The toddler is having a positive experience and is clearly interested in the object and is moving toward it. The initial use of language is very pleasurable to most toddlers. My intuition, which has not been studied in any systematic way, is that the left-hemisphere lateralization for language may actually be a byproduct of the left-hemisphere lateralization for positive emotion."

This intuition is, it would seem, the basis for a neuroanatomy of catharsis. Speech is positive; it remains positive. Speech is one of life's greatest pleasures, and the will to communicate is enormously powerful in all of us (including those who cannot produce coherent vocal sound and therefore use sign language, gesture, or writing to express themselves). People who are depressed lose interest in talking; people who are manic talk incessantly. Across broad cultural divides, the most consistent mood-enhancer is speech. Dwelling on negative events can be painful, but talking about current pain helps to alleviate it. When I am asked, as I am constantly, about how best to treat depression, I tell people to talk about it—not to work themselves up into hysteria about it, but simply to keep articulating their feelings. Talk about it with family if they'll listen. Talk about it with friends. Talk about it with a therapist. It may well be that Davidson and Crow are onto the mechanisms through which talk helps: it may well be that certain kinds of talking activate the same areas of the left brain whose underperformance is implicated in mental illness. The idea of articulation as release is absolutely fundamental to our society. Hamlet weeps that he "must, like a whore, unpack my heart with words"—and yet what we have evolved, along with our capacity for mental illness, is that capacity to unpack our hearts (or, as the case may be, our left prefrontal cortexes) with words.

Though effective treatments exist even for diseases we do not begin to understand, knowing how the components of a disease are related helps us to discern its immediate precipitants and address them. It helps us to understand a constellation of symptoms and to see in what ways one system may influence another. Most of the systems of explanation for illness—the biochemical, the psychoanalytic, the behavioral, and the sociocultural—are fragmentary and leave many things unexplained, and they suggest that even the combinatory approaches now in vogue are highly irregular and unsystematic. Why do particular feelings and particular actions correlate in illness but not in health? "Psychiatry's most pressing need," McGuire and Troisi write, "is to embrace evolutionary theory and to begin the process of identifying its most important data and of testing novel explanations of disorders. Attempts to explain behavior, normal or otherwise, without having an in-depth understanding of the species one is studying invite misinterpretation."

I am not persuaded that knowing the evolution of depression will be particularly useful in treating it. It is critical, however, to making decisions about treating it. We know that tonsils have a limited use; we understand what they are doing in the body; we know that fighting infection in tonsils is more trouble than removing them and that removing them does little harm to the body. We know that the appendix can be removed rather than healed. On the other hand, we know that an infection of the liver needs to be treated because if you remove someone's liver, that person will die. We know that it's necessary to snip off skin cancers but that pimples do not cause systemic inflammation. We understand the mechanisms of these different areas of the physical self, and by and large we know what kind and degree of intervention is appropriate in the event of dysfunction.

It is eminently clear that there is no consensus on when to treat depression. Should depression be removed like a tonsil, treated like liver disease, or ignored like a pimple? Does it matter whether the depression is mild or severe? To answer these questions correctly, we need to know why the depression is there at all. If depression served a useful function for hunter-gatherers but is irrelevant to modern life, then it should probably be removed. If depression is a misfunction of the brain that involves circuitry we need for other crucial brain functions, then it should be treated. If some milder depression is a self-regulating mechanism, then it should be ignored. Evolution may offer something of a unified field theory, revealing structural relationships among the other schools of thought that are used in studying depression; that will allow us to make decisions about whether, when, and how to treat the complaint.

CHAPTER XII

Hope

Angel Starkey has had a rough time of it. The youngest of seven children, she comes from a family in which she was seldom touched or hugged; she went on to be sexually abused by the janitor in her school; she was raped when she was thirteen. "I've been depressed since I was like three years old," she says. As a child, she used to lock herself in the closet under the stairs and draw tombstones on the wall. Her father died of pancreatic cancer when she was seven. At thirty-eight, "I can still hear him screaming sometimes. Like I'm laying in my bed or just sitting in my room and I hear it again and it scares the shit out of me." Her closest friend when she was little was a neighbor who hanged herself, it was subsequently revealed, while Angel was knocking on the front door. Angel has been hospitalized more or less full-time since she finished high school seventeen years ago, with brief moves out into supervised community housing. She has a schizo-affective disorder, which means that in addition to profound depression, she has hallucinations and hears voices instructing her to destroy herself. Panic blocks her from ordinary interactions in the world. No one can even remember how many times she has attempted suicide—but since she has been in an institution for most of her adult life, she has been saved over and over again, even when she has thrown herself in front of a car. Her arms are knotty with scars from the countless slicings; a doctor told her recently that she was out of pliable flesh, and that if she kept cutting herself, there would be no way to close the wounds. On her stomach, her skin is patchworked together because she has set herself on fire so many times. She has tried to strangle herself (with plastic bags, with a shoelace, with a blood-pressure cuff)—until "my head turned purple"—and she has the marks on her neck to prove it. Her eyelids are puckered where she has held lit cigarettes to them. Her hair is thin because she pulls it out, and her teeth have partly rotted as a side effect of her medications—

chronic dry mouth can lead to gingivitis. At the moment, her prescribed medications are Clozaril, 100 mg, five a day; Clozaril, 25 mg, five a day; Prilosec, 20 mg, one a day; Seroquel, 200 mg, two a day; Ditropan, 5mg, four a day; Lescol, 20 mg, one a day; BuSpar, 10 mg, six a day; Prozac, 20 mg, four a day; Neurontin, 300 mg, three per day; Topamax, 25 mg, one per day; and Cogentin, 2 mg, two per day.

I first met Angel at Norristown Hospital, the state facility I visited in Pennsylvania. She was a patient there. I was taken aback by the scarring, by the bloating her drugs caused, by the simple physical fact of her. But in a place where many eyes were as shallow as glass, she seemed to engage more. "She's very needy," one of her nurses told me, "but she's also very sweet-natured. Angel is special." Doubtless all people are special, but Angel has a moving quality of hopefulness that is extraordinary in someone with her biography. Underneath her suffering and its consequences is a warm, imaginative, and generous person, sufficiently appealing so that you are in the end distracted from the brutalized surface. Angel's personality is obscured but not destroyed by her illness.

I was to become intimate with Angel and her patterns of self-mutilation. Her favorite implement for slicing herself is the top of a can. She once shredded her arms so badly that she required four hundred stitches. "Cutting myself is the only thing that gives me any pleasure," she told me. When cans are not available, she has managed to uncurl the bottom of a toothpaste tube and use that to slice away ribbons of her flesh. She has done this even while she was going through a debridement—the surgical removal of devitalized tissue—for self-inflicted burns. In the small world of Norristown State Mental Hospital, "I've been going in and out of building fifty, the emergency center," she told me. "I have to go in there if I cut myself. It used to be building sixteen, but now it's building fifty. I'm living in building one, regular residential. For a break, I go to the karaoke nights in building thirty-three sometimes. I had to come into the hospital this time because I was getting these physical panic attacks constantly. And my mind wasn't working good, you know? It was like I kept skipping; it scared me. And I had to keep running to the bathroom—it's really weird the way my whole body reacts to just a little bit of anxiety! We went to the mall yesterday, and it was so scary. Even little stores. I had to take a bunch of Ativan and even that didn't do it. I'm so paranoid about losing it. Yesterday I went in and out of the stores real fast and went to the bathroom about ten times. I couldn't swallow. When I was leaving here to go there, I was afraid to go; but when it was time to come back, I was afraid to come back to the hospital."

Physical pain has always been indispensable to her. "I tell them not to stitch me up and make it so easy," she said. "Make it worse. It makes me feel better when it's hard. If I'm going to feel pain, I'd rather have physical pain than emotional pain. It's a purging thing for me when I get so worn-out I can't breathe. Stapling is nicer than stitches because it hurts more, but it doesn't hurt long enough. When I cut myself, I want to die—who's going to take care of me when I'm all ripped to pieces and burnt up and everything? See, I'm not a good person." Angel was on one-to-one supervision—no privacy even to use the bathroom—for three years in a particularly acute period. She has had times when she had to be tied to a bed. She has been held on locked wards, and she has spent her share of time in a body net—a big piece of webbing that swaddles a violent patient into total immobility. She describes that experience as unutterably terrifying. She has learned all about the medications she takes. She is an informed patient. "One more thought about Clozaril," she said, "and I'm going to start throwing them up, you know?" She has also had extensive ECT.

During a recent stay at Norristown, Angel told me she called her mother every day and went home to stay with her a couple of weekends every month. "I love my mother more than anything in the world. Much more than I love myself, you know. It's hard for her. Sometimes I think, she's got seven children, maybe she could do with six. It's not like I'd be leaving her by herself. I've tortured her long enough. She doesn't need me screwing up. I hurt her with the weight, the weight, and the embarrassment. My depression, her depression, my sisters' depression, my brothers', you know? It's never going to end, I don't think, until we all die. I just wish I could get a job and give her money. They say I worry about my mom too much, but you know, she's seventy-three years old. I go there and I clean stuff. I go home in a frenzy and clean. I'm cleaning and cleaning and cleaning and freaking out. I get fanatic about it. I like to wash things. And my mom does appreciate that."

The first time we met, Angel was clearly tense, and the memory problems that are endemic for her as a consequence of long-term ECT (she has had thirty rounds of treatment) and high dosages of medications were particularly disabling. She would forget herself halfway through a sentence. She talked about the little comforts of her small world. "I don't understand why people are so nice to me," she said. "I used to hate myself so bad. I hated everything I did. God must think something of me, because, I mean, I've gotten hit by two cars, and I've cut myself until I'd emptied out all my blood, and I'm still alive. I'm ugly. I'm very heavy. I can't—my mind's too messed up to even think sometimes. The hospital, that's my life, you know? The symptoms, they're not going to just end. The depression and the feelings of loneliness."

Acutely aware of the difficulties in our communication, she sent me, a few weeks later, a letter "to be clear." In it she wrote, "I've done so many things to kill and hurt myself. Everything is getting very tiring. I don't think I have a brain left. Sometimes if I start to cry, I'm afraid that I will never stop. I have lost and lost endlessly. There are so many people that I would love to help, even if it's just a hug. Just that in itself makes me happy. Sometimes I write poetry. It tells me and others how sick I have been. But it shows there is Hope. love, Angel"

In the year that followed, Angel moved out of Norristown, first to an intensive assisted-care setting and then on to a less intensive setting, in Pottstown, Pennsylvania. For more than fourteen months, she did not cut her arms. Her catalog of medicines seemed to be working to keep the dread voices away. Before leaving Norristown, she had told me, "What really scares me is that I'm not going to be able to get it together enough, do things like shopping, and the steps, three flights of stairs. And the people too. All of it." But she made the transition with surprising grace. "Right now," she told me about a month after her move, "I'm doing better than I've ever done." And then she just went on getting better bit by bit, acquiring a confidence she had never anticipated. She continued to hear a voice that called her name, but it was not the demonic, torturing voice she had heard before. "Mostly, I don't have any inkling of hurting myself. It was like a compulsion. And now, I think about it, but not like it used to be. Not at all like it used to be, the way if somebody sneezed, I'd cut myself. Now I feel like I want to be around, hopefully, for the rest of my life!" she told me.

I was struck that Angel, unlike many self-destructive patients, never sought to destroy anyone else. She never hit anyone in all her years in the hospital. She described once setting herself on fire by lighting her pajamas. Then she panicked that as she burned, she might set the building aflame. "I thought of the people I'd burn up and I put myself out real fast." She got involved with the Consumer Satisfaction Team at Norristown, the hospital's internal advocacy group for patient rights. She went out with her doctors, terrifying though she found it, to speak at schools about what life in the hospital was like. When I came to spend time with her in her supervised housing, I observed that she was the one who taught the others how to do things: she showed them how to cook (peanut-butter-and-banana sandwiches) with an almost infinite patience. "I've got to live life," she said to me. "I just so badly want to help people. And maybe in time, I'll feel, I'll be doing something for myself too. This woman who I'm sharing a room with now, she's got such a good heart. When you call and she answers, doesn't she sound like a little sweetheart? She's got a lot of problems; she doesn't even cook or clean. She doesn't do much at all. But she's sweet, you can't be mean to her. I've been trying to teach her for like two months how to peel a damned cucumber, but she can't get it."

Hope

Angel writes poems and is a true devotee of trying to give voice to her experiences:

> I wish I could cry
> as easy as the sky. The tears don't come
> as easily now. They're
> stuck inside my soul.
>
> It's empty and I am afraid
> Do you feel the emptiness? I guess
> it's my own fear from within. I should
> be brave and battle that fear
> but it's a war that's gone on
> for so damned long. I'm tired.
>
> The children are growing and the tears
> in my eyes are flowing. Missing the
> growth of them is like missing the seasons
> change, missing the roses that bloom
> in spring and missing snowflakes falling
> in winter. How many more years
> do I have to miss? The years won't
> stop for me or for them and why
> should they? They will continue to
> blossom and
> bloom and my life will continue
> to stand still like a silent pond.

I went to see Angel just before she moved from her supervised housing to her lower-supervision housing. She had made me a present—a birdhouse painted bright blue with a note tacked on the back that said, "Rent Due." We went for lunch at a Chinese restaurant in the shopping mall in Pottstown. We talked about *Pippin*, the show she had seen the one time she traveled to New York. We talked about her application for a job, part-time, helping out with sandwiches in a deli. She had been turned down and she was crestfallen; she had been so excited by the idea of working, though she was afraid of the cash register and of having to do the arithmetic of giving people their change. "I've got a third-grade math level," she confided. "It's horrible. And a pretty short attention span too, like a three-year-old. It's the medicines doing that I think." We talked about her favorite book—*The Catcher in the Rye*. We talked about the dreams she was having. "I dream about the ocean all the time," she said.

"It's like this room, and there's a wall. And in back of the wall, there's an ocean. And I can never get over on the beach in there, to the water. I struggle and struggle to get to the water, and I can't get in it. Other times I dream about this heat. The sun is starting to burn me and my hair is getting singed. I'm afraid of the heat of the sun. You know, even in real life I try to go to places where there are no windows during sunset, when the sun turns red. It terrifies me." We talked a little bit about the flaws in her memory. "I am godmother to one of my nieces," she said, "but I can't remember which one, and I'm too embarrassed to ask."

After that, I was in and out of touch for six months, and when we next met, Angel asked me what had been going on. I told her that I had had a little bit of a relapse. It was not long after the dislocated shoulder and my third breakdown. We were back at the Chinese restaurant. Angel rearranged the wilted bok choy on her plate. "You know," she said after a minute, "I was really worried about you. I mean, I thought you might have killed yourself or something."

I tried to comfort her. "Well, it wasn't really quite like that, Angel. It was horrible, but it probably wasn't that dangerous. Or at least it turned out to be not quite that dangerous. You know, I took the Zyprexa and shifted around a bunch of stuff and they turned it around really quickly." I smiled and spread my arms. "You see, I'm fine now."

Angel looked up and smiled. "That's great. I was so worried." We both ate. Then, "I'm never going to be fine," she said doughtily. I told her it was one step at a time, and that she was doing awfully well. I told her that she was a thousand times better than she'd been when I first met her two years earlier. I said to her, look, a year ago you couldn't even have imagined going out and living in a place like where you're going. "Yeah," she said, and for a minute she was bashfully proud. "Sometimes I hate the drugs so much, but they help me."

We got ice cream and went to a dollar store next to the restaurant. Angel bought some coffee and a few other things she needed. We got in the car to drive back to the place where she was living. "I'm really glad you came," she said to me. "I didn't think you'd come out here today. I hope you don't feel like I'm dragging you out here." I said that it was kind of exciting to see what was happening to her, and that I too was glad I'd come. "You know," she said, "if I could only get well enough to do stuff, I'd like to go on one of the big shows, like maybe *Oprah*. That would be my dream."

I asked her why she wanted to be on a talk show.

"I just want to get my message out to people," she said as we got back in the car. "I want to tell everyone: don't cut yourself, and don't hurt yourself, and don't hate yourself. You know? It's really so important. I wish I'd known that much sooner. I want to tell everyone." We drove for a little while in silence. "Will you try to tell people that when you write your book?" she asked me. And she laughed a little nervously.

"I'll try to tell people just what you said," I replied.

"Promise? It's so important."

"I promise."

We went to her new place then, the lower-supervision housing, and toured around it and looked through the windows, and I climbed a flight of outdoor stairs to see the view from a terrace affixed to the back of the building. It was so different from the slightly dilapidated place where she'd been living. Recently refurbished, it looked like a hotel: each two-bedroom apartment had new wall-to-wall carpeting, a big TV, an armchair and a sofa, a fitted kitchen. "Angel, this place is pretty great," I said, and she said, "Yeah, it's really nice. It's so much nicer."

We drove back to the location she was soon to leave. We both got out of the car, and I gave Angel a long hug. I wished her good luck, and she thanked me again for coming down to see her and told me how much my visit had meant to her. I thanked her for the birdhouse. "God, it's cold," she said. I got back in the car and watched her trudge slowly from the parking lot to her front door. I pulled out to go. "Good-bye, Angel," I said, and she turned around and waved. "Remember, you promised," she called to me as I left.

It seemed a happy picture, and it remains one in my mind—but within six months, Angel had lacerated her wrists and stomach, been returned to the hospital, and gone into intensive psychiatric care. When I drove down to see her back at Norristown, her arms were covered in volcanic-looking blood-filled blisters, because she had poured boiling coffee onto the gashes to alleviate an anxiety overflow. While we talked, she rocked back and forth in her seat. "I just don't want to live at all," she said over and over. I dug up every helpful remark I could think of from this book. "It won't always be like this," I said to her, even though I suspect that, for her, it will be like this much of the time. Heroism and light in your eyes are not sufficient in the depression business.

A schizophrenic woman kept joining our conversation, protesting that she'd killed a ladybug and not a lady and that her family had raped her because they'd misunderstood and thought it was a lady. She wanted us to set the record straight. A man with weirdly large feet kept whispering conspiracy theories in my ear. "Go *away*," Angel finally yelled at them. Then she wrapped her disfigured arms around herself. "I can't stand this," she said, angry and miserable and abject. "I'm never going to be free of this place. I want to just bang my head against the wall until it opens up and spills, you know?"

Before I left, one of the attendants said, "You optimistic?" and I shook my head. "Me neither," he said. "I was for a while, because she isn't acting crazy like most of 'em. I was wrong. She's pretty well in touch with reality at the moment, and she's still so sick."

Angel said to me, "They got me out of the worst once, so I guess they'll do it again."

Within six months, this storm had cleared and she was free again, back in the nice apartment. She was full of good cheer. She finally had a job—bagging groceries—and she was so proud. At the Chinese restaurant, they seemed glad to see us. We avoided words such as *always* and *never* when we chatted.

Why, people kept asking me, why are you writing a book about depression? It seemed to them incomprehensible that I would submerge myself in this unpleasant topic, and I must say that as I set about my research, it often seemed to me that I had been foolish in my choice. I came up with a number of replies that seemed to meet the occasion. I said that I thought I had things to say that hadn't been said. I said that writing is an act of social responsibility, that I wanted to help people to appreciate depression and to understand how best to care for those who suffer from it. I admitted that I had been offered a generous book advance and that I thought the topic might engage the public imagination, and that I wanted to be famous and beloved. But not until I had written about three-quarters of the book did my purpose fully reveal itself to me.

I did not anticipate the intense, shattering vulnerability of depressed people. Nor did I realize in what complicated ways that particular vulnerability interacts with personality. While I was working on this book, a close friend got engaged to a man who used his depression as an excuse for riotous emotional self-indulgence. He was sexually rejecting and cold; he demanded that she provide food and cash for him and run his personal life because it was too painful for him to take responsibility; he brooded for hours while she tenderly reassured him—but he could not remember any of the details of her life or talk to her about herself. For a long time, I encouraged her to put up with it, thinking it would clear with the illness, not recognizing that no cure on earth could transform him into a person of character. Later, another female friend of mine reported being physically attacked by her husband, who beat her head on the floor. He had been acting strangely for weeks—had responded in paranoiac ways to ordinary phone calls, and had been spiteful to the dogs. After his vicious physical attack, she called the police, terrified; he went into a mental hospital. It is true that he had some kind of schizo-affective disorder, but he is still culpable. Psychiatric illness often reveals the dreadful side of someone. It doesn't really make a whole new person. Sometimes the dreadful side is pathetic and needy and hungry, qualities that are sad but touching; sometimes the dreadful side is brutal and cruel. Illness brings to light the painful realities most people shroud in perfect darkness. Depression exaggerates character. In the long run, I think, it makes good people better; it makes bad people worse. It can destroy one's sense of proportion and give one paranoid fantasies and a false sense of helplessness; but it is also a window onto truth.

The fiancé of the first friend and the husband of the second have little place in this book. In and out of my research, I met plenty of depressed people for whom I had negative feeling or no particular feeling, and by and large I decided not to write about them. I have chosen to write about people I admire. The people in this book are mostly strong or bright or tough or in some other way distinctive. I do not believe that there is such a thing as an average person, or that by telling a prototypical reality one can convey overarching truth. The quest for the nonindividual, generic human being is the blight of popular psychology books. By seeing how many kinds of resilience and strength and imagination are to be found, one can appreciate not only the horror of depression but also the complexity of human vitality. I had one conversation with a severely depressed older man who told me that "depressed people have no stories; we have nothing to say." All of us have stories, and the true survivors have compelling stories. In real life, mood has to exist amid the clutter of toasters and atom bombs and fields of gazing grain. This book exists as a more protected environment for the stories of remarkable people and their successes—stories that I believe can help others as they helped me.

Some people suffer mild depression and are totally disabled by it; others suffer severe depression and make something of their lives anyway. "Some people can function through anything," says David McDowell, who works on substance abuse at Columbia. "That doesn't mean they're having less pain." The absolute measurements are difficult. "Unfortunately," Deborah Christie, a child psychologist at University College London, observes, "there's no such thing as a suicide-ometer or a pain-ometer or a sad-ometer. We can't measure in objective terms how sick people are or what their symptoms are. You can only listen to what people say and accept that that's how it feels to them." There is an interaction between illness and personality; some people can tolerate symptoms that would destroy others; some people can tolerate hardly anything. Some people seem to give in to their depression; others seem to battle it. Since depression is highly demotivating, it takes a certain survivor impulse to keep going through the depression, not to cave in to it. A sense of humor is the best indicator that you will recover; it is often the best indicator that people will love you. Sustain that and you have hope.

Of course it can be hard to sustain a sense of humor during an experience that is really not so funny. It is urgently necessary to do so. The most important thing to remember during a depression is this: you do not get the time back. It is not tacked on at the end of your life to make up for the disaster years. Whatever time is eaten by a depression is gone forever. The minutes that are ticking by as you experience the illness are minutes you will not know again. No matter how bad you feel, you have to do everything you can to keep living, even if all you can do for the moment is to breathe. Wait it out and occupy the time of waiting as fully as you possibly can. That's my big piece of advice to depressed people. Hold on to time; don't wish your life away. Even the minutes when you feel you are going to explode are minutes of your life, and you will never get those minutes again.

We believe in the chemistry of depression with a stunning fanaticism. In trying to tease out depression from the person who is depressed, we throw ourselves into the age-old debate about the boundary between the essential and the manufactured. In trying to separate the depression from the person and the treatment from the person, we deconstruct the person into nothingness. "Human life," writes Thomas Nagel in *The Possibility of Altruism*, "consists not primarily in the passive reception of stimuli, pleasant or unpleasant, satisfying or dissatisfying; it consists to a significant degree in activities and pursuits. A person must live his own life; others are not in a position to live it for him, nor is he in a position to live theirs." What is natural, or authentic? One would do better to seek the philosopher's stone or the fountain of youth than to seek the true chemistry of emotion, morality, pain, belief, and righteousness.

This is not a new problem. In Shakespeare's late play *The Winter's Tale*, Perdita and Polixenes debate the limits of the real and the artificial—the authentic and the created—in a garden. Perdita questions the grafting of plants as "an art which . . . shares / With great creating Nature." Polixenes replies:

> Yet Nature is made better by no mean
> But Nature makes that mean. So, over that art
> Which you say adds to Nature, is an art
> That Nature makes. You see, sweet maid. . . . This is an art
> Which does mend Nature—change it rather, but
> The art itself is Nature.

I am so glad that we have figured out all our ways to impose art on nature: that we have thought to cook our food and to combine ingredients from five continents on a single plate; that we have bred our modern breeds of dogs and horses; that we have forged metal from its ore; that we have crossed wild fruits to make peaches and apples as we know them today. I am glad too that we have figured out how to make central heating and indoor plumbing, how to build great buildings, ships, airplanes. I am thrilled by means of rapid communication; I'm embarrassingly reliant on the telephone and fax and E-mail. I am glad that we have invented technologies to preserve our teeth from decay, to keep our bodies from certain illnesses, to purchase old age for so large a part of our population. I do not deny that there have been adverse consequences of all this art, up to and including pollution and global warming; overpopulation; war and weapons of mass destruction. But on balance, our art has led us forward, and as we have adjusted to each new development, it has come to seem quite commonplace. We have forgotten that the many-petaled roses we love so much were once an ignominious challenge to nature, which had produced no such flower in the woods of the world until horticulturists meddled. Was it nature or art when the beaver first built his dam, or when monkeys with opposable thumbs peeled bananas? Does the fact that God made grapes that ferment into an intoxicant make drunkenness somehow a natural state? Are we no longer ourselves when we are drunk? When we are hungry, or overfed? Then who are we?

If grafting was the epitome of the seventeenth century's assault on nature, antidepressants and the genetic manipulation that will become ever more possible are the epitome of the twenty-first century's assault on nature. The selfsame principles articulated four hundred years ago apply to our newer technologies, which seem similarly to revise the natural order of things. If humanity is of nature, then so are our inventions. Whatever original life force made the first amoebas also made a human brain that could be affected by chemicals and made human beings who could ultimately figure out what chemicals to synthesize and to what effect. When we mend nature, or change it, we do so with techniques that are available to us through our particular combination of ideas from the natural world. Who is the real me? The real me is a person who lives in a world in which all kinds of manipulations are possible, and who has accepted certain of these manipulations. That is who I am. The ailing me is not a more or less authentic self; the therapized me is not a more or less authentic self.

Being good is a constant struggle. Perhaps my friend's fiancé had no choice but to behave like a jerk; perhaps he had moral turpitude hard-wired in his brain. Perhaps the husband of my other friend was born

431

cruel. I don't think it's quite so simple. I think that all of us have from nature a thing called will; I reject the notion of chemical predestination, and I reject the moral loophole it creates. There is a unity that includes who we are and how we strive to be good people and how we go to pieces and how we put ourselves back together again. It includes taking medication and getting electroshock and falling in love and worshiping gods and sciences. Angel Starkey, with a steely optimism, went out to give presentations in public on life in Norristown Hospital. With infinite blighted tenderness, she spent untold hours trying to teach her room-mate how to peel a cucumber. She took the time to write down her thoughts for me so that she could help me with this book. She scrubs her mother's house from top to bottom. The depression affects her func-tioning, but not her character.

One would like to demarcate clearly the boundaries of the self. In fact, no essential self lies pure as a vein of gold under the chaos of experience and chemistry. The human organism is a sequence of selves that suc-cumb to or choose one another. We are each the sum of certain choices and circumstances; the self exists in the narrow space where the world and our choices come together. I think of my father, or of the friends who came to stay with me through my third depression. Would it be possible to go into a doctor's office and have treatments and emerge capable of such generosity and love? Generosity and love demand great expenditure of energy and effort and will. Do we imagine that someday these quali-ties will be available for free, that we will be getting injections of char-acter, to make each of us effortlessly into so many Gandhis and Mother Teresas? Do the remarkable people have a right to their own splendor or is splendor too just a random chemical construction?

I read the science sections of newspapers hopefully. Antidepressants will give way to other magical potions. It is no longer inconceivable that we will map brain chemistry and be able to give someone a treat-ment that will cause him to fall madly in love with an appointed other under appointed circumstances. It is not so long until you will be able to choose between getting a talking cure for a bad marriage and having your infatuation renewed through the intervention of a pharmacologist. What will it be like if we unlock the secrets of aging and the secrets of all our failings and breed a race of gods instead of men, of beings who live for-ever free from malice and anger and jealousy, who act with moral fervor and practice passionate commitment to the ideal of universal peace? Perhaps all of this will happen, but in my experience, all the medicine in the world can provide no more than a way for you to reinvent yourself. The medicine will not reinvent you. We can never escape from choice itself. One's self lies in the choosing, every choice, every day. I am the one who chooses to take my medication twice a day. I am the one who chooses to talk to my father. I am the one who chooses to call my brother, and the one who chooses to own a dog, and the one who chooses to get out of bed (or not) when the alarm goes off, and the one who is also sometimes cruel and sometimes self-involved and often forgetful. There is a chemistry behind my writing of this book, and perhaps if I could master that chemistry, I could harness it to write another book, but that too would be a choice. Thinking seems to me less persuasive evidence of being than does choosing. Not in our chemistry and not in circumstance does our humanity lie, but in our will to work with the technologies available to us through the era in which we live, through our own character, through our circumstances and age.

Sometimes I wish I could see my brain. I'd like to know what marks have been carved in it. I imagine it grey, damp, elaborate. I think of it sitting in my head, and sometimes I feel as if there's me, who is living life, and this strange thing stuck in my head that sometimes works and sometimes doesn't. It's very odd. This is me. This is my brain. This is the pain that lives in my brain. Look here and you can see where the pain scratched this thing, what places are knotty and lumped up, which places are glowing.

It is arguably the case that depressed people have a more accurate view of the world around them than do nondepressed people. Those who perceive themselves to be not much liked are probably closer to the mark than those who believe that they enjoy universal love. A depressive may have better judgment than a healthy person. Studies have shown that depressed and nondepressed people are equally good at answering abstract questions. When asked, however, about their control over an event, nondepressed people invariably believe themselves to have more control than they really have, and depressed people give an accurate assessment. In a study done with a video game, depressed people who played for half an hour knew just how many little monsters they had killed; the undepressed people guessed four to six times more than they had actually hit. Freud observed that the melancholic has "a keener eye for the truth than others who are not melancholic." Perfectly accurate understanding of the world and the self was not an evolutionary priority; it did not serve the purpose of species preservation. Too optimistic a view results in foolish risk-taking, but moderate optimism is a strong selective advantage. "Normal human thought and perception," wrote Shelley E. Taylor in her recent, startling *Positive Illusions*, "is marked not by accuracy but positive self-enhancing illusions about the self, the world, and the future. Moreover, these illusions appear actually to be adaptive, promoting rather than undermining mental health. . . . The mildly depressed appear to have more accurate views of themselves, the world, and the future than do normal people . . . [they] clearly lack the illusions that in normal people promote mental health and buffer them against setbacks."

The fact of the matter is that existentialism is as true as depressiveness. Life is futile. We cannot know why we are here. Love is always imperfect. The isolation of bodily individuality can never be broached. No matter what you do on this earth, you will die. It is a selective advantage to be able to tolerate these realities, to look to other things, and to go on— to strive, to seek, to find, and not to yield. I watch footage of Tutsis in Rwanda or of starving hordes in Bangladesh: people who have, in many instances, lost all family and everyone they ever knew, who have no financial prospects of any kind, who are unable to find food, and who suffer from painful ailments. They are people for whom there is almost no prospect of improvement. And yet they go on living! Theirs is either a vital blindness that makes them keep up the battle of existence or a vision that is beyond me. Depressives have seen the world too clearly, have lost the selective advantage of blindness.

Major depression is far too stern a teacher: you needn't go to the Sahara to avoid frostbite. Most of the psychological pain in the world is unnecessary; and certainly people with major depression experience pain that would be better kept in check. I believe, however, that there is an answer to the question of whether we want total control over our emotional states, a perfect emotional painkiller that would make sorrow as unnecessary as a headache. To put an end to grief would be to license monstrous behavior: if we never regretted the consequences of our actions, we would soon destroy one another and the world. Depression is a misfiring of the brain, and if your cortisol is out of control you should get it back in order. But don't get carried away. To give up the essential conflict between what we feel like doing and what we do, to end the dark moods that reflect that conflict and its difficulties—this is to give up what it is to be human, of what is good in being human. There are probably people who don't have enough anxiety and sadness to keep them out of trouble, and it seems likely that they don't do well. They are too cheerful, too fearless, and they are not kind. What need have such souls of kindness?

People who have been through a depression and are stabilized often have a heightened awareness of the joyfulness of everyday existence. They have a capacity for a kind of ready ecstasy and for an intense appreciation of all that is good in their life. If they were decent people in the first place, they may well have become remarkably generous. The same might be said of survivors of other illnesses, but even someone who has miraculously emerged from the worst cancer does not have the meta-joy, the joy in being able to experience or give joy, that enriches the lives of those who have been through major depression. This idea is elaborated in Emmy Gut's book *Productive and Unproductive Depression,* which proposes that the long pause that a depression forces, and the rumination that goes on during that pause, often cause people to change their lives in useful ways, especially after a loss.

Our norm as human beings is not reality. What does it mean to develop medications and techniques that mitigate depression and that might ultimately affect even sadness? "We can now control physical pain much of the time," the evolutionary psychologist Randolph Nesse observes, "and how much of the physical pain that we experience do we really need? Maybe five percent? We need the pain that alerts us to injury, but do we really need persisting pain? Ask someone with chronic rheumatoid arthritis or colitis or migraine headaches! So this is only an analogy, but how much of the psychological pain we experience do we really need? More than five percent? What would it mean if you could take a morning-after pill the day after your mother died and be free of the agonizing and unproductive anguish of grief?" The French psychiatrist Julia Kristeva found a deep psychological function for depression. "The sadness that overwhelms us, the retardation that paralyzes us, are also a shield—sometimes the last one—against madness." Perhaps it is easier to say simply that we rely on our sorrows, more than we know.

The use of antidepressants is going up as people seek to normalize what is newly classed as aberrant, "popularizing and trivializing," as Martha Manning, who has written eloquently about her extreme depression, points out. More than 60 million prescriptions were written for the SSRIs in 1998—not to mention a substantial number for non-SSRI antidepressants. SSRIs are now prescribed for homesickness, for eating disorders, for PMS, for household pets who scratch too much, for chronic joint pain, and most of all, for mild sadness and ordinary grief. They are prescribed not only by psychiatrists but also by GPs, by OB-GYNs; someone I met had been put on Prozac by his podiatrist. When TWA flight 800 went down, families waiting for news of their loved ones were offered antidepressant drugs with the same palliative expression with which they might have been offered extra pillows or blankets. I have no argument with this broad use, but I think it should be done knowingly, deliberately, reflectively.

It has been said that everyone has the virtues of his flaws. If one eliminates the flaws, do the virtues go as well? "We are only at the dawn of pharmacological exuberance," Randolph Nesse says. "New medications that are being developed may likely make it quick, easy, cheap, and safe to block many unwanted emotions. We should be there within the next generation. And I predict we'll go for it, because if people can make themselves feel better, they usually do. I could imagine the world in a few decades being a pharmacological utopia; I can equally easily imagine people so mellowed out that they neglect all their social and personal responsibilities." Robert Klitzman of Columbia University says, "Not since Copernicus have we faced so dramatic a transformation. In centuries to come, there may be new societies that look back at us as creatures that were slaves to and crippled by uncontrolled emotions." If so, much will be lost; much will doubtless be gained.

When you have been depressed, you lose some of your fear of crisis. I have a million faults, but I am a better person than I was before I went through all this. I needed to have been depressed before I could want to write this book. Some friends tried to discourage me from entering relationships with the people about whom I was writing. I'd like to say that depression made me selfless and that I came to love the poor and the downtrodden, but that is not quite what happened. If you have been through such a thing, you cannot watch it unfold in the life of someone else without feeling horrified. It is easier for me, in many ways, to plunge myself into the sorrow of others than it is for me to watch that sorrow and stay out of it. I hate the feeling of being unable to reach people. Virtue is not necessarily its own reward, but there is a certain peace in loving someone that does not exist in distancing yourself from someone. When I watch the suffering of depressed people, it makes me itch. I think I can help. Not interfering is like watching someone spilling good wine all over the dinner table. It is easier to turn the bottle upright and wipe up the puddle than it is to ignore what is going on.

Depression at its worst is the most horrifying loneliness, and from it I learned the value of intimacy. When my mother was battling cancer, she once said, "Everything people do for me is wonderful, but it is still so awful to be alone in this body that has turned against me." It is at least as awful to be alone in a mind that has gone against you. What can you do when you see someone else trapped in his mind? You cannot draw a depressed person out of his misery with love (though you can sometimes distract a depressed person). You can, sometimes, manage to join someone in the place where he resides. It is not pleasant to sit still in the darkness of another person's mind, though it is almost worse to watch the decay of the mind from outside. You can fret from a distance, or you can come close and closer and closest. Sometimes the way to be close is to be silent, or even distant. It is not up to you, from the outside, to decide; it is up to you to discern. Depression is lonely above all else, but it can breed the opposite of loneliness. I love more and am loved more because of my depression, and I can say the same for many of the people I saw for this book. So many people have asked me what to do for depressed friends and relatives, and my answer is actually simple: blunt their isolation. Do it with cups of tea or with long talks or by sitting in a room nearby and staying silent or in whatever way suits the circumstances, but do that. And do it willingly.

Maggie Robbins, who has had such struggles with manic-depressive illness, said, "I used to get nervous a lot and I would just talk and talk. And then I started volunteering at an AIDS residence. They had teas there, and I was supposed to help get the tea and cake and juice for the patients, and to sit with them and chat, because many of them didn't have people to visit them and were lonely. I remember one day early on I sat down with some people and tried to kick off a conversation by asking them what they'd done for their Fourth of July. They told me, but they just weren't keeping up their end of the conversation at all. I thought, this is not very friendly or helpful of them. And then it hit me: these guys aren't going to make small talk. In fact, after those first, brief answers, they weren't going to talk at all. But they didn't want me to leave. So I decided, I'm here with them and I'm going to be with them. It's simply going to be an occasion where I'm a person who doesn't have AIDS and doesn't look really sick and isn't dying, but who can tolerate the fact that they do and they are. And so I just stayed with them that afternoon, without talking. The loving is that you are there, simply paying attention, unconditionally. If suffering is what the person is doing right then, that's what they're doing. You're being with that—not trying like crazy to do something about it. I've learned how to do that."

The survivors stay on pills, waiting. Some are in psychodynamic therapy. Some are receiving ECT, or having surgery. We go on. You cannot choose whether you get depressed and you cannot choose when or how you get better, but you can choose what to do with the depression, especially when you come out of it. Some people come out for a short time and know they are going to keep going back in. But when they are out, they try to use their experience of depression to make their life richer and better. For others, depression is just a total misery; they never get anything out of it at all. People who are depressed may do well to seek ways that the experience, after the fact, can lead to wisdom. In *Daniel Deronda*, George Eliot describes the moment when depression turns, the miraculous sensation of it. Mirah has been ready to kill herself and has let herself be saved by Daniel. She says, "But then in the last moment—yesterday, when I longed for the water to close over me—and I thought that death was the best image of mercy—then goodness came to me living, and I felt trust in the living." Goodness does not come living to those whose lives are utterly placid.

When I had the third breakdown, the mini-breakdown, I was in the late stages of writing this book. Since I could not cope with communication of any kind during that period, I put an auto-response message on my E-mail that said I was temporarily unreachable, and a similar message on my answering machine. Acquaintances who had suffered depression knew what to make of these outgoing messages. They wasted no time. I had dozens and dozens of calls from people offering whatever they could offer and doing it glowingly. "I will come to stay the minute you call," wrote Laura Anderson, who also sent a wild profusion of orchids, "and I'll stay as long as it takes you to get better. If you'd prefer, you are of course always welcome here; if you need to move in for a year, I'll be here for you. I hope you know that I will always be here for you." Claudia Weaver wrote with questions: "Is it better for you to have someone check in with you every day or are the messages too much of a burden? If they are a burden, you needn't answer this one, but whatever you need—just call me, anytime, day or night." Angel Starkey called often from the pay phone at her hospital to see if I was okay. "I don't know what you need," she said, "but I'm worrying about you all the time. Please take care of yourself. Come and see me if you're feeling really bad, anytime. I'd really like to see you. If you need anything, I'll try to get it for you. Promise me you won't hurt yourself." Frank Rusakoff wrote me a remarkable letter and reminded me about the precious quality of hope. "I long for news that you are well and off on another adventure," he wrote, and signed the letter, "Your friend, Frank." I had felt committed in many ways to all these people, but the spontaneous outpouring astounded me. Tina Sonego said she'd call in sick for work if I needed her—or that she'd buy me a ticket and take me to someplace relaxing. "I'm a good cook too," she told me. Janet Benshoof dropped by the house with daffodils and optimistic lines from favorite poems written in her clear hand and a bag so she could come sleep on my sofa, just so I wouldn't be alone. It was an astonishing responsiveness.

Even in the most desperate plea of the depressive—"Why?" or "Why me?"—lie the seeds of self-examination, a process that is usually fruitful. Emily Dickinson speaks of "that White Sustenance—Despair," and depression can indeed justify and support a life. The unexamined life is unavailable to the depressed. That is, perhaps, the greatest revelation I have had: not that depression is compelling but that the people who suffer from it may become compelling because of it. I hope that this basic fact will offer sustenance to those who suffer and will inspire patience and love in those who witness that suffering. Like Angel, I have a mission to bring the cure of self-regard to those who do not have it. I hope that they will perhaps learn not only hope, but also some love of themselves from the stories in this book.

There is great value in specific kinds of adversity. None of us would choose to learn this way: difficulty is unpleasant. I crave the easy life and would make and have made considerable compromises in my quest for it. But I have found that there are things to be made of this lot I have in life, that there are values to be found in it, at least when one is not in its most acute grip.

John Milton spoke in *Areopagitica* of the impossibility of appreciating good without knowing evil. "That virtue therefore which is but a youngling in the contemplation of evil, and knows not the utmost that vice promises to her followers, and rejects it, is but a blank virtue, not a pure; her whiteness is but an excremental whiteness." So the greatest knowledge of sorrow becomes the basis for a full appreciation of joy; so it intensifies that joy itself. Thirty years later, it was a wiser Milton who wrote in *Paradise Lost* of the wisdom that came to Adam and Eve after the fall when they learned the full spectrum of humanity:

> . . . since our eyes
> Opened we find indeed, and find we know
> Both good and evil, good lost and evil got,
> Bad fruit of knowledge.

There is some knowledge that, for all that it teaches, it would be better not to gain. Depression not only teaches a great deal about joy, but also obliterates joy. It is the bad fruit of knowledge, a knowledge I would prefer never to have contracted. Once one is given knowledge, however, one can seek redemption. Adam and Eve found:

> Strength added from above, new hope to spring
> Out of despair, joy.

And armed with this new, other human kind of joy, they set out to lead their short, sweet lives:

> They looking back, all th'Eastern side beheld
> Of Paradise, so late thir happy seat
> . . . .
> Some natural tears they dropp'd, but wip'd them soon;
> The World was all before them, where to choose

Thir place of rest, and Providence their guide:
They hand in hand with wand'ring steps and slow,
Through Eden took thir solitary way.

So lies the world before us, and with just such steps we tread a solitary way, survivors as we must be of an impoverishing, invaluable knowledge. We go forward with courage and with too much wisdom but determined to find what is beautiful. It is Dostoyevsky who said, "Beauty, though, will save the world." That moment of return from the realm of sad belief is always miraculous and can be stupefyingly beautiful. It is nearly worth the voyage out into despair. None of us would have chosen depression out of heaven's grab bag of qualities, but having been given it, those of us who have survived stand to find something in it. It is who we are. Heidegger believed that anguish was the origin of thought; Schelling thought that it was the essence of human freedom. Julia Kristeva bows before it: "I owe a supreme, metaphysical lucidity to my depression. . . . Refinement in sorrow or mourning are the imprint of a humankind that is surely not triumphant but subtle, ready to fight, and creative."

I take my mental temperature often. I have changed my sleeping habits. I give up on things more readily. I am more tolerant of other people. I am more determined not to waste the happy time I can find. A thinner and finer thing has happened to my self; it won't take the kind of punching that it used to take, and little windows go right through it, but there are also passages that are fine and delicate and luminous as egg. To regret my depression now would be to regret the most fundamental part of myself. I take umbrage too easily and too frequently, and I impose my vulnerabilities on others far too readily, but I think I am also more generous to other people than I used to be.

"The house gets messy," one woman who has battled depression for a lifetime told me, "and I can't read. When's it going to come back? When's it going to hit me again? Only my children keep me alive. I'm stabilized right now, but it never leaves you. You can never forget it, no matter how happy you are in a particular moment."

"I'm reconciled to a lifetime of medicine," says Martha Manning, suddenly fervent in a conversation. "And I'm thankful. I'm thankful for it. Sometimes I look at those pills and wonder, is this all that stands between torment and me? When I was little, I can remember, I wasn't unhappy, but I couldn't help thinking, I have to live my whole life, maybe eighty years of this or something. It seemed like such a burden. I wanted to have another child recently, but after two miscarriages, I realized I just couldn't bear the stress. I've cut back on my social life. You don't defeat depression. You learn to manage it and you make compromises with it. You try to stay in remission. You've got to have so much resolve, spend so much time not giving in. When you come so close to taking your life, if you get it back, you'd better claim it, you know?"

Striving to claim it, we hold on to the idea of productive depression, something vital. "If I had it to do over, I wouldn't do it this way," said Frank Rusakoff a few months after his brain had been lesioned to effect his cure. I had spent the afternoon with him and his parents and his psychiatrist, and they were discussing the grim reality: that his cingulotomy hadn't yet worked, and that he might have to have a second surgery. In his gently courageous way, however, he was making plans to be back up and running in six months. "But I think I have gained a lot and grown a lot because of it. I've become a lot closer to my parents, to my brother, to friends. I have this experience with my doctor that's been very good." The hard-won equanimity rang movingly true. "There really are up sides to depression; it's just hard to see them when you're in it." Later, after the surgery had worked, he wrote, "I said I would do it differently if I had it to do over again. And I guess I would. But, now that I feel like the worst is over, I'm grateful for having been where I've been. I do believe I am better off having been to the hospital thirty times and having had brain surgery. I've met a lot of good people along the way."

"I lost a great innocence when I understood that I and my mind were not going to be on good terms for the rest of my life," says Kay Jamison with a shrug. "I can't tell you how tired I am of character-building experiences. But I treasure this part of me; whoever loves me loves me with this in it."

"My wife, to whom I've been married just a few years, has never seen me depressed," says Robert Boorstin. "She hasn't. And I've walked her through it, and I've let other people talk to her about what it's like. I've done my best to prepare her, because doubtless I'll have another depression. Sometime, in the next forty years, I'm going to be crawling across the room again. And it scares me a lot. If somebody said to me, 'I'll take away your mental illness if you'll cut me off your leg'—I don't know what I would do. And yet, before I was ill, I was intolerant beyond comparison, arrogant beyond belief, with no understanding of frailty. I'm a better person as a result of having been through all this."

"The most important theme in my work is redemption," Bill Stein says. "I still don't know my role in things. I'm drawn to stories of saints and martyrs. I don't think I could endure what they have gone through. I'm not ready to set up a hospice in India, but depression put me on the right course. I meet people and I know that they don't have the level of experience that I have. The fact that I got through such a catastrophic illness has permanently changed my interior landscape. I was always drawn to faith and goodness, but I wouldn't have had the drive, the moral purpose, without the breakdowns."

"We walked through hell to find paradise," Tina Sonego says. "My reward is very simple. I am now able to understand things that I just could not understand before; and the things I don't understand now, I will in time, if they matter. Depression is responsible for making me who I am today. What we gain is so quiet but so loud."

"Our needs are our greatest assets," Maggie Robbins says. If it is through our needs that we come to know ourselves, that we open ourselves up to others, then neediness can breed intimacy. "I am able to just be there with people because of the stuff I've needed from people. I guess I've learned to give all the things I need."

"Mood is—another frontier, like deep ocean or deep space," Claudia Weaver says. "Having so much low mood gives you mettle; I think I deal with difficult losses better than most other people because I have so much experience of the feelings they entail. Depression isn't an obstacle in my path; it's a sort of part of me that I carry along down the path, and I believe that it's supposed to help me at various points. How? That I don't know. But I believe in my depression, in its redemptive power, nonetheless. I'm a very strong woman, and that's partly because of the depression."

And Laura Anderson wrote, "Depression has given me kindness and forgiveness where other people don't know enough to extend it—I am drawn toward people who might put off others with a wrong move or a misplaced barb or an overtly nonsensical judgment. I had an argument about the death penalty tonight with someone, and I was trying to explain, without being too self-referential, that one can understand horrifying actions—understand the terrible links between mood and job and relationships and the rest of everything. I would never want depression to be a public or political excuse, but I think that once you have gone through it, you get a greater and more immediate understanding of the temporary absence of judgment that makes people behave so badly—you learn even, perhaps, how to tolerate the evil in the world."

On the happy day when we lose depression, we will lose a great deal with it. If the earth could feed itself and us without rain, and if we conquered the weather and declared permanent sun, would we not miss grey days and summer storms? As the sun seems brighter and more clear when it comes on a rare day of English summer after ten months of dismal skies than it can ever seem in the tropics, so recent happiness feels enormous and embracing and beyond anything I have ever imagined. Curiously enough, I love my depression. I do not love experiencing my depression, but I love the depression itself. I love who I am in the wake of it. Schopenhauer said, "Man is [content] according to how dull and insensitive he is"; Tennessee Williams, asked for the definition of happiness, replied "insensitivity." I do not agree with them. Since I have been to the Gulag and survived it, I know that if I have to go to the Gulag again, I could survive that also; I'm more confident in some odd way than I've ever imagined being. This almost (but not quite) makes the depression seem worth it. I do not think that I will ever again try to kill myself; nor do I think that I would give up my life readily if I found myself in war, or if my plane crashed into a desert. I would struggle tooth and nail to survive. It's as though my life and I, having sat in opposition to each other, hating each other, wanting to escape each other, have now bonded forever and at the hip.

The opposite of depression is not happiness but vitality, and my life, as I write this, is vital, even when sad. I may wake up sometime next year without my mind again; it is not likely to stick around all the time. Meanwhile, however, I have discovered what I would have to call a soul, a part of myself I could never have imagined until one day, seven years ago, when hell came to pay me a surprise visit. It's a precious discovery. Almost every day I feel momentary flashes of hopelessness and wonder every time whether I am slipping. For a petrifying instant here and there, a lightning-quick flash, I want a car to run me over and I have to grit my teeth to stay on the sidewalk until the light turns green; or I imagine how easily I might cut my wrists; or I taste hungrily the metal tip of a gun in my mouth; or I picture going to sleep and never waking up again. I hate those feelings, but I know that they have driven me to look deeper at life, to find and cling to reasons for living. I cannot find it in me to regret entirely the course my life has taken. Every day, I choose, sometimes gamely and sometimes against the moment's reason, to be alive. Is that not a rare joy?

Notes

Many excellent general books on depression have influenced this book. Among these, I would particularly commend Peter Whybrow's dignified and accessible *A Mood Apart*, Kay Redfield Jamison's moving *An Unquiet Mind* and *Night Falls Fast*, Julia Kristeva's impenetrable but episodically brilliant *Black Sun*, Rudolph and Margot Wittkower's *Born Under Saturn*, and Stanley Jackson's rigorous *Melancholia and Depression*. I have identified all direct quotations from printed sources. All other quotations are from personal interviews conducted between 1995 and 2000.

9　The epigraph is from the closing paragraph of Mikhail Bulgakov's *The White Guard*, page 302.

A Note on Method

11　The *New Yorker* article appeared as "Anatomy of Melancholy" in the issue of January 12, 1998.

12　The quotation from Graham Greene comes from his *Ways of Escape*, page 285.

13　My father's company is Forest Laboratories. The company was not involved in the development of Celexa, though they have worked on producing its enantiomer.

13　The novel to which I allude is *A Stone Boat*.

13　Kay Redfield Jamison, Martha Manning, and Meri Danquah are among the authors who have discussed the toxicity of this subject matter.

Chapter I: Depression

15　The words *depression* and *melancholy* are grossly general and, despite the efforts of some authors to distinguish between them, are synonymous. The term *major depression*, however, refers to the psychiatric condition defined under the rubric "Major Depressive Disorder" in *DSM-IV*, pages 339–45.

16　I have taken the story of Saint Anthony in the desert from a lecture by Elaine Pagels.

16　The first quotation from *Jacob's Room* is on pages 140–41. The second is on page 168.

17　For a discussion of "legally dead," see Sherwin Nuland's *How We Die*, page 123.

19　Anhedonia is "the inability to experience pleasure," as defined by Francis Mondimore in *Depression: The Mood Disease*, page 22.

21   The depression formula comes from the 1989 edition of the *Comprehensive Textbook of Psychiatry,* page 870.

24   Both quotations come from Schopenhauer's *Essays and Aphorisms:* the first is on pages 42–43; the second is on page 43.

25   The number 19 million comes from the NIMH's Web site at www.nimh.nih.gov/depression/index1.htm. That approximately 2.5 million children suffer depression may be adduced through the compilation of a number of statistics. "The MECA Study," by D. Shaffer et al., in the *Journal of the American Academy of Child and Adolescent Psychiatry* 35, no. 7 (1996), found that approximately 6.2 percent of children age nine to seventeen had a mood disorder within a six-month period, and that 4.9 percent suffered a major depressive disorder. This latter percentage, applied to 1990 census statistics for children age five to seventeen (roughly 45 million) equals a rough estimate of 2.5 million. I thank Faith Bitterolf and the Sewickley Academy Library for their help with this matter.

25   The number 2.3 million comes from the NIMH's Web site at www.nimh.nih.gov/publicat/manic.cfm.

25   That unipolar depression is the leading cause of disability in the United States and worldwide for persons age five and up is taken from the NIMH Web site at www.nimh.nih.gov/publicat/invisible.cfm. The statistic ranking major depression as second in magnitude of disease burden in the developed world also comes from the NIMH at www.nimh.nih.gov/publicat/burden.cfm.

25   That depression claims more years than war, cancer, and HIV/AIDS put together is taken from the World Health Organization's *World Health Report 2000,* which can be viewed on-line at www.who.int/whr/2000/index.htm. The information is taken from Annex Table 4, and is valid for lung cancer and skin cancer, in some mortality strata in the Americas and Eastern Mediterranean, and in all mortality strata in Europe, Southeast Asia, and the Western Pacific. For Annex Table 4 specifically, see www.who.int/whr/2000/en/statistics.htm.

25   The idea that somatic illness masks depression is a commonplace. Jeffrey De Wester, in his article "Recognizing and Treating the Patient with Somatic Manifestations of Depression," *Journal of Family Practice* 43, suppl. 6 (1996), writes that while "it has been estimated that 77 percent of all mental health visits in the United States occur in a primary care physician's office . . . less than 20 percent of these patients complain of psychological symptoms or distress," page S4. Elizabeth McCauley et al., in "The Role of Somatic Complaints in the Diagnosis of Depression in Children and Adolescents," *Journal of the American Academy of Child and Adolescent Psychiatry* 30, no. 4 (1991), write that "somatization has been well documented as one way in which depression presents itself, especially in those individuals and/or cultures in which acknowledgment and expression of affect states is not acceptable," page 631. For more, see also Remi Cadoret et al., "Somatic Complaints," *Journal of Affective Disorders* 2 (1980).

25   The percentages given here may be found in D. A. Regier et al., "The de facto mental and addictive disorders service system. Epidemiologic Catchment Area prospective 1-year prevalence rates of disorders and services," *Archives of General Psychiatry* 50, no. 2 (1993). The study states, "Those with Major Unipolar Depression had an intermediate rate of mental health service use, in which almost half (49%) had some professional care, with 27.8% using the [specialty mental health/addictive] sector and 25.3% [general medical] sector care," page 91.

25   That over 95 percent of the general population suffering from depression are

treated by general practitioners is stated in Jogin Thakore and David John, "Prescriptions of Antidepressants by General Practitioners: Recommendations by FHSAs and Health Boards," *British Journal of General Practice* 46 (1996).

25 That depression is recognized only 40 percent of the time for adults, and only 20 percent of the time for children was set out by Steven Hyman, the director of the National Institute of Mental Health (NIMH), in an oral interview on January 29, 1997.

25 The estimated number of people on Prozac and on the other SSRIs is taken from Joseph Glenmullen's *Prozac Backlash*, page 15.

25 The mortality rates for depression have been studied extensively and the results are not fully consistent. The figure of 15 percent was originally established by S. B. Guze and E. Robbins, "Suicide and affective disorders," *British Journal of Psychiatry* 117 (1970), and was confirmed by Frederick Goodwin and Kay Jamison in a comprehensive review of thirty studies included in their book *Manic-Depressive Illness* (see the chart on pages 152–53). The lower rates are based on the work of G. W. Blair-West, G. W. Mellsop, and M. L. Eyeson-Annan, "Down-rating lifetime suicide risk in major depression," *Acta Psychiatrica Scandinavica* 95 (1997). This study demonstrated that taking current estimates of depression levels and applying the 15 percent figure would give an overall number of suicides at least four times as high as is currently documented. Some recent researchers have proposed a figure of 6 percent, but this is based on a population sample that seems to contain a deceptively high number of people treated as inpatients (see H. M. Inskip, E. Clare Harris, and Brian Barraclough, "Lifetime risk of suicide for affective disorder, alcoholism, and schizophrenia," *British Journal of Psychiatry* 172 (1998). The most recent work is by J. M. Bostwick and S. Pancratz, "Affective disorders and suicide risk: a re-examination," *American Journal of Psychiatry* (in press). This work establishes a rate of 6 percent for those who have been hospitalized for depression, 4.1 percent for those who have had inpatient treatment, and 2 percent for those who have had no inpatient treatment. It should be emphasized that the statistical problems involved in these calculations are extremely complicated, and that different methods of calculating proportionate mortality have given varying rates, mostly higher than those established by Bostwick and Pancratz.

25 The comparative rates of cumulative depression were taken from the Cross-National Collaborative Group, "The Changing Rate of Major Depression," *Journal of the American Medical Association* 268, no. 21 (1992); see Figure 1, page 3100.

26 The notion that depression is occurring in a younger population is taken from D. A. Regier et al., "Comparing age at onset of major depression and other psychiatric disorders by birth cohorts in five U.S. community populations," *Archives of General Psychiatry* 48, no. 9 (1991).

26 For a particularly eloquent exegesis on the supermodel's negative effects on women, see *The Beauty Myth* by Naomi R. Wolf.

27 Herman Spitz's *The Raising of Intelligence* states, "On the Wechsler Intelligence Scales mild retardation is encompassed by IQs of 55 to 69, and on the Stanford-Binet Intelligence Scale by IQs of 52–67," page 4.

30 The pills I see in these colors are BuSpar and Zyprexa (white); Effexor immediate release (pink); Effexor sustained release (dark red); and Wellbutrin (turquoise).

31 That skin cancer rates are rising is indicated by numerous studies. H. Irene Ball et al., "Update on the incidence and mortality from melanoma in the United States," published in the *Journal of the American Academy of Dermatology* 40 (1999), states,

"Over the past few decades, melanoma has become much more common; its increase in both incidence and mortality rates have been among the largest of any cancer," page 35.

31 Hippocrates' views on depression are discussed at length in chapter 8.

33 The horrors of the Khmer Rouge are extensively documented. For a vivid reenaction of the atrocities, I would commend the film *The Killing Fields*.

38 The quotation from Ovid I have taken from Kay Jamison's *Night Falls Fast*, page 66.

CHAPTER II: BREAKDOWNS

44 The story of my life with the Russians is told in my first book, *The Irony Tower*, and in these subsequent articles for *The New York Times Magazine:* "Three Days in August," published September 29, 1991; "Artist of the Soviet Wreckage," published September 20, 1992; and "Young Russia's Defiant Decadence," published July 18, 1993.

44 The rock band in question was Middle Russian Elevation.

45 The quotation from Gerhard Richter may be found in his poetical diary, published as *The Daily Practice of Painting*, on page 122.

47 The article I was closing during my kidney stones was published in the August 28, 1994, edition of *The New York Times Magazine* as "Defiantly Deaf."

48 The idea of hypothalamic and cortical function coinciding has been put forward on many occasions and is explicated in Peter Whybrow's *A Mood Apart*, pages 153–65.

48 The percentages are based, in my view, on difficult and still uncertain science and therefore show wide discrepancies. I have, nonetheless, taken these statistics, which reflect the general consensus, from Eric Fombonne's essay "Depressive Disorders: Time Trends and Possible Explanatory Mechanisms," published in Michael Rutter and David J. Smith's *Psychosocial Disorders in Young People*, page 576.

48 I have not treated manic-depressive illness at great length; it is a topic that warrants books of its own. For a scholarly examination of the specifics of the disease, see Fred Goodwin and Kay Jamison's *Manic-Depressive Illness*.

52 The remarks by Julia Kristeva are from *Black Sun* and occur on page 53.

52 The Emily Dickinson poem, which is among my favorite poems ever in the whole history of the world, is in *The Complete Poems of Emily Dickinson*, pages 128–29.

53 The quotation from Daphne Merkin appeared in *The New Yorker*, January 8, 2001, page 37.

54 The Elizabeth Prince poem is unpublished.

55 The quotation from Leonard Woolf may be found in his book *Beginning Again*, on pages 163–64.

55 The catalog of what is going on during depression is drawn from multiple sources too numerous to list, as well as from countless interviews with doctors, clinicians, and specialists. For superb and vivid descriptions of the basics of the majority of these processes see Peter Whybrow's *A Mood Apart*, pages 150–67. The April 1999 edition of *Psychology Today* offers another summary of the biologies of depression. Charles Nemeroff's summary of the neurobiology of depression, found in the June 1998 *Scientific American*, also provides a more detailed, nonacademic discussion of many of the complex issues brought up here.

56 The idea that raising levels of TRH can be a useful treatment in depression, at least temporarily, is spelled out in Fred Goodwin and Kay Jamison's *Manic-Depressive Illness*, page 465.

56 There is now a large body of work to support the idea that depressions become more severe during a lifetime. I have discussed the matter in particular detail with Robert Post of the NIMH and John Greden of the University of Michigan.

56 The quotation from Kay Jamison is taken from *Night Falls Fast,* page 198.

56 The insight about seizures in the animal brain comes largely from the work of Suzanne Weiss and Robert Post. For information on the "kindling" phenomenon and its use as a model for affective disorders, see their coauthored article "Kindling: Separate vs. shared mechanisms in affective disorder and epilepsy," *Neuropsychology* 38, no. 3 (1998).

57 The information on the lesioning of monoamine systems in animal brains comes from Juan López et al., "Regulation of 5-HT Receptors and the Hypothalamic-Pituitary-Adrenal Axis: Implications for the neurobiology of suicide," *Annals of the New York Academy of Sciences* 836 (1997). On depression and the monoamine system and cortisol, see Juan López et al., "Neural circuits mediating stress," *Biological Psychiatry* 46 (1999).

57 This explanation of stress responses in depression is based on the work of Juan López and Elizabeth Young at the University of Michigan, and Ken Kendler at the Medical College of Virginia in Richmond. There are as many explanations of depression as there are stars in the night sky, but I think the Michigan scientists' stress-based model is particularly convincing.

58 For the study using ketoconazole on an experimental basis, see O. M. Wolkowitz et al., "Antiglucocorticoid treatment of depression: double-blind ketoconazole," *Biological Psychiatry* 45, no. 8 (1999).

58 The studies on baboons were done by Robert Sapolsky and described to me in an oral interview with Elizabeth Young. The work on air traffic controllers may be found in R. M. Rose et al., "Endocrine Activity in Air Traffic Controllers at Work. II. Biological, Psychological and Work Correlates," *Psychoneuroendocrinology* 7 (1982).

58 That the heart is weakened after a myocardial infarction is a well-established idea. However, the severity of damage done to the heart depends upon the size of the area of dead tissue within the heart. While the data indicate that isolation lesions don't necessarily put one at a higher rate of relapse than controls, diffuse coronary disease almost certainly does. Nonetheless, close attention must be paid to the heart condition of anyone who has experienced a heart attack, and therapies to prevent relapse are in order for such a person. I thank Dr. Joseph Hayes of Cornell for his assistance with this matter.

59 Juan López's work with the stress systems of rats may be found in Juan López et al., "Regulation of 5-HT1A Receptor, Glucocorticoid and Mineralocorticoid Receptor in Rat and Human Hippocampus: Implications for the Neurobiology of Depression," *Biological Psychiatry* 43 (1998). The work on cortisol levels and adrenal enlargement postsuicide is found in Juan López et al., "Regulation of 5-HT Receptors and the Hypothalamic-Pituitary-Adrenal Axis: Implications for the Neurobiology of Suicide," *Annals of the New York Academy of Sciences* 836 (1997).

60 Work on the effects of continued stress on the brain may be found in a number of articles, a large majority of them headed by Robert Sapolsky. For information on the brain's response to stress, see Robert Sapolsky et al., "Hippocampal damage associated with prolonged glucocorticoid exposure in primates," *Journal of Neuroscience* 10, no. 9 (1990). For studies concerning the interaction of biological stress and social status, see Robert Sapolsky, "Stress in the Wild," *Scientific American* 262,

no. 1 (1990), and his "Social subordinance as a marker of hypercortisolism: Some unexpected subtleties," *Annals of the New York Academy of Sciences* 771 (1995). Greden's discussion of the epidemiology of major depression is in Barbara Burns et al., "General Medical and Specialty Mental Health Service Use for Major Depression," *International Journal of Psychiatry in Medicine* 30, no. 2 (2000).

60 The literature on antidepressants is based primarily on short-term studies and indicates that antidepressants take effect within two to four weeks and reach optimal function within six weeks. My own experience suggests strongly that it takes many months to get the full results of these medications.

60 That 80 percent of patients respond to medication but only 50 percent to any particular medication is spelled out in Mary Whooley and Gregory Simon's "Managing Depression in Medical Outpatients," *New England Journal of Medicine* 343, no. 26 (2000).

61 The friend to whom I allude here is Dièry Prudent, whose story is told in chapter 5.

62 That the first episode of depression is highly related to life events, with recurrent episodes being less dependent on such events is an idea first espoused by Emil Kraepelin in *Manic-Depressive Insanity and Paranoia.* This idea has been studied rather extensively with great consistency in the findings. One of the most recent studies—Ken Kendler et al., "Stressful life events and previous episodes in the etiology of major depression in women: An evaluation of the 'kindling' hypothesis," *American Journal of Psychiatry* 157, no. 8 (2000)—reviews the literature on the subject, while finding in its own research "strong and consistent evidence for a negative interaction. That is, with each new previous depressive episode, the association between stressful life events and onsets of major depression became progressively weaker."

62 George Brown's work on the relationship between depression and loss is published in a variety of academic journals, a small selection of which are referenced in the bibliography. For a particularly good introduction to his work I would recommend his essay "Loss and Depressive Disorders," published in *Adversity, Stress and Psychopathology,* edited by B. P. Dohrenwend.

63 This important idea from Kay Jamison is nicely summed up in a line from her book on suicide, *Night Falls Fast:* "The absolute hopelessness of suicidal depression is, by its nature, contagious, and it renders those who would help impotent to do so," page 294.

65 Thomas Aquinas's remarks on fear occur in his *Summa theologiae* I-II, q. 25, a. 4, vol. 6, page 187. For a reliable English translation, see his *Summa Theologica: Complete English Edition in Five Volumes,* q. 25, a. 4, vol. 2, pages 702–3. I thank Dr. John F. Wippel and Dr. Kevin White from the Catholic University of America for help in locating, translating, and interpreting these passages.

65 The overlap among affective disorders, alcoholism, and genetics is extremely complicated. For an excellent summary of current positions, studies, and conclusions see Frederick Goodwin and Kay Jamison's "Alcohol and Drug Abuse in Manic-Depressive Illness," beginning on page 210 in their book *Manic-Depressive Illness.* I would also highly recommend David McDowell and Henry Spitz's *Substance Abuse* and Marc Galanter and Herbert Kleber's *Textbook of Substance Abuse Treatment.*

65 This statistic on anxiety disorder is taken from Stephen Hall, "Fear Itself," *New York Times Magazine,* February 28, 1999, page 45.

65 For a more in-depth discussion of anxiety and sleep, see T. A. Mellman and T. W.

Uhde, "Sleep and Panic and Generalized Anxiety Disorders," in *The Neurobiology of Panic Disorder,* edited by James Ballenger.

66 The quote from Sylvia Plath is from *The Bell Jar,* page 3.

66 The Jane Kenyon quotation comes from "Having It Out with Melancholy" in the volume *Constance,* page 25.

77 The quotation from Daniil Kharms comes from *Incidences,* page 4.

78 The quotation from Artaud is taken from the title of one of his drawings. See the Artaud catalog from the Museum of Modern Art exhibition *Antonin Artaud: Works on Paper,* 1996.

78 The quotation from F. Scott Fitzgerald's *The Great Gatsby* occurs on page 66.

79 The Jane Kenyon quotation comes from "Back" in the volume *Constance,* page 32.

85 The standard textbook on emergency medicine is titled *Emergency Medicine: Concepts and Clinical Practice,* 4th ed., 3 vols., edited by Peter Rosen et al.

CHAPTER III: TREATMENTS

101 The quotation from T. M. Luhrmann is in her remarkable book *Of Two Minds,* page 7.

102 For the Luhrmann quotation, see *Ibid.,* 290.

103 The quotation from *The Years* may be found on page 378.

103 Russ Newman, the executive director for professional practice at the American Psychological Association, writes in a letter to the editor of *U.S. News & World Report,* April 26, 1999, "The research has been quite clear that in many cases of depression the treatment of choice is really 'treatments of choice': a combination of psychotherapy and medication," page 8. A recent study has found similar results. See Martin Keller et al., "A comparison of nefazodone, the cognitive behavioral-analysis system of psychotherapy, and their combination for the treatment of chronic depression," *New England Journal of Medicine* 342, no. 20 (2000). For a summary of this study in the popular press, see Erica Goode, "Chronic-Depression Study Backs the Pairing of Therapy and Drugs," *New York Times,* May 18, 2000. Ellen Frank has done a number of studies comparing talking and pharmaceutical therapies with different specific populations. Her geriatric study entitled "Nortriptyline and interpersonal psychotherapy as maintenance therapies for recurrent major depression," *Journal of the American Medical Association* 281, no. 1 (1999), concludes, "Combined treatment using both [treatment strategies] appears to be the optimal clinical strategy in preserving recovery." Initial studies in this area, such as Gerald Klerman et al., "Treatment of depression by drugs and psychotherapy," *American Journal of Psychiatry* 131 (1974), and Myrna Weissman and Eugene Paykel, *The Depressed Woman: A Study of Social Relationships,* also point toward the improved efficacy of combination therapy.

107 The basic description of the methodology of CBT can be found in Beck's seminal work, *Depression.* Among more contemporary publications, see especially Mark Williams's *The Psychological Treatment of Depression,* 2nd edition.

107 The phrase "learned optimism" comes from Martin Seligman and is the title of his 1990 book.

109 The basic methodology of IPT is described thoroughly in Myrna Weissman, John Markowitz, and Gerald Klerman's *Comprehensive Guide to Interpersonal Psychotherapy.*

111 The study concerning professors as therapists is Hans Strupp and Suzanne Hadley, "Specific vs. nonspecific factors in psychotherapy: A controlled study of outcome," *Archives of General Psychiatry* 36, no. 10 (1979). They write, "The results

of this investigation were consistent and straightforward. Patients undergoing psychotherapy with college professors showed, on average, quantitatively as much improvement as patients treated by experienced professional psychotherapists," page 1134.

111 My discussion of the neurotransmitter levels of depressed people was garnered from books, articles, and interviews too numerous to mention. Many of these ideas, however, are elucidated clearly in Peter Whybrow's *A Mood Apart*.

111 For a discussion of tryptophan and depression, see T. Delgado et al., "Serotonin function and the mechanism of antidepressant action: Reversal of antidepressant by rapid depletion of plasma tryptophan," *Archives of General Psychiatry* 47 (1990), and K. Smith et al., "Relapse of Depression After Rapid Depletion of Tryptophan," *Lancet* 349 (1997).

112 For an excellent and insightful examination of serotonin's synthesis and function, see Peter Whybrow's *A Mood Apart*, pages 224–27.

112 Receptor theory is fully explicated in David Healy's exceptional book *The Antidepressant Era*, pages 161–63; 173–77.

112 The notion of indirect function for the drugs that effect neurotransmitters, and the problem of homeostasis, are discussed provocatively in Peter Whybrow's *A Mood Apart*, pages 150–67.

113 The effects of the SSRIs on REM sleep was described in Michael Thase's presentation, "Sleep and Depression," at APA 2000, the annual conference of the American Psychiatric Association, delivered on May 14, 2000, in Chicago. The effects of the SSRIs on brain temperature is part of the larger chemistry of depression. It has been noted that in depression the body's temperature, especially at night, is often elevated. However, this elevation is only relative; the body's temperature simply drops less at night in depression than it normally would. This higher nocturnal temperature in depression goes along with other measures of hyperarousal, such as insomnia. That antidepressants reduce this elevated temperature is probably good—a normalization, so to speak. Some of these points are discussed in a review chapter entitled "Biological Processes in Depression: An Updated Review and Integration," by Michael Thase and Robert Howland in *The Handbook of Depression*, edited by E. Edward Beckham and William Leber, pages 213–79.

113 Most of the information regarding animal studies, maternal separation, aggression, and altered neurobiology comes from the NIMH-sponsored "Suicide Research Workshop" held November 14–15, 1996. Much, however, has been published in this area in general. I would particularly recommend Gary Kraemer et al., "Rearing experience and biogenic amine activity in infant rhesus monkeys," *Biological Psychiatry* 40, no. 5 (1996), as an introduction to the topic.

113 There has been much work on maternal separations and cortisol. See Gayle Byrne and Stephen Suomi, "Social Separation in Infant *Cebus Apella*: Patterns of Behavioral and Cortisol Response," *International Journal of Developmental Neuroscience* 17, no. 3 (1999), and David Lyons et al., "Separation Induced Changes in Squirrel Monkey Hypothalamic-Pituitary-Adrenal Physiology Resemble Aspects of Hypercortisolism in Humans," *Psychoneuroendocrinology* 24 (1999). That antidepressants can alleviate this condition is explicated in Pavel Hrdina et al., "Pharmacological Modification of Experimental Depression in Infant Macaques," *Psychopharmacology* 64 (1979).

113 The work on dominant vervet monkeys is in Michael Raleigh et al., "Social and Environmental Influences on Blood Serotonin Concentrations in Monkeys,"

Archives of General Psychiatry 41 (1984). That raising serotonin will alleviate these problems is discussed in Michael Raleigh and Michael McGuire, "Bidirectional Relationships between Tryptophan and Social Behavior in Vervet Monkeys," *Advances in Experimental Medicine and Biology* 294 (1991), and Michael Raleigh et al., "Serotonergic Mechanisms Promote Dominance Acquisition in Adult Male Vervet Monkeys," *Brain Research* 559 (1991).

114 The work on animal risk-taking, aggression, and serotonin can be found in P. T. Mehlman et al., "Low CSF 5-HIAA Concentrations and Severe Aggression and Impaired Impulse Control in Nonhuman Primates," *American Journal of Psychiatry* 151 (1994).

114 The work on monkey rank and serotonin is reviewed in Michael McGuire and Alfonso Troisi's *Darwinian Psychiatry,* pages 93–94; 172–74.

114 The evidence that SSRIs can reverse patterns of aggression is in C. Sanchez et al., "The role of serotonergic mechanisms in inhibition of isolation-induced aggression in male mice," *Psychopharmacology* 110, no. 1–2 (1993).

115 There is some controversy regarding the frequency of side effects from many of the SSRIs, most notably Prozac. Most doctors and clinicians feel that the frequency of many of the side effects, especially reduced sexual drive and anorgasmia, was radically underestimated by the pharmaceutical companies in their initial testings.

115 The information from Anita Clayton is drawn from her presentation "Epidemiology, Classification, and Assessment of Sexual Dysfunction" delivered on May 13 at APA 2000 in Chicago.

116 The statistic on the discontinuation of antidepressants after six months comes from Dr. H. George Nurnberg's presentation "Management of Antidepressant-Associated Sexual Dysfunction" delivered on May 13 at APA 2000 in Chicago.

116 For this catalog of pro-sexual drugs, see *Ibid.*

117 For Viagra's effect on nocturnal penile tumescence, see *Ibid.*

117 For the idea of taking Viagra daily, see *Ibid.*

117 Dr. Andrew Nierenberg presented his research in "Prevalence and Assessment of Antidepressant-Associated Dysfunction"; Dr. Julia Warnock presented her research in "Hormonal Aspects of Sexual Dysfunction in Women: Improvement with Hormone Replacement Therapy." Both presentations were delivered on May 13 at APA 2000 in Chicago.

118 Considerable care must be taken in prescribing antidepressants of any kind to people with manic-depressive illness. In general, people with manic-depressive illness need to take a mood stabilizer—lithium or an anticonvulsant—with antidepressants.

119 I thank Dr. David McDowell of Columbia University for his discussion regarding the problem of benzodiazepine addiction.

120 Numbers concerning the efficacy of ECT vary: Peter Whybrow in his book *A Mood Apart* cites a rate of 85–90 percent, page 216; Francis Mondimore, in his book *Depression: The Mood Disease,* estimates a higher rate of over 90 percent, page 65. The numbers I have given reflect an approximate average of many published efficacy rates.

121 That right unilateral ECT is less impairing than, while just as effective as, bilateral ECT is reported in Harold Sackein et al., "A Prospective, Randomized, Double-Blind Comparison of Bilateral and Right Unilateral Electroconvulsive Therapy at Different Stimulus Intensities," *Archives of General Psychiatry* 57, no. 5 (2000).

They report that right unilateral ECT, when given at 500 percent of seizure threshold, is as effective as bilateral ECT, but causes less than one-sixth of the cognitive side effects of bilateral ECT.

122 For a general discussion of the methods of ECT, see Francis Mondimore's *Depression: The Mood Disease,* and Elliot Valenstein's *Great and Desperate Cures.*

122 The statistic on death from ECT-based complications comes from Stacey Pamela Patton, "Electrogirl," *Washington Post,* September 19, 1999.

122 The quotation from Richard Abrams comes from his book *Electroconvulsive Therapy,* page 75.

123 Manning described these pickets to me, which included groups of people organizing together and handing out leaflets against "electronic mind control." Opposition such as this took place at an event sponsored by a private Northampton, Massachusetts, bookstore, but held at the Smith College library.

125 The passage from the Unabomber, Ted Kaczynski, is taken from his manifesto. I would like to affirm that I admire his insights and deplore his methods.

133 Charlotte Brontë's words appear in Juliet Barker's *The Brontës,* page 599. I thank the artist Elaine Reichek for calling my attention to this passage.

CHAPTER IV: ALTERNATIVES

135 I have taken the Chekhov quotation from the epigraph to Jane Kenyon's poem "Having It Out with Melancholy," in the volume *Constance,* page 21.

137 There are many studies on exercise and depression: one of the most rigorous is J. A. Blumenthal et al., "Effects of exercise training on older patients with major depression," *Archives of Internal Medicine* 159 (1999).

138 An extremely accessible discussion of the role of diet in combating depression may be found in *The Food Doctor,* by Vicki Edgson and Ian Marber, pages 62–65.

139 The relationship of fish oil and omega-3 fatty acids to depressive symptoms is described in J. R. Calabrese et al., "Fish Oils and Bipolar Disorder," *Archives of General Psychiatry* 56 (1999).

139 TMS and rTMS have been plagued simultaneously by low efficacy rates and high rates of depressive relapse. For a general introduction to the process, theory, and method of TMS, see Eric Hollander, "TMS," *CNS Spectrums* 2, no. 1 (1997). For more specific academic and research-oriented information, see W. J. Triggs et al., "Effects of left frontal transcranial magnetic stimulation on depressed mood, cognition, and corticomotor threshold," *Biological Psychiatry* 45, no. 11 (1999), and Alvaro Pascual-Leone et al., "Rapid-rate transcranial magnetic stimulation of left dorsolateral prefrontal cortex in drug-resistant depression," *Lancet* 348 (1996).

140 Norman Rosenthal lays out his views on SAD in his book *Winter Blues.*

140 The figures on light levels under artificial and actual light can be adduced from Michael J. Norden's *Beyond Prozac: Brain Toxic Lifestyles, Natural Antidotes and New Generation Antidepressants,* page 36. Calculations were based on 300 lux for domestic interior lighting; 10,000 lux for new light boxes; and 100,000 lux for a sunny day.

140 The literature on EMDR is spotty, but the best book on the subject as it relates to depression is *Extending EMDR,* edited by Philip Manfield.

141 My treatments in Sedona were at the Enchantment Resort.

142 Callahan's interesting ideas appear, summarized, in Fred Gallo's *Energy Psychology.*

For Callahan's discussion of his techniques in reference to trauma, see Roger J. Callahan and Joanne Callahan, *Stop the Nightmares of Trauma: Thought Field Therapy.* I am not persuaded that his work has real clinical significance, though his modes of thinking are useful to people practicing more conventional therapies.

142 The passage from Kurt Hahn is from *Readings from the Hurricane Island Outward Bound School,* page 71, a wonderful commonplace book published by Hurricane Island Outward Bound and sold through its store, the School Locker.

144 Michael Yapko has written an impressive and helpful monograph on the subject of hypnosis and mood disorders entitled *Hypnosis and the Treatment of Depression.*

144 For theories of sleep and depression, see the work of Michael Thase at the University of Pittsburgh and David Dingle of the University of Pennsylvania. Thomas Wehr at the NIMH is also an expert in the field. The description of altered sleep phases comes from a number of sources, both printed and verbal. See Thomas Wehr, "Phase Advance of the Circadian Sleep-Wake Cycle as an Antidepressant," *Science* 206 (1979); his "Reply to Healy, D., Waterhouse, J. M.: The circadian system and affective disorders: Clocks or rhythms," *Chronobiology International* 7 (1990); his "Improvement of Depression and Triggering of Mania by Sleep Deprivation," *Journal of the American Medical Association* 267, no. 4 (1992); and M. Berger et al., "Sleep deprivation combined with consecutive sleep phase advance as fast-acting therapy in depression," *American Journal of Psychiatry* 154, no. 6 (1997). For more on this topic, see also the review chapter entitled "Biological Processes in Depression: An Updated Review and Integration," by Michael Thase and Robert Howland in *The Handbook of Depression,* edited by E. Edward Beckham and William Leber, pages 213–79.

144 The quotation from F. Scott Fitzgerald comes from *The Crack-Up,* page 75. I thank the ever-vigilant Claudia Swan for suggesting this passage.

146 On arctic resignation, see A. S. Blix's material in *Symposium on Living in the Cold,* edited by André Malan and Bernard Canguilhem.

146 There is a vast literature on Saint-John's-wort, most of it repetitive, some of it sensationalist, and much of it goopy. I have drawn here on Norman Rosenthal's book *St. John's Wort.* The information regarding hypericum and interleukin-6 was taken from the National Institutes of Health's National Center for Complementary and Alternative Medicine's Web site at www.nccam.nih.gov/nccam/fcp/fact-sheets/stjohns wort/stjohnswort.htm.

147 I find Andrew Weil's writing intensely annoying and cannot recommend any of it. His views on these subjects are nicely summed up in Jonathan Zuess's *The Natural Prozac Program,* pages 66–67.

147 Dr. Thomas Brown of Tulane University has objected to Saint-John's-wort as "touted somewhat illogically by many as natural and therefore safe." See Thomas Brown, "Acute St. John's Wort Toxicity," *American Journal of Emergency Medicine* 18, no. 2 (2000). Like other antidepressants, the plant has triggered episodes of acute mania. See Andrew Nierenberg et al., "Mania Associated with St. John's Wort," *Biological Psychiatry* 46 (1999). There is evidence that the plant may cause skin sensitivities at high dosages in cows and sheep. See O. S. Araya and E. J. Ford, "An investigation of the type of photosensitization caused by the ingestion of St. John's Wort (*Hypericum perforatum*) by calves," *Journal of Comprehensive Pathology* 91, no. 1 (1981).

147 For information about Saint-John's-wort and drug interactions, see the NIMH's Web site at www.nimh.nih.gov/events/stjohnwort.cfm. A recent article also

reviews the current data on the subject; see A. Fugh-Berman, "Herb-drug interactions," *Lancet* 355, no. 9198 (2000).

147 The catalog of drugs whose efficacy is reduced when they are taken with Saint-John's-wort is from *Consumer Reports*, "Emotional 'Asprin'?" December 2000, pages 60–63.

147 For controlled studies of S-adenosylmethionine (SAMe), see G. M. Bressa, "S-adenosyl-l-methionine (SAMe) as antidepressant: Meta-analysis of clinical studies," *Acta Neurologica Scandinavica* 89, suppl. 154 (1994).

148 The tendency of SAMe to precipitate mania is described in *Consumer Reports*, "Emotional 'Asprin'?" December 2000, pages 60–63.

148 The information about SAMe and animal neurotransmitter levels may be found in Richard Brown et al., *Stop Depression Now*, pages 74–75.

148 The connection between SAMe and methylation is proposed in Joseph Lipinski et al., "Open Trial of S-adenosylmethionine for Treatment of Depression," *American Journal of Psychiatry* 143, no. 3 (1984).

148 The figure on annual American expenditure on acupuncture may be found on the National Institutes of Health's National Center for Complementary and Alternative Medicine's Web site at www.nccam.nih.gov/nccam/fcp/factsheets/acupuncture/ acupuncture.htm.

149 Claudia Weaver's homeopathic treatments were prescribed and administered by Pami Singh.

158 Hellinger's seminal book is *Love's Hidden Symmetry*. Reinhard Lier runs the Linderhof Therapy Center in Bavaria, which is where he conducts most of his practice. Reinhard Lier's visit to America was arranged by Regine Olsen.

162 The quotations from Frank Rusakoff's writings are taken from unpublished manuscripts.

166 For a discussion of the tradition of witchcraft among the Senegalese, see William Simmons's *Eyes of the Night*.

171 Reboxetine has passed all testing to date and awaits approval from the Food and Drug Administration. In a recent E-mail, Pharmacia writes: "With regard to reboxetine, we have not received Food and Drug Administration (FDA) approval in the United States, and we cannot speculate on a date when this medication may be available. Based on the approval letter Pharmacia received from the FDA on February 23, 2000, additional U.S. clinical trials must be conducted before the product can be approved." For further information, I recommend visiting Pharmacia's Web site at www2.pnu.com.

171 For more on substance P, see Merck's Web site at www.dupontmerck.com. An introduction to substance P as an antidepressant is provided by David Nutt, "Substance-P antagonists: A new treatment for depression?" *Lancet* 352 (1998).

172 I take the number "about thirty thousand" from Craig J. Venter, "The Sequence of the Human Genome," *Science* 291, no. 5507 (2001), which said, in part, "Analysis of the genome sequence revealed 26,588 protein-encoding transcripts for which there was strong corroborating evidence and an additional 12,000 computationally derived genes with mouse matches or other weak supporting evidence." I thank Edward R. Winstead for bringing this article to my attention. I thank Polly Shulman for her advice on the mathematical meaning of ten variations for each of thirty thousand genes.

Notes

CHAPTER V: POPULATIONS

173 That women suffer depression twice as often as men is repeated throughout the general literature. The statistical work to support this assertion was done and collated internationally by Myrna Weissman at Columbia University and was published as "Cross-National Epidemiology of Major Depression and Bipolar Disorder," *Journal of the American Medical Association* 276, no. 4 (1996).

173 That sex differences for depression begin at puberty is a fairly common idea, prevalent in most of the literature on the subject. See Susan Nolen-Hoeksema's *Sex Differences in Depression*.

173 While arguments about the biological components of women's depression are inconclusive, it is undeniably the case that mood effects result from fluctuations of estrogen and progesterone in the hypothalamic and pituitary hormone systems. A discussion of these phenomena may be found in Susan Nolen-Hoeksema's *Sex Differences in Depression*, pages 64–76.

174 The statistics on suicide among women who are pregnant or have just given birth are from E. Clare Harris and Brian Barraclough, "Suicide as an Outcome for Medical Disorders," *Medicine* 73 (1994).

174 This figure on postpartum depression reflects an extremely varied set of statistics on this issue. There are two problems in arriving at an accurate figure. First, how stringently one defines postpartum depression radically affects its apparent frequency. Second, many symptoms resembling those found in depression can in fact occur as physiological repercussions of childbirth. Susan Nolen-Hoeksema writes about one study in which "the seemingly high rates of depression in new mothers resulted from their acknowledgment of the aches and pains and problems in sleeping that come with pregnancy and having a new baby, rather than the presence of the full range of depressive symptoms." She continues, "Estimates of the prevalence of nonpsychotic depression in women during the postpartum period range from 3 to 33 percent." She provides an average of 8.2 percent. These quotations come from her book *Sex Differences in Depression*, pages 62–65. Verta Taylor, in her book on postpartum depression entitled *Rock-A-By Baby*, reports that 10 to 26 percent of new mothers experience this malady.

174 The statistics concerning severe postpartum and mild postpartum depression are taken from Susan Nolen-Hoeksema's *Sex Differences in Depression*, pages 62–64. Menopausal depression is described on pages 70–71.

174 The statistic on rate of serotonin synthesis is to be found in Simeon Margolis and Karen L. Swartz, "Sex Differences in Brain Serotonin Production," *The Johns Hopkins White Papers* (1998): 14.

174 The question of disenfranchisement as the source of women's depression is amply discussed in a number of books and publications, including Susan Nolen-Hoeksema's *Sex Differences in Depression*, Jill Astbury's *Crazy for You*, and Dana Crowley Jack's *Silencing the Self*.

174 The statistics on postpartum depression in stressed women are in Susan Nolen-Hoeksema's *Sex Differences in Depression*, page 68. Her quote is from pages 60–61.

175 On the parity of male and female rates of depression among college students, as well as proposed explanations, see *Ibid.*, 26–28.

175 The overall statistics on male-to-female depression rates are in Myrna Weissman's "Cross-National Epidemiology of Major Depression and Bipolar Disorder," *Jour-*

nal of the American Medical Association 276, no. 4 (1996), working on the basis of her epidemiological studies (see the first note for chapter five, page 173, above). That women have higher rates of panic disorders and eating disorders while men have higher incidences of autism, attention deficit hyperactivity disorder, and alcoholism was discussed in a personal correspondence with Steven Hyman.

175 The information on the nature of female disenfranchisement is not taken verbatim from any one source. Numerous authors have described and explained these various phenomena in different ways. My list is not meant to be either definitive or exhaustive. For the reader who would like more in-depth explanations of these ideas, I recommend Susan Nolen-Hoeksema's *Sex Differences in Depression*, Jill Astbury's *Crazy for You*, and Dana Crowley Jack's *Silencing the Self*. Professor George

175 The two feminist explanations of depression, as well as various summaries concerning the connection between depression and marital status, may be found in Susan Nolen-Hoeksema's *Sex Differences in Depression*, pages 96–101.

175 Brown has also done much interesting work regarding "the role of life events in the onset of depressive disorders." Various studies by him and his colleagues have found humiliation and entrapment to be key descriptive factors of depressogenic events for women. See "Loss, humiliation and entrapment among women developing depression: A patient and non-patient comparison," *Psychological Medicine* 25 (1995). Other scientists' findings on the importance of roles in defining depression are reported in numerous articles. That a woman's concern for her offspring should be a typical depressogenic event for her is consistent with traditional gender roles. However, one article states: "When in practice the man also had significant involvement in domestic roles this gender difference in onset did not occur." For more on this topic, see J. Y. Nazroo et al., "Gender differences in the onset of depression following a shared life event: A study of couples," *Psychological Medicine* 27 (1997): 9.

175 Myrna Weissman's evolutionary theories about depression and women I have taken from an oral interview.

176 The information about depression among adult survivors of childhood sexual abuse is in Gemma Gladstone et al., "Characteristics of depressed patients who report childhood sexual abuse," *American Journal of Psychiatry* 156, no. 3 (1999): 431–37.

176 For information about anorexia and depression, see Christine Pollice et al., "Relationship of Depression, Anxiety, and Obsessionality to State of Illness in Anorexia Nervosa," *International Journal of Eating Disorders* 21 (1997), and Kenneth Altshuler et al., "Anorexia Nervosa and Depression: A Dissenting View," *American Journal of Psychiatry* 142, no. 3 (1985).

176 Freud's description of Dora occurs in his essay "Fragment of an Analysis of a Case of Hysteria," in volume 7 of *The Standard Edition of the Complete Psychological Works of Sigmund Freud*. For a feminist discussion of Dora, see Jill Astbury's *Crazy for You*, pages 109–32.

176 For a discussion of ideas of femininity and depression, see Susan Nolen-Hoeksema's *Sex Differences in Depression*. For a discussion of the expectations of motherhood and postpartum depression, see Verta Taylor's *Rock-A-By Baby*, pages 35–58.

176 The quotations from Dana Crowley Jack may be found in her book *Silencing the Self*, pages 32–48.

177 Jill Astbury's analysis is in her book *Crazy for You*. The quotation comes from pages 2–3.

Notes

178 The comparative rate of male-to-female suicide is in Eric Marcus's *Why Suicide?*, in which he states, "Of the approximately thirty thousand people a year who take their lives, twenty-four thousand are men and six thousand are women," page 15.

178 The discussion of the rates of depression in single, divorced, or widowed men may be found in Myrna Weissman et al., "Cross-National Epidemiology of Major Depression and Bipolar Disorder," *Journal of the American Medical Association* 276, no. 4 (1996).

180 The statistics on depression among Jewish men may be found in Bruce Bower, "Depression: Rates in women, men . . . and stress effects across the sexes," *Science News*, June 3, 1995, page 346.

180 The qualities of children with a depressed mother are spelled out in Marian Radke-Yarrow et al., "Affective Interactions of Depressed and Nondepressed Mothers and Their Children," *Journal of Abnormal Child Psychology* 21, no. 6 (1993). Also see Anne Riley's NIMH grant proposal entitled "Effects on children of treating maternal depression," page 32.

181 Bruce Bower's "Depressive aftermath for new mothers," *Science News*, August 25, 1990, reports on a variety of studies that have found infant depression as early as three months of age.

181 The effects of a mother's depression upon her young appear immediate and grave. Tiffany Field, an expert in the field who has been publishing for over two decades, writes concerning an almost "neonatal" depression: "Infants show 'dysregulation' in their behavior, physiology, and biochemistry, which probably derives from prenatal exposure to a biochemical imbalance in their mothers," page 200. See Tiffany Field, "Maternal Depression: Effects on Infants and Early Interventions," *Preventive Medicine* 27 (1998). Unfortunately, these malignant effects also seem to endure. Nancy Aaron Jones et al., "EEG Stability in Infants/Children of Depressed Mothers," *Child Psychiatry and Human Development* 28, no. 2 (1997), describes a study in which the children of depressed mothers were followed from three months to three years of age. Seven of the eight children who had shown EEG asymmetry as infants still showed this pattern of dysregulation at three years of age. However, studies have also shown that even the most basic of maternal attention and interaction can alleviate much of the problem. Martha Peláez-Nogueras et al., "Depressed Mothers' Touching Increases Infants' Positive Affect and Attention in Still-Face Interaction," *Child Development* 67 (1996), claims that the calm and intimate interaction of a mother touching her infant can have drastically positive effects on the infant's mood and sociability. Other studies, such as Sybil Hart et al., "Depressed Mothers' Neonates Improve Following the MABI and Brazelton Demonstration," *Journal of Pediatric Psychology* 23, no. 6 (1998), and Tiffany Field et al., "Effects of Parent Training on Teenage Mothers and Their Infants," *Pediatrics* 69, no. 6 (1982), demonstrate that parent education can ameliorate much of the damage done by maternal depression.

181 The study of children of depressed mothers nearly one year after maternal improvement is Catherine Lee and Ian Gotlib's "Adjustment of Children of Depressed Mothers: A 10-Month Follow-Up," *Journal of Abnormal Psychology* 100, no. 4 (1991).

181 The information on a ten-year follow-up of social impairment, depression, panic disorders, and alcohol dependence is in Myrna Weissman et al., "Offspring of Depressed Parents," *Archives of General Psychiatry* 54 (1997).

181 The comparison of children with a depressed mother and children with a schizo-

phrenic mother is in Anne Riley's NIMH grant proposal entitled "Effects on children of treating maternal depression," page 32.

181 The problems of attention deficit disorder, separation anxiety, conduct disorder, and increased somatic complaints are described in Leonard Milling and Barbara Martin's essay "Depression and Suicidal Behavior in Preadolescent Children" in Walker and Roberts's *Handbook of Clinical Child Psychology*, pages 319–39. Also see Dr. David Fassler and Lynne Dumas's monograph on childhood depression entitled *Help Me, I'm Sad: Recognizing, Treating, and Preventing Childhood Depression*.

182 Sameroff's work on two-to-four-year-old children of depressed mothers is in Sameroff et al., "Early development of children at risk for emotional disorder," *Monographs of the Society for Research in Child Development* 47, no. 7 (1982).

182 The study on high blood pressure is in A. C. Guyton et al., "Circulation: Overall regulation," *Annual Review of Physiology* 34 (1972), edited by J. M. Luck and V. E. Hall. The information cited here is in the table on page 12.

183 Anaclitic depression is outlined by René Spitz, "Anaclitic Depression," *Psychoanalytic Study of the Child* 2 (1946). For a case example, see René Spitz et al., "Anaclitic Depression in an Infant Raised in an Institution," *Journal of the American Academy of Child Psychiatry* 4, no. 4 (1965).

183 My description of "failure to thrive" is taken from oral interviews with Paramjit T. Joshi at Johns Hopkins and Deborah Christie at the Adolescent Medical Unit at University College London and Middlesex Hospital.

184 The study that came up with the 1 percent statistic is E. Poznanski et al.'s "Childhood depression: Clinical characteristics of overtly depressed children," *Archives of General Psychiatry* 23 (1970). The study that came up with the 60 percent statistic is T. A. Petti's "Depression in hospitalized child psychiatry patients: Approaches to measuring depression," *Journal of the American Academy of Child Psychiatry* 22 (1978).

184 The figures on child suicide are taken from Leonard Milling and Barbara Martin's essay "Depression and Suicidal Behavior in Preadolescent Children" in Walker and Roberts's *Handbook of Clinical Child Psychology*, page 328. According to statistics for 1997, from the NIMH's Web site, suicide was the third leading cause of death for children aged ten to fourteen.

185 That tricyclics are not effective in children and adolescents is reported in N. D. Ryan et al., "Imipramine in adolescent major depression: Plasma level and clinical response," *Acta Psychiatrica Scandinavica* 73 (1986). There are fewer studies concerning MAOIs and child and adolescent depression, largely because, as Christopher Kye and Neal Ryan write in "Pharmacologic Treatment of Child and Adolescent Depression," *Child and Adolescent Psychiatric Clinics of North America* 4, no. 2 (1995), these drugs "require an especially high sensitivity for the impulsivity, compliance, and maturity of the depressed adolescent," page 276. The general idea held by most clinicians today is nicely summed up in Paul Ambrosini, "A review of the pharmacotherapy of major depression in children and adolescents," *Psychiatric Services* 51, no. 5 (2000). He writes that the studies to date "could suggest that affective disorders among children and adolescents represent a distinct biological entity that has a differing response pattern to pharmacotherapy," page 632.

187 The course of life depression for those who have been depressed as children is described in Myrna Weissman et al., "Depressed Adolescents Grown Up," *Journal of the American Medical Association* 281, no. 18 (1999), pages 1707–13.

187 Only in the post-Freudian world have many of the questions surrounding child-

hood depression finally been asked. While childhood depression is now well documented as a clinical reality, the numbers seem to surge during adolescence. Myrna Weissman et al. write in their article "Depressed Adolescents Grown Up," *Journal of the American Medical Association* 281, no. 18 (1999), "It is now clear that major depressive disorder often has an onset in adolescence." That approximately 5 percent of teens suffer from depression is an oft-cited statistic; I have taken it from Patricia Meisol's "The Dark Cloud," published in the May 1, 1999, edition of *The Sun.*

187 I recommend strongly the video *Day for Night: Recognizing Teenage Depression,* produced by the Depression and Related Affective Disorders Association (DRADA) working in cooperation with the Johns Hopkins University School of Medicine. It is an eloquent and inspiring record of the kinds of depression that afflict young people today.

187 That parents underestimate the depression of their children can be adduced from a number of studies and statistics. One such statistic, from Howard Chua-Eoan, "How to Spot a Troubled Kid," *Time* 153, no. 21 (1999), is that "57% of teens who had attempted suicide were found to be suffering from major depression. But only 13% of the parents of suicides believed their child was depressed." Pages 46–47.

187 The statistic for suicidal thoughts among high school students is from George Colt's *The Enigma of Suicide,* page 39.

187 Pioneering work done by Myrna Weissman and others has begun to shed light on the clinical reality of childhood and adolescent depression. Many researchers are beginning to look at the long-term effects of early diagnosis. The article "Depressed Adolescents Grown Up," coauthored by Weissman and published in *The Journal of the American Medical Association* 281, no. 18 (1999), notes: "The major findings are a poor outcome of adolescent-onset Major Depressive Disorder and the continuity and specificity of MDD arising in and continuing into adulthood." Page 1171.

188 The multiplicand for the correlation between early depression and adult depression is in Eric Fombonne's essay "Depressive Disorders: Time Trends and Possible Explanatory Mechanisms," in Michael Rutter and David J. Smith's *Psychosocial Disorders in Young People,* page 573.

188 The figure of 70 percent is from Leonard Milling and Barbara Martin's essay "Depression and Suicidal Behavior in Preadolescent Children," in Walker and Roberts's *Handbook of Clinical Child Psychology,* page 325.

188 The idea that sexual abuse causes depression is discussed in Jill Astbury's *Crazy for You,* pages 159–91. Gemma Gladstone et al., "Characteristics of depressed patients who report childhood sexual abuse," *American Journal of Psychiatry* 156, no. 3 (1999), discusses sexual abuse as an indirect cause of depression, pages 431–37.

188 The Russian orphanage adoption story was recounted in Margaret Talbot, "Attachment Theory: The Ultimate Experiment," *New York Times Magazine,* May 24, 1998.

189 That the elderly depressed are undertreated is indicated by a number of articles and studies, both academic and popular. Sara Rimer explores the various causes and consequences in "Gaps Seen in Treatment of Depression in Elderly," *New York Times,* September 5, 1999. In the article, Dr. Ira Katz, director of geriatric psychiatry at the University of Pennsylvania School of Medicine, is quoted as saying, "More than one in six older patients who go to a primary-care doctor's office have a clinically significant degree of depression, but only one in six of those get ade-

quate treatment." George Zubenko et al.'s "Impact of Acute Psychiatric Inpatient Treatment on Major Depression in Late Life and Prediction of Response," *American Journal of Psychiatry* 151, no. 7 (1994), explains, "It has been observed that recognition of major depression in the elderly is hampered because depressed mood seems less prominent in older patients than among younger adults. Moreover, the increasing burden of physical disorders with increasing age complicates the differential diagnosis of major depression in the elderly, especially when a cross-sectional assessment is made."

189 Emil Kraepelin's comments on the elderly depressed are in C. G. Gottfries et al., "Treatment of Depression in Elderly Patients with and without Dementia Disorders," *International Clinical Psychopharmacology*, suppl. 6, no. 5 (1992).

189 On the idea that older people in nursing homes are twice as likely to be depressed as those living in their own communities, see *Ibid.*

189 On the suggestion that one-third of nursing-home residents are depressed, see *Ibid.*

189 On the social dimensions of elderly depression and the importance of having a good friend, see Judith Hays et al., "Social Correlates of the Dimensions of Depression in the Elderly," *Journal of Gerontology* 53B, no. 1 (1998).

189 That levels of neurotransmitters are low in the elderly is confirmed in C. G. Gottfries et al., "Treatment of Depression in Elderly Patients with and without Dementia Disorders," *International Clinical Psychopharmacology*, suppl. 6, no. 5 (1992).

189 On the comparative levels of serotonin in the very elderly, see *Ibid.*

189 That the diminution of serotonin through natural aging does not necessarily have immediate dire consequences is proposed by a number of studies. B. A. Lawlor et al.'s "Evidence for a decline with age in behavioral responsivity to the serotonin agonist, m-chlorophenylpiperazine, in healthy human subjects," *Psychiatry Research* 29, no. 1 (1989), eloquently states: "The functional significance of alterations in brain serotonin (5HT) associated with normal aging in both animals and humans is largely unknown."

189 The information on the delayed response to antidepressants among the elderly is in George Zubenko et al., "Impact of Acute Psychiatric Inpatient Treatment on Major Depression in Late Life and Prediction of Response," *American Journal of Psychiatry* 151, no. 7 (1994).

190 On the success rate for treatment of depression among the elderly, see *Ibid.*

190 On prescription of short-term hospitalization for the elderly depressed, see *Ibid.*

190 The symptoms of depression among the elderly are described in Diego de Leo and René F. W. Diekstra's *Depression and Suicide in Late Life*, pages 21–38.

190 The term "emotional incontinence" is used in Nathan Herrmann et al., "Behavioral Disorders in Demented Elderly Patients," *CNS Drugs* 6, no. 4 (1996).

192 The role of depression in predicting Alzheimer's and senility is discussed in Myron Weiner et al., "Prevalence and Incidence of Major Depression in Alzheimer's Disease," *American Journal of Psychiatry* 151, no. 7 (1994).

192 On serotonin levels in Alzheimer's patients, see *Ibid.*

193 Work on whether lowered levels of serotonin may cause dementia is to be found in Alan Cross et al., "Serotonin Receptor Changes in Dementia of the Alzheimer Type," *Journal of Neurochemistry* 43 (1984), and Alan Cross, "Serotonin in Alzheimer-Type Dementia and Other Dementing Illnesses," *Annals of the New York Academy of Sciences* 600 (1990).

193 On the effect of SSRIs on intellectual and motor skills, see C. G. Gottfries et al., "Treatment of Depression in Elderly Patients with and without Dementia Disorders," *International Clinical Psychopharmacology,* suppl. 6, no. 5 (1992).

193 M. Jackuelyn Harris et al.'s "Recognition and treatment of depression in Alzheimer's disease," *Geriatrics* 44, no. 12 (1989), is my source on long-term use of low dosages of SSRIs. They write, "Generally, Alzheimer's patients require lower dosages of medication and longer drug treatment trials than younger patients treated for depression." Page 26.

193 Use of trazodone and benzodiazepines for depression in the elderly is described in Nathan Herrmann et al., "Behavioral Disorders in Demented Elderly Patients," *CNS Drugs* 6, no. 4 (1996).

193 On proposal of hormone therapies for sexual aggressivity in Alzheimer's, see *Ibid.*

193 For a discussion of and statistics related to depression and stroke, see Allan House et al., "Depression Associated with Stroke," *Journal of Neuropsychiatry* 8, no. 4 (1996).

193 For a review of the work on strokes in the left frontal lobe, see *Ibid.*

193 The anecdote of the weepy man is in Grethe Andersen, "Treatment of Uncontrolled Crying after Stroke," *Drugs & Aging* 6, no. 2 (1995).

193 For the anecdote of the man who returned belatedly to work, see *Ibid.*

194 The quotation from *Mad Travelers* is taken from the book's introduction, pages 1–5.

195 The quotation from *Willow Weep for Me* is on pages 18–19.

200 The Singapore magazine is *Brave,* and the article is by Shawn Tan and appeared in the 1999 final edition.

202 The passages on gay depression draw heavily from the work of Richard C. Friedman and Jennifer Downey, especially from their "Internalized Homophobia and the Negative Therapeutic Reaction," *Journal of the American Academy of Psychoanalysis* 23, no. 1 (1995), and their "Internal Homophobia and Gender-Valued Self-Esteem in the Psychoanalysis of Gay Patients," *Psychoanalytic Review* 86, no. 3 (1999). This work will ultimately be combined and augmented into a book to be called *Psychoanalysis and Sexual Orientation: Sexual Science and Clinical Practice.* I consulted with Richard Friedman at some length and he provided some supplementary information in anticipation of that book, and my quotations in several instances bridge the two articles with language approved by Friedman and Downey.

202 The 1999 study of male twins is in R. Herrel et al., "Sexual Orientation and Suicidality: A Co-Twin Control Study in Adult Men," *Archives of General Psychiatry* 56 (1999). They used a registry that had been set up during the Vietnam War and compared those who were exclusively heterosexual to those who had had same-sex partners. In addition to the shocking rates of suicide attempts, the study indicated that while straight men had a 25.5 percent rate of suicidal ideation, among gay people the proportion was 55.3 percent.

202 The 2000 study of suicide attempts in men between the ages of seventeen and thirty-nine was conducted by Cochran and Mays, and actually considered 3,648 randomly selected cohorts. It was published as "Lifetime Prevalence of Suicide Symptoms and Affective Disorders among Men Reporting Same-Sex Sexual Partners: Results from NHANES III," *American Journal of Public Health* 90, no. 4 (2000). The same researchers using a different database of 9,908 cohorts considered panic disorders in people who had had sex only with members of the opposite sex and those who had had same-sex partners during the previous year. This work was published as "Relation between Psychiatric Syndromes and Behaviorally

Defined Sexual Orientation in a Sample of the U.S. Population," *American Journal of Epidemiology* 151, no. 5 (2000). Of those considered for the latter study, 2,479 had to be turned away because they (rather depressingly, I think) had had no sexual partners during the previous year.

202 The New Zealand longitudinal study, which asked cohorts to comment on their sexual orientation and their sexual relationships from age sixteen onward, and showed risk factors for many complaint, was published by D. M. Fergusson, et al., "Is Sexual Orientation Related to Mental Health Problems and Suicidality in Young People?" *Archives of General Psychiatry* 56, no. 10 (1999).

202 The Dutch study conducted in 1999 had 5,998 cohorts, and in it both homosexual men and women were seen to have at least one *DSM-III-R* psychiatric diagnosis more frequently than heterosexuals. Gay men had increased rates of present and lifetime depression and anxiety; gay women had higher prevalence of major depression and alcohol drug dependence. See the study by T. G. Sandfort, et al., "Same-Sex Sexual Behavior and Psychiatric Disorders: Findings from the Netherlands Mental Health Survey and Incidence Study (NEMESIS)," *Archives of General Psychiatry* 58, no. 1 (2001).

202 The study of youth in Minnesota included 36,254 students from seventh to twelfth grades and was published by G. Remafedi, et al., "The Relationship between Suicide Risk and Sexual Orientation: Results of a Population-Based Study," *American Journal of Public Health* 88, no. 1 (1998). It indicated no variation for suicidal ideation between lesbians and straight women, but showed that while straight men had a 4.2 percent rate of suicidal ideation, gay males came in at 28.1 percent.

202 The study showing that homosexual males were 6.5 times as likely to make a suicide attempt as heterosexual males had 3,365 cohorts, and is found in R. Garofalo, et al., "Sexual Orientation and Risk of Suicide Attempts among a Representative Sample of Youth," *Archives of Pediatrics and Adolescent Medicine* 153 (1999).

202 The study that showed that 7.3 percent of homosexuals had made four or more suicide attempts as opposed to 1 percent of heterosexuals included 1,563 cohorts. Homosexual/bisexual students in this study showed greater incidence of suicidal ideation than straight students; 12 percent of homosexuals had attempted suicide as opposed to 2.3 percent of heterosexuals, and 7.7 percent of homosexuals had made a suicide attempt requiring medical attention in the previous twelve months as opposed to 1.3 percent of heterosexual youth. See the study by A. H. Faulkner and K. Cranston, "Correlates of Same-Sex Sexual Behavior in a Random Sample of Massachusetts High School Students," *American Journal of Public Health* 88, no. 2 (1998). The study showed that gay students were at elevated risk of injury, disease, death from violence, substance abuse, and suicidal behavior.

202 The finding that 10 percent of suicides in San Diego County were committed by gay men is in C. L. Rich et al., "San Diego Suicide Study I: Young vs. Old Subjects," *Archives of General Psychiatry* 43, no. 6 (1986). This was an uncontrolled study. D. Shaffer, et al., attempted to reproduce these results in the New York City area in 1995 in the article "Sexual Orientation in Adolescents Who Commit Suicide," *Suicide and Life Threatening Behaviors* 25, supp. 4 (1995), and were not able to do so, but these researchers were working on youth suicide only and took information about sexual orientation from family members and peers who are in many instances unlikely to know and in other instances unwilling to admit even to themselves the details of their children's sexual orientation.

202 The work on the socialization of gay men and children's upbringing in homophobic environments and the early incorporation of homophobic attitudes is in A. K. Maylon, "Biphasic aspects of homosexual identity formation," *Psychotherapy: Theory, Research and Practice* 19 (1982).

204 The study showing that gay students were likely to have their property stolen or deliberately damaged is in R. Garofalo et al., "The Association between Health Risk Behaviors and Sexual Orientation among a School-Based Sample of Adolescents," *Pediatrics* 101 (1998). The authors found that the homosexuals in the group were also more likely to engage in multiple drug abuse, high-risk sexual behavior, and other high-risk behaviors.

204 The fact that suicide rates were particularly high among Jews in Berlin between the wars is published in *Charlotte Salomon: Life? Or Theatre?* on page 10, though it is given more ample exposition in text panels that were mounted as part of the exhibition of Salomon's remarkable work at The Jewish Museum in early 2001. I thank Jennie Livingston for steering me toward this material, and for proposing the link between this Jewish suicidality in pre–Nazi Germany and gay suicidality in America.

205 The *New Yorker* questionnaire about parents' preferring unhappy straight-identified children to happy gay-identified children is in Hendrik Hertzberg, "The Narcissus Survey," *The New Yorker*, January 5, 1998.

208 Jean Malaurie's *The Last Kings of Thule*, though much maligned in recent years, gives a particularly stirring and passionate account of traditional Inuit life in Greenland.

208 The suicide rate in Greenland was published in Tine Curtis and Peter Bjerregaard's *Health Research in Greenland*, page 31.

213 The descriptions of polar hysteria, mountain wanderer syndrome, and kayak anxiety come from Inge Lynge, "Mental Disorders in Greenland," *Man & Society* 21 (1997). I must thank John Hart for providing the parallel to "running amok."

213 Malaurie's quote here is from *The Last Kings of Thule*, page 109.

CHAPTER VI: ADDICTION

217 That there are about twenty-five common substances of abuse was taken from the National Institute of Drug Abuse's Web site at www.nida.nih.gov/DrugsofAbuse.

217 The three-stage mechanism of substances of abuse is described in David McDowell and Henry Spitz's *Substance Abuse*, page 19.

217 Peter Whybrow provides a concise summary of the interactions between cocaine and dopamine in *A Mood Apart*, page 213. A more in-depth analysis is provided by Marc Galanter and Herbert Kleber's *Textbook of Substance Abuse Treatment*, pages 21–31.

217 Work on morphine and dopamine may be found in Marc Galanter and Herbert Kleber's *Textbook of Substance Abuse Treatment*, pages 11–19.

217 For work on alcohol's effect on serotonin, see *Ibid.*, 6–7, 130–31.

218 That levels of the neurotransmitter enkephalin are affected by many of the substances of abuse is indicated in Craig Lambert, "Deep Cravings," *Harvard Magazine* 102, no. 4 (2000).

218 The brain's response to increased levels of dopamine is explicated in Nora Volkow, "Imaging studies on the role of dopamine in cocaine reinforcement and addiction in humans," *Journal of Psychopharmacology* 13, no. 4 (1999).

218 The dynamics of addictive substances leading to addiction is discussed at some

length in Nora Volkow et al., "Addiction, a Disease of Compulsion and Drive: Involvement of the Orbitofrontal Cortex," *Cerebral Cortex* 10 (2000).

218 The statistics on proportions of addiction to specific substances are taken from James Anthony et al., "Comparative epidemiology of dependence on tobacco, alcohol, controlled substances, and inhalants: Basic findings from the National Comorbidity Survey," *Experimental and Clinical Psychopharmacology* 2, no. 3 (1994).

218 Work on substances of abuse and the blood-brain barrier may be found in David McDowell and Henry Spitz's *Substance Abuse*, pages 22–24.

218 The number of years it takes to develop dependence on alcohol and cocaine is described in H. D. Abraham et al., "Order of onset of substance abuse and depression in a sample of depressed outpatients," *Comprehensive Psychiatry* 40, no. 1 (1999).

219 The work with PET scans showing limited recovery even at the three-month period has been done by Dr. Nora Volkow. See, for example, "Long-Term Frontal Brain Metabolic Changes in Cocaine Abusers," *Synapse* 11 (1992). That chronic drug use has persistent neurological consequences is illustrated in Alvaro Pascual-Leone et al., "Cerebral atrophy in habitual cocaine abusers: A planimetric CT study," *Neurology* 41 (1991), and Roy Mathew and William Wilson, "Substance Abuse and Cerebral Blood Flow," *American Journal of Psychiatry* 148, no. 3 (1991). For information regarding cognitive impairment, including deficits in memory, attention, and abstraction, see Alfredo Ardila et al., "Neuropsychological Deficits in Chronic Cocaine Abusers," *International Journal of Neuroscience* 57 (1991), and William Beatty et al., "Neuropsychological performance of recently abstinent alcoholics and cocaine abusers," *Drug and Alcohol Dependence* 37 (1995).

220 A thorough review of the multiple causes of lesions in alcoholics is provided by Michael Charness, "Brain Lesions in Alcoholics," *Alcoholism: Clinical and Experimental Research* 17, no. 1 (1993). For a more general and recent review of alcohol and brain damage, see Marcia Barinaga, "A New Clue to How Alcohol Damages Brains," *Science*, February 11, 2000. That memory loss is a problem in this population is discussed in Andrey Ryabinin, "Role of Hippocampus in Alcohol-Induced Memory Impairment: Implications from Behavioral and Immediate Early Gene Studies," *Psychopharmacology* 139 (1998).

220 A description of the use of SSRIs to bring alcoholics off alcohol is in David McDowell and Henry Spitz's *Substance Abuse*, page 220. Mark Gold and Andrew Slaby, however, disagree with this position in their book *Dual Diagnosis in Substance Abuse*. They write, pages 210–11, "Antidepressant medication should not be prescribed for active alcoholics because the appropriate treatment is much more likely to be a period of sobriety."

220 Increased REM latency has long been established as a hallmark sign of depression. See Francis Mondimore's *Depression: The Mood Disease*, pages 174–78, for a good general discussion of depression and sleep. The work on REM sleep, alcoholism, and depression is taken from two studies: D. H. Overstreet et al., "Alcoholism and depressive disorder," *Alcohol & Alcoholism* 24 (1989); and P. Shiromani et al., "Acetylcholine and the regulation of REM sleep," *Annual Review of Pharmacological Toxicology* 27 (1987).

221 The statement on early-onset alcoholism and depression is taken from Mark Gold and Andrew Slaby's *Dual Diagnosis in Substance Abuse*, pages 7–10.

221 On work with tests to diagnose primary versus secondary depression, see *Ibid.*, 108–9.

221 The figures on the proportion of depressives who suffer from secondary alco-

Notes

holism and vice versa I take from Barbara Powell et al., "Primary and Secondary Depression in Alcoholic Men: An Important Distinction?" *Journal of Clinical Psychiatry* 48, no. 3 (1987). For more on this complicated topic, see Bridget Grant et al., "The Relationship between *DSM-IV* Alcohol Use Disorders and *DSM-IV* Major Depression: Examination of the Primary-Secondary Distinction in a General Population Sample," *Journal of Affective Disorders* 38 (1996).

221 That substance abuse often begins in adolescence is discussed in Boris Segal and Jacqueline Stewart, "Substance Use and Abuse in Adolescence: An Overview," *Child Psychiatry and Human Development* 26, no. 4 (1996). They write lucidly: "Considering the epidemiological factors further, one must notice that adolescence is the primary risk period for the initiation of use of substances; those who have not experimented with licit or illicit drugs by age twenty-one are unlikely to do so after." Page 196.

221 That substance abusers are more likely to relapse when depressed is indicated in Mark Gold and Andrew Slaby's *Dual Diagnosis in Substance Abuse:* "Alcoholics reporting depression during periods of sobriety return to drinking more frequently than those with normal mood," page 108.

221 R. E. Meyer's views here quoted come from *Psychopathology and Addictive Disorder,* pages 3–16.

221 The remission of apparently schizophrenic symptoms (paranoia, delusions, hallucinations, etc.) in patients with depression and stimulant-abuse problems is related to the fact that mania can often be precipitated by excess dopamine. Abstinence from stimulant use may help to control such excesses. For more on the relationships among stimulants, mania, and psychosis, see Robert Post et al., "Cocaine, Kindling, and Psychosis," *American Journal of Psychiatry* 133, no. 6 (1976), and John Griffith et al., "Dextroamphetamine: Evaluation of Psychomimetic Properties in Man," *Archives of General Psychiatry* 26 (1972).

221 The severity of each illness in dual-diagnosis cases is reviewed in Mark Gold and Andrew Slaby's *Dual Diagnosis in Substance Abuse.*

222 On the depression-engendering effects of withdrawal from cocaine, sedatives, hypnotics, and anxiolytics, see *Ibid.,* 105–15.

222 Work on the capacity of substances, especially alcohol, to exacerbate suicidality is summarized in Ghadirian and Lehmann's *Environment and Psychopathology,* page 112. Mark Gold and Andrew Slaby's *Dual Diagnosis in Substance Abuse* says "rates of self-reported suicide attempts increase progressively with increased use of licit and illicit substances." Page 14.

222 That depression often remits because of abstinence can be adduced from a number of studies. Mark Gold and Andrew Slaby's *Dual Diagnosis in Substance Abuse* says, "For the majority of these primary alcoholics, secondary depressive symptoms tend to remit by the second week of treatment and continue to decrease more gradually with three to four weeks of abstinence," pages 107–8.

222 Alcohol, in fact, causes all medications to be absorbed more rapidly; and it is a primary principle of antidepressant therapy that peaks of absorption exacerbate side effects.

222 Howard Shaffer's pithy remark about addictive dice was published in Craig Lambert, "Deep Cravings," *Harvard Magazine* 102, no. 4 (2000). Bertha Madras's comments appear in the same article.

223 Work on endorphin levels and alcohol use has been published in J. C. Aguirre et al., "Plasma Beta-Endorphin Levels in Chronic Alcoholics," *Alcohol* 7, no. 5 (1990).

224 The four origins of addiction I take from David McDowell and Henry Spitz's *Substance Abuse*.

224 The statistics on Irish and Israeli teetotalism were discussed in an oral interview with Dr. Herbert Kleber, March 9, 2000.

225 The quotation from Eliot appears in his poem "Gerontion," in *The Complete Poems and Plays*, page 22.

225 These remarks on substitution come from Mark Gold and Andrew Slaby's *Dual Diagnosis in Substance Abuse*, page 199.

225 The story of chili in the elephant's eye I take from Sue Macartney-Snape, who has spent much time in Nepal and has interviewed numerous howdah drivers.

225 Work on decreased oxygenation of the blood of smokers is reviewed in Marc Galanter and Herbert Kleber's *Textbook of Substance Abuse Treatment*, page 216.

225 Work on smoking and serotonin may be found in David Gilbert's *Smoking*, pages 49–59.

226 For a fuller account of my life with Russian artists, see *The Irony Tower: Soviet Artists in a Time of Glasnost*.

227 That the rationale behind alcohol taxes in Scandinavia includes the benefits of reduced suicide was discussed with Håkan Leifman and Mats Ramstedt of the Swedish Institute of Social Research on Alcohol and Drugs (SoRAD). Statistical information is provided in a study to be published in a forthcoming supplement of *Addiction* entitled "Alcohol and Suicide in 14 European Countries," by Mats Ramstedt. For more information on the relationship between alcohol consumption and suicide, see George Murphy, *Suicide in Alcoholism*, and I. Rossow, "Alcohol and suicide—beyond the link at the individual level," *Addiction* 91 (1996).

228 On serious alcoholism and cognitive impairment, see David McDowell and Henry Spitz's *Substance Abuse*, pages 45–46.

228 For alcohol's toxic effects on the liver, the stomach, and the immune system, see *Ibid.*, 46–47.

228 That the mortality rate is higher among alcoholics than among nonalcoholics is stated in Donald Goodwin's *Alcoholism, the Facts*, page 52.

228 The statistic that 90 percent of Americans have had alcohol and the figures on physiological addiction to alcohol in the United States are from David McDowell and Henry Spitz's *Substance Abuse*, pages 41–42.

228 The role of serotonin and cortisol in resisting alcohol consumption is discussed in Marc Galanter and Herbert Kleber's *Textbook of Substance Abuse Treatment*, pages 6–7 and 130–31.

228 Information on the GABA receptors I take from personal correspondence with Steven Hyman and David McDowell. For an in-depth discussion on alcohol, GABA, and other brain neurotransmitters, see Marc Galanter and Herbert Kleber's *Textbook of Substance Abuse Treatment*, pages 3–8. Work on serotonin's reinforcing alcohol consumption is in R. J. M. Niesink et al.'s *Drugs of Abuse and Addiction*, pages 134–37.

228 The superiority of psychodynamic therapies for dual-diagnosis patients seems more a clinical reality than a well-studied fact. Most of the clinicians I've spoken with have espoused a belief that for real recovery a dual-diagnosis patient must understand how the abuse affects the depression and vice versa. Marc Galanter and Herbert Kleber write in their *Textbook of Substance Abuse Treatment* that for "patients for whom affect regulation is an issue, psychodynamic psychotherapy may be especially valuable." Page 312.

228 The Columbia practice is in the S.T.A.R.S. (Substance Treatment and Research Service) Program.

229 A great deal has been published on Antabuse. For a detailed description of its mode of action, see David McDowell and Henry Spitz's *Substance Abuse*, pages 217–19.

229 On use of Naltrexone for withdrawal from alcohol and heroin, see *Ibid.*, 48–51.

229 For information on the history of marijuana, see *Ibid.*, 68.

230 Marijuana's lung toxicity is discussed in Marc Galanter and Herbert Kleber's *Textbook of Substance Abuse Treatment*, pages172–73.

230 The work on depression in the families of stimulant abusers is from Mark Gold and Andrew Slaby's *Dual Diagnosis in Substance Abuse*, page 18.

230 The percentage of cocaine users who become addicted is in David McDowell and Henry Spitz's *Substance Abuse*, page 93.

230 Work on lab rats choosing stimulants over food and sex is in R. A. Yokel et al., "Amphetamine-type reinforcement by dopaminergic agonists in the rat," *Psychopharmacology* 58 (1978). There have also been numerous studies involving rhesus monkeys, with the same results. See, for example, T. G. Aigner et al, "Choice behavior in rhesus monkeys: Cocaine versus food," *Science* 201 (1978).

230 The neurophysiology of the cocaine crash is expounded in Mark Gold and Andrew Slaby's *Dual Diagnosis in Substance Abuse*, pages 109–10.

230 The general effects of amphetamines and cocaine on the neurotransmitters are described in R. J. M. Niesink et al.'s *Drugs of Abuse and Addiction*, pages 159–165.

230 That acute craving can last for decades is indicated in Mark Gold and Andrew Slaby's *Dual Diagnosis in Substance Abuse*, page 110.

230 The use of a ten-week course of antidepressants to endure the drug crash is described in Bruce Rounsaville et al., "Psychiatric Diagnoses of Treatment-Seeking Cocaine Abusers," *Archives of General Psychiatry* 48 (1991).

231 The permanent effect of amphetamines and cocaine on the dopamine system is described in Mark Gold and Andrew Slaby's *Dual Diagnosis in Substance Abuse*, page 110. They write, "Animal studies have documented occasional dopaminergic neuronal degeneration with chronic stimulant administration."

231 The work on cocaine and CRF is in Thomas Kosten et al., "Depression and Stimulant Dependence," *Journal of Nervous and Mental Disease* 186, no. 12 (1998).

231 The figures on depression among opiate abusers comes from Ghadirian and Lehmann's *Environment and Psychopathology*, pages 110–11.

232 The high rate of depression among people on methadone is described in Mark Gold and Andrew Slaby's *Dual Diagnosis in Substance Abuse*, page 110.

232 The statistics on Vietnam veterans and heroin addiction are in Craig Lambert, "Deep Cravings," *Harvard Magazine* 102, no. 4 (2000): 67.

233 The work on ecstasy and serotonin axons is summarized in R. J. M. Niesink et al., *Drugs of Abuse and Addiction*, pages 164–65. That ecstasy reduces serotonin levels 30 to 35 percent may be found in U. McCann et al., "Serotonin Neurotoxicity after 3,4-Methylenedioxymethamphetamine: A Controlled Study in Humans," *Neuropsychopharmacology* 10 (1994). For more on ecstasy and the monoamines, see S. R. White et al., "The Effects of Methylenedioxymethamphetamine on Monoaminergic Neurotransmission in the Central Nervous System," *Progress in Neurobiology* 49 (1996). For a lively and varied discussion of ecstasy and neurotoxicity, see J. J. D. Turner and A. C. Parrott, " 'Is MDMA a Human Neurotoxin?': Diverse Views from the Discussants," *Neuropsychobiology* 42 (2000).

234 For my discussion of the benzodiazepines, I have relied on the work of Dr. Richard

A. Friedman of Cornell, and in particular on oral interviews conducted with him in the spring of 2000.

234 The dangers of excessive benzos are discussed in Mark Gold and Andrew Slaby's *Dual Diagnosis in Substance Abuse*, pages 20–21.

234 For a fuller description of roofies, see David McDowell and Henry Spitz's *Substance Abuse*, pages 65–66.

235 The origins of heroin with Bayer are discussed in Craig Lambert, "Deep Cravings," *Harvard Magazine* 102, no. 4 (2000): 60.

235 David McDowell and Henry Spitz's *Substance Abuse* provides a short history of ecstasy, pages 59–60.

235 Michael Pollan's piece appeared under the title "A Very Fine Line," *New York Times Magazine*, September 12, 1999.

238 Keith Richards's remark was discovered in Dave Hickey's brilliant book *Air Guitar*, before the title page. I thank the very hip Stephen Bitterolf for sharing it with me.

CHAPTER VII: SUICIDE

243 The idea that there is often no clear causal link between depression and suicidality is taken from a number of authors intimate with both phenomena. As George Colt writes on page 43 in *The Enigma of Suicide*, suicide is no longer thought of as "depression's last stop."

243 The quotation from George Colt is from *Ibid.*, 312.

243 That over 40 percent of the people in the general public who committed suicide had had psychiatric in-patient care is taken from Jane Pirkis and Philip Burgess, "Suicide and recency of health care contacts: A systematic review," *British Journal of Psychiatry* 173 (1998): 463.

244 A. Alvarez's remark on attempts at exorcism is from his *The Savage God*, page 96. His words about suicide and ambition appear on page 75.

245 These famous lines from *Hamlet* are in act 3, scene 1, lines 79–80; the second quotation is from act 3, scene 1, lines 83–85. There is of course no single and clear interpretation for this speech from Hamlet. I would point readers toward C. S. Lewis's *Studies in Words*, for example, which devotes a whole chapter to the relationship between "conscience" and "conscious." I would also emphasize the brilliantly lucid interpretation provided by Harold Bloom in *Shakespeare: The Invention of the Human*.

245 Albert Camus's notion that suicide is the one philosophical problem is in *The Myth of Sisyphus and Other Essays*, page 3.

245 Schopenhauer's remarks are from his essay "On Suicide" in *The Works of Schopenhauer*, page 437.

246 Santayana's statement comes from Glen Evans's *The Encyclopedia of Suicide*, page ii.

246 Freud's remark on having no way to approach suicide is taken from a speech he gave at a gathering of the Vienna Psychoanalytical Society on the subject of suicide, April 20 and 27, 1910. I have taken it as quoted in Litman's essay "Sigmund Freud on Suicide," in *Essays in Self-Destruction*, edited by Edwin Shneidman, page 330.

246 Albert Camus speaks of the illogic of postponing death in *The Myth of Sisyphus and Other Essays*, page 3.

247 Pliny's quotation is taken from *The Works of Schopenhauer*, page 433.

247 These lines are to be found in John Donne's *Biathanatos*, page 39.

247 The quotation from Schopenhauer is in the book *Essays and Aphorisms*, page 78.

247 The quotations from Thomas Szasz come from his book *The Second Sin,* page 67.

247 The Harvard study is described in Herbert Hendin's *Suicide in America,* page 216.

248 Edwin Shneidman's quotation about the split is from his book *The Suicidal Mind,* pages 58–59.

248 Edwin Shneidman's statement about the right to belch is quoted from George Colt's *The Enigma of Suicide,* page 341.

248 The assertion that someone commits suicide every seventeen minutes was calculated using statistics for total number of suicides per year, provided by the NIMH (31,000 for year 1996). The calculation: 524,160 minutes per year divided by 31,000 suicides per year equals one suicide every 16.9 minutes.

248 That suicide ranks number three among causes of death for young people is taken from NIMH Suicide Facts Web sites (statistics are for year 1996). That suicide ranks number two among college students is taken from Kay Jamison's *Night Falls Fast,* page 21. The comparative statistics on suicide and AIDS and the figure for suicide-attempt-related hospitalizations are both taken from Kay Jamison's *Night Falls Fast,* pages 23 and 24 respectively.

248 The World Health Organization (WHO) statistic on suicide comes from *The World Health Report,* 1999. The study that found suicide to have increased 260 percent within a geographic area is U. Åsgård et al., "Birth Cohort Analysis of Changing Suicide Risk by Sex and Age in Sweden 1952 to 1981," *Acta Psychiatrica Scandinavica* 76 (1987).

248 The statistics on suicide and manic-depression, and suicide and major depression, are taken from Kay Jamison's *Night Falls Fast,* page 110.

248 The connection between suicidality and first episode is in M. Oquendo et al., "Suicide: Risk Factors and Prevention in Refractory Major Depression," *Depression and Anxiety* 5 (1997): 203.

248 The figures on suicide attempts and completed suicides are in George Colt's *The Enigma of Suicide,* page 311.

248 The document containing the apparently conflicting statistics is Aaron Beck's *Depression.* On page 57, in a survey of suicide research, Beck cites two studies that claim radically different findings. The first study's findings "suggest that the risk of suicide in a patient hospitalized for depression is about five hundred times the national average." The second study, presented in the next paragraph, states, "The suicide rate for depressed patients, therefore, was twenty-five times the expected rate. . . ."

249 The NIMH position that "research has shown that 90 percent of people who kill themselves have depression or another diagnosable mental or substance abuse disorder" is on their Web site at www.nimh.nih.gov/publicat/harmaway.cfm.

249 That Monday and Friday have the highest rate of suicide is reported in Eric Marcus's *Why Suicide?* page 23.

249 The rate of suicide by hour of the day is in M. Gallerani et al., "The Time for suicide," *Psychological Medicine* 26 (1996).

249 The increase of suicide during spring is reported in David Lester's *Making Sense of Suicide,* page 153.

249 That women have a higher rate of suicide during the first week (menstrual phase) of their menstrual cycle is discussed in Richard Wetzel and James McClure Jr., "Suicide and the Menstrual Cycle: A Review," *Comprehensive Psychiatry* 13, no. 4 (1972). They also review studies that point to elevated rates of suicide attempts during the last week (luteal phase) of the menstrual cycle. There is, however, con-

troversy regarding the methodological validity of many of these studies. For a critical review of the literature, see Enrique Baca-García et al., "The Relationship Between Menstrual Cycle Phases and Suicide Attempts," *Psychosomatic Medicine* 62 (2000). The effect of pregnancy and childbirth on maternal suicidality is reported by E. C. Harris and Brian Barraclough, "Suicide as an Outcome for Medical Disorders," *Medicine* 73 (1994).

249 Émile Durkheim's watershed book was published in 1897 as *Le Suicide*. My discussion of Durkheim's classifications is taken from Steve Taylor's rigorous book *Durkheim and the Study of Suicide*.

250 The quotation from Charles Bukowski I got from a billboard on Sunset Boulevard. I have not been able to find its precise location within his work. I do not recommend driving on Sunset Boulevard during rush hour to locate this reference.

250 The quotation from Alexis de Tocqueville comes from his justly famous *Democracy in America*, page 296.

250 Émile Durkheim's extemporization on the social origins of suicide is discussed in Steve Taylor's *Durkheim and the Study of Suicide*, page 21.

250 The notion that adults, children, and people with psychiatric illnesses who commit suicide are at least two to three times as likely to have a family history of suicide as those who do not is compiled from over thirty studies and reported in Kay Jamison's *Night Falls Fast*, page 169.

250 Paul Wender et al., "Psychiatric disorders in the biological and adoptive families of adopted individuals with affective disorder," *Archives of General Psychiatry* 43 (1986), report higher rates of suicide among biological families than among adoptive families. For a review of studies on identical twins and suicide, see Alec Roy et al., "Genetics of Suicide in Depression," *Journal of Clinical Psychiatry*, suppl. 2 (1999).

250 The information on suicide clusters is in Kay Jamison's *Night Falls Fast*, pages 144–53 for locations, and pages 276–80 for recent epidemics.

251 The suicide epidemic following the publication of *The Sorrows of Young Werther* is described by Paolo Bernardini in his unpublished manuscript "*Melancholia gravis*: Robert Burton's *Anatomy* (1621) and the Links between Suicide and Melancholy."

251 The report that suicide rates go up when suicide stories occur in the media, and the report of a jump in suicides following the death of Marilyn Monroe, are in George Colt's *The Enigma of Suicide*, pages 90–91.

251 A discussion of how suicide-prevention programs may in fact inspire suicides occurs in Kay Jamison's *Night Falls Fast*, pages 273–75.

251 That suicide attempts predict suicide is reported in Rise Goldstein et al., "The Prediction of Suicide," *Archives of General Psychiatry* 48 (1991). They write, "We were able to demonstrate that not only a history of prior suicide attempts but also the *number* of attempts is critical, as the risk of suicide increases with each subsequent suicide attempt." Page 421.

251 The quotation from Maria Oquendo et al. is from "Inadequacy of Antidepressant Treatment for Patients with Major Depression Who Are at Risk for Suicidal Behavior," *American Journal of Psychiatry* 156, no. 2 (1999): 193.

252 That lithium is the drug most tested for its effects on suicidality is recorded in Kay Jamison's *Night Falls Fast*, pages 239–41.

252 That the rate of suicide among bipolar patients who discontinue use of lithium rises sixteenfold is indicated in Leonardo Tondo et al., "Lithium maintenance treatment reduces risk of suicidal behavior in Bipolar Disorder patients," in

Lithium: Biochemical and Clinical Advances, edited by Vincent Gallicchio and Nicholas Birch, pages 161–71.

252 That patients treated with ECT have lower suicide rates than those treated with medications is outlined in Jerome Motto's essay "Clinical Considerations of Biological Correlates of Suicide," in *The Biology of Suicide,* edited by Ronald Maris.

252 Freud's formulation of suicide as a murderous impulse toward the self is discussed in a number of his writings. In "Mourning and Melancholia," he writes, "We have long known, it is true, that no neurotic harbors thoughts of suicide which he has not turned back on himself from murderous impulses against others." See *The Standard Edition of the Complete Psychological Works of Sigmund Freud,* vol. 14, page 252.

252 Edwin Shneidman's description of suicide as murder in the 180th degree is reproduced in George Colt's *The Enigma of Suicide,* page 196.

252 Freud's formulation of the death instinct is described in Robert Litman's essay "Sigmund Freud on Suicide," in *Essays in Self-Destruction,* Edwin Shneidman, editor, page 336.

252 Karl Menninger's formulation is cited in George Colt's *The Enigma of Suicide,* page 201.

252 Chesterton's lines are in Glen Evans amd Norman L. Farberow's *The Encyclopedia of Suicide,* page ii.

252 The effects of chronic stress in depleting neurotransmitters have been researched by many people. An excellent summary of these ideas is provided by Kay Jamison's *Night Falls Fast,* pages 192–93. For more information on the brain's response to stress, see Robert Sapolsky et al., "Hippocampal damage associated with prolonged glucocorticoid exposure in primates," *Journal of Neuroscience* 10, no. 9 (1990).

253 The work on suicidality and cholesterol is summarized nicely in Kay Jamison's *Night Falls Fast,* pages 194–95.

253 The work on low levels of serotonin, high numbers of serotonin receptors, inhibition, and suicidality is summarized by John Mann, one of the pioneers in the area, in his "The Neurobiology of Suicide," *Lifesavers* 10, no. 4 (1998). Hermann van Praag's essay "Affective Disorders and Aggression Disorders: Evidence for a Common Biological Mechanism," in *The Biology of Suicide,* edited by Ronald Maris, is also an excellent review of the findings to date. For further reading, see Alec Roy's "Possible Biologic Determinants of Suicide," in *Current Concepts of Suicide,* edited by David Lester.

253 The information regarding low levels of serotonin in murderers and arsonists may be found in M. Virkkunen et al., "Personality Profiles and State Aggressiveness in Finnish Alcoholics, Violent Offenders, Fire Setters, and Healthy Volunteers," *Archives of General Psychiatry* 51 (1994).

253 There are countless studies of the relationship between low serotonin and animal risk-taking. One particularly strong essay is P. T. Mehlman et al., "Low CSF 5-HIAA Concentrations and Severe Aggression and Impaired Impulse Control in Nonhuman Primates," *American Journal of Psychiatry* 151 (1994). I have also drawn material from a number of articles published in the Across Species Comparison and Psychopathology *ASCAP* newsletters.

253 Levels of norepinephrine and noradrenaline in postsuicide brains have been studied by many researchers. Kay Jamison provides an excellent summary in *Night Falls Fast,* pages 192–93.

253 For more on low levels of essential neurotransmitters, see John Mann, "The Neurobiology of Suicide," *Lifesavers* 10, no. 4 (1998).

253 For an excellent report on Marie Åsberg's findings, see her "Neurotransmitters and Suicidal Behavior: The Evidence from Cerebrospinal Fluid Studies," *Annals of the New York Academy of Sciences* 836 (1997).

254 The work on tryptophan hydroxylase is in D. Nielsen et al., "Suicidality and 5-Hydroxindoleacetic Acid Concentration Associated with Tryptophan Hydroxylase Polymorphism," *Archives of General Psychiatry* 51 (1994).

254 Monkeys brought up without mothers have been studied by Gary Kraemer. I have looked specifically at his study "The Behavioral Neurobiology of Self-Injurious Behavior in Rhesus Monkeys: Current Concepts and Relations to Impulsive Behavior in Humans," *Annals of the New York Academy of Sciences* 836, no. 363 (1997), presented at the NIMH's Suicide Research Workshop, November 14–15, 1996.

254 Work on early abuse and lowered serotonin is in Joan Kaufman et al., "Serotonergic Functioning in Depressed Abused Children: Clinical and Familial Correlates," *Biological Psychiatry* 44, no. 10 (1998).

254 For more on the link between fetal neurological damage and suicidality, see Kay Jamison's *Night Falls Fast*, page 183.

254 Comparative male-to-female serotonin levels are described in Simeon Margolis and Karen L. Swartz, "Sex Differences in Brain Serotonin Production," *The Johns Hopkins White Papers: Depression and Anxiety,* 1998, page 14. For in-depth information regarding gender and brain monoamine systems, see Uriel Halbreich and Lucille Lumley, "The multiple interactional biological processes that might lead to depression and gender differences in its appearance," *Journal of Affective Disorders* 29, no. 2–3 (1993).

254 The quotation from Kay Jamison is from her book *Night Falls Fast*, page 184.

254 The link between availability of guns and suicide is published in a variety of studies. I have specifically looked at M. Boor et al., "Suicide Rates, Handgun Control Laws, and Sociodemographic Variables," *Psychological Reports* 66 (1990).

254 The information on gas-related suicide in England is in George Colt's *The Enigma of Suicide*, page 335.

255 That more Americans kill themselves with guns than are murdered with them every year is in Kay Jamison's *Night Falls Fast*, page 284. The suicide rates for states according to strictness of gun control laws, as well as the quotation by David Oppenheim, are from George Colt's *The Enigma of Suicide*, page 336.

255 The statistic for the number of Americans who kill themselves every year with guns was taken from the Centers for Disease Control. An on-line journal offered the following total, the source of which I could not find on the CDC's Web site: "Figures released on November 18 by the CDC show that the number of suicides using firearms [was] 17,767 in 1997." See www.stats.org/statswork/gunsuicide.htm. A rough estimate can also be calculated using information readily available on the CDC's Web site. Of the 30,535 people who committed suicide in 1997, the CDC estimates that "nearly 3 out of every 5" of these suicides was committed with a firearm. Calculations using this formula find the total number of firearm suicides to be 18,321. I have chosen 18,000 as an approximate average of these two figures. See the CDC's Web site at www.cdc.gov/ncipc/factsheets/suifacts.htm.

255 The information on modes of suicide in China is in Kay Jamison's *Night Falls Fast*, page 140.

255 The information on modes of suicide in Punjab is in *Ibid.*, 137.

255 For the rates of suicide among artists, scientists, businessmen, poets, and composers, see *ibid.*, 181.

Notes

255   The rate of suicide among alcoholics is taken from George Colt's *The Enigma of Suicide*, page 266.

255   Karl Menninger's quotation is from *Man Against Himself*, page 184.

257   The experiments on rats crowded together have been carried out by Juan López, Delia Vásquez, Derek Chalmers, and Stanley Watson and were presented at the NIMH's Suicide Research Workshop, November 14–15, 1996.

257   The work on rhesus monkeys reared without mothers has been carried out by Gary Kraemer. I have specifically looked at his study "The Behavioral Neurobiology of Self-Injurious Behavior in Rhesus Monkeys," presented at the NIMH's Suicide Research Workshop, November 14–15, 1996.

257   The story of the suicidal octopus I take from Marie Åsberg.

257   The work on suicide and trauma of early parental death comes from L. Moss and D. Hamilton, "The Psychotherapy of the Suicidal Patient," *American Journal of Psychiatry* 122 (1956).

257   The numbers on suicide attempts and those showing suicide to be the third leading killer among people fifteen to twenty-four in the United States are taken from D. L. Hoyert et al., "Deaths: Final data for 1997. National Vital Statistics Report," published for the National Center for Health Statistics. It is available on the Web at www.cdc.gov/ncipc/osp/states/10lc97.htm. Attempted suicide was estimated by using the NIMH's statistic that "there are an estimated eight to twenty-five attempted suicides to one completion." The figure of eighty thousand attempts is therefore, unfortunately, a modest estimate. The NIMH report may be found at www.nimh.nih.gov/publicat/harmaway.cfm.

257   The catalog of reasons for increased suicidality is taken from George Colt's *The Enigma of Suicide*, page 49.

258   The work on high-achieving adolescents and suicide is presented in Herbert Hendin's *Suicide in America*, page 55.

258   The notion that a protected view of death may lead to some young suicides is discussed in Philip Patros and Tonia Shamoo's *Depression and Suicide in Children and Adolescents*, page 41.

258   For information about suicide rates among men over sixty-five, see Diego de Leo and René F. W. Diekstra's *Depression and Suicide in Late Life*, page 188.

258   The notion that the elderly use particularly lethal technologies for suicide and are particularly secretive about it is from *Ibid.*

259   Higher suicide rates among divorced or widowed men are discussed in *Ibid.*

259   On the development of motor problems, hypochondria, and paranoia among the elderly as a consequence of depression, see *Ibid.*, 24.

259   On the elderly depressed and somaticization, see Laura Musetti et al., "Depression Before and After Age 65: A Reexamination," *British Journal of Psychiatry* 155 (1989): 330.

259   The comparative international suicide rates, which place Hungary at the top of the list with a suicide rate of 40 per 100,000 and Jamaica at the bottom with a rate of 0.4 per 100,000 can be found in Eric Marcus's *Why Suicide?* pages 25–26.

259   Kay Jamison's catalog of suicide techniques is in her book *Night Falls Fast*, pages 133–34.

263   The WHO position on suicide as a "suicidal act with a fatal outcome" is detailed in their report, *Prevention of Suicide*.

263   Kay Jamison's quotation is in *Night Falls Fast*, page 39.

263   A. Alvarez's quotation is in *The Savage God*, page 89.

Notes

263 Albert Camus's quotation is in *The Myth of Sisyphus and Other Essays*, page 5.

263 Julia Kristeva's quotation is in *Black Sun*, page 4.

263 Edwin Shneidman's formulation of the five causes of suicide is taken from his book *The Suicidal Mind*. The direct quotation is from pages 58–59.

264 The Kay Jamison quotation occurs in *Night Falls Fast*, page 74.

265 On Kay Jamison's description of her state of mind during her own suicide attempt, see *Ibid.*, 291. She has also published a memoir of her battles with manic-depressive illness, entitled *An Unquiet Mind*.

265 The suicide note is taken from Kay Jamison's *Night Falls Fast*, page 292.

266 The quotation from Edna St. Vincent Millay is from her "Sonnet in Dialectic," in *Collected Sonnets*, page 159.

268 I have written about my mother's death at some length in the past. I described it in a *New Yorker* story on euthanasia, and it was the basis for the eleventh chapter of my novel, *A Stone Boat*. I have chosen to write about it for what I hope will be the last time because it is part of my story as it exists in this book. I beg the indulgence of readers familiar with my earlier work.

268 The quotation from Fyodor Dostoyevsky's *The Possessed* is on page 96.

269 The British court finding on the diabetic anorexic was brought up in an oral interview with Dr. Deborah Christie, who worked on the case. See Deborah Christie and Russell Viner, "Eating disorders and self-harm in adolescent diabetes," *Journal of Adolescent Health* 27 (2000).

270 The quotation from Alfred Lord Tennyson's "Tithonus" is lines 66–71, in *Tennyson's Poetry*, page 72.

270 The lines from Eliot are in the epigraph to his poem "The Waste Land." *The Complete Poems and Plays* presents the Latin: "Nam Sibyllam quidem Cumis ego ipse oculis meis vidi in ampulla pendere, et cum illi pueri dicerent: Σίβυλλα τί θέλεις; respondebat illa: ἀποθανειν θέλω," page 37.

271 This poem by Emily Dickinson is in *The Complete Poems of Emily Dickinson*, page 262.

273 The quotation from E. M. Cioran is in his *A Short History of Decay*, page 36.

273 Virginia Woolf's suicide note is quoted from *The Letters of Virginia Woolf*, vol. 6, pages 486–87.

274 The quotations from Virginia Woolf's diaries come from *The Diary of Virginia Woolf*, pages 110–11.

278 Ronald Dworkin's remarks are in *Life's Dominion*, page 93.

278 The quotation from Rilke is from "Requiem for a Friend," in *The Selected Poetry of Rainer Maria Rilke*, page 85.

280 The quotation from A. Alvarez is from *The Savage God*, page 75.

281 The quotation from Nadezhda Mandelstam is in *Ibid.*, 151–52.

281 The quotation from Primo Levi is from the U.S. edition of *The Drowned and the Saved*, pages 70–71.

282 That medications may have been to blame for the suicide of Primo Levi is suggested in Peter Bailey's introduction to the British edition of *The Drowned and the Saved*.

283 Nietzsche writes in *Beyond Good and Evil*, maxim 157, page 103: "The thought of suicide is a powerful solace: by means of it one gets through many a bad night."

Notes

CHAPTER VIII: HISTORY

285 Though I was not able to find any secondary source that plumbed the history of depression in a fully convincing way, I wish to acknowledge my considerable debt to Stanley Jackson's *Melancholia and Depression*.

285 Etymology of the word *depression* is from *The Oxford English Dictionary*, vol. 3, page 220.

285 The Beckett quotation is from *Waiting for Godot*. I have taken it from *The Complete Dramatic Works of Samuel Beckett*, page 31.

286 For a general description of humoral theory as it existed among the Greeks, including the views of Empedocles on melancholy, see Stanley Jackson's *Melancholia and Depression*, pages 7–12.

286 The quotations from the Hippocratic Corpus, which, for the sake of simplicity, I have referenced as from Hippocrates, may be found in *Hippocrates*, W. H. S. Jones and E. T. Withington, trans. and eds., book 2, page 175. The information on his cure of King Perdiccas II is in Giuseppe Roccatagliata's rigorous *A History of Ancient Psychiatry*, page 164.

287 The suggestion that *chole* was conflated with *cholos* comes from Bennett Simon's *Mind and Madness in Ancient Greece*, page 235.

287 The use of black moods in Homer is from *Ibid.*

287 The quotation of Homer from *The Iliad* is in book 6, lines 236–40, page 202.

287 Hippocrates' attacks on the practitioners of sacred medicine is in Giuseppe Roccatagliata's *A History of Ancient Psychiatry*, page 162. That "all that philosophers have written on natural science no more pertains to medicine than to painting" is quoted in Iago Galdston's *Historic Derivations of Modern Psychiatry*, page 12.

287 Socrates' and Plato's opposition to Hippocrates, as well as Plato's model of the human psyche, are described in Bennett Simon's *Mind and Madness in Ancient Greece*, pages 224–27. A good comparison between Plato's and Freud's ideas exists in Iago Galdston's *Historic Derivations of Modern Psychiatry*, pages 14–16. Plato's ideas concerning the importance of childhood and family in the development of the child are discussed in Simon's *Mind and Madness in Ancient Greece*, pages 171–72.

288 Philotimus' prescription of a lead helmet is described in Giuseppe Roccatagliata's *A History of Ancient Psychiatry*, page 101.

288 The examples of Chrysippus of Cnidus' cauliflower remedy, Philistion and Plistonicus' basil mixture, and Philagrius' notion that excessive loss of sperm leads to depressive symptoms are from *Ibid.*, 102–3.

288 Aristotle's formulation of the mind-body relationship, his belief in the heart as the seat of the humors, and his disparagements of the brain are taken from *Ibid.*, 106–12.

288 Aristotle's famous words on the inspired character of the melancholic are in his "Problemata," book 30, page 953a. The following quote is taken from the same piece, pages 954a–b.

289 The lines from *The Sack of Troy* are quoted from Bennett Simon's *Mind and Madness in Ancient Greece*, page 231.

289 The lines from Seneca are in Rudolph and Margot Wittkower's *Born Under Saturn*, page 99.

289 Menander's grim line is from *Comicorum Atticorum fragmenta*, fragment 18.

289 For more on the Skeptics, including particularly relevant information on Medius,

Aristogen, and Metrodorus, see Giuseppe Roccatagliata's *A History of Ancient Psychiatry,* pages 133–35.

289 For more on Erasistratus of Juli see *Ibid.,* 137–38.

289 The line from Herophilus of Calcedonius, as well as the policies of Menodotus of Nicomedia, is from *Ibid.,* 138–40.

289 A lovely chapter on Rufus of Ephesus may be found in Stanley Jackson's *Melancholia and Depression,* pages 35–39. This provides the selected quotations I have used, as well as the recipe for the "sacred remedy."

290 The information on the use of dripping pipes and hammocks is from *Ibid.,* 35. The prescription of light-colored foods and human breast milk is in Barbara Tolley's unpublished dissertation "The Languages of Melancholy in *Le Philosophe Anglais,*" page 17.

290 The views of Aretaeus of Capidoccia are described in Giuseppe Roccatagliata's *A History of Ancient Psychiatry,* pages 223–32.

291 There is a great deal of material on Galen, both in general medical histories and in more specific accounts of early psychiatry. I have relied particularly heavily on Stanley Jackson's *Melancholia and Depression* and Giuseppe Roccatagliata's *A History of Ancient Psychiatry.* The quotations here are from the latter, pages 193–209.

291 The information on Aztec treatments is in Tzvetan Todorov's *The Conquest of America,* page 68. I thank Elena Phipps for leading me to this material.

292 The Stoic philosophers and their role in medical wisdom are in Giuseppe Roccatagliata's *A History of Ancient Psychiatry,* pages 133–43.

292 For a discussion of Saint Augustine, including the implications of his positions, see Judith Neaman's *Suggestion of the Devil,* pages 51–65.

292 Nebuchadnezzar is described in the King James Version of the Bible in Daniel 4:33.

292 The phrase "the noonday demon" occurs in the literature on this subject and seems to have been composed from several primary biblical sources. The passage in question is given in the King James Version of the Bible (Psalms 91:6), which sticks closely in this matter to the original Hebrew, as: "the destruction that wasteth at noonday." In the Catholic Douay version of the Old Testament (Psalms 90:6) we have the phrase "the noonday devil," which is a variant translation of the Latin *"daemonio meridiano"* of the Vulgate (attributed to Saint Jerome and commonly used in the medieval Latin West). The Latin phrase in turn derives from the old Greek or Septuagint Bible (Psalms 90:6) which has *"daimoniou mesembrinou."* This last may have been the basis for Cassian's translation of the phrase as "the midday demon" (cited by Stanley Jackson's *Melancholia and Depression* as coming from Cassian's *Institutes of the Conobia;* Jackson himself uses the phrase "noonday demon" in his discussion of Cassian). I thank Dr. Kevin White at the Catholic University of America for help with this matter.

293 Of Evagrius and the use of the term *noonday demon,* Reinhard Kuhn writes in *The Demon of Noontide* on page 43 that "Of the eight vices that Evagrius discusses in his *Of Eight Capital Sins,* acedia is given the longest and most detailed treatment. . . . Evagrius, like many of his followers, referred to acedia as the 'daemon qui etiam meridianus vocatur,' that is, as the 'noontide demon' of the Psalms. . . ." Kuhn seems to have come up with both *demon of noontide* and *noontide demon;* the phrase can, however, equally be translated as *noonday demon.* Stanley Jackson writes on page 66 of *Melancholia and Depression* that acedia, as described by Evagrius, "was characterized by exhaustion, listlessness, sadness, or dejection, restlessness, aversion to the cell and ascetic life, and yearning for family and former life."

293 On "madness" and the Inquisition, see Iago Galdston's *Historic Derivations of Modern Psychiatry*, pages 19–22.

293 For more on Thomas Aquinas in this regard, see *Ibid.*, 31–34. There has been a great deal—some might say more than is necessary—written on Aquinas and dualism.

293 The Parson's monologue was taken from Chaucer's *Canterbury Tales Complete*, pages 588–92.

294 On the distinction between *acedia* and *tristia*, see Stanley Jackson's *Melancholia and Depression*, pages 65–77.

294 Hildegard von Bingen's vivid remark is from *Ibid.*, 326.

295 On the artist Hugo van der Goes, see Rudolph and Margot Wittkower's *Born Under Saturn*, pages 108–13.

295 For an extensive discussion of Marsilio Ficino, see Paul Kristeller's *The Philosophy of Marsilio Ficino*. Many of the quotations I have used are taken from this text, pages 208–14. Additional information and quotations are taken from Winfried Schleiner's *Melancholy, Genius, and Utopia in the Renaissance*, pages 24–26, as well as Klibansky et al.'s *Saturn and Melancholy*, page 159; Barbara Tolley's unpublished dissertation "The Languages of Melancholy in *Le Philosophe Anglais*," pages 20–23; and Lawrence Babb's *The Elizabethan Malady*, pages 60–61.

296 On Agrippa, see Winfried Schleiner's *Melancholy, Genius, and Utopia in the Renaissance*, pages 26–27.

296 Vasari's comments on depressiveness among artists are presented erratically and esoterically in both volumes of his *Lives of the Artists*. In volume 1, Vasari discusses Paolo Uccello, whom he describes as ending up "solitary, eccentric, melancholy, and poor" because of "choking his mind with difficult problems," page 95. Correggio, he writes, "was very melancholy in the practice of his art, at which he toiled unceasingly," page 278. For an excellent secondary source on the tradition of melancholy and artistic genius, concerning especially the most supreme, Albrecht Dürer, and the German Renaissance, see Raymond Klibansky, Erwin Panofsky, and Fritz Saxl's truly inspired *Saturn and Melancholy: Studies in the History of Natural Philosophy, Religion, and Art*.

296 The "intercourse or meddling of euill angels" comes from Andreas Du Laurens's *Discourse*, as quoted in Lawrence Babb's *The Elizabethan Malady*, page 49.

297 The man who felt the "evil Spirit enter by his fundament" is described in Lawrence Babb's *The Elizabethan Malady*, page 53.

297 George Gifford's views are in Winfried Schleiner's *Melancholy, Genius, and Utopia in the Renaissance*, page 182.

297 Discussions of Jan Wier, who also appears under the name Johann Weyer, are from *Ibid.*, 181–87, as well as in Lawrence Babb's *The Elizabethan Malady*, pages 54–56.

297 Freud's remarks on Jan Wier are in his *Standard Edition*, vol. 9, page 245.

297 Reginald Scot's views on witchcraft and the story of King James demanding Scot's book be burned are described in detail in Lawrence Babb's *The Elizabethan Malady*, pages 55–56, and Winfried Schleiner's *Melancholy, Genius, and Utopia in the Renaissance*, pages 183–87.

297 The French case of the rumbling under the short ribs is described in Winfried Schleiner's *Melancholy, Genius, and Utopia in the Renaissance*, page 189.

298 The words from the synod of 1583 are from *Ibid.*, 190.

298 Montaigne on melancholy is a wonderful topic and warrants a long discussion of its own. For the material referenced here see *Ibid.*, 179, 184. A more in-depth discussion can be found in M. A. Screech's *Montaigne & Melancholy*.

298 Andreas Du Laurens is also known as Laurentius. For the sake of simplicity, I have stuck with his non-Latin name. The discussion, including quotations, is taken from Stanley Jackson's *Melancholia and Depression*, pages 86–91, and T. H. Jobe's "Medical Theories of Melancholia in the Seventeenth and Early Eighteenth Centuries," *Clio Medica* 11, no. 4 (1976): 217–21.

299 The doctor of the early seventeenth century to whom I refer here is Richard Napier, and his remarks may be found in Michael MacDonald's *Mystical Bedlam*, pages 159–60. John Archer wrote in his 1673 manuscript that melancholy is the "greatest enemy of nature," as referenced in *Mystical Bedlam*, page 160.

299 References to Levinus Lemnius, Huarte, Luis Mercado, and Joannes Baptista Silvaticus may be found in Lawrence Babb's *The Elizabethan Malady*, page 62.

300 The melancholic barber is in the play *Midas* by Lyly. His line is quoted as it appears in Michael MacDonald's *Mystical Bedlam*, page 151.

300 The physician whose melancholy patients tended to be titled is Richard Napier. The statistics are from *Ibid.*, 151. Napier's account of his practice is unusually thorough and is among the best materials of its period. He seems to have had an acute sensitivity to mental health complaints and is eloquent about them.

301 That those who were truly ill with melancholia had sympathy and respect is borne out in the writings of Timothy Rogers. In his *Discourse* of 1691 he writes extensively about the consideration and understanding that should be extended to the depressed. "Do not urge your Friends under the Disease of Melancholly, to things which they cannot do," he writes. "They are as persons whose bones are broken, and that are in great pain and anguish, and consequently under an incapacity for action . . . if it were possible by any means innocently to divert them, you would do them a great kindness." See *A Discourse Concerning Trouble of the Mind and the Disease of Melancholly*, sections of which are reprinted in Richard Hunter and Ida Macalpine's *300 Years of Psychiatry*, pages 248–51.

301 The quotes from "Il Penseroso" are lines 11–14, 168–69, and 173–76, from John Milton's *Complete Poems and Major Prose*, pages 72 and 76.

301 Robert Burton's *Anatomy of Melancholy* makes excellent reading and contains a great deal of wisdom that I have not been able to reproduce here. Commentaries on Burton abound. For a short and concise summary of his life and work, see Stanley Jackson's *Melancholia and Depression*, pages 95–99. For lengthier discussions, see Lawrence Babb's *The Elizabethan Malady*, Eleanor Vicari's *The View from Minerva's Tower*, Vieda Skultan's *English Madness*, and Rudolph and Margot Wittkower's *Born Under Saturn*. I have also relied heavily upon Paolo Bernardini's unpublished manuscript "*Melancholia gravis*: Robert Burton's *Anatomy* (1621) and the Links between Suicide and Melancholy." The quotations reproduced in the text come from Robert Burton's *Anatomy of Melancholy*, pages 129–39, 162–71, 384–85, and 391. The quotes used in the discussion of Burton and suicide are taken directly from Bernardini's manuscript.

304 The tales of Caspar Barlaeus and the man who had to be packed in straw, Ludovicus a Casanova on the butter man, the story of Charles VI, and the recent exemplar of the glass delusion in Holland are all in F. F. Blok's *Caspar Barlaeus*, pages 105–21.

306 On Descartes and mental health, see Theodore Brown's essay "Descartes, dualism, and psychosomatic medicine," in W. F. Bynum, Roy Porter, and Michael Shepherd, *The Anatomy of Madness*, vol. 1, pages 40–62. Selections of Descartes's *The Passions of the Soul* appear in Richard Hunter and Ida Macalpine's *300 Years of Psychiatry*, pages 133–34.

306 The passages from Willis may be found in his *Two Discourses Concerning the Soul of Brutes*, pages 179, 188–201, and 209. T. H. Jobe's "Medical Theories of Melancholia in the Seventeenth and Early Eighteenth Centuries," *Clio Medica* 11, no. 4 (1976), and Allan Ingram's *The Madhouse of Language* were both useful secondary sources.

307 The passages from Nicholas Robinson may be found in Allan Ingram's *The Madhouse of Language*, pages 24–25.

307 Boerhaave specifically rejected humoral theory and cultivated a notion of the body as a fibrous mass fed by the hydraulic action of the blood. The primary causes of melancholy were, Boerhaave believed, "all things, which fix, exhaust, or confound the nervous juices from the Brain; as great and unexpected frightful accidents, a great Application upon any Object whatever; strong Love, Waking Solitude, Fear, and hysterical Affections." Other causes to be considered were "immoderate Venery; Drink; Parts of Animal dried in Smoke, Air or Salt; unripe Fruits; mealy unfermented Matters." Those who allowed intemperate activity or consumption to imbalance their blood were likely to produce acidic materials, which Boerhaave called "acrids," and then their bile would undergo "acrimonious degeneration" to create a nasty burning liquid that went around causing trouble throughout the body. In the brain, a "coagulating acid" would solidify the blood, which would cease to circulate to certain essential areas.

307 Secondary sources on Boerhaave's theories abound. Among the best are Stanley Jackson's summary in *Melancholia and Depression*, pages 119–21, and T. H. Jobe's "Medical Theories of Melancholia in the Seventeenth and Early Eighteenth Centuries," *Clio Medica* 11, no. 4 (1976): 224–27. The quotations are taken from Boerhaave's *Aphorisms*, as well as selected quotes from T. H. Jobe's article, pages 226–27.

307 Boerhaave had many followers and disciples. It is interesting to look at how he influenced, for example, Richard Mead. In his magnum opus, published in 1751, Mead stuck with the idea of mechanics but moved them from the blood system to the "animal spirits" that move along the nerves. "Nothing disorders the mind so much as love and religion," he observed. For Mead as for Boerhaave, the brain is "manifestly a large gland" and the nerves are "an excretory duct," and whatever goes along the nerves is a "thin volatile liquor of great force and elasticity." Again, there are shadows of accuracy here: something does come from the brain and in a sense travels along the nerves, and that is the neurotransmitters. The first two quotations from Richard Mead may be found in his *Medical Precepts and Cautions*, pages 76 and 78; the last three quotations may be found in his collected works, entitled *The Medical Works of Richard Mead, M.D.*, page xxi.

307 Julien Offray de La Mettrie is described in some detail in Aram Vartanian's *La Mettrie's L'Homme Machine*. The quote is taken from Vartanian's book, page 22.

308 Friedrich Hoffman said in 1783 that blood became thick through "debility of the brain, from long grief or fear or love." He proposed, further, that mania and depression, long treated as two unrelated problems, "appear to be rather different stages of one; the mania being properly an exacerbation of melancholy, and leaving the patient melancholic in the calmer intervals." He picks up on Boerhaave's ideas in saying that melancholy was "a retardation of the circulation" and mania, "an acceleration of it." The passages from Friedrich Hoffman may be found in his *A System of the Practice of Medicine*, pages 298–303.

308 The quotations from Spinoza are from *The Ethics of Spinoza*, pages 139–40.

309 For a good discussion of Bedlam, see Marlene Arieno's *Victorian Lunatics*, espe-

Notes

cially pages 16–19. On Bicêtre and its most famous Dr. Philippe Pinel, see Dora Weiner's "'Le geste de Pinel': The History of a Psychiatric Myth," published as chapter 12 of *Discovering the History of Psychiatry*, edited by Mark Micale and Roy Porter.

309 Blake's complaint is from Roy Porter's *Mind-Forg'd Manacles*, page 73.

309 There are a multitude of general books on madness and the eighteenth and early nineteenth centuries. My discussion has been influenced by a variety of these including Andrew Scull's *Social Order/Mental Disorder*, Michel Foucault's *Madness and Civilization*, and Roy Porter's *Mind-Forg'd Manacles*.

309 The quotation from John Monro may be found in Andrew Scull's *Social Order/Mental Disorder*, page 59.

309 Depictions of some of the most alarming-looking torture devices of the early eighteenth century are to be found in *Ibid.*, 69–72.

309 Boswell's comments on mental illness, as well as his diaries and correspondence, may be found in Allan Ingram's *The Madhouse of Language*, pages 146–49.

310 Samuel Johnson on Burton is in Roy Porter's *Mind-Forg'd Manacles*, pages 75–77. Johnson on "the black dog" is in Max Byrd's *Visits to Bedlam*, page 127.

310 For Cowper on his depression, including the passages quoted, see Allan Ingram's *The Madhouse of Language*, pages 149–50. The lines of poetry are from his "Lines Written During a Period of Insanity," in *The Poetical Works of William Cowper*, page 290.

311 Edward Young's lines are in his *The Complaint, or Night-Thoughts*, vol. 1, page 11.

311 Tobias Smollett's description of himself as a hospital is in Roy Porter's *Mind-Forg'd Manacles*, endnotes, page 345.

311 The quotation from the Marquise du Deffand comes from Jerome Zerbe and Cyril Connolly, *Les Pavillons of the Eighteenth Century*, page 21.

311 Johnson on Scotland is in Max Byrd's *Visits to Bedlam*, page 126.

311 John Brown's fit disparagement of the British climate, as well as Edmund Burke's remarks, are in *Ibid.*, 126. One could go on for volumes with eighteenth-century comments on melancholy. Jonathan Swift, a splenetic fellow himself, had little mercy for these many accounts. He was very much of the pull-yourself-up-by-the-bootstraps mentality: "A fancy would sometimes take a Yahoo, to retire into a Corner, to lie down and howl, and groan, and spurn away all that came near him, although he were young and fat, and wanted neither Food nor Water; nor did the Servants imagine what could possibly ail him. And the only Remedy they found was to set him to hard Work, after which he would infallibly come to himself." This passage is from *Gulliver's Travels*, page 199.

311 The passage of Voltaire quoted here is from *Candide*, page 140.

311 Horace Walpole's charming prescription is in Roy Porter's *Mind-Forg'd Manacles*, page 241. The question of geography and depression first arose in this period. William Rowley wrote that "England, according to its size and number of inhabitants, produces and contains more insane than any other country in Europe, and suicide is more common. The agitations of passions, the liberty of thinking and acting with less restraint than in other nations, force a great quantity of blood to the head, and produce greater varieties of madness in this country, than is observed in others. Religious and civil toleration are productive of political and religious madness; but where no such toleration exists, no such insanity appears." William Rowley's remarks are in Max Byrd's *Visits to Bedlam*, page 129.

312 The line from Thomas Gray's "Elegy Written in a Country Churchyard" is num-

ber 36, to be found on page 38 of *The Complete Poems of Thomas Gray.* The lines from "Ode on a Distant Prospect of Eton College" are on pages 9–10 of the same volume.

312 Coleridge's remarks are to be found in *The Collected Letters of Samuel Taylor Coleridge,* Earl Leslie Griggs, editor, vol. 1, letter 68, page 123.

312 Kant's aphorisms are from his *Observations on the Feeling of the Beautiful and Sublime,* pages 56 and 63.

312 On mental health in the American colonies, see Mary Ann Jimenez's *Changing Faces of Madness.*

312 One example of the U.S. trend toward religious explanations of depression is William Thompson, a minister in seventeenth-century Massachusetts, who became so depressed that he had to give up his work and became "the lively portraiture of Death / A walking tomb, a living sepulcher / In which black melancholy did inter." The devil it was who "vexed his mind with diabolical assaults and horrid, hellish darts." The poem on William Thompson, written by his "family and friends," may be found in *Ibid.,* 13.

313 Cotton Mather on the depression of his wife is in *Ibid.,* 13–15.

313 The quotations from *The Angel of Bethesda* are on pages 130–33.

313 Henry Rose's remarks are in his *An Inaugural Dissertation on the Effects of the Passions upon the Body,* page 12. Other prominent Americans publishing treatises on the subject of depression include Nicholas Robinson, William Cullen, and Edward Cutbush. Nicholas Robinson was much read in the colonies, and his mechanical explanations of melancholy dominated thought there throughout the mid–eighteenth century. For more on Nicholas Robinson in the colonies, see Mary Ann Jimenez's *Changing Faces of Madness,* pages 18–20. William Cullen, publishing in Philadelphia in 1790, a humanist freed from some of religion's constraints, found that a "drier and firmer texture in the medullary substance of the brain" from a "certain want of fluid in that substance" causes melancholy. These words may be found in Cullen's *The First Lines of the Practice of Physic,* vol. 3, page 217. Edward Cutbush, in the colonies, speaks of melancholy as an "atonic madness" in which "the mind is generally fixed to one subject; many are cogitative, silent, morose, and fixed like statues; others wander from their habitation in search of solitary places, they neglect cleanliness, their bodies are generally cold, with a change of color and dry skin; all the different secretions are much diminished, the pulse slow and languid." He saw the brain as constantly in motion (much like the heart or lungs) and thought that all madness came from "an excess or defect of motion, in one or more parts of the brain." He then wondered whether such defects of motion come from the blood and the nervous fluid, as Boerhaave said, from chemical matters, as Willis suggested, or "an electric or electroid fluid" that could cause "the periodical attacks of insanity" in the event of "an accumulation of this electricity in the brain." Cutbush said that overexcitement of the brain could ruin it: "The first impression causes so great a commotion in the brain, that it will exclude, or draw into a vast vortex, every other motion, and insanity with her humerous train of attendants will usurp her way over sovereign reason." Edward Cutbush's views are in his *An Inaugural Dissertation on Insanity,* pages 18, 24, 32–33.

313 On "evangelical anorexia nervosa," see Julius Rubin's *Religious Melancholy and Protestant Experience in America,* pages 82–124 and 156–76. The phrase "starving perfectionists" is on page 158.

314 These words from Kant on the sublime are in *The Philosophy of Kant,* page 4.

Notes

314 The famous line is from Johann Wolfgang von Goethe's *Faust*, part I, scene 6, page 42.

314 Wordsworth's lines are from the poem "Resolution and Independence," in the volume *The Prelude: Selected Poems and Sonnets*, page 138.

314 Keats on easeful death is line 52 of "Ode to a Nightingale," in *The Poems*, page 202. The quotation from "Ode on Melancholy" is lines 21–25, in the same collection, page 214.

314 The quotations from Shelley are from his poem "Mutability," lines 1–4 and 19–21, in *The Complete Poems of Percy Bysshe Shelley*, page 679.

315 Giacomo Leopardi's lines are from "To Himself," in his *Poems*, page 115.

315 "Vanity of vanities" is Ecclesiastes 12:8.

315 The lines from *The Sorrows of Young Werther* are to be found on pages 95 and 120.

315 Baudelaire's lines are from *The Flowers of Evil*, pages 92–93.

316 The quotation from Hegel comes from his *Lectures on the Philosophy of History*, as quoted in Wolf Lepenies's *Melancholy and Society*, page 75.

316 Of course everything Kierkegaard wrote seems to be about depression at one level or another, but these passages come, respectively, from a quoted segment in Georg Lukács's *Soul and Form*, page 33, and from Kierkegaard's *The Sickness Unto Death*, page 50.

316 Schopenhauer's comments on melancholia are primarily in his essays rather than in his longer books. I would call attention particularly to his essays "On the Sufferings of the World," "On the Vanity of Existence," and "On Suicide." The quotations here are both from "On the Sufferings of the World," within the collection *Complete Essays of Schopenhauer*, pages 3–4.

317 Nietzsche's comments on health and illness are in *The Will to Power*, page 29.

317 The passages from Philippe Pinel may be found in his *A Treatise on Insanity*, pages 107, 132, and 53–54, respectively.

317 The quotation from Samuel Tuke is from Andrew Scull's *Social Order/Mental Disorder*, page 75.

318 The master of another asylum to whom I allude here is quoted in *Ibid.*, 77.

318 The statistics on the insane may be found in Marlene Arieno's *Victorian Lunatics*, page 11. The history of the Lunatics Acts is in the same book, pages 15–17.

318 The population of Bedlam in 1850 is in *Ibid.*, 17.

319 Thomas Beddoes's rather insightful quotation is in Stanley Jackson's *Melancholia and Depression*, page 186.

319 Benjamin Rush's ideas and words are in his *Medical Inquiries and Observations*, pages 61–62, 78, and 104–8.

319 J. E. D. Esquirol was among those who stuck quite closely to Pinel. He championed humane asylums in the very early nineteenth century, adding that patients should be treated with a "dry and temperate climate, a clear sky, a pleasant temperature, an agreeable situation, varied scenery," as well as exercise, travel, and laxatives. For the causes of melancholy, he gives a mind-boggling list that includes domestic troubles, masturbation, wounded self-love, falls upon the head, hereditary predisposition, and libertinism, among others. For the symptoms, he said that "this is not a complaint that agitates, complains, shouts, weeps; it is one that silences, that has no tears, that is immobile." Esquirol's quotations come from his *Mental Maladies*, page 226, and from Barbara Tolley's unpublished dissertation "The Languages of Melancholy in *Le Philosophe Anglais*," page 11. While some concentrated on the humanity of treatment, others focused on the nature of the illness

itself. James Cowles Prichard echoed Nietzsche in defining an illness much closer to sanity, setting up what would become the modern understanding of depression. "It is perhaps impossible," he wrote, "to determine the line which marks a transition from predisposition to disease; but there is a degree of this affection which certainly constitutes disease of mind, and that disease exists without any illusion impressed upon the understanding of reason. The faculty of reason is not manifestly impaired, but a constant feeling of gloom and sadness clouds all the prospects of life. This tendency to morbid sorrow and melancholy, as it does not destroy the understanding, is often subject to control when it first arises, and probably receives a peculiar character from the previous mental state of the individual." The passages here, quoted from James Cowles Prichard, are to be found in his *Treatise*, page 18.

319 Griesinger's ideas may be found in a variety of primary and secondary sources. His *Mental Pathology and Therapeutics* provides an excellent survey of his ideas. Stanley Jackson's *Melancholia and Depression* contains an enlightening summary of Griesinger's ideas.

320 Foucault's ideas are expounded in his famous *Madness and Civilization*, a book whose eloquent speciousness did significant damage to the cause of the mentally ill in the late twentieth century.

321 Most of Charles Dickens's work cries out for social reform. See, for example, *Nicholas Nickleby*.

321 For Victor Hugo on social injustice and alienation, see his *Les Misérables*.

321 Oscar Wilde gives voice to the spirit of alienation of his age in "The Ballad of Reading Gaol," from *Complete Poetry*, pages 152–72.

321 Joris-Karl Huysmans seems to indicate something of the alienated quality of late decadence in his famous *À Rebours* or *Against Nature*.

321 The first quotation from *Sartor Resartus* is on page 164; the second is taken directly from William James's essay "Is Life Worth Living?" in *The Will to Believe and Other Essays in Popular Philosophy*, page 42.

321 The views of William James on melancholia crop up throughout his writing. The passages quoted here come from his essay "Is Life Worth Living?" in *The Will to Believe and Other Essays in Popular Philosophy*, pages 43, 39, and 49, respectively. See also, of course, *The Varieties of Religious Experience*.

321 The lines from Matthew Arnold are from "Dover Beach," in *The Poems of Matthew Arnold*, pages 239–43.

322 Maudsley's quotations are taken from his *The Pathology of the Mind*, pages 164–68. John Charles Bucknill and Daniel H. Tuke took up Maudsley's theme in the United States—"a disorder of the intellect not being," they observed, "an essential part of the disorder." They went on to speak of the external treatments for melancholy, many of them age-old, as having a direct effect on the brain. "In all organs of the body, except the brain, great advances have been made into the knowledge of their physiological laws. But it is quite otherwise with the noble organ which lords it over the rest of the body. The physiological principle upon which we have to build a system of cerebral pathology is, that mental health is dependent upon the due nutrition, stimulation, and repose of the brain; that is, upon the conditions of the exhaustion and reparation of its nerve-substance being maintained in a healthy and regular state." And they enthusiastically suggest that opium may be effective in relaxing the brain. The passages from John Charles Bucknill and Daniel H. Tuke may be found in their *A Manual of Psychological Medicine*, pages 152

and 341–42. Richard von Krafft-Ebing also identified this mild illness. "When the innumerable slight causes that do not reach the hospital for the insane are taken into consideration, the prognosis of melancholia is favorable. Numerous cases of this kind pass on to recovery without the occurrence of delusions or errors of the senses." Richard von Krafft-Ebing is quoted from his *Text-Book of Insanity,* page 309.

322 George H. Savage's remarks may be found in his *Insanity and Allied Neuroses,* pages 130 and 151–152.

323 These remarks from Freud are from the "Extracts from the Fliess Papers," in *The Standard Edition of the Complete Psychological Works of Sigmund Freud,* vol. 1, pages 204–6.

323 Karl Abraham's 1911 essay is entitled "Notes on the Psycho-analytical Investigation and Treatment of Manic-Depressive Insanity and Allied Conditions," in *Selected Papers of Karl Abraham.* These passages are from this essay, pages 137, 146, and 156, respectively.

324 The passages quoted from "Mourning and Melancholia" have been taken from *A General Selection from the Works of Sigmund Freud,* pages 125–27, 133, and 138–39.

324 The article alluded to her is "Managing Depression in Medical Outpatients," *New England Journal of Medicine* 343, no. 26 (2000).

325 On Abraham's response to "Mourning and Melancholia," see his later essay "Development of the Libido," in *Selected Papers of Karl Abraham,* page 456.

326 For this material from Melanie Klein, see her essay "The Psychogenesis of Manic-Depressive States," in *The Selected Melanie Klein,* page 145. Other psychoanalysts writing on the topic include the great Freudian revisionist Sandor Rado. He put together a profile of the kind of person who is subject to melancholy, who is "most happy when living in an atmosphere permeated with libido" but who also has a tendency to be unreasonably demanding of those he loves. Depression, according to Rado, is "a great despairing cry for love." Depression therefore evokes once more that early demand for the mother's breast, the fulfillment of which Rado rather charmingly called "the alimentary orgasm." The depressed person, from infancy on, wants love of any kind—erotic love or maternal love or self-love are all reasonable fulfillments of his need. "The process of melancholia," Rado wrote, "represents an attempt at reparation (cure) on a grand scale, carried out with an iron psychological consistency." The quotations from Sandor Rado are from his essay "The Problem of Melancholia," in *Psychoanalysis of Behavior,* pages 49–60.

326 Hassoun's writing on depression is in his recently published book *The Cruelty of Depression.*

327 Kraepelin makes for some dull reading. The passages quoted here are from Stanley Jackson's *Melancholia and Depression,* pages 188–95. An excellent discussion of Kraepelin is also included in Myer Mendelson's *Psychoanalytic Concepts of Depression.*

328 The line from Sir William Osler is from his *Aequanimitas,* as quoted in Peter Adams's *The Soul of Medicine,* page 67.

328 Adolf Meyer is a delight to read. I am indebted to Stanley Jackson's *Melancholia and Depression* as well as Myer Mendelson's *Psychoanalytic Concepts of Depression,* and Jacques Quen and Eric Carlson's *American Psychoanalysis,* for much of my discussion of Adolf Meyer. The passages are quoted, in the order they appear in the text, from Myer Mendelson's *Psychoanalytic Concepts of Depression,* page 6; Jacques Quen and Eric Carlson's *American Psychoanalysis,* page 24; Myer Mendelson's *Psychoana-*

lytic Concepts of Depression, page 6; Adolf Meyer's *Psychobiology,* page 172; Adolf Meyer's *The Collected Papers of Adolf Meyer,* vol. 2, pages 598 and 599; Theodore Lidz's "Adolf Meyer and American Psychiatry," published in the *American Journal of Psychiatry* 123 (1966): 326; and from Adolf Meyer's *Psychobiology,* page 158.

328 On Mary Brooks Meyer, see Theodore Lidz's "Adolf Meyer and the Development of American Psychiatry," published in the *American Journal of Psychiatry* 123 (1966): 328.

329 The quotation on the goal of medicine comes from Adolf Meyer's late essay "The 'Complaint' as the Center of Genetic-Dynamic and Nosological Thinking in Psychiatry," *New England Journal of Medicine* 199 (1928).

329 The passages from Sartre come from his novel *Nausea,* pages 4, 95–96, 122, and 170.

329 The passagess byBeckett are taken, respectively, from *Malone Dies* and *The Unnamable,* and appear in the volume *Molloy, Malone Dies, The Unnamable,* on pages 256–57 and 333–34.

330 The story of the discovery of antidepressants is told over and over again. A nice version of it is in Peter Kramer's *Listening to Prozac,* and a more technical one in Peter Whybrow's *A Mood Apart.* I have relied on both of these, as well as on the detailed history that forms the backbone of David Healy's *The Antidepressant Era.* I have also incorporated information from oral interviews.

331 The Kline/Lurie–Salzer/Kuhn debate is in David Healy's *The Antidepressant Era,* pages 43–77.

331 The discovery of neurotransmitter theory and the early work on acetylcholine, as well as the discovery of serotonin and the link between substance and emotional function is from *Ibid.,* 145–47.

331 The 1955 article referenced is A. Pletscher et al., "Serotonin Release as a Possible Mechanism of Reserpine Action," *Science* 122 (1955).

331 The work on lowering serotonin levels is in David Healy's *The Antidepressant Era,* page 148.

332 The development of the MAOIs is in *Ibid.,* 152–55.

332 Axelrod's work on reuptake is in *Ibid.,* 155–161.

332 Joseph Schildkraut's original article is "The Catecholamine Hypothesis of Affective Disorders: A Review of Supporting Evidence," *American Journal of Psychiatry* 122 (1965): 509–22.

332 I am indebted to David Healy for his critique of Schildkraut.

333 The Scottish scientists who worked on receptor theory are George Ashcroft, Donald Eccleston, and team members, as is explicated in David Healy's *The Antidepressant Era,* page 162.

333 The story of Carlsson and Wong and serotonin is in *Ibid.,* 165–69.

334 The development of individual drugs is chronicled on the Web sites maintained by their manufacturers. For information on Prozac, see Lilly's Web site at www.prozac.com; for information on Zoloft, see Pfizer's Web site at www.pfizer.com; for information on drugs in development at Du Pont, see their Web site at www.dupontmerck.com; for information on Luvox, see Solvay's Web site at www.solvay.com; for information on drugs in development at Parke-Davis, see their Web site at www.parke-davis.com; for information on reboxetine and Xanax, see Pharmacia/Upjohn's Web site at www2.pnu.com; for information on Celexa, see the Web site of Forest Laboratories at www.forestlabs.com.

335 That the poor depressed tend to become more poor and depressed is indicated by a number of studies. Depression's effect on the ability to earn a living is reviewed in Sandra Danziger et al., "Barriers to the Employment of Welfare Recipients," published by the Poverty Research and Training Center of Ann Arbor, Michigan. This study indicates that among poorer populations, those with a diagnosis of major depression cannot in general work twenty hours or more a week. That they become increasingly depressed can be adduced by studies that show poor treatment records for poor and homeless populations, such as Bonnie Zima et al., "Mental Health Problems among Homeless Mothers," *Archives of General Psychiatry* 53 (1996), and Emily Hauenstein, "A Nursing Practice Paradigm for Depressed Rural Women: Theoretical Basis," *Archives of Psychiatric Nursing* 10, no. 5 (1996). For an excellent discussion on the relationships between poverty and mental health, see John Lynch et al., "Cumulative Impact of Sustained Economic Hardship on Physical, Cognitive, Psychological, and Social Functioning," *New England Journal of Medicine* 337 (1997).

336 On depression among women, see chapter 5.

336 On depression among artists, see Kay Jamison's *Touched with Fire*.

336 One example of depression among athletes may be found in Buster Olney, "Harnisch Says He Is Being Treated for Depression," *New York Times*, April 26, 1997.

336 On depression among alcoholics, see chapter 6.

336 That the poor have a high rate of depression can be adduced from the statistic that welfare recipients have an incidence of depression three times that of nonwelfare recipients, put forth in K. Olsen and L. Pavetti, "Personal and Family Challenges to the Successful Transition from Welfare to Work," published by the Urban Institute, 1996. Sandra Danziger et al.'s "Barriers to the Employment of Welfare Recipients," published by the Poverty Research and Training Center of Ann Arbor, Michigan, indicates that depressed welfare recipients are more likely to be unable to hold jobs, thus completing the circle of poverty and depression. Robert DuRant et al.'s "Factors Associated with the Use of Violence among Urban Black Adolescents," *American Journal of Public Health* 84 (1994), indicates a connection between depression and violence. Ellen Bassuk et al.'s "Prevalence of Mental Health and Substance Use Disorders among Homeless and Low-Income Housed Mothers," *American Journal of Psychiatry* 155, no. 11 (1998), reviews a number of studies indicating elevated levels of substance abuse among the depressed.

337 The efficacy of most pharmacological and psychodynamic treatments appears to be fairly consistent across populations. Depression among the indigent should therefore have the same efficacy rates as for a more general population. The difficulty with this population, in the current system, is of getting the treatment to patients.

337 The statistic that 85–95 percent of people with serious mental illness are unemployed in the United States is taken from two studies by W. A. Anthony et al.: "Predicting the vocational capacity of the chronically mentally ill: Research and implications," *American Psychologist* 39 (1984), and "Supported employment for persons with psychiatric disabilities: An historical and conceptual perspective," *Psychosocial Rehabilitation Journal* 11, no. 2 (1982).

337 On the early puberty of children of depressed mothers, see Bruce Ellis and Judy

Garber's "Psychosocial antecedents of variation in girls' pubertal timing: Maternal depression, stepfather presence, and marital and family stress," *Child Development* 71, no. 2 (2000).

337 Characteristic behavior of girls with early puberty is described in Lorah Dorn et al., "Biopsychological and cognitive differences in children with premature vs. on-time adrenarche," *Archives of Pediatric Adolescent Medicine* 153, no. 2 (1999). For a broad review of the literature on early puberty, promiscuity, and sexual activity, see Jay Belsky et al., "Childhood Experience, Interpersonal Development, and Reproductive Strategy: An Evolutionary Theory of Socialization," *Child Development* 62 (1991).

338 On medicaid programs and the mentally ill, see Lillian Cain, "Obtaining Social Welfare Benefits for Persons with Serious Mental Illness," *Hospital and Community Psychiatry* 44, no. 10 (1993); Ellen Hollingsworth, "Use of Medicaid for Mental Health Care by Clients of Community Support Programs," *Community Mental Health Journal* 30, no. 6 (1994); Catherine Melfi et al., "Access to Treatment for Depression in a Medicaid Population," *Journal of Health Care for the Poor and Underserved* 10, no. 2 (1999); and Donna McAlpine and David Mechanic, "Utilization of Specialty Mental Health Care among Persons with Severe Mental Illness: The Roles of Demographics, Need, Insurance, and Risk," *Health Services Research* 35, no. 1 (2000).

338 Examples of successful aggressive outreach programs may be found in Carol Bush et al., "Operation Outreach: Intensive Case Management for Severely Psychiatrically Disabled Adults," *Hospital and Community Psychiatry* 41, no. 6 (1990), and José Arana et al., "Continuous Care Teams in Intensive Outpatient Treatment of Chronic Mentally Ill Patients," *Hospital and Community Psychiatry* 42, no. 5 (1991). For information regarding outreach programs for homeless populations, see Gary Morse et al., "Experimental Comparison of the Effects of Three Treatment Programs for Homeless Mentally Ill People," *Hospital and Community Psychiatry* 43, no. 10 (1992).

338 L. Lamison-White's *U.S. Bureau of the Census: Current Populations Report* indicates that 13.7 percent of Americans are below the poverty line, as taken from Jeanne Miranda and Bonnie L. Green, "Poverty and Mental Health Services Research," page 4.

338 The study showing that 42 percent of heads of households receiving AFDC meet the criteria for clinical depression is K. Moore et al., "The JOBS Evaluation: How Well Are They Faring? AFDC Families with Preschool-Aged Children in Atlanta at the Outset of the JOBS Evaluation," published by the U.S. Department of Health and Human Services, 1995.

338 The study showing that 53 percent of pregnant welfare mothers meet the criteria for major depression is J. C. Quint et al., "New Chance: Interim Findings on a Comprehensive Program for Disadvantaged Young Mothers and Their Children," published by Manpower Demonstration Research Corporation, 1994.

338 That those with psychiatric disorders are 38 percent more likely to receive welfare than those without is shown in R. Jayakody and H. Pollack, "Barriers to Self-Sufficiency among Low-Income, Single Mothers: Substance Use, Mental Health Problems, and Welfare Reform." This paper was presented at the Association for Public Policy Analysis and Management in Washington, D.C., November 1997.

338 That the state and federal governments spend roughly $20 billion on cash transfers to poor nonelderly adults and their children, and roughly the same amount for food stamps for such families, is taken from the the U.S. House of Representa-

tives Committee on Ways and Means' *Green Book*, 1998. It cites, on page 411, government expenditures of $11.1 billion and state expenditures of $9.3 billion on Aid to Families with Dependent Children (AFDC) benefits. This does not count an additional $1.6 billion in federal administrative costs and $1.6 billion in state administrative costs. The federal costs for Temporary Assistance for Needy Families (TANF) benefits are cited as $23.5 billion on food stamp benefits and $2 billion on administration. State and local governments spent $1.8 billion on administration. TANF statistics are from page 927.

339 On the woes of the welfare system, in this example, the child welfare system, see Alvin Rosenfeld et al., "Psychiatry and Children in the Child Welfare System," *Child and Adolescent Psychiatric Clinics of North America* 7, no. 3 (1998). They write, "In contrast to the mental health system, nonmedical personnel usually run child welfare. . . . Most foster children probably need a psychiatric evaluation; few get one." Page 527.

339 Jeanne Miranda has been a real pioneer in this area. Her most notable publications include Kenneth Wells et al., "Impact of disseminating quality improvement programs for depression in managed primary care: A randomized controlled trial," *Journal of the American Medical Association* 283, no. 2 (2000); Jeanne Miranda et al., "Unmet mental health needs of women in public-sector gynecologic clinics," *American Journal of Obstetrics and Gynecology* 178, no. 2 (1998); "Introduction to the special section on recruiting and retaining minorities in psychotherapy research," *Journal of Consulting Clinical Psychologists* 64, no. 5 (1996); and Jeanne Miranda et al., "Recruiting and retaining low-income Latinos in psychotherapy research," *Journal of Consulting Clinical Psychologists* 64, no. 5 (1996).

340 That total costs per patient for all the mentioned treatment programs are under $1,000 a year was discussed in much correspondence with the researchers. The exact figures for such programs are of course extremely difficult to calculate and compare because of differences in treatment programs, protocol, and services. Jeanne Miranda estimated her costs at under $100 per patient; Emily Hauenstein provided total costs of $638 per person for treatment regimens that include approximately thirty-six therapeutic meetings. Costing for Glenn Treisman's work is based on figures he sent me in an E-mail of October 30, 2000. He estimated his operating costs at between $250,000 and $350,000 per year for an outreach service that provides care for twenty-five hundred to three thousand patients. Average cost per patient is therefore around $109.

343 That depression among the poor is not usually manifest in the cognitive arena of personal failure and guilt, but rather in somaticization, is indicated in Marvin Opler and S. Mouchly Small, "Cultural Variables Affecting Somatic Complaints and Depression," *Psychosomatics* 9, no. 5 (1968).

347 The article in *The New England Journal of Medicine* on economic hardship and depression is John Lynch et al., "Cumulative Impact of Sustained Economic Hardship on Physical, Cognitive, Psychological, and Social Functioning," vol. 337 (1997).

348 On the phenomenon of learned helplessness, see Martin Seligman's *Learned Optimism*.

353 The rate of schizophrenia among low-income populations is in Carl Cohen, "Poverty and the Course of Schizophrenia: Implications for Research and Policy," *Hospital and Community Psychology* 44, no. 10 (1993).

360 The antarctic ozone "hole" is defined as an "area having less than 220 dobson units

(DU) of ozone in the overhead column (i.e., between the ground and space)." As the Environmental Protection Agency's Web site points out, "The word *hole* is a misnomer; the hole is really a significant thinning, or reduction in ozone concentrations, which results in the destruction of up to 70 percent of the ozone normally found over Antarctica." I take from *One Earth, One Future: Our Changing Global Environment*, page 135: "The first unmistakable sign of human-induced change in the global environment arrived in 1985 when a team of British scientists published findings that stunned the world community of atmospheric chemists. Joseph Farman, of the British Meteorological Survey, and colleagues reported in the scientific journal *Nature* that concentrations of stratospheric ozone above Antarctica had plunged more than 40 percent from 1960s baseline levels during October, the first month of spring in the Southern Hemisphere, between 1977 and 1984. Most scientists greeted the news with disbelief." See the EPA's Web site dedicated to the ozone hole at www.epa.gov/ozone/science/hole/holehome.html. The British Antarctic Survey publishes yearly updates on the state of the antarctic ozone. For current information, see www.nbs.ac.uk/public/icd/jds/ozone/index.html.

Chapter X: Politics

361 For a general overview of changing government policies in the area of mental health, there are a number of informative Web sites focused on mental health advocacy, support, and education. I would particularly recommend the Web sites for the National Institute of Mental Health (www.nimh.nih.gov), the National Alliance for the Mentally Ill (www.nami.org), the Treatment Advocacy Center (www.psychlaws.org), the National Depressive & Manic-Depressive Association (www.ndmda.org), and the American Psychiatric Association (www.psych.org).

365 For Tipper Gore's remarks on her own depression, see her interview published as "Strip Stigma from Mental Illness," *USA Today*, May 7, 1999.

365 A plethora of articles have been published on Mike Wallace and his depression. See Jolie Solomon, "Breaking the Silence," *Newsweek*, May 20, 1996; Walter Goodman, "In Confronting Depression the First Target Is Shame," *New York Times*, January 6, 1998; and Jane Brody, "Despite the Despair of Depression, Few Men Seek Treatment," *New York Times*, December 30, 1997.

365 For William Styron's description of his depression, see his elegantly written first-person memoir *Darkness Visible*, which was one of the first open modern portraits of depressive illness.

366 The National Alliance for the Mentally Ill (NAMI) provides excellent information regarding the ADA, including summaries, consumer and advocate information, and contact information. This may be found at http://www.nami.org/helpline/ada.htm.

367 The Civil Aeromedical Institute (CAMI) is the medical certification, research, and education wing of the U.S. Department of Transportation Federal Aviation Administration. For the full FAA regulations, see the CAMI Web site at www.cami.jccbi.gov/AAM-300/part67.html.

368 The quotations from Richard Baron come from his unpublished manuscript "Employment Programs for Persons with Serious Mental Illness: Drawing the Fine Line Between Providing Necessary Financial Support and Promoting Lifetime Economic Dependence," pages 5–6, 18, 21.

369 For information on the NIH, as well as its various departments and budgets, see its Web site at www.nih.gov.

369 The six Nobel winners who spoke before Congress in the testimony mentioned here appeared before an annual hearing of the House Subcommittee on Labor, Health and Human Services, and Education, in the early 1990s. Representative John Porter, among others, has described the event in several oral interviews.

369 The figure that over 75 percent of health plans in the United States offer less coverage for mental health than for any other kind of physical health is from Jeffrey Buck et al., "Behavioral Health Benefits in Employer-Sponsored Health Plans, 1997," *Health Affairs* 18, no. 2 (1999).

371 The numbers for my own illness break down as follows: sixteen visits to the psychopharmacologist at $250 per visit; fifty visits to the psychiatrist (approximately three hours per week) at $200 per hour; and bills for medications that add up to at least $3,500 per year.

371 The statistics regarding the financial costs of depression in the workplace come from Robert Hirschfeld et al., "The National Depressive and Manic-Depressive Association Consensus Statement on the Undertreatment of Depression," *Journal of the American Medical Association* 277, no. 4 (1997): 335.

371 The Mental Health Parity Act of 1996 took effect January 1, 1998.

372 The statistic that four hundred thousand people fall off the insurance registers for every 1 percent increase in the cost is quoted in a letter from John F. Sheils, Vice President of the Lewin Group, Inc. to Richard Smith, Vice President of Public Policy and Research, American Association of Health Plans, November 17, 1997. Naturally this estimate will vary depending upon "the health policy being analyzed." The letter was provided to me by the Lewin Group, Inc.

372 The economic consequences of insurance parity are extremely complicated and rely on variables too diverse to be reflected in any one study. While many experts seem to agree that insurance parity will raise total insurance costs less than 1 percent—this statistic is quoted regularly in the professional and popular presses—various studies have found other numbers. The Rand Corporation Study found that equalizing annual limits would "increase costs by only about one dollar per employee." A report by the National Advisory Mental Health Council's Interim Report on Parity Costs found a number of possibilities—from decreases of 0.2 percent to increases of less than 1 percent. In a Lewin Group study of New Hampshire insurance providers, no cost increases were found. For more information on these various studies, see NAMI's Web site at www.nami.org/pressroom/costfact.html.

372 The figure on overall added costs for first year of parity is in Robert Pear, "Insurance Plans Skirt Requirement on Mental Health," *New York Times,* December 26, 1998.

373 That over a thousand homicides in 1998 were attributable to people with mental illness is stated in Dr. E. Fuller Torrey and Mary Zdanowicz, "Why Deinstitutionalization Turned Deadly," *Wall Street Journal,* August 4, 1998.

373 The extent of the discrepancy between the proportion of the mentally ill who are dangerous and the media coverage of those people is reported in "Depression: The Spirit of the Age," *The Economist,* December 19, 1998, page 116.

374 The recent study at MIT that showed that people who have major depression and lose work abilities can return to previous norms on medication is Ernst Berndt et al., "Workplace performance effects from chronic depression and its treatment," *Journal of Health Economics* 17, no. 5 (1998).

374 The two studies showing that supported employment for the mentally ill is the

most economically beneficial way of dealing with them are E. S. Rogers et al., "A benefit-cost analysis of a supported employment model for persons with psychiatric disabilities," *Evaluation and Program Planning* 18, no. 2 (1995), and R. E. Clark et al., "A cost-effectiveness comparison of supported employment and rehabilitation day treatment," *Administration and Policy in Mental Health* 24, no. 1 (1996).

376 The McCarran-Ferguson Act was passed in 1945. Dr. Scott Harrington, in his "The History of Federal Involvement in Insurance Regulation," quotes the act as stating "that no act of Congress 'shall be construed to invalidate, impair, or supersede' any state law enacted for the purpose of regulating or taxing insurance." This paper is in *Optional Federal Chartering of Insurance,* edited by Peter Wallison.

376 The statistics on Clinton's proposed budget for FY 2000 may be found on-line at the NIMH's Web site at www.nimh.nih.gov/about/2000budget.cfm. According to the NIMH, the final budget for FY 2000 will not be settled until early 2001.

376 That the Community Health Services Block Grant was increased by 24 percent is in *NAMI E-News* 99–74, February 2, 1999.

378 National-level suggestions for mandatory tuberculosis treatment are issued by the Center for Disease Control's Division of Tuberculosis Elimination's Directly Observed Treatment (DOT) program. This program proposes weekly meetings with health care workers who deliver treatment and verify compliance with treatment protocols. For more on the Center for Disease Control's recommendations, see: www.cdc.gov/nchstp/tb/faqs/qa.htm. While all fifty states recognize the DOT program, it is implemented at state and city levels according to local needs. In New York State, for example, mandatory tuberculosis treatment regulations are issued and enforced through the New York State Department of Health in conjunction with city and local governments. The New York State Department of Health stipulates a DOT program that provides for "directly observed administration of antituberculosis medications for people who are unwilling or unable to comply with prescribed drug plans." For more, see www.health.state.ny.us/nys-doh/search/index.htm. In New York State, more than 80 percent of people with tuberculosis are put into a DOT program. In New York City, the Commissioner's Orders for Adherence to Anti-TB Treatment states, "the Department of Health works with health care providers to facilitate patients' adherence to anti-tuberculosis treatment and to protect the public health. Most individuals adhere to treatment when they are educated about tuberculosis and receive incentives or enablers, assistance with housing problems, enhanced social services, and home or field programs of directly observed therapy (DOT). However, if these measures seem likely to fail or have already failed, the Commissioner of Health is empowered by Section 11.47(d) of the New York City Health Code to issue any order deemed necessary to protect the public health." See the New York City Department of Health's website at www.ci.nyc.ny.us/html/doh/html/tb/tb5a.html for more information. For a statistical analysis of mandatory tuberculosis treatment in New York City, see Rose Gasner et al., "The Use of Legal Action in New York City to Ensure Treatment of Tuberculosis," *New England Journal of Medicine* 340, no. 5, 1999.

379 The ACLU position on involuntary treatment of those with mental disabilities may be found in Robert M. Levy and Leonard S. Rubinstein's *The Rights of People with Mental Disabilities,* page 25.

380 For more on Willowbook, see David and Sheila Rothman's *The Willowbrook Wars.*

381 The budget breakdown for mental health spending in the Veterans Administra-

tion is in the testimony of the American Psychiatric Association to the Department of Veterans Affairs, April 13, 2000, and can be found on the APA's Web page at www.psych.org by clicking on "Public Policy and Advocacy," and then "APA Testimony."

381 I have taken from Representative Marcy Kaptur the anecdotal evidence that psychiatric disturbances may be the most frequent among veterans.

381 This statistic that 25 percent of veterans at VA hospitals suffer from mental illnesses is taken from the testimony of the American Psychiatric Association to the Department of Veterans Affairs, April 13, 2000, and can be found on the APA's Web site at www.psych.org by clicking on "Public Policy and Advocacy," and then "APA Testimony."

381 That more than half of all practicing physicians have had part of their education within the VA health-care system comes from the Veterans Administration Web site. They report: "The Veterans Administration currently is affiliated with 105 medical schools, 54 dental schools, and more than 1,140 other schools across the country. More than half of all practicing physicians in the United States have had part of their professional education in the VA health-care system. Each year, approximately 100,000 health professionals receive training in VA medical centers." From www.va.gov/About_VA/Orgs/vha/index.htm.

386 Kevin Heldman's piece is "7½ Days," published in *City Limits*, June/July 1998.

387 Estimates of the percentage of patients with depressive disorders within state and county mental health facilities are taken from Joanne Atay et al., "Additions and Resident Patients at End of Year, State and County Mental Hospitals, by Age and Diagnosis, by State, United States, 1998," published by the U.S. Department of Health and Human Services in May 2000. They report that affective disorders are the second most prevalent disorder among residents at 12.7 percent, page 53. For nonresidents this number increases to 22.7 percent, page 3.

391 The figures for the mental health budget for Pennsylvania were supplied by the Mental Health Association of Southeastern Pennsylvania. I thank Susan Rogers of the Mental Health Association of Southeastern Pennsylvania for her tremendous effort in tracking down this and several other statistics.

391 Regarding the effectiveness of community-based programs, one report declares that community services "are virtually always more effective than institutional services in terms of outcome" is reported in the *Amici Curiae Brief for the October 1998 Supreme Court Case of Tommy Olmstead, Commissioner of the Department of Human Resources of the State of Georgia, et al., vs. L.C. and E.W., Each by Jonathan Zimring, as Guardian ad Litem and Next Friend*, prepared by the National Mental Health Consumers' Self-Help Clearinghouse et al., in support of respondents, page 24. This report cites numerous studies supporting their findings, two of which are especially pertinent: A. Kiesler, "Mental Hospitals and Alternative Care: Noninstitutionalization as Potential Public Policy for Mental Patients," *American Psychologist* 349 (1982), and Paul Carling, "Major Mental Illness, Housing, and Supports," *American Psychologist*, August 1990.

393 Thomas Szasz's views are expressed in his numerous writings. His books *Cruel Compassion* and *Primary Values and Major Contentions* are a good place to start.

393 The story of the lawsuit against Thomas Szasz is told by Kay Jamison in *Night Falls Fast*, page 254.

393 The op-ed on denying care to the mildly mentally ill is Sally L. Satel, "Mentally Ill or Just Feeling Sad?" *New York Times*, December 15, 1999.

Notes

394 The education programs of the pharmaceutical industry run quite a range. At the annual meeting of the American Psychiatric Association (APA), industry-sponsored forums include presentations by some of the most prominent psychiatrists in the United States, many of whom have received independent research grants from pharmaceutical companies. Salesmen in the pharmaceutical industry often end up giving doctors the better part of their continuing education; their work keeps doctors up-to-date on available treatment, but their educative activities are, of course, biased.

394 On the strategies of research and "intellectual property" see Jonathan Rees, "Patents and intellectual property: A salvation for patient-oriented research?" *Lancet* 356 (2000).

397 The quotations from David Healey are from *The Antidepressant Era*, page 169.

397 The suggestion that mood disorders affect a quarter of the world's population is from Myrna Weissman et al., "Cross-National Epidemiology of Major Depression and Bipolar Disorder," *Journal of the American Medical Association* 276, no. 4 (1996).

398 These quotations from David Healy are from *The Antidepressant Era*, page 163.

398 The idea of taking antidepressants off prescription is in *Ibid.*, 256–65.

398 That the SSRIs are not particularly fatal or dangerous even in overdose is indicated in J. T. Barbey and S. P. Roose, "SSRI safety in overdose," *Journal of Clinical Psychiatry* 59, suppl. 15 (1998), in which they write, "Moderate overdoses—thirty times the common daily dose—are associated with minor or no symptoms." Only at "very high doses—seventy-five times the common daily dose"—do more serious events occur, "including seizures, ECG changes, and decreased consciousness."

Chapter XI: Evolution

401 The quotations from Michael McGuire and Alfonso Troisi are from their book *Darwinian Psychiatry*, pages 150 and 157.

403 The quotation from C. S. Sherrington I take from *The Integrative Action of the Nervous System*, page 22.

403 C. U. M. Smith's explanation of emotion and mood is in his article "Evolutionary Biology and Psychiatry," *British Journal of Psychiatry* 162 (1993): 150.

404 Jack Kahn's astute observation is quoted from John Price, "Job's Battle with God," *ASCAP* 10, no. 12 (1997). For more information, see Jack Kahn's *Job's Illness: Loss, Grief and Integration: A Psychological Interpretation.*

404 Anthony Stevens and John Price express their views in their book *Evolutionary Psychiatry.*

404 On the orangutan as a loner, see Nancy Collinge's *Introduction to Primate Behavior*, pages 102–4.

404 On the basic principle of the alpha male, see *Ibid.*, 143–57.

404 A large amount of literature exists on the general matter of depression and rank societies. Leon Sloman et al., "Adaptive Function of Depression: Psychotherapeutic Implications," *American Journal of Psychotherapy* 48, no. 3 (1994), is perhaps one of the first solid formulations of a coherent theory.

405 John Birtchnell's views are in his book *How Humans Relate.*

405 Russell Gardner's thoughts on altered dominance mechanisms in higher mammals are described in a variety of his publications. For the most comprehensive description of his ideas on depression and social interaction, see John Price et al.,

"The Social Competition Hypothesis of Depression," *British Journal of Psychiatry* 164 (1994). For more focused discussions, see Russell Gardner, "Psychiatric Syndromes as Infrastructure for Intra-Specific Communication," in *Social Fabrics of the Mind,* edited by M. R. A. Chance, and "Mechanisms in Manic-Depressive Disorder," *Archives of General Psychiatry* 39 (1982).

406   Tom Wehr on depression and sleep and energy-conservation strategy is in his "Reply to Healy, D., Waterhouse, J. M.: The circadian system and affective disorders: Clocks or rhythms," *Chronobiology International* 7 (1990).

406   Michael McGuire and Alfonso Troisi on the genome lag may be found in *Darwinian Psychiatry,* page 41.

407   J. H. van den Berg's book was originally published as *Metabletica,* a title I prefer. The ideas expressed here are developed throughout his text.

408   On the difficulties of freedom, see Erich Fromm's classic *Escape from Freedom.* Ernst Becker also has a pertinent discussion of freedom and its relationship to depression in *The Denial of Death,* beginning on page 213.

408   The description of the boy whose family had moved and who hanged himself is in George Colt's *The Enigma of Suicide,* page 50.

408   The statistics on the number of goods in the produce section of the supermarket is taken from Regina Schrambling, "Attention Supermarket Shoppers!" *Food and Wine,* October 1995, page 93.

409   The work of Paul J. Watson and Paul Andrews I have taken primarily from their unpublished manuscript "An Evolutionary Theory of Unipolar Depression as an Adaptation for Overcoming Constraints of the Social Niche." A shortened version of this paper was published in *ASCAP* 11, no. 5 (1998), under the title "Niche Change Model of Depression."

410   The principle that low mood keeps people from overinvesting in excessively difficult strategies is expounded in Randolph Nesse, "Evolutionary Explanations of Emotions, " *Human Nature* 1, no. 3 (1990). For his current ideas on depression and evolution, see his "Is Depression an Adaptation?" *Archives of General Psychiatry* 57, no. 1 (2000).

410   The musician is described in Erica Goode, "Viewing Depression as a Tool for Survival," *New York Times,* February 1, 2000.

410   The idea of depression as a means of soliciting altruism is described in the work of Paul J. Watson and Paul Andrews. I have taken their ideas from their unpublished manuscripts "An Evolutionary Theory of Unipolar Depression as an Adaptation for Overcoming Constraints of the Social Niche" and "Unipolar Depression and Human Social Life: An Evolutionary Analysis."

411   Edward Hagen's views are presented in his article "The Defection Hypothesis of Depression: A Case Study," *ASCAP* 11, no. 4 (1998).

414   On the link between depression and interpersonal sensitivity, see K. Sakado et al., "The Association between the High Interpersonal Sensitivity Type of Personality and a Lifetime History of Depression in a Sample of Employed Japanese Adults," *Psychological Medicine* 29, no. 5 (1999). On the relationship between depression and anxiety sensitivity, see Steven Taylor et al., "Anxiety Sensitivity and Depression: How Are They Related?" *Journal of Abnormal Psychology* 105, no. 3 (1996).

414   Paul MacLean's views on the triune brain are in his book *The Triune Brain in Evolution.*

415   Timothy Crow's views are expressed in a broad range of work, the relevant portion of which is cited in the bibliography. The most straightforward articulation of

Notes

his linguistic principles and his theories of brain asymmetry is in his article "A Darwinian Approach to the Origins of Psychosis," *British Journal of Psychiatry* 167 (1995).

415 On language as a function of brain asymmetry, see Marian Annett, *Left, Right, Hand and Brain: The Right Shift Theory,* and Michael Corballis, *The Lopsided Ape: Evolution of the Generative Mind.*

415 On deaf people and left-hemisphere strokes, see Oliver Sacks, *Seeing Voices.*

416 On deep grammar, see Noam Chomsky's *Reflections on Language.*

416 On the specific effects of right-brain strokes, see Susan Egelko et al., "Relationship among CT Scans, Neurological Exam, and Neuropsychological Test Performance in Right-Brain-Damaged Stroke Patients," *Journal of Clinical and Experimental Neuropsychology* 10, no. 5 (1988).

416 Timothy Crow's proposition that schizophrenia and affective disorders are the price of a bihemispheric brain is in "Is schizophrenia the price that *Homo sapiens* pays for language?" *Schizophrenia Research* 28 (1997).

417 For general information on prefrontal cortex asymmetries and depression, see Carrie Ellen Schaffer et al., "Frontal and Parietal Electroencephalogram Asymmetry in Depressed and Nondepressed Subjects," *Biological Psychiatry* 18, no. 7 (1983).

417 The work on blood flow abnormalities in the prefrontal cortex of patients with depression is in J. Soares and John Mann, "The functional neuroanatomy of mood disorders," *Journal of Psychiatric Research* 31 (1997), and M. George et al., "SPECT and PET imaging in mood disorders," *Journal of Clinical Psychiatry* 54 (1993).

418 On neurogenesis—the reproducing of adult brain cells—see, for example, P. S. Eriksson "Neurogenesis in the adult human hippocampus," *Nature Medicine* 4 (1998).

418 For a good general discussion of TMS, see Eric Hollander, "TMS," *CNS Spectrums* 2, no. 1 (1997).

418 On learned resilience, still an open field in which the hard data are just beginning to accumulate, see Richard Davidson's "Affective style, psychopathology and resilience: Brain mechanisms and plasticity," to be published in *American Psychologist* in 2001.

418 On left cortex activation and deactivation, see Richard Davidson et al., "Approach-Withdrawal and Cerebral Asymmetry: Emotional Expression and Brain Physiology I," *Journal of Personality and Social Psychology* 58, no. 2 (1990). For work on brain asymmetry and the immune system, see Duck-Hee Kang et al., "Frontal Brain Asymmetry and Immune Function," *Behavioral Neuroscience* 105, no. 6 (1991). For Richard Davidson's work with babies and maternal separation, see Richard Davidson and Nathan Fox, "Frontal Brain Asymmetry Predicts Infants' Response to Maternal Separation," *Journal of Abnormal Psychology* 98, no. 2 (1989).

418 In support of the assertion that the majority of people are left-side activated, see A. J. Tomarken's "Psychometric properties of resting anterior EEG asymmetry: Temporal stability and internal consistency," *Psychophysiology* 29 (1992).

418 The idea that right-frontal brain activation is often correlated with high levels of cortisol is explored in N. H. Kalen et al., "Asymmetric frontal brain activity, cortisol, and behavior associated with fearful temperament in Rhesus monkeys," *Behavioral Neuroscience* 112 (1998).

418 Timothy Crow's papers on handedness discuss the connections among language, hand skill, and affect. See "Location of the Handedness Gene on the X and Y Chromosomes," *American Journal of Medical Genetics* 67 (1996), and "Evidence for

Linkage to Psychosis and Cerebral Asymmetry (Relative Hand Skill) on the X Chromosome," *American Journal of Medical Genetics* 81 (1998).

419 Hamlet's line is in act 2, scene 2, line 561.

419 That evolution will cast light into the fog of modern psychiatry is one of the central arguments of Michael McGuire and Alfonso Troisi's book, *Darwinian Psychiatry.* The lines quoted here are from page 12.

Chapter XII: Hope

424 Angel's move had been from Norristown, which was a residential long-term-care facility or mental hospital, to Pottstown Community Residential Rehab (CRR), then to South Keim Street, which is defined as an Intensive Housing Program, or Supported Housing Arrangement, intended for graduates of the CRR program.

430 The quotations from Thomas Nagel are in his book *The Possibility of Altruism*, pages 126 and 128–29.

430 The lines from *The Winter's Tale* are from act 4, scene 4, lines 86–96.

433 On the matter of a depressive's perceived control over his circumstances, see Shelley E. Taylor's *Positive Illusions*. I also refer to a series of experiments related to me by the documentarian Roberto Guerra.

433 Freud's reference is from his seminal 1917 essay "Mourning and Melancholia," taken from *A General Selection from the Works of Sigmund Freud*, John Rickman, editor, page 128.

433 The quotation from Shelley E. Taylor is from *Positive Illusions*, pages 7 and 213.

435 Emmy Gut's thoughts are in *Productive and Unproductive Depression* and are sketched out in chapter 3.

435 The quotation from Julia Kristeva is from *Black Sun*, page 42.

435 These numbers on SSRI prescriptions have been taken from Joseph Glenmullen's *Prozac Backlash*, page 15.

435 The information on TWA flight 800 was given to me by a friend who had lost a relative on that flight in July 1996.

437 The quotation from *Daniel Deronda* is from page 251.

438 Emily Dickinson on despair is in poem 640 on page 318 of Thomas Johnson's edition of *The Complete Poems of Emily Dickinson*. Its first line is "I cannot live with You."

439 The quotation from *Areopagitica* is from *Paradise Lost*, page 384. The first quotation from *Paradise Lost* itself is from page 226 (Book IX, lines 1070–73); the second is from page 263 (Book XI, lines 137–40); and the third is from page 301 (Book XII, lines 641–49).

440 Fyodor Dostoyevsky's famous remarks are in *The Idiot*, page 363.

440 For more on Heidegger and the relationship between anguish and thought, see his monumental masterpiece *Being and Time*.

440 Friedrich Wilhelm Joseph von Schelling's words come from his "On the Essence of Human Freedom," in his *Saemmtliche Werke*, vol. 7, page 399. I thank Andrew Bowie for help in interpreting this passage. For more, see Andrew Bowie's *Schelling and Modern European Philosophy.*

440 The lines from Julia Kristeva on lucidity are from *Black Sun*, pages 4 and 22.

443 The words from Schopenhauer are from his essay "On the Sufferings of the World," in *Essays and Aphorisms*, page 45.

443 The flip remark from Tennesee Williams is from *Five O'Clock Angel: Letters of Ten-*

nesee Williams to Maria St. Just, 1948–1982, page 154. I thank the persistently studious Emma Lukic for finding this quotation for me.

443 *The Oxford English Dictionary* defines *joy* as "a vivid emotion of pleasure arising from a sense of well-being or satisfaction; the feeling or state of being highly pleased or delighted; exultation of spirit; gladness, delight," volume 5, page 612.

Bibliography

Abraham, H. D., et al. "Order of onset of substance abuse and depression in a sample of depressed outpatients." *Comprehensive Psychiatry* 40, no. 1 (1999): 44–50.

Abraham, Karl. *Selected Papers of Karl Abraham, M.D.* 6th ed. Trans. Douglas Bryan and Alix Strachey. London: The Hogarth Press Ltd., 1965.

Abrams, Richard. *Electroconvulsive Therapy.* 2nd ed. New York: Oxford University Press, 1992.

Adams, Peter. *The Soul of Medicine: An Anthology of Illness and Healing.* London: Penguin Books, 1999.

Aguirre, J. C., et al. "Plasma Beta-Endorphin Levels in Chronic Alcoholics." *Alcohol* 7, no. 5 (1990): 409–12.

Aigner, T. G., et al. "Choice behavior in rhesus monkeys: Cocaine versus food." *Science* 201(1978): 534–35.

Albert, R. "Sleep deprivation and subsequent sleep phase advance stabilizes the positive effect of sleep deprivation in depressive episodes." *Nervenarzt* 69, no. 1 (1998): 66–69.

Aldridge, David. *Suicide: The Tragedy of Hopelessness.* London and Philadelphia: Jessica Kingsley Publishers, 1998.

Allen, Hannah. "A Narrative of God's Gracious Dealings with That Choice Christian Mrs. Hannah Allen." In *Voices of Madness.* Ed. Allan Ingram. Thrupp, England: Sutton Publishing, 1997.

Allen, Nick. "Towards a Computational Theory of Depression." *ASCAP* 8, no. 7 (1995).

Altshuler, Kenneth, et al. "Anorexia Nervosa and Depression: A Dissenting View." *American Journal of Psychiatry* 142, no. 3 (1985): 328–32.

Alvarez, A. *The Savage God: A study of suicide.* London: Weidenfeld and Nicolson, 1971.

Ambrose, Stephen E. *Undaunted Courage.* New York: A Touchstone Book, 1996.

Ambrosini, Paul. "A review of pharmacotherapy of major depression in children and adolescents." *Psychiatric Services* 51, no. 5 (2000): 627–33.

American Psychiatric Association. *Diagnostic and Statistical Manual of Mental Disorders.* 4th ed. Washington, D.C.: American Psychiatric Association, 1994.

Andersen, Grethe. "Treatment of Uncontrolled Crying after Stroke." *Drugs & Aging* 6, no. 2 (1995): 105–11.

Andersen, Grethe, et al. "Citalopram for poststroke pathological crying." *Lancet* 342 (1993): 837–39.

Bibliography

Andrews, Bernice, and George W. Brown. "Stability and change in low self-esteem: The role of psychosocial factors." *Psychological Medicine* 25 (1995): 23–31.

Annett, Marian. *Left, Right, Hand and Brain: The Right Shift Theory.* New Jersey: Lawrence Erlbaum Associates, 1985.

Anthony, James, et al. "Comparative epidemiology of dependence on tobacco, alcohol, controlled substances, and inhalants: Basic findings from the National Comorbidity Survey." *Experimental and Clinical Psychopharmacology* 2, no. 3 (1994): 244–68.

Anthony, W. A., et al. "Supported employment for persons with psychiatric disabilities: An historical and conceptual perspective." *Psychosocial Rehabilitation Journal* 11, no. 2 (1982): 5–24.

———. "Predicting the vocational capacity of the chronically mentally ill: Research and implications." *American Psychologist* 39 (1984): 537–44.

Aquinas, St. Thomas. *Summa theologiae* I–II, q. 25, a. 4. In *Sancti Thomae de Aquino opera omnia.* Vol. 6. Rome: Leonine Commission, 1882–.

———. *Summa Theologica: Complete English Edition in Five Volumes.* Vol. 2. Trans. Fathers of the English Dominican Province. Reprint, Westminster, Md.: Christian Classics, 1981, I–II, q. 25, a. 4.

Arana, José, et al. "Continuous Care Teams in Intensive Outpatient Treatment of Chronic Mentally Ill Patients." *Hospital and Community Psychiatry* 42, no. 5 (1991): 503–7.

Araya, O. S., and E. J. Ford. "An investigation of the type of photosensitization caused by the ingestion of St. John's Wort (*Hypericum perforatum*) by calves." *Journal of Comprehensive Pathology* 91, no. 1 (1981): 135–41.

Archer, John. *The Nature of Grief.* London: Routledge, 1999.

Ardila, Alfredo, et al. "Neuropsychological Deficits in Chronic Cocaine Abusers." *International Journal of Neuroscience* 57 (1991): 73–79.

Arieno, Marlene A. *Victorian Lunatics: A Social Epidemiology of Mental Illness in Mid-Nineteenth-Century England.* Selinsgrove, Pa.: Susquehanna University Press, 1989.

Aristotle. "Problemata." *The Works of Aristotle Translated into English.* Vol 7. Oxford: Clarendon Press, 1971.

Arnold, Matthew. *The Poems of Matthew Arnold.* Ed. Kenneth Allott. London: Longman's, 1965.

Artaud, Antonin. *Antonin Artaud: Works on Paper.* Ed. Margit Rowell. New York: Museum of Modern Art, 1996.

Åsberg, Marie. "Neurotransmitters and Suicidal Behavior: The Evidence from Cerebrospinal Fluid Studies." *Annals of the New York Academy of Sciences* 836 (1997): 158–81.

Aseltine, R. H., et al. "The co-occurence of depression and substance abuse in late adolescence." *Developmental Psychopathology* 10, no. 3 (1998): 549–70.

Åsgård, U., et al. "Birth Cohort Analysis of Changing Suicide Risk by Sex and Age in Sweden 1952 to 1981." *Acta Psychiatrica Scandinavica* 76 (1987): 456–63.

Astbury, Jill. *Crazy for You: The Making of Women's Madness.* Oxford: Oxford University Press, 1996.

Atay, Joanne, et al. *Additions and Resident Patients at End of Year, State and County Mental Hospitals, by Age and Diagnosis, by State, United States, 1998.* Washington, D.C.: U.S. Department of Health and Human Services, May 2000.

Axline, Virginia M. *Dibs in Search of Self.* New York: Ballantine Books, 1964.

Babb, Lawrence. *The Elizabethan Malady: A Study of Melancholia in English Literature from 1580 to 1642.* East Lansing: Michigan State College Press, 1951.

Bibliography

Baca-García, Enrique, et al. "The Relationship Between Menstrual Cycle Phases and Suicide Attempts." *Psychosomatic Medicine* 62 (2000): 50–60.

Baldessarini, Ross J. "Neuropharmacology of S-Adenosyl-L-Methionine." *The American Journal of Medicine* 83, suppl. 5A (1987): 95–103.

Ball, H. Irene, et al. "Update on the incidence and mortality from melanoma in the United States." *Journal of the American Academy of Dermatology* 40 (1999): 35–42.

Ball, J. R., et al. "A controlled trial of imipramine in treatment of depressive states." *British Medical Journal* 21 (1959): 1052–55.

Barbey, J. T., and S. P. Roose. "SSRI safety in overdose." *Journal of Clinical Psychiatry* 59, suppl. 15 (1998): 42–48.

Barinaga, Marcia. "A New Clue to How Alcohol Damages Brains." *Science*, February 11, 2000, 947–48.

Barker, Juliet. *The Brontës*. New York: St. Martin's Press, 1994.

Barlow, D. H., and M. G. Craske. *Mastery of Your Anxiety and Panic: Client workbook for anxiety and panic.* San Antonio, Tex.: Graywind Publications Incorporated/The Psychological Corporation, 2000.

Barlow, D. H., et al. "Cognitive-behavioral therapy, imipramine, or their combination for panic disorder: A randomized controlled trial." *Journal of the American Medical Association* 283 (2000): 2529–36.

Baron, Richard. "Employment Policy: Financial Support versus Promoting Economic Independence." *International Journal of Law and Psychiatry* 23, no. 3–4 (2000): 375–91.

————. *The Past and Future Career Patterns of People with Serious Mental Illness: A Qualitative Inquiry.* Supported under a Switzer Fellowship Grant from the National Institute on Disability and Rehabilitation Research. Grant Award H133F980011.

————. "Employment Programs for Persons with Serious Mental Illness: Drawing the Fine Line Between Providing Necessary Financial Support and Promoting Lifetime Economic Dependence." Manuscript.

Barondes, Samuel H. *Mood Genes*. New York: W. H. Freeman and Company, 1998.

Barthelme, Donald. *Sadness*. New York: Farrar, Straus and Giroux, 1972.

Bassuk, Ellen, et al. "Prevalence of Mental Health and Substance Use Disorders Among Homeless and Low-Income Housed Mothers." *American Journal of Psychiatry* 155, no. 11 (1998): 1561–64.

Bateson, Gregory. *Steps to an Ecology of Mind*. Chicago: University of Chicago Press, 1972.

Batten, Guinn. *The Orphaned Imagination: Melancholy and Commodity Culture in English Romanticism.* Durham, N.C., and London: Duke University Press, 1998.

Baudelaire, Charles. *The Flowers of Evil*. Ed. Marthiel Mathews and Jackson Mathews. New York: New Directions, 1989.

————. *Les Fleurs du Mal*. Paris: Éditions Garnier Frères, 1961.

Beatty, William, et al. "Neuropsychological performance of recently abstinent alcoholics and cocaine abusers." *Drug and Alcohol Dependence* 37 (1995): 247–53.

Beck, Aaron T. *Depression: Causes and Treatment*. Philadelphia: University of Pennsylvania Press, 1967.

Beck, Aaron T., and Marjorie Weishaar. "Cognitive Therapy." In *Comprehensive Handbook of Cognitive Theory.* Ed. Arthur Freeman, Karen M. Simon, Larry E. Beutler, and Hal Arkowitz. New York: Plenum Press, 1989.

Becker, Ernst. *The Denial of Death*. New York: Free Press, 1973.

Beckett, Samuel. *The Complete Dramatic Works of Samuel Beckett*. London: Faber & Faber, 1986.

Bibliography

————. *Molloy, Malone Dies, The Unnamable.* New York: Alfred A. Knopf, 1997.

Beckham, E. Edward, and William Leber, eds. *The Handbook of Depression.* 2nd ed. New York: Guilford Press, 1995.

Bell, Kate M., et al. "S-Adenosylmethionine Treatment of Depression: A Controlled Clinical Trial." *American Journal of Psychiatry* 145, no. 9 (1988): 1110–14.

————. "S-adenosylmethionine blood levels in major depression: Changes with drug treatment." *Acta Neurologica Scandinavica* 89, suppl. 154 (1994): 15–18.

Belsky, Jay, Laurence Steinberg, and Patricia Draper. "Childhood Experience, Interpersonal Development, and Reproductive Strategy: An Evolutionary Theory of Socialization." *Child Development* 62 (1991): 647–70.

Benjamin, Walter. *The Origin of German Tragic Drama.* Trans. John Osborne. London: Verso, 1985.

Benshoof, Janet, and Laura Ciolkoski. "Psychological Warfare." *Legal Times,* January 4, 1999.

Berg, J. H. van den. *The Changing Nature of Man.* Trans. H. F. Croes. New York: Norton, 1961.

Berger, M., et al. "Sleep deprivation combined with consecutive sleep phase advance as fast-acting therapy in depression." *American Journal of Psychiatry* 154, no. 6 (1997): 870–72.

Bergmann, Uri. "Speculations on the Neurobiology of EMDR." *Traumatology* 4, no. 1 (1998).

Bernardini, Paolo. *"Melancholia gravis:* Robert Burton's *Anatomy* (1621) and the Links between Suicide and Melancholy." Manuscript.

Berndt, Ernst, et al. "Workplace performance effects from chronic depression and its treatment." *Journal of Health Economics* 17, no. 5 (1998): 511–35.

Bernet, C. Z., et al. "Relationship of childhood maltreatment to the onset and course of major depression." *Depression and Anxiety* 9, no. 4 (1999): 169–74.

Bickerton, Derek. *Language and Species.* Chicago: University of Chicago Press, 1990.

Birtchnell, John. *How Humans Relate.* Westport, Conn.: Praeger, 1993.

Blair-West, G. W., G. W. Mellsop, and M. L. Eyeson-Annan. "Down-rating lifetime suicide risk in major depression." *Acta Psychiatrica Scandinavica* 95 (1997): 259–63.

Blakeslee, Sandra. "Pulsing Magnets Offer New Method of Mapping Brain." *New York Times,* May 21, 1996.

————. "New Theories of Depression Focus on Brain's Two Sides." *New York Times,* January 19, 1999.

Blazer, Dan G., et al. "The Prevalence and Distribution of Major Depression in a National Community Sample: The National Comorbidity Survey." *American Journal of Psychiatry* 151, no. 7 (1994): 979–86.

Blok, F. F. *Caspar Barlaeus: From the Correspondence of a Melancholic.* Trans. H. S. Lake and D. A. S. Reid. Assen, Netherlands: Van Gorcum, 1976.

Bloom, Harold. *Shakespeare: The Invention of the Human.* New York: Riverhead Books, 1998.

Blumenthal, J. A., et al. "Effects of exercise training on older patients with major depression." *Archives of Internal Medicine* 159 (1999): 2349–56.

Bodkin, J. Alexander, et al. "Treatment Orientation and Associated Characteristics of North American Academic Psychiatrists." *Journal of Nervous Mental Disorders* 183 (1995): 729–35.

Boerhaave, Hermann. *Boerhaave's Aphorisms: Concerning the Knowledge and Cure of Diseases.* London: W. Innys and C. Hitch, 1742.

Bibliography

Boor, M., et al. "Suicide Rates, Handgun Control Laws, and Sociodemographic Variables." *Psychological Reports* 66 (1990): 923–30.

Bostwick, J. M., and S. Pancratz. "Affective disorders and suicide risk: A re-examination." *American Journal of Psychiatry* (in press).

Bottiglieri, T., et al. "S-adenosylmethionine levels in psychiatric and neurological disorders: A review." *Acta Neurologica Scandinavica* 89, suppl. 154 (1994): 19–26.

Bower, Bruce. "Depressive aftermath for new mothers." *Science News*, August 25, 1990.

———. "Depression therapy gets interpersonal." *Science News* 140 (1991): 404.

———. "Depression: Rates in women, men . . . and stress effects across the sexes." *Science News* 147 (1995): 346.

Bowie, Andrew. *Schelling and Modern European Philosophy*. London: Routledge, 1993.

Bowlby, John. *Loss: Sadness and Depression*. Vol. 3 of *Attachment and Loss*. London: Hogarth Press, 1980.

Braun, Wilhelm Alfred. *Types of Weltschmerz in German Poetry*. New York: AMS Press, 1966.

Breggin, Peter R., and Ginger Ross Breggin. *Talking Back to Prozac*. New York: St. Martin's Paperbacks, 1994.

Brenna, Susan. "This Is Your Child. This Is Your Child on Drugs." *New York* 30, no. 45 (1997): 46–53.

Bressa, G. M. "S-adenosyl-l-methionine (SAMe) as antidepressant: Meta-analysis of clinical studies." *Acta Neurologica Scandinavica* 89, suppl. 154 (1994): 7–14.

Brink, Susan. "I'll say I'm suicidal." *U.S. News & World Report*, January 19, 1998.

Brody, Jane. "Changing thinking to change emotions." *New York Times*, August 21, 1996.

———. "Despite the Despair of Depression, Few Men Seek Treatment." *New York Times*, December 30, 1997.

Brown, George W. "Clinical and Psychosocial Origins of Chronic Depressive Episodes. 1. A Community Survey." *British Journal of Psychiatry* 165 (1994): 447–56.

———. "Clinical and Psychosocial Origins of Chronic Depressive Episodes. 2. A Patient Inquiry." *British Journal of Psychiatry* 165 (1994) : 457–65.

———. "Life Events and Endogenous Depression." *Archives of General Psychiatry* 51 (1994): 525–34.

———. "Psychosocial factors and depression and anxiety disorders—some possible implications for biological research." *Journal of Psychopharmacology* 10, no. 1 (1996): 23–30.

———. "Genetics of depression: A social science perspective." *International Review of Psychiatry* 8 (1996): 387–401.

———. "Loss and Depressive Disorders." In *Adversity, Stress and Psychopathology*. Ed. B. P. Dohrenwend. Washington, D.C.: American Psychiatric Press, 1997.

Brown, George W., et al. "Aetiology of anxiety and depressive disorders in an inner-city population. 1. Early adversity." *Psychological Medicine* 23 (1993): 143–54.

———. "Aetiology of anxiety and depressive disorders in an inner-city population. 2. Comorbidity and adversity." *Psychological Medicine* 23 (1993): 155–65.

———. "Loss, humiliation and entrapment among women developing depression: A patient and nonpatient comparison." *Psychological Medicine* 25 (1995): 7–21.

———. "Social Factors and Comorbidity of Depressive and Anxiety Disorders." *British Journal of Psychiatry* 168, suppl. 30 (1996): 50–57.

———. "Single mothers, poverty, and depression." *Psychological Medicine* 27 (1997): 21–33.

505

Bibliography

Brown, Richard, Teodoro Bottiglieri, and Carol Colman. *Stop Depression Now: SAM-e.* New York: G. P. Putnam's Sons, 1999.

Brown, Theodore M. "Descartes, dualism, and psychosomatic medicine." In *The Anatomy of Madness*, vol. 1. Ed. W. F. Bynum, Roy Porter, and Michael Shepherd. London: Tavistock Publications, 1985.

Brown, Thomas M.. "Acute St. John's Wort Toxicity." *American Journal of Emergency Medicine* 18, no. 2 (2000): 231–32.

Bruder, G. E., et al. "Outcome of cognitive-behavioral therapy for depression: Relation to hemispheric dominance for verbal processing." *Journal of Abnormal Psychology* 106, no. 1 (1997): 138–44.

Buck, Jeffrey, et al. "Behavioral Health Benefits in Employer-Sponsored Health Plans, 1997." *Health Affairs* 18, no. 2 (1999): 67–78.

Bucknill, John Charles, and Daniel H. Tuke. *A Manual of Psychological Medicine.* Philadelphia: Blanchard and Lea, 1858.

Bulgakov, Mikhail. *The White Guard.* Trans. Michael Glenny. London: The Harvill Press, 1996.

Burns, Barbara, et al. "General Medical and Specialty Mental Health Service Use for Major Depression." *International Journal of Psychiatry in Medicine* 30, no. 2 (2000): 127–43.

Burton, Robert. *The Anatomy of Melancholy.* 3 vols. Ed. Thomas C. Faulkner, Nicolas K. Kiessling, and Rhonda L. Blair. Oxford: Clarendon Press, 1997.

Bush, Carol, et al. "Operation Outreach: Intensive Case Management for Severely Psychiatrically Disabled Adults." *Hospital and Community Psychiatry* 41, no. 6 (1990): 647–51.

Byrd, Max. *Visits to Bedlam: Madness and Literature in the Eighteenth Century.* Columbia: University of South Carolina Press, 1974.

Byrne, Gayle, and Stephen Suomi. "Social Separation in Infant *Cebus Apella*: Patterns of Behavioral and Cortisol Response." *International Journal of Developmental Neuroscience* 17, no. 3 (1999): 265–74.

Cadoret, Remi, et al. "Somatic Complaints. Harbinger of Depression in Primary Care." *Journal of Affective Disorders* 2 (1980): 61–70.

———. "Depression Spectrum Disease, I: The Role of Gene-Environment Interaction." *American Journal of Psychiatry* 153, no. 7 (1996): 892–99.

Cain, Lillian. "Obtaining Social Welfare Benefits for Persons with Serious Mental Illness." *Hospital and Community Psychiatry* 44, no. 10 (1993): 977–80.

Calabrese, J. R., et al. "Fish Oils and Bipolar Disorder." *Archives of General Psychiatry* 56 (1999): 413–14.

Callahan, Roger J., and Joanne Callahan. *Stop the Nightmares of Trauma: Thought Field Therapy.* New York: Professional Press, 2000.

Camus, Albert. *The Myth of Sisyphus and Other Essays.* Trans. Justin O'Brien. New York: Vintage International, 1991.

Caplan, Paula J. *They Say You're Crazy.* Reading, Mass.: Addison-Wesley, 1995.

Carling, Paul J. "Major Mental Illness, Housing, and Supports." *American Psychologist,* August 1990, 969–71.

Carlyle, Thomas. *Sartor Resartus.* Indianapolis: Odyssey Press, 1937.

Carney, Michael W. P., et al. "S-Adenosylmethionine and Affective Disorder." *American Journal of Medicine* 83, suppl. 5A (1987): 104–6.

———. "Switch Mechanism in Affective Illness and Oral S-Adenosylmethionine." *British Journal of Psychiatry* 150 (1987): 724–25.

Bibliography

Catalán, José, ed. *Mental Health and HIV Infection.* London: UCL Press, 1999.

Chagnon, Napoleon A. *Yanomamö: The Last Days of Eden.* San Diego: Harcourt Brace Jovanovich, 1992.

Chaisson-Stewart, G. Maureen, ed. *Depression in the Elderly: An Interdisciplinary Approach.* New York: John Wiley & Sons, 1985.

Chance, M. R. A., ed. *Social Fabrics of the Mind.* London: Lawrence Erlbaum Associates, Publishers, 1988.

Charness, Michael. "Brain Lesions in Alcoholics." *Alcoholism: Clinical and Experimental Research* 17, no. 1 (1993): 2–11.

Chaucer. *Canterbury Tales Complete.* Trans./ed. James J. Donohue. Iowa: 1979.

Chekhov, Anton. *Lady with Lapdog and Other Stories.* Trans. David Magarshack. London: Penguin Books, 1964.

———. *The Party and Other Stories.* Trans. Ronald Wilks. London: Penguin Books, 1985.

Chomsky, Noam. *Reflections on Language.* New York: Pantheon Books, 1975.

Christie, Deborah. "Assessment." Manuscript.

———. "Cognitive-behavioral therapeutic techniques for children with eating disorders." Manuscript.

Christie, Deborah, and Russell Viner. "Eating disorders and self-harm in adolescent diabetes." *Journal of Adolescent Health* 27 (2000).

Chua-Eoan, Howard. "How to Spot a Troubled Kid." *Time* 153, no. 21 (1999): 44–49.

Cioran, E. M. *A Short History of Decay.* Trans. Richard Howard. New York: Quartet Encounters, 1990.

———. *Tears and Saints.* Trans. Ilinca Zarifopol-Johnston. Chicago: University of Chicago Press, 1995.

Clark, R. E., et al. "A cost-effectiveness comparison of supported employment and rehabilitation day treatment." *Administration and Policy in Mental Health* 24, no. 1 (1996): 63–77.

Cochran, S. D., and V. M. Mays. "Lifetime Prevalence of Suicide Symptoms and Affective Disorders among Men Reporting Same-Sex Sexual Partners: Results from NHANES III." *American Journal of Public Health* 90, no. 4 (2000): 573–78.

———. "Relation between Psychiatric Syndromes and Behaviorally Defined Sexual Orientation in a Sample of the U.S. Population." *American Journal of Epidemiology* 151, no. 5 (2000): 516–23.

Cohen, Carl. "Poverty and the Course of Schizophrenia: Implications for Research and Policy." *Hospital and Community Psychiatry* 44, no. 10 (1993): 951–58.

Coleridge, Samuel Taylor. *The Collected Letters of Samuel Taylor Coleridge.* Ed. Earl Leslie Griggs. Vol. 1., letter 68. Oxford: Clarendon Press, 1956.

Collinge, Nancy C. *Introduction to Primate Behavior.* Dubuque, Iowa: Kendall/Hunt Publishing Company, 1993.

Colt, George Howe. *The Enigma of Suicide.* New York: Summit Books, 1991.

Colton, Michael. "You Need It Like . . . A Hole in the Head?" *Washington Post,* May 31, 1998.

Corballis, Michael. *The Lopsided Ape: Evolution of the Generative Mind.* New York: Oxford University Press, 1991.

Costa, E., and G. Racagni, eds. *Typical and Atypical Antidepressants: Clinical Practice.* New York: Raven Press, 1982.

Cowper, William, Esq. *Memoir of the Early Life of William Cowper, Esq.* Newburgh, N.Y.: Philo B. Pratt, 1817.

Bibliography

————. *The Poetical Works of William Cowper.* Ed. H. S. Milford. Oxford: Oxford University Press, 1950.

Coyne, James C., ed. *Essential Papers on Depression.* New York: New York University Press, 1985.

Craske, M. G., et al. *Mastery of your anxiety and panic: Therapist guide for anxiety, panic, and agoraphobia.* San Antonio: Graywind Publications/The Psychological Corporation, 2000.

Crellin, John K., and Jane Philpott. *Herbal Medicine Past and Present: A Reference Guide to Medicinal Plants.* 2 vols. Durham, N.C.: Duke University Press, 1990.

Cross, Alan. "Serotonin in Alzheimer-Type Dementia and Other Dementing Illnesses." *Annals of the New York Academy of Sciences* 600 (1990): 405–15.

Cross, Alan, et al. "Serotonin Receptor Changes in Dementia of the Alzheimer Type." *Journal of Neurochemistry* 43 (1984): 1574–81.

Cross-National Collaborative Group. "The Changing Rate of Major Depression." *Journal of the American Medical Association* 268, no. 21 (1992): 3098–105.

Crow, T. J. "Sexual selection, Machiavellian intelligence and the origins of psychosis." *Lancet* 342 (1993): 594–98.

————. "Childhood precursors of psychosis as clues to its evolutionary origins." *European Archives of Psychiatry and Clinical Neuroscience* 245 (1995): 61–69.

————. "Constraints on Concepts of Pathogenesis." *Archives of General Psychiatry* 52 (1995): 1011–15.

————. "A Darwinian Approach to the Origins of Psychosis." *British Journal of Psychiatry* 167 (1995): 12–25.

————. "Location of the Handedness Gene on the X and Y Chromosomes." *American Journal of Medical Genetics* 67 (1996): 50–52.

————. "Sexual selection as the mechanism of evolution of Machiavellian intelligence: A Darwinian theory of the origins of psychosis." *Journal of Psychopharmacology* 10, no. 1 (1996): 77–87.

————. "Is schizophrenia the price that *Homo sapiens* pays for language?" *Schizophrenia Research* 28 (1997): 127–41.

————. "Schizophrenia as failure of hemispheric dominance for language." *Trends in Neuroscience* 20 (1997): 339–43.

————. "Evidence for Linkage to Psychosis and Cerebral Asymmetry (Relative Hand Skill) on the X Chromosome." *American Journal of Medical Genetics* 81 (1998): 420–27.

————. "Nuclear schizophrenic symptoms as a window on the relationship between thought and speech." Manuscript.

————. "Relative hand skill predicts academic ability." Manuscript.

Cullen, William. *The First Lines of the Practice of Physic.* 3 vols. Worcester, Mass.: Isaiah Thomas, 1790.

————. *Synopsis and Nosology, Being an Arrangement and Definition of Diseases.* Springfield, Mass.: Edward Gray, 1793.

Curtis, Tine, and Peter Bjerregaard. *Health Research in Greenland.* Copenhagen: DICE, 1995.

Cutbush, Edward. *An Inaugural Dissertation on Insanity.* Philadelphia: Zachariah Poulson Jr., 1794.

Daedalus. "The Brain." Spring 1998.

Dain, Norman. *Concepts of Insanity in the United States, 1789–1865.* New Brunswick, N.J.: Rutgers University Press, 1964.

Damasio, Antonio R. *Descartes' Error.* New York: A Grosset/Putnam Book, 1994.

Danquah, Meri Nana-Ama. *Willow Weep for Me.* New York: W. W. Norton, 1998.

Bibliography

Danziger, Sandra, et al. "Barriers to the Employment of Welfare Recipients." Ann Arbor: University of Michigan, Poverty Research and Training Center, 1999.

Darwin, Charles. *The Expression of the Emotions in Man and Animals.* 3rd ed. Oxford: Oxford University Press, 1998.

Davidson, Park O., ed. *The Behavioral Management of Anxiety, Depression, and Pain.* New York: Brunner/Mazel Publishers, 1976.

Davidson, Richard J. "Affective style, psychopathology and resilience: Brain mechanisms and plasticity." *American Psychologist* (in press).

Davidson, Richard J., and Nathan Fox. "Frontal Brain Asymmetry Predicts Infants' Response to Maternal Separation." *Journal of Abnormal Psychology* 98, no. 2 (1989): 127–31.

Davidson, Richard J., et al. "Approach-Withdrawal and Cerebral Asymmetry: Emotional Expression and Brain Physiology I." *Journal of Personality and Social Psychology* 58, no. 2 (1990): 330–41.

Dean, Laura, et al. "Lesbian, Bisexual and Transgender Health: Findings and Concerns." Gay and Lesbian Medical Association (www.glma.org).

de Leo, Diego, and René F. W. Diekstra. *Depression and Suicide in Late Life.* Toronto: Hogrefe & Huber Publishers, 1990.

Delgado, T., et al. "Serotonin function and the mechanism of antidepressant action: Reversal of antidepressant by rapid depletion of plasma tryptophan." *Archives of General Psychiatry* 47 (1990): 411–18.

DePaulo, J. Raymond, Jr., and Keith Russell Ablow. *How to Cope with Depression.* New York: Fawcett Columbine, 1989.

DeRosis, Helen A., and Victoria Y. Pellegrino. *The Book of Hope.* New York: Bantam Books, 1977.

DeRubeis, R. J., et al. "Medications versus cognitive behavior therapy for severely depressed outpatients: Mega-analysis of four randomized comparisons." *American Journal of Psychiatry* 156, no. 7 (1999): 1007–13.

Devanand, D. P., et al. "Does ECT Alter Brain Structure?" *American Journal of Medicine* 151, no. 7 (1994): 957–70.

De Wester, Jeffrey. "Recognizing and Treating the Patient with Somatic Manifestations of Depression." *Journal of Family Practice* 43, suppl. 6 (1996): S3–15.

Dickens, Charles. *Nicholas Nickleby.* New York: Oxford University Press, 1987.

Dickinson, Emily. *The Complete Poems of Emily Dickinson.* Ed. Thomas H. Johnson. Boston: Little, Brown, 1960.

Diefendorf, A. Ross. *Clinical Psychiatry: A Text-Book for Students and Physicians.* Abstracted and Adapted from the Seventh German Edition of Kraepelin's *Lehrbuch der Psychiatrie.* New York: Macmillan, 1912.

Diepold, John H., Jr. "Touch and Breath (TAB)." Paper presented at Innovative and Integrative Approaches to Psychotherapy: A Conference. Edison, N.J., November 14–15, 1998.

Donne, John. *Biathanatos.* A modern-spelling edition by Michael Rudick and M. Pabst Battin. New York: Garland Publishing, 1982.

Dorn, Lorah, et al. "Biopsychological and cognitive differences in children with premature vs. on-time adrenarche." *Archives of Pediatric Adolescent Medicine* 153, no. 2 (1999): 137–46.

Dostoyevsky, Fyodor. *The House of the Dead.* Trans. David McDuff. New York: Penguin Classics, 1985.

———. *The Idiot.* Trans. Constance Garnett. New York: Modern Library, 1983.

Bibliography

———. *Notes from Underground.* Trans. Andrew R. MacAndrew. New York: Signet Classic, 1961.

———. *The Possessed.* Trans. Constance Garnett. New York: Heritage Press, 1959.

Dozier, Rush W., Jr. *Fear Itself.* New York: St. Martin's Press, 1998.

Dunn, Sara, Blake Morrison, and Michèle Roberts, eds. *Mind Readings: Writers' Journeys through Mental States.* London: Minerva, 1996.

Dunner, D. L. "An Overview of Paroxetine in the Elderly." *Gerontology* 40, suppl. 1 (1994): 21–27.

DuRant, Robert, et al. "Factors Associated with the Use of Violence among Urban Black Adolescents." *American Journal of Public Health* 84 (1994): 612–17.

Dworkin, Ronald. *Life's Dominion.* New York: Alfred A. Knopf, 1993.

Ebert, D., et al. "Eye-blink rates and depression. Is the antidepressant effect of sleep deprivation mediated by the dopamine system?" *Neuropsychopharmacology* 15, no. 4 (1996): 332–39.

The Economist. "Depression: The Spirit of the Age." December 19, 1998.

———. "The Tyranny of Time." December 18, 1999.

Edgson, Vicki, and Ian Marber. *The Food Doctor.* London: Collins & Brown, 1999.

Edward, J. Guy. "Depression, antidepressants, and accidents." *British Medical Journal* 311 (1995): 887–88.

Egelko, Susan, et al. "Relationship among CT Scans, Neurological Exam, and Neuropsychological Test Performance in Right-Brain-Damaged Stroke Patients." *Journal of Clinical and Experimental Neuropsychology* 10, no. 5 (1988): 539–64.

Eliot, George. *Daniel Deronda.* London: Penguin Books, 1983.

Eliot, T. S. *The Complete Poems and Plays.* New York: Harcourt, Brace & World, 1971.

Ellis, Bruce, and Judy Garber. "Psychosocial antecedents of variation in girls' pubertal timing: Maternal depression, stepfather presence, and marital and family stress." *Child Development* 71, no. 2 (2000): 485–501.

Epicurus. *A Guide to Happiness.* Trans. J. C. A. Gaskin. London: A Phoenix Paperback, 1995.

Eriksson, P. S., et al. "Neurogenesis in the adult human hippocampus." *Naure Medicine* 4 (1998): 1313–17.

Esquirol, J. E. D. *Mental Maladies. A Treatise on Insanity.* Fac. of English ed. of 1845. New York: Hafner Publishing, 1965.

Evans, Dylan. "The Social Competition Hypothesis of Depression." *ASCAP* 12, no. 3 (1999).

Evans, Glen, and Norman L. Farberow. *The Encyclopedia of Suicide.* New York: Facts on File, 1988.

Fassler, David, and Lynne Dumas. *Help Me, I'm Sad: Recognizing, Treating, and Preventing Childhood Depression.* New York: Penguin, 1998.

Faulkner, A. H., and K. Cranston. "Correlates of Same-Sex Sexual Behavior in a Random Sample of Massachusetts High School Students." *American Journal of Public Health* 88, no. 2 (1998): 262–66.

Fava, Maurizio, et al. "Folate, Vitamin B12, and Homocysteine in Major Depressive Disorder." *American Journal of Psychiatry* 154, no. 3 (1997): 426–28.

Feld, Steven. *Sound and Sentiment.* 2nd ed. Philadelphia: University of Pennsylvania Press, 1982.

Felman, Shoshana. *What Does a Woman Want? Reading and Sexual Difference.* Baltimore and London: Johns Hopkins University Press, 1993.

Ferber, Jane S., and Suzanne LeVert. *A Woman Doctor's Guide to Depression.* New York: Hyperion, 1997.

Bibliography

Fergusson, D. M., et al. "Is Sexual Orientation Related to Mental Health Problems and Suicidality in Young People?" *Archives of General Psychiatry* 56, no. 10 (1999): 876–86.

Ferro, Tova, et al. "Screening for Depression in Mothers Bringing Their Offspring for Evaluation or Treatment of Depression." *American Journal of Psychiatry* 157 (2000): 375–79.

Field, Tiffany. "Maternal Depression: Effects on Infants and Early Interventions." *Preventive Medicine* 27 (1998): 200–203.

Field, Tiffany, et al. "Effects of Parent Training on Teenage Mothers and Their Infants." *Pediatrics* 69, no. 6 (1982): 703–7.

Fischer, Joannie Schrof. "Taking the shock out of electroshock." *U.S. News & World Report*, January 24, 2000.

Fitzgerald, F. Scott. *The Crack-Up*. Ed. Edmund Wilson. New York: New Directions, 1993.

———. *The Great Gatsby*. New York: Charles Scribner's Sons, 1953.

Flowers, Arthur. *Another Good Loving Blues*. New York: Ballantine Books, 1993.

Flynn, John. *Cocaine*. New York: A Birch Lane Press Book, 1991.

Foucault, Michel. *Madness and Civilization*. Trans. Richard Howard. New York: Vintage Books, 1965.

Frank, Ellen, et al. "Nortriptyline and interpersonal psychotherapy as maintenance therapies for recurrent major depression: A randomized controlled trial in patients older than 59 years." *Journal of the American Medical Association* 281, no. 1 (1999): 39–45.

———. "The treatment effectiveness project. A comparison of paroxetine, problem-solving therapy, and placebo in the treatment of minor depression and dysthymia in primary care patients: Background and research plan." *General Hospital Psychiatry* 21, no. 4 (1999): 260–73.

Freeman, Arthur, Karen M. Simon, Larry E. Beutler, and Hal Arkowitz, eds. *Comprehensive Handbook of Cognitive Theory*. New York: Plenum Press, 1989.

Freud, Sigmund. *A General Selection from the Works of Sigmund Freud*. Ed. John Rickman. New York: Liveright, 1957.

———. *The Standard Edition of the Complete Psychological Works of Sigmund Freud*. 24 vols. Trans./ed. James Strachey, Anna Freud, et al. London: Hogarth Press, 1953–74.

Friedman, Raymond J., and Martin M. Katz, eds. *The Psychology of Depression: Contemporary Theory and Research*. Washington, D.C.: V. H. Winston & Sons, 1974.

Friedman, Richard C., and Jennifer Downey. "Internalized Homophobia and the Negative Therapeutic Reaction." *Journal of the American Academy of Psychoanalysis* 23, no. 1 (1995): 99–113.

———. "Internal Homophobia and Gender-Valued Self-Esteem in the Psychoanalysis of Gay Patients." *Psychoanalytic Review* 86, no. 3 (1999): 325–47.

———. "Psychoanalysis and Sexual Orientation: Sexual Science and Clinical Practice." Manuscript.

Friedrich, William N. *Psychotherapy with Sexually Abused Boys*. Thousand Oaks, Calif.: Sage Publications, 1995.

Fromm, Erich. *Escape from Freedom*. New York: Farrar & Rinehart, 1941.

Fugh-Berman, A. "Herb-drug interactions." *Lancet* 355, no. 9198 (2000): 134–38.

Galanter, Marc, and Herbert D. Kleber. *Textbook of Substance Abuse Treatment*. 2nd ed. Washington, D.C.: American Psychiatric Press, 1999.

Bibliography

Galdston, Iago, ed. *Historic Derivations of Modern Psychiatry.* New York: McGraw-Hill, 1967.

Gallerani, M., et al. "The time for suicide." *Psychological Medicine* 26 (1996): 867–70.

Gallicchio, Vincent, and Nicholas Birch, eds. *Lithium: Biochemical and Clinical Advances.* Cheshire, Conn.: Weidner Publishing Group, 1996.

Gallo, Fred P. *Energy Psychology.* Boca Raton, Fla.: CRC Press, 1999.

Gamwell, Lynn, and Nancy Tomes. *Madness in America.* Ithaca, N.Y.: Cornell University Press, 1995.

Garcia-Borreguero, Diego, et al. "Hormonal Responses to the Administration of M-Chlorophenylpiperazine in Patients with Seasonal Affective Disorder and Controls." *Biological Psychiatry* 37 (1995): 740–49.

Gardner, Russell, Jr. "Mechanisms in Manic-Depressive Disorder. An Evolutionary Model." *Archives of General Psychiatry* 39 (1982): 1436–41.

———. "Sociophysiology as the Basic Science of Psychiatry." *Theoretical Medicine* 18 (1997): 335–56.

———. "Mati: The Angry Depressed Dog Who Fought On and Won." *ASCAP* 11, no. 12 (1998).

Garofalo, R., et al. "The Association between Health Risk Behaviors and Sexual Orientation among a School-Based Sample of Adolescents." *Pediatrics* 101 (1998): 895–902.

———. "Sexual Orientation and Risk of Suicide Attempts among a Representative Sample of Youth." *Archives of Pediatrics and Adolescent Medicine* 153 (1999): 487–93.

Gasner, Rose, et al. "The Use of Legal Action in New York City to Ensure Treatment of Tuberculosis." *New England Journal of Medicine* 340, no. 5 (1999): 359–66.

Gazzaniga, Michael S. *The Mind's Past.* Berkeley: University of California Press, 1998.

George, Mark, et al. "SPECT and PET imaging in mood disorders." *Journal of Clinical Psychiatry* 54 (1993): 6–13.

———. "Daily repetitive transcranial magnetic stimulation (rTMS) improves mood in depression." *Neuroreport* 6, no. 14 (1995): 1853–56.

Ghadirian, Abdu'l-Missagh A., and Heinz E. Lehmann, eds. *Environment and Psychopathology.* New York: Springer Publishing, 1993.

Gilbert, David. *Smoking.* Washington, D.C.: Taylor & Francis, 1995.

Gillin, J. C. "Are sleep disturbances risk factors for anxiety, depressive and addictive disorders?" *Acta Psychiatrica Scandinavica Supplementum* 393 (1998): 39–43.

Gladstone, Gemma, Gordon Parker, Kay Wilhelm, and Philip Mitchell. "Characteristics of depressed patients who report childhood sexual abuse." *American Journal of Psychiatry* 156, no. 3 (1999): 431–37.

Gladwell, Malcolm. "Damaged." *The New Yorker,* February 24 and March 3, 1997, 132–47.

Glantz, Kalman, and John K. Pearce. *Exiles from Eden: Psychotherapy from an Evolutionary Perspective.* New York: W. W. Norton, 1989.

Glenmullen, Joseph. *Prozac Backlash.* New York: Simon & Schuster, 2000.

Gloaguen, V., et al. "A meta-analysis of cognitive therapy in depressed patients." *Journal of Affective Disorders* 49, no. 1 (1998): 59–72.

Goethe, Johann Wolfgang von. *Faust.* From a literary translation by Christa Weisman, updated by Howard Brenton. London: Nick Hearn Books, 1995.

———. *The Sorrows of Young Werther.* Trans. Bayard Quincy Jones. New York: Frederick Ungar Publishing, 1957.

Gold, Mark S., and Andrew E. Slaby, eds. *Dual Diagnosis in Substance Abuse.* New York: Marcel Dekker, 1991.

Bibliography

Goldstein, Rise, et al. "The Prediction of Suicide." *Archives of General Psychiatry* 48 (1991): 418–22.

Goode, Erica. "Federal Report Praising Electroshock Stirs Uproar." *New York Times,* October 6, 1999.

———. "Viewing Depression as a Tool for Survival." *New York Times,* February 1, 2000.

———. "Chronic-Depression Study Backs the Pairing of Therapy and Drugs." *New York Times,* May 18, 2000.

Goodman, Walter. "In Confronting Depression the First Target Is Shame." *New York Times,* January 6, 1998.

Goodwin, Donald W. *Alcoholism, the Facts.* 3rd ed. Oxford: Oxford University Press, 2000.

Goodwin, Frederick K., and Kay Redfield Jamison. *Manic-Depressive Illness.* Oxford: Oxford University Press, 1990.

Gore, Tipper. "Strip Stigma from Mental Illness." *USA Today,* May 7, 1999.

Gorman, Christine. "Anatomy of Melancholy." *Time,* May 5, 1997.

Gottfries, C. G., et al. "Treatment of Depression in Elderly Patients with and without Dementia Disorders." *International Clinical Psychopharmacology,* suppl. 6, no. 5 (1992): 55–64.

Grand, David. *Defining and Redefining EMDR.* Bellmore, N.Y.: BioLateral Books, 1999.

———. "EMDR Performance Enhancement and Auditory Stimulation." Manuscript.

———. "Integrating EMDR into the Psychodynamic Treatment Process." Paper presented at the 1995 EMDR International Conference and published in the June 1996 *Eye Movement Desensitization and Reprocessing International Association Newsletter.*

Grant, Bridget, et al. "The Relationship between *DSM-IV* Alcohol Use Disorders and *DSM-IV* Major Depression: Examination of the Primary-Secondary Distinction in a General Population Sample." *Journal of Affective Disorders* 38 (1996): 113–28.

Gray, Thomas. *The Complete Poems of Thomas Gray.* Ed. H. W. Starr and J. R. Hendrickson. Oxford: Clarendon Press, 1966.

Greden, John F. "Do long-term treatments alter lifetime course? Lessons learned, actions needed." *Journal of Psychiatric Research* 32 (1998): 197–99.

———. "Serotonin: How Much We Have Learned! So Much to Discover . . ." *Biological Psychiatry* 44 (1998): 309–12.

Greene, Graham. *Ways of Escape.* New York: Simon and Schuster, 1980.

Griaule, Marcel. *Conversations with Ogotemmêli.* London: Oxford University Press, 1965.

Griesinger, W. *Mental Pathology and Therapeutics.* 2nd ed. Trans. C. Lockhart Robertson and James Rutherford. London: New Sydenham Society, 1867; New York: William Wood & Co., 1882.

Griffen, Donald R. *Animal Minds.* Chicago: University of Chicago Press, 1992.

Griffith, John, et al. "Dextroamphetamine: Evaluation of Psychomimetic Properties in Man." *Archives of General Psychiatry* 26 (1972): 97–100.

Group for the Advancement of Psychiatry. *Adolescent Suicide.* Washington, D.C.: American Psychiatric Press, 1996.

Gut, Emmy. *Productive and Unproductive Depression.* New York: Basic Books, 1989.

Guyton, A. C., et al. "Circulation: Overall regulation." *Annual Review of Physiology* 34 (1972). Ed. J. M. Luck and V. E. Hall. Palo Alto, Calif.: Annual Reviews.

Guze, S. B., and E. Robbins. "Suicide and affective disorders." *British Journal of Psychiatry* 117 (1970): 437–38.

Hacking, Ian. *Mad Travelers.* Charlottesville: University Press of Virginia, 1998.

Hagen, Edward H. "Is Postpartum Depression Functional? An Evolutionary Inquiry."

Portion of paper presented at Human Behavior and Evolutionary Society Annual Meeting, Northwestern University, June 1996.

———. "The Defection Hypothesis of Depression: A Case Study." *ASCAP* 11, no. 4 (1998): 13–17.

Halbreich, Uriel, and Lucille Lumley. "The multiple interactional biological processes that might lead to depression and gender differences in its appearance." *Journal of Affective Disorders* 29, no. 2–3 (1993): 159–73.

Hall, Stephen S. "Fear Itself." *New York Times Magazine*, February 28, 1999.

Hall, Thomas S. *Ideas of Life and Matter: Studies in the History of General Physiology, 600 B.C.–1900 A.D.* 2 vols. Chicago: University of Chicago Press, 1969.

Halligan, Marion. "Melancholy." *The Eleven Deadly Sins.* Ed. Ross Fitzgerald. Port Melbourne: William Heinemann Australia, 1993.

Hamsun, Knut. *Hunger.* Trans. Robert Bly. New York: Noonday Press, 1967.

———. *Night Roamers and Other Stories.* Trans. Tiina Nunnally. Seattle: Fjord Press, 1992.

Hanna, E. Z., et al. "Parallels to early onset alcohol use in the relationship of early onset smoking with drug use and *DSM-IV* drug and depressive disorders: Findings from the National Longitudinal Epidemiologic Survey." *Alcoholism, Clinical and Experimental Research* 23, no. 3 (1999): 513–22.

Hannay, Alastair, and Gordon D. Marino, eds. *The Cambridge Companion to Kierkegaard.* Cambridge: Cambridge University Press, 1998.

Hantz, Paul, et al. "Depression in Parkinson's Disease." *American Journal of Psychiatry* 151, no. 7 (1994): 1010–14.

Harrington, Scott. "The History of Federal Involvement in Insurance Regulation: An Historical Overview." In *Optional Federal Chartering of Insurance.* Ed. Peter Wallison. Washington, D.C.: AEI Press, 2000.

Harris, E. Clare, and Brian Barraclough. "Suicide as an Outcome for Medical Disorders." *Medicine* 73 (1994): 281–96.

———. "Excess Mortality of Mental Disorder." *British Journal of Psychiatry* 173 (1998): 11–53.

Harris, M. Jackuelyn, et al. "Recognition and treatment of depression in Alzheimer's disease." *Geriatrics* 44, no. 12 (1989): 26–30.

Hart, Sybil, et al. "Depressed Mothers' Neonates Improve Following the MABI and Brazelton Demonstration." *Journal of Pediatric Psychology* 23, no. 6 (1998): 351–56.

Hassoun, Jacques. *The Cruelty of Depression: On Melancholia.* Trans. David Jacobson. Reading, Mass.: Addison-Wesley, 1997.

Hauenstein, Emily. "A Nursing Practice Paradigm for Depressed Rural Women: Theoretical Basis." *Archives of Psychiatric Nursing* 10, no. 5 (1996): 283–92.

Hays, Judith, et al. "Social Correlates of the Dimensions of Depression in the Elderly." *Journal of Gerontology* 53B, no. 1 (1998): P31–39.

Healy, David. *The Psychopharmacologists.* London: Chapman and Hall, 1996.

———. *The Antidepressant Era.* Cambridge: Harvard University Press, 1997.

Heidegger, Martin. *Being and Time.* Trans. Joan Stambaugh. New York: State University of New York Press, 1996.

Heldman, Kevin. "7½ Days." *City Limits,* June/July 1998.

Hellinger, Bert, et al. *Love's Hidden Symmetry.* Phoenix: Zeig, Tucker, 1998.

Hendin, Herbert. *Suicide in America.* New York: W. W. Norton, 1995.

Herrel, R., et al. "Sexual Orientation and Suicidality: A Co-Twin Control Study in Adult Men." *Archives of General Psychiatry* 56 (1999): 867–74.

Bibliography

Herrmann, Nathan, et al. "Behavioral Disorders in Demented Elderly Patients." *CNS Drugs* 6, no. 4 (1996): 280–300.

Hertzberg, Hendrik. "The Narcissus Survey." *The New Yorker,* January 5, 1998.

Hickey, Dave. *Air Guitar.* Los Angeles: Art Issues Press, 1997.

Hippocrates. *Hippocrates.* 4 vols. Trans./ed. W. H. S. Jones and E. T. Withington. London: William Heinemann, 1962.

Hirschfeld, Robert M. A., et al. "The National Depressive and Manic-Depressive Association Consensus Statement on the Undertreatment of Depression." *Journal of the American Medical Association* 277, no. 4 (1997): 333–40.

Hoffman, Friedrich. *A System of the Practice of Medicine.* 2 vols. Trans. William Lewis. London: J. Murray and J. Johnson, 1783.

Holick, Michael J., and Ernst G. Jung, eds. *Biologic Effects of Light, 1995.* New York: Walter de Gruyter, 1996.

Hollander, Eric, ed. "TMS." *CNS Spectrums* 2, no. 1 (1997).

Hollingsworth, Ellen Jane. "Use of Medicaid for Mental Health Care by Clients of Community Support Programs." *Community Mental Health Journal* 30, no. 6 (1994): 541–49.

Holloway, Lynette. "Seeing a Link Between Depression and Homelessness." *New York Times,* February 7, 1999.

Holy Bible. King James Version. London: Odhams Press Limited, 1939.

Holy Bible. Old Testament. Douay Version of the Latin Vulgate. Rockford, Ill.: Tan Books and Publishers, 1989.

Holy Bible. Revised Standard Version. New York: Thomas Nelson, 1972.

Homer. *The Iliad.* Trans. Robert Fagles. New York: Viking, 1990.

Hooley, Jill M., et al. "Predictors of Relapse in Unipolar Depressives: Expressed Emotion, Marital Distress, and Perceived Criticism." *Journal of Abnormal Psychology* 98, no. 3 (1989): 229–35.

Hooper, Judith. "A New Germ Theory." *Atlantic Monthly,* February 1999, 41–53.

Horgan, John. "Why Freud Isn't Dead." *Scientific American,* December 1996, 74–79.

House, Allan, et al. "Depression Associated with Stroke." *Journal of Neuropsychiatry* 8, no. 4 (1996): 453–57.

Hrdina, Pavel, et al. "Pharmacological Modification of Experimental Depression in Infant Macaques." *Psychopharmacology* 64 (1979): 89–93.

Hugo, Victor. *Les Misérables.* Trans. Charles E. Wilbour. New York: Modern Library, 1992.

Hunter, Richard, and Ida Macalpine, eds. *300 Years of Psychiatry: A History, 1535–1860. Presented in Selected English Texts.* London: Oxford University Press, 1982.

Huysmans, Joris-Karl. *Against Nature.* Trans. Robert Baldick. Suffolk, England: Penguin Classics, 1997.

Hyman, Steven E. "Statement on Fiscal Year 2000 President's Budget Request for the National Institute of Mental Health." Department of Health and Human Services. Washington, D.C. (1999), photocopy.

———. "Political Science." *The Economics of Neuroscience* 2, no. 1 (2000): 6–7.

Ingram, Allan. *The Madhouse of Language: Writing and Reading Madness in the Eighteenth Century.* London: Routledge, 1991.

Inskip, H. M., E. Clare Harris, and Brian Barraclough. "Lifetime risk of suicide for affective disorder, alcoholism, and schizophrenia." *British Journal of Psychiatry* 172 (1998): 35–37.

Ishihara, K., et al. "Mechanism underlying the therapeutic effects of electroconvulsive therapy on depression." *Japanese Journal of Pharmacology* 80, no. 3 (1999): 185–89.

Bibliography

Jack, Dana Crowley. *Silencing the Self: Women and Depression.* Cambridge: Harvard University Press, 1991.

Jackson, Stanley W. *Melancholia and Depression: From Hippocratic Times to Modern Times.* New Haven, Conn., and London: Yale University Press, 1986.

Jacobsen, Neil S., et al. "Couple Therapy as a Treatment for Depression: II. The Effects of Relationship Quality and Therapy on Depressive Relapse." *Journal of Consulting and Clinical Psychology* 61, no. 3 (1993): 516–19.

James, William. *The Will to Believe and Other Essays in Popular Philosophy.* Cambridge: Harvard University Press, 1979.

———. *The Varieties of Religious Experience.* Cambridge: Harvard University Press, 1985.

Jamison, Kay Redfield. *Touched with Fire.* New York: Free Press, 1993.

———. *An Unquiet Mind.* New York: Vintage Books, 1996.

———. *Night Falls Fast.* New York: Alfred A. Knopf, 1999.

Javorsky, James. "An Examination of Language Learning Disabilities in Youth with Psychiatric Disorders." *Annals of Dyslexia* 45 (1995): 215–31.

Jayakody, R., and H. Pollack. "Barriers to Self-Sufficiency among Low-Income, Single Mothers: Substance Use, Mental Health Problems, and Welfare Reform." Paper presented at the Association for Public Policy Analysis and Management, Washington, D.C., November 1997.

Jenkins, Philip. *Synthetic Panics.* New York: New York University Press, 1999.

Jensen, Peter S., et al. "Evolution and Revolution in Child Psychiatry: ADHD as Disorder of Adaptation." *Journal of the American Academy of Child and Adolescent Psychiatry* 36, no. 12 (1997) : 1672–79.

Jimenez, Mary Ann. *Changing Faces of Madness: Early American Attitudes and Treatment of the Insane.* Hanover, N.H.: University Press of New England, 1987.

Jobe, T. H. "Medical Theories of Melancholia in the Seventeenth and Early Eighteenth Centuries." *Clio Medica* 11, no. 4 (1976): 217–31.

Johnson, Richard E., et al. "Lithium Use and Discontinuation in a Health Maintenance Organization." *American Journal of Psychiatry* 153 (1996): 993–1000.

Jones, Mary Lynn F. "Mental health lobbyists say Capitol shooting avoidable." *The Hill,* August 5, 1998.

Jones, Nancy Aaron, et al. "EEG Stability in Infants/Children of Depressed Mothers." *Child Psychiatry and Human Development* 28, no. 2 (1997): 59–70.

Joseph-Vanderpool, Jean R., et al. "Seasonal Variation in Behavioral Responses to m-CPP in Patients with Seasonal Affective Disorder and Controls." *Biological Psychiatry* 33 (1993): 496–504.

Kafka, Franz. *The Metamorphosis and Other Stories.* Trans. Donna Freed. New York: Barnes & Noble Books, 1996.

Kahn, Jack. *Job's Illness: Loss, Grief and Integration: A Psychological Interpretation.* London: Gaskell, 1986.

Kalen, N. H., et al. "Asymmetric frontal brain activity, cortisol, and behavior associated with fearful temperament in Rhesus monkeys." *Behavioral Neuroscience* 112 (1998): 286–92.

Kang, Duck-Hee, et al. "Frontal Brain Asymmetry and Immune Function." *Behavioral Neuroscience* 105, no. 6 (1991): 860–69.

Kant, Immanuel. *Observations on the Feeling of the Beautiful and Sublime.* Trans. John T. Goldthwait. Berkeley: University of California Press, 1960.

———. *The Philosophy of Kant.* New York: Modern Library, 1949.

Kaplan, Bert. *The Inner World of Mental Illness.* New York: Harper & Row, 1964.

Bibliography

Kaplan, Harold I., and Benjamin J. Sadock, eds. *Comprehensive Textbook of Psychiatry.* 5th ed. Baltimore: Williams & Wilkins, 1989.

Karen, Robert. *Becoming Attached.* Oxford: Oxford University Press, 1998.

Karp, David. A. *Speaking of Sadness.* Oxford: Oxford University Press, 1996.

Katz, Jack. *How Emotions Work.* Chicago: University of Chicago Press, 1999.

Katz, Neal, and Linda Marks. "Depression's Staggering Cost." *Nation's Business,* June 1994.

Kaufman, Joan, et al. "Serotonergic Functioning in Depressed Abused Children: Clinical and Familial Correlates." *Biological Psychiatry* 44, no. 10 (1998): 973–81.

Keats, John. *The Poems.* Ed. Gerald Bullet. New York: Alfred A. Knopf, 1992.

Kee, Howard Clark. *Medicine, Miracle, and Magic in New Testament Times.* Cambridge: Cambridge University Press, 1986.

Keitner, Gabor I., et al. "Recovery and Major Depression: Factors Associated with Twelve-Month Outcome." *American Journal of Psychiatry* 149, no. 1 (1992): 93–99.

Keller, Martin, et al. "A comparison of nefazodone, the cognitive behavioral-analysis system of psychotherapy, and their combination for the treatment of chronic depression." *New England Journal of Medicine* 342, no. 20 (2000): 1462–70.

Kelose, John R. "The Genetics of Mental Illness." Department of Psychiatry, University of California, San Diego. Manuscript.

Kendler, Kenneth S. "A Population-Based Twin Study of Major Depression in Women." *Archives of General Psychiatry* 49 (1992): 257–66.

———. "A Longitudinal Twin Study of 1-Year Prevalence of Major Depression in Women." *Archives of General Psychiatry* 50 (1993): 843–52.

———. "The Prediction of Major Depression in Women: Toward an Integrated Etiologic Model." *American Journal of Psychiatry* 150 (1993): 1139–48.

Kendler, Kenneth S., et al. "Stressful life events and previous episodes in the etiology of major depression in women: An evaluation of the 'kindling' hypothesis." *American Journal of Psychiatry* 157, no. 8 (2000): 1243–51.

Kenyon, Jane. *Constance.* St. Paul, Minn.: Graywolf Press, 1993.

Kessler, Ronald C., et al. "Lifetime and 12-Month Prevalence of *DSM-III-R* Psychiatric Disorders in the United States." *Archives of General Psychiatry* 51 (1994): 8–19.

Kettlewell, Caroline. *Skin Game.* New York: St. Martin's Press, 1999.

Kharms, Daniil. *Incidences.* Trans./ed. Neil Cornwall. Cornwall, London: Serpent's Tail, 1993.

Kierkegaard, Søren. *The Sickness Unto Death.* Trans. Alastair Hannay. London: Penguin Books, 1989.

Kiesler, A. "Mental Hospitals and Alternative Care: Noninstitutionalization as Potential Public Policy for Mental Patients." *American Psychologist* 349 (1982): 357–58.

Klein, Donald F., and Paul H. Wender. *Understanding Depression.* Oxford: Oxford University Press, 1993.

Klein, Melanie. *The Selected Melanie Klein.* Ed. Juliet Mitchell. New York: Penguin Books, 1986.

Kleinman, Arthur, and Byron Good, eds. *Culture and Depression.* Berkeley: University of California Press, 1985.

Klerman, Gerald, et al. "Treatment of depression by drugs and psychotherapy." *American Journal of Psychiatry* 131 (1974): 186–91.

Klibansky, Raymond, Erwin Panofsky, and Fritz Saxl. *Saturn and Melancholy: Studies in the History of Natural Philosophy, Religion, and Art.* London: Nelson, 1964.

Klinkenborg, Verlyn. "Sleepless." *New York Times Magazine,* January 5, 1997.

Klitzman, Robert. *In a House of Dreams and Glass.* New York: Ivy Books, 1995.

Knishinsky, Ran. *The Prozac Alternative.* Rochester, Vt.: Healing Arts Press, 1998.

Kobler, Arthur L., and Ezra Stotland. *The End of Hope: A Social-Clinical Study of Suicide.* London: Free Press of Glencoe, 1964.

Kochanska, Grazyna. "Children of Normal and Affectively Ill Mothers." *Child Development* 62 (1991): 250–63.

Koestler, Arthur. *The Ghost in the Machine.* New York: Macmillan, 1967.

Kolb, Elzy. "Serotonin: Is there anything it can't do?" *College of Physicians and Surgeons of Columbia University* (spring 1999).

Kosten, Thomas R., et al. "Depression and Stimulant Dependence." *Journal of Nervous and Mental Disease* 186, no. 12 (1998): 737–45.

———. "Regional cerebral blood flow during acute and chronic abstinence from combined cocaine-alcohol abuse." *Drug and Alcohol Dependence* 50, no. 3 (1998): 187–95.

Kraemer, Gary. "The Behavioral Neurobiology of Self-Injurious Behavior in Rhesus Monkeys: Current Concepts and Relations to Impulsive Behavior in Humans." *Annals of the New York Academy of Sciences* 836, no. 363 (1997): 12–38.

Kraemer, Gary, et al. "Rearing experience and biogenic amine activity in infant rhesus monkeys." *Biological Psychiatry* 40, no. 5 (1996): 338–52.

Kraepelin, Emil. *Manic-Depressive Insanity and Paranoia.* Ayer Co. Pub., 1921.

Krafft-Ebing, R. von. *Text-Book of Insanity.* Trans. Charles Gilbert Chaddock. Philadelphia: F. A. Davis, Publishers, 1904.

Kramer, Peter D. *Listening to Prozac.* New York: Viking Press, 1993.

Kristeller, Paul Oskar. *The Philosophy of Marsilio Ficino.* Trans. Virginia Conant. New York: Columbia University Press, 1943.

Kristeva, Julia. *Black Sun: Depression and Melancholia.* Trans. Leon S. Roudiez. New York: Columbia University Press, 1989.

Kuhn, Reinhard. *The Demon of Noontide: Ennui in Western Literature.* Princeton, N.J.: Princeton University Press, 1976.

Kuhn, Roland. "The Treatment of Depressive States with G22355 (Imipramine Hydrochloride)." Paper read at Galesburg State Hospital, May 19, 1958.

Kye, Christopher, and Neal Ryan. "Pharmacologic Treatment of Child and Adolescent Depression." *Child and Adolescent Psychiatric Clinics of North America* 4, no. 2 (1995): 261–81.

Lambert, Craig. "Deep Cravings." *Harvard Magazine* 102, no. 4 (2000): 60–68.

Lamison-White, L. *U.S. Bureau of the Census: Current Populations Report.* Series P60–198. Washington, D.C.: U.S. Government Printing Office, 1997.

Lattal, K. A., and M. Perrone, eds. "Handbook of Research Methods in Human Operant Behavior." Manuscript.

Lawlor, B. A., et al. "Evidence for a decline with age in behavioral responsivity to the serotonin agonist, m-chlorophenylpiperazine, in healthy human subjects." *Psychiatry Research* 29, no. 1 (1989): 1–10.

Lear, Jonathan. *Love and Its Place in Nature.* New York: Noonday Press, 1990.

———. *Open Minded.* Cambridge: Harvard University Press, 1998.

Ledoux, Joseph. *The Emotional Brain.* New York: Touchstone, 1996.

Lee, Catherine M., and Ian H. Gotlib. "Adjustment of Children of Depressed Mothers: A 10-Month Follow-Up." *Journal of Abnormal Psychology* 100, no. 4 (1991): 473–77.

Lee, Soong, et al. "Community Mental Health Center Accessibility." *Archives of General Psychiatry* 31 (1974): 335–39.

Leibenluft, Ellen, et al. "Is Sleep Deprivation Useful in the Treatment of Depression?" *American Journal of Psychiatry* 149, no. 2 (1992): 159–68.

Bibliography

————. "Relationship between sleep and mood in patients with rapid-cycling bipolar disorder." *Psychiatry Research* 63 (1996): 161–68.

Lemley, Brad. "Alternative Medicine Man." *Discover,* August 1999.

Leopardi, Giacomo. *Poems.* Trans. Jean-Pierre Barricelli. New York: Las Americas Publishing, 1963.

Lepenies, Wolf. *Melancholy and Society.* Trans. Jeremy Gaines and Doris Jones. Cambridge: Harvard University Press, 1992.

Lester, David, ed. *Current Concepts of Suicide.* Philadelphia: Charles Press, 1990.

————. *Patterns of Suicide and Homicide in the World.* New York: Nova Science Publishers, 1996.

————. *Making Sense of Suicide.* Philadelphia: Charles Press, 1997.

Levi, Primo. *The Drowned and the Saved.* Trans. Raymond Rosenthal. New York: Vintage International, 1989.

————. *The Drowned and the Saved.* Introduction by Paul Bailey. Trans. Raymond Rosenthal. London: Abacus, 1989.

Levy, Robert M., and Leonard S. Rubinstein. *The Rights of People with Mental Disabilities.* Carbondale: Southern Illinois University Press, 1996.

Lewinsohn, Peter M., Julia L. Steinmetz, Douglas W. Larson, and Franklin Judita. "Depression-related cognitions: Antecedent or consequence?" *Journal of Abnormal Psychology* 90 (1981): 213–19.

Lewis, C. S. *Studies in Words.* Cambridge: Cambridge University Press, 1967.

Lewis, Ricki. "Manic-Depressive Illness." *FDA Consumer* 30, no. 5 (1996): 26–29.

Lidz, Theodore. "Adolf Meyer and the Development of American Psychiatry." *American Journal of Psychiatry* 123 (1966).

Light, Luise. "How Energy Heals." *New Age Magazine,* February 1998.

Linde, Klaus, et al. "St. John's wort for depression—an overview and meta-analysis of randomized clinical trials." *British Medical Journal* 313 (1996): 253–58.

Lindner, Robert. *The Fifty-Minute Hour.* New York: Rinehart, 1955.

Lipinski, Joseph F., et al. "Open Trial of S-adenosylmethionine for Treatment of Depression." *American Journal of Psychiatry* 143, no. 3 (1984): 448–50.

López, Juan F., et al. "Regulation of 5-HT Receptors and the Hypothalamic-Pituitary-Adrenal Axis: Implications for the Neurobiology of Suicide." *Annals of the New York Academy of Sciences* 836 (1997): 106–34.

————. "Regulation of 5-HT1A Receptor, Glucocorticoid and Mineralocorticoid Receptor in Rat and Human Hippocampus: Implications for the Neurobiology of Depression." *Biological Psychiatry* 43 (1998): 547–73.

————. "Neural circuits mediating stress." *Biological Psychiatry* 46 (1999): 1461–71.

Luhrmann, T. M. *Of Two Minds.* New York: Alfred A. Knopf, 2000.

Lukács, Georg. *Soul and Form.* Trans. Anna Bostock. Cambridge: MIT Press, 1971.

Lynch, John, et al. "Cumulative Impact of Sustained Economic Hardship on Physical, Cognitive, Psychological, and Social Functioning." *New England Journal of Medicine* 337 (1997): 1889–95.

Lynge, Inge. "Mental Disorders in Greenland: Past and Present." *Man & Society* 21 (1997).

Lyons, David, et al. "Separation Induced Changes in Squirrel Monkey Hypothalamic-Pituitary-Adrenal Physiology Resemble Aspects of Hypercortisolism in Humans." *Psychoneuroendocrinology* 24 (1999): 131–42.

MacDonald, Michael. *Mystical Bedlam: Madness, Anxiety, and Healing in Seventeenth-Century England.* Cambridge: Cambridge University Press, 1981.

Bibliography

MacLean, Paul D. *The Triune Brain in Evolution: Role in Paleocerebral Functions.* New York: Plenum Press, 1990.

Madden, Pamela A. F., et al. "Seasonal Changes in Mood and Behavior." *Archives of General Psychiatry* 53 (1996): 47–55.

Maj, M., F. Starace, and N. Sartorius. *Mental Disorders in HIV-1 Infection and AIDS.* Seattle: Hogrefe & Huber, 1993.

Major, Ralph H. *A History of Medicine.* 2 vols. Springfield, Ill.: Thomas, 1954.

Makanjuola, Roger O. "Socio-Cultural Parameters in Yoruba Nigerian Patients with Affective Disorders." *British Journal of Psychiatry* 155 (1989): 337–40.

Malan, André, and Bernard Canguilhem, eds. *Symposium on Living in the Cold.* (2nd, 1989, Le Hohwald, France.) London: J. Libbey Eurotext, 1989.

Malaurie, Jean. *The Last Kings of Thule.* Trans. Adrienne Foulke. New York: E. P. Dutton, 1982.

Maltsberger, John. *Suicide Risk: The Formulation of Clinical Judgment.* New York: New York University Press, 1986.

Manfield, Philip, ed. *Extending EMDR.* New York: W. W. Norton, 1998.

Mann, John. "The Neurobiology of Suicide." *Lifesavers* 10, no. 4 (1998): 1–7.

Mann, John, et al. "Toward a Clinical Model of Suicidal Behavior in Psychiatric Patients." *American Journal of Psychiatry* 156, no. 2 (1999): 181–89.

Manning, Martha. *Undercurrents.* San Francisco: HarperSanFrancisco, 1994.

———. "The Legacy." *Family Therapy Networker,* January 1997, 34–41.

Marcus, Eric. *Why Suicide?* San Francisco: HarperSanFrancisco, 1996.

Margolis, Simeon, and Karen L. Swartz. *The Johns Hopkins White Papers: Depression and Anxiety.* Baltimore: Johns Hopkins Medical Institutions, 1998–2000.

Marinoff, Lou. *Plato, Not Prozac!* New York: HarperCollins, 1999.

Maris, Ronald, ed. *The Biology of Suicide.* New York: Guilford Press, 1986.

Mark, Tami, et al. *National Expenditures for Mental Health, Alcohol and Other Drug Abuse Treatment.* Rockville, Md.: U.S. Department of Health and Human Services, 1996.

Marlowe, Ann. *How to Stop Time: Heroin from A to Z.* New York: Basic Books, 1999.

Mather, Cotton. *The Angel of Bethesda.* Ed. Gordon W. Jones. Barre, Mass.: American Antiquarian Society and Barre Publishers, 1972.

Mathew, Roy, and William Wilson. "Substance Abuse and Cerebral Blood Flow." *American Journal of Psychiatry* 148, no. 3 (1991): 292–305.

Maudsley, Henry. *The Pathology of Mind.* 3rd ed. New York: D. Appleton, 1882.

———. *The Pathology of the Mind.* London: Macmillan, 1895.

Maupassant, Guy de. *Selected Short Stories.* Trans. Roger Colet. London: Penguin Books, 1971.

May, Rollo. *The Meaning of Anxiety.* New York: W. W. Norton, 1977.

Maylon, A. K. "Biphasic aspects of homosexual identity formation." *Psychotherapy: Theory, Research and Practice* 19 (1982): 335–40.

Mays, John Bentley. *In the Jaws of the Black Dogs.* New York: HarperCollins, 1995.

McAlpine, Donna, and David Mechanic. "Utilization of Specialty Mental Health Care among Persons with Severe Mental Illness: The Roles of Demographics, Need, Insurance, and Risk." *Health Services Research* 35, no. 1 (2000): 277–92.

McCann, U., et al. "Serotonin Neurotoxicity after 3,4-Methylenedioxymethamphetamine: A Controlled Study in Humans." *Neuropsychopharmacology* 10 (1994): 129–38.

McCauley, Elizabeth, et al. "The Role of Somatic Complaints in the Diagnosis of Depression in Children and Adolescents." *Journal of the American Academy of Child and Adolescent Psychiatry* 30, no. 4 (1991): 631–35.

Bibliography

McDowell, David M., and Henry I. Spitz. *Substance Abuse: From Principles to Practice.* New York: Taylor & Francis Group, 1999.

McGuire, Michael, and Alfonso Troisi. *Darwinian Psychiatry.* Oxford: Oxford University Press, 1998.

McHugh, Paul R. "Psychiatric Misadventures." *American Scholar* 61, no. 4 (1992): 497–510.

McHugh, Paul R., and Phillip R. Slavney. *The Perspectives of Psychiatry.* Baltimore: Johns Hopkins University Press, 1986.

McKeown, L. A. "The Healing Profession on an Alternative Mission." *Medical World News,* April 1993, 48–60.

Mead, Richard. *Medical Precepts and Cautions.* Trans. Thomas Stack. London: J. Brindley, 1751.

——. *The Medical Works of Richard Mead, M.D.* London: C. Hitch et al., 1760.

Meisol, Patricia. "The Dark Cloud." *The Sun,* May 1, 1999.

Mehlman, P. T., et al. "Low CSF 5-HIAA Concentrations and Severe Aggression and Impaired Impulse Control in Nonhuman Primates." *American Journal of Psychiatry* 151 (1994): 1485–91.

Melfi, Catherine, et al. "Access to Treatment for Depression in a Medicaid Population." *Journal of Health Care for the Poor and Underserved* 10, no. 2 (1999): 201–15.

Mellman, T. A., and T. W. Uhde. "Sleep and Panic and Generalized Anxiety Disorders." In *The Neurobiology of Panic Disorder.* Ed. James Ballenger. New York: Wiley-Liss, 1990.

Menander. *Comicorum Atticorum fragmenta.* Ed. T. Kock. Leipzig: Teubner, 1888.

Mendelson, Myer. *Psychoanalytic Concepts of Depression.* New York: Spectrum Publications, 1974.

Menninger, Karl. *Man Against Himself.* New York: Harcourt, Brace & World, 1983.

Merkin, Daphne. "The Black Season." *The New Yorker,* January 8, 2001.

Meyer, Adolf. "The 'Complaint' as the Center of Genetic-Dynamic and Nosological Thinking in Psychiatry." *New England Journal of Medicine* 199 (1928): 360–70.

——. *The Collected Papers of Adolf Meyer.* 4 vols. Ed. Eunice E. Winters. Baltimore: Johns Hopkins Press, 1951.

——. *Psychobiology: A Science of Man.* Ed. Eunice E. Winters and Anna Mae Bowers. Springfield, Ill.: Charles C. Thomas, 1957.

Meyer, R. E., ed. *Psychopathology and Addictive Disorder.* New York: Guilford Press, 1986.

Miletich, John J. *Depression in the Elderly: A Multimedia Sourcebook.* Westport, Conn.: Greenwood Press, 1997.

Milgram, Stanley. *Obedience to Authority.* New York: Harper Colophon Books, 1974.

Millay, Edna St. Vincent. *Collected Sonnets.* New York: Harper and Row, 1988.

Miller, Alice. *The Drama of the Gifted Child.* New York: BasicBooks, 1994.

Miller, Ivan W., Gabor I. Keitner, et al. "Depressed Patients with Dysfunctional Families: Description and Course of Illness." *Journal of Abnormal Psychology* 101, no. 4 (1992): 637–46.

Miller, John, ed. *On Suicide: Great Writers on the Ultimate Question.* San Francisco: Chronicle Books, 1992.

Milton, John. *Complete Poems and Major Prose.* Ed. Merritt Y. Hughes. Englewood Cliffs, N.J.: Prentice-Hall, 1957.

——. *Paradise Lost.* Ed. Scott Elledge. New York: W. W. Norton, 1993.

Miranda, Jeanne. "Introduction to the special section on recruiting and retaining minorities in psychotherapy research." *Journal of Consulting Clinical Psychologists* 64, no. 5 (1996): 848–50.

———. "One in five women will become clinically depressed . . ." Manuscript.

Miranda, Jeanne, et al. "Recruiting and retaining low-income Latinos in psychotherapy research." *Journal of Consulting Clinical Psychologists* 64, no. 5 (1996): 868–74.

———. "Unmet mental health needs of women in public-sector gynecologic clinics." *American Journal of Obstetrics and Gynecology* 178, no. 2 (1998): 212–17.

———. "Current Psychiatric Disorders Among Women in Public Sector Family Planning Clinics." Georgetown University Medical Center. Manuscript.

Miranda, Jeanne, and Bonnie L. Green. "Poverty and Mental Health Services Research." Georgetown University Medical Center. Manuscript.

Mirman, Jacob J. *Demystifying Homeopathy.* New Hope, Minn.: New Hope Publishers, 1999.

Mondimore, Francis Mark. *Depression: The Mood Disease.* Baltimore: Johns Hopkins University Press, 1995.

Montgomery, S. A. "Suicide prevention and serotonergic drugs." *International Clinical Psychopharmacology* 8, no. 2 (1993): 83–85.

Montplaisir, J., and R. Godbout, eds. *Sleep and Biological Rhythms.* New York: Oxford University Press, 1990.

Moore, K., et al. "The JOBS Evaluation: How Well Are They Faring? AFDC Families with Preschool-Aged Children in Atlanta at the Outset of the JOBS Evaluation." Washington, D.C.: U.S. Department of Health and Human Services, 1995.

———. "The Association Between Physical Activity and Depression in Older Depressed Adults." *Journal of Aging and Physical Activity* 7 (1999): 55–61.

Moore, Thomas. *Care of the Soul.* New York: HarperCollins, 1998.

Mora, George, ed. *Witches, Devils, and Doctors in the Renaissance: Johann Weyer, De praestigiis daemonum.* (1583 ed.) Trans. John Shea. Binghamton, N.Y.: Medieval & Renaissance Texts & Studies, 1991.

Morse, Gary, et al. "Experimental Comparison of the Effects of Three Treatment Programs for Homeless Mentally Ill People." *Hospital and Community Psychiatry* 43, no. 10 (1992): 1005–10.

Moss, L., and D. Hamilton. "The Psychotherapy of the Suicidal Patient." *American Journal of Psychiatry* 122 (1956): 814–19.

Mufson, Laura, et al. "Efficacy of Interpersonal Psychotherapy for Depressed Adolescents." *Archives of General Psychiatry* 56 (1999): 573–79.

Murphy, Elaine, ed. *Affective Disorders in the Elderly.* London: Churchill Livingstone, 1986.

Murphy, George. *Suicide in Alcoholism.* New York: Oxford University Press, 1992.

Murray, Albert. *Stomping the Blues.* New York: A De Capo Paperback, 1976.

Murray, Michael T. *Natural Alternatives to Prozac.* New York: Morrow, 1996.

Musetti, Laura, et al. "Depression Before and After Age 65: A Reexamination." *British Journal of Psychiatry* 155 (1989): 330–36.

Mutrie, Tim. "Aspenite helps spread word on teen depression." *Aspen Times* 12, no. 169 (1999).

Nagel, Thomas. *The Possibility of Altruism.* Princeton, N.J.: Princeton University Press, 1970.

National Advisory Mental Health Council. "Minutes of the 184th Meeting." September 16, 1996. Manuscript.

———. "Bridging Science and Service: A Report by the National Advisory Mental

Bibliography

Health Council's Clinical Treatment and Services Research Workgroup." Manuscript.

National Institute of Health's Genetics Workgroup. "Genetics and Mental Disorders." National Institute of Mental Health. Manuscript.

National Institute of Mental Health. *Suicide Research Workshop: From the Bench to the Clinic.* November 14–15, 1996.

———. "Report to the National Advisory Mental Health Council Director of the NIMH." January 28–29, 1997.

———. *Depression: What Every Woman Should Know.* Depression Awareness, Recognition, and Treatment (D/ART) Campaign.

National Mental Health Association. "Tipper Gore Announces Major Mental Health Initiative." NMHA Legislative Alert.

National Mental Health Consumers' Self-Help Clearinghouse, et al. *Amici Curiae Brief for the October 1998 Supreme Court Case of Tommy Olmstead, Commissioner of the Department of Human Resources of the State of Georgia, et al., vs. L.C. and E.W., Each by Jonathan Zimring, as Guardian ad Litem and Next Friend.* Philadelphia, Pa.: NMHCSHC, 1998.

Nazroo, J. Y., et al. "Gender differences in the onset of depression following a shared life event: A study of couples." *Psychological Medicine* 27 (1997): 9–19.

Neaman, Judith S. *Suggestion of the Devil: The Origins of Madness.* Garden City, N.Y.: Anchor Books, 1975.

Nemeroff, Charles B. "The Neurobiology of Depression." *Scientific American,* June 1998.

Nesse, Randolph. "Evolutionary Explanations of Emotions." *Human Nature* 1, no. 3 (1990): 281–89.

———. "What Good Is Feeling Bad?" *The Sciences,* December 1991.

———. "Is Depression an Adaptation?" *Archives of General Psychiatry* 57, no. 1 (2000): 14–20.

Newton, Isaac. *Newton's Principia: The Mathematical Principles of Natural Philosophy.* Trans. Andrew Motte. New York: Daniel Adee, 1848.

Nicholson, Barbara L., and Diane M. Kay. "Group Treatment of Traumatized Cambodian Women: A Culture-Specific Approach." *Social Work* 44, no. 5 (1999): 470–79.

Nielsen, D., et al. "Suicidality and 5-Hydroxindoleacetic Acid Concentration Associated with Tryptophan Hydroxylase Polymorphism." *Archives of General Psychiatry* 51 (1994): 34–38.

Nierenberg, Andrew, et al. "Mania Associated with St John's Wort." *Biological Psychiatry* 46 (1999): 1707–8.

Niesink, R. J. M., et al., eds. *Drugs of Abuse and Addiction.* Boca Raton, Fla.: CRC Press, 1998.

Nietzsche, Friedrich. *Beyond Good and Evil.* Trans. R. J. Hollingdale. London: Penguin Books, 1990.

———. *Thus Spoke Zarathustra.* Trans. Walter Kaufmann. New York: Modern Library, 1995.

———. *The Will to Power.* Trans. Walter Kaufmann. New York: Vintage Books, 1967.

Nolen-Hoeksema, Susan. *Sex Differences in Depression.* Stanford, Calif.: Stanford University Press, 1990.

Norden, Michael J. *Beyond Prozac: Brain Toxic Lifestyles, Natural Antidotes and New Generation Antidepressants.* New York: ReganBooks, 1995.

Norton Anthology of Poetry. Rev. ed. Ed. Alexander W. Allison et al. New York: W. W. Norton, 1975.

Bibliography

Nuland, Sherwin B. *How We Die.* London: Vintage, 1997.

Nutt, David. "Substance-P antagonists: A new treatment for depression?" *Lancet* 352 (1998): 1644–45.

O'Connor, Lynn E., et al. "Guilt, Fear, and Empathy in College Students and Clinically Depressed Patients." Paper presented at Human Behavior and Evolution Society meetings, Davis, California, July 1998.

Olney, Buster. "Harnisch Says He Is Being Treated for Depression." *New York Times,* April 26, 1997.

Olsen, K., and L. Pavetti. *Personal and Family Challenges to the Successful Transition from Welfare to Work.* Washington, D.C.: Urban Institute, 1996.

Opler, Marvin, and S. Mouchly Small. "Cultural Variables Affecting Somatic Complaints and Depression." *Psychosomatics* 9, no. 5 (1968): 261–66.

Oppenheim, Janet. *Shattered Nerves.* Oxford: Oxford University Press, 1991.

Oquendo, M. A., et al. "Suicide: Risk Factors and Prevention in Refractory Major Depression." *Depression and Anxiety* 5 (1997): 202–11.

———. "Inadequacy of Antidepressant Treatment for Patients with Major Depression Who Are at Risk for Suicidal Behavior." *American Journal of Psychiatry* 156, no. 2 (1999): 190–94.

Osler, Sir William. *Aequanimitas.* London: H. K. Lewis, 1904.

Overstreet, D. H., et al. "Alcoholism and depressive disorder: Is cholinergic sensitivity a biological marker?" *Alcohol & Alcoholism* 24 (1989): 253–55.

Overstreet, S., et al. "Availability of family support as a moderator of exposure to community violence." *Journal of Clinical Child Psychology* 28, no. 2 (1999): 151–59.

The Oxford English Dictionary. 12 vols. Oxford: Clarendon Press, 1978.

Pagel, Walter. *Religion and Neoplatonism in Renaissance Medicine.* Ed. Marianne Winder. London: Variorum Reprints, 1985.

Papolos, Demitri, and Janice Papolos. *Overcoming Depression.* New York: HarperCollins, 1997.

Pascual-Leone, Alvaro, et al. "Cerebral atrophy in habitual cocaine abusers: A planimetric CT study." *Neurology* 41 (1991): 34–38.

———. "Rapid-rate transcranial magnetic stimulation of left dorsolateral prefrontal cortex in drug-resistant depression." *Lancet* 348 (1996): 233–37.

Patros, Philip G., and Tonia K. Shamoo. *Depression and Suicide in Children and Adolescents.* Boston: Allyn & Bacon, 1989.

Patton, Stacey Pamela. "Electrogirl." *Washington Post,* September 19, 1999.

Pear, Robert. "Insurance Plans Skirt Requirement on Mental Health." *New York Times,* December 26, 1998.

Peláez-Nogueras, Martha, et al. "Depressed Mothers' Touching Increases Infants' Positive Affect and Attention in Still-Face Interaction." *Child Development* 67 (1996): 1780–92.

Petti, T. A. "Depression in hospitalized child psychiatry patients: Approaches to measuring depression." *Journal of the American Academy of Child Psychiatry* 22 (1978): 11–21.

Phillips, Adam. *Darwin's Worms.* London: Faber & Faber, 1999.

Physicians' Desk Reference. 53rd ed. Montvale, N.J.: Medical Economics Company, 1999.

Pinel, Philippe. *A Treatise on Insanity, in Which Are Contained the Principles of a New and More Practical Nosology of Maniacal Disorders.* Trans. D. D. Davis. Sheffield, England: W. Todd, 1806.

Pirkis, Jane, and Philip Burgess. "Suicide and recency of health care contacts: A systematic review." *British Journal of Psychiatry* 173 (1998): 462–75.

Bibliography

Plath, Sylvia. *The Bell Jar.* New York: Harper & Row, 1971.

Pletscher, A., et al. "Serotonin Release as a Possible Mechanism of Reserpine Action." *Science* 122 (1955): 374.

Pollan, Michael. "A Very Fine Line." *New York Times Magazine,* September 12, 1999.

Pollice, Christine, et al. "Relationship of Depression, Anxiety, and Obsessionality to State of Illness in Anorexia Nervosa." *International Journal of Eating Disorders* 21 (1997): 367–76.

Porter, Roy. *Mind-Forg'd Manacles: A history of madness in England from the Restoration to the Regency.* London: Athlone Press, 1987.

Post, Robert M. "Transduction of Psychosocial Stress into Neurobiology of Recurrent Affective Disorder." *American Journal of Psychiatry* 149, no. 8 (1992): 999–1010.

———. "Malignant Transformation of Affective Illness: Prevention and Treatment." *Directions in Psychiatry* 13 (1993): 2–7.

Post, Robert M., et al. "Cocaine, Kindling, and Psychosis." *American Journal of Psychiatry* 133, no. 6 (1976): 627–34.

———. "Recurrent affective disorder: Roots in developmental neurobiology and illness progression based on changes in gene expression." *Development and Psychopathology* 6 (1994): 781–813.

———. "Developmental psychobiology of cyclic affective illness: Implications for early therapeutic intervention." *Development and Psychopathology* 8 (1996): 273–305.

———. "Rational polypharmacy in the bipolar affective disorders." *Epilepsy Research* suppl. 11 (1996): 153–80.

Powell, Barbara, et al. "Primary and Secondary Depression in Alcoholic Men: An Important Distinction?" *Journal of Clinical Psychiatry* 48, no. 3 (1987): 98–101.

Poznanski, E., and J. P. Zrull. "Childhood depression: Clinical characteristics of overtly depressed children." *Archives of General Psychiatry* 23 (1970): 8–15.

Price, John S. "Genetic and Phylogenetic Aspects of Mood Variation." *International Journal of Mental Health* 1 (1972): 124–44.

———. "Agonistic versus Prestige Competition." *ASCAP* 8, no. 9 (1995): 7–15.

———. "The Expression of Hostility in Complementary Relationships—Change due to Depressed Mood." *ASCAP* 9, no. 7 (1996): 6–14.

———. "Goal Setting: A Contribution from Evolutionary Biology." *ASCAP* 10, no. 10 (1997).

———. "Job's Battle with God." *ASCAP* 10, no. 12 (1997).

———. "Do Not Underestimate the Dog!" *ASCAP* 11, no. 12 (1998).

Price, John S., and Anthony Stevens. *Evolutionary Psychiatry.* London: Routledge, 1996.

Price, John S., et al. "The Social Competition Hypothesis of Depression." *British Journal of Psychiatry* 164 (1994): 309–15.

Prichard, James Cowles. *A Treatise on Insanity and Other Disorders Affecting the Mind.* London: Sherwood, Gilbert, & Piper, 1835.

Pritchard, C. "New patterns of suicide by age and gender in the United Kingdom and the Western World, 1974–1992; an indicator of social change?" *Social Psychiatry and Psychiatric Epidemiology* 31 (1996): 227–34.

Quen, Jacques M., and Eric T. Carlson, eds. *American Psychoanalysis: Origins and Development. The Adolf Meyer Seminars.* New York: Brunner/Mazel, 1978.

Quint, J. C., et al. *New Chance: Interim Findings on a Comprehensive Program for Disadvantaged Young Mothers and Their Children.* New York: Manpower Demonstration Research Corp., 1994.

Bibliography

Radke-Yarrow, Marian, et al. "Affective Interactions of Depressed and Nondepressed Mothers and Their Children." *Journal of Abnormal Child Psychology* 21, no. 6 (1993): 683–95.

———. "Depressed and Well Mothers." *Child Development* 65 (1994): 1405–14.

Rado, Sandor. *Psychoanalysis of Behavior: The Collected Papers of Sandor Rado.* 2 vols. New York: Grune & Stratton, 1956.

Raleigh, Michael, and Michael McGuire. "Bidirectional Relationships between Tryptophan and Social Behavior in Vervet Monkeys." *Advances in Experimental Medicine and Biology* 294 (1991): 289–98.

Raleigh, Michael, et al. "Social and Environmental Influences on Blood Serotonin Concentrations in Monkeys." *Archives of General Psychiatry* 41 (1984): 405–10.

———. "Serotonergic Mechanisms Promote Dominance Acquisition in Adult Male Vervet Monkeys." *Brain Research* 559 (1991): 181–90.

Readings from the Hurricane Island Outward Bound School. Rockland, Me.: Hurricane Island Outward Bound.

Real, Terrence. *I Don't Want to Talk About It.* New York: Scribner, 1997.

Rees, Jonathan. "Patents and intellectual property: A salvation for patient-oriented research?" *Lancet* 356 (2000): 849–50.

Regier, D. A., et al. "Comparing age at onset of major depression and other psychiatric disorders by birth cohorts in five U.S. community populations." *Archives of General Psychiatry* 48, no. 9 (1991): 789–95.

———. "The de facto mental and addictive disorders service system. Epidemiologic Catchment Area prospective 1-year prevalence rates of disorders and services." *Archives of General Psychiatry* 50, no. 2 (1993): 85–94.

Relman, Arnold S. "A Trip to Stonesville." *New Republic* 219, no. 24 (1998): 28–37.

Remafedi, G., et al. "The Relationship between Suicide Risk and Sexual Orientation: Results of a Population-Based Study." *American Journal of Public Health* 88, no. 1 (1998): 57–60.

Rich, C. L., et al. "San Diego Suicide Study I: Young vs. Old Subjects." *Archives of General Psychiatry* 43, no. 6 (1986): 577–82.

Richter, Gerhard. *The Daily Practice of Painting.* Trans. David Britt. Cambridge: MIT Press, 1998.

Ridley, Matt. *Genome.* London: Fourth Estate, 1999.

Riley, Anne W. "Effects on children of treating maternal depression." National Institute of Mental Health Grant #R01 MH58394.

Rilke, Rainer Maria. *The Selected Poetry of Rainer Maria Rilke.* Trans./ed. Stephen Mitchell. New York: Vintage International, 1989.

Rimer, Sara. "Gaps Seen in Treatment of Depression in Elderly." *New York Times,* September 5, 1999.

Ritterbush, Philip C. *Overtures to Biology: The Speculations of Eighteenth-Century Naturalists.* New Haven, Conn.: Yale University Press, 1964.

Roan, Shari. "Magic Pill or Minor Hope?" *Los Angeles Times,* June 14, 1999.

Robbins, Jim. "Wired for Miracles?" *Psychology Today* 31, no. 3 (1998): 40–76.

Robinson, James Harvey. *Petrarch: The First Scholar and Man of Letters.* New York: G. P. Putnam's Sons, 1909.

Robinson, Nicholas. *A New System of the Spleen, Vapours, and Hypochondriack Melancholy.* London: A. Bettewworth, W. Innys, and C. Rivington, 1729.

Roccatagliata, Giuseppe. *A History of Ancient Psychiatry.* New York: Greenwood Press, 1986.

Bibliography

Rodgers, L. N., and D. A. Regier, eds. *Psychiatric Disorders in America: The Epidemiologic Catchment Area Study.* New York: Free Press, 1991.

Rogers, E. S., et al. "A benefit-cost analysis of a supported employment model for persons with psychiatric disabilities." *Evaluation and Program Planning* 18, no. 2 (1995): 105–15.

Romach, M. K., et al. "Long-term codeine use is associated with depressive symptoms." *Journal of Clinical Psychopharmacology* 19, no.4 (1999): 373–76.

Rose, Henry. *An Inaugural Dissertation on the Effects of the Passions upon the Body.* Philadelphia: William W. Woodward, 1794.

Rose, R. M., et al. "Endocrine Activity in Air Traffic Controllers at Work. II. Biological, Psychological and Work Correlates." *Psychoneuroendocrinology* 7 (1982): 113–23.

Rose, William. *From Goethe to Byron: The Development of "Weltschmerz" in German Literature.* London: George Routledge & Sons, 1924.

Rosen, David H. *Transforming Depression.* New York: Penguin Books, 1993.

Rosen, Laura Epstein, and Xavier Francisco Amador. *When Someone You Love Is Depressed.* New York: Free Press, 1996.

Rosen, Peter, et al., eds. *Emergency Medicine: Concepts and Clinical Practice.* 4th ed. 3 vols. St. Louis, Mo.: Mosby, 1998.

Rosenfeld, Alvin, et al. "Psychiatry and Children in the Child Welfare System." *Child and Adolescent Psychiatric Clinics of North America* 7, no. 3 (1998): 515–36.

Rosenthal, Norman E. "Diagnosis and Treatment of Seasonal Affective Disorder." *Journal of the American Medical Assocation* 270, no. 22 (1993): 2717–20.

———. *Winter Blues.* New York: Guilford Press, 1993.

———. *St. John's Wort.* New York: HarperCollins, 1998.

Rosenthal, Norman E., et al. "Seasonal Affective Disorder." *Archives of General Psychiatry* 41 (1984): 72–80.

Rossow, I. "Alcohol and suicide—beyond the link at the individual level." *Addiction* 91 (1996): 1463–69.

Rothman, David J., and Sheila M. Rothman. *The Willowbrook Wars.* New York: Harper & Row, 1984.

Roukema, Representative Marge. "Capitol shootings could have been prevented." *New Jersey Herald,* August 16, 1998.

Roukema, Representative Marge, et al. "Mental Health Parity Act of 1996 (H.R. 4058)." House of Representatives.

———. "Mental Health and Substance Abuse Parity Amendments of 1998 (H.R. 3568)." House of Representatives.

Rounsaville, Bruce J., et al. "Psychiatric Diagnoses of Treatment-Seeking Cocaine Abusers." *Archives of General Psychiatry* 48 (1991): 43–51.

Roy, Alec, et al. "Genetics of Suicide in Depression." *Journal of Clinical Psychiatry,* suppl. 2 (1999): 12–17.

Rubin, Julius H. *Religious Melancholy and Protestant Experience in America.* Oxford: Oxford University Press, 1994.

Rush, Benjamin. *Benjamin Rush's Lectures on the Mind.* Ed. Eric T. Carlson, Jeffrey L. Wollock, and Patricia S. Noel. Philadelphia: American Philosophical Society, 1981.

———. *Medical Inquiries and Observations.* 3rd ed. 4 vols. Philadelphia: Mathew Carey et al., 1809.

———. *Medical Inquiries and Observations upon the Diseases of the Mind.* Philadelphia: Grigg and Elliot, 1835.

Bibliography

Rutter, Michael, and David J. Smith, eds. *Psychosocial Disorders in Young People.* England and New York: John Wiley & Sons, 1995.

Ryabinin, Andrey. "Role of Hippocampus in Alcohol-Induced Memory Impairment: Implications from Behavioral and Immediate Early Gene Studies." *Psychopharmacology* 139 (1998): 34–43.

Ryan, Neal, et al. "Imipramine in adolescent major depression: Plasma level and clinical response." *Acta Psychiatrica Scandinavica* 73 (1986): 275–88.

Sack, David, et al. "Deficient Nocturnal Surge of TSH Secretion During Sleep and Sleep Deprivation in Rapid-Cycling Bipolar Illness." *Psychiatry Research* 23 (1987): 179–91.

Sacks, Oliver. *Seeing Voices.* Berkeley: University of California Press, 1989.

Sackein, Harold, et al. "A Prospective, Randomized, Double-Blind Comparison of Bilateral and Right Unilateral Electroconvulsive Therapy at Different Stimulus Intensities." *Archives of General Psychiatry* 57, no. 5 (2000): 425–34.

Safran, Jeremy D. "Breaches in the Therapeutic Alliance: An Arena for Negotiating Authentic Relatedness." *Psychotherapy* 30 (1993): 11–24.

———. *Widening the Scope of Cognitive Therapy.* Northvale, N.J.: Jason Aronson, 1998.

———. "Faith, Despair, Will, and the Paradox of Acceptance." *Contemporary Psychoanalysis* 35, no. 1 (1999): 5–23.

Sakado, K., et al. "The Association between the High Interpersonal Sensitivity Type of Personality and a Lifetime History of Depression in a Sample of Employed Japanese Adults." *Psychological Medicine* 29, no. 5 (1999): 1243–48.

Saloman, Charlotte. *Charlotte Saloman: Life? or Theatre?* Zwolle, The Netherlands: Waander Publishers, 1998.

Sameroff, A. J., R. Seifer, and M. Zax. "Early development of children at risk for emotional disorder." *Monographs of the Society for Research in Child Development* 47, no. 7 (1982).

Sanchez, C., et al. "The role of serotonergic mechanisms in inhibition of isolation-induced aggression in male mice." *Psychopharmacology* 110, no. 1–2 (1993): 53–59.

Sandfort, T. G., et al. "Same-Sex Sexual Behavior and Psychiatric Disorders: Findings from the Netherlands Mental Health Survey and Incidence Study (NEMESIS)." *Archives of General Psychiatry* 58, no. 1 (2001): 85–91.

Sands, James R., et al. "Psychotic Unipolar Depression at Follow-Up: Factors Related to Psychosis in the Affective Disorders." *American Journal of Psychiatry* 151, no. 7 (1994): 995–1000.

Sapolsky, Robert. "Stress in the Wild." *Scientific American* 262, no. 1 (1990): 116–23.

———. "Social subordinance as a marker of hypercortisolism: Some unexpected subtleties." *Annals of the New York Academy of Sciences* 771 (1995): 626–39.

Sapolsky, Robert, et al. "Hippocampal damage associated with prolonged glucocorticoid exposure in primates." *Journal of Neuroscience* 10, no. 9 (1990): 2897–902.

Sartre, Jean-Paul. *Being and Nothingness.* Trans. Hazel E. Barnes. New York: Washington Square Press, 1966.

———. *Nausea.* Trans. Lloyd Alexander. New York: New Directions, 1964.

Satel, Sally L. "Mentally Ill or Just Feeling Sad?" *New York Times,* December 15, 1999.

Savage, George H. *Insanity and Allied Neuroses: Practical and Clinical.* Philadelphia: Henry C. Lea's Son & Co., 1884.

Schaffer, Carrie Ellen, et al. "Frontal and Parietal Electroencephalogram Asymmetry in Depressed and Nondepressed Subjects." *Biological Psychiatry* 18, no. 7 (1983): 753–62.

Bibliography

Schelling, Friedrich Wilhelm Joseph von. "On the Essence of Human Freedom." *Saemmtliche Werke.* Vol. 7. Stuttgart: Cotta, 1856–61.

Schiesari, Juliana. *The Gendering of Melancholy.* Ithaca, N.Y.: Cornell University Press, 1992.

Schildkraut, J. J. "The Catecholamine Hypothesis of Affective Disorders: A Review of Supporting Evidence." *American Journal of Psychiatry* 122 (1965): 509–22.

Schleiner, Winfried. *Melancholy, Genius, and Utopia in the Renaissance.* Wiesbaden: In Kommission bei Otto Harrassowitz, 1991.

Schopenhauer, Arthur. *Complete Essays of Schopenhauer.* Trans. T. Baily Sanders. New York: Willey Book Co., 1942.

———. *Essays and Aphorisms.* Ed./trans. R. J. Hollingdale. London: Penguin Books, 1970.

———. *The Works of Schopenhauer.* Ed. Will Durant. New York: Simon & Schuster, 1931.

———. *The World as Will and Representation.* Vol 2. Trans. E. F. J. Payne. New York: Dover Publications, 1958.

Schrambling, Regina. "Attention Supermarket Shoppers!" *Food and Wine,* October 1995.

Schrof, Joannie M., and Stacey Schultz. "Melancholy Nation." *U.S. News & World Report,* March 8, 1999, 56–63.

Schuckit, Marc. "A Long-Term Study of Sons of Alcoholics." *Alcohol Health & Research World* 19, no. 3 (1995): 172–75.

———. "Response to Alcohol in Daughters of Alcoholics: A Pilot Study and a Comparison with Sons of Alcoholics." *Alcohol & Alcoholism* 35, no. 3 (1999): 242–48.

Scott, Sarah. "Workplace Secrets." *MacLean's,* December 1, 1997.

Screech, M. A. *Montaigne & Melancholy.* London: Gerald Duckworth, 1983.

Scull, Andrew. *Social Order/Mental Disorder: Anglo-American Psychiatry in Historical Perspective.* Berkeley: University of California Press, 1989.

Searle, John. R. "Consciousness." Manuscript.

Segal, Boris, and Jacqueline Stewart. "Substance Use and Abuse in Adolescence: An Overview." *Child Psychiatry and Human Development* 26, no. 4 (1996): 193–210.

Seligman, Martin. *Learned Optimism.* New York: Simon & Schuster, 1990.

Shaffer, D., et al. "Sexual Orientation in Adolescents Who Commit Suicide." *Suicide and Life Threatening Behaviors* 25, suppl. 4 (1995): 64–71.

———. "The NIMH Diagnostic Interview Schedule for Children Version 2.3 (DISC-2.3): Description, acceptability, prevalence rates, and performance in the MECA Study. Methods for the Epidemiology of Child and Adolescent Mental Disorders Study." *Journal of the American Academy of Child and Adolescent Psychiatry* 35, no. 7 (1996): 865–77.

Shakespeare, William. *The Complete Works.* Ed. G. B. Harrison. New York: Harcourt, Brace & World, 1968.

———. *Hamlet.* New York: Penguin Books, 1987.

Shaw, Fiona. *Composing Myself.* South Royalton, Vt.: Steerforth Press, 1998.

Sheehan, Susan. *Is There No Place on Earth for Me?* New York: Vintage Books, 1982.

Shelley, Percy Bysshe. *The Complete Poems of Percy Bysshe Shelley.* New York: Modern Library, 1994.

Shem, Samuel. *Mount Misery.* New York: Fawcett Columbine, 1997.

Sherrington, C. S. *The Integrative Action of the Nervous System.* Cambridge: Cambridge University Press, 1947.

Shiromani, P., et al. "Acetylcholine and the regulation of REM sleep." *Annual Review of Pharmacological Toxicology* 27 (1987): 137–56.

Shneidman, Edwin S., ed. *Essays in Self-Destruction.* New York: Science House, 1967.

———. *The Suicidal Mind.* New York: Oxford University Press, 1996.

Bibliography

Shorter, Edward. *A History of Psychiatry: From the Era of the Asylum to the Age of Prozac.* New York: John Wiley & Sons, 1997.

Showalter, Elaine. *The Female Malady: Women, Madness, and English Culture, 1830–1980.* New York: Pantheon Books, 1985.

Shute, Nancy, et al. "The Perils of Pills." *U.S. News & World Report,* March 6, 2000.

Sickels, Eleanor M. *The Gloomy Egoist: Moods and Themes of Melancholy from Gray to Keats.* New York: Columbia University Press, 1932.

Silver, Cheryl Simon, with Ruth S. DeFries, for the National Academy of Sciences. *One Earth, One Future: Our Changing Global Environment.* Washington, D.C.: National Academy Press, 1990.

Simmons, William S. *Eyes of the Night: Witchcraft among a Senegalese People.* Boston: Little, Brown, 1971.

Simon, Bennett. *Mind and Madness in Ancient Greece: The Classical Roots of Modern Psychiatry.* Ithaca, N.Y.: Cornell University Press, 1980.

Simon, Linda. *Genuine Reality: A Life of William James.* New York: Harcourt Brace, 1998.

Simpson, Jeffry A., and W. Steven Rholes, eds. *Attachment Theory and Close Relationships.* New York: Guilford Press, 1998.

Skultans, Vieda. *English Madness: Ideas on Insanity, 1580–1890.* London: Routledge & Kegan Paul, 1979.

Sloman, Leon, et. al. "Adaptive Function of Depression: Psychotherapeutic Implications." *American Journal of Psychotherapy* 48, no.3 (1994).

Smith, C. U. M. "Evolutionary Biology and Psychiatry." *British Journal of Psychiatry* 162 (1993): 149–53.

Smith, Jeffery. *Where the Roots Reach for Water.* New York: North Point Press, 1999.

Smith, K., et al. "Relapse of Depression After Rapid Depletion of Tryptophan." *Lancet* 349 (1997): 915–19.

Snow, C. P. *The Light and the Dark.* Middlesex, England: Penguin Books, 1962.

Soares, J., and John Mann. "The functional neuroanatomy of mood disorders." *Journal of Psychiatric Research* 31 (1997): 393–432.

Solomon, Jolie. "Breaking the Silence." *Newsweek,* May 20, 1996.

Sontag, Susan. *Under the Sign of Saturn.* New York: Farrar, Straus & Giroux, 1980.

The Sorrow Is in My Heart . . . Sixteen Asian Women Speak about Depression. London: Commission for Racial Equality, 1993.

Spinoza, Baruch. *The Ethics of Spinoza.* New York: Citadel Press, 1995.

Spitz, Herman H. *The Raising of Intelligence.* Hillsdale, N.J.: Lawrence Erlbaum Associates, 1986.

Spitz, René. "Anaclitic Depression." *Psychoanalytic Study of the Child* 2 (1946).

Spitz, René, et al. "Anaclitic Depression in an Infant Raised in an Institution." *Journal of the American Academy of Child Psychiatry* 4, no. 4 (1965): 545–53.

Spungen, Deborah. *And I Don't Want to Live This Life.* New York: Ballantine Books, 1993.

Stabler, Sally P. "Vitamin B_{12} deficiency in the elderly: Current dilemmas." *American Journal of Clinical Nutrition* 66 (1997): 741–49.

Starobinski, Jean. *La Mélancolie au miroir.* Conférences, essais et leçons du Collège de France. Paris: Julliard, 1989.

Stefan, Susan. "Preventative Commitment: The Concept and Its Pitfalls." *MPDLR* 11, no. 4 (1987): 288–302.

Stepansky, Paul E., ed. *Freud: Appraisals and Reappraisals.* 3 vols. Hillsdale, N.J.: Analytic Press, 1988.

Sterne, Laurence. *The Life and Opinions of Tristam Shandy.* New York: Penguin Books, 1967.

Bibliography

Stevens, Anthony, and John Price. *Evolutionary Psychiatry: A New Beginning.* London and New York: Routledge, 1996.

Stone, Gene. "Magic Fingers." *New York,* May 9, 1994.

Stone, Michael H. *Healing the Mind: A History of Psychiatry from Antiquity to the Present.* New York: Norton, 1997.

Storr, Anthony. *Churchill's Black Dog, Kafka's Mice, and Other Phenomena of the Human Mind.* New York: Grove Press, 1988.

Strupp, Hans, and Suzanne Hadley. "Specific vs. nonspecific factors in psychotherapy: A controlled study of outcome." *Archives of General Psychiatry* 36, no.10 (1979): 1125–36.

Styron, William. *Darkness Visible: A Memoir of Madness.* London: Jonathan Cape, 1991.

Substance Abuse and Mental Health Services Administration. "House Appropriations Subcommittee Hearings." February 11, 1999.

Sullivan, Mark D., et al. "Depression, Competence, and the Right to Refuse Lifesaving Medical Treatment." *American Journal of Psychiatry* 151, no. 7 (1994): 971–78.

Summers, Montague, ed. *The Malleus Maleficarum.* New York: Dover Publications, 1971.

Sutherland, Stuart. *Breakdown.* Oxford: Oxford University Press, 1998.

Swift, Jonathan. *Gulliver's Travels.* New York: Dover Publications, 1996.

Szasz, Thomas. *The Second Sin.* New York: Anchor Press, 1973.

———. *Primary Values and Major Contentions.* Ed. Richard Vatz and Lee Weinberg. New York: Prometheus Books, 1992.

———. *Cruel Compassion.* New York: John Wiley & Sons, 1994.

Talbot, Margaret. "Attachment Theory: The Ultimate Experiment." *New York Times Magazine,* May 24, 1998.

Tan, Shawn. "Little Boy Blue." *Brave* (final edition), 1999.

Tannon, Deborah. *You Just Don't Understand.* New York: Ballantine Books, 1990.

Taylor, Shelley E. *Positive Illusions.* New York: Basic Books, 1989.

Taylor, Steve. *Durkheim and the Study of Suicide.* London: Macmillan Press, 1982.

Taylor, Steven, et al. "Anxiety Sensitivity and Depression: How Are They Related?" *Journal of Abnormal Psychology* 105, no. 3 (1996): 474–79.

Taylor, Verta. *Rock-A-By Baby: Feminism, Self-Help, and Postpartum Depression.* New York: Routledge, 1996.

Tennyson, Alfred Lord. *Tennyson's Poetry.* Ed. Robert Hill, Jr. New York: W. W. Norton, 1971.

Thakore, Jogin, and David John. "Prescriptions of Antidepressants by General Practitioners: Recommendations by FHSAs and Health Boards." *British Journal of General Practice* 46 (1996): 363–64.

Thase, Michael. "Treatment of Alcoholism Comorbid with Depression." Presentation at University of Pittsburgh, School of Medicine.

Thompson, Tracy. *The Beast.* New York: G. P. Putnam's Sons, 1995.

Thomson, James. *The City of Dreadful Night.* Edinburgh: Canongate Press, 1993.

Thorne, Julia. *A Change of Heart.* New York: HarperPerennial, 1996.

Thorne, Julia, et al. *You Are Not Alone.* New York: HarperPerennial, 1993.

Tiller, William A. *Science and Human Transformation.* Walnut Creek, Calif.: Pavior Publishers, 1997.

Tocqueville, Alexis de. *Democracy in America.* Trans. George Lawrence. New York: HarperCollins, 1988.

Todorov, Tzvetan. *The Conquest of America: The Question of the Other.* Trans. Richard Howard. New York: Harper & Row, 1984.

Bibliography

Tolley, Barbara. "The Languages of Melancholy in *Le Philosophe Anglais.*" Dissertation.

Tolstoy, Leo. *Anna Karenina.* Trans. Rosemary Edmonds. London: Penguin Books, 1978.

Tomarken, A. J., et al. "Psychometric properties of resting anterior EEG asymmetry: Temporal stability and internal consistency." *Psychophysiology* 29 (1992): 576–92.

Torrey, E. Fuller. *Nowhere to Go.* New York: Harper & Row, 1988.

Torrey, E. Fuller, and Mary Zdanowicz. "We need to ask again: Why do severely mentally ill go untreated?" *Boston Globe,* August 1, 1998.

———. "Why Deinstitutionalization Turned Deadly." *Wall Street Journal,* August 4, 1998.

Treisman, Glenn. "Psychiatric care of HIV-infected patients in the HIV-specialty clinic." Manuscript.

Triggs, W. J., et al. "Effects of left frontal transcranial magnetic stimulation on depressed mood, cognition, and corticomotor threshold." *Biological Psychiatry* 45, no. 11 (1999): 1440–46.

Tsuang, Ming T., and Stephen V. Faraone. *The Genetics of Mood Disorders.* Baltimore: Johns Hopkins University Press, 1990.

Turner, J. J. D., and A. C. Parrott. " 'Is MDMA a Human Neurotoxin?': Diverse Views from the Discussants." *Neuropsychobiology* 42 (2000): 42–48.

United States House of Representatives, Committee on Ways and Means. *Green Book.* 1998.

Valenstein, Elliot S. *Great and Desperate Cures.* New York: Basic Books, 1986.

van Bemmel, A. L. "The link between sleep and depression: The effects of antidepressants on EEG sleep." *Journal of Psychosomatic Research* 42, no. 6 (1997): 555–64.

Van der Post, Laurens. *The Night of the New Moon.* Middlesex, England: Penguin Books, 1970.

Vartanian, Aram. *La Mettrie's L'Homme Machine.* Princeton, N.J.: Princeton University Press, 1960.

Vasari, Giorgio. *Lives of the Artists.* 2 vols. London: Penguin Books, 1987.

Venter, Craig J., et al. "The Sequence of the Human Genome." *Science* 291, no. 5507 (2001): 1304–51.

Vicari, Eleanor Patricia. *The View from Minerva's Tower: Learning and Imagination in "The Anatomy of Melancholy."* Toronto: University of Toronto Press, 1989.

Virkkunen, M., et al. "Personality Profiles and State Aggressiveness in Finnish Alcoholics, Violent Offenders, Fire Setters, and Healthy Volunteers." *Archives of General Psychiatry* 51 (1994): 28–33.

Volk, S. A., et al. "Can response to partial sleep deprivation in depressed patients be predicted by regional changes of cerebral blood flow?" *Psychiatry Research* 75, no. 2 (1997): 67–74.

Volkow, Nora, et al. "Cerebral Blood Flow in Chronic Cocaine Users: A Study with Positron Emission Tomography." *British Journal of Psychiatry* 152 (1988): 641–48.

———. "Effects of Chronic Cocaine Abuse on Postsynaptic Dopamine Receptors." *American Journal of Psychiatry* 147 (1990): 719–24.

———. "Brain Imaging of an Alcoholic with MRI, SPECT, and PET." *American Journal of Physiological Imaging* 3/4 (1992): 194–98.

———. "Long-Term Frontal Brain Metabolic Changes in Cocaine Abusers." *Synapse* 11 (1992): 182–90.

———. "Imaging Brain Structure and Function." *Annals of the New York Academy of Sciences* 820 (1997): 41–56.

Bibliography

———. "Imaging studies on the role of dopamine in cocaine reinforcement and addiction in humans." *Journal of Psychopharmacology* 13, no. 4 (1999): 337–45.

———. "Addiction, a Disease of Compulsion and Drive: Involvement of the Orbitofrontal Cortex." *Cerebral Cortex* 10 (2000): 318–25.

Voltaire. *Candide.* Trans. John Butt. New York: Penguin Books, 1947.

Waal, Frans de. *Good Natured.* Cambridge: Harvard University Press, 1996.

Waddington, John, and Peter Buckley, eds. *The Neurodevelopmental Basis of Schizophrenia.* London: R. G. Landes, 1996.

Walker, C. E., and M. C. Roberts, eds. *Handbook of Clinical Child Psychology.* 2nd ed. New York: John Wiley & Sons, 1992.

Watson, Paul J., and Paul W. Andrews. "An Evolutionary Theory of Unipolar Depression as an Adaptation for Overcoming Constraints of the Social Niche." Manuscript.

———. "Niche Change Model of Depression." *ASCAP* 11, no. 5 (1998): 17–18.

———. "Unipolar depression and human social life: An evolutionary analysis. Manuscript.

Wehr, Thomas A. "Phase Advance of the Circadian Sleep-Wake Cycle as an Antidepressant." *Science* 206 (1979): 711–13.

———. "Sleep Reduction as the Final Common Pathway in the Genesis of Mania." *American Journal of Psychiatry* 144, no. 2 (1987): 201–4.

———. "Sleep Loss: A Preventable Cause of Mania and Other Excited States." *Journal of Clinical Psychiatry* 50, suppl. 12 (1989): 8–16.

———. "Reply to Healy, D., Waterhouse, J. M.: The circadian system and affective disorders: Clocks or rhythms." *Chronobiology International* 7 (1990): 11–14.

———. "Sleep-Loss as a Possible Mediator of Diverse Causes of Mania." *British Journal of Psychiatry* 159 (1991): 576–78.

———. "Improvement of Depression and Triggering of Mania by Sleep Deprivation." *Journal of the American Medical Association* 267, no. 4 (1992): 548–51.

Wehr, Thomas A., et al. "48-Hour Sleep-Wake Cycles in Manic-Depressive Illness." *Archives of General Psychiatry* 39 (1982): 559–65.

———. "Eye Versus Skin Phototherapy of Seasonal Affective Disorder." *American Journal of Psychiatry* 144, no. 6 (1987): 753–57.

———. "Rapid Cycling Affective Disorder: Contributing Factors and Treatment Responses in 51 Patients." *American Journal of Psychiatry* 145 (1988): 179–84.

———. "Treatment of a Rapidly Cycling Bipolar Patient by Using Extended Bedrest and Darkness to Promote Sleep." NIMH, Bethesda, Md., 1997.

———. "Melatonin Response to Seasonal Changes in the Length of the Night in SAD and Patient Controls." NIMH, Bethesda, Md.

Wehr, Thomas A., and Norman E. Rosenthal. "Seasonality and Affective Illness." *American Journal of Psychiatry* 146 (1989): 829–39.

Weiner, Dora. " 'Le geste de Pinel': The History of a Psychiatric Myth." In *Discovering the History of Psychiatry.* Ed. Mark Micale and Roy Porter. Oxford: Oxford University Press, 1994.

Weiner, Myron F., et al. "Prevalence and Incidence of Major Depression in Alzheimer's Disease." *American Journal of Psychiatry* 151, no. 7 (1994): 1006–9.

Weiss, Suzanne, and Robert Post. "Kindling: Separate vs. shared mechanisms in affective disorder and epilepsy." *Neuropsychology* 38, no. 3 (1998): 167–80.

Weissman, Myrna M. *IPT: Mastering Depression.* New York: Graywind Publications, 1995.

Bibliography

Weissman, Myrna M., et al. "Cross-National Epidemiology of Major Depression and Bipolar Disorder." *Journal of the American Medical Association* 276, no. 4 (1996): 293–99.

———. "Offspring of Depressed Parents." *Archives of General Psychiatry* 54 (1997): 932–40.

———. "Depressed Adolescents Grown Up." *Journal of the American Medical Assocation* 281, no. 18 (1999): 1707–13.

———. "Prevalence of suicide ideation and suicide attempts in nine countries." *Psychological Medicine* 29 (1999): 9–17.

———. *Comprehensive Guide to Interpersonal Psychotherapy.* New York: Basic Books, 2000.

Weissman, Myrna, and Eugene Paykel. *The Depressed Woman: A Study of Social Relationships.* Chicago: University of Chicago Press, 1974.

Weissman, S., M. Sabshin, H. Eist, eds. *21st Century Psychiatry: The Foundations.* Washington, D.C.: American Psychiatric Press, in press.

Wellon, Arthur. *Five Years in Mental Hospitals.* New York: Exposition Press, 1967.

Wells, Kenneth, et al. *Caring for Depression.* Cambridge: Harvard University Press, 1996.

———. "Impact of disseminating quality improvement programs for depression in managed primary care: A randomized controlled trial." *Journal of the American Medical Association* 283, no. 2 (2000): 212–20.

Wender, Paul, et al. "Psychiatric disorders in the biological and adoptive families of adopted individuals with affective disorder." *Archives of General Psychiatry* 43 (1986): 923–29.

Wender, Paul, and Donald Klein. *Mind, Mood, and Medicine: A Guide to the New Biopsychiatry.* New York: Farrar, Straus & Giroux, 1981.

Wenzel, Siegfried. *The Sin of Sloth: Acedia.* Chapel Hill: University of North Carolina Press, 1967.

Wetzel, Richard, and James McClure Jr. "Suicide and the Menstrual Cycle: A Review." *Comprehensive Psychiatry* 13, no. 4 (1972): 369–74.

White, S. R., et al. "The Effects of Methylenedioxymethamphetamine on Monoaminergic Neurotransmission in the Central Nervous System." *Progress in Neurobiology* 49 (1996): 455–79.

Whooley, Mary A., and Gregory E. Simon. "Managing Depression in Medical Outpatients." *New England Journal of Medicine* 343, no. 26 (December 28, 2000): 1942–50.

Whybrow, Peter C. *A Mood Apart: Depression, Mania, and Other Afflictions of the Self.* New York: Basic Books, 1997.

Wilde, Oscar. *Complete Poetry.* Ed. Isobel Murray. Oxford: Oxford University Press, 1997.

———. *Complete Short Fiction.* London and New York: Penguin Books, 1994.

Willcox, Monica, and David N. Sattler. "The Relationship Between Eating Disorders and Depression." *Journal of Social Psychology* 136, no. 2 (1996): 269–71.

Williams, J. Mark G. *The Psychological Treatment of Depression.* 2nd ed. London: Routledge, 1992.

Williams, Tennessee. *Five O'Clock Angel: Letters of Tennessee Williams to Maria St. Just, 1948–1982.* New York: Alfred A. Knopf, 1990.

Willis, Thomas. *Two Discourses Concerning the Soul of Brutes.* Facsimile of 1683 translation by S. Pordage. Gainesville, Fla.: Scholars' Facsimiles and Reprints, 1971.

Winerip, Michael. "Bedlam on the Streets." *New York Times Magazine,* May 23, 1999.

Winnicott, D. W. *Home Is Where We Start From.* New York: W. W. Norton, 1986.

Winstead, Ted. "A New Brain: Surgery for Psychiatric Illness at Massachusetts General Hospital." Manuscript.

Bibliography

Winston, Julian. "Welcome to a Growing Health Care Movement." In *Homeopathy: Natural Medicine for the 21st Century.* Ed. Julian Winston. Alexandria, Va.: National Center for Homeopathy, 1993.

Wirz-Justice, A., et al. "Sleep deprivation in depression: What we know, where do we go?" *Biological Psychiatry* 46, no. 4 (1999): 445–53.

Wittkower, Rudolph, and Margot Wittkower. *Born Under Saturn.* New York: Norton, 1963.

Wolf, Naomi R. *The Beauty Myth.* London: Chatto & Windus, 1990.

Wolkowitz, O. M., et al. "Antiglucocorticoid treatment of depression: Double-blind ketoconazole." *Biological Psychiatry* 45, no. 8 (1999): 1070–74.

Wolman, Benjamin B., ed. *Between Survival and Suicide.* New York: Gardner Press, 1976.

Wolpert, Lewis. *Malignant Sadness.* New York: Free Press, 1999.

Woolf, Leonard. *Beginning Again.* San Diego: A Harvest/HBJ Book, 1964.

Woolf, Virginia. *The Diary of Virginia Woolf.* Vol 3. Ed. Oliver Bell. New York: Harcourt Brace Jovanovich, 1980.

———. *Jacob's Room.* San Diego: A Harvest/HBJ Book, 1950.

———. *The Letters of Virginia Woolf.* 6 vols. Ed. Nigel Nicolson and Joanne Trautmann. London: Hogarth Press, 1980.

———. *To the Lighthouse.* New York: Harcourt Brace Jovanovich, 1981.

———. *The Years.* London: Hogarth Press, 1937.

Wordsworth, William. *Favorite Poems.* Canada: Dover Thrift Editions, 1992.

———. *The Prelude: Selected Poems and Sonnets.* Ed. Carlos Baker. New York: Holt, Rinehart & Winston, 1954.

World Health Oganization. *Prevention of Suicide.* Public Health Paper no. 35. Geneva: World Health Oganization, 1968.

———. *The World Health Report 1999.* Geneva: World Health Oganization, 1999.

Wortman, Marc. "Brain Chemistry." *Yale Medicine* 31, no. 1 (1996): 2–11.

Yapko, Michael D. *Hypnosis and the Treatment of Depression.* New York: Brunner/Mazel Publishers, 1992.

———. *Breaking the Patterns of Depression.* New York: Doubleday, 1997.

Yokel, R. A., et al. "Amphetamine-type reinforcement by dopaminergic agonists in the rat." *Psychopharmacology* 58 (1978): 282–96.

Young, Edward. *The Complaint, or Night-Thoughts.* 2 vols. London: 1783.

Zerbe, Jerome, and Cyril Connolly. *Les Pavillons of the Eighteenth Century.* London: H. Hamilton, 1962.

Zima, Bonnie, et al. "Mental Health Problems among Homeless Mothers." *Archives of General Psychiatry* 53 (1996): 332–38.

Zubenko, George S., et al. "Impact of Acute Psychiatric Inpatient Treatment on Major Depression in Late Life and Prediction of Response." *American Journal of Psychiatry* 151, no. 7 (1994): 987–93.

Zuess, Jonathan. *The Natural Prozac Program.* New York: Three Rivers Press, 1997.

Zwillich, Todd. "Mental Illness and HIV Form a Vicious Circle." International Medical News Group. Fax.

Acknowledgments

In late December of 1999, a friend found me in high spirits and asked what I was doing. I replied enthusiastically that I had just been given an appointment at a mental hospital in rural Poland for New Year's Eve and that I'd also found some suicide notes I'd feared were lost. She shook her head gravely and told me that this madness had to stop. It is with some considerable relief that I find my book complete. The madness has been arrested.

My agent, Andrew Wylie, has stood by me now for twelve years. He took me on before I had ever published a book and has guided all my adult efforts. He has been an unflagging partisan for me and for this work; I cherish his friendship and his discernment. I am also grateful to Liza Walworth, at the Wylie Agency, who made the beginning of all this so pleasurable, and to Jeff Posternak, who gracefully facilitated all the later arrangements. Nan Graham, my brilliant editor in the United States, has been consistently generous and wise and has worked entirely in concert with me; she has been the kind of radiant enthusiast I always hoped to find. Brant Rumble, her able assistant, has kept the idea of order alive in the face of chaos. Alison Samuel, my editor in the United Kingdom, has been a fantastically good reader and a staunch adherent. I am grateful to Pat Eisemann for her excellent and energetic leadership of the American publicity team, and to Giulia Melucci, Beth Wareham, and the others who have seen through the book's promotion, as well as Patrick Hargadon for his work on UK publicity. I also thank Christopher Hayes for coodinating the Internet component of *The Noonday Demon*'s public relations. I would also like to thank my lawyer, Chuck Googe, for his close attention to my contracts.

Portions of this book have previously appeared in *The New Yorker, The New York Times Magazine,* and *Food and Wine.* I owe thanks to Tina Brown for publishing "An Anatomy of Depression" in *The New Yorker* in 1998. My greatest real debt at that magazine is to my editor, Henry Finder. No one else in the world possesses his gentle tact, erudition, prudence, and loyalty. I would never have started on this difficult topic had I not been sure of his liberal forbearance. A smaller section of the book appeared in *The New York Times Magazine.* Jack Rosenthal gave me an invaluable base at the *Times,* and Adam Moss supported my protracted work on depression, poverty, and politics, helping me to pinpoint the truth behind diffuse anecdotes. Diane Cardwell also helped me as she edited that material. Dana Cowin, in the name of *Food and Wine,* sent me off at key times for the most pleasurable of the many cures I explored, and I thank her for her indulgence. Stephen Rossoff kindly invited me to pursue my research at the University of Michigan

Acknowledgments

for *The University of Michigan Alumni Magazine*. I wrote the opening parts of this book during a stay at the Villa dei Pini of the Bogliasco Foundation in Liguria in February 1998. I appreciate deeply the foundation's generous support.

For their assistance with my work on Cambodia, I thank Laurie Beckelman, Fred Frumberg, Bernard Krishna, and John Stubbs. For their assistance with my work on Greenland, I thank in particular René Birger Christiansen and Lisbet Lyager, as well as Flemming Nicolaisen, Johanne Olson, and the people of Illiminaq. I am also grateful for the assistance of Erik Sprunk-Janssen and Hanne Skoldager-Ravn, without whom I would have been unable to begin my Greenland project. For their assistance with my work in Senegal, I thank David Hecht and Hélène Saivet, whose efforts on my behalf went way, way beyond the call of duty or friendship. I am grateful to Anne Applebaum and Radek Sikorski for making arrangements on my behalf in Poland. I am indebted to Enrico Marone-Cinzano for helping me substantially with research for chapter 6. I also thank Mary Bisbee-Beek and Chris Hayes for their excellent help in getting the word out about this project.

Both friends and professionals in the field have taken time to comment on drafts of this book. For their truly extraordinary editing, I would like to thank my two closest readers: Dr. Katherine Keenum and Dr. Claudia Swan. Their extraordinary attentiveness was both uplifting and invaluable, and their insights and love allowed me to achieve some semblance of clarity in both my own thought and the expression of that thought. I am also grateful to those who read and commented on late versions of the manuscript: Dr. Dorothy Arnsten, Sarah Billinghurst, Mary Bisbee-Beek, Christian Caryl, Dana Cowin, Jennie Dunham, Dr. Richard A. Friedman, Dr. Richard C. Friedman, Dr. Rhonda K. Garelick, Dr. David Grand, John G. Hart, Dr. Steven Hyman, Eve Kahn, Fran Kiernan, Betsy Joly de Lotbinière, Sue Macartney-Snape, Dr. David McDowell, Alexandra Munroe, Dr. Randolph M. Nesse, Dr. Julie S. Peters, Margaret Robbins, Dr. Peter Sillem, Amanda Smithson, David Solomon, Howard Solomon, Bob Weil, Edward Winstead, and Helen Whitney.

I would like to thank Philippe de Montebello, Emily Rafferty, and Harold Holzer for their remarkable support of this project and their great generosity in giving me full access to the Metropolitan Museum of Art.

I would like to thank Chuck Close for his generosity in volunteering to take my author's photograph.

I am indebted to Eugene Cory, Carol Czarnecki, and Brave New Words for transcribing more than ten thousand pages of taped interviews. I appreciate the assistance of Fred Courtwright in arranging permissions for material quoted in this book. Emma Lukic was tireless at hunting down references and I appreciate her assistance with research.

I am grateful to the many professionals who took time to share their insights with me as I began my work on this project. Dr. Frederick Eberstadt spent a great deal of time with me and facilitated numerous introductions. Dr. Steven Hyman of the NIMH made himself and his staff wonderfully available. Dr. Kay Redfield Jamison gave me advice on early research and graciously invited me to her suicide conference in 1996. Dr. David McDowell was similarly generous and also guided me through the mysteries of the American Psychiatric Association—an invaluable service. Sally Mink of the Depression & Related Affective Disorders Association at Johns Hopkins Hospital was unfailingly generous with her numerous connections and her personal insight. Dr. Randolph Nesse first drew me into the field of evolutionary psychology and thereby had a profound influence on my project. Dr. Anne Stanwix provided lucid wisdom and offered many of the epigrams that I have incorporated here. Dr. Peter Whybrow was very generous in pointing me toward many of the general questions I address in this book.

It will be evident to any reader of this text how many others gave me of their time. It is not possible to list everyone whose ideas and views have been incorporated into my own, but I would particularly like to acknowledge those with whom I met in person to conduct extended taped interviews: Dr. Dorothy Arnsten, Dr. James Ballenger, Dr. Richard Baron, Agata Bielik-Robson, Dr. Poul Bisgaard, Dr. George Brown, Deborah Bullwinkle, Dr. René Birger Christiansen, Dr. Deborah Christie, Dr. Joyce Chung, Dr. Miroslaw Dabkowski, Hailey Dart, Dr. Richard Davidson, Dr. J. Raymond DePaulo, Senator Pete Domenici, Vicki Edgson, Laurie Flynn, Dr. Ellen Frank, Dr. Richard A. Friedman, Dr. Edward Gardener, Dr. David Grand, Dr. John Greden, Dr. Anna Halberstadt, Dr. Emily Hauenstein, Dr. M. Jabkowski, Dr. Mieczylsaw Janiszewski, Karen Johnson, Dr. Paramjit T. Joshi, Representative Marcy Kaptur, Dr. Herb Kleber, Dr. Don Klein, Gladys Kreutzman, Marian Kyner, Dr. Bob Levin, Dr. Reinhard Lier, Dr. Juan López, Sara Lynge, Dr. John Mann, Dr. Melvin McGuiness, Dr. Henry McCurtiss, Dr. Jeanne Miranda, Dr. William Normand, Phaly Nuon, Kristen Peilman, Representative John Porter, Dr. Robert Post, Dr. William Potter, Senator Harry Reid, Dr. Norman Rosenthal, Representative Marge Roukema, Dr. Arnold Sameroff, Senator Chuck Schumer, Dr. Sylvia Simpson, Dr. Colin Stine, Dr. Glenn Treismann, Dr. Elliot Valenstein, Dr. James D. Watson, Dr. Thomas Wehr, Senator Paul Wellstone, Dr. Myrna Weissman, Representative Bob Wise, and Dr. Elizabeth Young.

So many people opened up to me and told me their difficult stories as I worked in this book, and I enjoyed their confidence and have come to enjoy the friendship of many of them. No other enterprise in my life has been so sad, but no other one has so entirely convinced me that communication is possible and that the world is a place of intimacies. Tremendous thanks must go to the subjects who allowed me to tell their stories in this book: Laura Anderson, Janet Benshoof, Robert Boorstin, Brian D'Amato, Walt Devine, Sarah Gold, Ruth Ann Janesson, Amalia Joelson, Karen Johansen, Eve Kahn, Amelia Lange, Carlita Lewis, Betsy de Lotbinière, Martha Manning, Pearl Bailey Mason, Theresa Morgan, Dièry Prudent, Lynn Rivers, Maggie Robbins, Joe Rogers, Joel P. Smith, Tina Sonego, Angel Starkey, Mark Weiss, and the people I have called Sheila Hernandez, Frank Rusakoff, Bill Stein, Danquille Stetson, Lolly Washington, Claudia Weaver, and Fred Wilson. These men and women and numerous others magnanimously narrated their difficult stories for me; I only hope that I have been a sufficient conduit for all their courage.

Since this is a book about depression, I also thank the people without whom I would not have recovered far enough to write my story. I am grateful to the many doctors from whom I have received treatment for depression. I feel very fortunate to have had my mind in such capable hands. The doctors' work was complemented by the generosity of friends whom I will not catalog, but who know themselves to have created ways for me to stay alive. My formulary for depression would include, at the very top, such love as these many people have shown me; they are true and good to the core, and their gentle advice and empathetic good sense and rational control defined the space within which I could safely be crazy. I thank Juan and Amalia Fernandez, whose loving care and attention through the period of writing freed me to compose what I would.

I had never employed a research assistant until I started work on this book. I was wildly fortunate to find the gifted artist Stephen Bitterolf, who has taken hundreds of hours away from his canvases and has worked on *The Noonday Demon* as hard as I have. Whatever rigor I have achieved here would not have been possible without his rigor; and many of my ideas were formed by ideas of his. This book could not exist in any-

Acknowledgments

thing like its current form without his contribution. Furthermore, he has shown himself to be a man of character; his wit, affection, and kindness have been a source of constant pleasure to me.

My father was sixty-seven when I had my first episode of depression. He is to be praised not only for his love and generosity, but also for the flexibility of mind and spirit that has consistently allowed him to understand and arrest my illness over these last six years. I have never known anyone who so beautifully integrates the imaginative vitality of youth with the considered wisdom of age. He has been, always, my unfailing mainstay and my great inspiration. I have dedicated this book to him with all my heart.

Index

541

Index

alcohol consumption:
  anxiety relieved by, 226
  cultural differences in normal levels
    of, 226–27
  fetal neurological damage due to, 254
  medication absorption and, 467
Alcoholics Anonymous (AA), 228, 240,
  241, 365
alcoholism:
  antidepressant treatment for depres-
    sives with, 220, 222, 466
  of children of depressed parents, 181
  depression symptoms caused by, 219,
    227, 467
  dual-diagnosis cases of, 219–21, 228,
    238–42, 468
  endorphin levels and, 223
  genetic predisposition for, 65, 223, 450
  of men vs. women, 175
  physical debilitation due to, 228
  rates of, 218
  REM sleep patterns of, 220–21
  serotonin levels and, 217, 228
  suicidality and, 227, 255
  treatment options for, 219–22,
    228–29
  withdrawal from, 228–29
  see also substance abuse
alienation, late Victorian/early modernist
  sentiments of, 320–22, 329
allergies, 80, 139
alpha-2 antagonists, 116
altruism, 410–11
Alvarez, A., 208–9, 244, 263, 280
Alzheimer's disease, 192–93, 232, 463
amantadine, 116
Ambien, 119, 234
Ambrosini, Paul, 460
American Civil Liberties Union
  (ACLU), 379, 380
Americans with Disabilities Act (ADA),
  366, 370, 392, 491
amphetamines, 116, 222, 231
amygdala, 55, 60, 172
anaclitic depression, 183, 460
Anafranet, 118
Anafranil, 114
Anatomy of Melancholy, The (Burton),
  301–4, 310, 323, 480

Anderson, Laura, 92–98, 106, 262, 438,
  442
Andrews, Paul, 409–10
Angel of Bethesda, The (Mather), 313
anger:
  evolutionary role of, 413–14
  repression of, 197, 198
anhedonia, 19, 67, 445
animals:
  dominance in, 113–14, 404–6
  emotions of, 402–3, 412–14
  hibernation of, 406
  learned helplessness observed in, 348
  self-destructive behaviors of, 256–57
  serotonin studies conducted on,
    113–14, 253, 254
  short-term stress responses of, 407
animist ritual, Senegalese, 165–70
"Annabel Lee" (Poe), 359
anorexia nervosa, 313
Antabuse, 229, 469
Anthony, Saint, 16
antidepressant medications, 111–20
  adverse reactions to, 80–81, 98
  and alcoholics, 220, 222, 466
  atypical, 114, 118, 193
  basic principle of, 111
  body temperature and, 113, 452
  while breastfeeding, 83
  broad uses of, 435
  changing combinations of, 86, 87,
    93–94, 118–20, 121
  for children, 184–85, 460
  classes of, 114
  cortisol-reduction approach in, 58
  cost of, 60, 353
  cultural attitudes and, 195, 343
  current research on, 120, 171–72
  delays in responses to, 60, 112–13,
    120, 189–90, 237, 333, 450
  dependency concerns and, 235–36
  depressed substance abusers treated
    with, 220, 222
  developmental history of, 330–34
  directions of research on, 120
  disabling effects in high dosages of,
    423
  effectiveness of, 60, 86, 103–4, 120
  elderly and, 189–90, 192, 193

Index

atypical antidepressants, 114, 118, 193
atypical depression, 48, 114
Augustine, Saint, 292, 306, 478
autism, 175
autoreceptor agonists, 116
Axelrod, Julius, 332
Aztecs, hallucinogenic drugs used by, 291

B

Ball, H. Irene, 447–48
Ballenger, James, 65, 111, 119, 124, 406
Baltimore, Md., depression treatment
    study on indigent HIV/AIDS
    populations in, 340
Barbey, J. T., 495
barbiturates, 254
Barlaeus, Caspar, 304
Baron, Richard, 368
basil, 288
batterers, 178–79, 180
Baudelaire, Charles, 315
Bazelon Center, 381
Beck, Aaron, 107, 471
Beckett, Samuel, 285–86, 329–30
Beddoes, Thomas, 319
Bedlam, 309, 318, 481–82
behavioral control, 328–29
    see also cognitive-behavioral therapy
Bell Jar, The (Plath), 66
Benshoof, Janet, 109, 237, 438
benzodiazepines, 119, 193, 234, 469–70
Berger, M., 145
beta-adrenergic receptors, 333
bethanechol, 116
Biathanatos (Donne), 247
Bible, 292–93, 478
Bicâtre, 309, 482
Bielik-Robson, Agata, 201
Bingen, Hildegard von, 294
bipolar illness, see manic-depressive
    (bipolar) disorder
bipolar two, 92
birds, nesting behavior of, 406, 413
Birtchnell, J., 405
bisexuals, 202, 207–8
Bisgaard, Poul, 210

black bile, melancholy as excess of,
    286–87, 288, 290, 291–92, 298,
    306
black people, depression experiences of,
    195–200, 351
Blair-West, G. W., 447
Blake, William, 309
blood-brain barrier, 123
blood sugar levels, 136, 139
Bloom, Harold, 470
BMAP (Brain Molecule Anatomy Pro-
    ject), 171–72
body, mechanistic models of, 306–8
body net, 423
body temperature, 56, 452
Boerhaave, Hermann, 307, 308, 309, 481,
    483
Book of Common Prayer, 302
Boorstin, Robert, 370, 371, 441
Boorstin, J. M., 447
Boswell, James, 309–10
bowel problems, 65
Bower, Bruce, 459
brain:
    asymmetry of, 415–19
    autopsies of, 319
    blood circulation within, 307, 417, 418
    "decade of the," 369
    in imaging technology, 254, 362, 417
    magnetic stimulation of, 139, 418
    medical model of, 320
    nervous system supervised by, 289
    psychosurgery on, 137, 163–65, 441
    as seat of emotion/mental illness, 286,
        413–14, 418, 419
    triune model of, 414–15
brain chemistry, 20–22, 111–14
    anxiety problems and, 65, 111
    ECT effects on, 121, 123
    emotional mind vs., 102, 111
    neural electrical impulses vs., 330
    suicidality and, 252–54
    talking therapy effects on, 111
    theories of antidepressant actions on,
        331–33
    see also neurotransmitters; specific neuro-
        transmitters
brain function:
    adaptability of, 56, 112–13, 307

Index

Alzheimer's disease and, 192–93
cellular adaptive capacity in, 56
evolution of, 413–19
flexibility of, 416
genetic research project on, 171–72
impact of depressive episodes on, 55, 56
substance abuse effects on, 217–18, 219–20, 222–23, 231, 233
Brain Molecule Anatomy Project (BMAP), 171–72
breakdowns, 17, 39–99
cumulative causation of, 48–49
defined, 48
eating difficulties in, 50, 54, 55
immobility experienced in, 52–53
physiological functions affected by, 55–56, 448
sleep patterns in, 51
breastfeeding:
antidepressant medications and, 83
childhood loss of, 325, 326
Brecht, Bertolt, 321
breech birth, 40
bromocriptine, 116
Brontë, Charlotte, 133–34
Brown, George, 62, 63, 65, 175, 347, 450, 458
Brown, John, 311
Brown, Thomas, 455
Buckingham County, Va., depression treatment studied in women of, 339–40
Bucknill, John Charles, 485–86
Bukowski, Charles, 250, 472
Bulgakov, Mikhail, 7
bupropion, 116, 118
Burke, Edmund, 311
burns, self-inflicted, 421, 422, 424
Burton, Robert, 301–4, 310, 323, 480
BuSpar (buspirone), 78, 86, 87, 116, 119, 235, 383, 422, 447
B vitamins, 138–39

C

caffeine, 224, 225, 230, 397
Callahan, Roger, 142, 454–55

Cambodia, depression of trauma survivors in, 32–37
Cameron, Julia, 155
Camus, Albert, 245, 246, 247, 263, 321, 329
Candide (Voltaire), 311
Carlsson, Arvid, 333
Carlyle, Thomas, 321
Cartesian biology, 306
Casanova, Ludovicus a, 305
Cassian, 292–93, 478
catecholamine, 332–33, 397
Catholicism, 132–33
CBT, *see* cognitive-behavioral therapy
Celexa (citalopram), 13, 114, 118, 157, 191, 192, 333, 445, 487
celiac disease, 139
Center for Disease Control, 493
Cervantes, Miguel de, 304
Changing Nature of Man, The (van den Berg), 407
Charles VI (the Foolish), King of France, 305
Chaucer, Geoffrey, 293–94
Chavez, Cesar, 392
Chekhov, Anton, 135
Chesterton, G. K., 252
childbirth, maternal depression after, 138, 174, 176, 457
childhood depression, 181–89
of adolescents, 187–89, 461
adult depression rates after, 187–88, 461
assessments of, 184, 188–89
earliest manifestations of, 181, 421, 459
parental depression and, 180–83, 459
parents involved in therapy for, 183
physical illness and, 182, 187, 188–89
sexual abuse and, 349–50, 355, 421
suicidality and, 184, 254, 257–58, 261, 264–65, 356, 461
treatment of, 183, 184–89, 460
U.S. incidence of, 25, 446
children:
assertion of power developed by, 350
of depressed parents, 82–83, 180–83, 337, 345, 346–47, 349–50, 351–52, 356–58, 359, 383

545

Index

Index

Index

Index

Index

Index

Index

Netherlands, 202, 203, 464
neuronal tissue, long-term damage to, 60
neurons, excitability between, 55
Neurontin, 97, 422
neurotransmitters:
    and blood flow within brain, 417
    depressive episode impact on, 55
    ECT effects on, 123
    elderly diminishment of, 189–90
    exercise effects on, 138
    history of developmental research on,
        331–33
    indirect relationship of mood with,
        111–13
    interactions among, 113
    recovery time and, 417
    Saint-John's-wort and, 146
    seasonal light exposure and, 140
    in sleep states, 145
    substance abuse and, 217–18, 219,
        223, 228, 230–31
    suicidality affected by, 252–54
    see also dopamine; norepinephrine;
        serotonin, serotonin levels; *other*
        specific neurotransmitters
New Age treatments, 141–42
Newman, John, 310
Newman, Russ, 451
New York City, 464
New York State, 493
New Yorker, The, 11–12, 205, 363, 365
New Zealand, 202, 464
nicotine, 218, 202, 224, 225
Nierenberg, Andrew, 117
Nietzsche, Friedrich, 143, 283, 317, 476,
    484–85
Night Falls Fast (Jamison), 259–60
NIH (National Institutes of Health), 369
nihilism, 315
NIMH (National Institute of Mental
    Health), 368–69, 376
Nolen-Hoeksema, Susan, 174, 457
"noonday demon," history of term,
    292–93, 478
noradrenaline, 253
Norden, Michael J., 454
norepinephrine:
    antidepressant medication and, 117,
        118, 171

anxiety disorders and, 65
    early research on, 331–32, 333
    illegal stimulants and, 230
    in sleep, 145
    suicidality and, 253, 473
normality, standards of, 73, 89, 124
Normand, William, 102
Norpramin, 114
Norristown State Mental Hospital,
    386–89, 392, 422, 424, 427, 432,
    498
North America, colonial societies of,
    312–13
nortriptyline, 83, 184
Nyon Phaly, 34–37, 342–43, 351
nutrition, 138–39

O

obsessive-compulsives, irrational fears
    of, 305
octopus, suicide of, 257
"Ode on Melancholy" (Keats), 314
omega-3 fatty acids, 139, 454
opiates, 222, 231–32
opium, 231–32, 327
Oppenheim, David, 255
optimism, evolutionary selective advan-
    tage of, 433–34
Oquendo, Maria, 251
Osler, Sir William, 328
outreach treatment programs, 338, 341,
    349, 375, 390
Outward Bound, 142–44, 207
Ovid, 38
ozone layer, depletion of, 30, 31, 360,
    490–91

P

pain:
    benefits of, 24–25, 38
    emotional vs. physical, 422–23,
        435
    hospital procedures on medication
        for, 84–85
    self-infliction of, 422–23

Index

Index

Pol Pot, 32, 33
populations, 173–215
  child, 181–89
  elderly, 189–93, 461–62
  ethnic, *see* ethnicity
  female, 173–78
  gay, 202–5
  male, 173, 175–76, 177–80
  national cultural differences of,
    200–15
  prison, 380–81, 394
Porter, John, 362–63, 369, 372, 376, 492
Positive Illusions (Taylor), 433–34
Possessed, The (Dostoyevsky), 268
possession, depression as evidence of,
  293, 295, 297
Possibility of Altruism, The (Nagel), 430
Post, Robert, 56–57, 80, 124, 139, 449
postpartum depression, 138, 174, 176, 457
post-traumatic stress disorder (PTSD),
  141, 381
Potter, William, 26–27, 113, 120, 236, 395
poverty, depression in, 37–38, 335–60,
  488
  barriers to federal legislation on,
    375–76
  congressional policies on, 375–78
  emotional life repressed by, 350–51
  extremity of problems encountered
    in, 340, 355–60
  helplessness experienced by, 330, 348
  motherhood and, 337, 338, 342, 345,
    346–47, 351–52, 358, 359
  normality of, 347–48
  outreach programs and, 338, 341, 349,
    375
  passivity manifested in, 338, 344, 348,
    355
  physical symptoms presented in, 343,
    344, 345–46, 347
  public health studies of, 336, 339–40
  rates of, 336, 347
  recovery progress and, 340, 342–43,
    344–45, 346–47, 352, 358–60
  relief experienced in labeling of, 341,
    343
  socioeconomic assistance vs. psychi-
    atric remedies for, 337, 360
  symptom attribution and, 335–36, 343

  talking therapies employed in,
    341–42, 344, 351, 358, 359
  treatment of, 335, 336–60, 375, 488
  unemployment and, 337, 351
power, childhood development of, 350
prayer, 131, 133
prefrontal cortex, 59, 417–18
pregnancy, 174
  antidepressant medication and, 83, 93
  of daughters of indigent depressed,
    337
  ECT treatment in, 120–21
  low suicidality in, 249
  nutrition in, 138
presidency, 367
Price, John, 404
Prichard, James Cowles, 484–85
Prilosec, 422
Prince, Elizabeth, 54–55
Prince Georges County, Md., treatment
  study of women in, 339–40
Pritchard, James Cowles, 485
prisons, mentally-ill inmates of, 380–81,
  394
Productive and Unproductive Depression
  (Gut), 435
progesterone, 173, 457
prolactin, 55–56, 406
promiscuity, 337
protease inhibitors, 355
Protestantism, 311, 312–13
Prozac (fluoxetine), 83, 358, 422, 487
  adverse reactions to, 80
  for children, 184–85
  development of, 334, 395
  effectiveness of, 76
  emotional numbing in use of, 282
  excessive use of, 26–27, 337, 399
  imipramine vs., 331
  low side effects of, 115, 120
  negative sexual effects of, 115, 453
  1988 introduction of, 76
  popular criticism of, 81
  as SSRI, 25, 114
Prudent, Dièry, 196–200, 450
Prudent Fitness, 198
Psalms, Book of, 292–93, 478
psychiatry:
  categorical models used in, 398

Index

as dynamic therapy, 328

philosophical roots of, 287

as psychobiology vs. psychoanalysis, 322–28, 334

social context considered in, 328–29

talk therapy vs. psychopharmacology in, 101–2, 103–4, 451; *see also* antidepressant medications; psychoanalysis, psychoanalysts; psychopharmacology; talking therapies

trend shifts in, 171

psychoanalysis, psychoanalysts:

antidepressant medications disapproved by, 48, 50–51

cultic tendencies of, 328

theoretical development of, insights of, 323–26

time required by, 102–3

psychobiology, 322–28, 334

psychopharmacology:

addiction concerns of, 119

adjustment strategies in, 87, 89

broad usage of, 435

Hippocratic depression treatment vs., 285, 286–87, 288

personal responsibility vs., 432–33

prescription status of, 399

talking therapies integrated with, 101–2, 104

see also antidepressant medications

psychosomatic complaints, 20

psychosurgery, 137, 163–65, 441

puberty, onset age of, 337

Puritanism, 313

Q

Qigong, 148

R

racial prejudice, racism, 196, 197, 198, 199, 204, 351

Rado, Sandor, 486

Rand Corporation Study, 492

rank-based society, 404–6, 495

rape, 340–41

rapid eye movement (REM) sleep:

antidepressant suppression of, 113, 146, 452

depressive alterations in, 146

illicit drug/alcohol effects on, 220–21, 229

in primary illness diagnosis of alcoholic depressives, 220–21, 466

Reagan, Ronald, 373

reboxetine, 171, 456, 487

receptor theories, 112, 333, 487

Rees, Jonathan, 394–95

Regier, D. A., 446

Reid, Harry, 373, 375, 377

religious faith, 129–33

in colonial North America, 312–13

fasting and, 313

loss of, 82

modernist alienation from, 321–22

moral stigmatization of depression in, 285, 292–95, 312–13

recovery aided by, 76, 130–33

suicide prohibitions of, 132, 246–47, 259, 304

REM sleep, *see* rapid eye movement (REM) sleep

Renaissance, melancholic genius of, 285, 289, 295–96, 299, 300–301

repeated transcranial magnetic stimulation (rTMS), 137, 139, 418, 454

reptilian brain, 414

Republican party, 376

"Requiem" (Rilke), 278

research:

applied vs. basic, 369

federal expenditures on, 369, 376

by pharmaceutical industry, 395

residential services, long-term structured, 391

Restoril, 119

reuptake, 332

Rhodes, Tristan, 130

Richards, Keith, 238

Richter, Gerhard, 45

Rilke, Rainer Maria, 278

Rimer, Sara, 461–62

Risperdal, 118

ritual, power of, 170

561

oversimplification implied in name of, 396–97

pharmaceutical industry development of, 13, 333–34

post-stroke depression and, 193

reabsorption process blocked by, 112

side effects of, 80, 115–17, 120, 236, 453

in suicide prevention, 115, 252

U.S. usage of, 25, 447

varieties of, 114

see also specific selective serotonin reuptake inhibitors

self:

historical concepts of, 287, 300

sequential model of, 21, 432

self-consciousness:

brain asymmetry and, 415

mechanistic model of, 306

speech as origin of, 415

suicidality and, 245, 254, 256–57

self-hatred, gay shame and, 205

self-mutilation, 71, 151–52, 421, 422–28

Seligman, Martin, 451, 460

Seneca, 289

Senegal, *ndeup* ceremonies for mental illness in, 165–70

senility, 190, 191, 192–93

sensation, emotions triggered by, 402

separation anxiety, 182

Sérèr people, 165

serotonin, serotonin levels:

aggressive behavior and, 114, 253–54

alcoholism and, 217, 228

Alzheimer's disease and, 193, 463

in amelioration of depression, 22

in animal studies, 113–14, 253, 254, 473

anxiety and, 65, 119

atypical antidepressants and, 118

cortisol levels vs., 57, 59

dietary choices and, 138

elderly diminishment of, 189–90, 462

genetic determination of, 254

illegal substances and, 230, 233

impulsive behavior linked with, 253

initial isolation of, 331

melatonin derived from, 55

of men vs. women, 254

as monoamine, 332

multiple functions of, 112

nicotine use and, 225

oversimplification of popular beliefs about, 112, 362

prefrontal cortex and abnormalities in metabolism of, 418

in sleep, 145

suicidality and, 253, 254, 473

tricyclic effects on, 117

see also selective serotonin reuptake inhibitors

serotonin antagonists, 116

serotonin synthesis:

in men vs. women, 174

nutrition and, 138

in retina, 140

serotonin theory, 333

Seroxat/Paxil (paroxetine), 334

sertraline (Lustral/Zoloft), 51, 60, 78, 114, 118, 121, 236, 334

Serzone, 114, 118, 119

sexual abuse, 176, 188, 340–41, 348, 349, 350, 351, 355, 421

sexual behavior:

antidepressants' negative effects on, 91–92, 115–17, 157

mood disorder as risk factor in, 353–54

overabundance of public information on, 399–400

see also gay men and women, depression among

sexually transmitted diseases, 202

Shaffer, D., 464

Shaffer, Howard, 222

Shakespeare, William, 299–300, 301, 430

Shelley, Percy Bysshe, 314–15

Sherrington, Charles, 403

Shiels, John F., 492

Shneidman, Edwin, 248, 252, 263–64

shock treatments, *see* electroconvulsive therapy

shooting incidents, 373, 374

Shorter, Edward, 194

Short History of Decay, A (Cioran), 273

Silvaticus, Joannes Baptista, 299

Simpson, Sylvia, 104–5, 106, 185–86, 370

sin, depression as, 293–94, 295, 296–97

Index

Singapore, cultural attitudes on depression in, 200
Singh, Pami, 456
Skeptics, 289
skin cancer, 31, 447
skydiving, 261
Slaby, Andrew, 466, 467, 469
sleep:
    antidepressant suppression of REM phase of, 113, 452
    blood sugar fluctation as impediment to, 139
    caffeine and, 397
    disruption in patterns of, 144, 145–46, 190, 455
    insomnia and, 119, 146, 190
    neurotransmitter systems and, 145
    panic attacks in delta phase of, 65
    as primary illness diagnostic tool, 220–21, 466
    REM stage of, *see* rapid eye movement (REM) sleep
    as safe withdrawal, 406
sleep advancement, 145
sleep deprivation therapy, 137, 144
Sloman, Leon, 495
Smith, C. U. M., 403
Smith, Joel P., 268
Smith, Richard, 492
smoking, 202, 218, 225
Smollett, Tobias, 311
social ranking, dominance conflicts and, 404–6
Social Security Disability Insurance (SSDI), 368
societies, in transitional phases, 208, 407
Socrates, 287, 288
Solidarity movement, 201
Solomon, Andrew:
    alcohol reactions of, 227–28
    breakdowns experienced by, 42–43, 44, 45–48, 49–55, 61, 63–65, 67–69, 83–90, 91, 278–79, 325–26, 426, 432, 438
    childhood of, 39–42, 206
    costs of treatment for, 492
    homosexuality of, 206–8
    medications used by, 30, 60, 61, 63, 64–65, 70–71, 77–80, 86–92, 119,

123–24, 125, 234–35, 236–37, 242, 426, 432, 447, 492
    members of Congress interviewed by, 375–78
    personal value of depression experiences of, 78, 91, 436–37, 443
    in psychotherapy, 44–45, 48, 70, 105, 492
    suicidal thoughts of, 67, 68–69, 71–73, 77, 78, 85, 244, 247, 260–61, 265–66, 274–75, 278, 279, 280, 283, 443
    violent episodes of, 179–80
    writing career of, 40, 46, 49, 86–87, 89, 325, 397, 448, 448
Solomon, Carolyn, 206, 268, 271–73, 275–79, 476
Solomon, David, 277, 278
Solomon, Howard, 13, 278, 445
Sonata, 234
Sonego, Tina, 238–42, 438, 442
Sorrows of Young Werther, The (Goethe), 251, 315
Soviet concentration camps, 281
Special K (ketamine), 232
speech:
    as origin of self-consciousness, 415
    positive emotion allied with, 418–19
Spinoza, Benedict, 308
spiritual belief, *see* religious faith
Spitz, Henry, 466
spleen, 297, 300, 315
SSDI (Social Security Disability Insurance), 367, 368
SSI (Supplemental Security Income), 160, 368
SSRIs, *see* selective serotonin reuptake inhibitors
Stanley, Jonathan, 380, 381
Starkey, Angel, 421–28, 432, 438, 498
state mental hospitals, 385–89, 390–91
STDs (sexually transmitted diseases), 202
Stein, Bill (pseudonym), 73–77, 441–42
Stetson, Danquille (pseudonym), 351–52, 360
Stevens, Anthony, 404
Stewart, Jacqueline, 467
stimulants, illegal, 230–32
    see also substance abuse
Stoic philosophers, 292

Index

Index